RELIGION

PHILOSOPHY

YOGA

RELIGION PHILOSOPHY YOGA

A SELECTION OF ARTICLES
by
JEAN FILLIOZAT

translated from the French by
MAURICE SHUKLA

with Introduction by
PIERRE-SYLVAIN FILLIOZAT

MOTILAL BANARSIDASS PUBLISHERS
PRIVATE LIMITED • DELHI

First Edition: Delhi, 1991

ISBN: 81-208-0718-9

Also available at:
MOTILAL BANARSIDASS
41 U.A., Bungalow Road, Jawahar Nagar, Delhi 110 007
120 Royapettah High Road, Mylapore, Madras 600 004
16 St. Mark's Road, Bangalore 560 001
Ashok Rajpath, Patna 800 004
Chowk, Varanasi 221 001

PRINTED IN INDIA
BY JAINENDRA PRAKASH JAIN AT SHRI JAINENDRA PRESS, A-45 NARAINA INDUSTRIAL AREA, PHASE I, NEW DELHI 110 028 AND PUBLISHED BY NARENDRA PRAKASH JAIN FOR MOTILAL BANARSIDASS PUBLISHERS PVT. LTD., BUNGALOW ROAD, JAWAHAR NAGAR, DELHI 110 007

CONTENTS

Introduction vii

PART I—HISTORY OF RELIGIONS

Chapters

1. Charity in Indian Thought 3
2. Vaiṣṇava Devotion in the Tamil Country 19
3. About the Religion of Bhartṛhari 41
4. The Contribution of the Study of Indian Religions 47
5. Aśoka and the Spread of Buddhism 61
6. The Śaiva Āgamas 67
7. The Dates of Bhāgavatapurāṇa and Bhāgavatamāhātmya 79
8. Self-Immolation by Fire and the Indian Buddhist Tradition 91
9. Docetism in Christianity and in India 127
10. The Giving up of Life by the Sage: The Suicides of the Criminal and of the Hero in Indian Tradition 135
11. Traditional Religions and Modern Cultures 161
12. The Veda and Ancient Tamil Culture 179
13. The Respect of Life in Buddhism 193
14. Echoes of Sufism in India 199
15. Indian Religions and the Psychology of their Historians 215
16. Puṇya and its Semantic Field 233
17. The Historical and the Present Life of the Veda 253

PART II—PHILOSOPHY, PSYCHOLOGY, YOGA

18. On "Ocular Concentration" in Yoga 269
19. The Origins of an Indian Mystical Technique 293
20. The Unconscious in Indian Psychology 307
21. The Western Interpretation of Indian Thought 311
22. Continence and Sexuality in Buddhism and in the Disciplines of Yoga 327

23. The Limits of Human Powers in India 341
24. Thought and Efficiency in Ancient India 361
25. Yoga and its Underlying Doctrine 365
26. The Nature of Yoga in its Traditions 375
27. The Conception of Time and Space in the Indian World 415
28. The Oedipus Complex in a Buddhist Tantra 429
29. The Psychological Theories of India 439
30. Visions of the Spiritual Seekers of India 451
31. Science and Yoga I and II 461
32. Yoga and Psychotropic Substances 471
33. Psychic Tensions and Yoga 477

Index 481

INTRODUCTION

THE PRESENT COLLECTION of articles aims at acquainting the readers with a part of the Indological works of Jean Filliozat, a scholar of repute who, through the great originality of his thought and method, gave a new direction to Indology. He was much in advance of his times and pioneered research in such new fields that the impact of his effort and writings will be felt long after him, and in a field like historical ecology what he set in motion will be fully grasped only in the future.

Born on November 4th 1906, Jean Filliozat had his first taste of Indian culture in his schooldays through the writings of a 19th century French poet, Leconte de Lisle, who had adapted in verse some Vedic and classical myths and legends of India. He was also very keen on science and scientific research. After completing his higher studies in medicine, he became a doctor in 1930. Upto 1947 he practised medicine as an eye-specialist. His medical studies did not deter him from pursuing his desire to learn Sanskrit, Tamil and Tibetan. His first published works were about medical research: two books on ocular physiology and strabism (1930, 1932). Subsequently all his research and scientific study was devoted to Indology.

His principal teacher in this field and in Orientalism was Sylvain Lévi, a most versatile scholar who had made an exhaustive study of India's relations with neighbouring as well as other foreign countries like the Mediterranean and Central Asian ones. Under his guidance Jean Filliozat studied the Indo-European languages of Central Asia, Chinese and Tibetan, so that he could refer to Central Asian documents and manuscripts about India. Being basically a physician, he first took up the study of Indian medical literature. One of his first achievements was to bring to light many medical documents of Indian origin in Central Asia which demonstrated that along with Buddhism, India had also exported its system of medicine. He traced the movement of these ideas on physiology right up to Japan.

Jean Filliozat studied Indian medicine through its main texts and sought its origins in the earlier Vedic literature. In a major work *The Classical Doctrine of Indian Medicine* (1949) and in several other articles, he set out that many ideas on man and his physiology, for instance the conception of *prāṇa* as a regulating force of all physiological functions, were older than the systematic treatises of Caraka and Suśruta and were, as a matter of fact, rooted in Vedic texts as old as *Atharvaveda*, etc. He thereby helped in breaking the prejudice prevalent at that time in the West that Greece was the universal fount of all traditional science and revealing the originality of the Indian medical conceptions in the Indian context.

Towards the end of his life, Sylvain Lévi who had explored and worked on documents on India derived from Central Asia and China, realised that Indian culture could be better understood and explained through Dravidian sources. He, therefore, encouraged his disciple, Jean Filliozat to take up the study of Tamil Literature. His Tamil teacher was Jules Bloch, another French scholar of considerable intelligence and insight. Jules Bloch was primarily a linguist but he studied languages in their social and cultural contexts. Anthropology and ethnology also interested him. This also influenced Jean Filliozat and he directed his efforts not only at knowing languages and written documents but also understanding the country, its people and culture.

Jean Filliozat studied Sanskrit and Indology also with another distinguished French archaeologist, Alfred Foucher who had worked in India and Afghanistan and contributed a lot to the study of Gandhara art and Buddhism. He had also worked in close contact with some traditional pandits in Banares and other places. While teaching Sanskrit in Paris, he incorporated some of the elements and spirit of the traditional methods of Sanskrit teaching. His students were initiated into Sanskrit grammar through *Laghukaumudī* and into Indian philosophy through *Tarkasaṃgraha*. Jean Filliozat thus got acquainted with the traditional Indian methods of knowledge.

In his early years of Indological research, in addition to studying medicine he thoroughly explored Indian manuscripts available in France and initiated the cataloguing of manuscripts preserved in the Bibliothèque Nationale in the Société Asiatique etc. He knew all the Indian scripts well and became proficient also in Indian epigraphy. In collaboration with Louis Renou he prepared a general treatise entitled 'L' Inde Classique' about the different fields of Indology in two volumes (1949, 1953). His own contribution in this work was a history of India upto the 7th century and a lucid exposition of Buddhism.

From 1941 he was professor of Indology in the Ecole Pratique des Hautes Etudes in Paris, devoted to research in specific fields of science. He gave up his medical practice in 1947 in order to devote all his time to his personal researches and to the teaching and organisation of Indology in France and elsewhere. He became, in 1952, professor of the languages and literatures of India in the Collège de France, the highest academic institution for higher research in different sciences. In 1966, he became a member of the Académie des Inscriptions et Belles Lettres and soon thereafter an honorary member of the British Academy. In 1974 he became vice-president of the Société Asiatique in Paris of which he had been the secretary from 1945. He was also the secretary of the twenty first International Congress of Orientalists and organiser of the Indian classical section at the twenty ninth session of the same congress in 1973. He established two important international organisations for Indian studies: the International Association of Tamil Research in 1965 and became its president and the International Association of Sanskrit Studies in 1973 of which he was the vice-president. His last award was the degree of Doctor *honoris causa* conferred upon him by the University of Varanasi in 1981.

In 1947, he made his first trip to India. From then on he came regularly every year to organise in different fields Indological or Oriental studies from India upto Japan. There already existed at that time a French governmental institution devoted to scientific research on the cultures of different countries of Asia: The Ecole Française d'Extrême-Orient founded in 1901 and located in Hanoi, where it had an important library and even a museum. But its activities were not limited to this region. Missions were sent to other countries, like the famous mission of Paul Pelliot in Central Asia of Edouard Chavannes in China, of Alfred Foucher, Jules Bloch in India, of Noel Peri in Japan. After the agreements in 1949 between France, Vietnam, Cambodia and

Laos, Hanoi continued to be the repository of the Vietnamese, Chinese and Japanese collections, and new centres were formed in Cambodia and Laos. The Ecole opened other branches in Indonesia, Japan and India (in Pondicherry). Jean Filliozat who was instrumental in this reorganization became the director of this Ecole in 1956 and remained in this post till his retirement in 1977. The main centre of research was at first in Cambodia, site of the largest archaeological works in the world in recent years and conducted by Bernard-Philippe Groslier. The political turmoil in South-East Asia twice hampered the work undertaken by the Ecole Française d'Extrême-Orient, first due to the evacuation of Hanoi and North Vietnam in 1958 and then in 1975 due to the evacuation of Cambodia. The permanent missions in India, Indonesia and Japan continued their work uninterrupted.

The Pondicherry branch of the Ecole française d'Extrême-Orient had a special objective in inviting researchers to study the problems of the expansion of the Indian civilisation in South-East Asia, the Indian origins of ideas that inspired the construction of Cambodian monuments. In fact, this was one of Jean Filliozat's favourite subjects of study and where he attained some of his most notable scientific success in tracing the rules, processes, conceptions and images used in Cambodian architecture and art to the Sanskrit āgamas which are the basis of the religious life in India.

There was another reason for developing French Indology in Pondicherry. It was in Pondicherry that the first collaboration of Indian and French scholars toward a better, scientific knowledge of Indian culture took place. One such was Maridas Pillai, born in Pondicherry in 1721, a fine Tamil scholar who took up, in the course of his study, French and even Latin, worked with missionaries, with the professional astronomer Legentil and with others. His main achievement was a French translation of the Tamil Bhāgavata-Purāṇa a manuscript of which was transmitted to the French historian Deguignes who discovered therein dynastic lists, compared them with ancient Greek accounts of India and recognized in the name Sandragouten (a French transcript of the Tamil spelling of the Sanskrit Candragupta) the Sandrakottos of the Greek historians, a contemporary of Seleukos

Nikator (c. 305-280 B.C.). This identification placed India in a definite chronology and served as a basis for the integration of its ancient political history into world chronology. This discovery was published as early as 1777. Anquetil-Duperron, the first professional Indologist who succeeded in Surat in collecting, editing and translating the Zend-Avesta, had already in 1760 dreamed of establishing in Pondicherry an academy for the study of Indian languages and religions. In spite of ruling in Pondicherry for two hundred years, the French colonial government had never thought of setting up such an academy. A few individuals had, however, conducted some interesting researches but their work remained just a private initiative. At the time of the transfer of the French settlements to India an opportunity arose mainly due to the goodwill of a number of notable Frenchmen and Indians such as Sardar Panikar, a historian of the colonial period who had appreciated the work done by the Ecole Française d'Extrême-Orient, Homi Bhabha who was keen on encouraging collaborative scientific research, Pandit Nehru himself, Jean Filliozat and his colleagues, Louis Renou and others. India, therefore, decided to accept the French contribution in Pondicherry supported and sponsored by the French Government, in the sphere of scientific research and primarily in Indology. This led to the opening of the French Institute of Indology on March 20, 1955. A year later, a scientific section devoted to ecological studies of the vegetation was added. A branch of the Ecole Française d'Extrême-Orient was started in 1963, with the specific aim of studying the expansion of Indian civilization in South-East Asia.

European Indology has sometimes been criticised for distancing itself from Indian scholarship. And this was often its drawback in the 19th century and even in the first half of the 20th century. Jean Filliozat strongly advocated the collaboration with Indian scholars, traditional pandits and modern scientists. He had noticed that the most successful works of Indology were based on this collaboration. He also strove to turn Indology into a more rigorous, exact science. The first step in a scientific inquiry lies in collecting data, the totality of data. The scientist seeking for a theory which would disclose the hidden rationale behind extremely diverse data should when starting the process of collection, consider all facts equally and not neglect any of them. He should not modify anything so as to fit it into his theory which should not, in any case, be developed before all the data have been gathered. Texts are important as sources of facts that do not exist now and, therefore, cannot be known otherwise. But they are not the only source. The country itself is a significant source. And the data must be collected through direct observation of the country itself. A text cannot be divorced from the readers for whom it was written. Ancient Sanskrit texts are read even today by traditional pandits who are the direct heirs to the first readers. Their training and culture give them a deep understanding and enable them to make the best use of the ancient texts in their respective fields. On one side we have the letter of the text, on the other the consciousness of the intended reader, and the two are not separable. Both need to be examined and studied to get a correct understanding of the texts and their use in the civilization that produced them. A scientific research consists in collecting all the primary sources. In the study of Indian civilization we must, therefore, examine manuscripts of texts as well as the knowledge of traditional pandits.

Many pandits today are willing to collaborate with European researchers, to share their knowledge, and to show and explain their customs and the processes of their thought and acts. India has been able to preserve its ancient culture, and this preservation is sustained even today. Sanskrit is a perfectly living language, and, what is most important, it is still being taught according to the ancient methods. The pandits of today are, therefore, true heirs of the pandits of yore. These pandits have avoided the excesses of western influence and are not mere passive witnesses of an ancient culture, but its active interpreters and creators. In order to make this collaboration feasible between Indian and European scholars, to create the conditions in which a scientific inquiry can touch the true consciousness of the users of the languages and ideas being studied, it was necessary to have a well-equipped institution where European and Indian researchers could collaborate over long periods, and where the pandits could be given the same regard as given to the front-rank scientists to encourage them to work for collecting and utilising the documents of their own culture. It was with this aim that Jean

Filliozat started and directed the French Institute at Pondicherry from 1955 up to 1977. In the field of Indology he initiated an extensive research-programme on the living religions of India, especially of South India. The aim was and is to collect all the existing documents, manuscripts of sanskrit and tamil works about rituals, temple-construction, traditions, etc., in possession of temple priests, to make graphic and photographic surveys of temples, etc. and to do all this documentation in collaboration with Indian pandits.

Communication with pandits can be efficient and scientifically valuable if we are sufficiently capable of understanding them, and this becomes possible only by acquiring the basic elements of their culture. These elements, of a rational character, are the śāstras, vyākaraṇa, nyāya, mimāṃsa. Jean Filliozat, therefore, initiated another important endeavour for collecting documentation on these śāstras and making them generally accessible through translations and their studies.

The scientific ideal which inspired Jean Filliozat's organisational work is best expressed in his own publications on Indology. These cover the whole range of history and epigraphy, archaeology, history of religions, philosophy, psychology, yoga, science, medicine, languages and literatures, especially Tamiḷ studies, palaeography and manuscriptology, sociology and ethnology, history and the methodology of Indology. He mastered Sanskrit, Pāli, Tamil, Tibetan and some Indo-European languages of Central Asia such as tokharian. He could work on Chinese and with his colleagues, specialists of other Indian or Asian languages, he could usefully discuss and gather advanced and technical information. Besides his research, publications, organisational work, academic teaching, he also devoted a part of his energy to the popularisation of Indology through lectures meant for a general public, for amateurs of yoga and for anyone interested in any aspect of Indian art and civilization.

The present volume contains a selection of his articles on Indian religions, philosophy, psychology and yoga. This is to be followed by a selection of other articles on other subjects to which Jean Fillozat made an important contribution, the history of sciences and medicine, historical ecology, the expansion of Indian civilization, etc. But the present selection of articles on religion, philosophy and yoga gives us already a good picture of his knowledge and view of India.

The first focus of these articles is on methodology. On whichever subject he may have written, Jean Filliozat always thought it opportune to emphasize the points of methodology. He relentlessly underlined the need for exhaustive collection of data and handled the seemingly inexhaustible and overwhelming quantity of data very intelligently. The handling of data is, in fact, an art that consists in selecting what is relevant for establishing a theory which organizes the examined facts and enables us to have a global grasp. There is no mechanical method for handling data and establishing a theory. An intelligent use is the only safeguard from going astray. Jean Filliozat warned against the danger of too much theorizing. He criticised premature theories, especially those that were based on European or on other data foreign to India and did not take into account the relevant Indian background, a quality that radically differentiates the Indian facts from the foreign ones. For example he criticised the theory which identified yoga with the shamanism of Central Asia.

Jean Filliozat frequently cautioned against another danger of theorising, that is peculiar to the human sciences. In the natural sciences dealing with nature, a wrong theory does not generally affect the studied facts, but in case of human sciences a danger exists that a wrong theory might alter the observed facts in the future. Facts of language, of customs, of beliefs depend, at least partly, on human convention, they are human products. A theory which modifies facts, when describing them, is wrong. Such theories sometimes are passed off as valid by the group under study, because some non-scientific interest is found in them. The language and the customs of the group being studied are thus altered in accordance with the theory. Whether for good or for bad, that is another question. But such a procedure is hardly scientific. The scientist must not alter the object he studies, nor must he be a cause of any change in it. This highlights the great responsibility that rests on him while elaborating his theory.

For example, Jean Filliozat has rightly shown the rational character of yoga by taking into account all the ancient writings on this discipline and by studying them in their cultural context. He has shown that the practices were conceived in relation to a conception of the human body and mind prevalent among ancient Ayurvedic doctors. He noticed that yoga-practices were not at all documented before the emergence of this ancient literature. They were born with it. He believed, therefore, in an intellectual and rational origin of these practices. This subsequently led him and other medical scientists to look at yoga-practices with more seriousness and to start experimenting on yogins, in order to test the effects of the practices on the body and mind, for example in the case of stress. We see that this theory of the rational origin and nature of yoga led to further research. And this development is in harmony with the ancient view of yoga that was seen as the pursuit of salvation at the highest religious level, or, at a lower intermediary level, as an effort to making man more tranquil and perfect through a rational psychotechnical discipline. On the contrary, the theory of the shamanic origin of yoga, which confers an irrational and intuitive nature on it, has received a greater publicity and the attraction of the irrational has led to the proliferation of quackish yoga institutions in Europe and in India. This theory based neither on the fundamental ancient texts of yoga nor on what the authentic traditional yogins think of their art is, therefore, wrong. This development was a consequence of a faulty theory being accepted, because it offered an easier and a more colourful solution. And quackery does not go with ancient yoga, on the contrary, it completely alters it.

Jean Filliozat often told me that he had been lucky in his researches. Part of his good fortune was in having been a medical doctor which helped him start his indological researches with Ayurveda, a practice usually not followed by other indologists (in Europe they usually start with the Vedas or with literature). In this way, he got acquainted with the ancient conceptions of the human body and mind. That proved to be most revelatory for him because he soon understood that these conceptions were universally accepted in the whole of Indian culture even when it spread abroad. These concepts were clearly expressed only in medical literature. Elsewhere, though accepted, they were left implicit and consequently they were not understood clearly by the Indologists, a fact which has obscured the general understanding of Indian philosophy and religions. Jean Filliozat showed, for example, the place of ayurvedic conceptions in yoga. Wind (vāta) is considered to be one constitutive element of the body. It is not the mere phenomenon of respiration that is meant. It is the element which is the cause of all internal physiological activity in man. With this concept in mind yogins believed that by acting on the respiratory movements they could also act on the other functions of the same element. We can thus understand the development of the techniques of prāṇāyāma better.

Jean Filliozat pointed out the importance and the omnipresence of the concept of saṃskāras in the whole of Indian philosophy. This led him, thus, to bring out the psychological elements of the Buddhist doctrines which hold the human person to be a mere aggregate of saṃskāras. Some of them go as far as to deny the existence of a soul. The method of salvation in Buddhism appears more as a psychotechnique that aims at freeing the individual psyche of all impulses from the outside world as well as from the unconscious in himself, the unconscious being the result of past experiences organised in saṃskāras.

Jean Filliozat went far in the study of Indian metaphysics, by keeping to his method and never losing sight of the cultural background of the philosophers, especially of their knowledge of the sciences, medicine and psychology. He recognised in their philosophical pursuits the same rational character he had found in their sciences. He insisted on this rational and logical aspect of their expositions and quests even when they wanted to attain states considered to be beyond the human reach. He observed that intuition was never advocated by Indian philosophers. The only notion that corresponds to intuition could be that of pratibhā. It does not play any role in logic. It is left to poets and to yogins as a secondary psychic act. It appears merely in linguistic theory to explain the emerging knowledge of the meaning at the time of hearing the word. On the contrary, he found in Caraka Saṃhitā, a treatise of medicine, a full exposition of logic for the use of doctors, and he often quoted this fact as a remarkable example of the rational attitude of ancient Indian scholars.

He considered the Buddha and Nammāḻvār to be the most representative philosophers of India, even though the former is seen more as the founder of a religion and the latter as a saint or mystic. This was due to an intense personal predilection for Buddhism and due to his personal preference for the sublime, poetical and warm accents of the Tamil poet. It was also based on his observation of the pervasive presence of psychology in Buddhist doctrines and of ontology in mystic poetry. None has expressed more powerfully and directly than Nammāḻvār the concept of Being, which even while being an abstract idea, is also present in its humblest reflections in this world. None has expressed more sincerely the feeling of wonder that rises at becoming aware of their affinity. Nammāḻvār is a mystic, but in the object of his worship, even though it be material, localised and limited, he sees the universal Being. His mind does not interfere with his love, it nourishes it on the contrary, through rationalisation.

Jean Filliozat sometimes alluded to his personal belief in a few lofty Indian ideas, especially in the Ramanujian idea that the plenitude of Being is achieved by its immanence in the world that is accepted as a qualification of God. In times of suffering he found solace not in the Sankarian denial of the world, but by the conception of the world as a well-ordered structure, whether this conception was in the form of a scientific discovery of natural laws, or in the form of a mental construction of an order of things manifesting the plenitude of Being, and in the course of history the Indian genius has often created such remarkable constructions.

Pondicherry, 1988 PIERRE-SYLVAIN FILLIOZAT

PART I

HISTORY OF RELIGIONS

CHAPTER 1

CHARITY IN INDIAN THOUGHT*

ANY GENERAL ENQUIRY into a religious question must always start with the knowledge of the facet that it mirrors of the Indian world. This world, in itself so rich and by virtue of its influence on the Far-East, so vast, constitutes in the history of religion one of the prime domains, a domain that abounds in ancient documents and testimonies and which at the same time continues to hold sway, even today, on the minds of the people of that region. As regards the question of the concept of charity in India, it has already attracted much controversy, especially the notion of charity among the Buddhists. An equivalent of Christian charity has always been sought in Buddhism: in *maitrī*, which was even considered to be a more comprehensive virtue than its Christian counterpart since it embraced, beyond one's neighbour, all beings. This Buddhist idea of charity has also been contrasted with the 'indifference' of Brahmanism which, in its ancient form, was held to be basically a ritualism and in its classical, mediaeval and modern form as Hinduism was believed to hold individuality to be illusory. Therefore, according to this interpretation Hinduism does not believe that individuals should attract our feelings of charity. But these conceptions have been the butt of a great deal of criticism, much of which is often well-founded. However, this question was probed into often in a most partial way and the prematurely comparative method adopted in the probing did not take it far. The concept of charity in India should be studied in all its complexity and depth, within the context of the totality of Indian religions. In this article we shall limit ourselves to some key features of the concept of charity and their appraisal will be made within the philosophical systems of which they are a part and which lend them their actual significance.

***La charité dans le monde indien*, Cahiers de la vie spirituelle. L' Amour du prochain, Les éditions du Cerf. Paris, 1945, p. 327-45.

We shall follow the historical sequence of the testimonies that enable us to understand charity. What do we understand by 'charity'? We mean, on the one hand, love of another and of the Supreme Being; on the other, concrete manifestations of altruism: the former being the charity of love and the latter the charity of beneficence.

The oldest documents, those of the Vedic era, do not help us determine in any way what place either of these two forms had, but one feature is conspicuous: the importance attributed to the act of giving. It is true in most cases that what is meant is not simply a charitable giving, but the value of the giving, a point that is mentioned very early on, and is quite pertinent for explaining certain aspects of beneficence in the subsequent religious areas.

Munificence, much glorified in Vedic texts, is understood mainly as that which is bestowed for the good of gods and of the doer of the sacrifice, and it cannot be adequately explained simply in terms of the greed of the priestly class. If that had been the only reason, wouldn't it have been exposed in its true colours at once? On the other hand, this exhortation to free giving and the condemnation of avarice are clear pointers to the later glorification of renunciation; they lead us to consider the concept of the act of giving, as it actually prevailed in those very early times, as a means of self-perfection, as a virtue. Lastly and above all, in the early Vedic texts sacrifice is considered indispensable for the maintenance of the cosmic order, free giving is therefore deemed obligatory as it celebrates that order in an ample and uninterrupted way. It is the condition of universal well-being, and in this light it is altruistic. Moreover it confers on the doer of the sacrifice great merit.

The philosophy of the Upaniṣads in the Brahmanic period saw in all things and behind the physical and psychic personality involved in the world an underlying universal Being whose essence is pure self-existence but this did not take away from the belief in the cosmic utility of sacrifice. From then on, the Brahmanic ideal of life was to make contribution towards a stable order of the world even while one abstained from it in order to find oneness with the universal self. Man should strive for both at the proper time. In youth, one ought to cultivate a sense of duty through study and try to master passion through chastity. One should then fulfil the social duty of the householder and give oneself completely to works of sacrifice. Finally when one's posterity has been assured, one renounces the world to seek the Self common to all things and to oneself, unless one has already renounced the world for the supreme goal of life. It is detachment then that crowns life; it is ordained not only to those who can offer rich gifts to brahmins but mostly to the brahmins themselves. What is meant here is not just a renunciation of things that could be transferred to others but also the renunciation of personal joys: a total selflessness. In these conditions, the act of giving has a triple value: it confers merit, it leads to detachment and it contributes to the good of all. In the Brahmanic tradition the act of giving was of cardinal importance and it has been universally esteemed as above all virtues in the Indian perception, its usual expression being acts of welfare and especially a welfare leading to the perfection of oneself first and the happiness of others in consequence.

The act of giving and beneficence on such a basis clearly exists in ancient Brahmanism as expressions of sympathy and solicitude for beings. Total detachment is both an accomplishment and a limitation. It does not anticipate the elimination of the spontaneous sense of altruism and compassion, which are given the opportunity for expression when one is actively involved in life. Brahman himself, the Universal Self, is full of compassion when he assumes the form of God the Creator, that is to say when he is, in a way, actively involved in the world. Therefore, the Buddhists appropriately ascribe to the god Brahman four characteristic poises (*vihāra*): goodwill (*maitrī*), compassion (*karuṇā*), contentment (*muditā*) and undisturbed calm (*upekṣā*). It is also known on the basis of the experience of Brahmanic yogis (*Yoga-sūtra*, 1,33) that the feeling of goodwill occurs in relation to bliss, that of compassion in relation to suffering, those of contentment and imperturbability in relation to merit and demerit respectively. This information drawn from the Buddhists and from yogis could be dismissed as too belated in time to be applied to ancient Brahmanism but even in the Brahmanism of the Upaniṣads, Brahman's solicitude for the world is reiterated. There, one finds Brahman revealing the truth that shall be given to men and according to the *Chandogya Upaniṣad*, his mythical representative, Sanatkumāra, the 'perenially young man', saves the suffering beings through the revelation of Truth. The old Vedic religion itself clearly spoke of the 'saving' gods, the Aśvin twins. But charity, which is a human virtue, does not appear yet as the love of God.

In ancient Buddhism, Buddha who is human even though superior to all beings, is full of charity. His charity is not directed to any divine being, but it is altruistic in the sense that it is through compassion for others, through the discovery that suffering is joined to transient life, that he began seeking for the remedy to this universal suffering and finally became the Buddha, that is to say, "awakened" to the Truth that eliminates this suffering. However his compassion isn't merely love of others. According to the legend, which is often a reflection of his disciples' ideas, Buddha himself possessed all the worldly joys but he was moved on seeing the suffering of others though his own fate too moved him. It is the realisation that he too was subject to suffering that made him seek the secret of its cessation. He, therefore, acted out of charity both for himself as well as for others. And once he attained the goal he hesitated to reveal his supreme discovery to others, certainly not because of self-interest but because he wasn't quite sure that men would be able to understand it. Nevertheless he resolved upon imparting it to all, with the hope that at least a few would understand it. As the oft-repeated, fixed canonical saying goes: he did this 'for the good of the multitude, for the common well-being, as a gesture of compassion towards the world, for the interest, good and happiness of gods and men'. He even waved temptation aside, the temptation offered by the Evil Spirit to enter into the Repose of *Nirvāṇa* without waiting to establish firmly his Law among men. In a host of past-lives, both animal and human, he practised free giving which to Brahmanism was very important, and he carried it to its extreme. He offered everything to others regardless of all consequences: his wealth, his wife, his children, his body, his suffering, his life. He is, therefore, the hero of charity, but not the charity which is pure love and which Saint Paul compared to the heroism of Giving in his address to the Corinthians: 'And when I have distributed all my possessions and consigned my body to the flames, if I have no charity, it is of no use to me' (I, *Cor.* 13, 3). An examination of the Buddhist idea of love of others will make this clearer.

First of all, this love isn't founded on the love of God to which one may be led by loving another created in God's own image and therefore worthy of love because of our love of God. It consists in magnifying our natural feelings of sympathy and pity for sentient beings who are either happy or unhappy. Two states of being accompany these sentiments, two that are the first two attributes of Brahman: *maitrī* and *karuṇā.*

Maitrī is a feeling of affection or of friendly goodwill felt for all beings unconditionally, for all beings endowed with sensibility and who are not in a state of suffering—for suffering provokes the feeling of pity or *karuṇā. Karuṇā* is then merely a specific expression of the former. Ideally, *maitrī* is represented mainly by a father's or a mother's affection for their child and it can flow from a superior being to inferior ones. Considering that *maitrī* is compared to paternal or maternal love, it might seem a little strange to see it being applied indiscriminately and with the same intensity to any creature whosoever. It would seem reasonable to feel pity for a suffering creature but it is difficult to imagine an almost paternal kind of love bing bestowed on a serpent that apparently lives in a happy state. One could then be led to regard such a sentiment as unreal or unnatural, certainly inhuman, even though it might be considered sublime in its exaggerated form.

However, the ideal of *maitrī* can be understood when it is viewed in the light of the concepts of the spiritual milieu that extols it.

Firstly, there is no irrevocable antagonism between different categories of beings: groups of beings endowed with a soul and others who are without. All forms, whether they are human, animal, demoniac, infernal, divine are part of the same series of physical existence which the individual can embody depending on his past actions, as he transmigrates from one form into another. This individual being exists although schools differ in their views regarding his nature—some consider him to be a being with personality susceptible to merit or demerit while another more commonly held view sees him, not as a unitary personality but merely a specific amalgamation of psychic elements. These psychic elements are preserved imprints of ideas that accompanied particular actions and thus form a psychic entity linked to the physical body. This psychic entity does not die with the body but it reincarnates, in conformity with the tendencies of its actions, in a new physical body after the dissolution of the previous one. All species of beings assume the forms that are infused, in their turn, by the same psychic individualities and should, therefore, be regarded equally: they have equal rights to our compassion.

Secondly, the Buddhist must not discriminate between beings of the same species on the basis of his personal affinity with them as he has to renounce all attachment to the 'I' and 'mine' and, consequently, look upon those close to him as well as upon strangers with an equal eye. With such an uniformity of attitude being called for, Buddhism could have turned into a religion of general indifference but instead it turned into one of compassion.

The other alternative may have seemed more natural. In fact, the Buddhist's struggle against suffering, a struggle which provides his life with its very *raison-d'etre*, consists mainly in battling against all emotional attachment, against all passionate impulse which could leave another new imprint in the unconscious, psychic body whose individuality is made up of the totality of these imprints and which is what transmigrates and provides a mooring to suffering. As far as the Buddhist is concerned, this body has to be dissolved. The saint's ideal is to abolish it in order to escape rebirth, to reach the state of *Nirvāṇa*, the ultimate annihilation. Attachment to the 'I' and 'mine' and all other passion must, therefore, be eliminated, total indifference is the final objective of the Buddhist endeavour. In reality, it is not always so, because otherwise, the movement towards salvation would itself be arrested. The indifference that the Buddhist seeks is only in relation to temptation and aggression, in relation to all that could make him succumb to love and hatred. The virtue of energy continues to be uppermost for a Buddhist. However, even if total aloofness from activity was sought, it could only be realised after much struggle and such a struggle would bring into play forces superior to the passions to be conquered; or else it must shun the latter and retain their energy in order to use it for higher goals. Love of oneself in its present individuality is self-delusion for it is an unstable conjunction of phenomenal elements that are the playthings of suffering. It is most difficult to get rid of this self-delusion, this love of one's self and of others for oneself is one of the most perilous impulses. But its violence can be diverted away from oneself by a complete transfer onto others, without any discrimination whatsoever, without any preference for anyone, either one's neighbour or onto any other. He who wants to renounce the 'I' should no longer think of neighbour or stranger, for these exist only in relation to the 'I'.

Edifying Buddhist literature constantly extols *maitrī* for this reason, especially for creatures with whom man is least attached. Here too, it is compared to paternal or maternal love as this is made up of both ardour and self-abnegation, the force of protection from suffering and self-sacrifice. It is already quite evident that *maitrī*, love of all to the exclusion of oneself, cannot be identified with charity which is love of the neighbour as oneself.

The guarding virtue of *maitrī* which makes it similar to paternal love in its aspect of protection has actually, at its base, quite a unique connotation. It isn't so much a vigilant and thoughtful solicitude as a state of opposition to violence, and this state automatically confers invulnerability on the one who is propelled by *maitrī*, not on the person on whom this *maitrī* is bestowed, as if paternal love protected not the son but the father. Because of this quality egoism does not, in any way, take the upper hand, for, indirectly, it protects the child as well when the latter, under the father's influence, adopts the same attitude of *maitrī* towards those beings from whom some evil might come.

This will become clearer with a few examples taken from legend which although slightly exaggerated, are more clearly revelatory of the mind that imagined them.

We see in the accounts of Buddha's life that he overcame *Māra* and his hordes' attacks through *maitrī* (*Lalitavistara*, end of chap. 21). On the other hand, according to the Great Chronicle of Ceylon, a future king, the son of a lion and a princess, grew indignant at having a beast for father and wanted to kill him. Thrice, his arrows rebounded upon his feet because of the lion's attitude of *maitrī* (*mettacitta* in Pāli) As long as the lion was full of paternal love, nothing happened but when he was overtaken by anger the arrow pierced him through (*Mahāvansa*, 6, 28-30). In both these cases, *maitrī* acted as a protective spell without in any way mitigating the assailants. It is because *maitrī* is so radically opposed to violence that the latter cannot encroach upon its domain, no more than void can trespass into being. The whole of India has reiterated this up to our times, through a Tagore or a Gandhi: what can conquer hatred is not hatred but benevolence. But where existence or being vanishes, vacuity sets in, where *maitrī* yields violence takes over. Once the Buddha was told that a monk had been bitten by a serpent. The Buddha said the monk must not have radiated the feeling of *maitrī* for serpents (Cullavagga, 5,6). He did not want to foolishly imply that the monk should have looked upon serpents as his own children but through this accident he imparted a protective formula of *maitrī* against all beings, a formula that is effective in the name of excellence of the Buddha, of the Dharma and of Saṅgha, a formula of which *maitrī* must be the vector and power.

In this last instance the mitigating quality of *maitrī* is focused on, which was not the case in the preceding instances. There are many other instances where this virtue brings about the conversion of the wicked. In addition to its protective quality, benevolence has a communicative force. When Buddha miraculously directs his *maitrī* from a distance on the impious prince, Roja the Malla, the latter cannot but be drawn towards him. When a mad elephant is released to crush him, the Buddha meets the creature with *maitrī* and at once the beast calms down and kneels obediently. In another version, the elephant is said to follow him from that moment and he dies when he can no longer see him any more. These are some of the most well-known examples. They suffice to show that in popular Buddhist sentiment gentleness guides us towards the good, does not entangle us in existence and encourages renunciation—unlike passion which creates a craving for pleasure for oneself. This gentleness was considered an essential mode of *maitrī*.

In any case, in the strict ideal of the Buddhist *arhant*, i.e. the perfect technician of salvation in the ancient community, *maitrī*, compassion for all, and *karuṇā*, pitiful compassion, tended to be stripped of all gentleness, all warmth of feeling which elsewhere were equated with charity even though it is quite different from the Christian concept. For the *arhant* they almost ceased to be considered as qualities of love and became means of psychological purification. This is so because the *arhant*, even while emulating the Buddha, strives, above everything else, to attain a perfection built by a systematic elimination of all feeling and sensibility. In a radical effort at destroying the 'I' and its attachments, he is not content to divert from his own self onto others all natural impulse of sympathy in order to grant them the benefit; instead he stifles it. It is a difficult achievement that compels our admiration, for the *arhant* is 'one who has a right to respect'. The tradition of Buddhist schools, struck above all by the greatness of the battle he must fight, forgets the original meaning of the word *arhant* and explained it as 'one who kills his enemy' (*ari-han*) a meaning linguistically unjustified but illustrative of the idea that inspired it. Passion, hatred and stupidity are the enemies whereas he is ascetic, unflinching and clear. He is not charitable. Benevolence and pity in him are only the absence of hostility and ruthlessness. The legend mentions in addition some *arhants*, from among the most illustrious ones too, whom we might judge to be hard and pitiless. Kāśyapa the Great is one of these, a faultless master and an implacable defender of the Buddhist Law who took over as the Leader of the Community after Buddha's passing and treated even the pious and humane Ānanda harshly, the disciple who had served the Buddha till the very end of his life. In fact, Kāśyapa did so because Ānanda being absorbed in his love of and devotion to the Blissful one had not practised the difficult method of detachment which leads one to the state of an *arhant*; Kāśyapa excluded him from the council that was held to establish the Buddha's teaching and where Ānanda's participation as the principal witness was indispensable. He was kept out until he attained that perfection. We are even told about Kāśyapa hurling an unfortunate nun into hell with a mere look because on one occasion she wanted to intercede on Ānanda's behalf when Kāśyapa was reprimanding him.

It is certain that in the ancient Canonical Buddhist texts which are now usually termed *Hīnayāna*, the 'Little Vehicle' (it would be more correct to say 'the Lower Way of Progress') based on the name that was to be given to it by subsequent reformers, the ideal of the *arhant*, perfect saint but devoid of real charity, has played a leading role. However we do not think that this ideal was present at the origin or that it constituted an essential part. It did not prevail to such an extent as to obliterate charity in the form we inherited from the most ancient forms of the legend of the Buddha who is its supreme example. It seems more likely that it represents a tendency towards austerity felt in the practice of a thorough psychological technique but which could have emerged quite early on since the institution of this technique seems to go back to the time of the Buddha himself.

In any case, in the set-up of social living, ancient Buddhism has always encouraged the charity of welfare. We have its proof in the middle of the 3rd century B.C., during the time when the theoretical ideal of the *arhant* was in full sway, in the very region of the Buddha's preaching and in the country from which claims to originate the Buddhist school of Ceylon and Indochina, the school which extols best the ideal of the *arhant*; in the kingdom of Magadha in Central India. Aśoka, king of Magadha, but in fact ruler of almost the entire country except the Extreme South, gives us a proof about the existence of such a charity in his famous inscriptions found scattered everywhere.

Aśoka himself narrates how he was moved by the misery caused by his conquest of the Kalinga kingdom and renounced violence and strove from then on that all beings be provided security, mastery over themselves, equanimity and gentleness (XIII Edict on stone); he wanted happiness for them as he did for his own children (Ist Edict at Dhauli and Jauga). He abolished the slaughter of animals for his own consumption (Ist Edict on rock). He performed more and more deeds of solicitude and of benevolence. He took care of men and animals (it was formerly mis-translated: he got built hospitals for men and animals), he got wells dug and useful plants cultivated (II Edict on rock). For the good of beings all must, he declares, abide within the general Right Order and this can exist only if all beings are at peace and well-looked after. And he sent people to preach this Order, even to foreign countries, right up to the Greek kingdoms. The preservation of the Right Order and the protection of all creatures in their well-being are the most important duties of an Indian king whatever his personal religion. But Aśoka's extraordinary zeal for the good of others was prompted by his moral crisis during the conquest of Kalinga as well as by his conversion to Buddhism which took place at that time. At other times, too, the solicitude for institutions of welfare and the charitable 'giving' of the law through preaching, are testified to in the ancient schools of Buddhism.

In Jainism which developed simultaneously and in quite an analogous manner in several respects with Buddhism, the problem of charity arises in quite a similar way and goes back to very early times. Welfare has remained to this day one of the most striking features of this religion which unlike Buddhism is still alive and actively practised in India. It is in Jainism that the mindfulness to avoid harm is pushed to its highest degree. As in Buddhism, but much more severely, it is absolutely necessary to abstain from all violence towards others even involuntary violence. And one is to abstain from violence towards all beings and not merely towards one's neighbours. For preference to a neighbour too bespeaks of 'I'. A man free from I-consciousness cannot possibly entertain such preferences. It has been, therefore, established in the Jaina Canons for long time that it is not only important to abstain from killing and violence but, in a good number of cases, it is also essential to take all precautions to avoid killing even flies by sweeping the place where one sits and by filtering drinking water. The Jaina saints are expected to wear a veil which will protect minute creatures from drowning in the mouth or eyes. It is Jainism that founded a large number of charitable institutions and established hospitals for animals which are well-known in travellers' accounts.

Certain ancient sects that are known primarily through Buddhist and Jaina texts (which condemned them), were strictly fatalist. As a matter of principle they were not supposed to make any effort in favour of beings whose destiny was ineluctable. However, it cannot be ruled out that pity occupied a very strong place in these sects which by desisting from the fight against attachment to the 'I' could, as a matter of fact, give freer vent to the spontaneous feelings. The feeling of benevolence and pity was far too widespread in every part of India under various nuances and different names (we have but studied a part) to make it possible for a philosophy to uniformly abolish it from among all its adepts.

Compassion is tempered sometimes by the effects of a widely-held belief in the automatic retribution of actions. For those who do not consider happiness or unhappiness to be accidental but who believe that the fortunate or unfortunate circumstances of our successive lives are determined by the traces left in our psychic body by our acts, there is no guiltless sufferer. Pity for a sufferer might be great but then it is pity directed at an expiating criminal. The idea that he experiences only that which he deserves can mitigate the sense of pity it inspires and it encourages a rather vulgar kind of passivity vis-a-vis the suffering of others. It can, however, help in increasing our abhorrence for evil which is the inevitable catalyst of suffering and it can fortify the redeeming urge for goodness. Such a radical fatalism would turn charity into something futile by eliminating the sense of responsibility and by considering that everyone, even a criminal, merits his suffering. On the contrary, the belief in the automatic nature of retribution lends to charity the status of an enemy of evil and of suffering in general.

In the Buddhist reform of the *Mahāyāna* or 'the Great Way of Progress', taken up in the very first centuries of our era, a reform which moreover sometimes merely elaborated certain trends that were already present in ancient Budhhism, *maitrī*, *karuṇā* and free giving took on a predominant role in the ideal of conduct. The ideal saint is no more the *arhant* but the *Bodhisattva*, the transfigured replica of the Buddha as described by legend in the course of his long and sublime preparation for the Final Awakening. In the ancient tradition, it was only the *bodhisattva*, 'the being on the path of awakening', who dedicated himself unceasingly to other beings in the course of his preparatory lives and was destined to become the 'Awakened One', the Buddha. The ordinary saint was content to be the *arhant*. In the Mahāyāna, the seeker of sainthood aspired to emulate the Bodhisattva and a host of other mythological bodhisattvas. He would dedicate himself to others and sacrifice for them even the benefit of his own salvation, and he solemnly vowed to postpone his liberation to after theirs. From then on, for ordinary adepts, the great Bodhisattvas whose mythological representation was to a great degree inspired from Brahmanism and from aspects of Brahma himself, became helpful divinities and in this guise spread to a great part of the Far East. And although many adepts were, as elsewhere, seekers only of grace, in the case of bodhisattvas we can still speak of charity in the sense of love of God. But in theory love of oneself would always remain strictly excluded.

The disciple is not a creation of the bodhisattvas or of a multitude of Buddhas or of the one Buddha abiding above everything. He can love the bodhisattva who leans down to help him or the Buddhas who help him against his suffering. He can also love them for their infinite greatness. But he realises that his personality is only an illusion. It is devoid of its own self in the sense that it does not exist by itself, eternal and permanent; it is only a transitory collection of conscious and unconscious psychic phenomena, the unconscious phenomena being greater in number, and thus constituting a basic psychism which is not homogenous but composite in nature and subject to misery. The apparent autonomy of the personality and of visible beings is merely the product of a well-linked dream. As in ancient Buddhism, the liberation from the 'I' is a primordial necessity, the offering of all that one has and especially oneself, a cathartic operation. He who gives is like a convict who relinquishes his chains, but chains that would bring happiness to the other. Free giving in itself is, therefore, an agent of goodness; it opposes suffering which is its greatest enemy and helps in creating merit. Giving has enjoyed this prestige in the general Indian opinion from the time of ancient Brahmanism and Vedism. The giver helps the beneficiary either in a temporary way or permanently when it is the Buddhist Law that he gives and he unburdens himself of the 'I'. In this view, a well-ordered charity begins with the others. It is even directed exclusively to others without being a charity of 'investment', since any expectation of returns to oneself would cancel it out.

Therefore, ideally, giving must be totally selfless. As a consequence it can come into full play only after detachment from the self is complete and in that state one may wonder if it can still be called love. One could easily be led to think that in the logic of such a system it is no more than a generosity that is mechanical. When we are told that Nāgārjuna, the bodhisattva, because of a vow he had made never to refuse anybody anything offered his head to a young rogue who asked for it, we can think that bodhisattva proved not so much his love for the first person who turned up but rather his steadfastness to the rule of giving and his indifference for himself. What he gave, he had given up for long and did not need to feel any sense of benevolence in order to offer it to him. However, the motivation for giving and for the virtues of benevolence and pity is so close to love (*prema*), even according to the Mahāyānist thinkers themselves, that they often felt greatly concerned to know whether this love was indeed without peril and not of the nature which attaches one to life and thus thwarts one's liberation (*Mahāyānasūtrālaṅkāra,* 13, 20-23). The answer was negative. In *Mahāyāna*, the spiritual seeker is entitled to love others, theory does not prevail against go odness.

Love for others was similarly viewed in later Brahmanism and in Hinduism in most of its tendencies. Although the active aspects of the gods derive their profound being from the One Reality without any qualification or emotion, these aspects do not normally prevent them from helping men. The bulk of the teachings, not merely religious but technical and scientific as well, were said to be given by Brahma and Śiva out of compassion for humanity. And men, immersed in the sea of devotion, *bhakti*, which was so widespread in India, surrender themselves to God, particularly to Viṣṇu, leaning on him. There too, philosophical speculations might underrate benevolence and pity, as they underline the inconsistent nature of personality and therefore obliterate both the subject and the object of this benevolence and pity. But they dismiss them purely from the ontological point of view. If they deny them a self-existent, eternal reality, it concedes them a reality of appearance on the basis of a distinction which also exists in Buddhist doctrines and is in fact more explicitly present in them. If nature is but a fleeting illusion compared to the Self, within nature, in the universe, in society, in man, good and evil are not devoid of interest and love is a pre-eminent virtue.

The Bhagavadgītā, one of the oldest and most popular sacred texts on which the movements of *bhakti* were founded, speaks of the supremacy of the Absolute Self and prescribes detachment from the 'I'. But it reveals this Absolute to be present in all the forms of this world and advocates action in this world as a state-duty provided it is carried out in detachment from the fruit it can produce. The Supreme Self is the object of all devotion and is immanent in all beings and therefore the Gītā clearly declares that they attain this Self, those who joyfully seek the good of all beings. (12,4).

It is therefore for the love of the Supreme Self that love flows out to others, love of oneself being excluded or rather depersonalised and merged into love for the Supreme Self. Once again, the preservation of the altruistic and personal urge but without falling back on the ego seems to be the nature of Indian charity. The rejection of the 'I' as a goal results in this charity losing in ardour what it gains in serenity and wideness. In the movements of *bhakti*, the perception of the Supreme Self in all beings and even in all things culminates finally in distributing this benevolence and sympathy over the whole of nature. Even in its extreme form, love for God is the right of all things. Perhaps nowhere else except among the Tamil speaking Vaiṣṇava saints of South India has love of God in all ended in a more widely human charity, a charity which disdaining all rules of the Brahmanic social order, leads a saint to come to the aid of an untouchable.

Thus, under diverse forms in several religions, Indian charity appears to us as obviously different from Christian charity as it is associated with other views and other beliefs but comparable in some important features in several of its manifestations and characterised in general by the fact that it is led by a spontaneous feeling of joy in the happiness of others and of pain in their suffering, as well as by its philosophic refusal to discriminate among others the neighbour and the stranger, vis-a-vis the 'I', the egoism of which is condemned by morality and is dissolved by ontological thought.

CHAPTER 2

VAIṢṆAVA DEVOTION IN THE TAMIL COUNTRY*

SO FAR SANSKRIT philology and Buddhist studies have dominated Indological research, and this is quite understandable. Sanskrit culture by itself largely dominates the whole of Indian civilisation and is its uniting factor. It is again the same culture which got established in all the regions of India and thanks to its reputation of being a culture of great erudition, formed the crux of the Indian influence in Asia and the Far East. Even when Indian culture expressed itself in languages other than Sanskrit, its principal themes, or at least much of its material, were still provided by Sanskrit literature. Sanskrit is the Latin of Asia beyond Iran. On its part, Buddhism is one of the major religions of the world. Its study is indispensable in relation to Christianity or to Islam, as one of the great universal attempts to exceed the human condition. It is one of the essential factors in the spread of Indian culture and consequently of Indian history. And what interests us is not merely its actual role, and although Indologists must have been justly proud of having discovered this at a time when India herself had forgotten it, but also the nature of its doctrines and its methods that make of it a subject of exceptional interest and study. As it appears today—at least to my mind—Buddhism, more than being a religion, is a psychological discipline like several others India developed through yoga—even though it has given rise, up to this day, to great strictly religious developments. In the 19th century, when Buddhism was discovered, Europe could not reconcile itself to the increased appeal at Buddhism because she had too rudimentary a knowledge of psychology and, particularly, at psychological techniques that Buddhism had come to develop.

*Lecture delivered at the ISMEO at the invitation of Prof. Tucci, then Director of ISMEO and published under the title *La dévotion vishnouite au pays tamoul*, in *conferenze*, ISMEO, Rome, Vol. II, 1954, p. 81-109.

However, I would have certainly responded in a better way to the honour that Professor Tucci has kindly conferred on me by inviting me to address you if I had come to this important centre of Buddhist studies to share with you some reflections on a subject that is relevant to these studies. But I am well aware that I do not possess the knowledge of a specialist on the subject and I thought that I could make better use of this wonderful opportunity of a conversation between two schools of Indology in another way: To tell you about some new researches and to seek your encouragement as well as your useful cautionary suggestions.

Indeed, even if these studies of Sanskrit and Buddhism rightly dominate Indological studies, we are conscious that they do not embrace its entire range. In South India, Dravidian literature, and specifically Tamil literature, more ancient and richer than its sister-literatures, has stood for two thousand years,—or, probably, more,—as a permanent rival of Sanskrit literature. And we mean this not merely as a widely-accepted national literature that obstinately survived or may have even developed side by side with the erudite Sanskrit literature that was imported from the North. Tamil literature by itself contains an enormous quantity of scholarly works and covers the entire cycle of the traditional, classical teachings of the country. In this respect, Tamil stands out from among all other Indian languages, be they Indo-Aryan, Dravidian or of any other group. In no other province of India except in the Tamil country, has the local language been sufficiently rich and varied, even if possessing a splendid body of literature, to permit truly exhaustive studies in any branch of learning: everywhere the complete pandit could find fulfilment only through Sanskrit. This has legitimised, and quite often too, the feeling among some contemporary Tamils that their culture owes nothing to Sanskrit since it is complete in itself.

This feeling is certainly not totally justified. These Tamils could acquire, without learning Sanskrit, the same level of culture as that acquired by those who knew Sanskrit, but then precisely for want of its study, they are unaware that to a great extent their scientific books impart to them the same information as that found in Sanskrit books and by using mostly the same technical Sanskrit terminology, or at least, by expressing it in a manner that is very similar to that in Sanskrit.

The opposite illusion that the importance of Tamil literature is derived entirely from its having very freely robbed, adapted or imitated Sanskrit literature, was very widespread in the West during a time when it was believed that in India civilisation could have originated only among the peoples who possessed an Indo-Aryan language.

In reality, it is evident today that Tamil literature is partly a take-off on Sanskrit literature and partly altogether original. Taking up the same themes and teachings as contained in Sanskrit literature, it deals with them very thoroughly, leaving the Veda aside which cannot be conceived in any other language except Sanskrit. When it is original it lends classical and traditional forms to the works of the popular, national genius or to the feelings and ideas of its thinkers. And it is not in the beginnings of Tamil literature that Sanskrit influences are most profoundly felt. Almost all the ancient literary works have traces of the knowledge of Sanskrit traditions but they are often very insignificant. It is at a relatively later date that Sanskrit works greatly influenced Tamil literature—an example of it will be taken up shortly—and the fact that it did not get submerged was because this Tamil literature was already in full bloom.

What was more, the Tamil country provided to Sanskrit literature—at a time when Sanskrit studies were most in vogue there —front-ranking authors who drew much of their inspiration either directly or through tradition from the original Tamil literature which they transposed into Sanskrit. Rāmānuja is a case in point.

Hailing from Śrīperumbūdūr to the west of Madras, Rāmānuja became at Śrīraṅgam near Tiruchirapalli, the successor of Āḷavandār (Yāmunācārya in Sanskrit). The latter was one of the leaders of the Śrīvaiṣṇava sect and the grandson of Nāthamuni, the founder of the Śrīraṅgam centre, who around 1000 A.D., had piously collected the hymns of the illustrious Tamil saints, the Āḻvārs. It is these Āḻvārs, their doctrines and their devotion that we shall deal with briefly.

The poem of glorification (Māhātmya) (of Bhāgavatapurāṇa), the great text of Vaiṣṇava devotion, relates a brief story of

Kṛṣṇa-bhakti, the devotion to God Kṛṣṇa (I, 47-49). It is Bhakti herself who speaks. She declares Draviḍa to be her place of birth, Draviḍa being the Tamil country; she grew up in Karṇāṭaka, in Mahārāṣṭra and Gurjara she became old; there she was persecuted; but then she regained her youth in Vṛndāvan. We might be justified in doubting the authenticity of this tale, since being a devotee of Kṛṣṇa, Bhakti should have been born in the region where the epic Mahābhārata as well as Tamil tradition itself situates the descent of Viṣṇu as Kṛṣṇa, in the region where the Mahābhārata War takes place, i.e. in the heart of North and not South India. More precisely in North India among the Śūrasenas of Mathurā, a town neighbouring Vṛndāvana. At the end of the 4th century, Megasthenes was struck here by the cult of a God whom he called Heracles (Arrien, *Inde*, VIII, 5) but who should rather be identified with Kṛṣṇa although he confuses him with a god of the South, father of Pandaia who himself is Śiva according to the legend which corresponds best to the one which he relates and which has been preserved for us in the Tamil *Tiruviḷaiyāḍalpurāṇam*. There exist instances where the settings of Northern legends were transferred to the South and on the basis of which we may be inclined to think that the cult of Kṛṣṇa was borrowed by the South from Northern sources even if other indications tend to establish that it got mixed there with the cult of another young god with whom he might have been identified, even as this young god was also identified in Śaivaism with Śiva and chiefly with Kumāra.

Nevertheless, we can understand the error made by *Bhāgavatamāhātmya*, since, to my mind there does seem to be an error. In fact, the *Bhāgavatapurāṇa* itself reveals to us the basis of the idea that devotion to Kṛṣṇa was born in the Tamil country. According to it, those beings who lived in the ages of the world that were anterior to *Kaliyuga*, the worst of all ages, want to be reborn in it, however ruthless it might be; for it is in Kaliyuga and particularly in the Draviḍa country where flow the Tamraparṇī, the Kṛtamālā, the Payasvinī, the Kāverī, the Pratīcī and the Mahānadī, that men should become the devotees of Vāsudeva thus finding through him their supreme refuge in Nārāyaṇa (*Bhāg. Pur.*, XI, V, 38-40). This, according to Surendranath Dasgupta's indications (*A History of Indian Philosophy*,

III, 63) means that the *Bhāgavata* considers as models of Vaiṣṇava devotion the Tamil saints known as the Āḻvārs, the most important of whom are supposed to have lived, according to Tamil tradition, in the region watered by the rivers enumerated above. The *māhātmya* considers these saints to be the true founders of Vaiṣṇava *bhakti*.

But it should be noted that according to the *Bhāgavata*, it is in *Kaliyuga* that these saints were to be born—therefore after Kṛṣṇa's death, the point from which Kaliyuga started (*Viṣṇu-purāṇa*, IV, XXIV, 36; *Bhāg. Pur.* XI, VII, 4). However, other saints devoted to Kṛṣṇa could have been born before them. There is nothing in the information contained in the *Bhāgavata* that compels us to believe that if these Vaiṣṇava saints were the most admirable, they were also the first. We should rather suppose that, even if they gave an exceptional impetus to Kṛṣṇa-bhakti, it is precisely because some others from the North had propagated it among them.

However, there exists a tradition, relatively of a later date, of which the *māhātmya* might not have been ignorant and according to which the first Āḻvārs could have been born in the age that preceded the *Kaliyuga*, the *Dwāparayuga*, and only some of them were born in the beginning of *Kaliyuga*. This tradition that consists in preparing the biographies of the line of these saints' disciples, called *Guruparambarei* (Guruparampară), disagrees with the *Bhāgavata*, but the disagreement is not so very obvious from its outlook for it depicts the devotion of the saints as not strictly directed towards Kṛṣṇa but to the eternal Nārāyaṇa. The origin of this tradition which gives exact dates of the Āḻvārs (computing them on the basis of speculations of astronomical chronology), seems to be situated between the time of the writing of the eleventh book of the *Bhāgavata*, which does not know it, and the *māhātmya*, which seems to have accepted it. Whatever the case might be, the Āḻvārs' reputation remains totally unaffected. We can judge this from their works as well as from the power and vitality of the religious impetus they provided and which continues to impel people even today.

* * * *

There are twelve Āḻvārs in all, of whom one is a woman, Āṇḍāl. According to the *Guruparambarei,* four must have lived in the Dwāparayuga and they also belonged to the Pallava kingdom: Poygeiyār, Pūdattār, Pēyār and Tirumaḻicei. Pūdattār has in fact a Sanskrit name as well: Bhūdatta, and he must have been from Māmallai, i.e. Mahābalipuram, city of the Pallava king Narasiṃhavarman I, alias Mahāmalla, which places him actually at 650 A.D.

Three others belong to the Chola kingdom: Tiruppāṉ, Toṇḍāḍippoḍi and Tirumaṅgei. Only one bearing a Sanskrit name, Kulacēgarar, i.e. Kulaśekhara, is from the Cera country. And lastly four, Periyāḻvār, Āṇḍāl, Nammāḻvār and Madurakavi are from the Pāṇḍya country.

The works, in verse, which are attributed to them are of very unequal lengths, Nammāḻvār being by far the most prolific among them. Their language is not the most ancient form of Tamil as it is known to us today but it is closer to it than to modern Tamil. We can characterise it in short as the Tamil of the Early Middle Ages.

Nammāḻvār is indisputably the most important of these saints and his name means "Our Āḻvār", "Our Saint", but it was rather a nickname. His family name was Māṟaṉ or Kārimāṟaṉ, Kāri being his father. Several other names or nicknames are attributed to him, the most common one being Saḍagobaṉ, i.e. Śaṭhakopa in Sanskrit, "he who is enraged by falsehood".

Tradition describes him to be born at Teṉgurugūr, on the banks of the river Tamraparṇī, a village which came to be known as Āḻvārtirunagari, the 'sacred town of the Āḻvār'. Dumb in his childhood, he is said to have spent it in a temple seated steadfastly like a yogin under a Tamarind tree. At the age of sixteen, one day speech is said to have suddenly returned to him as the Āḻvar Madurakavi was passing by him and, blessed by visions of Viṣṇu, he supposedly sang his first hymns. His work, however, far from being that of an unlettered devotee, does not necessarily contradict the legend, for he could have educated himself by listening to discourses at the temple in the forced introversion of his speechlessness, or he could have in any case educated himself later. His hymns bear testimony to a profound knowledge of Vaiṣṇava tradition and of master-works in Tamil like the Kuṟal or in Sanskrit, like the *Bhagavadgītā* even though we have no proof that he read it in the Sanskrit original.

We are more or less certain of his time—thanks to some illuminating observations of T.A. Gopinatha Rao (*Sir Subramanya Ayyar Lectures on the History of Śrī-Vaiṣṇavas*, Madras, 1923): about the end of the 8th century in all likelihood. However a very small part of his work has been studied and we cannot vouchsafe that we have it today in the very form that he gave to it.

A gap seems to lie between the Āḻvārs and their school which was successively directed by different masters, *ācāryas*, who were inspired by the former's works. These *ācāryas* collected the hymns of the Āḻvārs sung by devotees and developed around them a prolific literature of exegesis, one part in Tamil, another in Sanskrit and a third section in a special technical jargon, the *Maṇipravaḷam* literally pearl and coral, which is a mixture of Sanskrit and Tamil. The structure of this jargon reveals a tendency of sanskritising the outpourings of the Tamil saints and to reduce their contents to the expression of Vedāntic doctrines. In general, in the texts in *Maṇipravaḷam,* the syntax is Tamil but the conceptual words are in Sanskrit and have a technical Vedāntic meaning. Such texts were useful in adapting the ideas expressed in Tamil stanzas to the taste of a people whose language was Tamil but who were conversant with the Sanskrit Vedāntic philosophy and whose culture was therefore different from that of the more purely Tamil and devoted milieus where these hymns had been composed.

As for the rest, tradition itself underlines the gulf which existed historically between the Āḻvārs and the *ācāryas*. Nāthamuni, the founder of the great school of *ācāryas*, could know only by accident the hymns of Nammāḻvār. He had not been educated at all in a tradition that taught them. It is at Vīranārāyaṇapuram, modern Kaṭṭumaṉṉārkōyil, that he probably first heard them being sung by the pilgrims and, struck by their beauty, must have wanted to have the text of these hymns but the pilgrims knew only a part. However, they told him where the poet lived and Nāthamuni proceeded to Āḻvārtirunagari: there he met Parāṅkuśadāsa who is supposed to have been a disciple of Madurakavi, a contemporary of saint Nammāḻvār and whose visit must have provided the latter,—dumb at the time—, with the determination of singing his hymns. But Parāṅkuśadāsa was obviously not a direct disciple of Madurakavi, or else this Madurakavi was not Nammāḻvār's contemporary, for Nāthamuni and Parāṅkuśadāsa are supposed to have lived around 1000, whereas we have just seen that Nammāḻvār and Madurakavi lived probably in the 8th century (besides, it is possible that Nammāḻvār and Madurakavi are nothing but a duplication of the same person; at least that seems to be the conclusion from an indication given by Kamban the poet in the 12th century).

In any case, the tradition of the hymns was not fully passed on to Parāṅkuśadāsa. What he possessed was never complete. But at the ceaseless chanting of those hymns he knew, Nāthamuni's piety grew more and more intense and, finally, Nammāḻvār himself must have given him the revelation of his works and those of the other Āḻvārs.

In the end we see therefore that it is perhaps futile to mull over the criticism of the chronology of this tradition. It accepts mystic interventions and seems to ignore the intervals of time which could have separated the alleged masters from the alleged disciples. But it bears testimony to the fact that Nāthamuni undertook a laborious rearrangement of this treasure of poignant, venerated, religious songs which had not yet been preserved in a fixed body of sacred scripture.

It is this body of sacred scriptures that Nāthamunī wanted to constitute. He called it the *Nālāyiradivyappirabandam*, the 'Divine bundle of four thousand'. It is composed, as a matter of fact, of four thousand stanzas of which almost twelve hundred are attributed to Nammāḻvār alone. We may certainly doubt the authenticity of texts collected through revelation. We might think Nāthamuni to have been deluded into believing that what was actually rising from his unconscious was a communication from outside. On the other hand, we may also doubt that Nāthamuni really believed that he had acquired these hymns of the Āḻvārs through revelation. An effort at literary arrangement which has nothing of the mystic inspiration, does in fact occasionally surface. The principal work attributed to Nammāḻvār, the *Tiruvāymoli* or the 'Utterance of the Sacred Mouth', is composed of a thousand stanzas, each of which begins with the last word or the preceding one. A text of which all the parts are so interlinked is not just the simple product of a collection of scattered fragments or a composition conceived in a flash in a mystic upsurge in that particular form. At least, it presupposes a work of structuring after a first highly inspired conception. Some would even suspect that it was a fake work of Nāthamuni or blame legend for having wrongly attributed some revelations to him.

In such a case, the hypothesis is often put forth that the compiler fabricated a fake by deliberately attributing his work to a well-known person in order to increase its prestige, and such a hypothesis is quite flattering to the critic who is proud to prove that he has not been duped. But often it is a simplistic hypothesis that ignores all possibility of another explanation, one that could be more probable, of the composition of this presumed forgery. The work may very well be the creation of a well-meaning mind but crossed by complex psychic movements, a mind that interprets its intuitions as revelations and holds to be genuine all that flows out of its system of representation of things. In our particular case, it is unlikely that Nāthamuni's collection was created entirely by him. In his time, texts of fervent devotion had existed for a long time all over the Tamil country, as much among the Śaivas as among the Vaiṣṇavas. We can suppose as tradition would want it that he had gained knowledge of these from the devotees who were familiar with one part and that later he collected them with such an enthusiastic communion with the spirit of these divinely inspired authors that he was able to complement them spontaneously without deviating from their inspiration. And this in no way stopped him from working further, at some later date, in order to add to the texts by means of reordering and retouchings, the regularity of a literary structure to which we referred and which must have been absent in the original composition. The retouchings did not go, however, so far as to wipe out the stylistic differences which mark out the different Āḻvāras.

We therefore have the works of the Āḻvārs in a restored form, no doubt but not without authenticity. The Sanskritised exegesis which was begun immediately after their collection, confirms that we are talking about works from another period and another inspiration and not these of the scholastic Vedānta in vogue then. These works could not have been conceived at that time and in that milieu. But by gaining spontaneous acceptance, because of their beauty, in that milieu, these works were taken up at the cost of an interpretation which made of them sacred texts like the Veda and the Upaniṣads, revelations of the Supreme Knowledge.

It was specifically Nammāḻvār's opera that was looked upon as a Veda and *Tiruvāymoḻi* was taken to be an Upaniṣad.

Nammāḻvār's works comprise four texts: the *Tiruviruttam*, the *Tiruvāymoḻi*, the *Tiruvāciriyam* and the *Periyatiruvandādi* which are said to be respectively like the *Ṛgveda*, *Sāmaveda*, *Yajurveda* and *Atharvaveda*. The *Tiruvāymoḻi* would correspond therefore to *Sāmaveda*. This analogy is very thinly justified because of the nature of the songs contained in the 1000 stanzas of the *Tiruvāymoḻi* and it is quite clear that Nammāḻvār had never intended to imitate the *Sāmaveda*. The theoretical identification with it is secondary: it belongs to a Sanskritising milieu which, when adopting the Tamil work, wished to confer a title of respectability on it of the same kind as the things it venerated. Moreover, the other texts which are extremely short do not have either any real links with the Vedas.

The *Tiruvāymoḻi* was also regarded as an *Upaniṣad* and called *Dramiḍopaniṣad*, the 'Tamil Upaniṣad'. The texts of the *Upaniṣads* are the most important authoritative sources upon which the Vedānta bases itself and from which it derives by way of its commentaries the teachings to which it is specially linked. The *Tiruvāymoḻi* has indeed been seen in this light, in Tamil, in Maṇipravaḷam and in Sanskrit. There are several commentaries that take up and explain it word by word and set out their technical Sanskrit equivalents. These commentaries are named according to the number of the elements of discourse they contain: 6000 for the Āṟāyirappaḍi of Tirukkurugeippirāṉ Piḷḷāṉ, 9000, 18000, 24000 and up to 36000 for others. The names of their authors are quite significant. Pirāṉ Piḷḷāṉ's is preceded by the information that he was from Tirukkurugei, one of the names of Nammāḻvār's home-town. Another is Periyaparakālaswāmi, 'he whose lord is the Great Transcendent Time', 'great' (*periya*) being expressed in Tamil, the rest in Sanskrit. Others for instance are Vedāntarāmānujaswāmi, 'he whose lord is the Rāmānuja of the Vedānta', and Śrīraṅgarāmānujaswāmi, 'he whose lord is the Rāmānuja of Śrīraṅgam'. The exegetical work on the *Tiruvāymoḻi* in Tamil and in Maṇipravaḷam,—which are the languages of these commentaries,—was therefore continued after Rāmānuja by those people themselves who were under the religious patronage of the former.

In Sanskrit an adaptation in verse of *Tiruvāymoḻi* was done by Vedāntadeśika, an author who may have lived for more than a century, from 1269 to 1371 A.D. This translation is titled *Dramiḍopaniṣattātparyaratnāvalī* and it was the basis simultaneously of a commentary (*vyākhyāna*) and a summary (*sāra*) by Veṅkaṭeśācarya. What developed was therefore a threefold literature about the time of Rāmānuja, on the works of the Āḻvārs, and above all on the *Tiruvāymoḻi*, and even today new commentaries on these works are brought out in modern Tamil.

* * * *

To our mind, the Tiruvāymoḻi seems to merit so much attention. The poet starts by an exhortation to either his heart or to his mind—which is the same thing in Indian thought that situates, like Aristotle, the mind in the heart. He urges it towards the Supreme Being, towards the Supreme Being that he first describes in its essence: all goodness, then in its manifestations as the all-comprehensive Grace which dissolves all troubles, as sovereignty over the Immortals and as the liberating image of adoration offered to the afflicted.

> 'He who, with nothing above, possesses the sublime Good,
> He who by eliminating all disturbance, bestows the grace of the Goodness of Intelligence,
> He who is the Sovereign of the Immortals without exception
> After having worshipped his luminous feet which put an end to suffering, raise thyself, my heart!' (I, 1.1)

But our exegetical scholars of the Vedānta were not content with such a simple interpretation. Some Sanskrit words borrowed very early by Tamil and which figure here, had only to be taken up by them, but, for instance, the Tamil word *nalam* meaning 'goodness' in a very wide sense was explained by them to be an equivalent of *ānanda* meaning 'beatitude'. It seems very likely that they wanted to find in the definition of Being, *Sat*, implied in the Tamil verses, the two other aspects of the essence of Being according to classical Vedānta: *cit*, the spiritual, and *ānanda*, the beatific. But this shows on their part, a tendency to arbitrarily ascribe to Tamil words meanings which are not attributed to them, which the poet could hardly have had in mind and which were necessary only to discover somehow in the text written by one they revered as a saint, the expression of some familiar doctrines. We see the intrusion into the exegetical framework of a pre-established conviction that the venerated text could have contained the truth only in the garb one was familiar with.

The Vedic commentators made attempts to interpret these works in different ways in accordance with their respective systems of thought. In the same stanza, *madinalam* which we translate as 'Goodness of Intelligence' (*madi*=Sansk. *mati*), has been interpreted by Śrīraṅgarāmānujaswāmi as being 'knowledge in the form of beatitude' (*ānandarūpajñāna*), whereas Vedāntarāmānujaswāmi saw in it 'knowledge and love', for he interpreted *nalam* no more as 'beatitude' but as *sneha*, 'love' or as *bhakti*, 'devotion'.

It would be proper to add before leaving these Sanskritising commentators, of whose methods an example was to be given, that their interpretations are not always arbitrary in this way, that they are mostly useful for understanding the text, often elliptical, and that they are, in any case, accurate testimonies of the state of Vedāntic ideas in the school that gave them currency.

However, as far as we are concerned, Nammāḻvār himself gives us an adequate idea about his conception of the Supreme Being, for his most important opening stanzas are an invocation to Him. For him, He is above everything supreme and transcendent, He is immanent at once in all things. Knowledge cannot fathom Him but He is known to be impartial, equal, immutable and yet helpful to those who surrender their hearts to Him for He becomes a frail human child to make Himself accessible to His devotees and, above all, He belongs to us, He is 'our Lord',

Emperumāṉ, literally 'our Great one'. What is more he is our very soul:

> 'When there is no more impurity in the heart, like a blossomed flower, he rises
> Unfathomable by spiritual knowledge, unfathomable by sensorial knowledge,
> (Always) unchanging, knowing, whole, and Goodness in future, present and past
> Peer he has none, (He) my soul, the One without-a-Second.' (I, 1, 2).

We cannot qualify him, because he transcends all qualification; he clothes himself with all forms and yet he is also the being of that which is formless; it is he that, while being our soul, perceives with our senses, but he does not fall to being an object in the clutches of these senses. He is eternal, infinite, perfectly good and yet we can reach out to him:

> When we say: "He is without this, he possesses that, he is difficult for thought (to seize)
> Similar to forms on the earth and in space, he is similar to the Formless,
> Accompanying the objects of the senses, he is not an object of the senses, he is infinite,
> He possesses Goodness. Towards (Him), Alone, we ourselves have indeed reached! (I, 1, 3)

The wonder is that he is Being of such a plenitude that non-being, as far as it exists, exists only by him. There where there is no form, where we see nothing, it does not mean that there is nothing; it means that he is there in the absence of form (if there were nothing, there would not be even non-being):

> If we say that he is, he has for his form, these things with forms before us.
> If He who is, is said not to be, it means that they are his absence of form, these things which we designate without form.

In the possession of these qualities which make us say "he is" or "he is not"
He has two natures, he who extends himself without limit."
(I, 1, 9)

Here, the saint touches on the philosophical argument and the commentator Pirāṉ Piḷḷāṉ believes that he intended to refute the doctrine of those who say that all is void, that there is no knowledge or object of knowledge or, rather, 'no criteria, no judgment' and no 'thing to judge' (*pramāṇa, prameya*), that there is no Veda, no Lord to be known with the help of the Veda, neither any world of which he is the sovereign (*Āṟāyirappaḍi* on *Tiruvāymoḻi* I, 1, 9).

We know who these 'upholders of the void' are; they are the Buddhist *śūnyavādins* who went one step further than the Buddha who had denounced the impermanent nature of compounds; the former deny the impermanent being of a self-existing thing and declared it to be void of all nature, since it is in continuous change. It is not absolutely certain that Nammāḻvār wanted specifically to contradict them. He could have very well, without any intention of creating a controversy, glorified his God, complete and infinite Being, as embodying at once form and formlessness, being and nothingness; as for its aspects, this nothingness was nothing but a negative form of being and not a non-existence at all unless it did not exist himself. It is of no lesser interest to observe that in a yet undetermined period of time but clearly later than the 11th century, a Tamil author of the Far-South declared the śūnyavādins to be his formidable adversaries who should have been attacked by the author he was commenting upon. He himself builds an argument against them which seems to him to correspond with Nammāḻvār's intentions. He criticises 'the upholder of the void' by reproaching him with denying the existence of the Lord and he asserts that existence and non-existence are two aspects of representing empirical reality, but the omnipresent Lord is in non-existence as he is in existence: "If we say 'He is', He is; if we say 'He is not', He is."

Perhaps 'the upholder of the void' would have accepted this for it is in the forms of the empirical world that he denounced the void of the self-existent nature, not in absolute Being. Yet, he certainly would not have accepted to bring absolute Being into the realm of forms, those of the sovereign and compassionate Lord. Severe like the ontology of the 'upholder of the void' and as fervent against the criticism of appearances, the Vedāntic doctrine of Śaṅkara too refrained from over-humanising the Absolute by making of it a God in accordance with human conception.

But Nammāḻvār and his followers, especially Nammāḻvār in his upsurge of love, rejected this ontological harshness. They did not hesitate in giving too great a value of being to changing phenomena of the external world. Assuming that the Lord is the sole absolute Reality and that he is everywhere, even in the apparent void, Nammāḻvār held on to these two principles without giving up his belief in his love of God. Since the Lord is the sole Reality, the apparent world in which we live enmeshed is without value; we must detach ourselves from it in order to consecrate to the Lord all the love we can offer to Him. But if the Lord is in everything, even if it be as a common ontological substratum, or as pure existence without an adorable form because it is utterly formless, then all things participate in this all-pervasive reality, and the humblest of existences takes on the infinite glory of the Absolute that is immanent in it. In this way, the Lord can embody the humblest form: he could incarnate himself as a little child, Kṛṣṇa, to come down at the level of appearances, closer to his devotee who knows how to find him there.

Nammāḻvār cries out:
'Surrender all!
When your soul has completed the surrender
To him, to whom belongs that which surrenders,
Surrender yourself!'
'No longer than the flash of lightning does it last
That which we call the bodies and of which the soul is stable.
Meditate awhile upon that!'
"You" and "Yours", destroy them from the roots
And draw near the Lord! For the soul there is
No plenitude that equals this. (I, II, 1-3)

It is then by abandoning all, by giving up the notions of 'me' and 'mine', these miserable limitations, that we will find the limitless plenitude of the Lord. To surrender all is to free oneself and to give oneself to him, a single word *viḍu* expressing this unique act, simultaneously in its two aspects of renunciation and offering.

Now, the Lord to whom the devotee by giving up his 'I' and his 'mine', surrenders in this way is undoubtedly beyond the limitations of existence and non-existence, being neither one or the other, but in their changing aspects, utterly Himself in his own form, which is infinite:

> 'That which is neither that which is not nor that which is:
> That is its real form.
> To this great, limitless good
> Ally yourself, having severed all attachment.'
> ' "Attachment is no more", when this we can utter
> the soul has attained liberation.
> If, by detesting (even) this you draw near to the Changeless One,
> Break away and seize the Lord.' (I, V, 4-5)

One should, therefore, give up all desire, even if it were that of liberation, for attaining him better. And in these stanzas, we have a simple expression of commonplace notions of all the religions of India. We see expressed what one ordinarily calls Indian pessimism: the world is bad because it is impermanent, subject to vicissitudes; one must detach oneself from it in order to unite with the fundamental stability of Being that is in everything and above all in oneself. In this regard Nammāḻvār has merely been faithful to his country and his age; he did not need to innovate. However, in a rhythm which unfortunately is lost in the translation, he has expressed these ideas with human passion quite differently moving than the usual, doctrinal sentences. But it is pure passion that is meant since it has only the Supreme Being for goal. What is meant is an impulse which at first sight we can take to be similar to that which leads towards worldly things. But there is a transmutation of the value of this impulse because there is a sublimation of these worldly things, the moment we see in them the Supreme Being. Indeed, this Supreme Being is immutable and impassive in its real nature but he is seductively splendid, attractive and accessible; his manifestation is redeeming to one who entirely surrenders himself to Him:

'Without attachment for any part, the Lord
Exists for all.
Being without attachment, in everything that belongs to Him

Surrender yourself!
'Beholding all splendour, all fortune,
By saying: "Of the Lord
That is all splendour,"
Surrender yourself to it!'
'Considering these three things which are
Mind, speech and action,
Destroy them and in the Lord
Surrender yourself!'
'Surrendered to him,
All restrictions
Once renounced,
Think of the moment of leaving the body.'
'(Of them that are) things of beauty
Through these excellences, in number infinite,
(Of them) whose praise is of boundless plenty
Of the immutable feet of Nārāyaṇa, draw yourself near!'
(I, II, 6-10)

'He is accessible to the devoted servitors, inaccessible to others.
He is wonderful, our Lord who is difficult to attain and who loves the Daughter-with-the-flower (his spouse Lakṣmī).
While stealing butter churned abundantly with the beater,
How, tied to the mortar, was he able to cry?' (I, III, 1)

For Nammāḻvār, this is the special quality of wonder of the Lord, the contrast which makes his devotion for Him more ardent, He who is inaccessible to common mortals, the divine groom of the goddess of Fortune, cried like a rebuked child because he had stolen butter! This is indeed recounted in a legend of Kṛṣṇa in the *Bhāgavatapurāṇa* (X, IX) inspired by the same devotion as that of the Āḻvārs to whom it alludes as we have seen. Viṣṇu-

Nārāyaṇa incarnated in the child Kṛṣṇa is brought up among shepherds, hidden among them so that he is not discovered by the tyrant who wished to get him killed from his birth and whom he is destined to kill. He is a child who performs prodigious feats at times but He is also like the others. One day his adopted mother who had just finished churning butter, had to hurriedly leave the churn to go to remove a pot of boiling milk from the fire. Meanwhile, the little Kṛṣṇa stole the butter and when the farmer's wife returned she scolded him, tied him to a mortar while he would not stop crying. Yet, beneath this child's countenance there is the God of the Universe, there is the Lord. This form of a child will awaken in the heart of the devotee a spontaneous sentiment of affectionate solicitude for the child but the knowledge that this child is the Lord will transport this human feeling onto the sole object that is worthy of all adoration. All said and done, to seek one's liberation from the ordinary human condition, one need not, contrary to what is sometimes said, suppress in oneself all human sentiment so as to coldly meditate on the problem of ontology. It is rather with the heart that one must relate to the Lord in his sublime form with human sentiments that one can concentrate on the adorable human form that he has deigned to take on.

Similarly,—and Kṛṣṇaite devotion finds its justification here—, the young grown-up shepherd Kṛṣṇa will be able to steal the hearts of the shepherdesses; their love for his human form will be justified because of this love's real object, the Lord embodied in this form.

It is love of Kṛṣṇa sublimated in this way that inspired one of the Āḻvār saints, Āṇḍāl. Legend says that Āṇḍāl was the adopted daughter of another Āḻvār, Periyāḻvār, who was the officiating priest in a Viṣṇu temple. One day the young Āṇḍāl adorned herself with a garland of flowers that was meant to adorn the divine image. As a consequence, this garland could not be offered anymore. But the god declared that he wanted the garlands first worn by Āṇḍāl who had dedicated herself to him. And the work of Āṇḍāl, the *Tiruppāvei*, a simple collection of thirty stanzas, glitters with this vocation of divine love in human manifestations.

The text of the *Tiruppāvei* is difficult; the commentators disagree in the interpretation of some important words, as in fact it often happens with ancient Tamil poetry, and there, in addition, the wealth of suggestions and their double meaning, mystic and human, have necessitated an endless exegesis over this short poem. But its basic themes are clear. In the morning Āṇḍāl calls her still-sleeping companions to the worship of the beloved Lord. She describes the practices of renunciation which all of them observed during a certain period and which have purified them. She runs to each one's house, rebukes her nonchalance and urges her on. Then she urges the guardian of the temple to open it. This is followed by an address to Kṛṣṇa and their young sister who is already Kṛṣṇa's spouse. She sings the glories of Kṛṣṇa and she tells him of her impatience. She reproaches the spouse with a touch of human jealousy which adds zest to the force of the feelings of love turned towards the Lord, with not wanting the groom to wake up so that she can keep him longer beside her. She concludes by devoting herself eternally to Kṛṣṇa with all her companions, and evoking, in reference to the chain of thirty strophes, the garland of flowers destined for Kṛṣṇa and which she herself had worn. She calls the sequence of these strophes a 'Tamil garland', Tamiḻ-mālai, because 'Tamil' (strictly Tamiḻ) designates the language and means 'suave'.

The *Tiruppāvei* is a poetic masterpiece and perhaps it gives us a glimpse of the path by which we would one day discover the prehistory of the cult of Kṛṣṇa in the Tamil country.

It is on a specific date, in the month of Mārgaḻi (December-January) that Āṇḍāl sings—she states this with the very first words of her first stanza—and she sings after a period of purificatory abstinence. This leads us to think that the young girls she wakes up and takes to the temple of the beloved God perform, along with her, a ritual ceremony on the assigned date and after the necessary preparation. The day is not arbitrarily selected, it is one of festivity and such a festivity is not fixed purely by a mystic improvisation. It can give free vent to the mystic upsurge, it can set it aflame, it is not created by it on a fixed date after a set preliminary rite. It is in answer to an organised cult which had survived and of which the goal was to acquire a husband for young marriageable girls. The *Bhāgavatapurāṇa* (X, XXII, 1) makes of it an occasion of prayer to Kātyāyanī (*Kātyāyanyarcanavrata*) done in the first month of the winter season (*Hemanta*, which is consistent with the Tamil dating of Mārgaḻi) by the shepherdesses asking him to grant them Kṛṣṇa as groom. And if the observance of such a rite is attributed to these shepherdesses, this is so because this rite for the acquisition of a groom existed in general; the shepherdesses practise it specifically to get Kṛṣṇa, it is not their own creation for the occasion. As for the rest, the rite is not inherent in the religion of Kṛṣṇa. The reference made by the *Bhāgavata*, which although is a Kṛṣṇaite work, that the rite is addressed to Kātyāyanī should suffice to warn us. Now, there exists a parallel of the *Tiruppāvei* in the religion of Śiva and of Śakti: the *Tiruvembāvei* by the Śhaivaite saint Māṇikkavācagar, similarly meant to be sung at the festival of *Mārgaḻi* by young girls.

We may now wonder whether this festival does not originate from a cult that was more widespread than that of Kṛṣṇa; that of the young God who appears here as Kṛṣṇa, there as Śiva or as the son of Śiva and Kātyāyanī, Skanda Kumāra. This figure of a young hero is of importance in the religions of the whole of ancient India. This figure reappears, in fact, as Sanatkumāra, the 'Eternally youthful one' of the *Chandogya-Upaniṣad* (VII, I, 1 and XXVI, 2), who in this text is Skanda, but the son of Brahman and not of Śiva, and who, as the protector of the afflicted as well as by his name seems to be simultaneously a prototype of the Brahman Sanaṃkumāra of Pāli Buddhism and of the two Bodhisattvas Avalokiteśvara and Mañjuśrī of Mahāyāna.[1] In the Tamil country, this supremely youthful god was Murugaṉ formerly and eventually thought to be identical with Skanda[2] and there is a marked preference for devotion to young gods; the much-loved Gaṇeśa, with an elephant's head and the body of a child is called by preference *Piḷḷeiyār*, the 'Child'.

We might therefore be led to believe that in Vaiṣṇavism tender love of the Āḻvārs for the child Kṛṣṇa corresponds to this form of devotion to *Piḷḷaiyār*, the son of Śiva, and above all that ardent love of an Āṇḍāl for the young shepherd who is the soul of the world is an extension of a ritualised devotion which formerly was directed at the youthful God of ancient times. Thus all the piety of the Āḻvārs for the Absolute Being, especially in Nammāḻvār, originated from a religious impulse which was first directed at a personal god. But this piety reconciles the survival of this ancient human impulse with the conviction, derived from the ontological thinking that the world and human sentiments are nothing beside the Immutable Being. The Āḻvārs share this conviction; they know that nothing is valid by itself, that nothing exists but by this Being; but then they see this Being in all and so feel justified in offering to him in the guise of a human manifestation of love, a boundless devotion.

The great thinker, Rāmānuja, held on to these ideas, and illustrated them in his philosophy. He was said to recite Āṇḍāl's Tiruppāvei three times everyday.

What is certain is that the devotional movement born with the Āḻvārs, which was given a doctrinal, Vedāntic form by Rāmānuja and which gave way to a scholarly overloading of ideas among the *ācāryas*, has remained quite alive to this day. Philosophers continue to scrutinize pandits' commentaries and devotees keep the saints' hymns alive by singing them. Nammāḻvār's *Tiruvāymoḻi*, along with its principal commentaries in Tamil, in *Maṇipravaḷam*, and in Sanskrit, has been published several times since the end of the 19th century, under the title of *Bhagavadviṣayam*, the 'Domain of the consciousness of the Blessed'. A few years back, the works of the Āḻvārs were re-edited with a literal explanation and a commentary, in modern Tamil by Aṇṇaṅgarācāriyar.[3] The Tiruppāvei, on its part, is frequently re-edited. In 1952 it was re-edited at least three times.[4]

But this wouldn't yet suffice to show the place that devotion to Āḻvārs occupies in the Tamil part of India today. Not only do the Vaiṣṇavas continue to popularise and sing their hymns but a lot of devotees in South India often give their attention, even though they are Śaivas, to all the religious potential which their fervour holds. There were formerly terrible quarrels, in South India, between Śaivas and Vaiṣṇavas. Although all the barriers have not disappeared yet, these quarrels are a thing of the past. Today it is the common beliefs and sentiments that are being enumerated by them. An ideal of ecumenism exists in both Śaiva and Vaiṣṇava groups, comparable to that which is felt in certain catholic and protestant circles and these openly refer to this example. They hope that one day they shall come together in love of the One Being.

Their respective literature already offers them a good number of texts that are so close to one another, as the *Tiruppāvei* and the

Tiruvembāvei, and the latter is included in the larger collection of *Tiruvācagam* of Māṇikkavācagar, which is comparable to the *Tiruvāymoḻi* of Nammāḻvār. A group of Vaiṣṇavas and Śaivas has recently constituted a *Tiruppāvei Tiruvembāvei Kamiṭṭi* (committee). This committee published the two texts last year with commentaries and a number of studies by numerous authors. Vaiṣṇava devotion in the Tamil country is not, therefore, dead, accessible only to the philologist through a forgotten literature. Alive like many others, it is based on an ancient literature full of brilliance and endlessly enriched by the tradition which has brought it up to us. It retains its place of a living portion of the extremely rich and variegated culture of present-day India.

NOTES

1. Cf. *Avalokiteśvara, d'aprés un livre récent, Revue de l'Histoire des Religions.* January-March 1950, pp. 44-58; *Manuel des études indiennes,* t. II, pp. 532, 573, 574.
2. P. Meile in *Manuel des études indiennes,* t. I, pp. 447–449.
3. Kanchipuram, 1944.
4. *Tirouppavai,* original Tamil text translated into French (alongside the Tamil text) by R. Dessigane, Pondicherry, *Cittirattiruppāvei* published by Sri C. Anna Rao, Tirupati. *Tiruvembāvei Tiruppāvei Tirumaṛei āṛaṅga magānāṭṭu* malar, Māyūram (Mayavaram), pp. VII-XV.

CHAPTER 3

ABOUT THE RELIGION OF BHARTṚHARI*

AT THE END OF the last century, Max Müller, along with Kasawara's and then Takakusu's help, brought to light some hints on Bhartṛhari by Yi-tsing that are at once illuminating and confusing. Illuminating, because they help in determining the death of the author of *Vākyapadīya* to 651-652. Confusing, because some of them do not correspond at first glance with what is known about the religious inspiration of Bhartṛhari through the Sanskrit works which are attributed to him. Two major questions remain unanswered despite their having been discussed quite often[1]: Was Bhartṛhari the grammarian a Buddhist as Yi-tsing has asserted? Was he the same as Bhartṛhari the author of the *Śatakas*?

It is true that one of the most important hints given by Yi-tsing could resolve the whole problem. Bhartṛhari may have entered the Buddhist Community seven times and seven times have given it up.[2] His various works, those that are known to us and those that are mentioned by Yi-tsing, may have been written, some while he was following the Buddhist path with fervour, the others during the periods when he became laic. Even though Yi-tsing asserts that in the end he remained a Buddhist as a lay believer, the changes in his feelings and in his life lead us to believe that he may have successively known quite a variety of both wordly experiences and religious upsurges. In such a case, it should not surprise us that he wrote Brahmanic works, the only ones that exist today, and that any taint of Buddhism they may have had earlier was rubbed out by the Brahmanic tradition that handed them down to us.

In any case, it is tempting to always want to look for new indications on the professed religious opinions in these works, with the hope that they may help resolve the twofold problem or at least throw some light on the ideas which either went into the

Á propos de la religion de Bhartṛhari, Silver Jubilee Volume of the Zinbun-Kagaku-Kenkyuso, Kyoto University, 1954, p. 116-120.

initial composition of the texts or which were later elaborated by tradition. Now, the introductory stanzas of works are often revelatory of the author's religion. We can, therefore, examine those found in the *Vākyapadīya* and the *Śatakas*.

One must not forget, however, that the introductory stanzas are not always penned by the author whose work they introduce. Their authenticity is subject to more uncertainty than any other part of the writing, because there exists at least one rule of poetics that requires that the introduction to a work should not be by the author himself of that work. This rule is formulated in the mediaeval literary Tamil art[3] and does not necessarily apply to the simple introductory stanzas of a work nor to the practice of Sanskrit authors. It is also clear that it was not always respected in Tamil, but some Tamil authors may have applied it in their Sanskrit works. The rule seems to explain why introductory stanzas do not always tally in different manuscripts of the same Tamil text. And this discrepancy is also found, in certain cases, in Sanskrit manuscripts, too.

Whatever the case might be, as regards the introductory stanzas of the three *Śatakas*, we are directly faced with a rather major problem.

First of all, the unity of the *Śatakas* and their composition by the same author is sometimes disputed. The common analogy of the *Śataka* group with that of the three books of the Tamil *Kuṟal* which are much more clearly the work of the same author, may prompt one to think that these *Śatakas* are written, all three of them, by the same poet, or they are composed by an arrangement of sentences of different origins, according to a system of classification in vogue for some time throughout India, in Sanskrit as well as Tamil traditions.[4]

On the other hand, the manuscript tradition is far from unanimous on the precise content of the *Śatakas*. The painstaking critical edition by D.D. Kosambi[5] shows this at once. The different manuscripts include only partially the same stanzas, arrange them differently and vary (the order of) the sequence of the *Śatakas*. The introductory stanzas given in common editions do not find a fixed place and are even of doubtful authenticity.

The introductory stanza of *Vairāgya* (*cūḍottaṃsita*.... St. 1, Kosambi ed.) is generally found in all the versions but without any invariable, fixed place. That of *Śṛṅgāra* (*Śaṃbhusvayaṃbhu*... Kosambi 112) is placed in the Northern version at the middle of the *Śataka*. That of *Nītiśataka* (*dikkālādy*.... Kosambi 256) appears among doubtful stanzas and Kosambi thinks it to be probably a later Vedic addition, because it is commonly found omitted in the manuscripts.

But this reason is truly not decisive and, in fact, it would also be difficult to establish by the criterion of unanimity its authenticity with certainty. The critical principles one is obliged to adopt do not offer absolute guarantee. An authentic passage might have been omitted or lost very early on from one or several of the important archetypes of the manuscript tradition which explains its absence from some and its presence in others. On the contrary, —difficult though it might seem—an inauthentic passage may have slipped into the archetype of all the preserved manuscripts, and this fact may seem to lend it authenticity but we cannot be sure whether the passage in question goes back to the origin. Critics are therefore, justified in considering these texts with suspicion, particularly those parts of the texts which are missing from the most important sources. Such is the case for *dikkālādy* ... a stanza which is found with variations at several places in the *Yogavāsiṣṭha* tradition as Kosambi has indicated. It is, in fact, in the southern version that the three stanzas in question serve as introductory and invocatory stanzas. But if this assigned role is secondary for them, it must nevertheless be admitted that it is legitimate: the introductory stanza of *Śṛṅgāra* is an invocation to Love, Makaradhvaja; that of *Vairāgya* is to the glory of Śiva, the beacon of Knowledge for yogins who burnt Love out; the *Nītiśataka* stanza alone is not specifically adapted to the purpose of the collection it introduces, because it is concentrated on the ultimate universal reality. In return, this last stanza denotes specifically a certain doctrinal state, even though it is usually inadequately translated without bringing out significant technical term that it contains.

The stanza, in its most common form, is as follows:

dikkālādyanavacchinnānantacinmātramūrtaye/
svānubhūtyaikamānāya namaḥ śāntāya tejase//[6]

'To him whose form is circumscribed by nothing that begins

by space and time, who is infinite and nothing-but-thought, to him whose only mode of knowledge is through self-perception, to him I bow, to him who is tranquil radiance!'

In this text, it is *cinmātra* that seems to be the important expression, the "nothing-but-thought", which echoes the teaching of the secondary *Upaniṣads*, the *Triśikhibrāhmaṇa* (II, 31), the *Tejobindu* (II, 24-41 and IV, 4), the *Kaivalya* (18), the *Sarva*-(3), the *Muktikā*-(II, 18; 50; 70), the *Nṛsiṃhottaratāpanī* (V, 3; IX, 17). In these different texts, *cinmātra* is only briefly mentioned except in *Tejobindu*- II, 24-41, where everything is referred to it, the unique and supreme reality. But in all the texts, it figures as the ultimate reality, being Sadāśiva, Brahman, Ātman; in any case, it is a form of the universal ontological substratum.

Now the concept of *cinmātra* is reminiscent also of the Buddhist *vijñānamātra* or *vijñaptimātra* or *vidyāmātra*, and it is to this Buddhist doctrine that Yi-tsing links Bhartṛhari.[7]

The two conceptions do not, in fact, cover each other because the theory of the *vijñaptimātra* does not take into account the *ātman*, as the theory of *cinmātra* does. But both agree to reducing the world to a psychic representation and their names correspond. It was easy and perhaps inevitable for Yi-tsing to get confused. If Bhartṛhari did profess the ideas that are contained in the doubtful stanza of *Nītiśataka*, it is understandable that Yi-tsing ascribes to him the doctrine of *vidyāmātra*. On the other hand, his changes of religious position may have been mere vacillations between different viewpoints of the doctrine of 'nothing-but-thought'. The doubtful stanza might, therefore be authentic: its particular idea agrees with the philosophy that is attributed to Bhartṛhari by Yi-tsing.

On another side, this particular idea is echoed well in the philosophy of the *Vākyapadīya*. Whatever may have been said, the *Vākyapadīya* is clearly Brahmanic in inspiration. The *Vākyapadīya* posits, at the very outset, Brahman as the essence of sound from which the universe is derived, through modulations which are caused by the 'intent' or the 'sense' of the primordial sound, the imperishable syllable (*akṣara*): *oṃ*. This is how it is expressed:[8]

anādinidhanaṃ brahma śabdatattvaṃ yad akṣaram/
vivartate 'rthabhāvena prakriyā jagato yataḥ// I, 1.

......

satyā viśuddhis tatroktā vidyaivaikapadāgamā/
yuktā praṇavarūpeṇa sarvavādāvirodhinī// I, 9.

'Without beginning or end, the Brahman is the essence of sound which transforms the imperishable according to the nature of the meaning and from where the activity of the world originates......

......

'The true purity is the science expounded here, whose tradition is only one word, condensed in the form of *praṇava* (*oṃ*), and which is in agreement with all words.'

Now the *Tejobindūpaniṣad* (III, 43) crowns the exposition of the Brahman-*cinmātra* identification by proclaiming that its inherent form is the meaning of *oṃ* (*oṅkārārthasvarūpa*), which is quite natural considering that Brahman is usually identified with *oṃ* but which shows that the speculations on *cinmātra*, such as those found in the later *Upaniṣads* and which are the same as the ones referred to in the *Nītiśataka* stanza, agree fully with the thought of *Vākyapadīya*.

It is impossible to affirm that the author of the *cinmātra* expounded the doctrine of 'nothing-but-thought' because of the inconstancy of the relevant stanza in the manuscripts of the *Śatakas*. It is good that we see the disappearance of the apparent contradiction between the Brahmanic nature of the works attributed to Bhartṛhari and the indication given by Yi-tsing according to which he is said to have professed the Buddhist doctrine of *vidyāmātra*: Yi-tsing's *vidyāmātra*, the *cinmātra* of *Nītiśataka* and the *praṇava* of *Vākyapadīya* could all three be one and the same.

NOTES

1. Cf. L. Renou, *La Durghaṭavṛtti de Śaraṇadeva*, vol. I, Paris, 1940, p. 37— *L'Inde classique, Manuel des études indiennes*, t. II, Paris, 1954, § 1532n, 1802.
2. J. Takakusu, *A Record of the Buddhist Religion...*, Oxford, 1896, p. 179.
3. *Naṉṉūl* 51 : *Taṉṉā cariyaṉ ṟaṉṉodu Kaṟṟōṉ*
   taṉmā ṇākkaṉ ṟagumurei kāraṇeṉṟu
   iṉṉōr pāyira miyambudal kadaṉē

'His master, his fellow-disciple, his student, an appropriate commentator, that these give the introduction is common practice.'

4. The analogy of the *Śatakas* and the *Kuṟals* is, in fact, not as great in the details as it is in the general arrangement. The differences of form, the form being shorter, simpler and sharper in the *Kuṟals*, are merely external. The fact that the *Kuṟals* englobe a greater gamut of human emotions is only because of their number, which is four times greater than that of the *Śataka* stanzas. But the identity of the parts is not total; if *poruḷ* and *iṉbam* correspond respectively to *nīti* and *Śṛṅgāra*; *aṟam* represents the natural and moral order and is equivalent of *ṛta* or *dharma* and not *vairāgya* at all. Considering the different views of things, the two groups of sentences are still ethical works of the same general form and which occupy the same place in literary traditions. Here, one can observe the popularity of both among the Jains.
5. *The Epigrams attributed to Bhartṛhari*, Singhi Jain Series 23, Bombay, 1948.
6. Principal variants: *dikpāla*, wrong variant, it would refer to the unencircled form by the guards of the cardinal points;—*aparicchinne=anavacchinna*; *ānanda* for *ananta*, plausible, 'who is bliss'; —*svānubhūtyekamānāya*, 'to him whose sole mode of knowledge is self-perception';—*bodhāya* for *mānāya*, '...consciousness...'; *cetase*, 'in the spirit';—*śambhave*, 'to Śambhu'; —*namaḥ somārdhamūrtaye*, 'adoration to the figure who bears the half-moon'.
7. Takakusu, p. 197.
8. Charudeva Shastri ed., Lahore 1934.

CHAPTER 4

THE CONTRIBUTION OF THE STUDY OF INDIAN RELIGIONS*

THE CONTRIBUTION of the religions of India to the scientific representation of human groups and of man in general is likely to be exceptionally great and significant.

It is great because Indian concepts are diffused over a very vast area of civilisation and gained currency in distant lands in foreign cultural domains. In addition, we come across these concepts as described in various literatures, some of which are among the richest in the world, spread over many centuries, preserving ancient evidence and providing the necessary elements for the understanding of certain developments across great stretches of time. India offers, therefore, a vast source of documentation which in its totality is spread over the whole of history even though there persist some very unfortunate chronological uncertainties. This material has grown with all that modern ethnological observation has supplied on the populations of India that are devoid of literary traditions and such populations are numerous and diverse even today.

The contribution of Indian documents is likely to be especially significant as a number of facts that can be elucidated by their traditional setting, which is preserved and determinable, are revealed to us along with their explanation. The explanation can be questioned as it might be the outcome of subsequent speculation which interferes with or even supplants the original ideas. Undoubtedly most often it is extremely valuable to be able to retrace without any hypotheses ancient conceptions which served as the basis,—of which the people are either fully aware or which they have forgotten but which are well attested to, in any case, in the past of the group—, for their practice and interpretations.

**L'apport de l'étude des religions de l'Inde à la science de l'homme*, Anthropologie religieuse, études publiées sous la direction de C.J. Bleeker (Supplement to *Numen II*, Leiden, 1955, p. 108-119.

This provides us then with a far more limited number of working hypotheses which often tend to be turned into preconceived ideas, and comparative and now authenticated elements become available which can be legitimately utilised in general ethnological research.

These comparative elements are useful at first typologically, in order to establish from a purely formal point of view certain analogies, contrasts, or variations but also to determine, eventually on the basis of known historic contacts, facts of cultural interaction.

A treasure-mine of facts and of critical elements of external facts, Indian religions thus enrich the science of man with a mass of information and are an important field of study, both quantitatively and qualitatively, of that science. At the same time they are in themselves a science of man in that they have conceived certain representations of him which they propound. A brief review of some of these representations in ancient Vedic Brahmanism or in classical Brahmanic culture, can evoke at the same time the speculative material that India offers for the study of cultural anthropology as well as furnish examples of how certain Indian data have contributed to the explanation of similar data outside India.

The preoccupation with the question of man, with his destiny and his liberation was present in India from very early times and has culminated in very divergent views of which only a few survived by eliminating the others. The ancient Canonical Buddhist (*Sāmaññaphalasutta*) and Jaina (*Sūyagaḍaṃga*, *Bhagavatī*) texts bear testimony in this regard to the multiplicity of rival teachings. The ancient Brahmanic texts also contain indications of divergent views. But their philosophy has contributed more than any other in narrowing this great variety of thought into a few key ones which became leading ideas.

The early quest for the Self of Man, the *ātman*, that is to say of man *himself* in his eternal and fundamental being, existing metaphysically in changing, physical forms and a variety of psychic behavioural patterns, has diverted, to a certain extent, the Indian mind from exploring the empirical man. In order to find the real man, it has set aside the man of appearance and it has discovered Universal Reality, which no longer has anything specifically human, because it is the basis of the world as well as of man.

This seeking is notably described in *Chāndogya Upaniṣad*, VIII, 7-15. Prajāpati indicates by stages what man in his real self is constituted of. He first states that he is the ordinary individuality, the bodily person, conscious and active in the normal state of wakefulness. The Asura, Virocana, is quite satisfied with this notion but not the leader of the gods, Indra, who returns to enquire further and to learn successively that the essential reality of man is the person who sees himself move about in dreams independently of the sleeping body, the person who exists as a latent presence in the state of deep sleep, independently of the body and the dreams, and finally that he is the universal reality, that underlying principle in all conscious activity, luminous, infinite space, the eternal field of all individualised existences, each distinguished by a combination of a name and a form (*nāmarūpa*). The fundamental reality which constitutes man is not therefore to be confused with any of the three states of empirical existence: wakefulness, dream and profound sleep: it is still beyond in a fourth state which is the only one that matters.

This conception can divert us from a deep analysis of the empirical states of man which are naturally devalued, but it doesn't however leave him out, it hitches him to a cosmic principle as speculation does as well with the nature of empirical man, speculation that, despite everything, is always present.

This last speculation describes and explains the body and the physiological and psychic life of man. The human body can be explained by the action of natural elements present in him as well as in the cosmos. (cf. esp. Chāndogya-Upan. III, 12-14) and these which lend him life and movement are the ones mentioned most often: Water that infuses him, Fire that inhabits him in the form of bile and Wind as breaths penetrate and move him.

Reciprocally the universe is explained as the body of a cosmic man (sometimes even as a cosmic horse or a bull). The exact origin of this marvellous set-up of cosmic man being similar to that of individual man, remains a mystery but we know that he is the result of a divine working, since the *Atharvaveda* asks merely which of the gods has assembled all his parts (AV, X, 2). So does the Kena Upaniṣad.

The connection between man and the cosmos is also evident in the correspondence established by the *Upaniṣads*—whose function is to 'seat' things close to one another—, between him on the one hand, and the Moon, an elemental part of the year, and Prajāpati, the demiurge, on the other. The *Upaniṣads* in fact state that it has fifteen vital parts which he can at the most lose through a fast of fifteen days without abstaining from water, and one in addition which is indispensable to its life and preserved by water and upon which he can reconstruct the others (*Chāndogya Upaniṣad*, VI, 7, 1-6). Thus he is like the Moon which is of aqueous essence and wanes and waxes again every fifteen days, and it participates in the nature of the fortnight, which is a basic unit of the calendar, one of the constituting periods of a year which itself is a form of the demiurge, Prajāpati, the orderer of the world (*Bṛhadāraṇyaka Upaniṣad*, I, 5, 14-15, cf. *Śvetāśvatara Upaniṣad*, I, 4, *Muṇḍaka Upaniṣad*, III, 2, 7).

Man's being's foundation is the Universal Reality, his physical structure is assembled by the gods, he is a replica of the universe and in harmony with the principle of arrangement of the world—from the Brahmanic point of view man is thus a product issued more from a cosmic design ruled by the gods than the terrestrial nature where he lives. Even in this terrestrial plan he is in close touch with the gods. The divinities are more specifically celestial powers but they also operate on the Earth, the cosmic grade inferior to the Heavens but a part of the world, and in man himself. The physiological activities of man are often called deva, 'gods', or 'devatā' 'divinities' as well as 'indriya', 'faculties' or 'powers' (more specifically it denotes 'sense', 'sense-organ') and are exposed to natural disturbances which are seen as attacks by the rivals of the gods, the Asuras, (*Bṛhad. Up.* I, 3, 6; cf. *Śat. br.* II, 5, 2, 2 and references in Böhtlingk-Roth s.v.° *devatā*; *Kauṣitakī* Up. II, 1, and 14; *Muṇḍaka Up.* III, 1, 8).

Therefore no chasm divides man from the gods, or even from God, if we use the name for the conscious, acting Universal Reality, for though this representation of reality does not admit of any natural or supernatural plan it does admit the existence of forces operating unchanged in all the stages of the world. The Greeks had understood this relationship between the human and the divine levels. They attributed very aptly to an Indian sage, who must have visited Socrates in Athens (according to Aristoxenes of Tarenta, end of IV cent. B.C.), the saying that we cannot know human things by ignoring the divine. Philostrate, too, in his *Life of Apollonius of Tyana*, quoted an Indian sage, Iarchas, as declaring that to know oneself is to know oneself as God. The *Elenchos* that came later and was attributed to Hippolytus (towards 235) summed up remarkably the doctrine of the Upaniṣads.

Naturally linked to the divine in a world where what we would call 'the supernatural' is dependent on nature, Man is, however, separate from the divine because of his earthly condition. According to Brahmanic legend the gods and men used to live together in the beginning, but then the gods, exasperated by the demands of men, left them (*Śat. Br.* II, 3, 4, 4) to live in Heavens which they won through 'sacrifice'. (*Śat. Br.* I, 6, 2, 1). From then on, man had to re-unite with the divine to get back, in part at least, his privileges. He can do this either individually through the knowledge of his real nature, or socially through his liturgical and royal duties.

Becoming conscious of the real Self leads one directly not only to the divine but also beyond the divine, to the transcendental Reality. Thus it is mostly the divine connection of liturgical and royal duties present in the Brahmanic society that specifically connects man to the world of gods.

The Brahmins and kings respectively assume these functions and are often seen as gods or representatives of the gods on the Earth.

The identification of the Brahmins with the gods is very common (cf. P. V. Kane, *History of Dharmaśāstra*, Poona, 1941, II, i, p. 37 & 135). According to the *Maitrāyaṇīsaṃhitā* I, 4, 6 the gods (*deva*) who enter the house of the Vedic sacrificer are of two kinds: the gods themselves, drinkers of *Soma* and eaters of fire-offerings, and Brahmins, who neither drink Soma nor eat the fire-offerings. The Brahmins can even receive an offering since the Brahmin is the Fire, *Agni Vaiśvānara* (*Taitt. Br.* III, 7, 3). They are the manifest gods, (*pratyakṣam, Taitt. S.* I. 7, 3, 1); as opposed to the real gods who are invisible (*pratyakṣadeva* as opposed to *parokṣadeva, Viṣṇudharmasūtra* XIX, 20). All the divinities inhabit the Brahmin, knower of the Vedas (*Taitt.,ār.* II, 15). The Brahmins are composed of all the gods (*Parāśara* VI, 53). The Brahmin is King *Soma* (*Śat. Br.* IX, 4, 3, 16) and Manu declares: 'Whether he is ignorant or full of knowledge, the Brahmin is a great divinity as is Fire a great divinity whether it is placed on the altar or not'. (*Manu*, IX, 317).

As for the king, his divine nature has been attested to in the same manner. With the help of the Brahmin whom he nominates as his chaplain (*purohita*), he maintains the right order of things (*dharma*), and for the maintenance of such an order a close collaboration between the *brahman* and the *kṣatra*, ritualistic efficiency and temporal authority, is indispensable. And this right order is not merely earthly, it is universal as it is common to all the worlds together. It is of interest to gods and fathers, inhabitants of different supraterrestrial worlds as well as to the king's subjects and foreigners. The *Rājadharmaparva* of the *Mahābhārata* expresses this very clearly:

'Both (king and chaplain) help subjects, gods, ancestors, foreigners, Fathers to prosper ... the *brahman* and the *kṣatra* are, in truth, the basis of all order (*dharma*)' (*Śāntiparvan*, LXXIV, 3, & 5).

The terrestrial and the divine worlds are ruled according to the same universal law; the former by the king and the Brahmin-priest, the latter by Indra and the gods. The king is to men what Indra is to the gods. He is popularly known as *narendra*, 'the indra of men' whereas Indra is the 'devarāja', 'the king of the gods'.

Their respective kingships were instituted in a similar way:

'He whose officers, chaplain, masters and others are known to be pandits, are honourable and honoured, is called the conqueror of the world and it is thus that the greatest of the gods (Indra) obtained the Earth (the entire world). And it is in his footsteps that the earthly (kings) wanted to achieve this Indra-like triumph (*aindra vijaya*, *Śāntip*. XCVII, 17-18).

'Activity (*utthāna*), said Bṛhaspati, is for the "Indras" of men, the foundation of a right, royal order and know the stanzas about this subject:

'Through activity, ambrosia was obtained, through action the Titans were beaten, through action great Indra achieved pre-eminence in Heaven and down here' (*Śāntip*. LVIII, 13-14).

But he is also similar to other divinities who collaborate to preserve the right cosmic and terrestrial order:

'The king is Yama (Master and Controller), supreme Lord of

all that is within the Order (*dhārmika*); he is master of lives, but when he isn't, he breaks the rules.

'When he receives the officers, the chaplain and masters perfectly, but honouring and not disdaining them, this is what is called the right order for the king.

'Yama is lord of all beings without distinction; the king must emulate him; the subjects must be contained according to the rules.

'The king is very much like the Thousand-eyed One (Indra), for the Order he desires is the Order (par excellence, the right, unique, universal Order)' (*Śāntip*. XCII, 38-41).

'The king is Indra, the king is Yama, the king is Dharma (the Right Order) too. The king embodies (their) aspects; all is in order (*dhṛta*) thanks to the king'. (*Śāntip*. LXXII, 26).

If man were to contemplate any evil of him, but only in his mind, he would be inevitably tainted down here, and once dead, he would fall into hell.

'One must not disdain the Guardian of the Earth too, by saying: "He is a man", for he is a great divinity in human form (= *Manu*, VII, 8, variant).

'He embodies five aspects and always according to the need of the hour: he is Agni (Fire), and the Sun, Death (Mṛtyu), Vaiśravaṇa, Yama.

'In fact, when the king is served badly he burns the wicked with his terrible radiance, then he becomes Fire (*Pāvaka*).

'When as a Guardian of the Earth he observes all things with the help of a spy and continues to provide security, then he is the Sun.

'When, irritated, he destroys corrupt men in hundreds with their sons and grandsons and their clients, he then becomes Death (*Antaka*).

'When he suppresses all disorder with severe punishment and promotes all things that are in harmony with Order, it is then that he is Yama.

'And when he rewards those who serve with a wealth of riches and strips the wrong-doers of all their precious possessions, he offers wealth to one and takes it away from the other, then in this world he is Vaiśravaṇa, the Guardian of the Earth.' (*Śāntip*. LXVIII, 39-47).

He is especially Indra's substitute on the Earth:

'It is Indra we select when we choose a king', says the Revelation; it is actually to Indra he pays obeisance while bowing to the king, he who desires prosperity.' (*Śāntip*. LXVII, 4).

And there is a necessary concordance between the regular action of Heaven and that of the king in order to achieve the happiness of the subjects:

'When Parjanya rains in time and the earthly king conducts himself according to the Order, then prosperity keeps the subjects in well-being." (Śāntip. XCII, 1).

'His conduct, which is so important, should at the same time, be full of gentle solicitude for he must be concerned with what is salubrious for the world as a future mother takes precautions for the child she bears. (*Śāntip*. LVI, 44-45).

The teaching of Manu is totally in agreement, except for a few variants. The Lord created the king for the preservation of the universe by setting apart the eternal elements of Indra, the Wind, Yama, the Sun, Fire, Varuṇa, the Moon, and the Lord of riches (Kubera). By his effulgence he surpasses all beings and one cannot look at him. Through his divinity he is all the forementioned gods and he is indeed a great divinity in human form (VII, 3-8). Moreover, according to the same Manu, his divine and cosmic nature becomes evident in the sequence of his activities, comparable, on the one hand, with the prevailing tendencies in the successive ages of the world, on the other, with the functions of the same eight divinities except for Kubera who is substituted this time by the Earth. His sleep corresponds to the Age of Kali when the Order is suspended and disorder reigns supreme; his waking up to the Age of Dvāpara, his rising to the Age of Tretā, his movement to the Age of Kṛta when the right Order is best maintained. He must then shower his good deeds as Indra sends down his rain, withdraw taxes as the Sun sucks in humidity, move about everywhere through his emissaries like the Wind, control like Yama, arrest the wicked like Varuṇa, rejoice like the full Moon, swallow misdeeds like Fire and sustain all creatures as the Earth bears them. (*Manu*, IX, 301-311).

It is therefore quite natural that literature and epigraphy speak of the king, popularly known as *deva*, god, and of the queen as *devī*, goddess. This latter term is used to designate the second wife of Aśoka (the Queen's edict, J. Bloch ed., p. 159) or the other queens of Aśoka (7th edict on Pillar, J. Bloch ed., p. 171). But '*deva*' is used in all addresses to the king whether in the vocative or other cases. But the title of *deva* joined to royal names doesn't always signify 'king' and, at the end of a compound, should often be understood to mean 'who has so-and-so for god'. The designation 'son of god', *Devaputra*, *devaputta* in Pāli, is frequently given to sons of kings (in the Pāli Canon especially), without at the same time losing the meaning of 'divine being' on (*devaputra*, cf. lastly F.W. Thomas, *B.C. Law Volume* II, Poona, 1946, p. 305-320).

The divine nature of kings is not such that it is always complete: its degrees may vary; it may even fade out completely. The king who moves according to the right Order becomes, after his death, a veritable god in Heaven, whereas he who doesn't move according to the Order goes to hell (*Śāntip.* XCI, 4). It remains true, however, that this aspect is stressed as strongly as possible in human nature and it is also reinforced by the legends about the origins of the royal lunar and solar races. According to these legends the king can not only be composed of divine elements but can also be an incarnation as is the case of a divine being as was, for example, the case with the first anointed Pṛthu, who was an incarnation of Viṣṇu.

The correlation of the functions of the king with those of the divinities of the world is also reiterated by the panegyrics which are not merely literary and adulatory compositions but also works of *kavis*, poets who are the creators of the 'body of glory' and in this light, true *prajāpatis*, lords of creatures (Rājataraṅginī, I, 3-4, cf. *Le symbolisme du monument du Phnoṃ Bakheṅ*, *BEFEO*, XLIV, p. 549 and foll.) Through these poets' utterances as through the monumental works of their symbolist architects, the Brahmanic and Hindu kings were able to establish their divine kinship. They did this in a particularly striking manner in ancient Hinducised Cambodia. It is likely that the most extravagant panegyrics are the magnification of real facts raised to divine proportions, or they are meant to serve the purpose of exhortations or prophecies. In fact, there exists a famous legendary prototype of songs of anticipated glory; those that were sung during the coronation of Pṛthu (*Viṣṇupur* I, XII, 53 and foll., *Bhāgavata Pur.* IV, 16).

Even in the Sanskrit tradition in the Far East, the king is

considered a god on earth because he is supposed to be the protector of the order on earth as the gods are its protectors in the cosmos as a whole. Similar is the case with non-Sanskrit tradition. The Tamil *Kuṟaḷ* 388, for instance, states:

"The master who by executing the Rule (*muṟei*) ensures protection is seen by people to be installed as God (*iṟei*)".

The actual adoration of the King as a divine being is testified to by the Greeks of the time of Alexander. Nearchus mentions that men not only bowed to him but also worshipped him in the manner of a divinity and that this custom seems peculiar to India. (*Strabo*, XV, 1, 67). The way Candragupta was made unapproachable as noted by Megasthenes, (*Strabo* XV, 1, 55) cannot merely be explained in terms of security; it can better be explained in terms of the preoccupation of holding the people away from their God (Cf. The "*Deva*" of Aśoka, "gods" or "divine majesties?" *J.A.* 1949, p. 225-247). Nearchus' testimony, in any case, confirms that from at least the end of the 4th cent. B.C., India was ready to promote the notion of the divinity of kings which she would later propagate to Indochina and Indonesia with Brahmanic conceptions and rituals. For these countries the history of the religions of India illuminates to a great extent the origins of their ideas and customs.

This history of religions sheds light even on aspects that are not so obvious like that of popular beliefs where the presence of an erudite religious contribution is not expected.

One of these beliefs is that of the plurality of souls which are to be held and tied down to the body, eventually to be called back. It is quite widespread in the whole of Southeast Asia and the neighbouring archipelago, contemporaneously in the most diverse environments whether the culture be Indian, Chinese or Islamic and it seems therefore to be a fact of a common substratum, the more so as it is to be also found in groups without any literary culture (cf. Jeanne Cuisinier, *Sumangat*, Paris 1951; Eveline Porée-Maspero, La cérémonie de l'appel des esprits vitaux chez les Cambodgiens, *BEFEO* XLV, p. 145-183).

Now, in India, such beliefs are found more or less pushed to the background by classical philosophical conceptions but still used by them and likely to have been taken outside India as rudimentary conceptions of man and therefore easily understood without the need of any explanation or scholarly speculations.

The notion of the materiality of the principle of life similar to a dwarf, big as the thumb, inhabiting the body and capable of being torn out from it, is clearly spoken of in the *Upaniṣads* (*Kaṭha*- IV, 12, 13; *Śvet*- V, 8; *Maitrī*- VI, 38, etc.) although in a figurative rather than a physical representation. The notion is more popularly mentioned in the famous myth of Satyavant whose life in the shape of a thumb-like man is caught in a lasso (*pāśabaddha*) by Yama and pulled out of the body (*Mahābhārata* III, 296, 17-18). But the idea is sometimes challenged by philosophers or identified with the theory of the subtle body, the liṅga, which confers on man his vital characteristics (cf. S.N. Dasgupta, *A History of Indian Philosophy* II, Cambridge 1932, p. 306, n.).

Elsewhere the notion of a soul (*asu*) or multiple souls in contact with the vital breaths and without a precise form which can escape but which can be called back and tied down, is spoken of even earlier in the formulae of the *Atharva Veda*.

V, 30, 1: *asum badhnāmi dṛḍham*, 'I firmly attach your soul.'

VIII, 1, 1: *antakāya mṛtyave namaḥ prāṇā apānā* te *ramantām ihāyam astu puruṣaḥ sahāsunā...*,' To the End, to Death, homage! May the breaths that are in front and those that are below be in harmony with you. Here let this man be with his soul...'

VIII, 1, 15: *mā tvā prāṇo balaṃ hāsīd asuṃ te 'nu hvayāmasi*, 'May the life-breath and the force not abandon you, we beckon your soul.'

VIII, 2, 26: *ma te hāsiṣur asavaḥ śarīram*, 'May your souls not leave your body.'

Such similarity of notions and expression of these notions that we find in the literature of India and that of the countries of South-east Asia, does not by itself imply the necessity of direct contact. This can be explained by a common simple way of dealing with the problem of life. But direct contact did take place and leaves, in some cases, unmistakable traces.

It is, thus, that the nineteen vital spirits accepted in Cambodia are called *praling*, a word where one can distinguish after *pra*, a probable distortion of the honorific *braḥ*, the word *ling*, generally interpreted as deriving from the Sanskrit *liṅga*. But Porée-Maspero prefers to see the Chinese word ling 'spiritual substance'. Now *liṅga* in the singular precisely designates in Sanskrit the soul which is the subtle body, *liṅgadeha* or *liṅgaśarīra*, strictly 'character-body', and in the plural the very characteristics of life. *Linga* is composed of eighteen elements according to the classical teaching of Sāṃkhya, namely, vide Aniruddha (*Śāṃkhyasūtravṛtti* III, 9): consciousness (*buddhi*), the idea of self (*ahaṅkāra*), the mind (*manas*, focaliser of sensations and feelings), the five subtle forms of the material elements (*bhūta*) and the ten sensory and motory faculties (*indriya*).

Elsewhere, the *Kāśyapasaṃhitā* (Hemraj Śarmā ed., Bombay, Nepal Sanskrit Series, no. 1 p. 45) which calls the soul '*kṣetrajña*', 'knower of the field', based on the current notion that equates the soul with the agent of knowledge, attributes to it thirteen *liṅgas*, 'characteristics' or 'signs', namely: ideation (*cetanā*), the idea of self (*ahaṅkāra*), the breath in front (*prāṇa*), the breath below (*apāna*), the opening of eyes (*unmeṣa*), their closing (*nimeṣa*), pleasure (*sukha*), pain (*duḥkha*), desire (*icchā*), repulsion (*dveṣa*), evoking memory (*smṛti*), the retaining memory (*dhṛti*), and consciousness (*buddhi*).

As they are known at present, the Cambodian notions of the nineteen *praling* do not fully agree with the eighteen elements of *linga* and the thirteen *lingas* of the soul. But India has elaborated yet other theories about the constitution of man and his soul. The *Sāṃkhyasūtras*, among others, allude to the theories that state that the body is composed of five elements, or of four, or just one (III, 17-19) and the Cambodian traditions, compiled so far, reveal some peculiarities resulting from the confusion in the interpretation of Indian documents. In fact, in addition to the nineteen *pralings*, these traditions ascribe to man four demons that inhabit him and are called by a name that corresponds exactly to *caturbhūta* (Porée-Maspero, p. 145) but here there is an evident confusion between two meanings of bhūta, 'spirit, demon' and 'elements'; the four elements that are present in the body are: earth, water, fire and air. But this confusion is fruitful for we have the example of an interpretation of a modern Cambodian reporter which represents the four *bhūtas* as miniature men which reminds us of the thumb-sized soul of the later Vedic texts and of the *Mahābhārata*. Thus we have here a clear example of the indispensable nature of a total exploitation of Indian sources for ethnological studies wherever the Indian influence could have made itself felt. It is only through a total understanding of the Indian data that a correct account could be drawn up about the original contributions of the numerous peoples, born out of an interaction with the vastly influential religions of India.

CHAPTER 5

AŚOKA AND THE SPREAD OF BUDDHISM*

BUDDHISTIC TRADITION readily considers next to the kings who favourably received the Buddha himself, Aśoka as the great benefactor of the Saṅgha and the king who strove to propagate its Doctrine. The numerous edicts of Aśoka, found engraved on rocks and on pillars from Afghanistan to Mysore, corroborate this tradition even as they enable us to understand better the activities of the great king who was certainly closer to the Buddhist community than to any other but this did not, in any way, take him away from his function of a guardian-prince of a general Right Order on the Earth, an Order not exclusively Buddhistic.

We do not have the full account of his reign through his inscriptions. We have only a part of it, but we have much more than simply a series of events: we have a firsthand report, a direct testimony, a confession and a declaration of intentions and of decisions. It is the sovereign's mind itself that unfolds itself before us directly and not, as happens in so many other cases, through official eulogies of a panegyrist on duty or the reports of a later annalist.

We know what he says in clear, straightforward words which he got engraved throughout his empire. When he had already been crowned king for eight successful years, he conquered the Kalinga province on the Bay of Bengal. He conquered through force but he was profoundly moved by the horrors of war. Laymen, brahmins, religious people from all communities, the virtuous and the good, everyone had to submit to killing, captivity and death or see others being subjected to these. Henceforth, he would wage no war of force but of *Dhamma*, a *dhamma* which consists in a good, universal Order and which he strives to establish in his kingdom and counsels other kings to do the same.

Despite the similitude of the word *Dhamma*, despite Asoka's

*Aśoka et l'expansion bouddhique in *Présence du Bouddhisme*, France–Asie, 1959, p. 427–431.

personal predilection for Buddhism, it is not, in effect, the Buddhist Law which is in question; nor does it deal with the organisation of states and of society. It consists in becoming conscious of the vanity of worldly things and in adhering to a discipline which shall break all craving for them. It implies all that a responsible king is required to do in this world to make it better even while it continues to remain vain; it requires of a king to let well-being and security take over from suffering. For, according to the Brahmanic social ideal, which Buddhism neither rejects nor substitutes, the king is on the Earth as the representative of the king of the gods in Heaven, gods who, according to Canonical Pāli texts, are shown to meet in an assembly each year under their chief and under a Brahmā, who manifests himself to them, to guarantee the good functioning of the world. In this the Buddhist Doctrine does not set out anything new in itself, but it presents itself as a means to realise this ideal. It does invent charity and compassion; but it does present them as deeply dear to Brahmā; it urges upon people to cultivate them in order to obtain temporal happiness even while they are waiting to break all links with existence. With Brahmā above them, the gods watch over the Buddhist Law as well as over the natural Order.

It is with this attitude that Aśoka conducted himself. Immediately after the conquest of Kaliṅga, he seemed to be convinced that Buddhism, which unceasingly denounces suffering in the world, was the path he himself had to take in order to escape from that suffering and he embraced it as a laic. He confesses that for a year he did not feel great zeal but then progressively he came close to the *Saṅgha*, and took up its practice; he went on a peregrination for the entire period that a Buddhist monk is ordained to, without however renouncing the world and his secular duties. He got his Brahmanic astronomers to calculate precisely the duration of his peregrination. He then gradually prohibited the slaughtering of animals for his food and on the important days of the Brahmanic calendar even in all his states. Occasionally he advised people to read Buddhist texts but he laid more emphasis on peace and good conduct. He undertook a pilgrimage to the place of Buddha's Enlightenment and ordered works of public utility to be carried out and instituted a control of the peaceful life of the country. His envoys went on a mission of conquering princes of foreign lands to the spirit of the *Dhamma* and we see in the instances that he has specifically mentioned that he also sent aid for men and animals. Everytime there is a reference to anything Buddhist in his edicts, it is connected with his personal activity except when he counsels others to read some particular scriptures. Everytime he speaks to his subjects or on their behalf, it is to propound an ideal of right conduct and not to ask them to adhere to a specific doctrine. In fact, he expresses his preoccupation with maintaining peace among all sects. Himself a Buddhist, he strives to be a good, impartial king to all his subjects.

But there is no doubt that he helped spread the Buddhist Law as he preached with his own example, through his example and belief, even while enforcing his measures for the reestablishment of a general, temporal Right Order. He favoured it indirectly by the position that he accorded, in his own capital, to the venerable Tissa Moggaliputta whose disciple he had become. Through the assembly of the third great Council at this capital, Pāṭaliputra, Tissa put an end to the sectarian disputes that were dividing the Saṅgha. From his side, the King promulgated an edict against monks who might disrupt the unity of the Saṅgha that they would have to wear white robes, that is to say, they would lose their right to wear the yellow robe of a true monk.

According to the 'Great Chronicle' of Ceylon, the *Mahāvaṃsa* (chap. XII), it was Tissa who, after his Council's success, took direct charge of the propagation of the Law beyond the territories where it already held sway. We have the list of names and destinations of these selected missionaries.

Majjhantika was sent to Kashmir and to Gandhāra, to the North-Western region of the empire; Mahādeva was sent to Mahisamaṇḍala, 'the district of the Buffalo', the present-day Maisūr in the South; Rakkhita to Vanavāsa, 'the Sojourn in the Jungles', also in the South in the Northern part of the Kannaḍa country; Dhammarakkhita, who was a 'Greek' (*yona*) to Aparāntaka, i.e. to Gujarāt in the West; Mahādhammarakkhita to the Maratha country in the South-West; Mahārakkhita to the 'Greek country'; Majjhima to the Himalayan regions; Soṇa and Uttara to the 'Land of Gold', probably Burma or may be the whole of Indochina and the Malay peninsula; and, finally, Mahinda to Ceylon.

Among the different countries in this list, some are under Aśoka's sovereignty, the others, foreign. In any case, as regards the 'Greek country', it can refer to the Greek country that was dependent on Aśoka rather than autonomous Greek kingdoms. The inscriptions refer to both. The second-rock edict lists, among the kings of the countries bordering the empire, the Greek king Antiochus and so does the thirteenth edict as well as four other Greek kings who came after him: Ptolemy, Antigone, Magos, and Alexander. These are precisely the kings of the kingdoms which divided the conquered territories of Alexander the Great. But the text goes on to add to the list of these foreign princes, the names of the Tamil kingdoms of the Extreme-south of the peninsula and Ceylon, and then continues with an enumeration of some peoples that it qualifies as being 'here within the royal domain' (*idha rājavi sayamhi*) and this enumeration is topped by the Greeks and the Kambojas: Yonakamboja.

It had seemed difficult for Hellenists like W.W. Tarn to accept that an Indian king could have subjugated the Greeks. W.W. Tarn expressed his doubts in this regard in 1938, even though 50 years earlier, Senart had already pointed out while publishing the Aśokan inscriptions that the Greeks referred to must have belonged to the territories which, according to the Greek geographer Strabo, Seleucus had conceded to Aśoka's grandfather, Candragupta.

The indications that Strabo provided were in fact categorical and precise. He had written (XV, 1, 10 and 2, 9) that the parts of riparian provinces of the Indus which Alexander had taken over from the Arianoi, and which he had peopled with colonies of the Greeks, had belonged from the time of Eratosthenes (276-194 B.C.) to India, having been ceded by Seleucus Nicator to Candragupta, as a guarantee for a matrimonial convention and in exchange for five hundred elephants. Jules Bloch too, writing in 1950, could repeat what Alfred Foucher had written in 1947, namely that it would not astonish him if the exploration of the Jāguḍa country were to demonstrate one day the correctness of Senart's finding. The Jāguḍa country is the valley of Arghand-āb, the river of Arachosia in Eastern Afghanistan where one could situate near the present-day Kandahar, the Alexandria of Arachosia founded by Alexander. And the discovery Foucher had sensed occurred exactly there in April, 1958 in the form of a bilingual inscription of Aśoka, in Greek and in Aramean, which has just been published in Serie *Orientale Rome* (tome XXI, 1958) and in the *Journal Asiatique* (1958, 1).

Erastothenes and Strabo were then right: during the former's lifetime, a slightly younger contemporary of Aśoka, the ancient Greek colony did in fact belong to India and Senart had rightly sought there Greeks who were dependent on Aśoka. Moreover, we see today, thanks to the new inscription which dates from the middle of the 3rd cent. B.C., that Hellenic culture had preserved itself very well since the time of secession by Seleucus, which went back to 305 B.C. But here Greek was not the only official language; Aramean, an Aramean that contained quite a good number of Iranian words, was also used there as in all the provinces which had been part of the vast Persian empire—where it had been the language of administration. According to Mr. Benveniste's guess, the Kamboja named concurrently with the Yonas by Aśoka, could allude to the people to whom the Aramean part of the inscription was destined, a part which comes immediately below the Greek section.

In both these versions, the inscription is totally consistent with the first rock-edicts of Aśoka, whom it calls in Greek *Piodasses*, even as the latter called it *Piyadasi*. It expresses the king's decision to show to men 'piety' (Greek) or 'Truth' (Aramean) and to establish general prosperity. The king calls upon people not to kill animals for the king's food, he calls upon those who were not master of themselves to become self-controlled; he respects obedience to one's ancestors and to elderly people and declares that such conduct would be more beneficial in every way. Here there is no specific reference to Buddhism. It is not a religious practice, neither a particular Buddhist discipline which is imposed or sanctified; it is civil ethics for the well-being of people and for all beings, a well-being which should be provided in a well-ordered kingdom. At the end of his life, twenty-six years after his coronation, the great king, in fact, clearly defined what he meant by the *Dhamma* which he had propagated and maintained in its purity with the help of his officers:

Dhamma is good, but what is *Dhamma*?

It is the absence of evil, the abundance of good, pity, generosity, truthfulness, purity.

2nd edict on Pillar

Although he had himself chosen the Buddhist path, Aśoka never wished to make use of his power to impose it. He specifies in the 5th rock-edict that the superintendents of *Dhamma* he had created thirteen years after his coronation, were supposed to look after 'all sects'.

The dates themselves of the edicts and the acts which are alluded to therein reiterate once again that it is necessary to distinguish between the propagation of *Dhamma*, the ideal of the Right Order, by the king as a sovereign, and the *Dhamma*, the Buddhist Law, to which the King owed personal allegiance but of which the propagation was the responsibility of the Community. In fact, it was at the time when Aśoka had been already king for eighteen years that, according to the Great Chronicle of Ceylon, Tissa sent his missionaries, whereas it was only after eight years of kingship that Aśoka started—with little zeal at first, as he himself tells us—to come close to the Community and that it was after thirteen years of rule that he created superintendents of the *Dhamma* in order to send them all over on trips every five years.

But nothing could have been more favourable to the propagation of Buddhism than the personal example of the king and the ideal of orderly right conduct which was set for all to follow and for the realisation of which Buddhism naturally seemed to be the perfect instrument.

CHAPTER 6

THE ŚAIVA ĀGAMAS*

THE ŚAIVA ĀGAMAS constitute a part of Sanskrit literature that has been very much neglected to this day. Numerous manuals do not make any mention of them. Such is the case, for instance, with A.B. Keith's work, *A History of Sanskrit Literature* (Oxford, 1928). Winternitz, on the other hand, could dedicate only one paragraph and a few notes in his large *History of Indian Literature*[1]. He was under the impression that out of the 28 traditionally listed Āgamas only 20 had been preserved in a fragmentary form. He was unaware that a number of texts had already been published in their entirety. They had been published in fact in "grantha" script editions which most Indologists were unfamiliar with.

In truth, these editions were not meant for them; they were used in Tamil country by the Śaiva devotees in whose midst the tradition of the Āgama doctrines and rituals was still alive. And it is precisely this that makes them important for understanding the still-practised Śaiva religion. These Āgamas were and continue to be used, especially by the officiating priests of Śaiva temples in Tamil country, the gurukkaḷ, since these texts describe, among other things, their liturgy.

Of these texts J.N. Farquhar gathered the maximum information but that information is quite scarce;[2] for even he was not aware of the existing editions. The works of Schomerus,[3] based on a crucial but badly analysed literature, have shed insufficient light on the Āgamas.

Their most important use to this day has been made by archaeologists and art historians. The literature of the Āgamas, in fact, contains detailed descriptions of the laws of the foundation and construction of temples and the making of divine images. Gopinatha Rao and Krishnasastri who had access to the grantha-editions and to manuscripts, have used them extensively in their

*Les Agama Çivaïtes, introduction to N.R. Bhatt, *Rauravāgama* I, I.F.I. no. 18, Pondicherry, 1961, p. V–XV.

classic works on iconography.[4] So has Acharya in his many works on the *Mānasāra* and on architecture.[5] Stella Kramrisch in her *Hindu Temple*[6] and other authors have often referred to them. D.N. Shukla recently translated numerous passages in his *Vāstu-Śāstra, Hindu Canons of Iconography and Painting.*[7]

The Āgamas are indeed cardinal sources for the identification of the types of temples and the divine images that adorn them. In South India, where, as we shall see, the Āgamas had their origin, the verification of the images themselves with their precise descriptions in the texts is indispensable in determining the nature and significance of most of these elements. They reveal between themselves certain differences of detail and the figured representations often differ from the prescribed standards but the agreements far outnumber the divergences. Śaiva iconography, on the whole, is in harmony with the data given in the Āgamas.

The expositions that describe the divine figures have a form that is analogous to those in *Agnipurāṇa* in Hindu literature, or to those in *Sādhanamālā* among Buddhist texts. This latter has enabled a number of writers since Alfred Foucher[8], to undertake an accurate study of Tantric Buddhist iconography.[9] And so the Āgamas are Tantras as well.

Āgama is opposed to *Nigama* as *Tantra* is to *Veda*. *Nigama* has been recognised as a synonymn of *Veda* since Pāṇini (VI, 3, 113). Although used much less, this term can always substitute *Veda*, even in a proper name like *Vedāntadeśika* who is also called *Nigamāntadeśika*. If *Veda*, 'Knowledge', is *Nigama*, it is because *nigama* is taken to mean either 'final establishing' and 'certainty' or, as in the *Śabdakalpadruma*, as 'that by which one learns, one knows' (*nigamyate jñāyate anena iti nigamaḥ*).

Āgama, in any case, is 'tradition'. The *Śabdakalpadruma* defines it thus: 'It has come from Him who has five mouths and it is in the mouth of Her who is born from the Mountain and it is that which is recognised by Vāsudeva, that is why it is *āgama*".[10] This definition applies specially to Śaivāgama taught to Pārvatī by Śiva with the five mouths. Vāsudeva, that is Viṣṇu-Kṛṣṇa, is assimilated in the Śaiva hierarchy but in the second rank.

These *Śaivāgamas* are in principle composed of four *pādas*: *Vidyāpāda*, the doctrine, *kriyāpāda*, the ritual, *caryāpāda*, the conduct and *yogapāda*, the psycho-physiological discipline. It is the same in principle with the *Tantras*. The term *Tantra* means strictly the linking of a cloth or a composition. It is interpreted in the *Āgamas* as if it was formed through the union of the roots *TAN* 'stretch', and *TRĀ* 'save'. 'It elaborates on the vast subjects connected with the essences and the formulae and helps in liberation; that is why it is called *tantra*'.[11]

In fact, the two denominations of *āgama* and *tantra* designate the same kind of texts and if *tantra* is more in use in the North and *āgama* in the South, the *Āgamas* in the South are also popularly given the designation of *Tantra*.

The two names are applied even today interchangeably to texts of the same nature that belong to the Vaiṣṇavas and which are usually called *Saṃhitā*, 'collection'.[12] *Āgama*, *Tantra* and *Saṃhitā*, distinct or intermingled, represent anyway the religious manuals of the techniques of Hinduism as distinct from the ancient Brahmanism with its Vedic ritual. Their importance is due to this, but this importance was neglected for much too long as a great number of scholars became interested first in the origins of Indian religions and in their most ancient forms rather than their state of development, of blossoming and of present living reality.

These texts are, in fact, technical treatises of religious beliefs and practice. In order to know and understand religions fully it is indispensable to study them deeply. The other categories of Hindu texts, much more well-known and generally more attractive, are insufficient, despite their great importance, to present all the aspects of Hinduism. These other categories of texts are firstly the *Dharmaśāstras* which contain *Smṛti*, mental remembrance and interpretation of a traditional knowledge of the order of things, and *Dharma*, which is as cosmological as it is social and ethical; then the *Purāṇas*, which are a collection of ancient stories describing the events and adventures that took place in the course of the play of the order of things in the world, among the Gods, the kings and the sages; also the epics, the *Mahābhārata* especially, narrating, in relation to the Order of things, heroic and human events and showing the part played by God in shaping those events; the works of philosophers, commenting on ancient texts which refer to the essence of things and disagreeing among themselves; finally the Vedic texts, *Śruti* or audition, *Veda* or strictly speaking 'Knowledge' and Brahmanic texts linked to the *Vedas*. But this literature, which is the most ancient, and, partially, of fundamental importance, is no more utilised in its totality and lives on in Hinduism only as a residual, though significant, element. The ancient Vedic and Brahmanic rites, aimed at maintaining the regularity of natural phenomena and the prosperity of mankind, especially the great solemn rites, are no more practiced. The shift of the human ideal, talked about from the time of the Upaniṣads, from pleasure to the knowledge of the Being and to knowledge of oneself as a participant in this Being, then the cultivation of the ardent inclination of *bhakti* towards the same Being as the Supreme God, gave way to new rituals, rituals of symbolism and adoration to which were appended methods of refashioning the psychic individuality. Everything that is connected with these rituals and these methods forms the subject of the *Āgamas*, the *Tantras* and the *Saṃhitas*. The other Hindu texts that are less technical—and thereby more attractive—set forth the philosophic ideas, religious beliefs and the corresponding legends, but only briefly refer to the practice of the religion or contain merely partial and infrequent descriptions of them. All these literatures therefore complement each other and should be studied simultaneously and compared constantly.

As the *Āgamas* and similar texts refer most of the time only briefly to legends which they illustrate through descriptive pictures, we have to take recourse to the *Purāṇas* which are the principal collections of these legends. Those that contain them are part of the great classical *Purāṇas*, such as *Liṅga-*, *Kūrma-*, *Vāmana-*, *Padma-*, or *Skanda-* and also the *Upapurāṇas*. They are found in addition in the vast literature of the *Sthalapurāṇas* or *Māhātmyas*, devoted to specific sacred places, and of which a part is incorporated in the great *Purāṇas* and the *Upapurāṇas*, and even in the *Mahābhārata*. They are found again in the *Purāṇas* and the *Māhātmyas* written in the language of the region where the corresponding sacred spot is situated.

In these circumstances the French Institute of Indology has undertaken in Pondicherry not only a research of the Āgamas and the preparation of a series of publications which the present work, *Rauravāgama*, inaugurates, but also a survey of Sanskrit and Tamil legends which provide a complement to the information given in the Āgamas, as well as a systematic photographic survey of the existing images. The first attempt at comparison of Āgamic and Purāṇic texts with the image-documentation is published in the *Arts Asiatiques*, with the study of the *liṅgodhbhavamūrti* to be followed immediately by that of the *bhikṣāṭana* and the *kaṅkālamūrti*.

But there is yet another interest in studying the Āgamas, especially the *Śaivāgamas*. The ancient kingdoms of Southeast Asia, Cam, Khmer or Javanese and Sumatranese, have considerably borrowed Śaiva concepts and rituals from India—concepts reflected in their culture by monuments created in their own style and not in imitation of those in India, but suggestingnevertheless, a profound Indian influence. Now the religions in these countries have changed and reduced Hinduism to merely some lingering vestiges. In Campa, the Chinese and Vietnamese cultures have replaced the Cam culture. In Cambodia, Theravādin Buddhism has replaced Hinduism and the Mahāyānic Buddhism. In Indonesia, Islam has covered up the past that was linked with Hinduism and Buddhism. The explanation of the monuments of these countries cannot therefore be found in the traditions prevailing today. The bulk of the ancient Sanskrit inscriptions scattered in the Indochinese peninsula, especially in Cambodia and in Campa and in Indonesia until Kelamantan (Borneo), largely compensates for the disappearances of the traditions connected with these monuments and with the culture of their builders. These are completed by the inscriptions which are found beside them and which are composed in the different languages of the ancient kingdoms. But epigraphical literature provides, in the main, references which need interpretation to be fully intelligible. As regards the principles of representation and the techniques of the cult, we have to turn only to India and to the specialised literature that corresponds to them, to get information likely to reveal to us the meaning of the archaeological observations. In fact, the Sanskrit inscriptions in Cambodia themselves indicate their sources. It is the texts of Hinduism that we know: the *Vedas*—but more as a general foundation of knowledge than in their textual form—, the *Dharmaśāstras*, the Epics, the *Purāṇas*, even the teachings of Śaṅkara[13] and the *Āgamas* to which several references are made. One of these references is specific. It is related to *Pārameśvara* which is mentioned several times in the context of Śaivaism and which must be *Pārameśvarāgama*. We haven't yet found this text itself. We only possess the *Vidyāpāda* of the *Mātangapārameśvara*, an *upāgama*, edited by Kṛṣṇaśāstrin at Devakottai in 1924. But the *Pārameśvara* is also one of the *āgamas* that the community of Lingayats mentions as one of the fundamental texts on which its founder or renovator Basava based himself in the 12th century, although they do not still possess it.

Besides the fundamental texts of the *Āgamas*, there still exists an abundant literature on Śaiva ritual which will be found to be frequently used in the notes to the publication which follows (by Aghoraśivācārya, Somaśambhu, etc.) and which is contemporaneous with a great flowering of Śaiva building and image-making in India as well as in Cambodia and it completes or clarifies the indications of the more ancient scriptural authorities.

The period in which the *Āgamas* were composed is uncertain, especially if we wish to consider the date for each *Āgama* separately. It seems, in fact, that their group, at least the part we know, was constituted of texts which, while possibly being composed independently from one another, were not preserved as such in their entirety but underwent modifications in their presentation when they were revised or classified. It does not seem that the texts were interfered with to such a point that the data of the different texts were brought together, but passages from a number of them mention or even enumerate the others. It is therefore obvious that at least these passages were written after they were unified in a classified body.

On the other hand, their classification is not always the same within the entire Āgamic school. The list given by the *Ajita* (*Kriyāp.*) which divided them according to the five mouths of Śiva that uttered them, is different from that which is current in the tradition of the Śaivasiddhānta school founded on the *Āgamas*. The list of the *Ajita*, in fact, is the following:

Uttered by the Sadyojāta mouth: *Vijaya, Pārameśvara, Niśvāsa, Prodgīta, Mukhabimba*

by Vāmadeva: *Siddha, Santāna, Śarvokta, Candrajñāna, Vimala*

by Aghora: *Svāyambhuva, Vīra, Raurava, Makuṭa, Kiraṇa*

by Īśāna: *Kāmika, Yogaja, Cintya, Kāraṇa, Ajita, Dīpta, Sūkṣma, Sahasra, Aṃśumat, Suprabheda.*

However in the *Pauṣkarabhāṣya* (page 1) the totality of the *Āgamas* is designated by: *Kāmikādivātulānta,* which refers not to the preceding list but to the next, that is commonly given:

Uttered by Sadyojāta: *Kāmika, Yogaja, Cintya, Kāraṇa, Ajita*
by Vāmadeva: *Dīpta, Sūkṣma, Sahasra, Aṃśumat, Suprabheda.*
by Aghora: *Vijaya, Niśvāsa, Svāyaṃbhuva, Anala, Vīra.*
by Tatpuruṣa: *Raurava, Makuṭa, Vimala, Candrajñāna, Bimba.*
by Īśāna: *Prodgīta, Lalita, Siddha, Santāna, Śarvokta, Pārameśvara, Kiraṇa, Vātula.*

This last order is followed in a list of *Āgamas* correlated to the different parts of the anthropomorphic body of Śiva. It will be noticed that those that it considers uttered by the mouth Sadyojāta are those that the list of *Ajita* ascribes to the mouth Īśāna, and that it attributes to the mouth Vāmadeva what the *Ajita* also ascribes to the mouth Īśāna, the series elsewhere having been disturbed in the attribution of the other texts to other mouths. The classifications reflect therefore the varying opinions of the Śaiva scholars and not a tradition fixed from the time of the elaboration of the texts. What has been really compiled is therefore not in its original form of presentation, which does not mean that their contents are not of ancient origin.

In order to evaluate the age of the teachings enshrined in the Āgamas, we have at our disposal some data which is unequally significant. The references made to the Āgamas or to the doctrines of the Āgamas in the Tamil texts were seen as indications of the period in which the *Āgamas* must have already existed, but the authors' opinions did not agree on the dates of the Tamil texts which would have implied or were supposed to imply the existence of the *Āgamas*. This problem has to be taken up and today with more hope than formerly. Some dates have been determined, as Karavelane has shown regarding *Kāreikkālammeiyār*[14] and one can foresee at least a partial reconstitution of the chronology of the Tamil texts of which the authors are known and linked to historical places and reigns.

Another observation becomes necessary. As we have ourselves pointed out in the introduction to the work of Karavelane on *Kāreikkālammeiyār*, a number of words that are used by the Śaiva saint to designate Śiva coincide with those that are found in texts such as the *Kumārasaṃbhava* of Kālidāsa. Now, these names can be related to the attitudes, attributes and the ornaments of Śiva. They show that from the 4th and 5th centuries A.D., aspects of Śiva that are the same that are described in detail in the *Āgamas* and which match the corresponding legends from a part of the *Purāṇas*, had already been conceived in the Śaiva tradition and known as much in Tamil as well as in Sanskrit literature. This does not necessarily mean that the Āgamas had already been composed but makes it probable that they could have been or, at least, it indicates the period in which their elaboration had the greatest chance of being accepted in order to codify the already very complex subject which the poets were familiar with. What we lack to be more accurate about the dates of the origin and of the elaboration of the texts, is, above all, the literature of the first periods of the making of Hinduism. We are suddenly face to face with the literature that Hinduism finally adopted in addition to the Vedic and Brahmanic literature. We do not have knowledge of the first attempts but only of their culmination, as the religious erudite milieus fixed them in their work of compilation and classification. Another fact finally enables us to situate in time at least some of the *Āgamas*, but it is more imprecise than the preceding ones and has mostly another utility: to show us the extent in terms of geography of the knowledge and the authoritativeness of these texts. In fact, the Śaiva tradition of Kashmir, the *Trika*, which began to get organised towards 800 into a separate school, refers to the *Āgamaśāstra*. The term *āgama* is interpreted there as referring to the passing on of teachings across the ages, from master to disciple, since the time of their revelation by Śiva. The *Āgamaśāstra* contains *Śivasūtras* which are considered to have been revealed by Śiva himself to Vasugupta at the beginnings of this school. This text is not part of the collection of *Āgamas* accepted in South India but several other works which are found in this collection are also contained in the *Āgamaśāstra* of Kashmir, as can be judged from their titles and also from the already recognized concordance of one of their texts, an *upāgama* and not an *āgama*, the *Mṛgendra*, which was edited in Kashmir as well as in Tamil country.

The other texts of which at least the titles are found in both schools are the *Mataṅga*, the *Naiśvāsa* (*Niśvāsa* in the Southern list) and the *Svāyambhuva*.[15] At least a partial knowledge of the literature of the *Āgamas* is testified to in Kashmir. Meanwhile it is essentially in South India and more specifically in Tamil country that the *Śaivāgamas* appear as constituting a body of scriptures that commands authority although, as we have already mentioned above, the Lingayats of Kannaḍa country were not unaware of them.

Their composition itself was surely done, at least in part, in Tamil country. As several notes of Mr. Bhatt in the present edition[16] will show, certain words of the Sanskrit text are in fact transpositions of Tamil words and certain unclear passages in Sanskrit become clear if we realise that they were conceived in Tamil and then transposed—rather than translated—into Sanskrit.

Moreover, as Mr. Bhatt has noted,[17] the Sanskrit of the *Āgamas* does not strictly follow the rules of Pāṇinian classicism. This is not true just of Sanskrit written in the South, for a number of other texts composed by the Tamils conform faithfully to the traditional norms of Pāṇini's school, and in numerous regions other than Tamil country, the divergences from this norm can be found. The most famous and striking example in this regard is that of Buddhist texts strongly contaminated by Middle-Indo-Aryan, to a point that their dialect came to be called hybrid, Buddhist Sanskrit. In the *Āgamas* the contamination is found to be Tamil but in a very slight measure; it is, relatively speaking, exceptional. Whatever the case, the divergences in relation to Pāṇini's rules are not usually accidental errors; they are fairly constant, indicating a usage of the milieu in which the texts were composed.

The comparison of *Raurava* with the other *Āgamas* has brought to light a number of divergences, breaking with the general concordance. Therefore Mr. Bhatt has deemed necessary to write abundant notes and to quote extracts from texts that are still unpublished or of difficult access.

The publication is therefore not simply the printing of a specific text, but represents the beginning of a systematic project to shed light on the totality of Āgamic literature. The point up to which it has been developed until today, this project and the considerable amount of material on which it bases itself, already show that it would be premature to presume to infer any conclusions rightaway on the numerous questions it raises. The first task that must be fulfilled is to gather and to classify the huge amount of material which is offered to us.

For instance, the relationships of Āgamic literature with the Śaiva school which dominates Tamil country today, the *Śaivasiddhānta*, are indisputable but they need to be specified. One of the fundamental classical treatises of this school, the *Śivañānapōtam* of Meykaṇṭa Tēvar, appears as an elaboration of twelve Sanskrit stanzas said to be taken from *Rauravāgama*. However these stanzas have not yet been found in any of the manuscripts of this text.

We have already seen that the links of the same literature with the totality of the works of the Tamil Śaiva saints still remain uncleared but that their study offers encouraging perspectives.

The position of Āgamic texts and of ritualistic Hinduism, devout and symbolic, in relation to Vedic tradition, needs also to be specified. As we shall see through Mr. Bhatt's notes[18] *mantras* belonging to the Vedic tradition are used. Elsewhere, the links with Brahmanic thought are evident in numerous places, although new ideas and practice are added and replace those of ancient Brahmanism. The later literature of *Śaivasiddhānta* has itself sometimes dealt with the question of the respective positions of Vedism and Śaivism and it has done this by bringing together selected excerpts from the *Āgamas* and from the relevant literature. This is the case with the *Varṇāśramacandrikā*[19] composed by the school of Dharmapuram which puts into evidence the preeminence of Śaiva Knowledge and Devotion, *jñāna* and *bhakti*, over Vedic scholasticism and which opposes *bhukti*, enjoyment of this world obtained through Vedic rites, to *bhakti*, devotion to God exalted by Śaiva practices and which gives to religion priority over birth.

In certain cases, important new notions are already coming into view. For instance, in the appendice II, page 195 and foll., Mr. Bhatt has been able to show that a few texts from our collection of the *Āgamas*, and a few only, treated the cult of the Sun as an integrating part of the daily cult of Śiva. Here is an example, among many others, of assimilation but of adaptation to its norms by Śaivism of cults which however had their origin and kinship outside itself.

The systematic research in the domain of the Śaiva Āgamas and in the totality of similar texts in other Hindu traditions, without giving up those texts that are usually studied and which are far from being explored, becomes indispensable today. The present book aims to initiate the necessary effort at their utilisation for a deeper and more complete knowledge of Hinduism in India and in other countries where her culture was known.

NOTES

1. The English translation revised by the author, Calcutta, 1927, t. I., p. 588.
2. *An Outline of the Religious Literature of India*, Oxford, 1920.
3. *Der Śaiva Siddhānta*, Leipzig 1912.
4. Gopinatha Rao, *Elements of Hindu Iconography*, Madras, 1914-1916, Krishnasastri, *South-Indian Images of Gods and Goddesses*, Madras, 1916.
5. Prasanna Kumara Acarya, *An Encyclopaedia of Hindu Architecture*, Vol. I-VII, Oxford, 1927-1946.
6. Calcutta, 1946.
7. Gorakhpur, 1959.
8. *Etude sur l'iconographie bouddhique*, Paris, 1905.
9. Mainly Benoytosh Bhattacharya, *The Indian Buddhist Iconography*, Oxford 1924.
10. *āgataṃ pañcavaktrāt tu gataṃ ca girijānane/*
    mataṃ ca vāsudevasya tasmād āgamam ucyate//
11. *tanoti vipulān arthān tattvamantrasamāśritān/*
    trāṇaṃ ca kurute yasmāt tantram ity abhidhīyate//
    Kāmika, Kumbakonam ed., p. 6. The same with slight variants in *Ajita*, *Kriyāp*. I.
12. The same composition in principle (and in fact with different divisions of the subjects) in chapters, in the Vaiṣṇava *Saṃhitās* as in *Śaivāgamas* and *Tantras*. Cf. O. Schrader, *Introduction to the Pañcarātra and the Ahirbudhnyasaṃhitā*, Madras, 1916, p. 22.
13. Cf. G. Coedès, *Inscriptions du Cambodge*, t. 1, 1937, p. 37 and preface to R.V. Joshi, *Le rituel de la dévotion kṛṣṇaite*, Pondicherry, 1959, p. iii note 3.
14. Publications of the French Institute of Indology no. 1, Pondicherry, 1956, new ed. 1982.
15. Titles taken from the list given by J.C. Chatterji, *Kashmir Shaivism*, Srinagar, 1914, p. 8.
16. Cf. p. 65 n.9; p. 79 n. 9; p. 86 n. 17; p. 92 n. 9; p. 99 n. 9.
17. Cf. esp. p. 69 n. 6.
18. For instance page 25 n. 20.
19. By Tiruvambala Deśika, Māyāvaram ed., 1930.

Chapter 7

THE DATES OF BHĀGAVATAPURĀṆA AND OF BHĀGAVATAMĀHĀTMYA*

The date of *Bhāgavatapurāṇa* has been very often discussed not just by modern Indologists but, before them, also by Indian authors of the preceding centuries[1] who challenged its being included in the group of the great *Purāṇas* compiled by Vyāsa and attributed it to Vopadeva. This opinion, although accepted by Colebrooke, Burnouf and Wilson, conflicted with the fact that Vopadeva lived in the 13th Century, whereas Madhva, his contemporary, perhaps more aged, looked upon the *Bhāgavata* as possessing venerable authority and disagreed particularly about the *Bhāgavata* being included in the list of *Purāṇas* that al-Bīrūnī[2] had reproduced in the 11th century,—as has often been pointed out.[3] On the other hand, it was not difficult to find reasons to suppose that the *Bhāgavata* could only be seen as one of the great, less ancient *Purāṇas*. Rāmānuja, who often alludes to the *Viṣṇupurāṇa*, does not quote from it. The reason for this cannot be that it did not exist during this time, since Rāmānuja was a younger contemporary of al-Bīrūnī. One is led to believe that he did not attribute to it the same authority as he gave to the *Viṣṇupurāṇa*, although the *Bhāgavatapurāṇa* improved upon the latter as regard the glorification of Viṣṇu and the devotion to Kṛṣṇa. Moreover, the *Bhāgavata* is clearly distinct from the other *Purāṇas* as a poetical work and, in this regard, rises well above the latter's colourless literature.

Now, Ālkoṇḍavilli Govindācārya, made a remark in 1902 which has often passed unnoticed or which has not been sufficiently exploited: in the prophetic form which the Purāṇas readily give to their expositions, the *Bhāgavata* (XI. 5. 38-41) refers to the devotees of the Tamil country; it refers in detail to the various regions of the country by enumerating the rivers from which the

*Les dates du Bhāgavatapurāṇa et du Bhāgavatamāhātmya, *Indological Studies in honour of N. Brown*, New-Haven, 1962, p. 70-77.

devotees take their water to drink. The greatest of these devotees are obviously the famous Vaiṣṇava saints: the Āḻvārs.[4] Govindācārya had no doubts that this was meant to be a real prophecy. But S. Krishnaswami Aiyangar[5], identifying the rivers and the saints belonging respectively to the regions watered by them, has underlined that the *Bhāgavata* must be of a date later than that of the Āḻvārs or else that the chapter must have been interpolated. In addition, he remarked, that in the case of an interpolation it must have been at a relatively early date as in the 14th century, Vedāntadeśika made use of the authority of this passage considering it to be that of the *Bhāgavata* itself. Finally he draws our attention to the fact that the *Padmapurāṇa* presents a text where Bhakti, in the form of a young lady in distress, declares to be born in Drāviḍa, to have grown up in Karnāṭaka and to have lived in Mahārāṣṭra and Gurjara.

S.N. Dasgupta has accepted the indications given by Krishnaswami Aiyangar[6] but, regarding the passage where Bhakti proclaims that she was born in Drāviḍa, he refers not to the *Padmapurāṇa* but to the *Bhāgavatamāhātmya* where this fact is also mentioned.

In 1913, R.G. Bhandarkar[7] did not know of the remark Govindacharya had made and which Krishnaswamy Aiyangar had yet to elaborate. About the Āḻvārs, he points out that the *Mukundamālā*, a Sanskrit work of Kulaśekhara, an Āḻvār, contains a verse from the *Bhāgavata* (XI. 2.36) and he supposes that Kulaśekhara is the same person as the 12th century king mentioned in an inscription of Narēgal, in the Dharwar district, under the name of Kulaśekharāṅka.

R.C. Hazra, in his important *Studies in the Purāṇic Records on Hindu Rites and Customs*[8], made a detailed study about the question of the dating of the *Bhāgavata*, but even while quoting Farquhar, he has kept silent about everything that points to a southern origin of the text and its reference to Tamil saints. For him the text cannot be later than the year 600 but it may have undergone some revisions.

The question deserves to be taken up again and examined in its chronological consequences.

Here is the passage from the *Bhāgavata*:

XI, 5.38. *kṛtādiṣu prajā rājan*[9] *kalāv icchanti saṃbhavam* /
kalau khalu bhaviṣyanti nārāyaṇaparāyaṇāḥ //
39. *kvacit kvacin mahārāja draviḷeṣu*[10] *ca bhūriśaḥ* /
tāmraparṇī nadī yatra kṛtamālā payasvinī //
40. *kāverī ca mahāpuṇyā pratīcī ca mahānadī*[11] /
ye pibanti jalaṃ tāsāṃ manujā manujeśvara //
41. *prāyo bhaktā bhagavati vāsudeve 'malāśayāḥ* /

38. 'In the cosmic ages, to begin with the Kṛta, the creatures, O king, wish to be born in the age of Kali.
In the age of Kali, in fact, they will become entirely devoted to Nārāyaṇa.
39. In all sorts of places, O great king, and among Dravidians in great numbers.
There where flow the rivers of Tāmraparṇī, Kṛtamālā, Payasvinī,
40. And the greatly sanctified Kāverī and the Western Mahānadī, the men who drink their water, O lord of men,
41. are pure-hearted, ardent devotees of the Blessed Vāsudeva.'
Vedāntadeśika begins thus his *Guruparamparāsāra*[12] which is the first part of his *Rahasyatrayasāra*:

gurubhyas tadgurubhyaś ca namovākam adhīmahe[13] /
vṛṇīmahe ca tatrādyau daṃpatī jagatāṃ patī //
poykaimuNi pūtattār pēyāLvār taṉ
porunal varuṅ kurukēcaN viṭṭucittaN
tuyya kulacēkaraNampāṇanātaN
Roṇṭaraṭippoṭi maLicai canta cōti
vaiyam elāmaRai viḷaṅka vāḷ vēl ēntu
maṅkaiyar kōN eNRivarkaṉ makiLntu pāṭuñ
ceyya tamiL mālaikaṇānteḷiyavōti t
teḷiyāta maRainilaṅkaḷ teḷikiNRōm ē //1//

'To the gurus and to their gurus, we bow! To this formula we bind ourselves and we first elect, here below, the couple ruling the world!
Poykaimuni, Pūtattar, Pēyāḻvār,
the Lord of Kuruku who has come to the fresh Tāmraparṇī (Nammāḻvār), He whose thought is Viṣṇu (Periyāḻvār).
the pure Kulaśekhara, our protector the Singer (Tirupāṇāḻvār).

he who is the dust of the feet of devotees (Toṇṭaraṭippoṭi),
the light which came to Maḻicai (Tirumaḻicaiyāḻvār), he who holding
the sword and the spear to irradiate the Veda over the entire world,
was the husband of the young girl (Tirumaṅkaiyāḻvār), in trying to understand the Tamil garlands composed and sung by them in joy,
we understand the obscure passages of the Veda.'

Vedāntadeśika, therefore, does not directly invoke the *Bhāgavata* but alludes to it by talking about Nammāḻvār, under the name of the 'Lord of Kuruku', his home town, and as having come to cool Porunal, whereas the *Bhāgavata* indicated him to be precisely there where flows the Tāmraparṇī. The commentator Vedāntarāmānuja (17th cent.) while explaining the *Guruparamparāsāra* in his *Bṛhadguruparamparāsvadinī*, quotes and discusses the passage of the *Bhāgavata*. He points out that the first three Āḻvārs of the *paramparā*, are not meant in the *Bhāgavata* since it speaks about the saints of the age of Kali whereas those three belong to the *Dvāparayuga*. He identifies Payasvinī with Pālāṟu and thinks that the passage from the *Bhāgavata*, a passage which he holds to be prophetic, refers to the *ācāryas* as the devotees of the Pālāṟu region, beginning with Śrībhāṣyakāra, that is to say Rāmānuja. He identifies the Kṛtamālā with the river of Madhurapurī, that is Vaikai. He does not talk of the Western Mahānadī but names the holy places celebrated by the Vaiṣṇavas on the banks of the Kāverī.[14] It is probable that Govindācārya has taken his data from him because he too does not quote the passage from the *Bhāgavata* beyond the point that speaks about the Kāverī.

The commentators of the *Bhāgavata* make few or no observation on this text. Only Vijayadhvaja, in his *Padaratnāvalī*[15], explains that the *pratīcī* Mahānadī is the Vetravatī flowing from Vārahakṣetra towards the Western Ocean after having traversed Sahyagiri.[16] Sahyagiri or Sahyādri is a chain of the Western Ghats. The Vetravatī, being a tributary of the Yamunā (Betwa in English maps) is out of the reckoning. It is Netravatī that one should read, as N.R. Bhatt pointed out to me, this Netravatī is, in fact, known in the region of south Kannaḍa as Kittel points out in his dictionary. But there it is the river of Maṅgalūr and we cannot identify it with the 'great western river' of the Draviḍa country. Therefore, we cannot agree with Vijayadhvaja in his identification and this praticī Mahānadī of Draviḍa country must be identified as Periyāṟu, a Tamil name synonymous with 'Mahānadī' which translates it. And it is the river of Kulaśekhara's country.

The identification of Kṛtamālā with Vaiyai or Vaikai, though made by Vedāntarāmānuja, may seem to pose some problem, because the Vaiyai is ordinarily called Vegavatī in Sanskrit.[18] The *Maturaittamiḻppērakarādi* (1956) under Kirutamālai—(ā) does not make the identification but restricts itself by giving in Tamil the indication of the Purāṇas according to which the Kṛtamālā flows from Malaya.[19] But it would be strange for the *Bhāgavata* not to have named Vaiyai[20] next to Tāmraparṇī and Kāverī and point out some other less important river in its place. One must admit that the two names of *Kṛtamālā* and *Vegavatī* have been used interchangeably in Sanskrit to designate Vaiyai.

The correlation of Payasvinī, the 'Milky one' with Pālāṟu, the 'river of milk' is obvious.

The promoters of Vaiṣṇavabhakti in the Draviḍa country where these rivers flow are indeed the Āḻvārs; it is truly therefore with the latter in mind that the passage of the *Bhāgavata* which refers to the bhaktas of this country was composed, after the time when they had all flourished, that is after the 10th century. It is possible *a priori* that this passage was added later to the text that as a whole was composed much earlier. The elements of the legend of Kṛṣṇa to which the Āḻvārs refer, notably Periyāḻvār, are exactly as the *Bhāgavata* presents them. These elements are borrowed from North India, since for the Āḻvārs, the play of Kṛṣṇa unfolds itself on the banks of the Yamunā and the *Bhāgavata* could have been the source of inspiration of the Āḻvārs, in which, later, one might have incorporated a reference to these devotees themselves. It could have been a book of the religious group of the Bhāgavatas whose existence had already been certified around 100 B.C. by the famous inscription of Heliodoros. One can note in favour of this hypothesis that the knowledge in Tamil country of Sanskrit texts cannot be doubted, especially of the Vaiṣṇava saints, considering the number of Sanskrit expressions which appear in their vocabulary. Meanwhile it is simpler to admit—disregarding the hypothesis of interpolation which is not necessary at all—that the *Bhāgavatapurāṇa* was composed in the Tamil country in the period when bhakti had been exalted by the hymns of the Āḻvārs and when the vogue of Sanskrit literature was spreading, which in the Vaiṣṇava circles appears towards 1000 with Nāthamuni, the compiler of the works of Nammāḻvār, and which grew with Rāmānuja, a native of Śrīperumputūr between Mayilapūr and Kāñcipuram and an admirer of the Āḻvārs and their philosophic interpreter, who wrote only in Sanskrit. The most likely date of the *Bhāgavata,* therefore, seems to be the 10th century. It is late enough for the poet of the *Purāṇa* to know about the Āḻvārs whose fervent poetry was truly such that it inspired him. It is early enough so that in the 11th century a text as admirable as the *Bhāgavatapurāṇa* was already incorporated in the list of the great purāṇas compiled by al-Bīrūnī.

As for the passage of the *Bhāgavatamāhātmya* included in the Uttarakhaṇḍa of the *Padmapurāṇa* or accompanying some editions of the *Bhāgavatapurāṇa,* a passage where Bhakti takes up her story, it can be dated in a more conclusive manner and the sketch of the story it gives is exactly confirmed.

Nārada recounts there that he had wandered everywhere and observed the pitiful state of religion. Finally on the banks of the Yamunā he met, next to two boys who seemed to be dead, an unconscious girl over whom a hundred women were sprinkling water to revive her. He asked her who she was and who these boys and these women were. She then replied:

Padma- Uttarakhaṇḍa 189.51, *Bhāgavatamāhātmya* 1, 45-50.
Bālovāca //
ahaṃ bhaktir iti khyātā imau me tanayau matau //
jñānavairāgyanāmānau kālayogena jarjarau //
gāṅgādyāḥ saritaś cemā matsevārthaṃ samāgatāḥ /
tathāpi na ca me śreyaḥ sevitāyāḥ surair api //
idānīṃ śṛṇu madvartām[21] *sacittas tvam tapodhana* /
vārtā me vitatāpy asti tāṃ śrutvā sukham āvaha //
utpannā drāviḍe sāhaṃ vṛddhiṃ karṇāṭake gatā /
kvacit kvacin mahārāṣṭre gurjare jīrṇatāṃ gatā //

tatra ghorakaler yogāt pākhaṇḍaiḥ khaṇḍitāṅgakā |
durbalāhaṃ ciraṃ jātā putrābhyāṃ saha mandatām[22] *||*
vṛndāvanam punaḥ prāpya navīneva surūpiṇī |
jātāhaṃ yuvatī samyakpreṣṭharūpā nu[23] *sāṃpratam ||*
imau tu śayitāv atra sutau me kliśyataḥ śramāt |
idaṃ sthānaṃ parityajya videśaṃ gamyate mayā ||

'The girl said: "My name is Bhakti, these two here are known to be my sons, their names are Jñāna and Vairāgya (Knowledge and Absence of Desire). They decay with time.

"And these here are the rivers, Gaṅgā and others, assembled here to serve me, but I could not be better served, not even by the gods.

"Hear now my story with all your heart, O jewel of asceticism. I have a long history. Having heard it secure for me well-being.

'Born in Drāviḍa, I grew up in Karnāṭaka. Here and there in Mahārāṣṭra, and in Gurjara I grew old and weak.

"There, because of the effects of Kaliyuga, I was mutilated by heretics. I grew weak and languished for a long time and so did my sons.

"But now on coming to Vṛndāvana, I have become new again, young and beautiful, with the most perfectly endearing beauty.

"But my two sons are lying here and I am overwhelmed with fatigue. Leaving this place, I go to a foreign land."'

The rest of the text shows that *Jñāna* and *Vairāgya* are revived by the recitation of the *Bhāgavatapurāṇa.*

The short description of Bhakti's career which these lines give is usually cited just to point out that there exists a tradition pertaining to her origins in the Tamil country. But these lines deserve to be studied more.

Their date can be fixed as later than the re-emergence of Bhakti in Vṛndāvana; now this re-emergence is well-known: it was mainly due to the initiative of Caitanya (1485-1533). It is his disciples, mainly Rūpagosvāmin, Sanatānagosvāmin and Jīvagosvāmin, who at his urging, settled at Vṛndāvana, looked for the forgotten sites that were connected with the legend of Kṛṣṇa, in the Mathurā region and offered them for the devotion of the pilgrims, built over with new temples. They succeeded in doing this, after Caitanya's passing, during the reign of Akbar, and it is thanks to the tolerance of the latter and even because of his sympathy that the re-establishment of the cult of Kṛṣṇa in places famous for his feats and his love-play with the gopis, could actually take place. Akbar himself paid a visit to these disciples at Vṛndāvana in 1573. Formerly it was Mahmūd of Ghazni who, in the 11th century, pillaged Mathurā and its sacred places.

The prolonged stupor in which Bhakti had fallen before this regaining of youth corresponds to the intermediary period when under Muslim princes, hostile to 'infidels' and during times of great difficulties, no religious revival of the Kṛṣṇa cult had been possible. Meanwhile it does not seem likely that the text was referring to the attacks of Mahmūd when it makes Bhakti say that she was mutilated by heretics. Normally the term *pāṣaṇḍa* does not apply to foreigners who are labelled *mlecchas*, and in a preceding verse (37 in P., 34 in *Bh.M*) it is by the name Yavana that the Muslims, who hinder the social order of the *āśramas* or stages of life, are designated. In the literature of the school of Caitanya,[24] as in classical Sanskrit, the *pāṣaṇḍa*(*-in*) are sectarians that one reproves. Besides, it is not Vṛndāvana that the text considers to be the place of mutilation. It situates it in Gurjara, otherwise in Mahāraṣṭra. Gurjara, being adjacent to Mahārāṣṭra, designates Gujarāṭ. It is also an ancient name for Rājpūtāna. Now, at the time when Caitanya revived Bhakti in Vṛndāvana, the great poet Narasiṃhadāsa Mehtā (1415-1481), had himself already glorified it precisely in Gujarāṭ, where ancient legend had situated Kṛṣṇa's capital at Dvārakā. On the other hand, at the time of Caitanya, it was in Rājpūtāna, as later at Vṛndāvana and Dvārakā, that the Rajput princess Mīrābāi sang her devotion to Kṛṣṇa in Hindi and Gujarati. It was also in Rājpūtāna that she fell a victim to her brother-in-law's hatred, he being a zealous Śaiva. In Nārada's address preceding the words ascribed to Bhakti, one of the worst evils of Kaliyuga is the fact that 'people with tall spears, brāhmaṇas with spears of Śiva, ardent women for whom hair is a burden[25], are seen all over the world.'[26] Actually whether Gurjara was just Gujarāṭ alone or Rājpūtāna and Gujarāṭ together, the author, in saying that Bhakti had been mutilated by heretics in Gurjara, had mainly the Śaivas in mind who, like the Jainas, did not allow devotion to Kṛṣṇa to manifest before the time of Narasiṃhadāsa Mehtā[27] and who persecuted Mīrābāi.

The rest is self-evident. The Tamil movement of bhakti is the most anciently and richly documented one. It expresses itself in the brilliant and noteworthy work of the Āḻvārs which bears testimony to their knowledge of the *Bhagavadgītā* and to the legend of Kṛṣṇa localised in the North and in the West. Now, the literature of the Āḻvārs is preceded by no other literature which has been preserved till today and which can be compared to it. It is this Tamil movement of devotion, of which Caitanya himself could ascertain the force during his voyage to the south and which provided him with the Sanskrit text of *Kṛṣṇakarṇāmṛta* which he brought back to Bengal. It is on this text the religious school of Rāmānuja was founded. He carried its fervour to the Kannaḍa country, to Mēlukōṭe where he exiled himself during the Chola persecution which was raging in Śrīraṅgam. It is from that that the *Bhāgavatapurāṇa* itself seems to draw inspiration.

It is in fact in this Kannaḍa country, in Karṇāṭaka, that the Vaiṣṇava Devotion bloomed after having flowered in the Tamil country, in Drāviḍa. It was during the reign of Vīra Ballala II of the Hoysalas (1173-1220) that Rudrabhaṭṭa, a smārta Brahmin, composed his *Jagannāthvijaya* on the life of Kṛṣṇa. In the 13th century, the philosophic movement of Madhva also favoured, although with a less ardent upsurge, the Vaiṣṇava devotion in the Kannaḍa country. The third successor of Madhva, Naraharitīrtha sang, in 1281, about Viṣṇu in Kannaḍa.

Finally, in Mahārāṣtra, the Viṭhobā[28] cult, the Viṣṇu of Paṇḍharpūr, which is a holy place in a region linked in ancient times with Karṇāṭaka, represented a powerful movement of Vaiṣṇava bhakti from the 13th century onwards, particularly towards the end of the century, at the time when Jñānadeva composed his *Jñāneśvarī* (1290) and his prayer to Viṣṇu, *Haripāṭha*. This movement was rendered famous by a number of devotees like Muktābāi (1279-97), sister of Jñānadeva and Nāmdev (1270-1350).

We find then the perfect accuracy with which the *Bhāgavata-māhātmya* gives us a glimpse of the history of Bhakti from the time of its flowering in the Tamil country to its resurgence on the banks of the Yamunā by the disciples of Caitanya. We are dealing here with a text which is later than this resurgence, which took place in the middle of the 15th century, a text that does not contain any tradition related to the first origins of Vaiṣṇava bhakti, but a text well-documented as to the successive stages of its history during a period of which the major texts are preserved.

NOTES

1. Cf. Eug, Burnouf, *Le Bhāgavata Purāṇa*, tome I, Paris 1840, p. LXI-XCVI. Around 1400, Śrīdhara while commenting on the text, had already betrayed his disagreement with those who challenged that this text had the same authority as the other great *Purāṇas*. Cf. also Winternitz, *A History of Indian Literature*, t. I, Calcutta, 1927, p. 555.
2. Cf. Sachau, I, p. 130.
3. Cf. especially J.N. Farquhar, *An Outline of the Religious Literature of India*, Oxford, 1920, p. 231. Pusalker has summed up the opinion of a number of writers on the date of the *Bhāgavata* and has given the corresponding bibliography in *Studies in Epics and Puranas of India*, Bombay, 1955, p. 214-16.
4. A. Govindacarya, *The Holy Lives of the Azhvârs or the Drâvida Saints*, Mysore, 1902, p. XXI 191 and foll.
5. *Early History of Vaishnavism in South India*, Madras, 1920, p. 7-11.
6. *A History of Indian Philosophy*, t. III, Cambridge, 1940, p. 62 and note 1. Das Gupta does not refer to K.A's work but reproduces the facts contained in it and adds some of his misunderstandings: he has substituted the rivers Kṛtamālā and Mahānadī with regions of Kṛtamāla and Mahānada which do not exist and he has repeated by mistake the name of Periyāḻvār by reproducing a hint given by K.A. where Peṛiyāru is meant. In the note he has followed K.A. who wrongly states that Vedāntadeśika has 'quoted' the passage of the *Bhāgavata* in the *Rahasyatrayasāra*. He has added that the *Prapannāmṛta* mentioned three other saints having preceded the Āḻvārs, but actually the first three Āḻvārs of the classical lists are meant.
7. *Vaiṣṇavism, Śaivism and Minor Religious Systems*, Grundriss der Indoarischen Philologie, Strassburg, 1913, Collected works, Vol. IV, Poona, 1929, p. 68-71.
8. Dacca, 1940, p. 52-57.
9. The address is to the King of Mithilā Nimi.
10. Variant: *draviḍeṣu*. Sridhara: *dravileṣu*. Vijayadhvaja: *dramiḷeṣu*. Viraraghava: *dramiḍeṣu*.
11. Vīrarāghava's Commentary: *pratīcī suravartmagā*.
12. Śuṃḍappāḷaya's edition, 1910, with Bṛhadguruparamparāsvadinī by Vedāntarāmānuja.
13. The commentator indicates another reading *adhīmahi* which he considers to be problematic and rejects. The *adhīmahi* form would be the middle imperfect voice of DHĪ but the present is expected as in *vṛṇīmahe*. It is the root *I* with *adhi* which is meant.
14. P. 18: Tirukkutantai, that is to say Kumbakonam and Tiruvālitirunakari, about 10 kilometres from Cirkāli.
15. Kṛṣṇaśāstrī ed., Bombay, 1892. R.V. Joshi has kindly pointed out that a

Hindi commentary remarks on this passage that Śaṭhakopa (that is Nammāḻvār) and Rāmānuja are actually from these regions.

16. *Pratīcī mahānadī nāmnā vetravatī vārahakṣetrāt sahyagiriṃ bhittvā paścimasamudraṃ syandamānā.*
17. In their translations, A. Roussel and J.M. Sanyal have both misunderstood *pratīcī* to be the name of a distinct river, whereas what is meant is an adjective used to distinguish this western Mahānadī from the more well-known Mahānadī of Orissa. S. Subbarau, on his part, has translated correctly.
18. Particularly everywhere in Hālāsyamāhātmya translating in Sanskrit the Tiruviḷaiyāṭaṟpurāṇam of Parañcōti.
19. *Brahmāṇḍa-* II, 16.36; *Viṣṇu-* II, 3.12 (*Kṛtamālātamraparṇīpramukhā malayodbhavāḥ*).
20. The Vaiyai form is the more ancient. Vaikai is found only after the period called Sangam. In the *Tamil Lexicon* the cross reference to Vaikai from Vaiyai and the etymology of Vaikai as deriving from the Sanskrit Vegavatī are therefore not legitimate.
21. Var. *madvākyam.*
22. Var. *sammatam.*
23. Var. *tu.*
24. Cf. Śriharidās Dās, *Śrīśrīgauḍīya-vaiṣṇava-abhidhāna*, Calcutta, undated (recent).
25. One can understand 'donning hair and spears', but it wasn't the custom with women. N.R. Bhatt points out to me that it could suggest women who have shaved off their heads when joining a heterodox sect like Jainism where hair is sometimes even pulled out. In the *Padma-* edition, a verse that was added within brackets tries to explain differently: by stating the respective meanings for *aṭṭa, śūla, śiva* and *keśa* to be *anna, vikraya, veda* and *bhaga*, he reduces the verse of the text to refer to (which is quite common, in fact, in the description of the evils of Kaliyuga) the sale of food by people, to the sale of the Veda by the brahmins and to prostitution by women.
26. *Padma-, Utt.* 189.39: *aṭṭaśūlā janapadāḥ śivaśūlā dvijātayaḥ |*
    kāminyaḥ keśaśūlinyo dṛśyante bhuvi sarvataḥ ||
    Var. (adopted also in Bh. M. 1.36): ......*keśaśūlinyo saṃbhavanti kalāv iha.*
27. Before his time there is hardly any testimony of great religious activity of the Vaiṣṇavas in Gujarāṭ, cf. Krishnakumari J. Virji, *Ancient History of Saurashtra*, Bombay, 1955, p. 169.
28. G.A. Deleury, *The Cult of Viṭhobā*, Poona, 1960.

CHAPTER 8

SELF-IMMOLATION BY FIRE AND THE INDIAN BUDDHIST TRADITION*

A REMARKABLE ARTICLE written recently by Jacques Gernet made a study of Self-immolation by fire among the Buddhist Chinese from the 5th to the 10th century.[1] One such recent suicide (in June 1963) in Saigon by a Vietnamese Buddhist monk caused quite a flutter and amazement. Since then several other monks as well have burnt themselves to death in Saigon.

Gernet has taken up the study of quite a number of cases of self-cremation or of self-mutilation by fire that took place in China and which are advocated or of which there are instances in legend described in sacred texts. These texts also describe other methods of voluntarily giving up one's body: giving oneself up to tigers, jumping off a cliff, drowning oneself, submitting oneself to the violence of dacoits, etc. Gernet has analysed the conditions in which such self-cremations are described; he has not tried to unravel the historicity of the tales, he has rather rightly studied them as an expression of the beliefs and sentiments of the milieus which provoke such phenomena. He finds that in spite of the Sanskrit origin of the Buddhist texts which glorify these acts, some typically Chinese traits show up in the motivations and the execution or in the expositions which deal with them. He has, moreover, given a general, sociological interpretation. He admits that we are dealing here with a ritual act of sacrifice preceded by an act of self-purification, collective participation and perhaps the taking upon oneself through martyrdom of the sins of other beings, (although, as he points out on p. 558, there is no clear indication that leads us to confirm such an interpretation). He has also studied the objections raised by a Chinese writer of the 6th century against such methods of suicide which he found to be marred by vain glory and as being against the Buddhist ethic.

*La mort volontaire par le feu et la tradition bouddhique indienne, in *Journal Asiatique* 1963, p. 21-51.

The texts that inspired the cases of self-cremation referred to are the Chinese version of the *Vyāghrīparivarta*, the 17th chapter of *Suvarṇabhāsasūtra*, and, the most important, the 22nd chapter of *Saddharmapuṇḍarīka*, entitled *Bhaiṣajyarājapūrvayogaparivarta*, 'The Elaboration on the ancient yoga of Bhaiṣajyarāja', where Bhaiṣajyarāja, the 'King with Remedies' in the form of the Bodhisattva Sarvasattvapriyadarśana, 'He whose vision is precious to all beings', burns his body and, in his next life, burns his arms.

Gernet points out that this last text was the origin, in China, of the rites (pp. 541–42) corresponding to the events in the tale and adhered to by the monks who burnt themselves from the 5th to the 10th centuries: the vow to burn oneself, diet, use of perfumes, covering oneself with oil-soaked sheets, the gathering of relics. He believes that the burning of the fingers is a practice linked to the cult of relics (p. 543) for it is performed frequently before the Buddha's relics. He also notes (p. 544) that when the whole body is cremated on a pyre, then the pyre is in the shape of a *stūpa*, or a cave or a niche where the monk who is burning himself is seated like the Buddha, for according to him, the transformation of the monk into the Buddha is one of the principal aims of self-cremation. Finally, he believes that self-cremation is 'meant to commemorate and to fulfil a myth, the death or the birth of the Bodhisattva or the Buddha (death and birth being one and the same thing)'.

The reference to the original Indian texts and to the Indian Buddhist tradition helps us to pinpoint, above all, the psychological motivations of the cremations for the Indians in conformity with the doctrines that were passed on to the Chinese. It will also enable us to review, in the light of these doctrines, Gernet's interpretations of the Chinese data themselves.

A text similar to *Saddharmapuṇḍarīka* which was even translated into Chinese quite early,[2] but which does not seem to be mentioned among the documents surveyed by Gernet, offers some additional precisions. We refer to chapter XXXIII of the *Samādhirāja*, the chapter entitled *Kṣemadattaparivarta*, 'Elaboration on Kṣemadatta'. Here is the translation except for a few passages that have been summarised.[3]

Bhagavant recounts to his usual interlocutor the ancient feat of mastery of the Bodhisattva Kṣemadatta one of his own former incarnations. Tathāgata Ghoṣadatta has just passed away; King Śrīghoṣa wanting to worship the Tathāgata (*pūjārtham*), got eighty-four thousand tens of million stūpas containing relics (*dhātugarbha*) with numberless lamps of honour (*dīpārghya*, Tibetan: *mar-me'i yon*), music, flowers, incense, etc. as was the practice. The Bodhisattvas chanted the Order (*dharma*).[4]

'And at the time, during that period, it was in this assembly that was born the Being on the Path of Awakening, the Great Being named Kṣemadatta, a little child with black hair. Although he was in the joyous time of full-blown youth, he did not give himself up to games. With regard to desires he had the juvenile Brahmic (i.e. chaste) conduct. He had been ordained for a year.'

The king had requested the Bodhisattvas to sing the six *pāramitās* in order to gain the great fixation on the group of the Beings on the Path of Awakening (*bodhisattvapiṭakamahādhāraṇī*) and after having worshipped, he installed himself with his harem and his court on a terrace.

'And the large divine and human gathering had assembled wanting to hear the Order. And the Bodhisattva, the Great Being Kṣemadatta beheld these hundreds of thousands of hundreds of millions of tens of millions of lamps of honour which shone. It was bright because of the luminosity of these lamps. Knowing that the divine and human multitude had gathered to hear the Order, the thought crossed his mind: 'May I, fully established in the great way of progress, be capable by aspiring to the *positioning* of psychism, to offer homage to Tathāgata! May the world along with the gods, humanity and the Titans marvel[5] at such a homage, may the world thus enthralled in spirit be joyous, full of gaiety and euphoria, may it obtain the brilliance of the Order and may I surpass all this homage to Tathāgata offered by King Śrīghoṣa. And may king Śrīghoṣa marvel in an enthralled spirit, joyous, full of gaiety and euphoria, along with his harem and his court.'

'And so in truth, the Bodhisattva, the Great Being Kṣemadatta who was thinking thus, full of gaiety and euphoria, knowing that the great body of the mass of auditors of the Order had gathered, stood in front of the monument of Tathāgata at nightfall, and soaking his robe which he held around his right arm with oil, he set fire to it. And so in truth, the Bodhisattva, the Great Being

Kṣemadatta, aspiring with resolve to a perfect and total Awakening with nothing above, while his right arm was burning, did not waver in thought, nor did his countenance change colour. And so, young man, as soon as the arm caught fire, the arm of the Bodhisattva, the Great Being Kṣemadatta, all blazing and luminescent, became a single flame; and just then, in truth, a great earthquake occurred. By the brilliance of his burning arm, the many hundreds of thousands of hundreds of millions of tens of millions of lamps of honour were eclipsed. And the radiance spread in all directions. By this radiance all the illuminated directions became bright in all parts. He, full of gaiety and euphoria, illustrated that positioning of psychism, where the identity of the inherent self of all things is manifest, by revealing it to the whole assembly all along, with remarkable speech and in a graceful, enthralling voice, the consonants of words well linked to one another. There were gathered to hear the Order twelve thousand gods of the body of Thirty-three. Full of gaiety and euphoria, they offered the divine homage in every manner. And the choirs of apsaras celebrated with celestial songs. King Śrīghoṣa, who after having climbed up to his terrace leading his people and surrounded by his harem, had consecrated himself to the vigil of the eight articles, saw the Bodhisattva, the Great Being Kṣemadatta illuminating with his arm, radiant with a divine light that was superhuman and surpassed all radiance. And beholding him the thought came to him: "He must have attained the supreme Knowledge! This Kṣemadatta, the Bodhisattva, this Great Being!" And having felt an intense love, serenity and respect, he flung himself down from the terrace, along with his escort, his eighty wives, sustained by the fullness of benefit derived from the great roots of good, in order to see, to felicitate in joy the Bodhisattva Kṣemadatta. By virtue of the root of good issued from respect and having once seen the Order, he obtained along with his escort the privilege of being received[6] by the gods, the *nāgas*, the *yakṣas*, the *gandharvas*, the *asuras*, the *garuḍas*, the *kinnaras* and the *mahoragas*. Then, received by the gods, the *nāgas*, the *yakṣas*, King Śrīghoṣa along with his escort, fell from the terrace, a height of a hundred thousand cubits. And he suffered no injury on the body or on the mind or any crushing.

'So, in truth, King Śrīghoṣa, stretching his arms, uttered together with the great body of people, a huge, resonant, loud lamentation. Indeed, on seeing the burnt, blazing arm of the Bodhisattva, the Great Being Kṣemadatta, the king together with the great body of people cried out in tears:

'So, in truth, the Bodhisattva, the Great Being Kṣemadatta, asked King Śrīghoṣa: "Why do you, O great king, together with the great body of people, utter this huge, resonant, loud lamentation, and weep and shed tears?" And here, in truth, is what King Śrīghoṣa answered to the Bodhisattva Kṣemadatta, by uttering the following stanzas:

1. 'Knowing that Kṣemadatta of the great intelligence, wise, proclaimer of the Order, is mutilated, it is for this that these people cry.
2. 'Knowing that such a form erect like a mass of radiance has lost an arm, yes, I too am even more afflicted.
3. 'The arm that you have kindled, the brilliance radiating in all directions, these lamps eclipsed by your divine force!
4. 'This earth has been shaken! and your mind does not swoon! The thought that arises is : this is not a sage without excellence.
5. 'Yes, I fell from a tower a hundred thousand cubits high, here, along with my harem, and my body suffered no pain!
6. 'Bravo! for your marvellous knowledge! Bravo! for your thought which is topped by nothing! And bravo! for your spontaneous energy! And bravo! for your great determination!
7. 'He whose hands have burnt, did not for once wince! And what is more, you proclaim the Order full of gaiety and gladness!
8. 'Like the Moon when it is full or the Sun on a bed of clouds, or like Sumeru, the king of mountains, you irradiate, O venerable one!
9. 'May I too in wisdom, fulfil such an engagement (*praṇidhi*)! And, after having given up love for the body, may I too be able to do good to living beings!
10. 'And by love of the Order I am transported in joy and my gaiety on this account is unimaginable. That you should, in addition, suffer mutilation is my greatest pain.'
11. 'Kṣemadatta, in truth, adored by the gods and the *nāgas*, with infinite lucidity, spoke these stanzas to the king:
12. 'He who has no arms cannot be thus mutilated. But he is mutilated, O king, for whom there is no observance.

13. 'The Tathāgatas adored by this corrupt body of mine are for the whole world inconceivable, honourable, sacred objects (*caitya*).
14. 'The infinities of the three thousand (worlds) packed with jewels, he can offer to the Protectors of the world, he who aspires to the knowledge of the Awakened:
15. 'That is common adoration. The other adoration is inconceivable: those who know things to be void abandon their corporeal life.
16. 'I will make the declaration of truth, great king, harken to me ! And all this multitude (that you are), all of you shall know this stanza:
17. 'In virtue of the truth by which truth I myself shall become the Awakened One, a sacred object for the world, let the Earth tremble in six ways!'
18. 'These words were uttered and the Earth shook. A miracle! Overcome by this prodigy, the tens of millions of gods were transported with joy.
19. 'Transported with joy, the gods and men received the thought of Awakening. Measureless, inconceivable (in number) they were established in the distinguished way of progress.
20. 'Moreover, from among all of them the monk Kṣemadatta performed this good, there where the knowledge of the Awakened is cultivated, imperishable and inconceivable.
21. 'In virtue of the truth, by which truth this thing called arm does not exist, my arm will soon be as before.
22. 'In virtue of the truth by which truth this thing that Kṣemadatta is does not exist, because of the vacuity, those who search in the ten directions do not perceive it.
23. 'Even the sound you produce, you know it to be void. Sound is comparable to an echo, you know that things are thus.
24. 'He becomes an expert for ever, he who has arrived at the understanding that touches the void, by whose truthful speech the entire world is not burnt.
25. 'As many as there are beings in the three worlds, be they gods or men, all take on the psychic poise thanks to the radiance of ominiscience.
26. 'As many as there are accidents, be they divine or human, all of them are prevented thanks to him who must not return (to existence).

27. 'And these stanzas were spoken and the arm was raised once again and the body of Kṣemadatta was embellished with the signs (of the Great Man).

28. 'And the tens of millions of gods who were stationed in the air covered the monk with mandara flowers.

29. 'This Jambudvīpa, in truth, was covered with flowers that are not of the world of men. Songs were sung by hundreds of millions of tens of millions of *apsaras*.

30. 'At that very moment, as Kṣemadatta uttering these words, thousands of tens of millions of Awakened Ones beheld this prodigy.

31. 'In each one's own domain, he who is of immense glory, may he shine for the monks and the nuns, for men and women-zealots!

32. 'Kṣemadatta, indeed, this wise monk with the great force! He who kindled the arm thanks to the knowledge of the Awakened Ones.

33. 'By him, thousands of domains as numerous as the grains of sand of the Ganges, were illumined, by his light, like at the time of the conflagration of the cosmic age.

34. 'And all the fields bloomed with flowers and powder of sandal, bloomed from the soil up to the knees.

35. 'The domain of the Awakened One bloomed with all the precious gems and with all the flowers. For the adoration of Kṣemadatta the nāgas rained pearls.

36. 'This domain was decorated with exhibits made with all the precious gems, studded with precious gems and pearls in adoration of Kṣemadatta.

37. 'The gods and the *nāgas* and the *yakṣas*, the *kinnaras*, the *apsaras* and the *mahoragas* turned towards the distinguished awakening in as great a number as the grains of sand of the Ganges.

38. 'The Totally Awakened One, the Lion among the Śākyas, he too, standing on the Vultures' Peak facing the community of monks, roared the roar of the lion, he the Victorious One.

39. 'I was Kṣemadatta. As for Śrīghoṣa, it was Ajita (Maitreya) coursing the path of the total Awakening across thousands of tens of millions of cosmic ages.

40. 'By the very sight of the monk Kṣemadatta, at that very

instant, the feminine nature was abandoned by the women inconceivable (in their number).

41. 'These women were the subject of an announcement made by the Chief of men: "For these (beings) there is no return. Free now, they will all become the Guides of the world.

42. 'May he who knows, after he has heard this text, which reveals the nature of the practices of the one who is delivered, may he have no more love for the body, being well-instructed in the Order in this matter.'

This text does not obviously give the relation of a historical event but it has a far greater bearing than what it would have then: it expresses clearly the representation regarding the psychological states of the hero of the legend—the representation that the milieu from where it originated conceived of it and passed it down to tradition. Now, these states are those that this milieu aimed at ideally and taught that they be acquired. This teaching bore fruit, since acts similar to those that it glorified have taken place in history and since texts such as *Saddharmapuṇḍarīka*, shorter and undoubtedly more popular but less explicit, rise, as we shall see, from the same psychological current or, better still, from the same psychotechnical goals.

Several salient features stand out:

1. Kṣemadatta is no ordinary devotee: he is predisposed to be one. From his behaviour since his childhood, he had been a *bodhisattva*, a 'Being on the path of Awakening', that is to say engaged on the path that leads to waking up to the consciousness of the true Order of things, as the Buddhas, the 'Awakened ones' know it;

2. Men and gods have been gathered to worship (*pūjā*) the relics of one of these Awakened ones, precisely because he has revealed the true Order of things which they want revealed to them on this occasion;

3. On this occasion too, Kṣemadatta, who is conscious of being fully established in the great way of progress towards the 'Awakening' (*mahāyānasaṃprasthita*) thinks of participating in the collective worship by aspiring to be in the state of total positioning of the psychism in the truth (*samādhim ākāṅkṣant*), which is a participation not only in the worship of the relics but more and above all in the true Order of things to which his psychic self will

adhere for ever. In this way, the act of worship will surpass that of the king and of the divine and human multitude, but not in a spirit of rivalry in order to vanquish them, for he will be a source of wonder and beatitude for the king and for the universe;

4. Kṣemadatta sets fire to his arm aiming for the Awakening with resolve (*adhyāśayena...paryeṣamāna*) and without showing any sense of pain, showing on the contrary, quiet and euphoria and describing the positioning of psychism that consists in the conviction of the identity of the essential being of all things (*sarvadharmasvabhāvasamatā*). What is meant, according to the general doctrine of the text, is the conviction that all things are identically devoid of an essential being (*svabhāvaśūnya*) which is the same thing as saying that vacuity itself is the essence of their own being or, more commonly, that their fundamental constituent is no more than empty space and that their apparent being is in truth a non-being.[7]

5. The King, wonder-struck and moved to tears with the whole assembly, believes that Kṣemadatta has attained the 'supreme knowledge' (*abhijñā*), that is to say mastery in the integral knowledge of the worldly phenomena (divine sight and hearing, knowledge of the sequence of the thoughts of others and of the past situations of individuals) as well as the knowledge of the techniques of getting a wondrous power over these phenomena and the knowledge of the destruction of impulsive currents which pull psychic individualities into the world. It is obviously the fifth 'supreme knowledge', the knowledge of the techniques of a wondrous power (*ṛddhividdhi*) that Kṣemadatta manifests directly but the possession of one of the aspects of 'supreme knowledge' implies the possession of all the others. This wondrous power is, therefore, considered not as a miracle in the sense of a happening that is contrary to the laws of nature but as a prodigious act of a hero fully positioned in the natural Order of things;

6. Supreme adoration does not consist in the mundane ceremony of homage; it is the illustration, through the giving up of the bodily life, of a complete adherence to the real doctrine of the void of things (st. 15);

7. The burnt arm was actually a mere unreal appearance. Now, truth exceeds the appearance and controls it and that is why through the 'utterance of truth' (*satyavākya*) by the hero,

the arm resumes its actual form in the eyes of the assembly (st. 21-27);[8]

8. The purpose of the act of cremation is to lead to the renunciation of the love (*preman*) of the body (st. 9-10, 42).

Kṣemadatta's act, therefore, is the fruit of a total mastery of individuality, of body and of mind, through a psychological integration of a representation that devalues the goal of all desires and through a neutralisation that correlates all impulsive movement except that which tends towards this representation itself, and the individualities that reinforce it. The hero is, therefore, hardly a martyr suffering on account of his faith; he is an unimpressionable yogin by virtue of a psychosomatic training towards impassivity, of detachment from all that is not connected with the real Order of things and the propagation of its knowledge.

Such a training is truly that of a yogin. The *Samādhirāja* incidentally clearly states this:

42. *asvabhāvā ime dharmāḥ svabhāvaiṣāṃ na labhyate |*
yogināṃ gocaro hy eṣa ye yuktā buddhabodhaye ||
43. *ya evaṃ jānāti dharmān sa* (*na*) *dharmeṣu sajjate |*
asajjamāno dharmeṣu dharmasaṃjñāprabodhayī ||

'These things are without any essential being: one cannot find in them any essential being. Indeed, it is there that lies the field of the yogins' thoughts, yogins who are prepared for the Awakening of the Awakened.

'He who knows things thus is no more attached to things. Not being attached to things anymore, he helps in the awakening to the perception of the Order of things. (*Samādhirāja*, XXXII, 42-43.'

The psychic state in which the act of cremation is executed is actually *samādhi*, a supreme culmination of yogic discipline. In this particular case, it is the *samādhirāja* itself, the 'king among *samādhis*' which is the subject of the *sūtra*. This *samādhi* is constantly qualified as *śānta*, 'tranquil'. Such a state is obtained by a neutralisation of all perception (*saṃjñā*) except that of the real which is the vacuity of essential being in things and it involves the disappearance of the unconscious, psychic constructions (*saṃskāras* or *abhisaṃskāra*) which are the ordinary results of actions and tie us down to existence by their residual influence. For those who are thus engaged only in the Awakening to the Reality, the Positioning of psychism, conscious and unconscious, has become stable and automatic; they are not preoccupied by it. This is how the *Samādhirāja* expresses itself:

XXXII, 121. *na teṣām abhisaṃskāraḥ samādhī riddhikāraṇam /*
vipāka eṣa śūrāṇāṃ nityakālaṃ samāhitaḥ //

'For them there is no psychic superconstruction, the positioning of psychism is the instrument of the wondrous power. For the heroes, this ripening is forever psychically established.'

130. *strīsaṃjñā puruṣasaṃjñā ca sarvasaṃjñā vibhāvitāḥ /*
sthitā abhāvasaṃjñāyām deṣenti bhūtaniścayam //

'They do not create the perception of woman, the perception of man, or any other perception. Firmly established in the perception of non-being, they manifest the certainty of the real.'

269. *samāhitaḥ sa carati sajjate na samādhiṣu /*
asaktaś cāpramattāś ca nāsau lokeṣu sajjate //

'He moves in a poised spirit. He is not attached to the positioning of psychism and detached and undistracted, he is not attached to the worlds.'

If we now go back to *Saddharmapuṇḍarīka*, connected through the language, the hybrid Sanskrit, we find the same ideas again.

The narrative of chapter XXII is similarly that of an ancient example of yogic mastery as the title of this chapter indicates.[9] It is *samādhi*, a positioning of psychism, analogous to the *samādhi* of Kṣemadatta that has been realised by Sarvasattvapriyadarśana and which is called *sarvarūpasaṃdarśanasamādhi*, 'a positioning of psychism in total vision of all appearances', that is to say, as in the *Samādhirāja*, in total vision of the ontological non-existence of appearances, for the *Saddharmapuṇḍarīka* also teaches incidentally the doctrine of the vacuity along with the absence of cause and of end (*SP*, chap. V, Kern ed., pp. 136-37; Wogihara-Tsuchida, pp. 126-27). In both the texts, the Bodhisattvas who burn their bodies or their arms have reached this state of mastery after a long path through transmigrations, but those who witnessed their acts were led all together to the Awakening. The *SP* adds an important detail: total renunciation of the self, that is of one's corporal individuality (*ātmabhāvaparityāga*), excels all worship (*pūjā*) and any other renunciation such as that of a kingdom or of a loved wife and son and all these renunciations are *dāna* or *pradāna*, acts of 'giving' (*SP*, Kern ed. p. 406, l. 13; 408, l. 1-4; W.T., p. 341, l. 7-9; l.27 and foll).

We observe that in these conditions, if we can truly say that this self-cremation by Buddhist yogins is a sacrifice—a sacrifice of the body or of a part of the body, we are not talking about an act that belongs to the sociological type of ritual sacrifice, which is moreover quite vague. From the standpoint of the concerned milieu itself, it is part of the type called *dānapāramitā*, that is the 'utmost of giving', and it is born from a spirit of total renunciation of all good; it is charity if the renunciation benefits another being, but in every case, it is the perfect test and an inspiring example of absolute detachment. The tales illustrating *dānapāramitā*, where we see the Bodhisattva in all sorts of existences giving up his flesh or his head or his body to the flames (the story of the hare who throws himself into the brazier)[10] for the good of a being or again, in order to serve a Buddha or to pay his homage, are among the most common in any Buddhist literature. They were popularised in China by collections like the *Lieou tou tsi king*[11] translated by K'ang Seng-houei who lived in China from 247 to 280. In this collection *dānaparamitā* is, as elsewhere, the first *pāramitā*. One of the examples given is that of a Brahmin disciple who, in order to participate in the service of a Buddha whom his master has welcomed, soaks his cloth-covered, clean-shaven, washed head with oil and then sets fire to it in order to act as a lamp and later becomes, as a result of this act, the Buddha Dīpaṃkara, 'He who acts as a lamp'. During the period of the combustion, the head does not suffer and the young man keeps his attention fixed on the sacred books.[12]

To interpret such acts, even within the Chinese context, as a ritual sacrifice is not justified, even less so to make the hypothesis put forward by Gernet although he points out that it is not confirmed by the texts that such acts could imply the taking upon oneself the sins of other beings. A sacrifice done in pain for the atonement of sins is primarily a Christian idea, not a Buddhist one, and which in any case does not apply here.

It must also be remarked that self-cremation, at least as far as it is depicted in the original Buddhist legends, is not a common suicide for the one who performs it—even when it entails his death. In fact the hero who burns his body does not believe in the real existence of this body (see above, *Samādhirāja*, XXXIII, stan. 21-23). His act differs totally from that of the one who commits the common suicide. The latter, in attacking life in which he believes, does it out of a sudden impulse of despair: he is seized with the idea of destruction. The Buddhist, on the other hand, gets deliberately rid of an appearance he knows to be just that and from which he is emotionally released. His death is a voluntary death without there being any will to death and it overcomes an envelope from which his psychic training has separated him.

The distinction is clearly made in Buddhist tradition between the suicide by an ordinary man and the giving up of the body by the being who has attained the culmination of the psychosomatic discipline of psychic detachment and corporeal equanimity which are part of Buddhist training.

La Vallée Poussin pointed this out a long time ago.[13] He drew our attention especially to the story of the *thera* Vakkali and the *ayasmā* Godhika beheading themselves and whom Māra could not seize since this self-killing was not an ordinary one. He also reminded us that Śākyamuni himself had 'released his vital energies'. As for Śākyamuni, the tales of *Mahāparinirvāṇa* actually state that he let go (*ossaji, utsṛjati*) his vital, psychic construction (*āyusaṃkhāra, āyuḥsaṃskāra*).[14] However, we do not have there a definite act of the destruction of the body.

As for Vakkali, some of the various legends that deal with him[15] and the commentaries made on them are much more significant. For he was at the head of the monks who were 'supremely consecrated to their faith' (*saddhādhimutta*,[16] *śraddhādhimukta*).[17] His faith leads him to contemplate untiringly the body of the Buddha and the Buddha tries to divert him to the contemplation of the Order by telling him that fixing his attention on the Order is the same as fixing it on him but that his own material body is subject to decay.[18] But later, sent away by the Buddha, he wants to throw himself into a precipice. The Buddha, meanwhile, knowing the state of his dejection[19] manifests himself to him, utters a stanza that promises him beatitude born out of the appeasement of psychic constructions, holds out his hand and beckons him. Transported with joy, he is freed from the state of depression, rises in the air and transcending delight attains the state of the *arhant* endowed with discernments.[20]

The accounts about this Vakkali in *Apadāna* (PTS ed., II, 465) and in *Divyāvadāna* relate that he hurls himself down from a rock not to kill himself but in an elan towards the Buddha. He suffers no pain like King Śrīghoṣa hurling himself towards Kṣemadatta from the terrace out of 'love'. It is the same in other legends dealing this time with real attempts at suicide, where the dejected are saved by the Buddha or by their favourable antecedents from past lives,[21] which confirms that an impulsive attempt against the bodily life is seen by Buddhism as a misfortune for the one who commits it.

It is the *Saṃyuttanikāya* which recounts in the greatest detail how Vakkali killed himself (PTS ed. III, pp. 119-24). He is very ill. The Buddha asks him if he has any remorse or regrets (which would imply a persistent attachment to the world). Vakkali regrets having remained for a long time without seeking the vision of the Bhagavant. The latter makes him shift his craving from the contemplation of the material body which is a body subject to decay, to the contemplation of the Order, or as Buddhaghosa says in his commentary of the text, to the "body of the Order", *dhammakāya*, which is *lokottaradhamma*, 'the Order transcending the world'. He reminds him that this Order consists in the impermanence of the elements of the psychosomatic individuality (the five groups *khandha*, appearances, sensations, perceptions, unconscious psychic constructions, thoughts). From this moment Vakkali wants to get rid of this individuality now that he is released (*vimutta*) from it by the conviction of its vanity. The Bhagavant rids him of all misgiving: 'Do not fear Vakkali, do not fear Vakkali, your death will be sinless, sinless the fulfilment of your time!'[22] He answers that he has no doubts regarding the impermanence of appearances, etc. and neither does he feel attracted to it nor does he feel any impulse, passion or love (*chanda, rāga, pema*). Then 'he took the dagger' (*sattham āharesi*). The Bhagavant approaches his body and showing to his monks a black cloud moving in all directions, he declares: 'There is the Evil Māra, monks. He seeks the thought of the noble son Vakkali, wondering: "On what then is fixed the thought of the noble son Vakkali?" The noble son Vakkali is fully extinguished, with a thought that is not fixed.' The story of Godhika (*Saṃyutta*, I, 120), less detailed, ends in the same way.

The thought in question, *viññāṇa*, is the fifth of the *Khandhas*, the psychological set-up which crowns all the other constituents of individuality. An ordinary person who has committed suicide would have fixed his thought on some object and the psychic individuality would have remained subject to the demon of Love and Death. But Vakkali was certainly liberated by virtue of the removal of all the *Khandhas* (*vivattakkhanda*) including *viññāṇa*. There was no thought in him that strained towards any worldly object. The Canonical text of *Saṃyuttanikāya*, therefore, fully justifies Vakkali's act.

Buddhaghosa, while commenting on this text in the *Sāratthappakāsinī*, had however a doubt which he explained away with a hypothesis. According to him, the *thera* was undoubtedly presumptuous (*adhimānika*) in believing himself to be free from impulses (*khīṇāsava*) since he still retained the impulse to kill himself.

'Not seeing anymore the course of affects, downcast by his positionings of psychism and searches, believing himself to be free from impulses, he wondered: 'Of what use is this unhappy life to me? I shall end my life with a dagger.' And he slit the canal of his throat (the trachaea) with a sharp dagger. Then he had a painful sensation Realising at that moment his ordinary human condition, by falling into an inclination to uninterrupted action, he swiftly entered into a concentration by assuming the fundamental inclination to action and it is by raising himself to the state of the *arhant* that he fulfilled his time of life.'[23]

It is clear that Buddhaghosa has to admit that Vakkali did enter the state of *nibbāna* even though seeming to be still caught in the worldly sensibility, since it is mentioned in the canonic text he was commenting on. But he does not agree that at the moment when he slit his throat, he was already a saint fit for the Extinction. He therefore had to become such a saint between this moment and the moment of his death; and this is the reason for analysing, evidently hypothetically, the psychic activity during that time.

The account of *Saṃyuttanikāya* and this analysis show us clearly the similarity of opinions of the Theravāda and the Mahāyāna of the *Samādhirāja* regarding the voluntary, legitimate death as opposed to impulsive suicide. All of them demand the positioning of all the individual psychism on the conviction about the insignificance of the body and the psychological elements of the individuality, elements which finally include the body which exists for the latter as a representation or appearance (*rūpa*), next to the other psychological categories which are: sensations (*vedanā*), perceptions (or notions, *saṃjñā*), unconscious psychic constructions (*saṃskāra*) and thoughts (*vijñāna*).

The witnessing public, even the Buddhists, have expressed different opinions on the value of voluntary death and in particular death by fire. Gernet showed—as we mentioned—that they were sometimes censured in China and that the public authorities sometimes accepted them and, at other times, expressed concern and prevented them.[24] De Groot also stated this.[25] La Vallée Poussin, on his part has spoken about the censure of voluntary death by Yi-tsing.[26] Gernet rightly remarked that the practice of self-cremation seems to be linked with amidism. The *Samādhirāja* seems to confirm it since the Sukhāvatī, the paradise of Amitābha, plays there the same part as in the *Saddharmapuṇḍarīka* and it is there that the example of an absolute detachment from the apparent body brings about the rebirth of the converts. It is in one milieu accepting these beliefs, at least in China, that an abridged practice of cremation in the living state was incorporated in the rites of admission into the community in the form of the rite of burning the scalp by allowing small cylinders of paste to burn slowly on the clean-shaven head.[27] We can say that this practice is technically linked to the application of *moxas*, popular in Chinese medicine.

One of the qualities of total or partial self-cremation, or of the application of *moxas* on the scalp is not to provoke visible reactions of pain. Both the legends and the observation of real cases testify this fact. It is a sign of the required mastery. It is probable that in many cases the prior, psychological training really eliminates pain. We are familiar today with some kinds of psychosomatic training completely independent of all religious beliefs, such as autogenous training or painless child-delivery, that can lead to a real anaesthesia of pain. A similar anaesthesia can be realised so much the more by means of a yoga that strives to disconnect the consciousness from the sensorial organs, a disconnection that is set off by a conviction about the insignificance of the representations connected with the body but subsequently converted into a psychological automatism.

Naturally, European writers, ill-equipped to judge such facts, often failed to understand them. De Groot, for instance, after translating the chapter from the Chinese version of the *Saddharmapuṇḍarīka* connected with self-cremations, added, in conformity with the theories of his time, theories smitten with the solar myth: 'In our view, it is either some sort of mumbo-jumbo full of sheer absurdities, or else a solar myth...'[28] At the beginning of this century, Matignon,[29] although a physician, believed like Mac Gowan before him—whom he cited[30]— that it was nothing but 'religious folly'. Actually it is a case of feats of a rigorous psychosomatic technique founded on a specific philosophy.

In India, such feats were not peculiar only to Buddhism. We know about the voluntary giving up of life by Jains through starvation. We also know, from the time of Greek Antiquity, the self-cremations by the gymnosophist Kalanos in the time of Alexander[31] and of the sramana 'Khegas', as his name is transcribed in Greek (Zarmanochegas), in the time of Augustus.[32] In both the cases, either Hindus or Buddhists must have been meant—not Jains who do not practise self-cremation and it does seem that by 'gymnosophists', 'naked philosophers', the Greeks designated any Indian philosopher, since they were struck by the near nudity of these men.

In any case, it is not possible to dwell on the reasons that prompted these gymnosophists to burn themselves before the Greeks, considering that the information that has come down to us from antiquity is of varying and contradictory nature in this regard, as Strabo complained.[33] But the very same Strabo points out also that according to Megasthenes, the Indian philosophers generally condemned suicides.

This is indeed what the tradition of the *Dharmaśāstra*, of the epics and the *Purāṇas* teaches. It allows however for some exceptions.[34] For the sake of atonement, the killer of a Brahmin can get himself killed by flinging himself in the midst of a battle of archers or rush headlong into the fire. To die voluntarily in certain sacred places can guarantee liberation from rebirth. According to some, it is an acceptable practice for someone who is very old or incurably ill (as was the case with Vakkali) on condition that one is free from all desire, or one has exhausted one's activity (*kṛtakarman*), or if one no longer wishes to live a vain life (*vṛthā necchet tu jīvitam*), because he is no more capable of fulfilling the duties prescribed by the *Śāstras*.[35] We know of historical instances on the basis of epigraphy of the giving up of the body in such conditions.

The opinion of Brahmanic scholars is therefore eventually often the same as that of the Buddhists: the attempt on one's own life is a serious sin but it is not the same when one gives up the body that has lost its utility and from which one is totally detached. In this regard, Kane has mentioned a significant passage of *Mahābhārata* (*Anuśānaparvam*, XXV, 62-64). After a brief eulogy of Himavant, the text continues:

Śarīram utsṛjet tatra vidhipūrvam anāśake /
adhruvaṃ jīvitaṃ jñātvā yo vai vedāntago dvijaḥ //
abhyarcya devatās tatra namaskṛtya munīṃs tathā /
tataḥ siddho divaṃ gacched brahmalokaṃ sanātanam //

'Yes, the twice-born who has gone to the end of the Veda can abandon through starvation his body ritually prepared previously, once he has realised his life to be unstable, after adoring the divinities and bowing to the sages. After this he, the perfect, can leave for the eternal world of Brahman.' (63-64)

But Nīlakaṇṭha's commentary gives to this passage an interesting yet restrictive annotation to the śloka no. 63:

Vidhipūrvakam ātmaśrāddhādikaṃ kṛtvā / *anāśake* anaśanavrate kṛte sati buddhipūrvakam *atraiva śarīram utsṛjet* / tīvrarogādyanabhibhūtasyāpy etan maraṇaṃ vidhīyate / *adhruvam* iti vākyaśeṣāt / tad api *vedāntagasya* jñātatattvasya śarīradhāraṇe prayojanam apaśyata eva itareṣāṃ tv iha maraṇaṃ rogādimahānimittaṃ saty eva mahāpātakaprāyaścittārthaṃ vā ucitaṃ nānyatheti vyākhyātaṃ prāg eva vanaparvaṇi //

'*Previously prepared ritually*: having performed his own funerary rite, etc. *Through starvation*: having vowed to abstain from food, it is here that he can abandon his body after his mind.[36] Even for the one who does not constantly suffer violent pain, such a death is prescribed. *Adhruvam*: the word *iti* is understood. When there are no more motivations to preserve the body, for *the one who has reached the end of the Veda*, for whom the truths are known. But for others, death is indicated here, when it is mainly prompted by pain, etc. or for the sake of atonement of a great wrong, not otherwise. This is what is explained earlier in the *Vanaparvan*.'[37]

The Vedāntin of the *Mahābhārata* who considers life to be *adhruva* 'unstable', is in the very same psychological condition that issues from his philosophy, as the Buddhist who holds the body to be *anicca* 'impermanent', or *svabhāvaśūnya* 'empty of an essential being'. But the legitimacy of his voluntary giving up of the body is far from being unanimously accepted in Hinduism. It is the ordinary doctrine of the *Dharmaśāstra* and of the other passages from the *Mahābhārata* itself which are the most important, for it is this doctrine that Nīlakaṇṭha considers to be contrary to the one expressed in the passage that he is commenting on. In addition there is no question at all that such a death be considered edifying and conducive to inspiring the eventual witnesses to renunciation nor, for even stronger reasons, to lead them to eternal peace. The Vedāntin goes alone to Brahmaloka. He does not take with him crowds as do the Bodhisattvas of the *Saddharmapuṇḍarīka* or of *Samādhirāja* and he does not go there through fire.

If the doctrinal justification for the giving up of the body, for the Vedāntin as well as for the Buddhist, consists in the depreciation of the body, then the secondary aims and the methods of this giving up are different in both.

The choice of starvation or fire could be influenced by the way Hindus and Buddhists traditionally represented the being who has attained the summit of knowledge. Among the former, one of the most well-known images that illustrates the state of this being shows him renouncing his body like the serpent who sloughs, renounces his skin.[38] And this liberation is purely individual. For others it can have the value of an example to be emulated; it is not meant directly for their good. Among the Buddhists, the oldest schools are accustomed to qualifying eminent beings, especially the saints, with the metaphor *aggikkhandha* or *agnikhandha* 'mass of fire'[39] and it is for the good of many (*bahujanahitāya*) that they act in accordance with the teaching of the Buddha himself.

The giving up of the body over a dagger, resorted by the Buddhist saint Vakkali when he was ill, is related to the suicide permissible in case of a fatal illness in the *Dharmaśāstras*. It is not an inspiring example set by the Bodhisattvas who burn in utter insensibility the body that is so much cherished by humanity and of which they have recognised the vanity.

Meanwhile Hinduism also knows of a voluntary death by fire which leads to the celestial world: death of the virtuous widow, *satī*.[40] The origins of this practice continue to remain obscure. Its supporters advocate the theory that it guarantees a heavenly sojourn. In the vedic ritual, an animal put to death through a bloody sacrifice was also promised life with the gods.[41] It is possible that the burning of the living widow was more or less a direct continuation, during the time and in milieus where the burning of the dead was systematically practised, of an ancient custom of burying the wife along with her husband. Such a custom seems to be attested to in fact in the proto-historic civilisation of Gujarāt where tombs of couples were excavated from the site of Lothal. We can relate this with the Arab accounts of burying the living partner with the dead one, the tale of the fourth voyage of Sindbad the sailor being a typical one. In fact, in India there existed descriptions of the burial of the woman with the husband.[42]

Whatever it may be, these cases differ from the cases of voluntary renunciation of the body by liberated Vedāntins and mostly by Buddhists who have succeeded in establishing their psychic individuality in the conviction that the body is insignificant. The calm countenance of the widow before the ordeal, a countenance that often astonished those witnessing the *satī*, could not be the result of the same psychosomatic preparation as that of the philosophers. Besides it is not certain that the oft-mentioned impassiveness of the *satī* before the lighting of the pyre lasted even when she was engulfed by the flames, as it did in the recent case of self-cremation in Saigon according to the witnesses and the photographs. The descriptions of the *satīs*' cremation we have at our disposal point out, in fact, that in most cases, the wood or the smoke prevented the *satī* from being seen.

These descriptions however point to one fact: the forms of the pyre were different and so were the positions taken by the *satī* inside the pyre. Depending on the region, the women was at times tied to a post over the pyre, at times the pyre was shaped like a hut made of fuel and the body of the husband and the living wife were placed inside. Elsewhere the pyre was substituted by a burning pit.[43] One must not, therefore, try to seek a ritual symbolism in these technical circumstances. Similarly the practice in certain self-cremations of making pyres in the form of a niche or a heap within which a small cabin was set up does not necessarily imply a symbolic stūpa or a niche with a Buddhist statue, even though Gernet found sufficient indications of the incorporation of the pyre of Chinese monks to a *stūpa* in several cases.[44] It can simply mean, when the accounts do not refer clearly to these *stūpas* or niches, certain technical arrangements for a more complete combustion. Besides, according to these accounts, such arrangements are not regular.

As for the seated position, it does not necessarily reveal the identification of the monk undergoing this self-cremation, with certain 'Buddhist divinities'.[45] This position, more specifically a posture of meditation, is usually the one given to mummified bodies[46] and to statues of dead monks as they continue to be erected in certain monasteries of Thailand. But it is a question of a posture of self-collectedness, of even *samādhi*, nay of a common sitting position taken equally by the Hindu *satī* and the Buddhist monk. In the case of the latter, it is not necessary to posit an identification with some 'divinity' whose posture was being imitated. It would seem to mean simply the adoption of the same posture of meditation often seen in Buddhist statues because it mirrors the same self-collectedness as that of the iconographic Buddhas or Bodhisattvas.

The self-cremation of a Buddhist monk, considered to be a feat of yoga, as the original Indian tradition leads us to suppose, should not be compared to the Brahmanic sacrifice, its Indian origin notwithstanding. Brahmanic sacrifice is meant to nourish the gods, it is not therefore right that the sacrificer who invites the gods should eat before them. That is the reason for prior fasting (which can be broken however by taking any food that is not part of the offering to the gods).[47] A Brahmanic fast in itself is an offering of the substance of the sacrificer who has thinned due to the fast.[48] The fast that precedes self-cremation is altogether different and it does not disallow the eventual taking in of non-alimentary substances, but they should be fragrant and combustible.[49] It is less a matter of purification[50] than a preparation for the mastery of the body by the mind, thanks to a willed and methodical curtailment of organic functions. Fasting is, in fact, a common element in any preparation for an effort of psychic tension which is intense and concentrated, and of which the principal somatic activities would divert a part. Now it is particularly necessary to neutralise these activities for the sake of an act where the neutralisation of these, right up to the sensibility, is a must in order to succeed in this encounter with fire.[51]

In addition, self-cremation, as we have seen, is not a sacrifice of an offering or an atonement offered to some divinities but an act of adoration by the striking and exemplary demonstration of total adhesion to the doctrine of the vanity of things and in particular of that which the ordinary man holds most dear: the body.

The self-cremation of Buddhists and the cremation of widows are still echoed, though faintly, in the practice of fire-walking which can be frequently witnessed in numerous parts of the South. This fire-walk which deserves a separate description is performed by groups of men, even a hundred or a hundred and fifty, who jog over a three-metre long bed of burning coal. Sometimes it takes place among the Muslims during the mourning of the massacre of Kerbela and more commonly among the Hindus at the close of the festival of Draupadī in which the daily preparatory ceremonies last over two weeks and involve the reading of long passages of *Pāratam* (*Mahābhārata*) in Tamil by Villiputtūrār (15th cent.). It is performed by the Vaṉṉiyar caste which claims to belong to the Kṣatriya class and to the *agnikula*, 'the race of fire' (*vaṉṉi* is the transcription of the Sanskrit *vahni*). The collective training that consists in fasting, some rites and participation in a number of religious meetings which prepare for the festival is, for most, not a yogic training. Sometimes there is no preparation at all and any random spectator finds himself called, at the last moment, to follow the others. There is no intention of destroying one's flesh in order to demonstrate an absolute detachment from the body. Here, the major motivation is the faith that this walk on fire, on the very grounds of that faith, will be accomplished without pain or any damage. And indeed everything happens according to their resolution, without any evidence of pain or any serious burn as a consequence. The thick skin on the soles of the subjects accustomed to walking barefoot is a relative protection and if any fragment of live coal were to stick to the sole it would be extinguished in a muddy pit at the end of the bed of fire. However, nothing protects the top part of the foot, the articulations and the leg from the radiating heat. No oil is applied to the teguments. However, in case of an accident, due to jostling that may impede the walk for some, or due to a fall, deep burns do occur. The fact remains that without a psychological preparation, the teguments exposed to the heat will feel the beginning of an intense sensation of burning. However, when the walk is performed in normal conditions, the participants do not feel any such sensation. At the most, one may see some walkers sometime nervously nudging those in front, even though the pace of the group may seem correct to others. They are those who are frightened, those whose attention is not entirely diverted away from the preoccupation with the fire.

In any case, if we were to speak about this practice of resisting the burning sensation and the dread of fire, it would be clear that any connection with the Buddhist practice of self-cremation is but a distant one. Such a practice can be found among different peoples, not only in Japan but also in Greece and Oceania where no Buddhist influence seems to have reached.

Self-cremations can, therefore, be compared much less to the other Indian practices of fire-exposure as the cremation of widows, fire-walking and ordeals of fire, than to other methods of giving up the body prompted by the belief in its insignificance and which do not consist in the use of fire: starvation, drowning, hanging or, as in the case of Vakkali and Godhika, jumping into a precipice or slitting the throat.

This is clearly confirmed by going through chapter XVIII of the *Suvarṇabhāsasūtra* which, according to Gernet, was recited by Fa-yu at the time of setting fire to himself in the way described in the *Saddharmapuṇḍarīka*.[52] In fact, this chapter recounts on two occasions and in detail, once in prose and the second time in verse, how the prince Mahāsattva who was to become in his final life

Śākyamuni Buddha, gave up his body to a starved tigress who was ready to eat up her own cubs. Here although it is not a matter of fire the feat is not in any way different in nature from self-cremation: it involves 'total self-renunciation' (*ātmaparityāga*). Mahāsattva believes that such a self-giving is not difficult for men of goodness who are better adapted to the good of others. He contrasts, as did the Buddha in the story of Vakkali, the 'body of decay' (*pūtikāya*) with the 'body of the Order' (*dharmakāya*). Therefore he offers himself to the tigress but as he is full of goodwill (*maitrī*), the beast does not attack him. To enable the tigress to devour him he slits his throat before her with a piece of bamboo.[53] His bones are recovered and a *stūpa* is erected to contain these relics. The Buddha, while recounting this story, will give his disciples a glimpse of this *stūpa* and then make it disappear again.

The theme of slitting the throat with a piece of bamboo used as a knife, reminds us of a legend related by Hiuan-tsang, about the death of Nāgārjuna. It is said he had chopped off his head with a plant in order to hand it without delay to someone who had desired his death knowing that a bodhisattva never refuses anything.

The instances of the giving up of the body that multiplied thanks to the Indian influence on China are therefore essentially forms of an absolute renunciation of all attachment to the body which illustrates the doctrine by which the saint is liberated from all personal sentiment and consequently from all feeling of physical or moral pain, retaining, nevertheless, on the one hand, a motivation of helpfulness and pity in regard to individual beings whose suffering it alleviates by his self-giving, and on the other, by a motivation of adoration of the true Order of things and all that awakens one to It, namely: The Awakened Guides of the world, their teaching, the monuments commemorating them, their relics and those of their disciples, even their images. In the latter motivation, the body is offered in homage of adoration. In both the cases, it is offered and his killing is not consequential since it was already abandoned. But for this very reason, in principle, no pain at all is felt.

The act of self-cremation as that of slitting one's throat to let oneself be devoured by a tigress, is therefore in theory an act of heroism only in appearance: for it is done for the satisfaction of the benevolent sentiment for others and does not imply suffering for oneself. However the one who accomplishes it is truly a hero (*vīra*). He is not a hero at the moment of the dramatic giving up of the body which means nothing to him. He is a hero for having made himself fit to do it. His final act is an outcome and a test. It is the long and difficult psychological discipline of acquiring the mastery of detachment which makes his heroism and which bears its glory.

It is also due to 'the knowledge of the Awakened Ones' in which he became 'learned', that an act like that of Kṣemadatta in the *Samādhirāja* (see above, stan. 32) could be accomplished. That is why the Being on the path of Awakening, the *bodhisattva*, too, should not seek glory for himself. There are texts that greatly censure those monks who seek the admiration and acclaim of the world and praise those who live like the powerful and solitary rhinoceros, to take up a common comparison.

It is no less true that the world is moved by the sublime horror of their shows of mastery and impassiveness and that they become in people's eyes *caityas* or 'sacred objects' such as the places to which is connected the memory of some event concerning the Awakening to the right Order of things, or else and more commonly, the monuments commemorative of these events or containing sacred relics. The Buddhist method of conversion has always profitably utilised the emotion born in men from the evocation of some pious memories. The *Mahāparinibbānasutta* attributes to Śākyamuni the exhortation to build *stūpas* at the places of his birth, his Awakening, his Sermon and his Extinction so that men may come there and wonder: 'Here, the Blissful One was born; here He got the Awakening...'[54] Everywhere in a Buddhist country, to whatever school the community may belong, the *stūpas* and the *caityas* are distinctive monuments. It is, therefore, natural to know through legends and biographies of heroes who undertook self-cremation or other ways of giving up their body that *stūpas* were erected in their memory and thereby became holy places. This is true not only of China but also of India. In China, sites where partial or total self-cremation took place Gernet informs us, often became new sacred sites—these sites corresponded with the Chinese concepts of the holy sites and were thought fit to be sanctified with the rites—unless, of course, they had already been so sanctified and held sacred. It is certain that these concepts are in harmony with the Buddhistic concepts that prevailed in India and facilitated the acceptance of Indian practices there.[55] We cannot, for this reason, consider them to be specifically Chinese. Some of them, such as the preference for mountains, belong not only to Buddhism but to all Indian religions as well. The belief in the benignant effect of the victories of the Dharma, in nature and for prosperity, is equally current in India and China. The prosperity or the ruin of the kingdom too depended, as in China, on the conduct of the king vis-a-vis the Dharma.[56]

Gernet also mentions, in order to explain the vogue of sacred places marked by acts of self-cremation, the Chinese idea of the consecration of a place by the sacrifice of a human being. It is true that this is not an exclusively Chinese idea, it exists in South-east Asia although we are not certain if it came from China. It also exists in India where classical texts on architecture, without prescribing any human sacrifice strictly speaking, place in the foundations of an edifice an ideal being: *vāstupuruṣa* 'the man of the site'. Whatever it may be, the widespread belief in China could only encourage there the conversion of the sites of self-cremations into sacred places even if the latter were not performed with any such view in mind.

We do not have sufficient details about the Buddhist monk who recently burnt himself to death, turning his petrol-soaked body into an almost unwavering living torch. We cannot, therefore, analyse his motivations. It has been termed a political protest by contemporary journalists. At first glance this would connect this self-cremation to the suicides by vengeance, well-known in China, and above all to the sacrifices for pressurising others, creditors or public authorities, which in India assume the form of 'hunger-strikes' where the person on fast is supposed to practice *satyāgraha*, 'clinging to truth' until his death, of which his adversary will be held responsible.[57] The self-cremation of another monk mentioned by Moura[58] to have taken place formerly in Cambodia would also seem to suggest a political protest. If it is so, these acts are nonetheless accomplished in conformity with the tradition of Buddhistic yoga which guarantees an impassibility in the resolve and in the execution and which basically bear witness to the insignificance of the body and, even more so, of worldly material things in contrast with the true Order of things.

This tradition seems to have been developed essentially in milieus that advocated the absence of an essential being in things (*śūnyavādin*) and more particularly in tune with the doctrines of *Amitābha* and of the *Sukhāvatī*. Although the vanity of the body and of all things is taught in all the Buddhist schools and that the giving up of the body, as we have seen, is perfectly legitimate among the theravādins and also among the liberated Vedāntins, self-cremation does not seem to have been practised in all the Buddhistic circles. Among the theravādins, total or partial self-cremation practiced by igniting the whole body or the hand (wrapped in cloth) soaked in oil is mentioned on several occasions in the Pāli canon. They are respectively called: *jotimālikā*, 'garland of light' and *hatthapajjotikā*, 'the setting fire to the hand'[59] but these were tortures inflicted by kings. It is unlikely that *bhikkhus* submitted themselves to them voluntarily.

From the point of view of psychiatry and modern psychology, it would be easy to find an interpretation, or at least some diagnosis in these cases of disdain for the body and this will to be self-destruction attitudes which seem to be natural to those who undertake self-cremation or any other voluntary death that is prompted by the conviction that the body as well as all things are insignificant.

The legend of Kṣemadatta in the *Samādhirāja*, however fantastic it may seem, brings to the forefront a type of a person who recalls at once a real case of schizophrenia or premature insanity. Kṣemadatta is, in fact, described as a very young man who was ordained to become a monk a year before and who made himself conspicuous by abstaining from all play from his earliest childhood. He showed signs, therefore, even before his Buddhistic indoctrination of an attitude of self-contemplation. On the other hand, among the legendary or real cases of Buddhists wanting to give up their body, several made repeated attempts at committing suicide, which leads us to think at once to the ordinary suicidal tendencies that psychiatry is familiar with.

It is certain that some psychopathological tendencies, universal in nature, may have triggered the Buddhist practice of depreciating the body—especially among those who were particularly predisposed to it. The Buddhist doctrine itself may have pushed into self-destructive action some subjects who, without Buddhism, would have merely leaned on a proneness to self-destruction.

Nevertheless, a pathological explanation cannot be upheld as a general explanation of the Buddhistic acts of self-destruction. The pathological cases can be recognised at once by their antagonism to the norms of the life of the milieus and societies in which they are born. The acts that are accomplished are in contradiction with all acts expected by the environing society considering the education and the actual personal standing of the subject who undertakes them. They are manifest results of impulses foreign to the motivations usually set forth by the milieu of his existence. The conditions for the creation of Buddhistic representations of the insignificance of the body and for the acts of self-destruction that are based on these representations are altogether different. It is a question of representations acquired through a precise psychotechnical method.

One of the best illustrations at our disposal occurs twice in the Pāli canon of the theravādins: in the *Dīghanikāya*, sutta no. 22 entitled *Mahāsatipaṭṭhānasutta*, and in the *Majjhimanikāya*, sutta no. 10 called *Satipaṭṭhānasutta*. They give a detailed description of the psychic representations which are born only in him who is autonomous, not dependent on anything (*anissita*, Skr. *aniḥśrita*), who 'does not take possession of anything in the world' (*na kiñci loke upādiyati*). The prescribed psychic operation is called *satipaṭṭhāna* and the corresponding name in Sanskrit texts is *smṛtyupasthāna*, 'stabilising the presence in the consciousness'. In the system of conventional translation of technical Buddhist terms he adopted, Sylvain Levi[60] chose 'aide-mémoire' to render this expression and he was followed by Lin Li-kouang who made an important analytical study of the various Buddhist theories of *smṛtyupasthāna*.[61] But this translation is unfortunate, *sati* in Pāli, *smṛti*[62] in Sanskrit is not just 'memory' but 'awareness in the mind', consciousness, and it can be that of a memory but, precisely in the case of a psychic operation called *satipaṭṭhāna*, it is that of a series of representations created voluntarily in the course of instantaneous observation. Neuman's translation 'Einsicht'[63] and J. Bertrand-Bocandé and W. Rahula's translation 'attention'[64] are more adequate but the former refers to the operation that achieves this awareness in the consciousness, and the latter to the operation that conditions such awareness rather than to the 'awareness in the consciousness' itself.

In fact, it is a matter of a series of creations of representations concerning successively the body (*kāya*), the sensations (*vedanā*), the mind (*citta*), and things (*dhamma*) which means that according to the Pāli canon there are four *satipaṭṭhāna*. The solitary secluded bhikkhu, while sitting, breathes in and out and becomes conscious of his respiration. He shortens and lengthens it and 'instructs himself' (*sikkhati*) by saying to himself: 'I breathe in long, I breathe out long', etc. Then he observes himself standing, walking, etc. instructing himself all the time, as if to learn his lesson, saying to himself: 'I am walking, I am standing up' etc. Then he observes the different anatomical parts of the body[65] and its constituting substances. He visualises the dead body, then the stages of its decomposition. Similarly he observes his sensations, then his thought in all its manifestations, then again the visible, audible things, etc. He concludes by visualising in succession the elements of the Awakening (*bojjhaṅga*) and the four noble truths (*ariya-sacca*).

He thus situates himself in relation to all sensible things, starting with the body, as objects. Thus he dissociates himself from the body, from the sensations, from the mind and the sensible things. The body, sensations and ideas are no longer for him instruments of pleasure and elements of his psychic individuality: they become strange devalued images in his consciousness by this exclusive visualisation of their corruptibility. The eventual attachment to these representations or to some among them is, from the very beginning of the exercise, removed. In each paragraph related to one of the representations prescribed, it is specified that 'for him the awareness in his consciousness is established only as far as it is for knowledge, for the representation and (that) it remains autonomous, by not taking possession of anything in the world.'[66]

Such is the methodical exercise prescribed in order to objectivise the body and the perceiving and the feeling mind and to liberate oneself from all attachment through the Awakening to the insignificance of the subjective consciousness. What pathology would be able to explain only in some particular cases, which would be foreign to the Buddhist practice, the latter explains it by its fine and rigorous psychotechnical methods which eventually prepare the upsurges of faith and of charity towards the suffering world for which the *bodhisattva* can sacrifice his body and his individuality which no more hold any significance for him.[67]

NOTES

1. Les suicides par le feu chez les bouddhistes chinois du Ve au Xe siècle, in *Mélanges publiés par l'Institut des Hautes Etudes chinoises*, t. II, Paris, 1960, pp. 527-58. A study on the same problem containing a personal observation of the ritual burning of the skull and translation on the basis of the Chinese version by Kumārajīva of chapter XXII of the *Saddharmapuṇḍarīka* (there marked chap. XXIII) included in J.J.M. De Groot's *Le code du Mahāyāna en Chine*, Amsterdam, 1893, pp. 217-31.
2. The two translations of *Saddharmapuṇḍarīka* are dated 300 or about 400, respectively by Tchou Fa-hou and by Kumārajīva (Gernet, p. 537). Of the *Samādhirāja*, a translation seems to have been done by Ngan Che-kao in the 2nd century, but whether it actually exists is very uncertain like everything else that is ascribed to this translator. Another partial translation, by Sien-kong, is from the period of Song (420-79). The most common one is by Narendrayaśas and dates from 557 (*Hôbôgirin*, fasc. an., Nos. 639-41; Bagchi, *Canon bouddhique*, I, pp. 271, 406). The Chinese title, *Yue teng san mei king*, corresponds to *Candra-pradīpa-samādhisūtra*. Nalinaksha Dutt & Shiv Nath Shastri ed., *Gilgit Manuscripts*, vol. II, parts 1-3, Srinagar-Calcutta, 1941–1954.
3. Dutt-Shiv Nath ed., pp. 455–67. Tibetan translation, Tibetan Tripitaka Research Institute, Tokyo–Kyoto, 1958, t. 32, p. 9, text 5, 1.7-11, t. 5, 1.4.
4. I translate *dharma* with 'Order', *saddharma* with 'Right Order' or 'true Order' rather than with 'Law' although there is little difference between the two notions. Less succinctly it should be the 'Order of things' or the 'Law of things' for what is really meant is the arrangement of the whole universe as the Buddhas visualise it and not some religious law belonging to Buddhism. The *dharmas* are 'things arranged according to this Order'.
5. *Citrīkāra*, Tib. *ṅo-mchar*, 'wonder'. The same translation in Tibetan of *citrīkāra* in *Lalitavistara*, Leffman ed., p. 287, 1.8, in Rgya-cher rol-pa, Foucaux ed., pp. 245, 1.10.
6. *Parigraha*, Tib. *yoṅs su bzuṅ pa*.
7. Cf. *Samādhirāja:*
   XXXII, 40: *agrāhyaṃ gaganaṃ proktaṃ grāhyam atra na labhyate |*
   eṣa svabhāvo dharmāṇām agrāhyo gaganopamāḥ ||
   'Unseizable is said to be space: we find nothing seizable in it. The essential-being of things is unseizable: things are comparable to space.'
   XXXII, 112: *yo bhāvaḥ sarvabhāvānām abhāva eṣa darśitaḥ |*
   evaṃ bhāvān vijānitvā abhāvo bhoti darśitaḥ ||
   'The being that belongs to all beings is manifest as non-being. When one knows the beings thus, then non-being is manifest.'
8. An old Brahmanic idea of the omnipotence of the utterance of truth, truth

being the real order of things, Cf. on truth (*satya*) according to the *Brāhmaṇas*, Sylvain Lévi, *La doctrine du sacrifice dans les Brâhmanas*, Paris, 1898, pp. 39, 109.

9. Burnouf (*Lotus*, p. 242) translated *yoga* as 'meditation', which he also used for *samādhi*. This is inaccurate in both cases and takes away all their specificity from the technical notions expressed in the original terms. Kern (*The Saddharmapuṇḍarīka*, in SBE, XXI, 1884, p. 419) translated most unfortunately *pūrvayoga* as 'ancient devotion' while adding in a note 'rather ancient history' and by referring to another passage of his translation (p. 159, n. 1) in which he tried to trace *yoga* as a derivative of *yuga*. This last attempt is totally unacceptable, although also echoed by Rhys Davids-Stede (PTSD, s.v. *pubbayoga*) who translated *pubbayoga* by 'former connection, i.e. connection with a former body or deed, former action (and its result)'. Senart (*Mahāvastu*, I, p. 615) made *yoga* to be an equivalent of *bhava* and spoke about the 'existence in some particular society from which nirvāṇa alone can liberate men'. Edgerton (BHSD, s.v. *pūrvayoga*) has followed Rhys Davids-Stede: 'Former connexion, i.e. deeds, adventures, lives in former incarnations'. But it is utterly futile to deviate in this way from the meaning of *yoga*. Its strict meaning of a discipline for self-control is quite adequate. The beginning of *Milindapañha*, where the antecedents of Milinda and of Nāgasena are dealt with and from which Kern selected this passage: *pubbayogan ti tesam pubbakammam*, does not prove that *yoga* is a synonym of *kamma*. The preceding activity, *pubbakamma*, of the two heroes is defined as having consisted in a *pubbayoga* an ancient discipline of self-control, characterised, according to the account given at that time, by the wishes articulated by the two heroes about their future conduct and their goals.
10. Cf. among others, J.J.M. de Groot, *Le code du Mahâyâna en Chine*, p. 231.
11. T. 152, translated by Chavannes, *Cinq cent contes*, I, pp. 1-346 Cf. P. Demiéville in *Inde classique*, t. II, pp. 413-14.
12. Chavannes, No. 24, t. I, pp. 85-6.
13. *Le dogme et la philosophie du bouddhisme*, Paris, 1930, pp. 48, 77-79, 194-95, and especially *Quelques observations sur le suicide dans le bouddhisme ancien* in *Acad. roy. de Belgique. Bull. de la Classe des Lettres*, séance du ler décembre 1919, Bruxelles, 1930, pp. 685-93.
14. Cf. texts compiled in Ernst Waldschmidt, *Das Mahāparinirvāṇasūtra*, Berlin, 1951, p. 212.
15. Cf. Malalasekera, *Dict. of Pali Proper Names*, s.v. *Vakkali*.
16. *Aṅguttaranik.*, I, XIV, 2. Commenting on this text, the *Manorathapūraṇī* (*Mp.*, PTS ed., I, p. 248) qualifies Vakkali as being a *thera* among the *bhikkhus* and adds: *aññesaṃ hi saddhā vaḍḍhetabbā hoti, therassa pana hāpetabbā jātā*; *tasmā so saddhādimuttānaṃ aggo ti vutto*, 'for the other (*bhikkhus*), in fact, faith has to be developed, for the *thera* however, it has become unimportant; that is why he is said to be the first among those who are supremely established in faith'. Thus it is because he radiates the most ardent faith, even though as a *thera* he has transcended this stage, that Vakkali is in this respect the most remarkable of all the *bhikkhus*'.

17. *Divyāvadāna*, Cowell-Neil ed., p. 49, 1.18.
18. *Pūtikāya, Mp.*, I, p. 249, About *pūtikāya* and *dhammakāya*, cf. La Vallée Poussin, *Siddhi*, p. 764 and foll.
19. *Kilamanabhāva, Mp.*, 250.
20. *Pītim vikkhambhatvā saha paṭisambhidāhi arahattaṃ patvā, Mp.*, 251, 1.1-2.
21. *Avadānaśataka*, VIII, 10, the case of Virūpā; X, 2, the case of Sthaviraka, and X, 8, the case of Gaṅgika.
22. *Mā bhāyi Vakkali mā bhāyi Vakkali apāpakaṃ te maraṇam bhavissati apāpikā kālakiriyā* SN, III, p. 122.
23. *Sāratthapakāsinī*, Siam ed., I, p. 383: *Thero kira adhimāniko ahosi / so samādhivipassanāhi vikkhambhitānaṃ kilesānaṃ samudācāram apassanto khīṇāsavo mhīti saññī hutvā kiṃ me iminā dukkhena jīvitena satthaṃ āharitvā marissāmīti tikhiṇena satthena kaṇṭhanāḷaṃ chindi / athassa dukkhā vedanā uppajji / so tasmiṃ khaṇe attano puthujjanabhāvaṃ ñatvā avisaṭṭhakammaṭṭhānatta sīghaṃ mūlakammaṭṭhānam ādāya samasanto arahattaṃ pāpunitvā va kālam akāsi /*
24. Gernet, p. 550 and foll.
25. De Groot, p. 227 and foll.
26. *Le dogme et la philosophe du bouddhisme*, p. 78.
27. De Groot, p. 219.
28. De Groot, p. 225.
29. J.J. Matignon, *Superstition, Crime et misére en Chine*, 5th ed., Lyon-Paris, 1909, pp. 143-56.
30. D.J. Mac Gowan, *Self-immolation by Fire*, Chinese Recorder, 1888.
31. Strabo, *Geographie*, XV, 1, 4 & 68; Arrian, *Anabase* VII, 1; Diodore de Sicile, XVII, 107.
32. Strabo, XV, 1, 4, & 73. The Name of Khega would signify in Sanskrit 'Gone to Heaven'. It is probable that a proper name is not meant but that Zarmanochegas designates 'the śramaṇa who has gone to heaven', the designation his companions must have given him after his death on the pyre.
33. XV, 1, 68. He presents these variations as an example of the lack of consensus among historians.
34. On these questions: Hopkins, *Hindu customs of cremation*, in *JAOS*, 1900, pp. 149, 159; Hillebrandt, *Die freiwillige Feuertod in Indien und die Somaweihe*, in *ZBAW*, München, 1917; P.V. Kane, *History of Dharmaśāstra*, vol. II, part II, Poona 1941, pp. 924-28. The references are numerous. Add notably the *Mitākṣarā* on *Yājñavalkyasmṛti*, III, 6 and *Śaivapurāṇa* quoted in *Kriyādīpikā* by Śivāgrayogendra, Muttukumārat Tampirān ed. Madras, 1929, p. 262.
35. Kane, p. 926 and n. 2137, quoting Vivasvant and Gārgya according to Aparārka.
36. *Buddhi* as a major psychic element according to the Sāṃkhya.
37. Nīlakaṇṭha alludes here to his own commentary on the *Vanaparvan*, LXXXV, 83 (which corresponds in the critical edition of Poona to LXXXIII, 78) The censure of the one who gives up his body (*ātmatyāgin*)

is also mentioned by way of allusion in the text itself of the *Vanaparvan*, CCLII, 2 (=Poona CCXL, 2).

38. *Bṛhadar. Up.* IV, 4, 7; *Praśna Up.*, V, 5.
39. *Vinaya*, *Mahāvagga*, I, 26, 27 (Sakka and the four mahārājas); *Dīpavaṃsa*, VI, 38 (Nigrodha); *Samanātapāsadikā*, I, 36 (the saints of the second Council), I, p. 67 (*Dhammarakkhita*); *Paramatthadīpanī*, II, 189.
40. Kane, *Hist. of Dharmaś.*, II, p. 624 and foll.
41. *ṚV*, I, 162, 20-21, a hymn addressed to the sacrificial horse in the *aśvamedha*. The woman is supposed to confirm not only her personal felicity but that of her husband too even if he is not worthy of it. Abraham Roger, *La Porte ouverte, pour parvenir à la connaissance du paganisme caché*, trans. by La Grue, Amsterdam, 1670, p. 135 and foll.
42. For example: *Voyage de M. Thevenot*, Paris, 1684, p. 253.
43. A Roger, p. 129 and foll.; Thevenot, p. 251 and foll.
44. Gernet, pp. 544-45.
45. Gernet, p. 544.
46. Gernet, pp. 548, 556.
47. S. Lévi, *La doctrine du sacrifice....*, pp. 82, 83 and 83, n.1.
48. About this subject Gernet, refers to p. 548, n.3. to Hubert & Mauss, *Essai sur la nature et la fonction du sacrifice* (the quoted passage is to be found in *Année sociologique*, t. II, 1899, p. 50, n. 2 and in the 2nd edition, in *Mélanges d'histoire des religions*, Paris, 1929, p. 25, n. 8).
49. Gernet, p. 548.
50. In the passage quoted by Hubert and Mauss and taken up by Gernet, the attribute 'pure' applied to the emaciated sacrificer is not quite accurate. The word in the text is *medhya* which is actually frequently translated by 'pure'. But that is not its real meaning which is 'sacrifiable, worthy of sacrifice' or 'sacrificial' as Hubert and Mauss have explained within parentheses. In order to be 'worthy of sacrifice', it is necessary to be pure no doubt but the term does not mean that directly.
51. Gernet has pointed out on p. 558, n. 1, the existence of some techniques of eliminating sensibility and mentioned in the case of the monk, Seng-yai, interiorisation, the stoppage of breathing and immobilisation into a 'wooden statue' that are practiced before the burning of the arms.
52. Gernet, p. 531 and n.6, 542 and n.1, where a summary of the chapter is given as per the Chinese version. The event took place between 394 and 415 and the translation of the Sūtra was done only between 414 and 421. Gernet observes that these dates can be reconciled with difficulty. If they are quite exact, it would mean either that the event and the distribution of the translation happened both in 414 or 415, or else that Fa-yu had already known the Sanskrit text or some earlier translation. It should be noted that this Fa-yu, according to the note translated by Gernet, 'was the disciple of Houei-che who had instituted a method of asceticism and culture of the dhutas'. Gernet has explained *dhuta* as referring to purificatory practices, but the *dhuta* or *dhūta* (written also *avadhūta*) is the 'detached one', the one who is freed of all attachment for the well-being of the body, for the habits of life that are not strictly indispensable to

survival. The practices of the detached one are not exactly practices of purification but of abstinence: eating only once a day, sleeping anywhere, etc. Fa-yu had therefore undergone a training to be indifferent to bodily demands.

53. *Maitrī* works actually like a charm of invulnerability, cf. *Maitreya l' Invaincu* in *JA*, 1950, p. 147 and foll. A similar account of the *Suvarṇabhāsasūtra* is to be found in the *Divyāvadāna* (chap. XXXII, p. 478), the hero being Brahmaprabha who acts like Mahāsattva in the same circumstances and for the same purpose, being full of *maitrī* and realising that the tigress will not attack him as long as his body contains thought (*vijñāna*).
54. Cf. E. Waldschmidt, *Das Mahāparinirvāṇasūtra*, pp. 388-90.
55. Gernet, p. 554. In his hypothesis that self-cremation is a sacrifice, Gernet admits that the creation of a sacred place was one of the principal outcomes, that the radiance of this sacred place had a beneficent influence over the entire surrounding area—which sounds quite likely—but that even the self-cremations carried out on the outskirts of the ramparts aimed precisely to reinforce the religious protection of the city itself. We can also admit that they were such in the mind of the Buddhists but not that of the monks who wished to burn themselves. In n. 3 Gernet also believes that sacrifice is power of life and in this connection the sprouting of a strong *sterculier** at the site of the cremation is characteristic (biography of the Houei-chao, p. 532) or in the cell of the burnt monk (the case of Seng-yu p. 533). But the biography of Seng-yu is not very conducive to such an interpretation for it points to another which is aptly Buddhist. The *sterculier** growing in Seng-yu's cell is double, it is compared to *śāla* (*Shorea robusta* ROXB.) and is taken as evidence of the monk's realisation of *Nirvāṇa*. It is, therefore, identified with the twin *śālas* under which Śākyamuni's Parinirvāṇa took place. For the Buddhists, it referred to a testimony not of life but of the final extinction of life. *Sterculier** and Shorea robusta are characterised by a tall and straight growth.
56. It is commonplace in Buddhist tales that under a *dharmarāja*, the good order prevails and rice, sugarcane, cows and buffaloes abound. Cf. Leon Feer, *Avadâna-Sataka*, A.M.G. XVIII, Paris, 1891, p. 4; *Divyāvadāna*, p. 435, where the two kings are contrasted and consequently the two peoples of North and South Pañcāla.
57. Cf. L. Renou, *Le Jeune du créancier dans l'Inde ancienne*, dans *JA*, 1943, 45, pp. 117-30.
58. Information got from Professor P. Huard.
59. *Majjh. nik.*, I, 87; *Aṅg. nik.*, I, 47 (on which *Manorathap.*, II, 89) and II, 122, *Mahānid.*, I, 154, *Cullanid.*, 604, *Milinda*, 197. Cf. Warren, *Buddhism in translations*, in *HOS*, III, Cambridge, Mass., 1906, pp. 436-40.
60. *Mahāyānasūtrālaṃkāra*, t. II, Paris, 1911, index. La Vallée-Poussin has also wrongly interpreted *smṛti* by "memory" in *smṛtyupasthāna* which he translated by 'application of memory, *Kośa*, VI, 153.
61. *L'Aide-mémoire de la Vraie loi* (*Saddharma-smṛtyupasthānasūtra*), Paris, 1949, p. 118 and foll.

62. *Smṛti*, in classical logic, is opposed to *anubhava* which is the new cognition.
63. *Die Reden Gotamo Buddhos*, 2nd ed., München, 1921, t, I, p. 98 ('Die Pfeiler der Einsicht').
64. *Majjhimanikāya*, I, Paris, 1953, p. 137 ('The bases of attention').
65. Discrimination of anatomical elements of the body is spoken of, even outside Buddhism, in classical Indian medicine, as suitable for developing the awareness of the impermanent nature of the composition of the body in order to detach oneself emotionally from the body. Cf. *Carakasaṃhitā*, Śārīr. and commentary by Cakradatta (11th Cent.) on this text.
66. *assa sati paccupaṭṭhitā hoti yāvad eva ñaṇamattāya patissatimattāya anissito ca viharati na ca kiñci loke upādiyati.*
67. The *Samādhirāja*, chap. XXXV, brings into focus compassion which prevents the bodhisattvas from enjoying any felicity as long as they see the misery of beings. It is a common trait but it was propounded by the Buddha after he asked Ānanda if in his opinion a man whose body was aflame could at the same time feel the qualities of desire (*kāmaguṇa*). Ānanda answered in the negative but the Buddha replied that he could do so except if, as a compassionate bodhisattva, he was moved by the misery of beings.

Chapter 9

DOCETISM IN CHRISTIANITY AND IN INDIA*

The Reverend Father de Lubac made several comparative studies of the Christian texts of the Alexandrian period and the Buddhist texts of the same period.[1] The findings of such studies of two different religious traditions are significant regardless of the reasons that attempt to explain the parallels. Either it is due to historical influence, in which case, the reason is revealed or localised, or it is due to an identity of sentiment in two separate settings, in which case, what we find is a commonness of the same natural, psychological response. However, both these reasons are not mutually exclusive, they often intermingle.

Moreover, similar ideas which can be recognised in different religions acquire a particularly significant bearing when they meet. They serve as starting-points to a coming together but also to a divergence. Missionary Christianity, on sometimes meeting in other religions notions similar to its own, often looked upon them as instruments to be used by its apostolate and in some cases tried using these points of doctrinal similitude to rally round the non-Christians. But the same ideas belonging to different systems can be superimposed: they do not necessarily reveal an identity of the two systems. It is rather their incompatibility that is exposed. When the similitude is emphasised, it often pushes the interlocutors not to yield to the other's interpretation, because although conforming on one point, the interlocutors will continue to see it within a context with which they are familiar or which they traditionally and readily accept, there may even be a sense of shock or of surprise at each other's interpretation. Similar ideas do not actually have the same bearing everywhere. On the one hand they can play a fundamental part in the doctrine, and on the other, be just a minor detail. And thus the interlocutors are unable to agree on the value to be ascribed to them.

*Docétisme chrétien et docétisme indien, in Mélanges de Lubac, III, Paris, 1964, p. 7-13.

The corresponding attitudes in regard to docetism both in Christianity and in the principal religions of India provide one such example of convergence and divergence at the same time.

The conceptions about the manifestations of the Supreme Being in a human body or in other material forms in Brahmanism, the manifestation of the Buddha, the Being, liberated from existence in the world, as a human sage subject to sickness, old age, and death, and the manifestation of God in Christ have raised respectively, among the Brahmanists, the Buddhists, and the Christians, the question about the contradiction of the infinity of the embodied Being and the suffering of the manifested body: how or in what way could the Supreme Being actually incarnate in the body of an ordinary being?

Many have answered that the material body in question could only be an 'appearance', dokēsis, a 'manifestation', *vyūha*, or a 'fabricated body', *nirmāṇakāya*; in any case it is a form created by the Supreme Being but neither does it contain His essence nor share His nature.

From the Christian and the Buddhist side, the answer however could have been different. In Christianity man could be redeemed out of his decrepitude by the sacrifice of a human victim. The victim could be worthy of Him only by being Himself and thus God became Man.

Among the first Buddhists, the Buddha, the 'Awakened' one, is a psychic individual who in the course of a succession of numberless lives accumulated the conditions necessary for the final realisation of the real nature of things and the unreality of their phenomenal being. He 'awoke' in human condition and in it he annihilated himself forever, but during his transmigrations he did incarnate himself in other bodies, both animal and human. The body in which he became the Buddha was an ordinary body subject to accidents and infirmity. The earliest Buddhists were not docetists.[2]

Those who believed in docetism were those who identified the Buddha with the *Dharma*, the Right Order of things, 'Reality par-excellence' (*Paramārthasatya*), i.e. a total absence of an objective, self-existent reality in things which, thereafter, were mere subjective representations. For these the body with which the Buddha had preached to humanity could not be more 'substantial' than ordinary bodies and belonged, like the latter, to the phenomenal plane. In fact at the phenomenal level, in the "Reality of the envelope" (*samvṛtisatya*), the body is an amalgamation of elements animated by a psychic individuality, which, without possessing a personal nucleus distinct from its parts, is a specific amalgamation of psychic events derived from some psychological experiences of the past (*saṃskāra*). Therefore the Buddha, conceived as the 'Reality par excellence', could not be a psychic individuality of a phenomenal nature nor could he be a finite being: the body in which men imagine to see him, is not inhabited by him like their own bodies are inhabited by their psychic individuality; it can only be a fantasmatic form, a 'fabricated body', the *nirmāṇakāya*. Another body, that in which the manifestations of glory take place, the 'body of sheer Delight', the *saṃbhogakāya*, does not contain the essence of the Buddha also; this essence is found only in the *dharmakāya*, the body of the Right Order of things.

For the Brahmanists or the Hindus, the divine presence in a material body, not merely human but in any body at all, is popularly considered to be possible. First of all, any thing that exists, by that very reason participates in the One Universal Existence. Then God, Whose essence consists precisely in being that Existence and the aspect the Existence takes vis-a-vis the world, manifests Himself in varying degrees in the material nature itself. He can 'descend' or incarnate as *avatāra* in the world in various ways. He can appear in a body specially created for a particular circumstance: that is the case with the animal or semi-animal *avatāras* of Viṣṇu, tortoise, fish, boar, man-lion. He can manifest Himself as the son of a man and woman, as Rāma who was the son of King Daśaratha and Queen Kauśalyā, or as Kṛṣṇa, son of Vāsudeva and Devakī, who was killed by an arrow. He can also manifest a part (*aṃśa*) of Himself in men.

He can assume human shapes that brusquely appear and disappear: a common phenomenon in the legends of Viṣṇu who wanders about incognito with his consort, the goddess Lakṣmī, amidst the cities where there exists a Viṣṇu temple. This is also common in the legends about Śiva. God can also cause certain manifestations, *vyūha*, in various cosmic forms and functions. He has some 'representations' *mūrti*, which correspond to his divine aspects or to forms he assumed according to the legends of his feats among men or among secondary gods. These *mūrtis* are represented by 'images', *pratimā*, made of different materials: statues, reliefs, paintings, but every image can become a legitimate object of adoration only after a ritual consecration by which the deity descends to inhabit it in the aspect that corresponds to its representation. Otherwise the image is nothing more than a piece of sculpted material. After the consecration this real presence in the image can be lost by accident, breaking, or profanation. As a consequence, in Hindu eyes, the Christian adoration of the sacred host is perfectly natural, whereas the worship of the Cross or icons, even the blessed ones, is mere gross idolatry.

In these conditions, the question about the material body or of the body apparition of God has little importance in Hinduism. The divine essence can incarnate in matter as well or appear in a vision. Besides, matter itself is considered by several philosophic schools, notably that of Śaṃkara, as a product of a universal worldly illusion, *māyā*. And if, on the contrary, like with the Vaiṣṇava doctrine of Madhva, material nature is not illusory but co-existent with God, the Unique sovereign Being, on Whom it is dependent and Who uses it at His Will for His creations, then no other causal essence interferes with them except that of God, Viṣṇu, and none other exists except Him.[3] In both the cases and with greater reason in the intermediary viewpoints[4], whether God be Pure, Unique Existence without attributes (all qualification, personalisation, or materialisation being illusory), or He be Pure, Unique Force (all qualification, personalisation or materialisation being then real but dependent on Him). He can be felt by man in all things, be it a dreamlike or a hallucinatory representation. It is ignorance that prevents us from seeing His immanence; by knowledge one can discern Him in matter. The wonder that impels the devotee to prostrate himself at the feet of His images, is precisely the joy of discovering Him there even while knowing Him to be transcendent. The miracle of incarnation is only an individual reflection of the miracle of immanence.

However, the pure essence of God being transcendent in itself, infinite and eternal, it is opposed to his temporary manifestations in the phenomenal world and in representations that are visible to man. However grandiose those may be, they temporarily limit the divine aspect, they do not contain therefore the full Godhead. It is from this that we derive our notions about the descent of a greater or a smaller "portion" of Him. According to Vālmīki's *Rāmāyaṇa* (I, 16), for instance, Viṣṇu took a human form by means of a drink that was meant for the wives of King Daśaratha and which he distributed to them unequally. These queens gave birth to four sons, Rāma among them, who took upon parts of Viṣṇu according to the portions they had received. Rāma's mother received half of the drink, the other queens shared the other half. Ultimately, if nothing exists except by God and consequently if his indivisible reality is present in all, no aspect including the one which invokes Him with the greatest force represents Him in all his fulness: His transcendent essence is necessarily beyond the field of representation. Immanent in that field of delimitations, he overflows it with his infinity.

Even though these conceptions render ultimately irrelevant, for most of the Brahmanic milieus, the question of knowing whether the bodies or the aspects they believe to be assumed by God are in the eyes of man real or apparent, Brahmanism is docetist, in the sense that these bodies or these aspects, while assuming His presence and turning it into a manifest one, are merely partial appearances that never embrace His plenitude which, in His all-inclusiveness, is beyond all.

Unfortunately we know but little on the first Christian predications in India faced with such theological and Buddhistic conceptions. We could, however, have some idea of the different kinds of doctrines that they might have introduced.

Even if we accept the historical reality of a predication by St. Thomas the apostle in the North-West of India, then on the Coromandel coast, where he gave up his body, even if we accept that Eusebes reference (V, 10) was to India, according to which Bartholomew the apostle also preached the Gospel in India, we cannot imagine what form their predication must have taken. If it was true that Pantene, at the end of the 2nd century, completed a mission to India and took back to Alexandria a gospel of St. Matthew in Hebrew left by Bartholomew, we can only conclude that both of them mixed with the Jewish trading community in India during a time when Indian commerce with Western countries was known to be active and continuous. The notably correct report that the *Elenchos*, written by St. Hippolytus or by an author of his Roman circle, has given of the doctrines of the Brahmins of the Dekkan, establishes that extremely enlightening contacts, direct or indirect, between Christian circles and a Brahmanic community had taken place at the beginning of the 3rd century. However it does not inform us about the Christian doctrines that could have been expounded in India.[5] All the aspects that were discussed in Christian milieus were likely to have been taken to India but more probably those that issued from Eastern Christianity—especially from Lower Mesopotamia and Iran, two regions which were regularly trading with the Western part of India. It is in fact from Basra that David, bishop of this city, set out to evangelise in India between 310 and 340[6] and it was because of the Persian Church, according to the accurate testimony of Cosmas Indicopleustes, that a Christian community could have established itself in Ceylon at the beginning of the 6th century.

Now the relationship between the Persian Church and Western Christianity was not always very close. The homilies of Afraat, between 337 and 346, ignored the Council of Nicaea that was held in 325[7]. The Persian Church seems to have stayed clear of the controversies about arianism. It fought against the Jewish opinion that challenged the divinity of Christ and this last controversy seems to have been taken to India where Jews and Christians coexisted. In Afraat's view, his faith consisted in believing simply in a God who was Creator and Master, who had fashioned man in His own image, who sent His spirit into the prophets and Christ in the world, and in believing in the resurrection of the dead and the mystery of baptism[8]. If such a faith had been propagated in India in the 4th century, it could not have exercised much fascination. As the transcendence of the God was not affirmed, a transcendence which implies His creative sovereignty but which exceeds it too, it could not gain currency among the Brahmanists. The Buddhists were even further from any Christian conception about the redemption of the human condition since they only strove to go beyond it.

Later, during the time of Cosmas, the Christian community of Ceylon depending on the Persian Church must have been Nestorian as is generally believed. It is not certain whether it won to its fold converts from the local population, since Cosmas has pointed out that his Church was for foreigners. These foreigners must have been a colony of Persian traders. The two religions already established in Ceylon then were the Theravādin school of Buddhism, which accepts the human nature of the body of the Buddha even while it confers on it superhuman powers, and Tamil Hinduism, especially Śaivism, that believed, on its part, in multiple apparitions of God in human forms as well as in the images (*mūrti*) of his own manifestations, his characteristic symbol being the *liṅga*, a phallic symbol for some but generally for Tamil Śaivism a representation of the infinite. It recalls a legend in which Śiva appears as a column whose ends cannot be measured by either Brahman or Viṣṇu.

There does seem to exist a certain parallelism between the simultaneously human and superhuman nature attributed to the Buddha by the Theravādins and the double nature, human and divine, of Christ in a single figure (*prosōpon*) according to the Nestorians[9]. But the parallels stop as soon as these similar conceptions are put back in their respective framework, the Buddha being superhuman by individually going beyond the human condition and not by the union of the divine nature with the human. Similarly, every *mūrti* of Śiva can be compared to a prosōpon, and more fully than in the preceding example, for it is indeed the Supreme Being which animates the human or the humanised figure in question. But this meeting of conceptions does not lead to a convergence of the systems to which they belong. Apart from the prosōpon being unique and the *mūrtis* multiple, the union of the divine and the human nature in the *mūrtis* differs from the union of the two natures in the prosōpon. In the Indian docetist view, the nature of God is truly present in the *mūrti* itself, but does not contain the totality of the Being that animates it: it evokes the transcendent without containing it.

The Christian missionaries of former times were frequently astonished to see the Indians agree with them about certain points and then refusing to follow them into the consequences that they drew from them. For want of a knowledge of the interlocutors' train of thought, they sometimes suspected them of being blind, illogical, even servile vis-à-vis a clergy that held them back in order to retain control over the adherents. They did not suppose that the currents of thought that have similar points, if pursued logically, diverge naturally beyond the point of their meeting.

NOTES

1. *Textes alexandrins et bouddhiques. Rech. de. Sc. Rel.* 1937; no. 27, pp. 336-51. *Aspects du Bouddhisme*, Paris, 1950, p. 93 and foll., (*Les apparences diverses du Christ et du Buddha*).
2. For the opinions on the principal schools of the different periods see E. Lamotte, *L'enseignement de Vimalakīrti*, Louvain, 1962, p. 416 and foll.
3. Cf. Suzanne Siauve, *Les noms védiques de Viṣṇu*, Publ. Institut français d'indologie no. 14, Pondicherry, 1959, p. VII.
4. The most important among the intermediary viewpoints between Śaṅkara and Madhva is that of Rāmānuja. Śaṅkara propounded 'the Oneness of the Isolated Being' *kevalādvaita*, i.e. the Unique real existence is the Transcendent who is 'isolated' from the phenomenal world. Madhva believes in the 'duality' *dvaita* of Nature and of the Transcendent. Rāmānuja preaches 'the Oneness in what is qualified', *viśiṣṭādvaita*, i.e. the unique real existence is within the domain of qualifications which in this way is part of the reality.
5. Cf. J. Filliozat, *Relations exterieures de l'Inde*, I, Publ. Institut français d'indologie, no. 2, Pondicherry, 1956: *La doctrine brahmanique à Rome au III siècle*, p. 31 and foll.
6. Cf. F. Nau, *L'expansion nestorienne en Asie*, Ann. Musée Guimet, Bibl. de vulg., t. 40, Paris (1913), p. 208, referring to *Patr. Or.* IV, pp. 292-93.
7. Cf. J. Labourt, *Le christianisme dans l'Empire Perse*, 2nd ed. Paris, 1904, p. 32.
8. Labourt, p. 35.
9. The Christians of 'St. Thomas' as they are called, transcribed in their tongue, Malayālam of Kerala, the word *prosōpon* in the form of *parsūppa* and call the two natures the two *svabhāvas* 'essential nature'. Cf. a quotation of Mar Dionysios (1892) in L.W. Brown, *The Indian Christians of St. Thomas*, Cambridge, 1956, p. 292.

CHAPTER 10

THE GIVING UP OF LIFE BY THE SAGE: THE SUICIDES OF THE CRIMINAL AND THE HERO IN INDIAN TRADITION*

SINCE ANCIENT TIMES, India has been wedded to scorn for life and for pain, by virtue of philosophical pessimism, of frenzied asceticism, almost of ostentation. Indian philosophers, like Kalanos in the time of Alexander and Zarmanochegas in the time of Augustus, were famous among the Greeks for having burnt themselves alive.[1] Basing himself on Megasthenes' account, Strabo wrote in detail about the kinds of death that certain Indian philosophers readily embraced, and for which they attracted the censure of some others; the methods of self-immolation included throwing oneself on swords, jumping off rocky heights, drowning, strangling or death by fire.[2] He also mentions the customary practice by certain Indian widows of burning themselves on the funeral pyre of their husbands,[3] a custom that was quite widespread until it was forcefully abolished by the British viceroy, Lord William Bentinck, in 1829, although even then it did not completely disappear. The act of burning herself with her dead husband transformed the woman into a *satī*, literally a 'true one' or a 'good one'; in brief, the consummately virtuous wife.

These accounts have formed, for a long time, the Western opinion on Indians and their utter readiness to offer themselves to death. Marco Polo confirms this in two passages on South India, passages that are quite elaborate but do not give a very global idea of the facts. He says that one who is condemned to death is entitled to ask to be 'occire il mesme por le oner e por l'amor de tiel ydules' 'permitted to kill himself in honour of or out of love of his *idols*'.[4] We observe that thus he transforms his punishment into a courageous religious sacrifice, and Indian documents tell us about the various motives of such sacrifices.

*L'abandon de la vie par le sage et les suicides du criminel et du héros dans la tradition indienne in Arts Asiatiques, t xv, 1967, pp. 65-68.

Marco Polo recounts that at first the men in question hacked themselves with a knife, braved the resultant pain and finally cut off their head with a violent slash of a very sharp knife placed behind the neck. In the second passage, Marco Polo relates how the Queen-mother of the Pāṇḍya country threatened her sons to cut off her own breasts and kill herself if they refused to stop a violent quarrel.[5] More recent travellers have recounted a number of other events of this kind. They have mostly written—and profusely too—about the self-immolation of widows and suicide by the devotees throwing themselves under Lord Jagannath's chariotwheels at Puri, although the recurrence and even the truth of these last kinds of suicides were vehemently challenged by W. Hunter, a specialist on Orissa, according to whom it was always due to some accident in the huge, uncontrollable masses of people around a juggernaut chariot which was not very easily manoeuverable.[6]

I. THE GIVING UP OF LIFE BY THE SAGE

As a matter of fact, the texts on the Right Order, *Dharma*, and the major religious texts generally denounce suicide or accept it only in some specific circumstances or conditions,[7] as even Megasthenes hinted at by stating that some of the Indian philosophers who had killed themselves were denounced by others.

The suicidal act is impulsive which is naturally criticised by philosophers who profess detachment from all emotion. He who is freed from all worldly bondage will no more be subject to rebirth after death, all impulse to be reborn for further activity having been eliminated, but he will not act to hasten that death. He is liberated but a living-liberated, *jīvanmukta*, and the course of his life after the removal of impulses is comparable to the rotation of the potter's wheel which keeps turning but as soon as the effort that produced the movement ceases, it too stops.

Meanwhile, it has often been accepted that it was desirable for those who had completed their spiritual journey to decide to let their life come to an end, nay, to hasten the dissolution of their body which, overcome by old age or illness, falls into a state of decrepitude. This is expressed by a well-known text of Manu about a Brahmin who after having paid his debt to society by begetting a son, retires into the forest and practices the Upaniṣadic traditions for an integral self-perfection (*ātmasaṃsiddhaye*, VI, 29). He (on conditions, add the commentators, that he is suffering from some incurable disease) heads (*āsthāya*) towards the North-east (the region of the 'Lord', Īśāna), and by means of yoga (*yukta*), nourishing himself with water and air, can walk on until his body drops dead (VI, 31). This is what is called *mahāprasthāna*, the 'great departure'. It is this great departure of the heroes of the *Mahābhārata* that is described at the end of that mighty epic: Yudhiṣṭhira, his brothers and their wife, through the exercise of yoga (*yogayukta*, 1st stanza and *yogadharmin*, stanza 3 of *Mahāprasthānikaparvan* 2) head towards the North[8] (*āsthita*, st. 1) and walk on and successively collapse, except for Yudhiṣṭhira followed by his faithful dog whom he refuses to abandon. Yudhiṣṭhira finds them back in heaven where he arrives in his mortal body which he relinquishes there.

The great departure is not an act of suicide, a violent attempt on life, it is a renunciation of the physical condition that has become futile. Those who commit ordinary suicide, go to hell: 'Whether it be in water, or on firm ground, with the help of a dagger or by hanging, they go directly to hell who kill themselves.'[9]

There are numerous testimonies of cases, and all apparently very genuine ones, of such renunciation of the physical state in legends and epigraphy. But, strictly speaking, there are no genuine accounts of the practice of the 'great departure'. People generally gave up their bodies at holy places, specially in the places of sacred baths (*tīrtha*). And so, according to the *Mahābhārata*, Yayāti, after annointing Puru as King, retires to the Bhṛgutuṅga and practices asceticism (*tapas*) there for a long time, and when his time comes, ceases to nourish himself and attains heaven (*svarga*) along with his wives.[10] Ruṣaṅgu, on aging, abandons his body at Pṛthūdaka on the Northern bank of the Sarasvatī, there where 'he who renounces his body while being fully immersed in reciting (some mantra) is not tormented by the imminent death.'[11] According to the *Rāmāyaṇa*, the Brahmin Śarabhaṅga, a hermit of the forest who merited Brahmaloka by virtue of his askesis, is invited by Indra to come there; he gets into the fire which consumes his old body and there re-emerges a young man who ascends to *Brahmaloka*.[12] In order to reach there, he crosses three series of worlds which according to Rāma's commentary are those that belong to the Fathers (*pitṛ*), and gravitate around the Moon; those that belong to the *ṛṣi* and gravitate around the Sun and those that belong to the gods by birth: Brahmā, Viṣṇu and Rudra around whom the Pole star (*dhruva*)[13] does the circumambulation keeping them on the right. The *Brahmaloka* he attains is a fourth world where Brahman, the Ancestor, Pitāmaha, dwells in the aspect that reunites all the three, Brahmā, Viṣṇu and Rudra.

Kālidāsa has immortalised Aja, the King of Kośala, whose heart was rent by pain at the loss of his wife, 'like a stucco terrace is cracked by a ficus shoot', and this pain fills him with an incurably fatal hurt which he welcomes as a means of rejoining his wife faster. In such a situation, Aja, after properly educating his son in the art of war and of administration, contemplates embracing death (*prāyopaveśana*) which requires abstinence from food, and he reaches the confluence of the Ganges and the Sarayū and abandons his body there and is 'listed as one of the immortals', regaining felicity near his wife.[14]

Such traditional examples are quite common in popular literature and they explain the giving up of life in holy places or on the banks of sacred rivers through starvation or drowning. Numerous inscriptions bear testimony to this.[15]

These cases, whether legendary or not, are about sages or about princes who have fulfilled their state-duties, completed their temporal and spiritual work and whose bodies cannot be of any use anymore. They, therefore, give it up as a serpent would shed off its skin, but they have to be prepared for this, not merely by fulfilling their duties enjoined by the Right Order (*dharma*) and ritual (*karman*), but also by the knowledge of the culmination of the Vedas, the Vedānta.

An ancient text, the *Praśnopaniṣad*, had already spoken of it. The question is asked: Which world can he attain, he who meditates on the syllable *OM* until death (*prāyaṇāntam* V, 1) and the final answer (V, 5) is that he merges in the radiance at the Sun, that he liberates himself from evil as a serpent sheds off its skin[16] and that he is led to the world of Brahman (*Brahma-*

loka). The *Mahābhārata* states it even better and explains the prevailing classical opinion.

'Yes, the twice-born who has gone to the end of the Veda (*Vedāntaga*) can give up there (on the Himavant), through starvation, his body prepared previously by rites, once he has realised life to be impermanent, after adoring there the divinities and bowing to the sages. After which, become perfect, he can go to the eternal world of Brahman.' (*Anuśāsana Parvan* 25. 62-64).[17]

We have just seen that instead of letting oneself die through abstinence from food, one could also give up one's body in fire.[18] The *Mitākṣarā*, a widely accepted text by Vijñāneśvara (11th century), while commenting on a passage from the *Yājñavalkyasmṛti* (III, 55) which enjoins, like Manu the great departure (VI, 31), points out that according to one tradition 'the *vānaprastha* can take the path of the heroes (i.e. iron), entry into fire or water or fall into a precipice.'[19]

Vijñāneśvara then adds: 'even for him, the rules of bathing, cleaning of the mouth, etc. enjoined for the *brahmacārin* (*Yājn.* I, 16 and foll) are not incompatible (with his state of *vānaprastha*). 'For the people of the North it is compatible', says the tradition of Gautama. Thus, he who adopts an end through the giving up of the body by starting with *aindava* (*cāndrāyaṇa*, a vow that essentially involves the reducing of food progressively with the waning moon) spoken of earlier and ending with the consecration and the great departure, requires the right to be worthy of homage, in the world of Brahman.'[20] This is what Manu says: 'Among those who follow the practice of the *maharṣi*, the Brahmin whom all fear of pain has left is glorified in the world at Brahman once he has given up his body in any other way (besides the great departure)'.

But voluntary death through an act of violence is not approved by all, even if it occurs in sacred places where according to numerous texts, death is considered to be desirable, although they do not specify the kind of death they had in mind. Nīlakaṇṭha, while commenting on the *Mahābhārata* (*vanaparvan*, 85-83) wherein it is said that one must never abandon the idea of dying at Prayāga whether on the word of the Veda or under the influence of the world (that is to say one must always keep the hope of dying at the confluence of the Ganges and the Yamunā), declares that, according to the Easterners, 'a violent death, prohibited by the world and the Veda, attracts censure in the same way as the sacrifice of a victim for reasons related to the rule of non-violence'. Now, what the text means, in fact, is the eventual death, he adds, as in the case of death at Vārāṇasī; he does not advocate a violent death.[21] He then affirms that the prohibition of suicide in water, with iron or by hanging is absolute and is not waived at Prayāga since it is not different from a violent death. He concludes: 'It needs to be said that this (death) does not lessen the gravity of the transgression because of the fact that it is desirable. In fact, even when there is no express prohibition, it is a grave error to imagine and say that it is different from a violent death and that the rule has a new interpretation. Or else, if one admits it, this rule that makes an exception of Prayāga, is aimed at those who are non-Brahmins, for the Tradition states: 'Death by falling from a precipice, etc...except for the Brahmin.'[22]

As for the *Brahmaloka*, the world of Brahman, the destination of those who abandon their body in the conditions of preparation that we have seen, opinions vary with texts but less in actual fact than in appearance.

In the *Atharvaveda* (19.71), it is the abode where one wishes to go after a full and prosperous life. But it is mostly in the much later Vedic speculation and then in all the subsequent traditions, that it is frequently mentioned and at times described. A long passage is devoted to it in *Kauṣītakyupaniṣad* (I, 3-7) which says that the one who enters it identifies himself with Brahman himself,[23] but this world is described as a place of glorious material sojourn. The *Bṛhadāraṇyaka* (IV, 3. 32-33) and the *Taittirīya-upaniṣad* (II, 8) make of it a sojourn of supreme felicity (*paramānanda*). It is indeed the ultimate world in which all reposes (*Bṛhad.* III, 6.1), a world from which those who know do not return (*Bṛhad.* VI, 2, 15), where one obtains liberation (*vimokṣa, Bṛhad.* IV, 3, 33), where one can enter through the knowledge of the ātman-brahman (*Bṛhad.* IV, 3, 33.34, 25). 'It is towards it (the Self) that go those who lead a life of wandering (*pravrājin*) aspiring for Its world.'[24]

The *Chāndogyopaniṣad* states that it can be attained through *brahmacarya* (the Brahmic practice of the student given to work, chastity, and surrender to the master).[25] The gods who live there know the Self (VIII, 12, 6). When one attains to it, one can say: 'Shaking evil like a horse shakes his mane, shaking the body like the Moon freeing itself from Rāhu's jaws, I enter, having created the Self, in the uncreated world of Brahman.'[26] From there one does not return (*Chānd.*, VIII, 15, 1).

For the *Mahābhārata* (*Śāntiparvan*, 185, 3-6) as for *Bṛhad.* IV, 4, 22, *brahmaloka* is the destination of wandering ascetics or *parivrājakas*, but it is not the last world. Beyond it in the North, there is still the *Paraloka* (*Śāntip*. 185. 7-8), the 'superior world'. For the *Bhāgavatapurāṇa* (II, 5, 39), on the contrary, *Brahmaloka* is the highest world: it corresponds to the heads of Cosmic Man (Puruṣa) and it is also the 'world of truth', *Satyaloka.*

The philosophers of the Vedānta have dwelt on the question whether the Brahman of the *Brahmaloka* is the Supreme Brahman (*parabrahman*) transcending all form or its specialised manifest-ation, the *Kāryabrahman*, the 'Brahman who is created' or who is *saguṇa, saviśeṣa* 'with qualities, with particularities'. The classical manual of the *Brahmasūtras* states contradictory opinions: that of Bādari (IV, 3.7) who thinks that we can strive towards the *Kāryabrahman* and that of Jaimini (IV, 3.12) who thinks that we strive towards the *Parabrahman.*

Bādarāyaṇa, who is said to be the author of the *Sūtras* themselves, thinks that those who are led to the world of Brahman are those who do not take appearances to be objective realities.[27] His own conclusion about the validity of the two forementioned opinions remains uncertain, because the text that was intended to formulate it, is expressed in a self-contradictory manner by the two greatest commentators, Śaṅkara and Rāmānuja.[28] But if, as both the philosophers agree,—and rightly, it seems—the *kārya*, the 'product' is the Brahmaloka (*Br.* S. IV, 3, 9 or 10), it is a transient abode, because the *sūtra* says: 'When the product is destroyed, we go from there along with its ruler, to the superior one, according to the Word (of the texts).'[29]

And so we have here the same conception as in the *Mahābhārata* and it is also the one supported by Vijñāneśvara, in his *Mitākṣarā*, on the basis of the passage referred to above.

This is what he says: 'The world of Brahman is a sort of a place but not the (neutral) Brahman who is Eternal. Since we do not call the latter, a 'world', and as the promise of liberation can only be given in the fourth stage of life (the *sannyāsa* of the *parivrājakas*), not before, not even, it seems, by the practice of yoga, it (liberation from rebirth) is altogether uncertain as regards its realisation for not being in conformity with the rule of consecrating oneself to Brahman and (it is uncertain) even as regards its conformity with the intention of obtaining an access to the same world (as Him).[30] He continues by taking up and elaborating upon a passage of the *Chāndogyopaniṣad* according to which there are three branches of the Right Order (II, 23. 1-2) which correspond to the three stages of life: that of the student, that of the householder and that of the ascetic settled in the forest, and all these three are 'worlds of benefit' (*puṇyaloka*), i.c. wherein one can reap the fruit of one's actions, whereas it is the man 'that holds himself in Brahman who attains immortality.'[31] And therefore Vijñāneśvara concludes: 'It is to him who leads a life of wandering (*parivrājaka*), holding himself in the Brahman, that the immortality of liberation is given. Even if it is said that the householder too who performs the rites for his ancestors, and whose word is the Truth, is liberated, it must be understood that the gaining of salvation is also for the householder when he has taken up a life of wandering in another existence.'[32]

The opinion expressed in this text and which ultimately is the prevalent one in general tradition is that *Brahmaloka* is an abode of great felicity, which is reached only by the meritorious conduct of the Brahmins in the three stages of life which are specific to them,[33] but it is enjoyed only temporarily and it is only the wandering *sannyāsins* who can attain permanent liberation. This did not stop certain philosophers from considering *Brahmaloka* as a specific place, for Brahman is everywhere for the one who conceives him as Universal Reality underlying all things. And therefore one can interpret the compound *Brahmaloka* either as *tatpuruṣa*, having the ordinary meaning of 'the world of Brahman', or as a *karmadhāraya* in which case it means 'the world that is Brahman.'[34]

Among the Jains, as among the Hindus, it is only the saint

who can legitimately commit suicide and that too only by discontinuing its upkeep. But then there exists a whole systematised and exclusive process for leading to this final salvation or at least to considerably shorten the course of new births that are necessitated by the consequence of actions accomplished in the past. In this process, death is the culmination of total fasting, to which a long prior preparation is made by other fasts and by exercises of meditation and psychosomatic discipline. This practice called *saṃlekhanā* (*ardhamāgadhī*: *sallehaṇā* or *saṃlehanā*) is an ancient and long-standing one. Jain tradition tells us that Candragupta gave up his throne, retired to Śrāvaṇabeḷagoḷa with the patriarch Bhadrabāhu and there starved himself to death. This could be a legend. In any case, numerous examples of *saṃlekhanā* are cited in Jain epigraphy. Fifty years ago Guérinot mentioned a certain number of these, mostly from the South.[35] Only a few years ago Louis and Marie-Simone Renou found yet another case among the Terāpanthī.[36] *Saṃlekhanā* can be accomplished by laymen as well as monks, men as well as women. It is usually practiced preferably at a holy place, as in Hinduism, but rather on a mountain than near a river.[37] It demands, in any case, a total annihilation of desires and impulses, a total detachment from all except the aspiration for liberation. Now, this aspiration, at the moment when a final decision is taken to undertake a fast unto death, is not an impulse but an inclination that has been cultivated for a long time and has now become an automatism that no longer requires any active willing. This clearly distinguishes such giving up of life from the common suicide which is denounced outright.

The kind of judgment and motivations can be compared with those of the Buddhists. Any act of an attempt on life is wrong according to the Pāli tradition of the Theravādins. One Megalaṇḍika, who was a monk only by his dress (*samaṇakuttaka*) prompted by an evil divinity who was diverting him from his remorse, began killing those monks, who, extremely impressed by Buddha's speeches advocating detachment from life, wanted to do away with life itself. It was a matter of scandal and the Buddha promptly rebuked it.[38] But it was not merely the killing of desperate men he rebuked; his rebuke was also aimed at suicide, strictly speaking, and as regards even the saint's act of voluntary death he accepted it only as a last resort. The two cases, those of the *thera* Vakkali and the *āyasmā* Godhika, especially the former, have clearly shown at least the reluctance of the ancient Buddhist tradition to grant legitimacy to wilful death on the part of one who as a saint ought to be detached from all interest in anything whatsoever. In words attributed to the Buddha himself, it is clearly stated that if Vakkali had been a saint and ill, his suicide would have been sinless and would have caused no rebirth. For he would have given evidence of the fact that he had no attachment of any kind for appearances. But the great commentator Buddhaghoṣa did not think it totally futile to argue out this exceptional case in order to justify it.[39]

In the tradition of the subsequent Buddhist schools voluntary death, particularly by fire, is admitted and even glorified but only in the case of those who are convinced, through an integral revolution in their habitual psychic individuality, of the basic unreality of the phenomenal world.[40] It is this tradition which has permitted the recent self-immolation by fire of the Vietnamese monks, who in their turn, by their example have inspired others, Buddhist and even non-Buddhists, and in widely different countries, to commit similar acts but with altogether other motivations, as a mark of protest or as an affirmation of faith.

II. THE EXPIATORY SUICIDE OF THE CRIMINAL

Suicide in honour of or out of love for an idol, permitted to the condemned convict in India, as Marco Polo pointed out, is obviously neither the suicide by a sage nor by a hero. But it seems to be actually accepted by law in some cases that a condemned convict can commit suicide instead of getting executed and his death is akin to the suicide of a hero which will be studied below and which is meant for the regaining of lost honour or as a sacrifice to a divinity. Killing oneself requires, in any case, courage, which distinguishes him from the one who commits suicide because he is led to the scaffold.

According to Manu, he who has killed a Brahmin voluntarily (the commentators say that it is a kṣatriya who commits such a murder) can offer himself for being the target of archers or throw himself headlong into fire for a maximum of three times (XI, 73). The murderer of a Brahmin can also sacrifice, or at least imperil, his life to save a cow or a Brahmin (XI, 79-80).[41] But there exist yet other ways of atoning for a similar crime which do not require the death of the guilty. The criminal law contained in the *dharmaśāstras* is extremely varied and if the victim happens to be of a lower class the law was even less strict. We thus see that he who commits adultery with his guru's wife has to sleep on a bed of red-hot iron or embrace a column of hot metal or cut off his sexual organs himself and then holding them walk towards the region of *Nirṛti* (the South-West) until be falls dead (Manu XI, 103-04).

These prescriptions by Manu are found in the chapter dealing with expiation (*prāyaścitta*). In fact, justice in India tends to be not merely coercive. It does not merely wish to set an example, it also strives to redeem the criminal and that is why the punishment can take the form of expiation. In the middle of the 3rd century B.C. already Asoka prescribed in the 4th Edict on Pillar that the condemned convicts be given three days to let others intercede on their behalf or at least give them the time to practice charitable acts and take up fasting for the sake of the beyond (*pālattika*) since the king would want to see them reach it.[42] This concern for the salvation of criminals is not peculiar only to Asoka and to Buddhism which he followed. Manu himself expounds that criminals punished by the king go effortlessly to heaven like the good and the doers of good deeds.[43] We can then understand better that the king could grant them the favour of acquiring merit by themselves choosing the punishment which was expiatory and redeeming.

III. *Suicide by the hero*

As for the suicide of the hero, it is mostly ancient Tamil literature which gives us its first instances and their motivations.

The *Tolkāppiyam*, in its repertory of poetic subjects, mentions among those that refer to *kāñci*, the instability of things, and they are tragic situations: 'the courage with which one ends up lacerating a wound, after having weighed how much this would contribute to attaining excellence'.[44] He also mentions 'the horror of the spouse ranting on the spear left by her husband who has been given up by life'[45] and the commentator Ilampūraṇar (12th century) thinks that she kills herself on this spear[46] but such an interpretation is not very likely. It is however interesting that it is mentioned because it is not borne out by the text and if it has been suggested, it is probably because there were known examples of wives killing themselves in order to reunite with the hero, killed in combat, as revealed by the sculptures that we shall see. The same passage of the *Tolkāppiyam* also mentions the mother who dies of pain as her son has fled and forfeited the 'distinction' of dying in battle. The 'quality' *paṇpu*, and the 'distinction' *ciṟappu* both correspond here to honour.

The poems of *Akanāṉūṟu* and of *Puṟanāṉūṟu* refer to a prince, who on being wounded in the back, probably without having fled, but in any case, forfeiting thus his honour, positioned himself facing the North and killed himself with his sword.

Akanāṉūṟu (55. 9-12) calls this warrior Cēral Ātaṉ, i.e. Ātaṉ from Cēra or Kerala and says about him:

'Fighting on the battle field, of Veṇṇi with Karikāl in fertile country, ashamed of his wound, Cēral Ātaṉ positioned himself facing the North, with the sword in his abdomen at the site of his defeat.'[47]

Puṟanāṉūṟu (65. 9-11) does not name him but the colophon calls him Cēramāṉ Peruñcēralātaṉ which means 'the King of Cēra, great Cēral Ātaṉ' and the same person is meant[48] of whom it is said:

'Vanquished, although he had thought he was facing a sovereign who was equal to him, ashamed of a wound in the back, the King with a natural heroic bent positioned himself facing the North with his sword.'[49]

Puṟanāṉūṟu (66. 5-8) eulogises Karikāl (the Cola) in the fertile country and says:

'You have won. He is unequal to you, he who on the battle-field on the ever-prosperous Veṇṇi, acquired a lot of glory in the world when, ashamed of a wound in the back, he positioned himself facing the North.'[50]

One notes that if the wound in the back is dishonourable, the hero recuperates glory in the world by killing himself the way he does. But it is not only glory that he regains. In fact, he turns towards the North, i.e. towards *svarga*, India's abode where heroes who die in war go, as Sanskrit tradition tells us in a number of texts such as the following ones:

Mahābhārata, Śāntiparvan 98.31: 'Ready for the supreme sacrifice of himself, every combatant who loses his life like a hero without showing his back, attains the same abode as that of Indra.'

Mahābhārata Śāntiparvan 99.45: 'Thousands of select *apsaras* rush towards the hero killed on the battlefield, exclaiming: 'May he be my husband'.

Arthaśāstra, 10.3.30 (a stanza given as a quotation from an earlier text): 'The heroes who lose their lives in fine battles instantly exceed even (the worlds where) Brahmins aspiring for heaven (*svarga*) go by virtue of a host of sacrifices, of asceticism and by filling the bowls (of religious mendicants).'

Manusmṛti VII, 89: 'The kings who desire mutual self-destruction in battle, fighting with supreme energy without turning away, go to heaven.'

Yājñavalkyasmṛti I, 324 (Stenzler ed. 323): 'Those who die in battle without losing ground and without turning away, with loyal arms, these go to heaven with the yogins.'

The Sanskrit poets while describing battles often depict the scene of the ascent to *svarga* of warriors killed in battle. Apsaras wait for them in heaven unless they go to the battlefield itself to quarrel over these warriors. Māgha amused himself immensely in describing this in his *Śiśupālavadha* (7th century):

XVIII, 58: A (warrior), who had received a terrible blow fell unconscious; doused with fresh drops of water by an elephant, he began to breathe. The celestial nymph came down desiring to take him but her hope shattered, she fell unconscious.

59. The head of another warrior flying very high above in the sky, the neck severed by an arrow, resembled the son of Siṃhikā (Rāhu) with the terrible face: it was dread that darkened the innocent, moon-like faces of the *Apsaras*.

60. One of them embracing a hero fallen over in combat, rushed rapidly towards a thicket of the Meru in order to enjoy him before his wife could reach, his wife who, all of a sudden, unable to bear being separated from him, had offered her body to the fire.

61. On seeing a dead person in battle while she (herself) was (near the battlefield) sitting on an elephant, his own wife, losing at once her life for her love and obtaining the integral, divine condition because she was virtuous, embraced him.

In the part of the *Kumārasambhava*, generally considered to have been added to the unfinished earlier work of Kālidāsa, the celestial women are all equally desirous to lay hold on the soldiers sent to heaven (XVI, 36) and there, two of these warriors who died at the same time and who found only one apsaras to receive them start fighting again (XVI, 48).

The Tamil texts of the *Sangam* quoted above which refer to the hero's committing suicide facing the North, in order to win back his tarnished honour, do not speak about divine nymphs but these women are spoken of elsewhere in the same *Sangam* literature. *Puṟanāṉūṟu* 229 is a poem sung by Kūṭalūr Kilār on the death of a king of Kerala, different from Cēral Ātaṉ and who bears the names and titles of Kōccēramāṉ Yāṉaikkaṭcēey Māntarañ Cēral Irumpoṟai. The poem describes some evil omens that have appeared in the sky, foreshadowing the death of this king and which in fact has just happened. Desolation reigns: the king's elephant remains listless, his trunk hanging limply, the king's drum has cracked and fallen, his white parasol torn, the shaft broken, his proud horse has lost its frisky gait and the text says about the dead king:

'He has attained the world of those above! Has he, therefore, in the company of numerous girls wearing brilliant bracelets, forgotten the court of his own companions?'[51]

The king in question is dead and has reached the heavenly dwelling where the divine women wait for him. However, there is nothing in the whole poem that suggests that he died in battle. His attributes, his elephant, his drum, the white umbrella and his horse could be from the war but are also used in a parade. Tamil poetry from the kind to which this text belongs loves descriptions of war. The poet could not have let this chance go by without evoking at least the heroism of the killed king to the enemy, if such had been the case. We must, therefore, believe that he set out on the premisse that the king had gone to his heavenly abode in his capacity as king and that one could attain it by a predestination of class or through a meritorious act. This is clearly confirmed by later literature, nay by another text from the same *Puṟanāṉūṟu*.

The poem no. 74 begins thus:

'A dead child although born as a mass of flesh, by those saying all the while: "It is not a person" shall not be missed by a sword.'[52]

And this implies that a child from the royal stock, even though still-born, will be pierced by a sword so as to be killed, as it were, with a weapon. Tamil tradition, in fact, desires that a warrior-prince die in this way and the king dying of illness should end his life with iron or be pierced with it if he has already died a natural death.[53]

One of the last poems of the *Sangam* period of Tamil Literature, the *Cilappadikāram*, tells us in two passages that warriors offered their head or the blood from their neck as the price of victory. James C. Harle has already used one of these passages and rightly related it with sculptures where one can see men taking swords to their neck in front of images of Durgā.[54] Some of these representations have been known for a long time and were studied by Coomaraswamy, Vogel and P. R. Srinivasan. One can find the bibliography in the article of Harle who also recapitulates the references given to *Kathāsaritsāgara* and to the *Hitopadeśa* in which there are accounts in Sanskrit of warriors who sever their head as an offering to Durgā. One of these accounts,[55] about Vīravara 'the Best among Heroes', describes him severing his son's head as an offering to the goddess, followed by his wife who also severs her head and finally he himself does the same (and in fact all three are finally resuscitated). The main interest of this tale lies in depicting a woman accomplishing the same suicide as that by a hero.

The text from *Cilappadikāram* quoted by Harle from V. R. Ramachandra's Dikshitar's translation, would lead us to believe, in this translation, that what is spoken of here is that warriors do cut their neck but, as Harle remarks, it is only to offer blood from the neck, since these warriors make this offering before leaving on an expedition and pray to the goddess to grant them victory. Actually the text does not really say anything else:

'We have served the two Feet which have the compassion to remove the pain of those who wander with the Sun, the sages and the immortals. This debt offered at Thy Feet by the energetic warriors Eyiṉar, this blood poured from their neck, accept! This is the price that brings victory.'[56]

As the images studied by Harle depict warriors, one knee on the ground and pulling back the hair with the left hand and taking with their right hand the sword to their nape, these warriors seem ready to sever their head as in the legend. But here it is merely a question of a simulation of the act by executing what would constitute its beginning, if that were really possible. Now, it is obvious that a man who could cut his throat cannot sever his neck by starting with the cervical column. He can only blood his nape. It represents here an offering of blood from the neck, as Harle so rightly remarks, an offering made in a symbolic gesture of decapitation.

But the offering of the head itself with the victory of the king in view is testified to in another passage of the *Cilappadikāram*. The scene is set at Kāviripumpaṭṭiṉam, the 'Flowery Port of Kāveri', which does exist on the Coromandel Coast at the Delta of the Kāveri (in Sanskrit Kāverī).

'76. In the region of the fragrant city, the heroes endowed with bravery,
77. And in the region of the port, the numerous men of the army,
78. Moved forward towards the oblatory altar,
79. To end their life for the king with the nature of fire,
80. They desired to offer it as an oblation, an oblation of their utmost energy,
81. Those who had slings for hurling stones,
Those who, with their shield of black skins where flesh hung still,
82. pointed their jagged spears; those who by piercing the bodies,
83. had conquered, combatting on the battlefield in the midst of the raging battle,
84. when, their black heads with rolling eyes, all red and burning,
85. excliming: 'May the king triumph and achieve victory!'
86. they placed them on the altar of beautiful offerings, to gain excellence, and so

87. when their life was offered with a resounding of thunder
88. from the drum made of raw skin,[57] the great sacrifice was accomplished!'[58]

The passage that Harle himself made use of applies to the Eyiṉars who belong to Maṟavas, and Harle concluded that the custom of offering blood from the neck to Durgā was peculiar to the Maṟavars, but the offering of the head of the victorious hero for the ultimate victory of their king does not seem to be peculiar to the Maṟavars and the iconography relating to the suicides by the heroes which we shall now study shows by its different locations, that such a custom did not belong only to a warrior class of the Tamil country but it had been equally prevalent, if not more, in Karnāṭaka and Andhra, considering the profusion there of such iconography and epigraphic texts.

In the whole of South India we find an abundance of *vīrakkal* 'stones of Heroes' as they are called in Tamil. They are also called *naṭukkal* in Tamil, 'stele' and '*vīrakallu*' in Kannaḍa.

A number of voluntary deaths, by fire or by iron, or by yet other means, are commemorated in the form of inscriptions and representations. The warriors' loyalty to the king till death in which they accompany him has gone hand in hand in Kannaḍa country with sacrifices of *satī* and one finds 'stones of *satī*' as we find 'stones of heroes'. The *satī*-stones represent the *satī* symbolically by a woman holding the right arm horizontally and raising the palm of the right hand facing out or simply by a pillar out of which an arm in that gesture is extended to its right.

The different conditions in which the cases of suicides by heroes took place during the Kadamba, Gaṅga and Vijayanagar dynasties and the examples given by the inscriptions have been frequently studied.[59] The French Institute of Indology has elsewhere collected a file of photographic documents containing a few scores of documents emanating from the Museums of Golconda and Hampi or from the regions of Karnāṭaka and Andhra, on the subject of suicides by heroes.

The *vīrakkal* represent the hero in various conditions, the principal among them being:

1. During the exploit which qualified him, walking over the enemy's body and in the midst of arrows shot at him (fig. 3), attacking an elephant (fig. 4);

2. Marching into battle (fig. 5), on foot or on horseback and carrying arms;

3. The stele which shows him walking to the battlefield or fighting may include another panel above where he is represented seated in heaven, flanked by two standing *apsaras* (fig. 6).

4. A more complete representation consists of three levels. On the bottom one he accomplishes his feat. In the example reproduced here (fig. 7), he is represented as an archer who has bewildered the stealers of cows, the recovered cattle is seen behind him, the fallen thieves are in front of him. On one upper panel, he is held by the arms and lifted up by two celestial women flying towards heaven. Above he is installed in a heavenly *maṇḍapa*, placed on a seat, with a heavenly woman standing on his either side.

5. The hero is depicted flanked by the *satī* raising his right hand (fig. 8).

6. Some pieces of sculpture show the hero cutting his nape with a dagger or a long sword held with both hands (fig. 9). This attitude echoes the classical representation where the hero is next to Durgā (fig. 1 & 2).

7. The hero severs his neck. Two *apsaras* wait for him with their fly-whisk at the top of the stele (fig. 10 & 11); heavenly palaces near which *apsaras* are flying can sometimes be represented on top of the stele and there are also two *apsaras* below, on either side of the hero (fig. 12).

8. The hero plunges his sword into his abdomen and even severs himself into two; divine women still await him in heaven (fig. 13).

9. The women sever their heads (fig. 14 & 15).

10. The sacrifice of heads at the sanctuary of Śiva is depicted at Śrīśailam (fig. 16).

Many of the images are very rough, some extremely clumsy in execution. But their clumsiness apart, the abundance of images, particularly of decapitation (18 out of 70) bear testimony to the importance that was attached to the sense of honour and the scorn for death as well as to the distinction of bravery not simply among princes but also among the general populace, especially in rural circles. This is borne out by the fact that the hero represented was often a simple cowherd.

Fig. 1—Durgā and the hero severing his neck. Puñcai (Māyuram tāluk, Tañjavur dist.) Temple of Śrīnaṟṟuṇaiyīśvarar. IFI 890-10, see pages 149and 152, 6°.

Fig. 2—Durgā and the hero severing his nape. Piḷḷaimaṅkai, Pacupatikōvil (Pāpanāsam tāluk) Temple of Brahmapurīśvarar. IFI, See pages 149 and 152, 6°.

Fig. 3—Hero-stone. Vijayanagar. Museum of Hampi. IFI 2029-2, see page 151, 1°.

Fig. 4—Hero-stone. Hanamakoṇḍa (Warangal tāluk, Andhra Pradesh) Temple of Śiva Śrī Siddheśvara. IFI, see page 151, 1°.

Fig. 5—Hero-stone. Museum of Bangalore. IFI 2061-6, see page 152, 2°.

Fig. 6—Hero-stone. Kulpak (Bhonagiri tāluk, Karṅāṭaka) IFI, see page 152, 3°.

Fig. 7—Hero-stone from Begur, Bangalore Museum. IFI 2061-5 see page 152, 4°.

Fig. 8—Hero-stone and satī. Vijayanagar, Hampi Museum. IFI 2036-1, see page 152, 5°.

Fig. 9—Hero-stone severing his nape. Kālahasti (Andhra Pradesh) Temple of Śiva Kālahastīśvarar, IFI 3233-3, see page 152, 6°.

Fig. 10 & 11—Hero-stones severing their throat. Golconda Museum. IFI, see page 152, 7°.

Fig. 12—Hero-stone. Hero severing his throat. Museum of Haiderābād. IFI, see page 159, 7°.

Fig. 13—Hero-stone. Hero severing his trunk into two. Golconda Museum. IFI, see page, 159, 8°.

Fig. 14—The hero's wife severing her head, Haiderābād Museum. IFI 3060-5, see page 152, 9°.

Fig. 15—Hero's wife severing her head. Celestial women wait for her in heaven. Haiderābād Museum. IFI 3060-1, see page 152, 9°.

Fig. 16—Offering of heads severed in front of a Śivaliṅga. Bas-relief from the compound wall of Śrīśailam (Andhra Pradesh). Photo J.F. see page 152, 10°.

Whether they are extremely varied and profuse images or texts, all the documents illustrate what was already hinted at by the testimonies of the Greeks of the time of Alexander—namely that the Indians gave themselves up to death with extraordinary ease and courage. They show, in addition, the continuity of this tendency and its propagation, along with that of Buddhism, outside India. They finally reveal its manifold motivations too.

At first sight, the main motivation had to be disdain, nay, disgust of life in the world, endlessly preached by the religions and disciplines of renunciation. It is certain that their predication and the examples they set forth have played an important part in the depreciation of life, even the human life considered to be the best since it grants the capacity of attaining the knowledge of the supreme value of detachment which leads to liberation through a release from the cycle of rebirth. But it is not certain, as a more serious study of the data shows us, that the desire for liberation through renunciation was the only factor that was responsible, nor even that it was the principal one.

We have in fact seen that the most ardent disciplines of renunciation disapprove of suicides, as not being an act of renunciation but of a strong impulse and accept the giving up of life only when it has become useless and above all naturally exhausted. The story of the Buddha reacting to the folly of the monks who, out of their great disgust for life, got themselves killed by one among them is quite typical in this regard. The moment a man comes to know and realise that his life has little significance or importance, he will have no will left to destroy it. For to have such a will would imply being 'interested', which is contrary to renunciation. One can therefore let life extinguish itself slowly, by simply abstaining from its upkeep, like the Jains, or put oneself in conditions that bring it to an end, in water, in fire, into a precipice, why even stabbing oneself with a knife—but then this last form is the most criticised, as is evident in the story of Vakkali, for then there arises immediately the suspicion that the will is 'interested'.

Finally, one can end one's life in order to pay homage to the Buddha or for the edification and good of others, but this is allowed only in total personal detachment, through an utterly disinterested will since it is directed towards others and for the doer himself is merely an act of phenomenal illusion. It is not therefore essentially renunciation that prompts one to abandon life, it enables one to do it only in specified conditions which are difficult to fulfil. It does not encourage suicide, it prohibits it. The one who is liberated through renunciation has no need to die, he remains a 'living-liberated'. And then renunciation is not an absolute renunciation. It is applicable to existence and its incidental suffering and limitation. It does not apply to the Self it strives to attain—and this is done through a superior will which is sustained and not abandoned—to attain It in all its Infinite purity and imperturbability, the purity and imperturbability of the supreme world of Brahman. Nor does renunciation apply to the will to transcend this organised world.

The capital punishment of the criminal is more a method of redemption than a punishment and that is why the criminal can sometimes gain the favour of inflicting this punishment himself, in an act of courage which redeems his death and brings it closer to that of the hero.

As for the hero, if he scorns death, it is not out of renunciation; on the contrary, it is to fulfil his secular-duty as a king, warrior or guardian. It is this secular duty that both the *Gītā* and the *Dharmaśāstras* (though with less brilliance) have placed above all other duties. Such a death is also undertaken out of devotion for a being or for something lost that the hero regains at the cost of his life. Sometimes it is to win back tarnished honour. For the warrior, finally, it is to surrender himself entirely to the Goddess in return for victory. In all these cases, it is for an entry into a heavenly life, for supreme bliss. The sage dies in order to attain the Transcendent, the hero, or the wife of the hero, to attain felicity.

A Buddhist text from the beginning of our era, presents in its own way a summary of the general ideas about the death of the sage. We mean the collection of edifying tales lost in Sanskrit except for some fragments, and which is called either *Sūtrālaṅkāra* by Aśvaghoṣa, according to its Chinese version, or *Kalpanāmaṇḍitikā dṛṣṭāntapaṅkti* by Kumāralāta, according to the Sanskrit fragments.

The tale no. 24[60] is about a village-chief who is prompted by Brahmins to burn himself alive in order to go to heaven. He prepares himself when one of his friends, a Buddhist monk, intervenes and tells him that the Brahman who had convinced him to burn himself to gain heaven will have to accompany him into the fire and gain heaven for himself as well. But the brahmin refuses to enter the fire and it becomes clear that he was trying to cheat the village-chief in order to get paid for his advice. The village-chief adandons the idea and becomes a Buddhist. The monk utters some stanzas which state that formerly *ṛṣis* who had lived for a long time ended up getting tired of living. They would then immerse themselves into meditation (*dhyāna*), liberate themselves from the world of desires and they knew that by renouncing their life they would be reborn in the world of Brahman. But it was not because they ended their life by jumping into a precipice or by throwing themselves into the fire, that they were reborn in the world of Brahman. It was only thanks to their practice of meditation and detachment from all bonds which entangle one to existence. He finally adds that the belief in the immediate effectiveness of death for gaining heaven was born from forgetting the indispensable need of meditation. One might blindly consider the manner of physical giving up of life chosen by the sage, not his wisdom, to be the prerequisite of liberation.

The Buddhist author, therefore, admits the effectiveness of the practices employed by the *ṛṣis* to attain the world of Brahman, practices which culminate in the giving up of life, but placing on top the Buddhist method of liberation, and he expresses well the most widespread idea in all Indian milieus of thought which admits the giving up of the body on condition that a spiritual detachment has been established but which denounces the idea of suicide.

NOTES

1. Strabon XV, 1, 4; 64; 65; 68; 73. Diodore de Sicile XVII, 107.
2. Strabon XV, 1, 68.
3. Strabon XV, 1, 30 and 62.
4. Text of the Société de Géographie, Paris 1824, chap. CLXXIV, p. 202. Moule-Pelliot, chap. CLXXV Translation by L. Hambis, Paris, 1955, p. 255.
5. Soc. de Géogr. chap. CLXXIX, p. 220, Hambis, p. 275.

6. William W. Hunter, *Orissa*, vol. 1, pp. 132-36, 306-08 and *The Indian Empire*, 3rd edition, London 1982, pp. 274-75.
7. P.V. Kane, *History of Dharmaśāstra*, vol. II, 2, pp. 924-29, vol. III, pp. 939, 949, vol. IV, pp. 603-14.
8. Kashmiri manuscripts of the *Mahābhārata* (Poona ed., *Mahāprasthānikap.* 2, p. 9, col. 2) add verses according to which the great departure was preceded by the worship of Īśāna-Śiva, by baths in the *tīrtha* of Prayāga and of Kedāra, and by funerary rites. The difference between the North-East and the North respectively indicated as directions of the great departure by Manu and the MBh. is due to the fact that with Manu it is in reference to the great departure of the *vānaprastha* Brahmins towards the supreme abode, whereas in the *MBh* it is in reference to the departure of *kṣatriyas* who first go towards the world of Indra which is on the Meru at the North Pole and finally attain *svarga*, the paradise of glory, not of the Absolute. In fact, on arrival, Yuddhiṣṭhira sees Govinda (Kṛṣṇa-Viṣṇu) in the Brahmic body (*govindaṃ brāhmeṇa vapuṣānvitam, Svargārohaṇa parvan*, 4.2) while his companions are integrated in the different divine classes (*Svarg.* 4, 5).
9. *Jale vāpi sthale vāpi śastreṇodbadhya vā punaḥ* /
narakaṃ te prayānty āśu ātmānaṃ ghātayanti ye // stanza quoted by Nīlakaṇṭha while commenting on *MBh.*, *Vanaparvan* 85, 83. Other texts: Kane, II, p. 924.
10. *Ādip.* 75. 57-58 (Poona ed., 70. 46; there, the last verse is put at the foot-note along with its variants).
11. *Śvomaraṇa. Mbh.*, *Śalyap.* 39. 27-34.
12. *Araṇyak.* V 38-42 (Bombay), IX, 33-37 (Gorresio).
13. *Dhruva* means 'fixed', but here what is meant is its slow actual movement in the astronomical field.
14. *Raghuvaṁśa*, VIII, 93-95.
15. Kane, II, p. 925.
16. Cf. also *Bṛhadāraṇyakop.* IV, 4, 7.
17. Cf. J. Filliozat, Self-immolation *by Fire and the Indian Buddhist tradition*, p. 108, where this text is reproduced with Nīlakaṇṭha's commentary. (Nīlakaṇṭha was a Maratha Brahmin of the 16-17th century).
18. Contrary to what I marked on p. 109 of the article cited in the preceding note. The fact remains that this case is more rarely mentioned (except when we refer to a condemned convict who is left free to kill himself (cf. p. 108 of the same article) and that the choice of fire is more common with the Buddhists and corresponds there to the metaphorical representation of saints as 'masses of fire'.
19. *Vānaprastho vīrādhvānaṃ jvalanāmbupraveśanaṃ bhṛgupatanaṃ vānutiṣṭhet.*
20. *snānācamanādidharmā brahmacāriprakaraṇādyadhihitaś cāvirodhino' syāpi bhavanti/ uttareṣāṃ caitad avirodhīti gautamasmaraṇāt / evaṃ prāguditaindavādidīkṣāmahāprasthānaparyantaṃ tanutyāgāntam anutiṣṭhan brahmaloke pūjyatāṃ prāpnoti/ yathāha manuḥ /, āsāṃ maharṣicaryāṇāṃ tyaktvānyatamayā tanum/ vītaśokabhayo vipro brahmaloke mahīyata iti //*
21. *Lokavedaviruddhasya haṭhamaraṇasyāpavādo 'yam ahiṃsāvidher iva*

paśvālambhavidhir iti prāñcaḥ || vastutas tu vārāṇasīmaraṇavad yādṛcchikamaraṇaviṣaya evāyaṃ grantho na haṭhamaraṇapratipādakaḥ ||

22. *kāmyatvāc ca nāyam ullaṅghane pratyavāyāvaha iti vācyam | ukte'rthe bādhakābhāve' pi vākyasya haṭhamaraṇaparatvam apūrvavidhyarthatvaṃ ca kalpayato gauravāpatteḥ | abhyupagame vā brāhmaṇavyatiriktaviṣaya evāyaṃ vidhiḥ | bhṛgvādipatanena maraṇam anyatra brāhmaṇād iti smṛteḥ |*
23. *K.U.*, I. 7 ... *sa brahmeti hi vijñeya ṛṣir brahmamayo mahān iti:* 'Verily, he is to be known as being Brahman, the great *ṛṣi* who is Brahman'.
24. *Bṛhad.* IV, 4, 22: ...*etam eva pravrājino lokam icchantaḥ pravrajanti.* The *pravrājin* are the wandering ascetics, the *parivrājaka*, who have renounced the worldly life and have adopted *pārivrājya* as Śaṅkara calls it while commenting on this passage.
25. *Chānd.* VIII, 4, 3-5, 4.
26. *aśva iva romāṇi vidhūya pāpaṃ candra iva rāhor mukhāt pramucya dhūtvā śarīram akṛtam kṛtātmā brahmalokam abhisambhavāmi* (*Chānd.* VIII, 13).
27. *Apratīkālambanān nayatīti Bādarāyaṇa* (Br. S. IV, 3, 15 in Śaṅkara's Text, 16 in that of Rāmānuja).
28. The continuation of the same *sūtra* is in fact *ubhayathā 'doṣāttatkratuś ca* in Śaṅkara's version who finds the two opinions discussed earlier to be faultless, and *ubhayathā ca doṣāt tatkratuś ca* in Rāmānuja's who finds fault with both.
29. *kāryātyaye tadadhyakṣeṇa sahātaḥ param abhidhānāt.*
30. *Brahmaloko sthānaviśeṣo na tu nityaṃ brahma | tatra lokaśabdasyāprayogāt| tatra turīyāśramam antareṇa muktyanaṅgīkārāc ca | na ca yogābhyāsena vā punar iti brahmopāsanavidhyanupapattyā tadbhāvāpattipariśaṅkanīyā | sālokyādiprāptyarthatvenāpi tadupapatteḥ | Mitākṣarā* on *Yājñavalkyasmṛti* III, 55.
31. *brahmasaṃstho 'mṛtatvam eti. Chānd.* II, 23, 2.
32. *parivrājakasyaiva brahmasaṃsthasya muktilakṣaṇāmṛtatvaprāptir abhihitā | yad api śrāddhakṛt satyavādī ca gṛhastho 'pi vimucyata iti gṛhasthasya mokṣapratipādanaṃ tadbhāvāntarānubhūtapārivrajyasyety avagantavyam|| Mit.* III, 55.
33. Actually only the Brahmins can go through the three stages and in addition be *sannyāsins*, the *kṣatriyas* go through only the three stages, the *vaiśyas* through two: *brahmacarya* and *gārhasthya*, the *śūdras* can only be householders. Cf. Kane, II, 923-24. This is according to the *dharmaśāstras* though not always in practice.
34. *brahmaiva loko brahmaloka uktaḥ.* Śaṅkara on the *Chānd.* VIII, 4, 1—*brahmaiva loko brahmaloka iti.* Rāmānuja on the *Br. S.* IV, 3, 11.
35. Cf. *Répertoire d'épigraphie jaina*, Publ. of the E.F.E.O., vol. X, Paris 1908, No. 117, 119, 140, 163, 183, 289, 298, 420, 427, Cf. especially S.R. Sharma, *Jainism and Karṇāṭaka Culture*, Dharwar, 1940, pp. 192-94 and the references in the index.
36. *Une secte religieuse dans l'Inde contemporaine* in *Etudes*, March 1951, pp. 343-51.
37. Notably mount Kalbappu, alias Candragiri or Kaṭavapra at Śravaṇabeḷa-

goḷa in Karnāṭaka. See specially Guérinot, *Répertoire....* no. 805, 820, 830 and Sharma, *Jainism....* p. 6.

38. *Vinaya* III, 68.
39. Cf. J. Filliozat, *Self-immolation by Fire......*p. 104 and foll.
40. Cf. *ibid.* and for Buddhist China J. Gernet, *Les suicides par le feu chez les bouddhistes chinois du V au X siècle*, in *Mélanges publiés par l'Institut des Hautes Etudes Chinoises*, t. II, Paris, 1960, pp. 527-58.
41. All these are acts of devotion which, independently of all expiation of crimes, grant heaven to those who accomplish them. (*Viṣṇudharmaśāstra*, quoted by Kane III, 949).
42. Jules Bloch, *Les inscriptions d'Asoka*, Paris, 1950, p. 165.
43. *Nirmalāḥ svargaṃ yanti santaḥ sukṛtino yathā* // Manu, VIII, 318.
44. *paṇpuṟa varūum pakuti nōkkip*
puṇkilittu muṭiyu maṟattu... Tol. Poruḷ. 79, 3-4.
45. *...nītta kaṇavaṟ ṟirtta vēliṟ*
pēetta maṉaivi kāñci ...Tol. Poruḷ. 79, 12-13.
46. Cf. R. Vasudeva Sharma, *Tolkāppiyam*, Trichinopoly, 1934, p. 171. Vasudeva Sarma does not adopt this view himself (contrary to S. Ilakkuvanar, *Tholkāppiyam*, Madurai 1963. p. 170) and thinks that she is lamenting. But *pēetta* means '*talk in an incoherent way*', and therefore '*ranting*'. There exists a variant of *pēetta, peyartta* 'pulling out' (*Puliyūrk Kēcikan ed*, Madras, 2nd ed., 1964, p. 284, 1.8).
47. *Karikāl valavaṉoṭu veṇṇi paṟantalai*
porutu puṇṇāṇiya cēralātaṉ
aḻikaḷa maruṅkiṉ vāḷvaṭakkirunteṉa
48. In spite of P.T. Srinivas Iyengar's doubt in *History of the Tamils*, Madras, 1929, p. 337.
49. *taṉ pōl vēntaṉ muṉpukuṟit teṟinta*
puṟappuṇṇāṇi maṟattakai maṉṉaṉ
vāḷvaṭakkiruntaṉaṉ...
50. *Veṉṟōy niṉṉiṉu nalla ṉaṉṟē*
kalikoḷ yāṇar veṇṇi paṟantalai
mikappukaḻ ulakam eytip
puṟappaṇ ṇāṇi vaṭakkiruntōṉē.
51. *Mēlōr ulakam eytiṉaṉ ākiliṉ*
oṇ toṭi makaḷirkkuṟu tuṇai y ākit
taṉṟunai y āyam maṟantaṉaṉ kollō. Pur. 229, 22-24.
52. *kuḻaviy iṟappiṉum ūṉṟaṭi piṟappiṉum*
āḷ aṉṟ eṉṟu vāḷiṟ ṟappār. 74, 1-2.
53. *Puṟanāṉūṟu* 93, 4-11, *Maṇimēkalai* 23, 11-16. Cf. P.T. Srinivas Iyengar, *History of Tamils*, p. 413 and 480; R. Vasudeva Sarma, *Tolkappiam*, p. 168.
54. *Durgā, Goddess of Victory* in *Artibus Asiae*, XXVI, 3/4, 1963 pp. 237-46.
55. *Hitopadeśa* III, 9.
56. *cuṭaroṭu tiritaru(m) muṉivarum amararum*
iṭar keṭa v arulu(m) niṉ iṇai y aṭi toḻutēm
aṭal vali y eyiṉar niṉ aṭi totu kaṭaṉ itu

miṭaṟ uku kuṛuti koḷ viṟal taru vilaiyē. Cilap. XII, V. Cāminātaiyar ed., Madras, 1892, p. 296.
The French translation, very beautiful though quite free, by A. Daniélou and R.S. Desikan, *Le Roman de l'annean*, Connaissance de l'Orient, coll. UNESCO, Paris, 1961, improves further (p. 105) upon the already very free translation of V. R. Dikshitar by expressing thus: 'Accept now the blood that flows in torrents from our severed heads.'

57. Literally 'of a skin with hairy pores' (where one can still see hairy pores).
58. 76. *muruvūr maruṅkiṉ maṟaṅkoḷ vīrarum*
 77. *paṭṭiṉamaruṅkiṟ paṭaikeḻu mākkaḷu*(*m*)
 78. *muntac ceṉṟu muḻuppali pīṭikai*
 79. *ventiṟaṉ maṉṉar kuṟṟatai y oḻikkeṉap*
 80. *palikkoṭai purintōr valikku varam pākeṉak*
 81. *kallumiḻ kavaṇiṉar kaḻippiṇik kaṟaittōṟ*
 82. *palvēṟ parappiṉar meyyuṟat tīṇṭi*
 83. *yārttu k kaḷaṅkoṇṭōr āramar aḻuvattu*
 84. *cūrttu k kaṭai civanta cuṭu nōkku k karuntalai*
 85. *veṟṟi vēntaṉ koṟṟaṅ koḷḷeṉa*
 86. *naṟpali pīṭikai n^{a}laṅ kola vaittāṅ*
 87. *kuyir p pali y uṇṇum urumu k kuraṉ muḻakkattu*
 88. *mayirkkaṇ muracoṭu vāṉpali y ūtti*... *Cilap*. V, 76-88.
59. B. Lewis Rice, *Mysore and Coorg from the Inscriptions*, London, 1909, pp. 185-88.—R.S. Mugali, *The Heritage of Karnāṭaka*, Bangalore, 1946, pp. 71-80.
60. E. Huber, *Sūtrālaṃkāra*, Paris 1908, pp. 126-31. Cf. also tale 77, pp. 437-41. The same text expresses equally well the classical conception of Brahmanism about the effect of askesis, of *tapas*, which was practiced in order to obtain all kinds of powers and felicities and was a temporary renunciation, motivated by lust, in relation to the normal life and was opposed to any kind of spiritual renunciation. From the Buddhist point of view, it condemns asceticism as a suicide, see. tales 5-8, pp. 35-53.

CHAPTER 11

TRADITIONAL RELIGIONS AND MODERN CULTURES*

WHEN RELIGIOUS TRADITIONS deal with the organisation of nature and lay upon man certain specific duties of conduct they can come into conflict, on the one hand, with the new developed cosmologies thanks to the advance in the knowledge of Nature, and on the other with the needs for new activities in societies.

It is not for the first time that such a situation has been created, as it is nowadays by the accelerated thrust of the current scientific discoveries and technical achievements and the changes in societies brought about by industrial and economic development.

It is quite a common situation in history.

As an example of conflicts between traditional religions and scientific advances, it is enough to recall the trial of Galileo and the disputes over transformism. As for the conflicts between religious rules that traditionally govern society and the evolutionary tendencies of the same society, they are particularly evident in the domain of sexuality but are not of recent origin: birth-control, the celibacy of priests, divorce, etc. At every change, whether it is religious or not, and it is far from being always religious, the normal established order offers some sort of a resistance.

The conflicts which ensue can, at that time, get impassioned and violent, but it must be observed that they are eventually resolved and often for the common benefit of the antagonists. Science is the victor if one of its findings is finally accepted and religion rids itself of a superstition which does not seem to actually belong to its core. There are a good many sacred texts which, while alluding to the organisation of nature, assert things

*Religions traditionnelles et cultures modernes (Rapports et perspective d'études), in *Numen*, vol. XIV, fasc. 2, July 1967, pp. 87-103. Reproduced in *Proceedings of the XIth International Congress for the History of Religions*, t. I, Leiden, 1969, pp. 39-54.

about it that are literally incompatible with the series of scientific findings of more recent times. Certain believers seem forced to admit that human science, which is universally accepted to be still imperfect, is mistaken and that, for example, the Bible or the Purāṇas were right. In order to consolidate their own convictions, they underline the assertions made by these texts which themselves agree with the scientific findings. Others maintain that the language of the sacred texts is not to be taken literally, in its outward meaning, but needs to be symbolically interpreted. And they proceed to offer with much difficulty an interpretation of these texts in a manner that is compatible with scientific thought. They can, above all, maintain without great effort that the divine utterance as found in the texts, and revealed for the use of men, was adapted to their capacity of understanding at the time of the revelation, that is to say, to their knowledge of Nature, imperfect as it might have been then. Religious truth which is of a theological and metaphysical nature, may have been revealed exactly as it was worded but the affirmations relating to Nature would have conformed, not to a Reality of a physical level without any religious bearing, but to the prevalent provisional opinion of that time. Faith, in its supernatural realm, is beyond the reach of any contradiction directed against it in the domain of nature and reciprocally, it can withstand any change and any advance in the knowledge of this domain of nature. Metaphysics, on its part, can always dismiss as one-sided and even blind, the denial of its legitimacy by exclusivist 'scientists' for they do not realise that by opposing all metaphysics on principle, they are making a choice which itself is metaphysical.

In any case, the conflicts between supernatural faith and the knowledge of nature, are superficial conflicts. They occur only when the opponents are in a state of confusion about their respective domains. It is so, at least, when many scientists feel a clear demarcation between their religion and their science and without feeling any internal contradiction in their mind, they maintain simultaneously a basic traditional faith and an unquestioning conviction in the validity of modern science and its technical applications. And that is why, in fact, the universal spread of science undermines the traditional opinions associated with religious traditions but not the religions themselves, or it undermines these only to the extent that their adherents are confused between the basic religious principles and the secondary cosmological views that they are unable to separate because both are received from tradition.

In Asian countries, and notably in India, which possess great general religious cultural traditions, it is not surprising then to find simultaneously and among the same people a deep attachment to traditional religions and a strong assimilation of modern culture, particularly the scientific one.

The variety in personal attitudes in a country as vast and as diversely populated as India is bound to be great. Between those who remain attached exclusively to their opinions and to their ancestral customs and those who completely reject them, we find the bulk of people who represent all the degrees of transition between the ancient and the modern tendencies.

There is still a widespread belief in the West, at least outside the circle of Indologists, that India is changeless. Since it venerates scriptures that are very ancient and whose antiquity in fact it readily exaggerates, one is easily led to believe that it has never changed and that it should remain opposed to all innovation in the name of religion and that it cannot evolve without first discarding its religious traditions. But, however, when one sees its present activities of modernisation one imagines it to be either merely superficial, more artificial and formal than deeply rooted and sustained by a deep-felt need of people or that it is a phenomenon noticeable only among classes free from religious constraints. One of the foremost of these constraints is the famous caste system, legally abolished by the constitution but which in reality continues to strongly persist in society. The political thinkers who are of a colonial or communist bent of mind generally also agree in considering that Hinduism is an obstacle to the social and economic evolution of India. The former are of the opinion that it ought to have abandoned its culture and should have become anglicised as Macaulay and William Bentinck had dreamt of in 1835. For the others, salvation lies only in Marxism.

But the real situation isn't what it is ordinarily made out to be. In the ordinary scheme of things, there are indeed quite a few true elements but all the facts do not conform to the interpretation. Confusion reigns in the minds, even among many Indians as well as foreign observers, between what is born from religion, strictly speaking, and that which is based only on concomitant and secondary beliefs and customs.

In order to appreciate better the real state of things and feelings, one must therefore deepen one's enquiry.

The numerous works published in English, specially in India and by Indian philosophers and religious men, works which strive to define and to explain the fundamental traits of Hinduism as the major religion of India, can be of great utility for this study. However, too often they have the disadvantage of being conceived for giving an idea of Hinduism that while remaining genuine is aimed at drawing the Westerner's appreciation of it. They emphasise the points of concordance between the facts set out by ancient Hindu scriptures and the religious, philosophical or moral ideas of the West, and tend to disregard the others. They present the Hindu concepts not so much to delineate the specific cultural frame-work but more to win the foreigner's understanding. At its extreme, we get authors who naively wish to discover in their ancient traditional texts the findings of modern science already foretold, but who decipher in the latter those facts alone which correspond to their own times and with which they are familiar and not the conclusive truths their tradition is thought by them to actually contain. These writings are futile; they only serve to prove the existence and activity of a milieu which, far from repudiating modern cultures, claims to incorporate them, without, however, making use of them, except to reassert the greatness of their heritage.

The scientific results of classical Indology, however, fundamental they may be, are not yet suitable in themselves to serve as the starting points for the study of the problem of contact between the traditional religions of India and the modern cultures that it is adopting today.

While the frequent and extended contacts between the interested European observers and India in the 17th century had, in fact, encouraged the former to describe the religions of the country as they saw them being practised around them, the organisation of the science of Indology has tended, since the end of the 18th century, to concentrate on the investigation of ancient texts and the original forms of religions.

This was but natural and necessary. It was not only the interest in exploring the origins of the first stages of a civilisation that led to the study of the remotest past but also and specially a study of the sacred books, declared by the Indian scholars themselves to be the revered sources of their beliefs, assumed primary importance. To understand Christianity one studies the Bible and the Gospels before studying the churches and the later sects. This does not mean that Indologists have totally neglected modern Indian religions. The remarkable work of Horace Hayman Wilson *Sketch of the Religious Sects of the Hindus*, which came out first in 1828 and 1832 in *Asiatic Researches*, bears testimony to the interest he took in it. But the *Ṛgveda* and the *Viṣṇupurāṇa* were also translated by him. It was indispensable to start at the very sources before following the tributaries. But Wilson's work on the sects wasn't taken up until much later and it is only today that monographs of some of them have begun to appear. Besides, the study of these sects concerns only certain local, specific groups, often numerous, and, had the study included all present-day sects as well, it would still not have given a complete picture of general Hinduism today. This Hinduism, even today, is best depicted in its main current, by texts that are common to a large number of varied groups: the *Bhagvadgītā* or the *Manusmṛti*, for instance. But, however great their authority might be, such texts cannot reveal by themselves the present psychology of those who venerate them, any more than the Bible reveals the psychology of its present-day followers.

The comparison of ancient sources of religious traditions with modern cultures is anachronistic and unjustified. One comparison which is most important comprises, on the one hand, the total present culture of the possessors of religious tradition,—and not merely the religious aspect of their culture—, and on the other, modern culture as those very possessors of traditions see it, not as the research-scholars do. In fact, any contact of traditional religions with modern cultures can really consist only in an inner link of the subject between his own representations of religion and modern culture. It is, therefore, the specific psychology that pertains to the human group being studied that has to be known in all its aspects and not merely the ancient or modern sources from which it can draw.

It is, therefore, indispensable to make the most thorough sociological enquiry. But sociology is not yet ready to fully exploit the domain it seeks to explore. It endeavours to do this forcefully and courageously with results, but it is pulled between two equally legitimate tendencies which, at the present stage of the research, are unfortunately still difficult to reconcile into common results.

On the one hand, descriptive sociology, akin to ethnography as a science of observation, should make its researches more specialised. This would lead to an increase of branches of sociology according to the kind of facts they want to investigate: economic, political, juristic, religious, urban, rural or industrial ...to name only a few and which are among the more specialised ones. But each society is a whole whose components are, by nature, linked and interdependent, and such societies are innumerable about which our knowledge is rather unequal. It would be vain to generalise the conclusions obtained from some specific aspect, artificially separated because of the requirements of the study, when the study may have touched only a limited number of societies. It does not follow that such systematic enquiries in question are futile. On the contrary, these researches collect indispensable basic material and we need to increase such studies in order to probe constantly deeper. Besides, the disadvantage of specialised research on artificially dissociated aspects is negligible when a sociologist works on his own society with which he is familiar in its totality since he is part of it. When he turns his attention to a category of social facts for a specific enquiry, the global environment remains present for him and he can correctly interpret these facts in relation to the unified milieu of which they are a part. It is a totally different story when he works on a society that is foreign to him not only on grounds of nationality, but more and particularly so because of a different education and upbringing. He may belong to the country where his research is being conducted but if he is a stranger to the particular milieu he is studying, even though he might be on vantage ground because he knows the local language and can communicate with the people capable of providing information, he will find it hard to reset the results of his specialised enquiry within the whole context from which they derive their real value. This is often the case in a country like India where different milieus are often like islands that remain inaccessible to direct entry from outside.

On the other hand, there has naturally been an effort at a global sociological approach for a long time. Sociology is quite aware that as long as it possesses only incomplete facts about most societies, its findings are only provisional. Physics and biology are in a more advanced stage because they have been making an inventory of matter, of species, of phenomena in nature from a long time, but an inventory of facts about man has remained incomplete almost up to the present day, because the classical values in the study of man have predominated. The national, literary, religious cultures, whether in Europe, in India or in China, have justly sought to deepen and to enrich themselves but in this effort, they have always ignored or disdained the others. The minds of one nation have been fixed to its ideal of man, without orienting themselves towards finding an objective knowledge of all men in all their activities, brilliant and obscure.

In the middle of the 18th century, Joseph Deguignes, the Sinologist historian of the Huns and the Tartars, helped in firmly establishing the important role of all the peoples of the world in order to have a general knowledge of man but it wasn't universally recognised and one had to wait for a long time still for sociology to prove the significance and necessity of such a knowledge. When it finally did so, it first sought to discover in the most primitive human groups the first forms of all human activity in society, to distinguish the principles of social structures which tended to disappear in the profusion of forms at the heart of the great civilisations. But the so-called 'primitives' are not simple and it is often more difficult to understand them than the civilised who, to a great extent, can make themselves understood. The findings or the hypothetical interpretation of the facts culled from these 'primitives' are not necessarily applicable to others, they do not provide any definite general laws of structures of the life and thought of societies. It is only at the cost of haphazard reasonings based on analogies that we can make use of them to understand the nature and the visualised pattern of facts that are discovered about new groups being studied, especially at different levels.

When we deal particularly with traditional religious data, typological and phenomenological similarities may seem to indicate a mistaken identity of nature between the observed facts in different kinds of civilisations or areas but without ascribing a similarity of motive, for the religious forms that can be observed from outside are far less varied than all the possible inner motives. We require positive testimonies on traditions to interpret these in a valid way and they outstrip all theoretical linking with independently conceived elementary laws.

We are finally, therefore, led to acknowledge the insufficiency of data available to us at present to understand the relationships between traditional religions and modern cultures and what happens when they clash.

But there is a capacity of self-adaptation and self-completion in the science of religions. It can fill in the gaps that we stumble upon while considering the question of the encounter in question. If the ongoing study of the major sources of traditions is inadequate to reveal the state of these traditions in the present minds where the intermingling with modern culture occurs, one needs to study what they precisely mean to these minds. One mustn't proceed only by retracing the origins of these traditions. One should come down to the present by following the course of their life till the present day. It isn't sufficient either to undertake a research solely on their present condition which is only a culmination. A tradition, by nature, is a continuous movement, and a movement cannot be studied only at its point of culmination.

A complete study of religious traditions rests then on three elements: the substance itself of these traditions from their source, their evolutionary stages historically attested, and their final status in the opinion of their adherents.

Only those historical civilisations which possess a well-preserved written literature can provide the stuff for such a study. As for the others, only an ethnographical investigation is possible and has a bearing only on the final stage of an evolution which itself remains inexplorable. It can retrace the past only with the help of occasional historical evidence arising from civilisations with fixed traditions. It is true that it can use oral traditions but then these offer only a semblance of an authentic continuity. In fact, a lot of personal fabrications of an uncertain date gets mixed up because certain people claimed to be inspired and thus acquire some sort of an authority. Modern psychological observation abounds in examples of thinkers who, depending on their religious beliefs, either consider themselves inspired or not and who construct, in good faith,—often in the good faith of paranoids—very coherent systems that they either present as being altogether independent or they link up with some secret tradition of which they claim to have the key.

Written traditions are not immune from such interference but it is impossible to make such intrusions through interpolations in all the copies of sacred books that were accepted in the past. They can only create new works or commentaries which, in case of successful acceptance become instruments of change and evolution of the traditional current, but then they are rooted to the place of their historic emergence. They become milestones in traditional evolution without disturbing the whole content of the tradition by mixing up all the various strata.

We cannot rely on oral tradition for yet another reason. In case some details have been forgotten, the informing subject can insert the forgotten part by means of a reconstructive hypothesis thought of in the very course of his explanation. One at once becomes aware of the frequency of such an accident while listening to a narrator recounting a written legend, of which he has forgotten a part. He invents the missing elements which he omitted through conjecture and on going back to the text which he claimed to sum up, one notices that he didn't hit on the right element. It is impossible to verify informations gathered from a purely oral tradition.

The best case for conducting a meaningful research is, therefore, the one where there exists behind the present forms of traditions within a homogeneous human group, a continuity of written traditions and of historical testimonies which inform us about what preceded the contemporary stage.

We frequently experience this in Asia, at least in the great and ancient civilisations that have survived. As far as India is concerned, one needs to separate, as in fact they are in society, the groups that emerged from the major Pan-Indian culture and those that exist outside its ken, locally scattered. The major Pan-Indian culture has certainly absorbed in the course of the ages a number of local groups which were primitively isolated. But those that still remain isolated today are not so much the surviving witnesses of those that were assimilated but rather opponents of such assimilation. We cannot, therefore, expect from them a valid representation of those who, by behaving contrarily to them, joined the mainstream culture.

They are not to be neglected for this and as a matter of fact greatly merit the ethnographical and linguistic studies that have been undertaken on them and which are most urgent. But these studies themselves should take into account the quite imperceptible influences exerted by the highly civilised neighbouring societies which allegedly have always kept the external groups at a distance, even while they appeared hostile to all interaction. However, in the case of the Santals, for example, whom Bodding studied so well, it was easy to show that while Bodding thought to discover among them unique, 'primitive' ideas on disease and illness, in fact, many of these ideas had been recently borrowed from classical *Āyurveda* and Bengali magic. If they were looked down upon and kept apart by the Bengali community, some of its members being at logger-heads with it were able to approach them, and it is clear that they passed on to them some of their ideas. Besides, since Sir Alfred Lyall's studies in the 19th century on the spread of Hinduism and the movement of Brahminisation within the aboriginal tribes, we have always been led to accept that in spite of the orthodox rules of the segregation of social classes, Hinduism was not as closed to the outside world as it might have appeared from the *Dharmaśāstra*. The adoption of Hinduism in ancient times by many South-East Asian countries, mainly in Campa, Cambodia and Indonesia, clearly shows that it hasn't shied away from communicating itself abroad where it often encountered peoples who were less hostile to assimilating it than many of the groups in the Indian territory itself. And, therefore, one seeks to discover even in the most orthodox Brahmanic traditions some probable traces of an aboriginal sub-stratum that it must have overlain.

It is already clear from these observations that traditions in

India and South-East Asia, especially religious traditions, even when fixed in strict orthodoxy—as we have often observed them to be—were in the past permeable to the influence of foreign cultures and mutual borrowings. These contacts resulted in as much of assimilation as of shocks and recoils, depending on circumstances. A historic study of these contacts, as far as possible, should enable us to reset the question of the present encounter of religious traditions and modern cultures in the course of the long chain of similar events. Only thus can we hope to arrive at some general observations. And that is why, hand in hand with the extension and deepening of the studies on the present state of human thinking, we should also endeavour to complete our knowledge of traditions of all times.

Uptill now, Indology has mainly studied the basic ancient sources of religious and social traditions. One of its most urgent tasks today is to update itself by providing the data to fill the gap that remains between the ancient past and the present. It should thus be able to determine what really lives on in the content of the ever-revered sources and what the recent times have brought in addition. It should, therefore, find out about the nature of evolution and the profound reasons for the observable human responses and the perspectives that are opening out in the present stage of that evolution.

More precisely, it should collect and survey the traditional literature of beliefs, cults and religious techniques on which faith and current practices actually rest. This literature consists of texts that are used by believers and of liturgical books used by officiating priests.

The texts used by believers are different, depending on the facet of Hinduism, the region and the language. They vary also with social class and the educational level.

Sanskrit texts, whether ancient or modern, belong more specifically, but not exclusively, to the Brahmin class, in any case, to the educated class. Only a section of this class takes up a profound study of the philosophical works. Traditional Brahmin education consists in, along with a great training of the memory which is developed from a young age, the study of grammar, of logic and of literature. Except for logic which is part of the basic learning, philosophy is an optional subject, varying according to school. The complete traditional studies, followed particularly by orthodox Brahmins and non-Brahmins who wish to be like them, are long and engrossing. They are, nevertheless, compatible with a solid study of English through which the students are put in touch with modern cultures. The most common attribute of the Brahmin class is its intellectual vocation. Traditional family-custom, therefore, impels a person to acquire all sorts of knowledge, which increases in these minds the possibility of conscious interaction between religious traditions and modern cultures.

It is, then, an activity that is most often divided into the traditional and the modern, traditional for all that is concerned with metaphysical beliefs and certain religious practices, and modern, for all that is concerned with the science of the physical and biological world as well as the practice of a profession. The lack of inevitable incompatibility between religious tradition and modern culture is, therefore, present in India, in conditions which seem quite similar to those prevalent in the West. This absence of incompatibility manifests particularly among those who are educated best in the two cultures at the same time. But, as in the West, it is again in the educated class that we often meet the most zealous supporters of one or the other culture, when exclusivism arises, in general accompanied with a political choice, and at times repudiates the national culture as being outdated, or at others, the modern one for being an inadequate innovator to the needs and sentiments of the nation. The proportion of exclusivists, particularly the anti-religious exclusivists seems less in India than in the West, either because the religious beliefs and practices, by themselves, hold for the former a greater attraction, or because they have been reinforced for a long time in a movement of self-defense against cultures of foreign origin introduced into the country under a foreign rule. What is certain is that the educated Indian class has always sought to demonstrate that it contained within its own folds what the foreign modern culture was bringing in. The same phenomenon took place under the moghuls when the national traditions got crystallised in order to face up to the Islamic intrusion and when the highly qualified Hindus, like Toḍarmal, strove, even while serving the Moghuls, to reinforce Hindu tradition. Toḍarmal, who served Akbar, in fact, had a whole encyclopaedia of Hindu wisdom compiled.

The most frequently published books on religion and put on sale show what readers prefer. Besides, the *Bhagavadgītā* and the *Bhāgavatpurāṇa*, there are mainly devotional hymns, particularly those that are recited during the rites of worship. Many Sanskrit texts are published today with a passage by passage translation in different modern languages.

The *Sthalapurāṇa* or *Māhātmya* published from sanctuaries and pilgrimage-centers narrate and glorify the legends connected with the sacred place. These works, neglected uptill now, as mere later works of propaganda, are in fact very important because they tell us about the subject matter that sustains the present religion.

A large number of these texts are in modern or in ancient languages, other than Sanskrit, particularly in Tamil, Kannaḍa and Telugu in the South, where literatures rivalling Sanskrit literature had flourished from ancient time or during the medieval period, depending on the language. When it is a question of ancient texts or of scholarly poetic art, they are made available to the public in certain versions or in regular translations in the current form of the language.

Those who undergo a primary education or only an English education, even if it is higher studies, cannot understand Sanskrit texts and are not always capable of understanding ancient texts in their mother-tongue. Nevertheless, they are familiar with at least some excerpts or know a few quotations and proverbs that typically reflect their traditional environment. As for the illiterate, they are not always uncultured. In a country where education has always been traditionally mainly oral right up to its highest levels, where memory, developed from a young age takes the place of a library, where the pandit is 'the one who has heard a lot', one can, without knowing to read and write, be well-versed in legends, in stories and in the vast ethical literature. One is familiar, in any case, with popular songs and those which accompany rhythmic work. Now, a number of these songs have a strong religious colouring. The uneducated mass of Indians is, therefore, not a soul-less body. Psychologically, it is conditioned by traditional education which the Westernised kind of statistician does not take into account when he simply records the ratio of attendance in the official schools.

For this mass of people, the contact with modern culture is purely material, it experiences its effects, it benefits from it, uses it in its applications. It does not possess it intellectually in the same way as it possesses religious traditions. Therefore, in its mind, the two do not come into conflict, neither do they get any occasion to. It does not offer any specific resistance to modern culture, as one often presumes, out of fanaticism or inertia. It utilises its creations when it needs them and when it is capable of procuring them for itself—which explains, for example, the immense success of cinema—but otherwise it scarcely bothers about it.

This state of things easily leads the outside superficial observer to believe that the bulk of Indians is indifferent and passively follows an unchanging tradition which stands in the way of all progress. Among them, there are those who are perplexed, who cannot conceive of progress except in the forms they are used to themselves and who truly despair of those who live differently from them. Then there are those who get irritated, as they wish for the population a development that would bring them consumers of their own technical production. But both panic without reason even while they remain discontented. The Indian religious tradition isn't generally opposed to change, specially to material change with which it isn't concerned. But, precisely because the material changes don't concern it, this tradition doesn't have to obliterate itself to make way for them, and they bring nothing to the psychological level which could be compared to what the tradition possesses and which is rich and living. Many Indians think that their national culture is spiritual and that modern culture, exclusively materialist, but they accept the achievements of technology that are not thought to be prejudicial to spirituality. Religious tradition doesn't prevent India from accepting modern culture but in most milieus India is familiar with it only in its technical achievements which aren't always very useful to her.

The works of liturgy, of prayers and in general of all that deals with doctrines and religious practices used by the priests, form quite a large body of literature: the *Āgamas*. This word, strictly speaking, means 'tradition' and, in this general sense, it has been used in Sanskrit by Buddhists as well as by Hindus. In Bali, religion profoundly inspired by India, is even called by this name. The Sanskrit inscriptions of Cambodia also use it but to specifically designate Indian texts, that specifically include it in their titles, like the *Pārameśvarāgama* mentioned in a 10th century inscription.

It is in the different kinds of literatures connected with the cult of Śiva that the word *Āgama* is most often used to designate these treatises on religion. But they are also known as *Tantra* and similar works among the Buddhists also bear this last designation, applicable to the whole class of these writings. Among the Vaiṣṇavas, they are known as *saṃhitā* and similar writings are also found among the Jains.

To whichever religious trend they may belong, these doctrinal and practice-manuals, when complete, deal with four subjects which are complementary and equally necessary: science or knowledge (*vidyā* or *jñāna*), ritual (*kriyā*), conduct (*caryā*) and psychosomatic training (*yoga*).

The *Āgamas* as a whole are opposed to the *Nigamas* which designate the *Vedas*. It is readily believed that they issue from a current that is different from the religious Vedic one, a current which dates back to the pre-history of the pre-Aryan substratum, for a long time covered up by Aryan Vedism and which may have re-surfaced. This theory is a hypothesis and not the fruit of any findings. It would imply that nothing new can ever be created in the course of time in the religions of India and that all that they profess comes from outside, as would be the case for the Vedic contribution of the Aryan invaders, or that it comes from the native pre-historical past. And this is hardly plausible. A scrutiny of the totality of Indian literature including the ancient Tamil literature, leads us rather to believe that the development of scientific ideas and the theories of representation of the order of the world, of body-functions and of the human mind have given place to innovations in religious thought and conduct. The techniques of yoga appear only as a result of the experimental applications of psycho-physiological theories. The disciplines of conduct similarly correspond to the scientific concepts on the modes of the conditioning of psychism.

The relative positions of the *Vedas* and the *Āgamas* conform to the definitions of the *Āgamas* themselves: the *Vedas* teach the rites which lead to the enjoyment of the world (*bhukti*), the *Āgamas* fulfil the same role, but in addition they open up the path of liberation from this world (*mukti*), which can only be conceived in the belief in a reality that transcends the world.

However, in South India, where Hinduism has remained more sheltered from the Islamic influence than in the North, it is the texts of the Śaiva *Āgamas* and the Vaiṣṇava *saṃhitās* which always dictate the religious practice. The doctrines and devotions are perpetuated and glorified by devotional Tamil literature, by the legends of holy places, by the representation of gods and sacred stories in the temples as well as by philosophical writings. In Śaiva circles specially, there predominate in this field works said to be of the *Śaivasiddhānta* whose doctrines have been attested to at least since the 7th century and are still in vogue.

Here lie the real and direct sources of the religious mentality of today. Their study, therefore, allows us to know how this mentality was formed and to understand what they mean today. It is aimed at filling the gaps of knowledge that still remain between the venerated but dead past and the life of today.

Such a study cannot be conducted by individual researchers. Nobody can simultaneously collect and publish the unpublished texts, study the current edited texts in several languages as well as in different but connected fields, compile the legends, compare them to their depiction in art, and undertake researches in temples and at the numerous levels of society. But this task becomes possible through a coordination of efforts on the part of researchers and here within India. It was with the aim of contributing to this task, as far as its means allowed, that a French Institute of Indology was founded in Pondicherry ten years ago. It cannot promise a solution to the problem of the meeting of religious traditions and modern culture but its initial efforts may have been able to define the data and to focus attention on a great void of information about the truly active religious traditions really comparable to modern cultures either in opposition or in reconciliation with them.

In any case, a more definite study of the conditions in which religious traditions get established and evolve should lead to discern better in these traditions that which truly springs from religion and that which is merely fixed on to it by an insufficiently formed opinion.

To take an example, we can consider what is called the 'caste system'. It is noteworthy that the present divisions correspond only incompletely—and in certain regions not at all—to the definitions of the *Dharmaśāstra* and in particular that of Manu which is more well-known. However, as the *Dharmaśāstras* encompass religious norm as well as civil law, and as the division of society into four major classes goes back to the *Ṛgveda*, we normally suppose that the divisions into numerous castes within the four main classes have a religious basis and that the customs and the prohibitions recognised by the member of each caste are rules imposed by religion. Many Hindus think that too. Therefore, we hold religion responsible for the compartmentalisation of Indian society.

If, however, we do not limit ourselves to the study of the *Ṛgveda* or of Manu, if we examine to what extent the official texts of the *Dharmaśāstras* are actually followed, it becomes difficult to uphold this theory in its present form.

We observe at first that the 'system' is theoretical and ideal, that it is described in the books but that the facts of division although real, do not correspond to any system, considering that they are infinitely variable according to the local opinion across India and even according to the opinions of different groups within the same locality. Outside the large class of Brahmins, the other classes are not represented or are only presumed to be represented by the rest of the population, especially in the Tamil country where the divisions don't correspond to those of Manu and where the major classes of Kṣatriyas and Vaiśyas are represented only by the groups that claim to be part of these classes and who are accepted by others only on the ground of tolerance.

The real divisions seem mostly based on the necessity of safeguarding professions in a country where there is bitter competition for jobs and over sentiments of honour, even group-pride, which are very strong even among the most humble, who, as a matter of fact, often do not have any other possession to claim or defend. It's the social psychology which explains the acceptance of castes, not a religious rule which does not even list them as they are known.

The current religions, particularly the Śaivasiddhānta of the Tamil country, the doctrine of the Vīraśaivas of Mysore as well and others still which are prevalent in certain regions, have moreover, for centuries, opened up the path of religious salvation to all followers, whatever social class they may belong to.

Rāmānuja, the Vaiṣṇava Brahmin, was already using *Tirukul-attar* to designate the 'untouchables', 'those of the family of fortune', foreshadowing with this name the one used today 'Harijan' or 'people of God'.

But religion did not claim to decree equality in society from which it exhorted man to liberate himself and which it could not govern and could neither prevent, in this domain which wasn't its own, the conservative elements from taking religious tradition as a pretext for the maintenance of a social tradition that in reality was independent.

In any case, the study of the history of religions in India and in the whole of Asia under Indian influence stands only to benefit from any research which has as its aim, even while continuing its exegesis of ancient sources and carrying on the present studies, to restore as far as possible between the origins and the culmin-ations, the full continuity of a tradition that is widely documented and whose field is without end.

CHAPTER 12

THE VEDA AND ANCIENT TAMIL LITERATURE*

The controversy continues about whether ancient Tamil literature is original. The opinions do not always rest on a complete and an objective analysis of the sources of information. They are often coloured, both in the West and in India, by racial prejudice, systematic hypotheses or some parochial idiosyncrasy. Many of the opinions were formed much before the sources on which they should have been based became available.

The Sanskrit texts composed in North India often betray some sort of contempt towards the Dravidians of the South. Manu thinks that the Dravidians as well as the foreigners who surrounded India, the Yavanas, the Pahlavas, the Cīnas etc., were kṣatriyas who had fallen because of ignoring the *saṃskāras* and for not keeping the company of Brahmins. (X, 44) In the *Carakasaṃhitā*, Agniveśa, according to Ātreya, announces the most dreadful misfortunes for the man 'who, in his dream, is surrounded by vultures, owls, dogs, crows, etc., rakṣas, the dead, piśācas, women, caṇḍālas, draviḍas and āndhrakas', the last two being the Tamils and the Telugus who are listed here after the Caṇḍālas, the 'Brutes', that is after those who are considered to be the untouchable savages.[1] Bāṇa, in *Kādambarī*, offers an unfavourable description of the *draviḍadhārmika*, 'the one who follows the order of the Dravidians'.[2]

A number of Western Indologists have postulated, on their part, the hypothesis that if the Dravidian languages constitute a linguistic family which is different from Sanskrit, then Dravidian culture, starting with its most ancient representative, Tamil, was merely a southern adaptation of the Aryan and Sanskrit culture of the North. The Aryans must have subjugated or pushed the Dravidians down to the South and eventually partly educated

*Le Véda et la littérature tamoule ancienne, in *Mélanges d'indianisme à la mémoire de Louis Renou*, Publ. I.C.I. no. 28, Paris, 1968, pp. 289-300.

and Brahmanised them. Any Dravidian culture worth the name must have come from the Aryans. The Dasyus or Dāsas, mentioned in the Veda as the enemies of the Āryas, have often been interpreted to mean the Dravidians. Authors like Macdonell and Keith[3], after several others, have interpreted *anas*, an epithet of the Dasyus or Dāsas, to mean 'without nose' (but which can also mean 'without mouth', mute) and which, they said, corresponds perfectly to the flat nosed aboriginal Dravidians. In their conviction they forgot that the *Ṛgveda* (X, 99, 6) also depicted the Dāsas as having six eyes and three heads and that the Dravidians are not flat-nosed. The Greeks of the time of Alexander had already noted that the South Indians were dark like the Ethiopians but that they were not as snub-nosed[4]; and they are in fact mesorhinians.[5]

Numerous scholars from the South have reacted against such unwarranted disdain and these hypothesis founded on incorrect facts which judged them without knowing them. They often carried this to the other extreme. Some go as far back as the geological eras or to some cosmic epoch prior to the present one, in trying to explain the origins and a part of Tamil literature. Many deny all influence from the North on Tamil literature or accept it only for the relatively later periods where it is seen as a colonial intrusion on the part of the Northern Brahmins. In these last years, the plan to adopt Hindi as a Pan-Indian language of national unity (whereas in reality it is a source of discord) and the confusion that is common among the ignorant politicians of both the North and the South between Hindi and Sanskrit, have only aggravated the opposition and on the political level led to exchanges of inflamed and poor cultural and linguistic arguments, between the North and the South.

This has not always been the case. In the time of the greatest glory of Tamil literature and culture, Sanskrit was rather readily embraced than despised and rejected. Sanskrit as a means for the spread of the ideas of the men of the South whose work was of universal interest, was actually utilised by them for enriching Indian culture and for the South it is a matter of glory not to have refused Sanskrit but to have produced such first-grade national philosophers in that language like Diṅnāga, Kumārila, Śaṃkara, Rāmānuja, Madhva and several others even while continuing to produce authors of Tamil masterpieces like the ones by the Nāyaṉmār, the Āḻvārs, Māṇikkavācakar or Kampar. It is also to be noted that sometimes in certain Tamil milieus of the Middle Age, there existed an excessively servile tendency towards sanskritisation which ended in giving rise, on the one hand, to absurd legends like the one about Agastya who came from the North in order to teach Tamil grammar in Madurai[6], and on the other, to inadequate imitations of Sanskrit grammar to bring out the Tamil one, as is the case with the Vīracōḻiyam. It is rather the twofold mastery revealed by some of the Dravidians that should be appreciated—the Dravidians, that is the Tamils, Telugus, Malayālis and the Kannaḍigas— a mastery in two cultures and literatures at once, their own and Sanskrit. The Sanskrit culture and literature, despite its far-off origins in pre-history, has been the property not just of the North but that of the whole of Bhāratavarṣa for two thousand years at least.

Fortunately, since the end of the last century, the untiring work of several Tamil pandits who were philologists and epigraphists, beginning with V. Cāminātaiyar among the philologists who gradually made available a considerable volume of original documents for research, have enabled us to come to some factual findings rather than baseless judgments that are either prejudiced or premature. Their publication has been completed. A scrutiny and a critical edition of these ancient Tamil texts, said to be of the most ancient period called 'Sangam', is in progress.[7] The interpretation and therefore any criticism of the texts is often quite difficult. Our understanding is assisted by commentaries done during the Medieval period without which many of the texts would remain unintelligible. However, they are relied upon too blindly by some, even to the extent that sometimes the literal tenor of the commentaries is substituted for the original texts themselves thereby imputing to these texts ideas and observations which are coloured with the dominant beliefs and principles of the period in which the commentaries were written. Nevertheless, thanks to the availability of original documents and the various studies to which they have given rise, it is possible to make an in-depth study of a number of problems, problems that were either misinterpreted or whose solution was not yet clear.

One of the most important of these problems is related to the references in the ancient 'Sangam' literature to Vedic ritual and science and the solution to this problem would throw light on the real relationship between the North and the South during the first centuries of our era.

Most of these references have been frequently brought up but usually simultaneously with references to divinities of the post-vedic cults, and both together are seen as a testimony of the Aryan contribution in general to the Dravidian country. Now, in this regard, it is only the Vedic facts that are meaningful, because a partially identifiable part of post-Vedic facts does not definitely originate in the North. It is only the basic Vedic tradition along with the Vedic language that is of a definite Northern origin. On the contrary, the Prakrit and classical Sanskrit traditions, once they were adopted in the South next to the Dravidian languages, were the fruit of the efforts of men both from the South and the North. It is not enough that we find concepts expressed in Sanskrit in Tamil texts to make them of 'Aryan' origin or imported by the Aryans: in Europe, it is not enough for an idea to be expressed in Latin to make it of Italian origin. The use of Indo-Aryan words in Tamil only proves the knowledge and adoption of Indo-Aryan cultural elements and nothing more.

There are no truly long texts in ancient Tamil still preserved which are totally free of any Indo-Aryan borrowings. It has often been suggested to classify Tamil texts in a relative chronology according to the proportion of Sanskrit words which are found in them. If we believe that the Sanskritisation happened progressively then the Tamil texts that would contain fewer worlds of Sanskrit would be considered more ancient. But the value of such a statistical criterion is very limited and for two reasons. First, the frequency in the use of Sanskrit words can depend on the subject being dealt with as well as on the date of the text, and it can also depend on the personal habits of each author who had at his disposal two sets of equivalent terms, Sanskrit and Tamil, and who could choose either at will. Secondly, we have not given due weight to words borrowed from the Middle Indian which were not always recognised as such and which consequently were considered to be purely Tamil.[8]

In any case, the use of Prakrit words is somewhat more significant vis-à-vis the chronology than the frequency or the uncommonness of Sanskrit words. Before Sanskrit had become the customary language of exchange between different regions of India and even with foreign countries, it was preferred to borrow more from the Prakrit dialects than from Sanskrit. The Tamil texts that contain Prakrit words and few or no Sanskrit words at all can, therefore, be considered to belong to a more ancient and more popular layer than those texts that abound in Sanskrit terms. More so because once these Prakrit terms entered the current usage, they became part of the language and remained so right upto the advent of the modern language. The rarity of equivalent Sanskrit words concurrently used can, depending on the case, be due to both the subject of the text as well as the date of its composition and to the strong or weak Sanskritising tendencies of the authors.

We cannot, therefore, base a detailed relative chronology that is definite on the basis of the frequency of words borrowed from the Indo-Aryan into the Tamil texts. These are all posterior to the early spread of a vast amount of knowledge of literatures of Northern origin in the South. At first we see only the language being influenced, right up to its common usage, by a Prakrit vocabulary, especially by the *ardhamāgadhī* of the Jains who lived in great numbers in the Tamil country. Later we see it accepting Sanskrit words, erudite or popular, which were all the more common as Sanskrit was used more and more as the language of culture and general communication and that more authors from the South themselves wrote in Sanskrit.

But the borrowing of specific technical terms, especially Vedic terms, is on the contrary, revelatory about the adoption in Tamil country of rituals and beliefs of the North and it is all the more noteworthy because it is possible to find at least one dated document of reference to situate in time one of the first instances of their usage.

The collection of poems called 'The Four Hundred about the Feats' *Puṟanāṉūṟu*, or in short *Puṟam*, contains some indications that were obviously added as colophons to the poems when they were put together in this collection and which give the names of poets and persons in whose honour they were written. These indications are not part of the texts themselves and may contain some errors but it would be unjust to think that they were completely invented. They derive from notions that were preserved along with the texts. We cannot strip them of all value *a priori*, all the more so as we do not know the reasons for which they may have been falsified.

A few of these colophons mention corresponding poems as the ones that were sung in honour of the Pāṇḍya Palyākacālai Mutukuṭumi Peruvaḻuti. The texts themselves call him Kuṭumi (*Puṟ*. 6.26, 9.8). We know that elsewhere he is mentioned in the inscription of Vēḷvikkuṭi.[9] This reference is extremely important for it enables us to establish as shown by P. T. Srinivas Iyengar[10], if not its precise period then at least the time prior to which one must situate it.

The Vēḷvikkuṭi chart is bilingual, Sanskrit and Tamil. It presents a genealogy of the Pāṇḍyas which starts in a legendary time, in a cosmic period prior to the present one. At the end of this period there ruled a Pāṇḍya king whose *purodhas* was Kumbhodbhava, that is Agastya. This king was reborn at the beginning of the present *kalpa* and was coronated again. He had a son, a Pururavas, in whose lineage was born Palayākacālai. The latter offered a *brahmadeya* to a certain Naṟkoṟṟaṉ of Koṟkai[11] who was a *kēḷvibrāhmaṇa*, that is a *śrotriya*.[12] There came later one of the Kalabhrar[13] kings, the Kalabhrars being usurpers who abolished the donation. The Pāṇḍya dynasty was re-established by Kaṭuṅkoṉ (590-620).[14] From this prince onward, the historical dynasty is listed until Parāntaka Neṭuñcaṭaiyaṉ, named in the Sanskrit section Jaṭilaparāntaka (Tam. *caṭai* = Skr. *jaṭā*) who bestows the chart once again to re-establish the ancient foundation of Palyākacālai. Jaṭilaparāntaka offers this chart in the third year of his reign, either in 768 or 769, his reign having lasted from 765 to 815.

Now we know from other sources that Buddhadatta, a Tamil Buddhist and commentator of the Pāli canon and author of the *Abhidhammāvatāra* and *Vinayavinicchaya* in Pāli, is said to have lived around 400 A.D. and that he wrote at Kāverīpaṭṭanam under the reign of Accutaccutavikkanta Kalabbhakulanandana (*Vin.* 3178). The verse that says this, sometimes has another reading: *kaḷambha* instead of *kalabha*. As observed by P. T. Srinivas

Iyengar,[15] this can be due to a remembrance of the Kaḍambas which must have infiltrated into *kalabha* in the mind of the scribe. *Kalabha*, in any case, corresponds in Pāli to *Kalabhrar* and resembles it with greater probability than with *kaḷambha* alone.

Buddhadatta, the Pāli author prior to Buddhaghosa, was from Uṟaiyūr (Uragapuranivāsika) according to the colophon of *Abhidhammāvatāra*. Uṟaiyūr and Kāverīpaṭṭanam traditionally belonged to the Coḷa kingdom, to the North of the Pāṇḍya where Palyākacālai had reigned, but the usurpation by the Kalabhrars must have affected the whole of the Tamil country. The Vēḷvikkuṭi inscription unfortunately does not mention the time that passed under this usurpation, neither that between Palyākacālai and the start of this usurpation. Nevertheless we are obliged to situate the Pāṇḍya king in question, some time before 400. It is possible that the donation he is said to have made and which Jaṭilaparāntaka was to have re-established after a lapse of more than four centuries, was assumed by alleged descendants of the first beneficiaries but the fact remains that Jaṭilaparāntaka expressed his faith in it and that the existence of Palyākacālai before the Kalabhrars was definite according to the dynastic tradition in force in the 8th century in the country that it governed.

Now, among the rather numerous references to the Vedas, to the Vedic brahmins and Vedic things that are found in the 'Sangam' literature, those that allude to Palyākacālai are the most important.

Yākacālai is the Tamil transcription of the Sanskrit *yāgaśālā* and *pal* signifies 'numerous'. The king in question is, therefore, one who has got numerous 'halls for sacrifices' built (if we accept, according to the current practice, the rough translation of 'sacrifice' for *yāga* which designates more precisely the oblatory ceremonies).

A poem of Kārikilār (*Pur.* 6) first evokes all the world that is known, as if the king truly dominated it, then he glorifies the successes of this king over his enemies, the king's piety and generosity. He ends with the wish that this king live as long as the Moon and the Sun. The panegyrist's theme has already become current in royal inscriptions not merely in India but right up to Cambodia.

The whole poem can be literally translated thus:

6.1. 'That which is in the North, is the North with a chain of mountains which hold the snows,[16]

2. That which is in the South, is the South with the Terrible Virgin,[17]

3. That which is in the East, is the East with the Ocean which advances beating against the shore.

4. That which is in the West, is the West with the primeval ocean of antiquity.

5. That which is at the bottom is in the first group in a regular succession of a series of three.[18]

6. The bottom at the level of the abode of waters.[19] That which is above

7. is that which does not end even with the world of the cows.[20]

8, 9, 10. By claiming a fortune which stretches in the form of fear and renown, may you not let one side stoop, like the beam of a balance. May your side prosper!

11. Among the enemies who are opposed to the work you have undertaken,

12, 13. having gathered their army which is an ocean, to submerge it, you have joyously commanded the elephants with small, dark-brown eyes.

14. From the side of the low-lying green lands, you have offered many a rugged (conquered) rampart,

15, 16. You have offered as gifts to people, according to their rank, beautiful ornaments won while fighting to conquer these ramparts.

17, 18. May you incline your parasol to circumambulate around the city of the three-eyed One, (the god of) the sages (*Muni*).

19, 20. May you bow your head, O Great One, before the extended hand[21] of the sages of the four, excellent mysteries!

21, 22. May you wilt, O Lord, your garland of the head, by the violence of the odorous smoke that burns the enemy country!

23, 24. May you drive away your wrath before the luminous

sulking faces of women with all their adornments intact (undefiled by other men)!

25. And there, bearing all your victories in your heart, after having conquered,
26. O King Kuṭumi of an infinitely generous heart,
27, 29. May you abide like the Moon with the cold beams, like the Sun with the dazzling beams whose heat is over powering, O Great One who sit on the summit of the Earth!'

Verses 17 and 18 refer to the *pradakṣiṇā* of the temple of the three-eyed god of the *munis*, therefore, of Śiva; verses 19 and 20 refer to the blessings the king should receive from the *munis* of the four Vedas, which are alluded to here according to a common practice as the 'Mysteries' (*Maṟai*). The king, therefore, practices this cult according to Śiva worshipping *munis* even while he reveres the Vedic *munis*. This suggests duality and a coming together of two traditions that are still in force, that of the Āgamas and the Vedas, and shows this duality to be well entrenched already in the far South of India during the time of Palyākacālai. On the one hand we have the temple and the cult of the supreme God, and on the other the recitation of the Veda and the performance of Vedic ceremonies. Palyākacālai's preference for these ceremonies is confirmed by other poems from the *Puṟanāṉūṟu*, the 9th and the 15th, attributed to Neṭṭimaiyar who expresses himself thus (first in the *Pur.* No. 9):

1. 'O cows, multitudes of Brahmins (*pārppaṉa makkaḷ*) of the same essence as the cows and
2. women, he has protected you, you who suffer,
3, 4. you who did not have any son (valuable) like gold in order to perform the painful duty for those who will dwell in the South (the dead),
5. when he said: "We shall soon shoot our arrows, rally round your ramparts!",
6. by virtue of the courage of announcing the path of the right order.
7. The sky darkened with the numerous standards flying on top of massacring elephants,
8. May he live on, our Lord Kuṭumi, Lord of himself!
9. He gave to the dancers, more new, liquified red-gold,

10. during the festival of the sea, He who is Great,
11. than there is sand in the clear-watered Paḥṟuli.'

Pur. 15 is dedicated thanks to its final word, *niṉkē*, 'To you!', to Kuṭumi, and is to be sung during the march towards the enemy called *vañci*, from the appellation of the garland that is worn as an emblem. It is in this poem that reference is made to a great number of sacrificial areas set up by Kuṭumi which explains his title of Palyākacālai:

1. 'There where the roads were dug through by speeding chariots,
2. harnessed by small groups of white-mouthed asses,
3. you destroyed the high-peaked ramparts belonging to people there,
4. in the fields resounding with multitudes of birds teeming in well-known abundance,
5. under the round hooves of proud white-maned horses,
6. you who led the chariots into your enemies' country.
7. The elephants with brilliant tusks,
8. in a crushing humour and with puissant neck,
9. huge-legged and with eyes of fury,
10. you bathed them in ponds that were under the protection of these people.
11. And such is the consequence if you are enraged.
12. With shields bright with the brilliance flashed by burnished gold,
13. under cover of such protection holding their long spears, the enemies,
14. striving to have the upper hand over the thin force of the vanguard of (your) brilliant army,
15. they who had come with this aim but now having failed in it,
16. suffering contempt, are there many who (still) live? Of the flawless,
17. fine treatises and of the four Vedas,
18. greatly conscious of the singular excellence,

19, 20. ceremonies abounding in oblations rich with butter, that have manifold excellence, you have fulfilled with an immortal glory.

21. They are indeed numerous, the vast areas planted with sacrificial posts!
22. Indeed they are numerous! O Great One! Carefully englobed
23. the paste-covered[22] drums by taut joints in the form of straps,
24. for the battle-song towards the enemy which the singers will sing on their rhythm.
25. O Thou endowed with admirable strength, this is in your glory!'

In this last poem, in verse 17, we find 'fine treatises', naṟpaṉuval being mentioned next to the Vedas (under that very name), the word paṉuval which literally means 'good threads', corresponds exactly to the Sanskrit word *sūtra* and here it is obviously ritual Vedic *sūtras* that are meant. A little further, *yāga* appears under the name of *vēḷvi* used elsewhere as an equivalent of *kratu*.[23] The oblations of *ghee* referred to in verse 19 are called *āvuti* (Sanskrit *āhuti*). The 'posts' and the 'areas' of verse 21 are respectively *yūpa* and *kaḷams*. This last word corresponds to *śālā*. The poet has, therefore, used Tamil and Sanskrit terms freely even while referring to things that are specifically Vedic. This is clearly an indication that we must not attach too much importance to the greater or lesser proportion of Sanskrit words in these 'Sangam' texts, in order to date them.

We shall also translate poem 224 of the *Puṟanāṉūṟu*, one among those of 'Sangam' literature that refer to Vedic ritual, as it gives some supplementary information which is precise. In this poem, Karuṅkuḻālataṉār is lamenting the death of the Coḷa King Karikāṟperuvaḷattāṉ, and mentions his martial power, his magnificence as the patron of the bards in the assemblies where he drinks freely with them and as a patron of the Right Order (*aṟam* which corresponds to the Sanskrit *ṛta* and *dharma*) perpetuated by Vedic rites:

1. 'Without any thought for the combat, he destroyed the fortresses.
2. In the midst of the gathered assembly he emptied the pots.
3. The bards and all their relatives he patronised in large numbers.

4. With the great counsel that has always the way of the Right Order in mind,
5. the profound knowers of the procedures led the worthy,
6. women to the nature of purity, irreproachable in their vows, in whose company,
7. within the precincts of multiple circular walls,
8. with a high pillar that is a post (planted at a place) where the kite swallows,
9. he performed the Vedic rite.
10. Undoubtedly, he knew, he was a man endowed with knowledge.
11. He is the one who is dead! This world here is to be regretted!
12. When the fountains have dried up, when it is terribly hot,
13. during the summer abounding in great famines,
14. to offer to useful flocks, to famished groups,
15. the cowherds with sharp-edged knives chop the flowers down,
16. they pluck them and the veṅkai[24] loses its bloom.
17. (like the tree) the gentle-natured women have removed their ornaments!'

The 'Vedic rite', *vetavēḷvittoḻil,* was performed, then, with the participation of the wives led by the specialists of the Right Order to a circular area made with piled-up rings (probably with earth) where there was a post (*yūpa*) planted in front of the beak of a representation of a kite, that is the *garuḍa* depicted on the ground and forming a raised pillar (*tūṇ*, Sk. *sthūṇa*). In fact *eruvai* 'kite' is especially pertinent to the Tamil country as the brick-red bird with a white neck that is called *karuṭaṉ* (Sanskrit *garuḍa*) and is considered the bird of Viṣṇu. Meanwhile *eruvai* can also designate another predatory bird, called in Tamil *kaḻuku* and which might remind us of the *śyena* in the form of which Vedic altars are built.

One could go on citing other texts that mention in the same conditions Vedic rites in the poems of the 'Sangam' period but the most notable reference seems to us to be the one we have just quoted above and according to which the cult of Śiva and the Vedic ritual were observed simultaneously by the king before the year 400. The Vedic ritual is essentially present in all subsequent traditions in the Tamil country and is said to promote *bhukti* or prosperity. It was, therefore, patronised by the kings for the general good of the kingdom but religion, which according to the Āgamas consists in the adoration of God, guarantees both *bhukti* and *mukti*, material prosperity and liberation.

Besides, it is evident that the ancient Tamil poems represent a literature that is original as much by its nature as by its language. This literature is not inspired from Sanskrit models but it had already begun expressing a culture that is pan-Indian and in which the Veda plays an important role. And as far as we understand, it developed after the period, going far back in time, when the North and the South of India had begun to interact and understand each other.

NOTES

1. *Gṛdhrolūkaśvakākādyaiḥ svapne yaḥ parivāryate / rakṣaḥpretapiśācacaṇḍāladraviḍāndhrakaiḥ // Carakasaṃhitā, Indriyasthāna*, V, 28 (Jamnagar ed., 1949, t. III, p. 1218). There exists a variant *dravitān-dhakaiḥ* for the last two terms of the enumeration (Narendraśāstrī ed., Lahore, 1929, t. I, p. 674). A Bengali translation (without the Sanskrit text) contains: *dhāvita andha* (Carakasaṃhitā, Śrī Devendranāth Sengupta and Śrī Upendranāth Sengupta ed. Kalikātā, 1898, p. 520) which does not give a satisfactory meaning. But Vāgbhaṭa taking up the text in *Aṣṭāṅga-saṃgraha* (Śārīrasthāna, XII, Ganeśaśarman ed., t. I, p. 254) and in *Aṣṭāṅgahṛdaya* (Śār. VI, 49) does give *draviḍāndhra*. *Aṣṭāṅgasaṃgraha* follows the text of the *Carakasaṃhitā* more closely than *Aṣṭāṅgahṛdaya*. It says: ....*pretapiśācarakṣodraviḍāṃdhrastrīcaṇḍālādyair*, whereas the *Aṣṭāṅgahṛdaya* reads:.........*pretapiśācastrīdraviḍāṃdhragavāśanaiḥ*. The Tibetan version of this last text, translates as is the usual Tibetan practice, *preta* as *yi-dags*, interprets *piśācastrī* as the feminine of *piśāca* by translating it as *śa-za-mo*, renders *gavāśana* 'feeding on cow-meat' as *rme-śa-čan* 'having an unclean diet' and replaces *draviḍāṃdhra* with *byad-ma* 'enemy' which in the translation of *Bodhicaryāvatāra* corresponds to *ḍākinī* (Fr. Weller, *Tibetisch-Sanskritischer* Index Zum B., Berlin, 1955, t. II, p. 343, and Lokesh Chandra, *Tibetan-Sanskrit Dictionary*, New Delhi, 1960, p. 1642). Jäschke and S.C. Das interpret the group *byad-ma-rme-śa-can* as designating 'a wicked demon'. In any case, the agreement between the two Sanskrit works ascribed to Vāgbhaṭa ensures their reading as *draviḍāndhra* and in the *Carakasaṃhitā*, their source, the reading *draviḍāndhraka*.
2. *Kādambarī*, Kāśīnāth Pāṇḍuraṅg Parab ed., Bombay, 1921, Pūrvabhāga, pp. 398-401.
3. *Vedic Index*, I, 348; II, 391 n. 38.

4. Arrian, *Inde*, VI, 9.
5. G. Olivier, *Anthropologie des Tamouls du Sud de l'Inde*, Paris, 1961, p. 120.
6. Cf. R. Dessigane, P.Z. Pattabiramin & J. Filliozat, *La Légende des jeux de Śiva à Madurai*, Publ. of the I.F.I. no. 19, Pondicherry, 1960, p. XII.
7. The Institut Français d'Indologie at Pondicherry has completed on index-cards (over 300.000) a survey of all the words of the 'Sangam' literature in all their instances of occurrence, under the supervision of Kandaswamy Pillai. This work is meant to facilitate the interpretation of texts and the morphological, lexicographical and statistical study of the language as well as the investigation of the data supplied by this literature on the ancient society and its culture. The University of Kerala has, on its side, published a complete index of the *Puṟanāṉūṟu:* V.I. Subramoniam, *Index* of *Puranaanuuru*, Trivandrum, 1962, 628 pages, with translation of each word into modern Tamil and in English and with a grammatical identification of the forms. The University has also published in a similar way, the index of *Cilappatikāram* which is preceded by a grammatical study: S.V. Subramaniam, *Descriptive Grammer of Cilappatikāram*, Madras, 1965, 88 pages, Part II, *Index of C.*, 308 pages.
8. J. Filliozat, *Chronique bibliographique. Travaux récents sur les langues dravidiennes*, J.A. 1963, p. 267 and foll.
9. E.I., XVII, No. 16, pp. 291-309.
10. *History of the Tamils from the earliest times to* 600 *A.D.*, Madras, 1929, pp. 439, 535.
11. Ptolemy: Kolkhoi, L. Renou ed. I, 10, p. 6. *Periplus* 58.
12. Cf. Krishnaswamy Aiyangar, *Ancient India and South Indian History and Culture* vol. I, Poona, 1941, p. 471, n. 1.
13. Kalabhrar has a plural ending which is also used as a honorific. Nevertheless the plural is needed. Some wonder whether the usurpation of the Pāṇḍya kingdom by the Kalabhrar was not the Kaḷḷar's doing (Krishnaswami Aiyangar, *Ancient India...*). It would then refer to a particular group of these Kaḷḷars, otherwise they would have been designated by their usual appellation. The form of Kalabhrar is not Tamil (*bhra* is a Sanskrit or a Sanskritised form).
14. Nilakanta Sastri, *History of South India*, Oxford-Madras, 1955, p. 164.
15. *History of Tamils...* p. 532.
16. The Himālaya.
17. Kaṉṉiyakumari (Cape Comorin).
18. The Earth, the first whole in the group of the three planes successively listed as being the Earth (*nilam*), space (*ākāyam*) and the sky (*cuvarkkam*). It refers to lower Central Pāṇḍya country.
19. The ocean.
20. The Goloka. That which is above goes even beyond the Goloka.
21. The outstretched hand is to bless.
22. The drums are covered with a black paste at the centre of their taut skin.
23. Cf. *Tirumurukaṟṟuppaṭai* 155-56 where Indra is called *nūṟupalvēḷvi* which corresponds to *śatakratu*.
24. Butea frondosa Roxb.

CHAPTER 13

THE RESPECT OF LIFE IN BUDDHISM*

One of the fundamental tenets of Buddhism is 'do not kill'. The respect of life must, therefore, be absolute with the Buddhist and it extends to animal life as well as human.

This extension to both animal and human life is often seen as based on the belief in transmigration which can lead men to be reborn after their death in animal bodies. And so, finally, it would be out of concern for the human person that animal life should be respected. In reality, such an explanation ought not to be formulated on the basis of some European ideas considered to be valid universally and especially in ancient India. The explanation must be sought within thc Indian doctrines themselves. Now the Indians, from very early times, represented the psychic individuality as being constituted of the accumulation and organisation of dynamic imprints of the psychological experiences one has gone through and this representation was common to all its milieus, including the Buddhist. These imprints are not mere traces but retain in the unconscious mass that they form, the nature of the activity that provoked them. They are organised in psychic constructions which are coherent by their affinity and their associations. Whether we accept or not the existence of a soul that forms, in addition, the nucleus of these acquisitions of experience, these acquisitions themselves are a subtle psychic body involved in the gross body and using its organs. This psychic body does not dissolve at the death of the physical body, but disembodied, it returns once again into the embryo of another physical body according to the impulses it might have retained from its preceding empirical origins.

This is how the theory of transmigration is explained. But the theory also indicates that some particular psychic formations constituting the psychic individuality can be destroyed by others

*Le respect de la vie dans le bouddhisme, in *Axes*, April-May, 1973, pp. 13-18.

of an opposite kind and that generally it is possible by a conscious choice of psychic experiences to constitute or to reform the psychic body according to one's liking.

And, therefore, the Indian religious practice, aiming for liberation by breaking this chain of transmigration, requires a strict psychological discipline and not merely the building up of faith and respect for ethics. One must abstain particularly from any action that can leave in the psychic self an undesirable trace whose dynamism would lead one to a further action whose consequences would be equally undesirable. And that is why one must refrain from all violence, and must respect life, not only out of charity for the living being, although charity is valued, but more out of precaution for oneself.

Buddhism demands for the same reason, along with the abstention from killing life, four other abstentions: of taking anything that is not given, being unchaste, speaking lies and drinking alcohol. By implication anything that can enslave the psychic self to pleasure or self-interest and make it lose its self-control, is to be shunned. This self-control is, in fact, necessary to stand firm against desire that entangles one to existence and prevents the breaking off of the unavoidable chain of fatal transmigrations.

The individual's transgressions of the five obligatory abstentions are all equally serious and undermine his psychic conditioning on the Buddhist path. But it does not follow that the acts corresponding to each transgression are considered morally as equally serious. Otherwise it would be as criminal to procreate by transgressing the rule of chastity as committing a murder. Thus, the monk, totally committed on the Buddhist path, is expected to observe strict chastity, but domestic life and procreation are not condemned for the secular members of society without whom the community of monks would not even be able to survive. What is more, the sexual act, even when not meant for the propagation of the species, is not considered a sin in itself. The divine states to which the meritorious devotees can attain after their death while waiting to attain the final liberation in the course of rebirths, offer them all kinds of pleasures, while gods and goddesses as couples do not procreate. With the ripening of their previous life's acts, gods and goddesses appear and disappear in a flash in full youth into various paradises.

While theft or falsehood or even drunkenness are in no way tolerated, the sexual act is permissible in some conditions and even the butchering of animals, deplorable as it is, is however officially admitted by the casuistry. A monk, and even the Buddha himself can or could have received meat in alms, when the animal was not specially killed for them. If it was, they would become the indirect but real cause of its death.

Casuistry also permits, as in Brahmanism and Jainism, a voluntary and conditioned giving up of life while prohibiting common suicide which is an attempt triggered by passion. From the moment the sage achieves a total emotional detachment from his body he can let it perish through starvation, like the Jains and sometimes the Brahmanists do. He can even get rid of his body by withdrawing the 'structure of longevity' which sustains the body for its use by holding on to the psychic individuality, like the Buddha did according to legend, before entering into Total Extinction. More often the body can be consigned to the flames, or hurled down an abyss, or drowned, or even decapitated. In any case, the sage will not kill a fully conscious living being, he will only come out of the material envelope from which he has withdrawn its life as the serpent who slowly sloughs off his dead skin. In a more special case he can immolate himself by fire to uplift the masses as can be seen from the very first centuries of our era, in several fundamental texts of Buddhism that are termed 'Mahāyānic', that is 'the Great Way of Progress' and as it has been done in our days in Vietnam in the same Mahāyānic tradition.

It is certain that psychologically the giving up of the bodily life by the sage differs completely from the suicide of the desperate and in fact from any kind of suicide which, without despair, would be a deliberate or impulsive act of self-destruction: one does not destroy oneself when one situates oneself outside the body that is being destroyed.

However, there are cases where the theoretical distinction between suicide and the giving up of life by the sage is almost uncertain. The Pāli Buddhist canon in Ceylon and Western Indo-China as well as the commentaries on it mention numerous instances where sages are very near committing personal suicide but break away only at the very last moment from this impulse for self-destruction which would make the killing of their body an ordinary attempt on life. The great commentator Buddhaghosa, speaks about a canonical text according to which a devotee named Vakkali, being very ill, killed himself, but did this only after the Buddha himself had helped him to drive away his worldly thoughts and Buddhaghosa supposes that Vakkali had already slit the trachea when he became aware through the pain that he was still an ordinary man and he had to sever at once this link before dying (about these questions, see above chp. 8, p. 91-125 and chp. 10, p. 135-159).

In any case, and however remarkable the famous cases in legend and in history may be of voluntary deaths that were considered justified, the Buddhist rule remains that all life should be respected, but respected not so much for itself as for a psychological discipline.

In fact, the living being is an amalgamation not only in its body where the constructive elements of the universe are in their solid, liquid, caloric, pneumatic forms, but also in its psychic nature made up of aggregates of psychic experiences preserved and organised in multiple constructions. But every composite is subject to dissolution, does not enjoy permanence and is not a stable being. Life in this world does not belong to the domain of being, it belongs to the domain of having, because it is a fleeting possession of the transmigrating psychic self, not an autonomous existence. Certain Buddhist schools reduce it even to its being merely a subjective representation of psychic individualities and devoid of any objective reality. Therefore, theoretically, it would not be more respectable in itself than a mirage or in any case only a haphazard, phenomenal amalgamation doomed anyway to destruction. If this life has to be respected it is, therefore, mainly for oneself and not for itself, for oneself so as not to burden oneself with any act in its regard which the very act of attacking it would recognise and of which one would retain within oneself the corrupting dynamism.

It would however be incorrect to conclude from this that respect of life ordained by Buddhist doctrine is purely egoistic. It would mean forgetting the positive compensation for prohibition, namely, charity to which we have already alluded. In fact if in absolute truth phenomenal life is without ontological consistency, in empirical truth, even though illusory, phenomenal life is endowed with sensibility and particularly painful sensibility which awakens compassion. The Buddha, understanding the vanity of existence, was tempted not to preach. However, he overcame this temptation through compassion for beings in need of succour. His whole doctrine glorifies the states of mind called 'Brahmic' and which are: benevolence for all beings, compassion for the suffering, happiness at the sight of the good, imperturbability before the wicked. The function of a Buddhist community is to lead the laity to detach itself from the world but this is done through charity for them and the function of the community is also to work for its well-being, even the present one.

In its solicitude, Buddhism tends to embrace even the dead of this world and who have taken form in other worlds, in heavens or hells or who still linger between two existences. The Buddhist can and must accomplish, in the name of the dead, meritorious acts which benefit these dead in the beyond. Here, it is not a question, as one often tends to believe, of a simple magical transfer of merit to the acquisition of which the beneficiary is a stranger. The merit of the act goes indeed to him who accomplishes it and is not strictly transferred from the agent to the receiver. The participation of the dead in the merit gained for him by the charitable believer occurs in a different way. The dead person who in the intermediary existence or in a conscious but not human rebirth, generally a rebirth given as punishment, may have, prior to his death, desired the accomplishment of an act of merit or else, when it is a question of a damned person, the instructive legends declare that he may have the chance of communicating with a believer and asking him to accomplish in his name an act of merit. In these cases the dead person who is incapable of any human act outside the human condition is however the initiating cause of the act of which another person takes responsibility in his name and it is natural that the merit should come back to him, the charitable third person also acquiring the merit of his charity. Even if they have remained unconscious and did not themselves wish for the act of merit it is not impossible that the non-human beings benefit from this

Buddhist benevolence. The act which is accomplished for them even if it is without their knowledge, makes of them, though involuntarily, the cause of this act and they can still share its merit. The development of goodness is universally beneficent: the damned are relieved when a Buddha appears in the world.

All these ideas have an important corollary. If chastity was practised by all Buddhists, the Buddhist community, as we have already said, would not only be unable to survive but what is more, chastity to the extent it is actually practised, would be an obstacle to the propagation of life, a condemnable practise from the point of view of Buddhist charity. In fact, there is a risk of depriving the psychic individualities, transmigrating out of the human condition, of all chance of reincarnation in a human matrix. Now, liberation, the realisation of *Nirvāṇa* or 'Extinction' is only possible in the human condition (more particularly in the masculine condition). It is, therefore, the very liberation of the transmigrating being which can be compromised by the ascetic's fault. In this perspective, birth control is obviously condemnable. A Buddhist legend illustrates these ideas: an eminent monk who believed he had severed all link with desire, all of a sudden attempted to violate a woman. The latter defended herself successfully and the monk explained that he was indeed detached from all desire. But he had seen, thanks to an extraordinary power he had acquired, the psychic body of a dead, wandering friend who was seeking a chance to reincarnate himself. He had wanted to give him a chance of a human reincarnation. He failed because the wrong actions of his friend did not allow him to enjoy such a privilege.

One must also note the existence of medieval Buddhist sects whose adherents like the licentious gnostics of classical antiquity took the opposite standpoint of morality and Buddhist prescriptions after having, at first, conformed to them. The adept knows the precepts and then considers himself released from them once they have been mastered and submits in thought to all crimes, murders, incests etc. and to all sorts of repugnant acts and above all considers the sexual act in a symbolic and real way as representative of the awakening of the true knowledge. It does not seem that murder was actually committed in these sects and in any case the respect of life in all its forms is certainly one of the fundamental tenets of Buddhism.

CHAPTER 14

ECHOES OF SUFISM IN INDIA*

The main texts that deal with the analogies between Sufism and the spiritual doctrines and practices of India are two works attributed to Muhammad Dārā Śukoh, the first in Persian, *Majma-'al-Baḥraīn*, the other in Sanskrit, *Samudrasaṅgama*, and the titles mean respectively, 'The Mingling (or the Confluence) of the two Oceans' and 'The Meeting of Oceans'.

The Persian text composed in the 1065th year of the Hegira, that is 1657 A.D., was published in the Bibliotheca Indica at Calcutta by Mahfuz-ul-Haq in 1929 along with an English translation, notes and variants.

A French translation was recently published in Paris in 1979 by Daryush Shayegan in the work entitled *Les relations de l'hindouisme et du soufisme d'après le Majma-'al Bahrayn de Dârâ Shokûh.*

The Sanskrit text which is based on a unique manuscript conserved at the Bhandarkar Oriental Institute at Poona, was edited at Calcutta by Jatindra Bimal Chaudhuri and translated simultaneously by Roma Choudhuri in *Prācyavāṇī-Mandira, Comparative Religion and Philosophy Series*, vol. 2, *A Critical Study of Dārā Shikuh's 'Samudrasaṅgama'*, in 1954.

Dārā's work was known even in his own life-time. He was the son of the emperor Shah Jahan, born on March 20th in 1615 and suffered the same fate as his two other brothers, at the hands of his brother Aurangzeb who usurped power and executed him in 1659 for being a heretic because of his sympathies for Hinduism.

His intellectual work has been mainly known for his translation of the *Upaniṣads*, translated first in French but published in Latin by Anquetil-Duperron. His work is also well-known because of the summarised report about his talks with Bābā Lāl

*Sur les contreparties indiennes du soufisme, *Journal Asiatique*, 1980, pp. 259-73.

in 1862 by H. H. Wilson in his *Essays and Lectures chiefly on the Religion of the Hindus* (vol. 7, p. 348 and foll.) published and translated in our *Journal Asiatique* in October-December 1926 by Cl. Huart and L. Massignon, under the title of *Entretiens de Lahore*. His whole work has been dealt with by Bikramajit Hasrat, *Dārā Shikūh: Life and Works* Vishvabharati, Calcutta, 1953. But Hasrat could not include *Samudrasaṅgama* which was published only the following year. He came to know about it through P. K. Gode's discovery but he did not know the grounds upon which Gode affirmed that it was a Sanskrit work of the prince whereas he thought it to be merely a translation (p. 213).

Daryush Shayegan does not seem to have had any knowledge of the *Samudrasaṅgama* and neither of the works of the two Choudhuris.

Incidentally, Roma Choudhuri published at Calcutta in 1945, at the beginning of her series of *Prācyavāṇī-Mandira*, Sufism and Vedānta and *Part II: Some Prominent Sufis and their Doctrines*, in 1948.

A big work has recently been published: Saiyid Athar Abbas Rizvi's *A History of Sufism in India*, vol. I: *Early Sufism and its History in India to 1600 A.D.* (New Delhi, 1978, 467 pages). He stops before the period of Dārā but does describe its antecedents amply, particularly from the Persian side. He summarises, however, various works in Indian languages that he cites in footnotes in *nāgarī* script. Rizvi identified some 1500 Sufis in his book but does not dwell much on their Hindu homologues, the chronology of the latter being, in fact, far more uncertain, although some of the miracles attributed to both are generally comparable.

The *Majma-'al-Baḥraīn* and the *Samudrasaṅgama* continue to be the most significant texts about the comparison of the Sufi movements and their Indian counterparts in the 17th century. However, this comparative study between the *Samudrasaṅgama* and the *Majma-'al-Bahraīn* has only been done by Roma Choudhuri. This study must, therefore, be picked up again, the more so as the recent study of Daryush Shayegan does not take it into account even while looking through the classical commentaries on the Vedānta for finding the sources of Dārā's information.

The authenticity of *Samudrasaṅgama* as a personal work of

Dārā, had been challenged, as we mentioned, by Bikramjit Hasrat, at the mere announcement of the finding of the manuscript which like the *Majma-'al-Baḥraīn*, says the work to have been composed in 1065 of the Hegira, that is 1657 while the manuscript itself is dated 1765 samvat, i.e. 1708-09 A.D.

The *Samudrasaṅgama* and the Persian text seem to almost always agree as far as the parallels between the data of Islam and of India are presented.

Actually they are two versions of the same text and the Sanskrit one could be a translation of the Persian. But in the Sanskrit version, Dārā expresses himself in the first person while in the Persian one, in the third. The Sanskrit sentences are then not always a literal translation of their Persian content. They might have very easily been composed by Dārā himself whose personal competence in Sanskrit culture is confirmed by the *Majma-'al-Baḥraīn* itself. However, even if it be certain that the *Samudrasaṅgama* had been translated from the Persian by someone other than Dārā, it would not be any less important a document for a comparative study of Sufi and Indian doctrines, since it is clear that it is the voice of an expert that speaks in both the cultures.

I shall give here only the introduction from the Sanskrit text of *Samudrasaṅgama* along with its translation which could then be compared with the Persian text and its translations.

Introduction to Samudrasaṅgama

sarvatra prakaṭaḥ sa sarvāvabhāsaḥ sa ādiḥ so'ṃtas tadatiriktaṃ vastu nāstīti /

prativeśī savāsī ca sahagaḥ sarvam eva saḥ /

paṭaccare daridrasya kṣaume rājñaḥ sa sarvataḥ //

bhāti saṃsadi bhedo yam abhedo rahasi sphuṭaḥ /

īśasya śapanam bhūyas tacchapaḥ sarvam eva saḥ //

praṇāmānām ānantyaṃ paramaprakāśaprakāśake jagat-sṛṣṭinimitte'smākaṃ siddhānāṃ siddhe parameśvareṇa satkṛte saṃmātite ca tathā pavitratame tatparivāre mahattare tatpratinidhirūpe ca atha kathayati vītarāgavigataśokasaṃdohamahammada dārā śukoha // *evaṃ yad vijñāya sakalatattvatattvaṃ nirṇīya ca satyaikātmavādatātparyam āsādya ca bhagavanmahāprasādaṃ tad anu caitad vicāramadhye praviṣṭaṃ mayā yad aṃtaṃ prāpnuyām abhiprāyasya siddhānāṃ niścetṝṇāṃ vaidikānām anādikulajānām iti atha ca kaiścikaiścit paripūrṇaiḥ vaidikaiḥ saha viśeṣataś caitanyasvarūpajñānamūrttisadguruvābālāla aṃtaṃ tapasyāyā jñānasya sauvudhyaphalasyeśvaraprāpte* (:) *śāṃteśca prāptavān tena ca saha punaḥpunah saṃgatīr goṣṭhīś cākaravaṃ paribhāṣābhedātiriktaṃ kam api bhedaṃ svarūpāvāptau nāpaśyam ataś ca dvayor apy ekavākyatām akaravaṃ* (*ta*) *tas'ca satyāvāptyadhikāribhir avaśyaṃ jñātavyānāṃ saphalānāṃ katipayavākyānāṃ sārasya saṃgraham akaravaṃ jñāninor dvayor api matasamudrayor iha saṅgama iti nāma cāsthapayam samudrasaṅgama iti itthaṃ kilopadeśo mahānubhāvānām yan nirmatsaratayā tattvavivecanaṃ sakalavedāṃtānāṃ prayojanam ato yaḥ kaścid vivekī jñānī ca sa eva jānāti tattvanirṇayatalasparśe kīdṛśaḥ śrama iti niścayena vidvāṃso jñā*(*n*)*inaś ca bahutaraṃ sukhamitayāpsyaṃti na prāpsyaṃti na bhedivādinaḥ kuṃṭhitamataya iti/svānubhavānusāreṇa ca nirṇīya tattvārthaṃ svakuṭumbeṣv anukampayā kṛto'yam ārambhaḥ na punar ajñāninor vibhinnamatasaṃbamdhinor bodhanena mama prayojanam iti anyac ca mahāpuruṣaḥ ṣvājai aharār nāmā śuddhāṃta*(*ḥ*) *karaṇaḥ kila ajñaptavān yady ahaṃ jñānīyāṃ kaś cana nirīśvaro'pi kathākhyadeśasthito'pi mano'nuraṃjakaśabdais tattvavārttam vadatīti tarhi tatra gatvāśroṣyāmi śiṣyāmi anuneṣyāmi ca tam atra ca parameśvarādeva mama sāmarthyaṃ parameśvara eva me sahāya.*

'Manifest in all, he is the manifestion of ALL,
He is the Beginning, he is the end, nothing exists outside of him.

> "Neighbour, co-resident and companion, he is All.
> In the pauper's rags, in the king's finery, he dwells equally.
> To the outside he appears in diversity, but in the secrecy he is manifest non-diversity.
> The oath (to be sworn) about the Lord is greater still: the oath to be sworn about him is: All is Himself."[1]
>
> Infinite salutations to illuminer of the supreme light, of the cause of the emanation of the world[2], of the Perfect (*siddha*) among our Perfect Beings, favoured (*satkṛta*) and shaped (*sanmatita*) by the Supreme Lord; (salutations) in the same way to the purest and thereby the vastest accompaniment of his representatives.'

'Muhammad Dārā Śukoh, whom passions have left[3], from whom the load of afflictions has vanished, now expounds: "After having recognised the reality of all reality, and after having understood the meaning of the real doctrine of the One Self and obtained the immense grace of the Blissful One[4], may I now reach the final goal, immersed in my Self, in the contemplation of the thoughts of the Perfect Ones who decide and speak of the Veda, men of a line without beginning." And then: "I attained peace along with other altogether perfect Vedic seers, especially in nearness to the true guru, an image of the form itself of spirituality and of knowledge, Bābā Lāl[5], who by the Lord, has attained the utmost of askesis, of knowledge, of the fruit of right understanding, and with him I met and conversed frequently. I perceived no difference, except in the terminology, regarding the realisation of one's own form (*svarūpa*).[6] And so I expressed both in the same way. And then I collected numerous fruitful expositions to be known by those who are engaged in the realisation of the Real. And here, under the name of a 'reunion' of the two oceans of the doctrines of the two upholders of knowledge, I established the *Samudrasaṅgama* (the Meeting of the Oceans)".

"And in this way, without doubt, the information on the great obvious truths, the discrimination of realities, when it is untouched by jealousy, becomes the means for the attainment of the ultimate ends of all Knowledge.[7] Therefore, whoever possesses discrimination and knowledge is aware of the kind of difficulty that exists in regard to the level of the determination of Reality. Undoubtedly the scholars and those who have the knowledge will realise much more in terms of happiness; they shall attain nothing, the dull minds who declare that these (oceans) are separate. After having confirmed the sense of the Reality in accordance with my own direct perception (*anubhava*), this enterprise was fulfilled out of sympathy for my own household.

Two kinds of ignorant people clinging onto the distinctness of the doctrines, I do not yet possess the means of giving them understanding."

"And besides, the great man with the truly pure heart, and named Khvājai Ahrar[8], thought likewise: 'If I can know someone, whether he be an atheist or from a place spoken of in a fairytale, who declares the truth about Reality in words that enthuse the spirit (*mano'nurañjakaśabdaiḥ*), I shall go there then, listen and become his disciple and I shall ally myself to him.'

'And down here, it is from the Supreme Lord that I draw my strength, it is the Supreme Lord who is my companion (*sahāya*).'

We notice a sustained concordance between the two Sanskrit and Persian versions but with a few differences that arise evidently because of the adaptation made for the milieu the author wished to address, milieus that were culturally different but which he wanted to bring together.

In his entire work, Dārā quotes verses from the Koran which are translated into Sanskrit in the *Samudrasaṅgama*. In the Persian version he gives the equivalent Sanskrit terms for the Arabic-Persian expressions not only from Sufism but from the Koran itself, exactly as the Arabic-Persian terms corresponding to the Sanskrit are given in the Sanskrit version, phonetically transcribed. We have, therefore, in both the places, the authentic forms of the words and their respective equivalents. This sometimes allows us to suggest useful corrections. For instance, a numerical name in an Indian language, appearing under the same form in the various manuscripts of *Majma-'al-Baḥraīn*, has bothered the translators of this text. It is spelt *anj*. Mahfuz-ul-Haq has not suggested, as he usually does, a Sanskrit restoration of the word. Daryush Shayegan has offered various explanatory conjectures. But in the Sanskrit text we have *abja* which means lotus and is equivalent for *padma* which has the same meaning, both signifying 10 billion in number. Roma Choudhuri has translated *abja* in the normal way without consulting the Persian text which we can now correct by simply shifting at the requisite place the point of the second Arabic letter and then reading it as *abj*.

Other comparisons of the two versions enable a reciprocal improvement of the Sanskrit edition as we have seen in the case of a translation of a quatrain by Jāmī. At times they too raise some questions regarding the competence of the author or the editor of one or the other text.

In certain cases, Dārā indicates some trivial correspondences between Persian and Indian data: the knowledge of cardinal points or of stars is found on either side without making that significant in any way and it is important only for the correspondence in the vocabulary. Besides, we find the Persian side to be in the wrong on this point (if the text is truly the original one and if its translations are accurate).

In Section XV which deals with the skies (*āsmānhā* corresponding to the Sanskrit *gagana*) the Persian text says that the seven planets are called *nicchattar* in Indian languages which is wrong as the *nakṣatras* are the 27 or 28 fixed constellations which mark the course of the planets and the Sanskrit version, on the other hand, is totally correct. It does not, therefore, translate the wrong Persian wording or, more probably, the Persian wording distorted in the traditional manuscript.

The translators of the two texts have discussed extensively the statements of Dārā, less in relation to the Arabic and Persian texts which are cited than in relation to the classical Indian teachings to which Dārā himself refers or seems to refer. The views of the different philosophical Sanskrit schools were raised by Roma Choudhuri and by Shayegan who also set out the Buddhist viewpoints (outdated then) and utilised to a great extent and rightly too, mainly the *Upaniṣads*, including some later ones which happened to be well-known during Dārā's time.

Now that we have both the versions together and on the Indian side, a whole lot of new documentation as well, we can try to deepen our studies on the sources of Dārā and to rightly ascertain the real value of his effort.

While welcoming the inclusion of *Majma-'al-Baḥraīn* in the Bibliotheca Indica, Johan van Manen, then secretary of the Asiatic Society of Bengal, wrote that 'the purely artificial individual endeavours of an Akbar and a Dārā Sukoh to introduce Hindu thought and speculation into Persian literature have remained almost completely isolated and sterile.'[9] It would be impossible to uphold such a view after a scrutiny of the texts today. First of all, nothing shows that Dārā wanted to introduce Indian thought into 'Persian literature'. He wanted to find a certain convergence of the theological conceptions and aspirations quickening the two vast communities that were distinct but coexisting, of the spiritual seekers practicing the same ideal of rejection of all worldly attachment in order to realise the One God. Moreover Dārā was not isolated, he simply aided the movement of a spiritual coming-together and of general cultural exchanges (notably in science) which had existed before him,—quite independently from the short-lived endeavour of Akbar—, and which have continued up to our day, even though the multitudes were never so inclined towards any kind of ecumenism and which, in fact, was never proposed to them.

A scrutiny of the terminology itself employed to show equivalences between technical Islamic terms (and not merely *sufi*) and Indian terms is revelatory of the care taken to establish this terminology and we can discover quite a number of elements far away from Dārā and from Delhi in the whole of India.

We shall mention here only a few important terms.

Muhammad is designated in Sanskrit in the introduction of the *Samudrasaṅgama* as *paramaprakāśaprakāśakaḥ*, 'the illuminer of the supreme light', *jagatsṛṣṭinimittaḥ* 'the cause (or sign or causal manifestation) of the world',[10] *asmākaṃ siddhānāṃ siddhaḥ*, 'the Perfect among our Perfect Ones', 'favoured' and 'shaped' *satkrta* and *sanmātita*, by *Parameśvara*, the Supreme Lord, God.

Among these expressions, *asmākāṃ siddhānāṃ siddhaḥ* is the most remarkable. *Siddha* signifies 'Perfect' and particularly 'he who has succeeded' but it is not a common term. It designates in Sanskrit and in most Indian languages, more precisely someone who possesses extraordinary powers, the *siddhis*. *Siddhi* is 'success' but, par excellence, the success which is the highest of all on a spiritual plane. The acquisition of extraordinary powers such as levitation, metamorphosis, or of the realisation of all desires may be a stage in elevation above the human condition—the saints perform miracles—and this acquisition of powers may be sought by the psychosomatic exercises of yoga, but it is not the ultimate goal, the ultimate goal remains the integral knowledge of the ontological reality, God, through direct experience.

However, Dārā uses the word *siddha* freely in his text, either to designate the Prophet as we have seen or to speak of the Indians whose teachings he refers to.

In order to designate the Prophet, he uses it in the same form signifying 'the Perfect One among the Perfect' in Section I (Skr.

ed., p. 2, 1.7) or *siddhānāṃ siddhasya tattvam*, 'The Reality of the Perfect One among the Perfects' echoing *haqīqat-ī-Mohammadī*, the 'Mohammedan Reality' and also under the equivalent form of *paramasiddha* 'the supreme Perfect One'. Here is the entire passage in Sanskrit:

Cidākāśāt prathaman ⟨⟨iṣk⟩⟩ iti padārthaḥ abhūt sa vaidikamunibhir māyety ucyate | yad āha paramasiddho bhagavadvākyam ahaṃ guptākāraḥ sthitas tataḥ prasiddhaḥ syām itīcchayā sṛṣṭiṃ kṛtavān iti | tasya māyāyāḥ sakāśāt jīvātmā prādur babhūva | sa eva siddhānāṃ siddhasya tattvam iti vadanti |

'Out of the spiritual space was first born the thing that is called *iṣk* ('Love'). It is called illusion (*māyā*) by the Vedic sages. The utterance of the Blissful One (God) brought down by the Supreme Perfect One (the Prophet) : "I was a hidden treasure, then by desire (*icchā*) saying 'May I be known!' I effected the creation."

In the presence of this illusion there appeared the living Self (*jīvātman*). He it is who is known to be the Reality of the Perfect One among the Perfects.'

It is not only the Prophet who is designated as *siddha*, *siddhatva* means prophecy. The Section XII in Persian deals with *Nubuwwat wa Walāyat* which in Sanskrit is *siddhatva-ṛṣīśvaratva*, 'the fact of being a Perfect One and the fact of being a lord among the seers', the *ṛṣis* or 'seers' being the Vedic authors and the *ṛṣīśvaras* having been introduced already in the preceding section as the equivalent of the *Walis* of the Islamic tradition.[11] Islamic tradition itself is called in Sanskrit in the *Samudrasaṅgama, asmadveda*, 'our Veda', that is our 'knowledge'; it is obviously to suggest Koran as a symmetrical counterpart to the Sacred Book of Brahmanic India. The Vedic authors or the venerated sages are often called in our texts *munis*, but the most common word to designate the Indians whose ideas Dārā wanted to make known is still *siddha*. He has in fact quoted it in Indian languages in *Talks at Lahore* (16 and 35), under the form of *siddh* which, as pointed out by La Vallée Poussin to Massignon, was connected to *siddhi* as well as to *siddha* (J.A. 1926, p. 318, n. 1) but it was used to designate the supreme level of Being and was represented by the syllable *OṂ* (35).

Whereas about the senses (*ḥawās, indriya*) in Section II, Dārā correlates the senses with the elements to which they are applied. He says notably according to the Sanskrit text:

śravaṇendriyaṃ bhūtākāśaśabdagrāhakatvāt | anāhataśabda-śravaṇadvārā ca siddhānāṃ cidākāśatattvaṃ prakaṭaṃ jāyate siddhair vinānyair jñātum aśakyatvāt | idaṃ śravaṇarūpaṃ dhyānam asmadīyānāṃ siddhānāṃ ca sādhāraṇam eva | idaṃ ca dhyānam asmadekātmavādino nirantaraśravaṇam iti vadanti | tad eva siddhair dhvanir ity ucyate |.

'The faculty of audition depends on the fact of perceiving the sound of the material space. As for the reality of the spiritual space, thanks to the audition of the uncaused sound, it becomes evident to the *siddhas*, none else besides the *siddhas* can know it. And this meditation in the guise of audition is common to our *siddhas*. And our monists say that this meditation is the audition of the Eternal. This is what is called *dhvani* (resonance) by the *siddhas*.' (cf. Shayegan, p. 30)

It is indeed *oṃ* that is the uninterrupted sound produced by no impact of any instrument or body whatsoever, the sound of the ocean, that which we hear within caves or inside sea-shells, the uncreated sound, without beginning or end, the heard image of eternity.

And we know thereby who the siddhas really are and that they are monists like the sufis ('our own siddhas') as opposed to the ordinary followers of Islam who are theologically monotheistic but philosophically dualistic since they distinguish God from His creation.

Besides, classical Indology which, outside the general Brahmanic literature, has mainly studied classical Sanskrit philosophy as well as Buddhism and its philosophies, does not yet know much about the *siddhas*, even though their presence in all forms of Indian spirituality and their literature is quite considerable.

In Sanskrit texts we find them mentioned mainly among the trains of attendants of Śiva in his manifestation on Mount Kailāsa. They are depicted in iconography as anonymous amidst the flying genii. We know of 84 *mahāsiddhas* who are sometimes called the 'great sorcerers' in Buddhist literature. They are qualified as 'Tantrics' and they do appear also in the Śaiva and

Vaiṣṇava Tantras, that is in the technical texts of religious practice, but of science as well: medecine, astronomy, alchemy even magic.

They are, in any case, those who have 'succeeded', those who have attained perfect knowledge. Dārā terms *siddhas* not only those who have attained the supreme knowledge but also the specialists of cosmography and cosmology, for instance. The general Indian culture did lead one to this knowledge since the spiritual seekers in India who make use of Yoga, in particular, are considered to be those who realise the Truth in all its forms. As a matter of fact, texts on astronomy are usually called *siddhānta* which literally means 'established end, conclusion', but Dārā read in it 'the ultimate (science) of the *siddhas*' as we have in the Vedānta, 'the ultimate in Veda'.

Nevertheless, the *siddhas* who are attributed with the teachings and works are from the whole of South Asia. The most well-known are from Nepal, Matsyendranātha and Gorakṣanātha, who are considered to be originally from Nepal but whose diverse teachings are known right up to South India, in Karnāṭaka and Tamilnāḍu. The different languages of the texts that are ascribed to them or which they make use of are: Sanskrit, apabrahṃśa, old Hindi, old Bengali, other regional languages and mainly Tamil and Kannaḍa in the South. The Sanskrit texts which express their ideas are themselves very varied. The most ancient Sanskrit sources from which they draw inspiration are the *Upaniṣads*, *Upaniṣads* from all the periods, such as those that Dārā translated in *Sirr-i-Akbar*. Shayegan was justified in quoting in his commentary certain *Upaniṣads* said to be of *yoga*, since *yoga* is especially important for the *siddhas*, as it leads to the worldly *siddhis* but also enables us to realise by virtue of detachment (*vairāgya*) supreme knowledge.

However, the *sufis* do not use yoga and regulated psychological exercises to the same extent. They were familiar with them. They translated texts on yoga into Persian but the *Majma-'al-Baḥraīn* does not go beyond the concepts and the knowledge of God, of the world and of man. Translators of Dārā have sought for the Indian sources of his writings in the Vedānta. And these are mainly in Sanskrit.

But the major part of the texts of the *siddhas* known today are in fact in Tamil and in Kannaḍa although they are closely linked to the general Sanskrit tradition.

In Tamil the *Tirumantiram* of Tirumūlar contains more than 3000 quatrains; in Kannaḍa, the work of Allamaprabhu which has just been edited and translated into English, comprises four fat volumes.

Similar works, philosophical and devotional at the same time, are from the *siddhānta*[12], 'The Utmost Limit of the Perfect One', which extends and surpasses the ancient Vedānta, 'The Utmost Limit or Knowledge'.

It was believed in the last century that the Tamil *siddhas* (*cittar*) must have been influenced by Christianity and Islam. They were influenced by Islam because some of them were alchemists and that the name itself for alchemy is of Arabic origin (no precise reason was given). They were influenced by Christianity according to Bishop Caldwell who was an excellent Tamil scholar and linguist (he initiated the comparative grammar of Dravidian languages) but was insufficiently familiar with the spiritual aspects of Indian religions. He was struck by monotheism and the strong devotion in the poems of the *siddha* Koṅkaṉar. On noticing that this name apparently designated someone from the Konkan, the region of Goa, he thought that he had picked up monotheism from the Portuguese. He was unaware that the Indian monotheism, despite the multiplicity of secondary *devas*, dates back to the Veda and is above all the essential doctrine of the *siddhas*. Unfortunately Caldwell's opinion was re-echoed for a hundred years in a good number of manuals. It fitted in with the idea that the Dravidians formed a race apart that was civilised by the Aryans and remained dependent on Aryan and Sanskrit literature of the North. But when one is astonished to find in South India a religious evolution of a Pan-Indian nature, it is because one forgets that the five principal Sanskrit authors of the commentaries on the Vedānta, starting with Śaṃkarācārya, were all Dravidians.

In fact, the devotional movements, founded on a transcendent spiritual experience and on psychosomatic technique, are not based on race but are Pan-Indian and even simply human. They are akin, in truth, not only to Sufism but to all the spiritual movements of the world which at their height are the same. The surrender of one's self in God is as ardent in Mme. Guyon or Fénelon as it is in the *siddhas* or the *sufis*.

It is evident that in the milieus as that of Dārā, reciprocal influences were possible but they are not necessary; Dārā's work draws parallels and convergences, it does not imply a pre-existing syncretism.

The spread of the movements of the *siddhas* is well anterior to Islam, but it does not seem to have touched the ancient *sufis*. We have a biography, or rather a collection of anecdotes on the Life of Abu Saïd. It is attributed to one of his relatives, Monawar, and it has been recently translated into French by Muhammad Achena. It seems that Abu Saïd developed in Khorassan an important Sufi movement in the 12th century, which spread during the time of the Islamisation of Afghanistan into several cities of the region, notably in Cist from which we have the famous Sufi order of the *ciṣṭis* in India. But one perceives nothing in the tradition of Abu Saïd which reveals an Indian influence. In the whole book India is mentioned only once regarding some object that was so hard that it could be cut only with an Indian sabre. It is a recognition of the Indian metallurgical science, not of its spiritual culture.

The psychosomatic techniques of the *sufis* and the *siddhas* are identical in goal and regarding certain effects but they differ on the essentials. Abu Saïd made his dervishes dance whereas Jalaluddin Rūmī made them turn around. The Indians do yoga. However the sessions of what is called *bhajans* consist incidentally in going round and whirling which could be compared to the turning dervishes, and yoga is not unknown to all Muslims. But what is truly common to the *sufis* and the *siddhas* is the rejection of the ego out of this phenomenal world and the offering of all one's being to the sempiternal stability which is God. This is what is expressed in some Persian verses quoted without any reference by Dārā[13] and which might be by Him. Here is the translation based on the Sanskrit version:

yad rūpaṃ svasvarūpaṃ pradarśya ceto harati /
tat kālas tvaddṛṣṭer dūraṃ nayati /
ata manas tatra deyaṃ yat tava saṅge sthitaṃ vartate sthāsyati ca /

'All representation that having appeared as a representation in itself, ravishes the thought, is carried by Time out of thy sight. Thus, your heart is to be offered there where what is immutable in your company is present and will remain immutable.'

NOTES

1. A quatrain by Nūruddin Abdurrahman Jāmī (born 1414) quoted by Dārā. Jatindra Bimal Chaudhuri reads *śayanam* 'couch' and *tacchayaḥ* which do not mean anything. Roma Chaudhuri, therefore, considers the text to be altered but the Ms. carries *śapanam* 'oath' and *tacchapaḥ* 'oath on him' which conveys the original well. However, the meaning in Sanskrit would be: 'The oath of the Lord is much more: his oath is All.' Such an interpretation would be forced, even inappropriate, for the original Persian text but it would be in harmony with Indian ideas according to which God (in the Veda, Prajāpati, elsewhere Śiva or Viṣṇu) not wanting to remain alone creates the universe by His Word which is the starting point of the cosmic realisation.
2. Or 'of the sign (*nimitta*) of the emanation of the world'. *Nimitta* is mostly 'presage', a sign of what will necessarily happen, from which we use it for 'cause'.
3. Vītarāga which translates *faqir* from the Persian text.
4. Literally: the great serenity in the Blissful One (God) called Bhagavant, 'The Blissful One' by the Vaiṣṇavas such as Bābā Lāl. At the end of the *S. Saṅg.* in a passage that does not have a Persian counterpart and which corresponds to certain practices of Sanskrit poetry, the research-work of the data which constitute the subject-matter of the work is compared to the churning of the ocean which Viṣṇu carried out in order to extract ambrosia; the spirit of Dārā is, therefore, compared to Viṣṇu himself.
5. Bābā Lāl is not mentioned in the Persian version at this point but he is mentioned elsewhere at the end of the section 12 where the Sanskrit version does not speak of him.
6. Of the real Essence.
7. Sakalavedāṃtānāṃ prayojanam, that is the final revelations of the Veda, i.e. *Vedānta* (For Dārā, Vedānta consists above all in the *Upaniṣads* of which 52 have been translated under the title of *Sirr-i-Akbar*).
8. From Samarkand at the beginning of the 15th century. (born in 806 of the hegira). The spelling *ṣvājai* in the Sanskrit text results from the common equivalence in Sanskrit between *ṣa* and *kha* (cf. *Upanikhat, Oupnekhat* used by Anquetil for *Upaniṣad*).
9. *Majma-'al-Bahrain*, p. v.
10. Shayegan: 'cause of the existentiation of the universe'.
11. At the end of the section II, the *M.a.B.* writes *rikhi* for *ṛṣi* which corresponds to the common equivalence in North India between *ṣa* and *kha*. At the same place the *Sam.sang.* calls the *nabī siddha* and according to the two translations, the M. a-B. would call it *Mahasudh* which would correspond to *mahāśuddha*. But the Persian text writes this word with a

ḍammah which signifies *u*, p. 99, 1.14. But as we would expect a *kasrah* below the letter instead of a *ḍammah* on top and in that case we will have *mahāsidh* which means 'the great siddha' and is a common term, we can suggest this correction.

12. The obvious designation of the Śaiva form of the *siddhānta*: *śaivasiddhānta* appears in the Rājasiṃha inscription of the Kailāsanātha temple at Kāñcipuram (end of 7th century) where the king is called śaivasiddhānta-mārge śrīmān atyantakāmah, 'the Fortunate One moved by a transcendent desire on the path of the śaivasiddhānta'. (although R. Nagaswamy, *New Light on Mamallapuram.* The Archaeological Society of South India, Silver Jubilee Volume, 1962, p. 23 has translated *atyantakāma* as 'of unlimited fancies' by neglecting *śaivasiddhāntamārge*). But the *siddhas* and the *siddhānta* are as much respected by the Vaiṣṇavas as by the Śaivas (cf. *Ahirbudhnyasaṃhitā* XV, 14) as also by the Jains.
13. Section XII, Persian ed. p. 100, Sanskrit ed. pp. 9, ll, 14-15.

CHAPTER 15

INDIAN RELIGIONS AND THE PSYCHOLOGY OF THEIR HISTORIANS*

The current portrayals of Indian religions by present-day scientific research depend, like all portrayal, on the observed facts as well as on the psychology of the observer. Now, because of the vast range of sources of information in India, written sources from all periods or oral ones of today, an exhaustive observation of Indian religions escapes all their historians. To make up for the lack of access to data these historians are often led to making conjectures. This is specially the case when they are strangers not only to these religions but to India itself. This can also happen when they are Indian and accept the classical views of international Indology.

In these conditions the subjective element which infiltrates into the portrayals of Indian religious thought and practice is considerable. It can be harmful to their validity. It is, therefore, important to ask oneself about the personal equation of the Indologists who look into, describe and judge the religions of India and about the background of the ideas that are formed on them.

It is necessary for this to first refer to the time of the European discovery of Indian societies and their beliefs, that is to say to the 17th century and particularly to the 18th. In fact, some of the opinions of this period continue to persist, having been unanimously acknowledged as fundamental and definitive. They become then indispensable data, in some set-ups of Indian beliefs that are still put forth and no more subject to a fresh critical evaluation.

The first European attempts at understanding and describing Indian religions were made by some travellers, but essentially by Christian missionaries: Jesuits, Friars, priests of Foreign

*Les religions de l'Inde et la psyhologie de leurs historiens, in *Journal de pshchologie*, no. 2-3, 1980, pp. 133-49.

Missions, evangelic Lutherans, etc. Some like the Jesuit Roberto de Nobili and the Lutheran Abraham Roger in the 17th century, or the Jesuits Pons, Calmette and Coeurdoux in the 18th century, had the knowledge of the monotheistic characteristic of the main Indian theologies. Because of the large number of secondary divine forms about which legends abound, the Indians were considered by most of them as well as the Muslims to be pagan, polytheistic and idolatrous, bound only to superstition. In spite of the discovery at the end of 18th century of the *Upaniṣads* by Anquetil-Duperron and of the *Bhāgavadgītā* by Charles Wilkins, the East India Company, interested in taking upon itself the duty of governing the Indians in order to lift them out of ignorance, favoured or decided itself to publish two works on the Indians, the first a Protestant work by the Rev. Ward, the other, Catholic, by Abbé Dubois. Ward clearly depreciated Indian thought, and even denied the existence of a rational Indian philosophy. Dubois, less negative, accepted the existence of such a philosophy in ancient times, but believed it was now corrupt. Similar judgments no more hold, but they have influenced these studies for long. In 1839, in spite of the earlier works by Colebrooke Barthélemy Saint-Hilaire[1] while translating and commenting on a classical treatise of Indian logic, strove to depreciate it in relation to the Aristotelean logic, which, he was translating alongside. At the beginning of this century, one of our most illustrious Indologists, Louis de la Vallée Poussin, while making an admirable study of some of the Indian philosophies, described them only as 'philosophoumena'. My own guru, Sylvain Lévi, thought that the Indian mind, unlike our own, did not recognise the principle of contradiction. In fact it is quite common to catch thinkers blatantly contradicting themselves, but this is not peculiar only to India. Now, in Indian philosophies, when it is stated that something is at the same time real and unreal, it is, in general, in relation to different views of reality, or to uphold the ontological emptiness of representations. And Sylvain Lévi rightly affirmed that apart from this one exception, which he acknowledged, the Indian mind proceeded in the same way as ours. He knew also, and he demonstrated, that the most abstruse of philosophic conceptions could pass without alteration from one linguistic structure into another that is altogether different. It is the case of philosophical Sanskrit texts which have been translated into Tibetan with such rigour that often it has been possible to restore the original Sanskrit text from the sole extant Tibetan version and the exactitude of this restoration was confirmed by the later discovery of the original.

But this demands the use of a conventional vocabulary, where the word in the translation is taken as the mechanically employed substitute on the translated word. So the translation reproduces the original without explaining it. The problem of the interpretation of the concept expressed in the translation is referred back to the interpretation of the original. There is no passing from a traditional system of conceptual references to a foreign system, European or American, in the case of the present international study of Indian religions. This explains the difficulty of translators and of the readers of these translations. This also explains the ever existent prejudice about the heterogeneity of the 'oriental' and the 'western' mind.

This prejudice goes back at least to the 18th century and to a period when, it was, however, rightly challenged. The Jesuit missionaries, who strove at that time to preach Christianity among the Siamese Buddhists, were struck by the latter's frequent refusal to believe their reasonings and to accept their propositions which, to the missionaries, who were Christian and French, contained an obvious truth. They sought help from abbé de Fleury who, as the author of *L'Histoire ecclésiastique*, had the opportunity to study the conditions of Christian preaching and of its success among the pagans of Antiquity. They published his reply at the end of the Lyon edition (1819) of the *Lettres édifiantes*.

Fleury adviced them to verify whether in geometry the Siamese agreed with the same demonstration as they. He added that if they did not agree with the philosophical arguments we placed before them, one must ask oneself whether these arguments did not rest upon a prejudice. Fleury's observation is still pertinent, but everyone is not familiar with it. Some continue to believe that the ideas they have received, that is to say those which they do not question, are the fruit of ineluctable logic, that the ideas of foreign religions which oppose it, Indian in our case, are absurd. But, at present more often, others believe that the ideas, either in the texts or in the statements of the reporters, of which they cannot follow the line of thought nor understand the reasonings, are not in themselves absurd but arise from a social mentality peculiar to the people who profess them, or even from an aboriginal substratum which might be covered up by the historic culture of these peoples. They generally stress the fact, that in these conditions, one cannot understand them in the light of one's own ideas, but still they never hesitate to compliment themselves on explaining them on their own.

As a matter of fact, when we deal with speculation and beliefs, speech by itself never expresses the thought completely. It presupposes, in the listener, the general culture of the one who speaks. It suggests ideas in relation to this implicit culture which serves as an echo-chamber without which the isolated sound, lacking its own environment, loses its natural range.

Whether one is a philologist working on written sources, ancient or present, or a collector of oral information, which is limited to the present, one should above all, be familiar with the education of the authors one is reading and the interpreters one listens to, and moreover be prepared, in the case of the latter, for a possible incomprehension on their part of the questions as well as their desire to satisfy the researcher who is often interested not in observing the reality but in verifying his working hypothesis.

Knowledge of Indian religions, therefore, demands caution when the data comes from translators who are merely grammarians, from philosophers working only on translations of major texts, and from field-researchers using only English or a very elementary form of the local language. Even the missionaries who speak or even write these languages currently have often missed the real understanding of Indian religions, for want of having studied the entire range of culture of those who give it expression in their rich literature, in their symbolic monuments and their explained iconographies.

As for the professional Indologists, they were, very early on divided into two categories on the basis of their methods of research. Everyone has considered the study of Sanskrit necessary, but one group asserted that it had to be learnt from the contemporary men of Letters, the pandits, who had mastery of the language as well as of the culture of which Sanskrit was the instrument. The others have challenged the teaching by the pandits,[2] especially their personal interpretations of vocabulary in the most ancient texts, the Vedas. The comparative grammar of Sanskrit and the classical languages, ignored by the pandits, offered in fact valuable information on the linguistic and even cultural pre-history of India.

The analysis, in fact, of Sanskrit which the ancient Indian grammarians had made served, at first, as a model for a new analysis of the classical languages, but a comparison of Sanskrit with these soon served at arriving at a more general linguistic interpretation than the one of the Sanskrit tradition.

Jointly with comparative grammar, comparative mythology has rapidly become a basic means of enquiry into Vedic religion, and, in the renewal which it has enjoyed today in the works of Georges Dumézil, it has continued to gain in importance. But it concerns the pre-history of the proto-history of the historic Indian civilisation, not the latter directly, even when it uncovers traces of the Indo-iranian or Indo-european past in the legendary medieval or even modern data.

The religions of India have been able to preserve quite a good number of features of their lost pre-history, but what formed and evolved these religions is the mass of conscious and classically taught ideas which India has effectively conceived and developed in the course of history, and it is these living ideas that India has propagated in the entire range of its cultural expansion from east Iran to Japan and Indonesia.

Now, if the Veda, especially the Ṛgveda, could, in fact, only be understood thanks to Sāyaṇa's commentary which is as recent as the 14th century A.D., but which explains quite a few unknown archaic grammatical forms of classical Sanskrit ignored by the grammatical tradition of Pāṇini, this commentary was and still is often neglected for being too late to have been able to conserve the original religious sense of the text. Bergaigne who only wished to make an analytical inventory of the Ṛgveda and who did it admirably, asserted that he had ignored Sāyaṇa. The last complete translation of the text, by Geldner, made use of it, but in a general manner, the data of the historical tradition were left out in favour of hypotheses based on the tendencies that were successively in vogue in the modern science of religions. Even the use of hymns in the ancient ritual has often been overlooked, as has been recently pointed out by the present master of Vedic studies, J. Gonda, who rightly explains this lacuna in research to be due to specialisation.[3] That is why the use of Vedic texts in the popular Indian rituals today, as those related to the planets, has passed off unnoticed[4] till today in the same way as other uses of Vedic texts in the rituals of potters.[5] However these uses appear today as facts which, along many others that were ignored for two long, invalidate one of the most popular prejudices, even today, about the religions of India.

Many believe that everything is religious in India, that the whole of life, in all its details, is ruled by religion, that astronomy, medicine and even technology are of religious origin, and particularly that the social state and law are regulated by a religion based on mythology. If it were so, life in India would have been nothing but applied mythology.

This idea of the universality of a religious presence in all things in India goes back again to the missionaries who saw in the 17th and 18th centuries, a period in which the existence and the distinct nature of India became known, religious superstition in all the acts of the 'pagans'. And there followed the famous quarrel over the 'malabar rites' during which the daily custom of bath in India had to be defended by justifying the act as a hygienic and not a religious practice.[6]

It is true that the practices of the adherents of Śaivism as of Vaiṣṇavism prescribe also the repetition of religious formulae even during the most common activities of life and that naturally this may have affected the minds of the observers.[7]

In reality, the reason for this practice is psychotechnical in nature and not in the least superstitious at its roots. When one accepts the general theory of the psychic functioning which is common to the whole of Indian culture, and consequently to all the religions of the country and even of the whole of oriental Asia, we believe that the psychic individuality forms a subtle body in the material one, which does not die with the latter, but, surviving it, tends to reincarnate in a new body.

This subtle body, or psychic individuality, is formed through the simple play of the psychic process itself. Every state of consciousness, even though transitory, is an act (*karman*) which leaves in the psychic individuality an active imprint, a *vāsanā*, literally a 'perfuming', and these active imprints organise themselves through an affinity of nature into more complex 'constructions', the *saṃskāras*. The Indian philosophers speculated since ancient times to find out if the individuality thus fashioned by conscious acts had, as basis, a self (*ātman*), constituting the nucleus of its existence into which the 'perfumings' would accumulate and in which the unconscious 'constructions' would be stored, or whether the individuality was only an aggregate of the elements which constituted it, even as a car is an assembly of parts and possesses an individuality without being a person and without having a self or a soul. In other words, the psychologists, in India as elsewhere, are divided between spiritualists and materialists in their metaphysical conceptions, but generally they agree upon the mechanism of the formation of the psychism. The common conception they have of its functioning is the learned explanation of the theory of transmigration: one transmigrates according to the automatic tendencies and urges which result from consciously accomplished acts.

From this standpoint it is possible to mould oneself, by means of a constant vigilance, one's unconscious psychic individuality according to an ideal model, and thereby prevent the intrusion of undesirable elements into the psychic individuality. This explains the detailed prescriptions given to those who aspire to be constantly turned in all their being towards the divinity. So these prescriptions are evidently used for religious ends, but they are in themselves simple means of psychotechnical realisation. They do not nourish the mysterious superstitions of primitive people and in them there is no clear presence of a hypothetical aboriginal substratum which would go back to pre-history.

Besides, the psychological theory in question and the doctrine of action, *karman*, and of transmigration, do not appear in the earliest times, but only during the period of development of the rational theories of scientific Indian medicine.[8] But the notion of *karman* persists in the popular mind of India and in countries that were brahmanised or became Buddhist, as an established fact whose origin one does not question. The modern oral investigations have, therefore, not revealed to foreigners the origin and the theoretical reasons for the practices and beliefs. On its part, the study of philosophical and technical texts began establishing a translator's vocabulary since the beginning of the 19th century, at a time when the unconscious or subsconscious psychic life was still unknown to European psychology which was then purely intellectualist. The Indian ideas on the unconscious were also not understood, and the dictionaries explaining Sanskrit in European languages, having been practically completed since 1875,[9] could not correctly interpret the technical terms of Indian psychology expressed in Sanskrit. Now, these dictionaries determined and popularised a host of equivalences of terms, accepted but not always exact, between European and Indian languages, Sanskrit and the others. The glossaries of a hundred years ago have fixed the representations of Indian notions into conceptions of that time.

It is only today and rather slowly too, that a more adequate knowledge of the real Indian ideas on the unconscious psychism and the psychic functioning are being developed. Not only does seem to be retarded by the lexicographical conservatism, but some historians still continue to reason on the religious conceptions of Indians by considering only the specific speculations of metaphysics and of soteriology which their schools evolved. Now, the Indian authors always expected their readers to be familiar with the psychological views that belong to the general classical culture of their country and to know this culture completely. They were not strictly specialised in metaphysics; they too were Indians like the others.

In order to fully understand philosophers such as Śaṅkara or Rāmānuja, to mention only the ones that are most commonly studied, it is not sufficient to analyse, as with European philosophers, only the texts of their specific doctrines; one must also possess the full knowledge which, by virtue of the classical education that everyone followed, formed their minds. It is this knowledge, along with the prejudices it involves that, in their statements, are briefly alluded to, or even remain latent, but they are not any less real component of the ideas formulated in these statements. Everywhere, these expositions are dominated by a grammar[10] which is not only pragmatic but also speculative and by a formal logic, both rigorous and compulsorily studied. The specialisation in the study of different philosophical viewpoints comes into picture only secondarily. But the conceptions related to the universe and related to life with their elementary data of astronomy and medicine, belong to the general common culture.

A misunderstanding of this culture has often been responsible for the incomprehension of Indian arguments, and has led the historians to believe that Indians opined rather by intuition than by reason.

One has deemed their thought to be illogical, but this is due to a lack of knowledge of the in-built models which could have, in fact, lent logical substance and form to their theses. Now, among them, logic was not only an intellectual exercise limited to a few specialists. As a compulsory subject in the classical studies, as we have already remarked, it constituted, as a system of the correct arrangement of the expressions of these concepts and their relations, the framework of the statement and of discussion of any kind of knowledge. We find it to be a part of the teaching in one of the principal manuals of medicine of the beginnings of our era, the *Carakasaṃhitā*, in its most anciently known developed form, but which presupposes that it was used metaphysically and eschatologically previously, because one typical example of reasoning given there is the proof of the existence of the self (*ātman*) as the ontological substratum of the individual psychic being (*sattva*). This demonstration itself has become classical, and all the great Indian religions, Buddhist, Jain, as well as Brahmanic never ceased to explore and discuss among themselves the logical basis of their faith.

With increasing frequency modern students seem to take up for study the Indian schools of logic and their teeming literature, which went beyond India, having been partially translated into Chinese, Japanese and Tibetan. But very few have worked on the school which from the standpoint of the complexity of the problems and their rigourous treatment, has gone furthest, i.e. the *Navyanyāya* or the 'New logic', founded by Gaṅgeśa in the 13th century in the North-East of India. Many historians leave the study of the rational foundations of Indian religions to a small number of specialists and restrict the field of their investigations to ancient data, to socio-economic aspects and to comparisons. But this comparative study is often limited to a mere juxtaposition of data pertaining to a same theme in different civilisations. The specialists of each field willingly meet but without an interchange of their knowledge at a deeper level.

In such a situation, the following sketch of the religions of India is given in manuals of classical Indology:

'The Vedic religion, in ancient Sanskrit, was heir to the Indo-European religion, which was also prehistoric, the Vedic religion belonging to a less ancient layer. It is that of the Aryans. In India the Aryans met with peoples who spoke foreign languages: the Mundas without any script and the Dravidians using scripts of Aryan origin and influenced by Sanskrit culture. But the Aryans, Mundas, and Dravidians were all influenced by a central Asian and prehistoric (that is also hypothetical) shamanism.

All these contributions, inheritance and borrowings having intermingled in India, were taken into consideration by the Aryan class of Brahmins who created a unity of norms that gave society a structure.

'Structured by the Brahmins according to the activities necessary to its life, this society is dominated by religion, the Brahmins being the priests.

'The texts of this religion are *Śruti* or 'revelation', and *Smṛti* or 'tradition'. The first includes the *Vedas*, to which are linked the *Brāhmaṇas*, texts of ritualistic exegesis, as well as the *Āraṇyakas* and the *Upaniṣads* which are the *Vedānta* or 'culmination of the Veda'. As for the *Smṛti*, it contains the teachings of the structured system of Dharma which is the 'standard', that is at once cosmic, social and legal.

'The observance of the norms of *Smṛti* constitutes the Brahmanic orthodoxy.

'But in opposition to this orthodoxy there exist some movements that defy this Brahmanic society and its classes and castes. Such are Buddhism and Jainism, which have their own founder and Scriptures, but also 'tantrism' which has neither founder, nor any scriptural homogeneity.

'As to the term Hinduism, it means in Persian the religion of the 'hindus' (*Hindu* is the Persian form of the Sanskrit *Sindhu*) as opposed to the religion of the Muslims. We see here a collection of a multiplicity of sects, more or less heterodox, some relatively of a later date or even recent, which maintain links with the collections of legends known as the Epics and the Purāṇas or 'Antiquities', but which bring out the prehistoric and non-Aryan substrata.

'Hinduism deviates from the Brahmanic, and, even more so from the Vedic cult. It replaces the ancient ritual of sacrifice with a bloodless ritual of homage, pūjā. Or again it tends towards 'Tantrism', which uses formulae, symbolic characters, magical diagrams, psychosomatic practices of yoga, towards a tantrism which exists as a movement in Buddhism and Jainism, as well as in Hinduism. This movement has a predilection for the cult of the feminine Energy, Śakti, and for deliberately breaking the orthodox Brahmanic observances.

'Another trend in Hinduism, since the last century, has been an effort at a return to the Vedāntic sources and at an interpretation of the ancient Sanskrit culture, as a forerunner of the philosophical, religious and scientific thought of the modern western world.'

The general characteristic of this current representation of the Indian religions is that it perpetuates some of the prejudices which we indicated earlier, that it gives primacy to ancient sources to the detriment of those that trace the evolution till today, and that it favours the ethno-sociological speculations on the origin and structures rather than on the study of its evolution.

In fact, there are two present currents of ethno-sociological research on India: one, leaning towards the ancient period, which attempts to interpret the ancient sources in the light of the current philosophical and political theories, the other, modernist, which makes field enquiries.

The first plunges into pre-history and takes recourse to some working hypotheses, compares Indian data with those of other countries, ignores or challenges those of the medieval Indian tradition, but in the current observations it readily picks out those traits that are considered to be authentic remnants, since they suit the adopted hypothesis. The second, when it doesn't limit itself to mere description, is familiar only with a superficial pattern of tradition, but follows the results of the other movement or props it up with some working hypotheses. Both bring together protohistoric research and present ethnography, skipping the whole mass of intermediary traditional documentation. This last element, however, is essential. It is the expression of the psychology of the people of India since the post-Vedic development of Indian culture till today, and without a break throughout the period of its great expansion.

No doubt the survival of the ancient classical tradition through the centuries justifies its place in the first rank given to it by Indologists, but it doesn't authorise them to neglect the development and interpretations which the Indians have given to it in the successive centuries. These developments could be excessive, these interpretations could be erroneous, but they are historical realities of Indian psychology, effective realities which count more than the possible remnants of forgotten norms.

And if we take these realities into account, we can judge how far from them is the opinion of Indologists bound not to Indian tradition, but to their own, in the ideas we mentioned earlier.

Specialisation, although unavoidable because of the vast scope of Indian studies, hinders increasingly a global vision of data. One who is exclusively concerned with Vedism, with Buddhism, with Jainism or with a particular form of Hinduism will have very few opportunities to reflect on the complexity of the latter. Its literary and epigraphic sources are among the most abundant and, because of the diversity of the languages in which they are composed, they stretch the philological capacities of each of these languages. But it is these sources which governed and continue to govern the state of Hindu religion that has retained only some basic but pruned remnants of ancient Vedism and Brahmanism, has allowed a solid but side-lined Jainism to survive and has eliminated Buddhism altogether.

Now, apart from the sources of the general culture which we have already indicated, they include, specially on religion:

1. The *Mahābhārata* with the *Bhagavadgītā*, the *Rāmāyaṇa*, the *Purāṇas* (particularly the *Purāṇas* connected with the pilgrim centres, the *Māhātmyas*);

2. The *Dharmaśāstras* or *Smṛti* which conserve the norms of 'orthodoxy' and the *Subhāṣitas*, the 'well-said words' which spread the national wisdom as do the *Smṛtis*, but better than the latter;

3. The commentaries on the *Vedānta*;
4. Texts of devotion (*Bhakti*);
5. The *Tantras* or *Āgamas*.

The Tantras or Āgamas are still the sources that are most often ignored or held to be sectarian and heterodox and in any case expressing an altogether different religious movement. In reality, *tantra* simply means 'text' and is used in the scientific or technical literature only in that connotation. *Āgama* signifies 'tradition' and refers to the technical literature of religious practice. This literature comprises four sections presented together or separately: doctrine (*vidyā* or *jñāna*), ritual (*kārya*, including the construction of temples and the making of the images), conduct (*caryā*) and *yoga*. It is this literature which, from Kashmir and Nepal in the North to Śrī Laṅka in the South, regulates the public cult, with variations depending on the divine form chosen to be adored, within the temples and without; it also regulates the private cult and the life of the devotee. It is this which has regulated even the Śaiva and Vaiṣṇava practices in South-East Asia, in Cambodia, Campā, Java and Bali. Even in the country of Pali Buddhism, as in Thailand and Cambodia, where the Buddhist religion does not prescribe rules for state ceremonies, it is again *Āgama* that has governed the execution of these ceremonies.[11]

It is no doubt true that some Buddhist *tantras*, which are equivalent to the texts of the licentious gnostics of European Antiquity, do teach the violation of morality, but their reputation cannot be applied to the totality of the technical work of the *Tantras* and the *Āgamas*. It is in these texts that one must try to discover the psychology of the real Hindu religious practice of the majority, as also in the various literatures, be they Sanskrit or regional, which throw light on some aspect of this psychology.

In this regard, it is necessary to realise the profound unity of ideals and techniques which the diversity of languages had hidden from the specialists, to the extent that classical Indology has pictured religious India in such a way as to minimise the importance of its living evolving reality and delineate it only vaguely.

However this unity had already been felt, well before us, in the 17th century, and a Muslim thinker who was conscious of it, saw it not only among all spiritual seekers in India, but also among the Muslim spiritual seekers, the *sufis*. Prince Dārā Śukoh, eldest son of Shah Jahan and who would have been the 'Great Moghul' had his brother Aurangzeb not killed him in 1659 like his two other brothers. Prince Dārā Śukoh composed in Persian the *Majma-'al-Baḥraīn*, the 'confluence of two Oceans', with a Sanskrit counterpart, the *Samudrasaṅgama*, 'Meeting of Oceans'[12], which recognises in Hinduism the same monotheism and the same surrender in God as in Islam and specially among the *sufis*. He called the monotheist Indians *siddhas* in Sanskrit, which signifies 'the perfect ones', but essentially designates those who have attained, precisely by the observance of Tantric teachings, extraordinary powers, the *siddhis* or 'successes', but who have surpassed them by the acquisition of the knowledge of the Supreme Self beyond the workings of the ego, transcendent knowledge which is the supreme *siddhi*.

From our side, we should note that the notion of the one Being with multiple forms and names had already existed in the Veda (*Ṛgveda*, I, 164, 46) and in the *Brāhmaṇas* (Śat. Brāh. VI, 2, I, I), that its quest in oneself is justified by Vedāntic thought, favoured by the psychological mastery, the technique of which is regulated by *yoga*, and that success of this quest, the *siddhi*, is given by the Divine grace to devotion. So the *siddhi* is not only a magical achievement, it is a psychological state of being.

The *siddhas* are alchemists or magicians when they look for powers in this world, but devotees (*bhaktas*) and possessors of knowledge (*jñānin*) when they aspire for the transcendent reality.

The Sanskrit literatures which glorify them or which are attributed to their disciples are above all the *Tantras* or *Āgamas*, the texts of *Haṭhayoga* and the *Upaniṣads* that are said to be 'of yoga', but many of the poems written by the *siddhas* are also found in various other languages. The most ancient in Indo-Aryan languages apart from Sanskrit are in *apabhraṃśa* or in regional forms of *apabhraṃśa*: old-bengali or old-oriya, and they are Buddhist and translated into Tibetan. They are the *Caryā-gīti*, 'songs on conduct' and the *Dohākoṣa*, 'treasury of couplets'.[13] But the psychological attitude of their authors is the same as that of the Śaiva, Vaiṣṇava or Jaina *siddhas*, who continued to flourish after the Buddhists had disappeared. It is also the same attitude which made Dārā integrate into the *sufi* fold all these *siddhas* and which allowed different communities of the 15th-16th centuries, including the Muslim, to claim the poet Kabīr as one of their own.

But the richest literature of the *siddhas* is found in the South, using simultaneously Sanskrit and the Dravidian languages. It is there that the study of the *Vedānta* 'Culmination of the Veda' was developed with the Śaṃkaras, the Rāmānujas, the Madhvas, and many others, but also of the *Śaivasiddhānta* 'fulfilment of the knowledge of Śiva', known under this title in Sanskrit since the 7th century. And if these studies are the philosophical, logical and even scholastic justifications of the religion, the actual practices of these religions, regulated, as we have said, by Sanskrit texts, are expressed in devotion in the outpourings of the *bhaktas* or the *siddhas*. And this time, it is in the South and in Tamil and Kannaḍa that these spiritual outpourings constitute the most ancient and vast collections. The *Tirumuṟai* of the Śaivas and the *Nālāyirappirapantam* of the *Vaiṣṇavas* constitute twenty volumes containing works, most of which were composed between the 6th and the 11th century. The *Tirumantiram* by the legendary *siddha* Tirumūlar is a part of the *Tirumuṟai*, but the 3000 quatrains which are attributed to him are all replete with a complete knowledge of Sanskrit and Tamil cultures, of the psychological and psychosomatic mastery of yoga and of the faith in the oneness of the transcendent Being in the world. And numerous other *siddhas* in the Tamil country (*cittar* in Tamil) have constantly proclaimed this oneness as well as charity towards men, compassion of God (*karuṇā*), who is this Being.

They have done this to such an extent, even like others, such as Allamaprabhu in Kannaḍa, that eminent Indologists who were convinced that in India there could only be polytheism and idolatry, wanted to separate their works from the authentic Indian tradition, seeing in them the effect of later and minor borrowings from Christianity and from Islam. This was possible only by ignoring Vedic and Brahmanic testimonies and by misrepresenting the profound spiritual unity that the *siddhas* stressed in all the languages throughout India and propagated beyond it and which forms the summit of religious Indian psychology.

It is in the study of their texts, as well as of the present psychology of the living religious seekers who find inspiration in these texts, that dwells the future of our true knowledge of the religious Indian psychology, which is inseparable from the entire general culture of the Indian world and which must be freed from the interpretative psychology, so characteristic of its foreign historians.

NOTES

1. Mémoire sur la philosophie sanscrite, Le Nyāya, in *Mémoires de l'Académie des Sciences morales et politiques*, tome III, sessions of 21 September and 26 October 1839.
2. Cf. A.W. Von Schlegel, *Réflexions sur l'étude des langues asiatiques adressées à Sir James Mackintosh, suivies d'une lettre à M. Horace Hayman Wilson*, Bonn-Paris, 1832. Schlegel does not agree with Wilson for having followed the pandits, but today it is only Wilson's works that have merited republication.
3. J. Gonda, *Hymns of the Ṛgveda not employed in the solemn ritual*, Amsterdam, 1978, p. 5.
4. Special collections of stanzas from the *Ṛgveda* and formulae from the *Yajur* were made especially in Kashmir (cf. J. Fillioat, *Bibliothèque Nationale, Catalogue du fonds sanscrit*, fasc. II, 1970, pp. 60-74). Similar collections exist in South India.
5. Marguerite E. Adiceam, Contribution à l'étude D'Aiyaṉar-Śāstā, Pondicherry, 1967, pp. 107-14.
6. Cf. Pierre Dahmen, *Robert de Nobili, l'apôtre des Brahmes-Première apologie 1610*, Paris, 1931, pp. 146-48.
7. Cf. Hélène Brunner, *Le rituel quotidien dans la tradition śivaite de l'Inde du Sud selon Somaśambhu*, Pondicherry, 1963-78. For the Vaiṣṇavas, it is the great philosopher, Rāmānuja, himself who expounded the daily permanent rites, *Nityagrantha*, cf. Anne-Marie Esnoul, *Journal Asiatique*, 1972, pp. 39-78.
8. Cf. Arion Rosu, *Les conceptions psychologiques dans les textes médicaux indiens*, Paris, 1978.
9. The basic dictionary of Sanskrit is *Sanskrit-Wörterbuch* by O. Böhtlingk and R. Roth, published from 1855 to 1875. The most common one, frequently re-edited today, is *A Sanskrit-English Dictionary* by Monier Williams which is nothing but an abridged translation of the former. *Die Philosophie des Unbewussten* by E. von Hartmann is only from 1869.
10. Cf. Louis Renou, *Prolégomènes au Vedānta*, Paris, p. III.
11. Neelakanta Sarma, *Sanskrit-and Tamil Texts of Thailand*, a publication of the *Insti. Fr. d'Indologie*, no. 47, Pondicherry, 1972.

12. Mahfuz-ul-Haq, *Majma-'al-Baḥraīn*, Calcutta, 1926, Daryush Shagevan, *Les relations de l'hindouisme et du soufisme d'après le Majma-'al-Bahrayn*, Paris, 1979. —Dr. Roma Chaudhuri, A critical study of ...*Samudrasaṅgama*, First critical edition of the Sanskrit Text, in *Prācyavāṇīmandira*, vol. II, Calcutta, 1954.
13. M. Shahidullah, *Les chants mystiques de Kaṇha et de Saraha*, Paris, 1928, and lastly Per Kvaerne, *An Anthology of Buddhist Tantric Songs*, Oslo, 1977.

CHAPTER 16

PUNYA AND ITS SEMANTIC FIELD*

The meanings of the word *puṇya*, the etymology of which remains uncertain[1] although Indian grammarians derive it from the root PŪ,[2] are listed in detail in all the dictionaries. They are found there in different orders according to the author's ideas, in a way that their relative frequency is uncertain and more so as the related meanings are often interchanged in the translations. We notice also that there exist certain clear preferences of usage in the languages of the different circles that have adopted the term and even in milieus of diverse religions which use or have used Sanskrit. Some observations follow from such a conclusion.

The word *puṇya* is ancient. We know that it figures in the *Ṛg-Veda* in the wording of a prayer to Śakuni the prophetic bird, asking him to announce good fortune. There it is found along with *bhadra* and both carry the same meaning of good fortune or good.

...*sarvā́to naḥ śakune bhadrám ā́ vada*
Viśvato naḥ śakune púṇyam ā́ vada // II. 43.2.
'...from all quarters, O Śakuni, proclaim to us good fortune! from everywhere, O Śakuni, proclaim to us well-being.'

In a compound and in its function of an adjective, *puṇya* is mentioned again in the *Ṛg-Veda* with the general meaning of 'good' and more specifically of 'agreeable': ...Stríyo yā́ḥ púṇyagandhās tā́ḥ sárvāḥ svāpayām asi... 'those women with agreeable fragrance, you shall put them all to sleep'. VII, 55.8 and A.V. IV, 5.3.

The *Atharva Veda* has not only adopted the same text but describes once again the image of agreeable fragrance, VIII, 10. 27: When Virāj went to the Gandharvas and to the Apsaras while she was being beckoned thus: "Come, Puṇyagandhā, you who are of agreeable fragrance!", then Vararuci, son of Sūryavarcas, was milking it: he was milking the agreeable fragrance.

* First published in *Indianisme et bouddhisme, Milanges offerts á Mgr. Etienne Lamotte* Louvain 1980, pp. 101-10.

The Gandharvas and the Apsaras lived on this agreeable fragrance. He who knows thus becomes endowed with the Agreeable fragrance (puṇyagandhin). Elsewhere the *Atharva Veda* qualifies the world of Aja (IX, 5.16) which in the *Chandogya upaniṣad* VIII, 12.6. is the Brahmaloka, as *puṇya*, 'agreeable' or 'happy'. It qualifies similarly the happy worlds (*puṇyā lokās*) which are on the earth, in space, in the sky, the happy worlds of the fortunate (*púṇyānāṃ púṇyā lokāḥ*, XV, 13. 1-4).

The *Śatapathabrāhmaṇa* (IV, 5.4.1) declares that at the origin, the gods were all alike, all 'good' (or 'happy', *sárve púṇyāḥ*) and it takes up the idea of the happy worlds beyond: 'To Agni belongs this ritual (*yajña*). As Light, Agni is the burner of evil: He burns evil in this (ritual). Here below, He is Light: through Fortune, through Glory He becomes Light in the beyond because of the nature of the happy worlds (of this beyond)'.[3] 'He who has practiced this ritual has [for destination] the happy worlds' (*púṇyaloka ījāna iti* III, 6.2.15). In this last passage, H. de Willman-Grabowska[4] rightly admits that *puṇyaloka* is a *bahuvrīhi* that qualifies *ījāna* but translates it with: 'who has the world of merit'. Eggeling, on his part, understood it to mean: 'He who has sacrificed shares in the world of bliss', which is more correct for the worlds in question are indeed the happy worlds and not 'of merit', although good and bliss can be the reward of merit and although many other modern translators got accustomed to translating *puṇya* roughly as 'merit'. It is probable that the happy worlds promised to the practitioner of the ritual are 'those that are on the Earth' in AV. XV. 13.1.

In classical literature *puṇya* has the general meaning of 'advantageous', 'good', 'convenient', 'beneficent', 'purifying' according to what it qualifies. A few examples will suffice to call this back to mind.

In Manu II, 68 *puṇya* qualifies the rule of the initiation of the twice-born (*aupanāyaniko vidhiḥ*) which marks the (second) birth and which is *puṇyaḥ*, 'good'. In II.26 it qualifies as 'good' the vedic rites (*vaidikaiḥ karmabhiḥ puṇyair* Kulluka: *puṇyaiḥ śubhair*). In XI, 186 we have: *snātvā puṇye jalāśaye*, 'after having bathed in the beneficent pond', Kulluka annotates: *pavitre jalādhāre*, 'in a reservoir of water which is purifying' and it is not the purity or the limpidity of water that is directly suggested.

It is the same with *Meghadūta* 1;...*janakatanayāsnānapuṇyoda-keṣu...rāmagiryāśrameṣu*... 'in the retreats of Rāma's mountain with waters rendered beneficent by the baths taken by the daughter of Janaka' (Mallinātha: *snānair avagāhanaiḥ puṇyāni pavitrāṇy udakāni*, 'waters beneficent, purifying because of the baths, the immersions...'

The opposite of *puṇya* is *apuṇya* 'disadvantageous', 'bad', 'unsuitable', 'maleficent'. In Manu II.57, we have the meaning of 'unsuitable': 'excess of food is contrary to health, to longevity, to the sky, unsuitable, repugnant to people and it must be completely avoided.'[5]

In all rituals a *puṇyāha* has to be chosen, a beneficent 'or favourable', 'suitable, auspicious' day, or quite simply a 'good day'. It is the same for lunar days (*tithi*), nights, constellations where the Moon is present, the signs of the zodiac traversed by the Sun. Ritual formulae are also 'beneficent' such as the *Mahāvyāhṛtis* produced by Hiraṇyagarbha (*Hariv*. 12434).

In all these cases one cannot translate *puṇya* by 'merit' or 'meritorious' or by their opposites the word *apuṇya*. However the transfer to the meaning of meritorious is often natural in the same texts.

In Manu II, 106 where interruptions of Vedic recitation are dealt with, it is said that even in these cases what is offered in oblation in the *brahmāhuti* is *puṇya* (*brahmāhutihutam puṇyam*) and one usually translates *puṇya* here with 'meritorious'. But this translation is not obligatory and 'beneficent' or 'good' can be used as in most of the other passages.

In Manu VIII, 91 Yama Vaivasvata, who resides in the heart is qualified as *puṇyapāpekṣitā muniḥ*, 'the wise observer of good and evil', meaning the thinking activity of the individual whose heart is but the seat of the mind. But one could also understand 'observer of merit and demerit'. However, this is neither necessary nor appropriate here. In fact, *pāpa* which is often translated as 'sin', does not have this connotation in the most ancient period, where it signifies an evil whose appearance does not necessarily implicate the responsibility of the person it lays hold on; he can only be its innocent victim. As we shall see it is only with the development of the doctrine of the retribution of acts through successive lives that the good and evil we experience get mixed up with merit and demerit. It is quite possible, though uncertain, that this confusion was already complete in the text relating to Yama Vaivasvata.

In any case, we can see that the Vedic notion of happy worlds being qualified as *puṇya* was preserved in the *Āyurveda,* as we have seen it preserved also in Manu and in relation to health. Eulogising surgery the *śalyatantra,* Suśruta who praises specially the promptness of action in the art of curing, makes Brahman say: 'It is this (*śalyatantra*) which is permanent, beneficent (*puṇya*), good for heaven (*svargya*), for glory, for longevity and it produces means of subsistence.'[6]

A remarkable derivative meaning of *puṇya* is its changing from adjective connoting rites which are good or beneficent to the substantive form to designate corresponding ceremonies (*puṇya* and *puṇyaka, Anuśāsanap,* 95.2 and 3 and *puṇyatā,* 5). A twofold evolution seems to have taken place from this meaning of beneficent ceremony. On the one hand *puṇyaka* takes the more specialised meaning of 'ceremonial fast' (*upavāsa,* Amara, II, 7.37) which also exists in Prakrit.[7]

On the other hand, outside India but borrowed from her, *puṇya* in lao (written as *pun* and pronounced *bun,* or written as *punyaḥ*) has taken on the meaning of 'festival' as well as those of 'merit' and 'good' and such related meanings.

In Sanskrit, *Amarakośa,* which was just quoted in regard to the meaning of a 'ceremonial fast', gives at other places (I, 3.24) for synonymns of *puṇya*: *dharma* 'right order, happy arrangement', *śreyas* 'good', *sukṛta* 'good action' and *vṛṣa,* literally 'bull' but because the bull symbolises *dharma.*

The big Hindi dictionaries enumerate quite a great number of synonyms of the semantic field of good, of beautiful, of right and of good fortune, this last originating from right *karman.*[8] The abridged dictionaries limit themselves to the most current interpretations. The *Student's Practical Dictionary containing Hindi words with Hindi and English meanings* gives: 'adj. *nek* /virtuous; pure; righteous, n.m. *dharm, acchā kām*/virtue; a good action, moral or virtuous merit.'[9]

Another dictionary for students gives for the Sanskrit *puṇya* as equivalents the parallel Marathi and Gujarati expressions, and for *puṇyaka*: 1. 'A religious or virtuous act, *dharmakārya.*

2. Religious rite, *dharmavidhi*'; the expressions which actually are Sanskrit are the same in both languages.[10]

In the most ancient texts of Tamil literature, which is the most ancient of the present-day languages in India, we find 25 times[11] the *puṇṇiya* form, which is a simple transcription of the borrowed word *puṇya*. The word is found separately only five times, in the other cases it appears as the first member of a compound. Used separately under the form of *puṇṇiyaṉ* it applies once to God (*Maṇimēkalai* 5, 98) and means 'happy', or if one prefers 'sacred'. Under the *puṇṇiyam* form it appears as a neuter four times. It is found for the first time in one of the principal texts of the 'Sangam' literature, the *Paṭṭiṉappālai* (204) which is part of the *Paṭṭupāṭṭu* collection, the 'Ten Idylls', but its occurrence is unique in this literature. It is also found only once in the gnomic stanzas of the *Nālaṭiyār* (264-1) and of *Ācārakkōvai* (41-2) and only once separately in *Maṇimēkalai* (16.49) which, along with *Cilappatikāram*, contains all the occurrences of *puṇṇiya* at the beginning of compounds. It follows that the frequency of the use of *puṇṇiya* in Tamil appears only in the latest part of the ancient literature.

Its unique occurrence in *Paṭṭiṉapālai* (204) deserves study. The text describes the Cola country. A long series of verses refers to the external trade of the country and to the merchants. The merchants lead a 'life of delights without any want of *puṇṇiyam*', *puṇṇiya muttā t taṇṇiḻal vāḻkkai*. Moreover, a famous Buddhist text, the *Mahāvastu*, recounts the story of a merchant, Dharma-labdha of Vārāṇasī, who had made successful voyages on ship (*siddhayānapātra*) despite a dangerous stopover at an island of Rākṣasī. Five hundred merchants wanted to go with him on the same oceanic route, thinking that the path he took to travel is good and his journey fast and happy, his ship being in perfect condition[12] and above all that he possesses *puṇya* and he keeps collecting more *puṇya*. By accompanying him they want to amass as much *puṇya* as him.[13] The *puṇya* in question here is, therefore, surely of commercial value. In fact, the verses in hybrid Sanskrit which follow start thus: 'After having amassed goods, the merchants, starting from Jambudvīpa, launched into the ocean which is a mine of wealth and jewels.'[14] It is obvious that the goods meant here is a cargo destined for barter in the South Seas.

If now we go back to the Tamil text which dates back to the same period of maritime Indian commerce, we are led to understand that in their life of delights the *puṇṇiyam* that the Cola merchants did not lack is the same material benefit that was sought by the merchants of Vārāṇasī. However the context suggests, even demands a less hasty interpretation. In fact, the Cola merchants referred to are described as being honest and pious. They respect all life, raise bulls and cows, honour the knowers of Veda. They, therefore, practice *aṟam*, the equivalent of the Sanskrit *dharma* and this is what Nacciṉārkkiṉiyar points out in his commentary which renders *puṇṇiyam* by *aṟattoḻilkaḷ*, 'activities in harmony with the Right Order'.[15] Their happiness is the sign of their virtue and in the *Mahāvastu* it is the same with the joy of Dharmalabdha who is none other than the future Buddha and whose name signifies precisely 'He who has attained the Right Order'.

It is, however, clear that in the uses of *puṇya* as in *Paṭṭiṉappālai* and in *Mahāvastu* that we have just considered, one must translate the word by 'good' or 'goods' but one can observe that the meaning of 'merit' is at hand, a meaning which became current in most translations of the Buddhist texts, especially of the texts in Pāli. 'Merit' is the main and almost the only meaning given by the most recent Pāli dictionaries (PTS, Buddhadatta and even CPD s.v. *apuñña*).

But it is not so with the earlier dictionaries. The *Abhidhānappadīpikā*[16] writes: (*paddhake sukate*) *puññam* (*manuññe pāvane tisu*), '*puññam* is in (the sense of) good useful action; in the three (genders) in (the sense of) agreeable purifying.' The Sinhalese version translates the natural substantive with *kusal*, 'well' and the adjective with *sundara* 'beautiful', and *pavitra* 'purifying'. The equivalents given in English are: 'Virtue or merit; pleasing; pure.' The Childers Dictionary (1872) has for the adjective: 'Good, virtuous, just, righteous, meritorious, pure, holy', and for the noun: 'good works, goodness, virtue, pious act, righteousness, merit'. We thus see that the use of the word 'merit' to render *puṇya* became current in a secondary way and to a point that it became almost the only meaning and tended to eliminate the first meanings.

There is even a general misuse of the word 'merit' or 'meritorious' and which goes back at least to Senart (*Mahāvastu* 1. p. XXVIII) who translates *duṣkara* by 'merit' referring to great acts of disinterestedness of the Bodhisattvas which the text (I. 83, 12) simply says are 'difficult to perform'. These actions no doubt are meritorious but the translation unnecessarily modifies the original conceptual character.

It is not so most of the time when one translates *puṇya* by 'merit' in cases where one could retain this meaning of 'good' or more precisely of 'moral benefit' or even use the meanings of 'fortune' or 'good luck' or simply 'good fortune'. Translating it as 'merit' has, in fact, often the advantage of expressing an inherent notion in the original texts. This is true not only in Buddhism as we know and as we shall underline, but also in current Indian usage: for example if one felicitates someone for some gain or good fortune that has come his way, one would tell him admiringly: 'What *puṇya* you must have!' and it means literally 'what good fortune!' or 'What good luck!'. But it signifies more deeply that this good fortune or luck are not fortuitous but are held to be the fruit of good acts that have been performed, in a way that the most exact equivalent of the Indian expression would be: 'What merit you must have had to get so much good fortune!' It is undoubtedly for this reason that in *Mahāyānasūtrālaṃkāra*, Sylvain Lévi used to translate *puṇya* and *śubha* similarly as 'merit'.

In any case, a number of Buddhist texts remind us that *puṇya* is above all 'well-being' but it is linked to the merit of works. The *Madhyamakavṛtti* (chap. XVII) does precisely this. In the seven kinds of acts of the *kārikās* 4-5, Mgr. Lamotte translates: 'the merit (*puṇya*) resulting from enjoyment (*paribhogānvaya*) and the demerit (*apuṇya*) of the same nature.' At first sight one would be astonished that an enjoyment can produce some merit but the *vṛtti* explains: 'merit (*puṇya*) is well-being; resulting from enjoyment (*paribhogena anvayo'sya*). Enjoyment (*paribhoga*) is the fruition by the community, etc. for a given thing. The result (*anvaya*) that is the consequence (of this enjoyment) is an accumulation of well-being in the *series* of the donor. Demerit of the same nature is the demerit resulting from enjoyment; thus, for instance, the erection of a temple, etc. where creatures will be killed.'[17]

From this text it follows that well-being or merit, like misfortune and demerit, do not depend only on the intentions and the direct actions of the subject but also on the secondary effects of these acts, effects of which he is not necessarily aware but of which he is the initial cause.

Moreover, many other Buddhist texts show clearly that well-being or benefit obtained as the fruit of actions is not directly proportional to the responsibility of the agent and it is possible that consequently there is a dissociation between this goodness and merit. In such a case, the automatic translation of *puṇya* by 'merit' is no more justified.

Louis de La Vallée Poussin showed a long time back that even an *arhant*, a *puṇyakṣetra*, 'a field of well-being', could without his knowledge be the cause of a stranger's misfortune, precisely because of the great good that is due to his merit. Any offence towards him, even though minor in itself, can be of the greatest importance: good or evil resulting from an action is proportional to the dignity of the object to which it is directed, whether the agent is aware or not. A young monk who was sweeping badly is called the 'son of a slave' by a monk. This young monk was however an *arhant*. The monk did not know this but regardless of this he had to be reborn from a slave five hundred times.[18] The misfortune that struck him was commensurate with the greatness of the *arhant*, not with the weakness of his responsibility and of his demerit. This is why the *arhants*, although free from the retribution of acts, but in order to remove all risk of a third party offending them, build up around themselves a zone of 'non-hostility', *araṇa* and 'live according to non-hostility'; they are *araṇāvihārin*.[19]

These facts should draw our attention on certain aspects of Buddhist notions of individual responsibility and therefore of the conditions in which this responsibility is set in motion and on the causality of the retribution of acts. The idea that the good fortune or bad fortune resulting from a performed action do not depend only on the voluntarily assumed responsibility to undertake the action but also and essentially on the quality of the eventual beneficiary: this is a popular assumption in Buddhist society. The teaching diffuses this notion, particularly the teaching about the fruit of offering which seems to be constantly dwelt upon. The *aṭṭhakathās* of the *Dhammapada*, the *Jātakas*, the *Thera-* and *Therīgāthās*, the *Petavatthu*, the *Vimānavatthu* and many others contain uplifting stories which exalt the benefit of offering to the Community, to the *arhants*, to the simple monks. The value of this benefit is measured on the dignity of the donor.

All the literature of the *ānisaṃsas* takes up these texts and includes others. It comprises several collections of themes of sermons in Pāli like those that the monks use in Sri Lanka and the whole of Western Indo-China for their addresses in the local languages. Such are *Rasavāhinī* and the group of texts which preceded it, the *Dasavatthuppakaraṇa*,[20] the *Sahassavatthuppakaraṇa* and the *Sīhaḷavatthuppakaraṇa*.[21] According to all these literatures that go to form the general opinion among Buddhist peoples, the misfortune that befalls on anyone who causes harm to the community and its members, in any manner it may be, or even abstains himself from helping them this misfortune is also proportionate to their dignity. It matters little that the author of the action was conscious or not about what he was doing for the fact takes precedence over the intention. It is enough that the act in itself was accomplished consciously for it to bear fruit but its fruit will ripen according to the ground where the grain was sowed, not according to the initial intention of the sower. Fortune or misfortune, *puṇya* or *apuṇya*, will be really caused by the sower through the working of the action and of this he is responsible but the form and the importance of this *puṇya* or this *apuṇya* will have their determining causes outside his person: they will not reflect his moral merit or his demerit. The general idea of an absolute correspondence between the act and the retribution is unanimously accepted, but its application culminating in the confusion of 'good' and 'merit' is undoubtedly too simplistic.

To take but one example among a host of others we will recall the story of the man who in a great sacrifice makes an offering to a monk. We could say equally that he acquires merit or that he confirms his good fortune. But the monk realises the greatness of the donor's sacrifice and deems it his duty, he who is the beneficiary, to increase the fruit by making himself greater. To do this he hastens through quick efforts to break off the last shackles that separate him from the state of the *arhant*. From now on, without the donor's merit having in any way changed, the good he will receive will be magnified.[22] The donor's merit will always have had only one cause but the good will have two, including that which consists in the beneficiary's intent.

To sum up, the created good or *puṇya*, is not merit but the good fruit of two combined merits.

This leads us to consider what has been decided to be called 'transfer of merit'. The simplest case is the case wherein someone does a good deed so that the benefit goes to his dead parents or to a *peta,* an unfortunate person incapable of accomplishing any action whatsoever.

Another case is that wherein it is a mother who through the good actions she has done protects her son. Rarer than that, where parents or *petas* are the beneficiaries, is the typical case of Maitrāyajña, who in order to embark into the ocean despite his mother, struck her on the head and who merited his head being cut off by a dreadful disc. He takes the vow to remain in this infernal state for the good of all beings. He thereby wishes for them the compensation of the suffering he will undergo but he is delivered because his mother utters on his behalf a word of blessing (*āśis*): 'If I possess any fruit of goodness because of an offering, a religious vow or continence, or fidelity to my husband then by that fruit of goodness let no evil befall my son, wherever he may be.'[23]

One can say that she transfers her merit to her son: nevertheless, the power of her wish is also derived according to ancient Indian tradition from the force of *satyavacana*, from the utterance of truth pronounced by a perfectly faithful woman, and besides her son realised his errors and the greatness of Buddhist charity that he intended to practise as a bodhisattva. He has, therefore, himself gained merit through an awakening of his mind.

Several new works have appeared in these last few years on various aspects of this merit-transfer.

Mr. Minoru Hara in *Transfer of Merit*[24] does not deal with its Buddhist aspects. It is the notion of *dharma* (good deeds) and *tapas* (asceticism) that he renders mainly by 'merit' and which are linked to the idea of *tejas*, transferable or exchangeable force. Transfers or exchanges are not necessarily willed. In many cases they are automatic: the good (*puṇya*) or 'good deed' (*sukṛta*) by a man who refuses to give, passes on to the one he has disappointed and reciprocally he finds himself burdened with the 'evil deed' (*duṣkṛta*) of the other. Similarly, the evil (*pāpa*) that a sage might have merited is passed on to his future detractor. According to these ideas the Brahmin *pāśupata* who willingly submits himself to people's contempt could have had the intention of gathering the others' merit by abusing them.

But that does not seem to be the case: by suffering contempt the *pāśupata* wants to cultivate his patience.

We shall observe that, in any case, in this example as well as in that of the disappointed guest, the good and evil appearing in one and disappearing in the other correspond neither in nature nor in greatness to a personal 'merit' of the one who is supposed to be the ultimate beneficiary of it.

Nothing justifies the belief that it was thought that if the disappointed guest had committed a crime it is the one who had misled him who would suffer the consequences and that the beggar would gain the fruit of all the virtues of the other person for having been disappointed. The good and evil in play in these instances result from conscious, responsible actions but are not in themselves 'merits' or 'demerits'. It is not even certain that one should strictly consider them 'transferred'. They could be considered as mutually triggered. In any case the people involved are the initial causes for this good or this evil being set in motion but what they would experience or undergo will depend not on their own intentions but on the quality of their partner as in the cases that we have mentioned with the Buddhists.

Quite recently, at least two other articles have appeared on merit-transfer. Mr Myōhō Igarashi has studied two kinds of merit-transfers distinguished in the literature pertaining to the Sukhāvatī, Amitābha's paradise.[25] 'The first is a transfer of merit for all beings so that they are born in Sukhāvatī. The second is for a fortunate one who resides in Sukhāvatī and who must return to the world of senses in order to guide others there. But there it seems to refer to charity and to apostolate rather than a transfer of merit. Even in the Theravāda Buddhism the Buddha bestows good on men but does not transfer to them his merit.

It is this problem in Theravāda Buddhism that Jean-Michel

Agasse[26] has just taken up. He examines particularly *pattidāna* and its equivalence.

The free rendering of *pattidāna* by 'transfer of merit' has been accepted since Childers who justifies it by quoting an explanation given to him in Pāli by Subhūti and according to which *pattidāna* is *puññadāna*, the offering by someone to another of *puñña* accumulated by himself. It is, therefore, a classical translation which corresponds to the feeling of the eminent Buddhist scholar, Subhūti, which is largely confirmed by the present-day Buddhists. For a long time, however, a contradiction has been put forward between this idea and the canonical principle of a strictly personal salvation. If one can achieve one's salvation only through one's own actions how can one attain it through the actions of another? It is principally this question that Agasse deals with, finding that the texts he quotes enlighten only imperfectly but he thinks that the contradiction can only be apparent. He quotes appropriately the commentary of Tirokuḍḍasutta[27] where it says that the action of one cannot bear fruit in another but can provide him with the necessary conditions to perform a profitable action.

Agasse also thinks that the profitable action will consist in rejoicing in the virtuous act that has been accomplished.

This observation is certainly correct. It is certified not only in Pāli but also in Sanskrit, that the mere act of rejoicing in relation to the Buddha or in relation to the Community offers a portion of *puñña* even without anyone having thought of transferring it. The awakening of the mind to a confident serenity (*prasāda*) is by itself a good and a root of the supreme good. Thus the *Mahākarmavibhaṅga*[28] tells of a poor man who while watching the Bhagavant and his followers taking their meal has a thought of pious and confident serenity (*...bhuñjānaṃ dṛṣṭvā cittam prasāditavān*) and the Blessed One utters this *gāthā*:

ye tatrābhyanumodante vaiyāvṛtyakarāś ca ye /
anūnā dakṣiṇā teṣāṁ te'pi puṇyasya bhāginaḥ //

'Those who rejoice in this and who fulfil their responsibility, nothing is found wanting in their earning and they have their share of *puṇya*.'

Here one can take *puṇya* in the derivative meaning of 'merit' as in its original meaning of 'good'. But the thought of serene confidence, however meritorious its conceiving may have been and whatever the circumstance that may have triggered it, is an individual, psychological act, a 'disposition of the mind', or *dharma*,[29] peculiar to the individual and of which the consequences are for the individual. This same *Mahākarmavibhaṅga* expresses it clearly too and according to a very common widespread doctrine in Buddhism, declaring thus:

manaḥpūrvaṃgamā dharmā manaḥśreṣṭhā manojavāḥ /
manasā cet prasannena bhāṣate vā karoti vā /
tataḥ taṃ sukham anveti chāyā vā anuyāyinī //[30]

'The dispositions controlled by the mind are at their best through the mind. They are swift through the mind. If one speaks or acts with the mind impressed with confident serenity, there follows well-being like the shadow that accompanies.'

The same text shows us also that even a deliberate utterance is capable not of giving merit to the individual, but of laying down for him, by the will of another, a first cause of his salvation.

The Bhagavant tries to tempt a child with insatiable desires with sugarcane. He offers sugarcane on condition that he pronounce the words 'I do not desire'. Through greed he utters them and the Bhagavant declares that this utterance, that has never been pronounced before, when said in a burst of joy will be that cause.[31]

Here there is neither merit nor transfer but an individual ripening of good for the unconscious person in question.

This instance, although extreme, is not an isolated one in the Indian sense of charity. Vis-à-vis the insatiable child it is obviously *brahmavihāra* that one calls *karuṇā* (compassion) which the Bhagavant bestows.

We do have much more well-known examples of the compassion of Śiva or of Viṣṇu. They are recounted in well-known legends. An Indian Oedipus, a brahmin who loved his mother and killed his father, receives from Śiva the means of his salvation. Śiva answers to the astonished Umā that this unfortunate person could not achieve salvation by himself and, therefore, it was necessary to provide him with a genuine protection.[32] Viṣṇu, on his part, tempts a notorious thief by taking on the disguise of the bridegroom in a brilliant wedding. The thief comes to steal all the jewels of the wedding but is unable to lift his loot. In order to make it light Viṣṇu makes him utter a magic formula, a beneficent formula of adoration. Here is the first cause of the thief's conversion: the thief became a Vaishṇavaite, the Tamil poet-saint, Tirumaṅkaiyāḻvār[33]. The beneficent formula of adoration happens to be 'Oṃ Nārāyaṇāya namaḥ' which contains the divine Name charged with omnipotence but the parallel with what the Buddha asks the insatiable child to utter shows that the formula containing no divine Name could have been considered equally efficacious for salvation according to Indian psychology.

A verbal allusion to the Good made even unwillingly but linked to a surge of enthusiasm leaves in the psychic individuality a *vāsanā*, an unconscious imprint whose residual dynamism will operate in the future towards the destination that has been decreed: Good or the rejection of the Thirst. The Good that will follow will not be a reward awarded to merit, but the culmination of right psychological conditioning beginning in the individual himself. This good will develop in him when he will become conscious of the value of the utterance that he has been made to pronounce in enthusiasm for another goal, an enthusiasm he will then redirect to the real goal.

Thus, even where the beneficent act has been imposed, it is finally by an inner linking of his psychological acts, of his own *karman*, that the individual will attain salvation.

In those instances where merit-transfer takes place the solution is even simpler according to the Indian notions of psychology and of causality.

If the *pretas* or the *petas* are incapable of acting themselves, the mere fact that they ask a third person to perform a good deed in favour of the Community, manifests the confidence that they have gained in the power of this Community. They become the first cause of the good deed to be performed and which would not take place without them. This thought of the recourse to the Community would be the first cause (*hetu*) of the good which shall accrue to them. Even if they have not thought about this recourse and have only been the object of a believer's compassion who works in their favour, this time too, they would not have been any less the first cause of the good deed and it is for this reason that they would taste themselves the fruit by becoming conscious of it in an upsurge of grateful and admiring joy (*anumodana*) towards the Master or the Community.

The greatness of the fruit will then be immense since it would correspond to the greatness of the Master and of the Community which are the final object of the good thoughts.

In these conditions it is very natural that the author of the good deed performed in favour of a *peta* should also have his share of good at the same time, and even increase it by his own charity,[34] which would not fail in further increasing the rights to the good that is due to the *peta* who is the cause for the good deed.

There is, therefore, not necessarily and always a 'transfer of merit', as has been made to appear in the Western world and in the portrayal of Buddhism to the Westerners, by the analogy with the idea of the 'indulgences' that a believer can obtain for the souls in Purgatory.

No doubt in a good number of cases, including in the one where we spoke about the guilty son who is saved by his mother who makes a vow in his favour, everything happens as if the good accomplished or the merit acquired by a person is transferred from him to another. But in fact, both of them experience individually and simultaneously the happiness that is born from their different respective acts: one of incitement, the other of execution.

One is the cause of the good, the other, its realiser. They only exist interdependently but they are possible because of distinct individuals, each of whom derives the fruit for himself, all the while helping each other in order to obtain and to increase it.

There is no transaction from one account to another.

In fact, the common translation of *pattidāna* by 'transfer of merit' is an analogous interpretation. Literally, the term means 'the donation of the acquisition'.[35] It is understood that what is meant is the acquisition of essentially good dispositions (*dharma*) or of *puṇya*, good fortune or merit, but the word *prāpti/patti* does not itself have the meaning of 'merit'. In any case, the play of the donation of the means of this acquisition is explained on the basis of the Buddhist conception of the causality of actions rather than on the basis of our common notions of moral responsibility and charity towards the sinners.

Ultimately *puṇya* is happiness through the right disposition which produces merit or which results from it, rather than the merit itself, and this is the way the Chinese and the Tibetans understood it and their translations retain the old and general meaning of the word without directly suggesting the idea of merit.

In Chinese the usual translation is *fou-te*, 'happinesss-virtue', *bsod-nams* in Tibetan where *bsod* signifies 'felicity, good-luck'. In Lao it also means 'festival'.

The meaning of 'merit' for *puṇya/puñña*, very often legitimate for those who explain all good fortune of life by acts performed in previous lives, should not, therefore, make us forget even in its current usage the old meanings of the word which suggest the good and the good fortune that accompanies it.

The wish to extend this good to others, this good that one has gained oneself through difficult and consequently meritorious acts, is intended usually for the whole world, and it is merit and good fortune merged in the single word *puṇya* which are connected with it as we see, for instance at the end of the *Madhyāntavibhāgabhāṣya*:[36]

vyākhyām imām upanibadhya yad asti puṇyaṃ
puṇyodayāya mahato jagataḥ tad astu /
jñānodayāya ca yato'bhyudayaṃ mahāntaṃ
bodhitrayaṃ ca na cirāj jagad aśnuvīta //

'After this commentary has been written, may all that is good (/meritorious) be for the manifestation of good (/merit) for the vast world and for the manifestation of knowledge and through that may the world attain soon prosperity and the triple great Awakening!'

NOTES

1. See lastly Manfred Mayrhofer, *Kurzgefasstes etymologisches Wörterbuch des Altindischen*, Heidelberg, 1963, II. pp. 302-3.
2. *Śabdakalpadruma*, s.v. Puṇyam.
3. āgneyo'yáṃ yajña ḥ/jyótir agniḥ pāpmáno dagdhā so'sya pāpmā̆naṃ dahati sa iha jyótir evá śriyā yáśasā bhavati jyótir amútra puṇyalokatvá̆ (Śat. Br.

II, 2.3.6.). Puṇyalokatvā was found to be difficult, cf. A. Minard, *Trois Enigmes sur les Cent Chemins*, Paris, 1949, p. 187, note 542b: 'the moderns have doubted it (wrongly, no doubt, but it must be admitted that the obtained meaning is inadequate)'. The meaning Eggeling gives is indeed inadequate: 'becomes a light of prosperity and glory in this, and a light of bliss' (in footnote: 'lit. a light by (Way of) blissful state in yonder world' (vol. I, p. 315)'. Minard: 'light in this world (Agni) becomes through fortune and glory, light in yonder world through felicity'. But the reference to the Vedic *puṇyalokas* which are of the yonder world becomes necessary. Moreover the *Upaniṣads* distinguish solar and lunar light of this world and the *tejas* of the Ātman.

4. H. de Willman-Grabowska, Les composés nominaux dans le *Śatapatha-brāhmaṇa*, Ist part, Cracow, 1928.
5. anārogyam anāyuṣyam asvargyañ cātibhojanam /
apuṇyaṃ lokavidviṣṭan tasmāt tat parivarjayet //
asvargya, 'opposed to heaven', obviously means hindering the attainment of the *puṇyalokas* which are referred to earlier above.
6. Suśr., Sūtr. I, 19: *tad idaṃ śāśvataṃ puṇyaṃ svargyaṃ yaśasyam āyuṣyaṃ vrttikaraṃ ceti* //
7. H.D. Seth, *Pāia-sadda-mahaṇṇavo*, s.v. puṇṇa: 1. *subh karm*, 2. *upavās*, 3. *pavitr*.
8. Cf. for instance: *Bṛhat hindī koś*, by Kālikā Prasād, Rāj Vallabha Sahāy and Mukundi Lāl Śrīvāstava, 2nd ed., Banāras, 1956, s.v. Puṇya, (p. 823) sukarm se utpann śubh adṛṣṭ.
9. Allahabad, Ram Narain Lal, 6th ed., 1931, pp. 748-49.
10. Dr. G.V. Devasthali, Y.B. Joshi and G.R. Kulkarni. *The student's New Sanskrit Dictionary, Sanskrit into English, Marathi and Gujarati*; 2nd ed., Bombay, 1955, p. 618.
11. Cf. Index des mots de la literature tamoule ancienne, vol. III. Inst. Fra. d'Indologie, Pondicherry, 1970, p. 1037.
12. *ayaṃ dharmalabdho vāṇijako śobhanena mārgeṇa mahāsamudraṃ gacchati kṣemena gacchati kṣemenāgacchati laghuṃ cāgacchati siddhapātro ca āgacchati*/III, 287, 7-9.
13. III, 287, 10-14.
14. *puṇyaṃ samudānetvāna jambudvīpāto vāṇijā/mahāsamudraṃ prasthihensuḥ yaṃ dhanaratanākaram* // Mv. III, 288, 16-17.
15. Ve. Cāminataiyar, *Pattupāṭṭu mūlamum maturaiyāciriyar pārattuvāci Nacciṉārkkiṉiyaruraiyum*. 5th ed., Cennai, 1956, p. 553.
16. By Mogallāna Thero, Waskaduwe Subhuti ed., Colombo, 1865, 2nd ed., 1883, p. 260, no. 976.
17. *Melanges chinois et bouddhiques*, IV, pp. 269-70.
18. *La morale bouddhique*, Paris, 1927, p. 130 and *Kośa* VII, p. 86, n.2.
19. La Vallee Poussin, ibidem and *Kośa* VII, p. 86 where *araṇa* is interpreted as 'the power to withhold another's passion', on the basis of the explanation : *raṇayati kleśayatīty arthaḥ*, but it does not follow that *raṇa*, 'battle, hostility', is a synonymn of *kleśa* which in fact does not strictly mean 'passion' but 'impurity'. The sentence referred to means: 'he develops hostility: he tarnishes; that is the meaning.'

20. Ed. and Trans. Jacqueline Ver Eecke, Paris, 1976, cf. p. xi, references, footnote 2 and foll.
21. Budhadatta ed., Colombo, *Sahas.* 1959, *Sīhala*, 1959 (ed. and trans. J.V. Paris, 1980, Sahas, in preparation).
22. *Sīhalavatthu*, stories VIII, XXXV, XLV, LVI, LVII, LXI, LXXX, LXXXI. In the last story, two brothers who have become *arhants* go to see their mother but without revealing their identity so that the alms she may give them remain pure as alms, given to monks and thereby generating for her great good which she would not obtain by giving to her children. In the story no. VIII, king Saddhātissa, who wants to make an offering which is particularly difficult to make and is therefore meritorious, gets himself employed as a paid worker in order to offer what he has earned himself. His moral merit is very great, the Thera Tissa increasing its fruit by sending a monk endowed with wonderful powers to receive his alms. It is only in the end that the greatness of the fruit is revealed to the donor-king.
23. Sylvain Lévi, *Mahākarmavibhaṅga*, Paris, 1932, pp. 55, 127. *yady asti mama kiṃcit puṇyaphalam pradānena vā śīlena vā brahmacaryeṇa vā pativratatvena vā tena puṇyaphalena mama putrasya yatra tatra sthitasya mā kiṃcit pāpam bhavatu.*
24. *The Adyar Library Bulletin*, vols. 31-32, 1967-68 (Dr. V. Raghavan Felicitation Volume), pp. 382-411.
25. *On the Reliefs of Eternity and Presence in the Two Kinds of Merit-transference in 'Ōsō' and 'Gensō'.* Journal of Indian and Buddhist Studies (Indogaku Bukkyōgaku Kenkyū), Tokyo vol. XXVI, no. 2 March 1978, pp. 1041-47.
26. *Le transfert de mérite dans le bouddhisme pāli classique.* J.A., 1978, p. 311-32.
27. Ibid., p. 328.
28. Sylvain Lévi, *Mahā-Karmavibhaṅga*, Paris, 1932, text on p. 57, trans. p. 128 (here slightly modified).
29. One is often confused about whether to translate *dharma* in the singular or in the plural, but the ancient meaning of the term is 'organisation', 'arrangement' (Cf. L. Renou, *Sur deux mots du Ṛgveda*, J.A., 1964, p. 159-67, 1. *dhárman, vīdharman*, pp. 159-63. What is meant here is a cosmic arrangement, an arrangement or law set forth by the Buddha, legal and regulatory arrangements, dispositions of the mind. Examples of the latter are clear in the *Samādhirājasūtra*: the *bodhisattvadharmas* (XXXVII, p. 562, 1.3) and *buddhadharmas* (XXXVIII, 59) are the dispositions of the Bodhisattvas and of the Buddhas.
30. S. Lévi ed., XXVa and XXXIIg. The first quotation is in XXVa, preceded by its counterpart where *praduṣṭena* appears in place of *prasannena* and *duḥkham anveti cakraṃ vā vahataḥ padam* in place of *sukham...*
31. XXXVI...*na kadācit uktapūrvaṃ tad etasya vacanaṃ tasya necchāmīti hetubhūtam bhaviṣyati... necchāmīti prakarṣeṇa yaiṣā vāk samudīritā hetur alpecchatā...*

32. Cf. R. Dessigane, P.Z. Pattabiramin and J. Filliozat, La Légende des Jeux de Çiva a Madurai, Pondicherry, 1960, pp. 41-42.
33. Âlkoṇḍavilli Govindâchârya, *The Holy Lives of the Âzhvârs or the Drâvida Saints*, Mysore, 1902, pp. 161-65.
34. Agasse on p. 326 has rightly stressed this notion that has been clearly attested to.
35. On the *prāptis* cf. La Vallée Poussin, Kośa, esp. II, 179-195, E. Lamotte, *Histoire du Bouddhisme indien*, p. 672.
36. G.N. Nagao ed., Tokyo, 1964, p. 77.

CHAPTER 17

THE HISTORICAL AND THE PRESENT LIFE OF THE VEDA*

Western Indologists commonly consider the Veda to be a sacred text that originated in a very remote past, it was fundamental to ancient Brahmanism but fell into misuse in medieval and modern Hinduism, despite being talked about with the same reverence. Our late fellow-researcher, L. Renou, had, in fact, remarked at the conclusion of a detailed and profound analysis of the references to the Veda in classical, Sanskrit literature: 'the Vedic world, whose essence had passed through a transformation into the very heart of Hindu practice and thought, was now merely a distant thing, left to the hazards of a veneration stripped of the substance of the text.'[1]

Renou, therefore, rightly remarked that the essence of the Veda had survived although in a changed form, in the general substance of the living religion of India. He rightly observed that there was a loss of the substance of the Vedic text but this loss affected only the original tenor of the basic Vedic collections. One should not confuse it with the evolutionary modifications which occurred in the letter and in the interpretation in the course of time.

The word *Veda*, which means 'knowledge', designates, depending on the context, a more or less large body of Sanskrit literature. Without including the art of medicine, *Āyurveda*, 'The knowledge of life', or the military art, *Dhanurveda*, 'the knowledge of the bow', the Veda as a group of sacred texts, designates either only the *Ṛgveda* or the four collections or Vedic *saṃhitās* or also these same collections along with all the literature that is connected with them: *brāhmaṇa*, *āraṇyaka*, *upaniṣad* and the supplementary texts which are the *vedāṅga*. All this adds up to

*Text of a lecture delivered in 1980 at the A.I.B.L., published under the title: La vie historique et actuelle du Veda, in Comptes rendus des séances de l'année 1980. Académie des Inscriptions et Belles-Lettres, Paris, 1980, pp. 516-27.

500 works; and the index of words contained in them and brought out along with the references to all their occurrences totals up to 16 fat 4° volumes in 3-column[2]. But in certain religious schools, the Veda also includes texts in classical Sanskrit and not necessarily Vedic or Brahmanic, but which are the principal sources of devotion such as the *Bhagavadgītā* or the *Bhāgavatapurāṇa.*

In this study, both for us and for L. Renou, the Veda will designate only the most ancient texts as it is from these texts themselves that we must endeavour to trace the living evolution in history of the Indian religious life right up to our present day.

The observations made by Renou, in 1960, about literature are correct. Dr. V. Raghavan who presided over the International Association of Sanskrit Studies until his death last year, did not challenge any of these observations but only underlined in 1962, during a 'Vedic convention' held in Delhi, the work done in schools of Vedic chanting[3] and which was visible all over India. If the Vedic rituals for great ceremonies have not been in vogue for many centuries, except for reasons of historical reconstitution, the basic texts of the Veda are, however, still memorised in specialised schools for children and very young boys.

One could play down the importance of this fact by declaring that recitation does not necessitate comprehension and that it is simply a question of parrotry and superstitious attachment to an outdated tradition. In fact, Indian and not merely European scholars, have acknowledged that the reciters often do not worry about the meaning of the text. The prestige that lay in the personal recitation of the Veda in ancient times, *svādhyāya*, which was studied recently by Charles Malamoud,[4] today consists merely in a mechanical habit lacking both the right spirit and the right faith.

It is indisputable that since time immemorial children who were sent to school by parents did not find any interest at all in the recitations that were thrust on them, but in India, the development and training of the memory from the age of four or five, by learning long texts and even the whole Sanskrit dictionary, is a classical method of education. This method consists in developing the memory and enriching it with a voluminous quantity of material. But this is only preparatory.

It must obviously be followed by lessons of grammar and logic and in their light by an explanation of the texts learnt by heart. The mind has at its permanent disposal and for ready use, a huge amount of material. It is not burdened anymore by the need of interrupting its thought-process for the sake of gleaning more data. The mind may become lazy at times or too hasty in its judgments because of such facility but the vastness and the precision of memory from which it can draw are most valuable aids. And so, the recitation of the Veda, for the Vedic students, is a means of psychically storing what they perceive as the Universal word. By virtue of possessing its formulae, they can compare them, find points of similarity, complement them mutually, interpret them. And they actually did so all through history.

We may doubt this at first sight as the commentaries on the Veda in the ancient times are few and the bulk of them preserved only in parts. Only the commentary by Sāyaṇa, an author of the 14th century, is complete and quite extensive. It follows that apparently Vedic exegesis wasn't all that active as compared to the exegesis on grammar, on logic and on Vedānta, that is the concluding part of the Veda. These gave birth to a mass of literature of commentaries and their survey, started a hundred years ago, is still not over. New works are frequently discovered.

Meanwhile, in addition to the fact that the commentaries on the Vedānta always continued to quote the basic Vedas and to interpret them, there is a whole collection of technical works which testify to the persistence in the continuous use of Vedic texts in the religious practice not only of the Brahmins who were considered to be the unique upholders of the Vedic tradition, but also of the other classes of society. Now, these works have been ignored and neglected because they were set forth not as literary or philosophical works but as manuals of liturgy and of the principles of handicraft meant for the use of the officiating priests of the cults current at that time, of builders of temples or of sanctuaries and of sculptors of statues. They included a good number of sections related to the doctrines on the one hand, and to the discipline of yoga on the other. But these sections, without any evident guarantee about their antiquity, were said to have been produced at a later age by sects that were alien to the great classical civilization.

These were, moreover, called *Āgama* which means simply 'Traditions', or *Tantra*, literally 'Texts', but referred particularly to technical texts. However, a certain number of Buddhist *Tantras* were supposed to advocate a violation of some of the most sacred principles of Buddhist ethics, on the ground of a Gnosis that transcended the Good and the Evil. These *Tantras* are reminiscent, in a wider scope, of some of the ideas of the licentious gnostics of the West. The contempt for them has wrongly spread to the entire group of the other *Tantras*. On the basis of the cult of the *liṅga*,—a phallic symbol of Śiva—, and that of his consort, Śakti 'Energy' or *Mātā*, the 'Mother', found in some of these *Tantras*, it was imagined that there existed a 'Tantrism' that was opposed to 'Vedism' and which was said to have been born from an extraneous substratum that emerged later against the Veda of the conquering Aryans, who were the authors of the classical civilization. Therefore, we have not sought to look into these books in order to find living remnants of the Veda.

In reality, they are the books which regulate the practice of Hinduism itself in all its entirety. There are variations among them, which are the result of certain preferences for the invocation and the legends of the supreme Lord in one form or another, either Śiva or Viṣṇu, and which are also due to the subdivisions of communities within Śaivism and Vaiṣṇavism itself. But their teaching is based on the same theological, cosmological and soteriological conceptions. Their attitude vis-à-vis the Veda is perfectly lucid. The Veda bestows on man temporal well-being, *bhukti*; the *Āgama* leads him to temporal well-being as well as salvation, *mukti*. This *mukti* is attained, being the ultimate good, both through ontological knowledge and by good conduct, through the ritual of adoration and through the discipline of yoga which crowns and fulfils the right conditioning of the individual. We can also attain it through devotion, *bhakti*. The *Āgama*, therefore, goes beyond the Veda: it does not either deny or criticise it. It ascribes to it its supreme importance in the bygone ages of this world and recognises and utilises its eternal elements which evidently are pertinent to the present.

Although the āgamic ritual, whether Śaiva or Vaiṣṇava is basically a ritual of *pūjā*, a rite of homage, which differs completely from the Vedic sacrificial rites and has substituted them, the *Āgamas* may use Vedic formulae either in their integrally preserved form or in a modified version and sometimes even interpreted in a new way. Sometimes there are schools that even refer to some Vedic formulae as the original fount of their inspiration. Here are some such instances.

Reverence is almost universal for the Vedic formula called the *gāyatrī*, because of the name of the metre in which it is composed, or *sāvitrī* because of the god Savitṛ it invokes (ṚV, III, 62,10). It is imparted ritually during the ceremony of initiation, especially to a young *smārta* Brahmin, that is of those who venerate the Veda and the Vedānta, follow the *Smṛtis* that lay down the principles of Brahmanism. These Brahmins may be and generally are either Vaiṣṇava or Śaiva. And often they are so without excluding the other. In any case, the manifold gods are for them as for the vast majority of the Hindu believers, specific manifestations of the Supreme Lord who is the universal basis of all existence.[5]

It is through the imparting of the *sāvitrī* that the young brahmin receives a new birth in this world. *Sāvitrī* is, therefore, his mother (*asya mātā sāvitrī*, *Manu*, II, 170). But it is under the name of *gāyatrī* that she is glorified by the *Chāndogyopaniṣad* (III, 12) as being all that exists down here, the Word which 'sings' (*gāyati*) and 'saves' (*trāyate*) all things in their reality. We have here a verbal interpretation of functions suggested by the name. The linguists see therein an erroneous etymology, but it does not claim to be the original formation of the word. It is simply trying to bring out and explain some inherent significances in the concept associated with the word. Such an interpretation is not to be dismissed as an error or a linguistic fancy but should be studied as evocative of a psychology of the concept that is familiar to the whole of Indian culture.

Furthermore, the *Chāndogyopaniṣad* text holds the *gāyatrī*, in its aspect of the Earth for the world and of the body for Man, to be the support of all things and by quoting the *Ṛgveda* (X, 90, 3) which speaks about the *Puruṣa*, the Unique Self, places this self in the Universal space and at the same time within the human heart.

In principle, the *gāyatrī* and such ideas are reserved for the Brahmins. The formula has, in fact, served as a model for a great number of invocations that can be utilised by any devotee whatever his social standing.

The original formula is the following:

tát savitúr várenyaṃ bhárgo devásya dhīmahi| dhíyo yó naḥ pracodáyāt ||

'May we receive that excellent radiance of God Savitṛ who must stimulate our thoughts !'

The grammarians have discussed this text to find out whether the word *yó* which has been translated with 'who' refers to the radiance (*bhárgas*) or to the God himself. The difficulty lies in the fact that radiance (*bhárgas*) is of the neuter gender, whereas the relative pronoun *yó* 'who' is in the masculine like the name of the god. It was left to one of the greatest Indian Vedic scholars of our times to come up with an explanation based on what he calls 'palaeo-etymology' that supposes an earlier reading of *yad* which is neuter in place of *yó*.[6] But the common, traditional interpretation accepts the text as it is: for it, it is the god who is invoked and the radiance is merely his instrument. In addition it links up *dhīmahi* to *DHYAI* 'to think' and not to *DHĀ* and translates: 'May we think about' rather than 'May we receive'.[7]

But there is another point of argument. The name of the god Savitṛ 'the Inciter', is appropriate and is applied to the Sun and the Western upholders of the solar mythology are certain that the formula is a prayer to the Sun. But the historic Indian tradition does not give such an interpretation. The Sun is merely a specific manifestation of the One Being and it is the latter that is invoked in the prayer, the Supreme Lord who brought out the world, who is the principle of all forward urging since he has the nature of being the inner guide (*antaryāmin*) of all individuals.[8] This is what Sāyaṇa, the commentator, actually suggests in the 14th century but it is in perfect agreement with the ancient text from the *Chāndogyopaniṣad* that we have quoted. And it is this which, long before the 14th century, enabled one to invoke this same Supreme Being under its multiple specific forms by adapting the *gāyatrī*. The adaptations did not respect the metrical form *gāyatrī* but continued to preserve the name of *gāyatrī*. We find in the *Mahānārāyaṇa*[9] *Upaniṣad gāyatrīs* for Rudra, Danti, Nandi, Ṣaṇmukha, Garuḍa, Brahman, Viṣṇu, Narasiṃha, Āditya, Agni and Durgi (for Durgā): they are addressed to both Śaiva and Vaiṣṇava divinities.

In the Vaiṣṇava *Lakṣmītantra* we have a *cakragāyatrī*[10] and the invocation is to the disc which is an attribute of Viṣṇu; in the Śaiva *Āgamas*, there is an increase in the number of *gāyatrīs*. The *Ajitāgama* uses in addition to the usual *gāyatrī*, the *Vṛṣabha-gāyatrī*, the *Gaurīgāyatrī* and the *Skandagāyatrī*.[11]

The Gayatris are not merely found in texts from another age that we are publishing today. They abound even today in recent texts and are brought out in popular editions for the use of devotees and not of international philologists. One such publication is a Sanskrit book published in 1977 which is related to one of the most important Śaiva temples in South India, at Cidambaram, 80 km. south of Pondicherry. The work is called *Cidambarakṣetra-sarvasvam*,[12] 'Everything about the sacred place of Chidambaram.' It contains a *Cidambareśvarani-tyapūjāsūtra* in 27 parts, that is 'a Text of perpetual adoration of the Lord of Cidambaram'. We find here a *Viṣṇugāyatrī* and a *Brahmagāyatrī* (I, p. 97), others on the *haṃsa* of Brahman (II, p. 115) or of Viṣṇu's *śaṅkha* (II, p. 119) but particularly on Śiva in his different aspects: Tatpuruṣa (I, p. 9), Maheśa, Sadāśiva and Śiva (I, p. 58), Ratnasabhāpati (I, p. 57), Rudra (I, p. 59) and a *gāyatrī* of the Sun as well (I, p. 36) which is explicitly called thus. This last could serve as an example of how the formula was adapted. It goes like this:

bhāskarāya vidmahe mahādyutikarāya dhīmahi |
tan no ādityaḥ pracodayāt ||

'We offer our gratitude to the creator of light, may we be able to join our thought to the great creator of light so that the son of Aditi (the Sun) may inspire us.'

The 22nd part is almost entirely constituted of Vedic quotations given without any mention of their original sources and some-times in an abridged form with their first and last words. It is presumed that they are already known.[13] They are generally in concordance with the vulgates, though not always, and in this case, they do not seem to have been copied mechanically but adapted to the purpose for which they were joined together in a homogeneous series. In the present case the group forms an *annasūkta*, 'Hymn to food'. The adaptation consists mainly in a simple substitution of *anyam* 'other' by *annam*, 'food' in the original text:

paśyanti dhīrāḥ pracaranti pākāḥ /
jahāmy anyaṃ na jahāmy anyaṃ /
aham annaṃ vāsam ic carāmi /

'The sages see, the simpletons run about. I reject something, I do not reject something else. Myself, I go towards food with mastery.'

In the new reading, one must understand 'I reject one kind of food and not another'. The alteration is insignificant since food is meant in any case but by underlining the word 'food', this variant reading stresses an inherent evocation which gives to the text all its meaning. It is the evocation of a passage that is common to the *Ṛgveda* and the *Atharvaveda* and which is taken up not only by the *upaniṣads* but also by devotional texts such as the *Bhāgavatapurāṇa*[14]. Two birds are perched on the same fruit-tree, one who symbolises the Supreme Soul, watches, the other, who is the individual soul, involved in the world of desire, nourishes itself.[15]

We find another hymn in the appendix, the *Sarasvatīsūkta*, made up of different stanzas from the *Ṛgveda*.[16] We find then an *Agnikārya*, a ritual of Agni (Fire, but particularly the unique cosmic, vital element of which fire is a visible form). There the Vedic formulae that are used—still without any explicit reference—belong to the *Taittirīyasaṃhitā* and to the *Ṛgveda*.[17]

The modern work where we come across so many quotations, wholly Vedic or modified, is a publication of South India but the Far-North, Kashmir, has also brought out the same type of technical literature applying to medieval and modern rituals the ancient knowledge.

The Bibliothèque Nationale at Paris possesses a whole pile of manuscripts in *śāradā* script which it acquired at the end of the last century through the intermediary of Aurel Stein and Alfred Foucher. One of these manuscripts (Sanskrit 1661) is an *Agni-*

kāryapaddhati, a 'Manual of the ritual of Agni', which deals with a Śaiva ritual as does the South Indian work. It begins with a salutation to the 'seed of the tree of Veda' (the syllable *Oṃ* is meant), whose branches are infinite, as well as the fruit that is obtained from it.[18] There also exist in the same collection from the same source, eleven manuscripts entitled *Ṛcaka*,[19] forming together 918 folios and which are collections of stanzas from the *Ṛgveda* and formulae from the *Yajurveda* meant for rituals which are specified. I have given in the 2nd volume of my catalogue published in 1970, the identifications of all the Vedic texts mentioned without any references. They were found to be generally in agreement with the readings of *Vedic Concordance* by Bloomfield, taken from the vulgates. Their abundance and variety show that the whole mass of Vedic literature was at the disposal of the authors who chose these texts. But the prescribed uses are connected with Hindu ritual of the *Āgamas* and the *Tantras*. It is particularly remarkable that a number of these manuscripts apply Vedic texts to the cult of the nine planets (*navagraha*). Now, the Veda and even ancient Brahmanism have never spoken of nine planets. In our manuscripts, the most visible planets are classified according to the days of the week, this last having been borrowed from Greek astrology. Two others are supposed to be knots of the Moon. Of these two, Ketu was included much later. In the Veda his name designates any meteor.[20] We are, therefore, confronted with a modern utilisation of the Veda and with the proof of the abiding faith in the efficiency of its formulae.

In South India we have similar collections of Vedic formulae for the cult of the *navagraha*[21] which is popular even today. We even have some authentic Vedic formulae for a ritual of potters in Tamil Nadu.[22]

India did not merely preserve her Veda in its current religion, it also introduced it, along with its living religions, into foreign lands not very long ago. Sylvain Lévi, while visiting Bali, recognised there the *gāyatrī* and collected the texts of the *Upaniṣads* and of the āgamic ritual which he published in 1933 at Baroda. The *Textes sanskrits et tamouls de Thailande* published in Pondicherry by Neelakanta Sarma in 1972 contain number of Ṛg-Vedic formulae, formulae from the *Taittirīyasaṃhitā*, from the

Taittirīyabrāhmaṇas and from the *āraṇyakas.*[23] Similar texts were in use in Cambodia. Today they have been given up both in Thailand and in Cambodia but it is not too long ago that they were taken from South India, certainly not earlier than the 15th century.

In any case in India the life of the Vedas never ceased. Several current movements use the Vedas as an object and instrument of their activity. In the last century the *Brahmasamaj* and the *Āryasamaj* in particular, based their teaching of a Hindu 'theism' on the Veda. The former did so particularly on the basis of the Vedānta. The *Āryasamaj* was founded in 1875 in Bombay by Dayānanda Sarasvati. Dayānanda published in English *Satyârtha Prakâsh* which was translated into French in 1940 by Louise Morin and later re-edited in Mauritius in 1975 on the occasion of the centenary of the founding of the *Āryasamaj.* In 1974 already, a Mauritian Sanskrit scholar, B. Bissoondoyal, had published the first volume of a new French translation of the *Ṛgveda* done in the spirit of the *Āryasamaj* which looked upon the Veda as an expression of absolute truth as well as modern scientific and technical theories but which naively ignored the fact that modern theories were never meant to represent absolute truth.

From a philosophical point of view, the Veda in the 19th century, was a field of study for such masters as Ramana Maharṣi and Śrī Aurobindo among others. The former is less known since he wrote only in Tamil but he is closer to the tradition of the Veda and of Vedānta. Śrī Aurobindo, on the contrary, wrote directly in English and his interpretation is very personal and independent. However, both have inspired in different milieus in France great interest. Two books came out on Ramana Maharṣi in 1975 and 1978. The first is by Maria Burgi-Kyriasi; the second is a posthumous work of a Benedictine, Henri Le Saux: *Souvenirs d'Arunachala: Récit d'un ermite chrétien en terre hindoue.*[24] As for Śrī Aurobindo, his considerable work includes among others *Secret of the Veda* published in English (in 1956 entitled *On the Veda*) and in French in 1975.

The philologists and linguists in the west do not make much of this survival of the Veda in contemporary thought. In fact, it brings nothing new to the interpretation of the original text. In the West, particularly in Europe and in the Orientalist milieus in

India, the Veda is studied essentially in its origins and its pre-history. It is a valuable mine of comparative grammar and mythology where the indispensable task is the investigation of pre-history, not the evolving history. Even classical tradition is of little use in the study of the origins and therefore there is even less reason to study the contemporary lines of thinking on the Veda. The scholarly bibliographies also ignore the publications which are not of scientific bearing. However, these publications bear testimony to the fact that the Veda continues to exercise interest among an important group of the living Indian public. They deserve to be taken notice of at least and it is to be remembered that All India Radio continues to broadcast Vedic recitations.

Bibliographies mention a number of translations of the Veda in Marathi, Bengali, Telugu, Hindi and also the 64 volumes brought out by a publishing group since 1942 of commentaries on the *Ṛgveda.* They omit another enterprise which published 30 in-quarto containing the different forms of the text along with the translation in Kannaḍa both of the text and the classical commentary.[25] They also omit an edition of a Tamil translation of the *Sāmaveda* which gives a literal explanation of each word and therefore has a present pedagogical purpose.[26]

Such works, entirely in Indian languages, reveal to us that there exists a public that is still interested. Our science must not ignore these works. It cannot ignore the living faith that accounts for their success. A naive scientific attitude believed too prematurely—and this not only in the case of India—that the coming of rationalism will announce the end of religions in thought, and that technical advance would abolish their practice.

This scientific temper does not trip only in its predictions of the future but in its hypotheses on the Vedic past as well. It follows the doctrine of Evhemerus: It denies the existence of gods and demons; it is then obvious according to it that everything that is magical in religious texts was human at its source. There exist at present at least two theories that are still upheld by some. The *Ṛgveda* gives an account of beings that are hostile to Indra, the god who liberates the celestial waters. These beings have three heads and six eyes. Tradition would want them to be demons but scientism which knows that demons do not exist and therefore do not suppose that the authors of the Vedas could have believed in their existence, sees instead un-Aryan peoples vanquished by the Aryans taking control of the country. As these demons are black, it is obvious that they are the melanodermous peoples of the South and it follows that the unknown and the undeciphered script of the Indus Valley seals must be Tamil.

Another theory refers to the nature of *soma*. *Soma* is an inebriating drink from the heavens. A celestial plant called *haoma*, of which the name is related to *soma*, is also known in ancient Iran. But as celestial plants do not exist, *soma* must be a terrestrial hallucinogenic which was subsequently apotheosised. As elsewhere, people of Siberia, discovered only in the 17th century but said to be 'primitives', have used the psychotropic juice of the fly-killing amanita, the *soma* of the Veda must have been in the beginning this mushroom. It does not grow in India but may have been imported into the primitive country of the Veda, since the ritual indicates that it was bought from the mountain people and squeezed during the ceremonies. It is enough in that case to suppose that the Veda had been composed at a high latitude in Central Asia. It was enough to believe the ancient theorists who said that the Veda knew about the borealis constellations that are invisible in India and to ignore the fact that these theorists were wrong. In a similar way, we can, even today, develop such hypotheses said to be 'working' hypotheses.

But it would seem more appropriate for a study of the Veda to understand that the Veda is not a fossilised book, that it continues to inspire religious faith and that the evolution of this faith and its applications in history offer today a vast field for Vedic studies that has not been sufficiently explored.

NOTES

1. Louis Renou, *Le destin du Veda dans l'Inde*, Etudes védiques et paninéennes, t. VI, ICI Publ. fasc. 10, Paris, 1960, p. 77.
2. *A Vedic Word Concordance*, *Vaidika-padānukramakośaḥ*, by Vishvabandhu, Lahore, then Hoshiarpur, 1935-65.
3. Dr. V. Raghavan, *The Present Position of Vedic Recitation and Vedic Sakhas*, The Veda Dharma Paripalana Sabha, Kumbhakonam, 1962.
4. Ch. Malamoud, *Le Svādhyāya, récitation personnelle du Veda, Taittirīya-Āraṇyaka*, Book II, ICI Publ. fasc. 42, Paris, 1977.

5. This monotheism is already Vedic: Ṛ.V. I, 164, 46... ékaṃ sád viprā bahudhā vadanty agníṃ yamáṃ mātaríśvānam āhuḥ. 'The Unique Self, the sages speak of Him in various ways; they call Him Agni, Yama, Mātariśvan.' See also II, 1, 1-16; x, 121. The idea of I, 164, 46 is clearly taken up in the living Hinduism of the *Bhāgavatapurāṇa* I, 2.12; V, 18, 32; V, 19, 26.
6. Vishva Bandhu, *The Gāyatrī, its Grammatical Problem*, Research Bulletin (Arts) of the University of the Punjab, No. XIII (I), 1954.
7. Cf. Sāyaṇa's commentary, especially *Sūtasaṃhitā* IV, 6, 36 and the related commentary by Mādhava, *Sūtasaṃhitā with Tātparyadeepīka*, Vol. II, Madras, 1914, p. 374 (chap. 6; Gāyatrīvivaraṇam).
8. Sāyaṇa on *ṚV.*, III, 62, 10: *devasya savituḥ sarvāntaryāmitayā prerakasya jagatsraṣṭuḥ parameśvarasya*;—see also *Tripurātāpinyupaniṣad* (14th paragraph) for a commentary on this part of the *gāyatrī*.
9. *Mahānārāyaṇa-Upaniṣad*, 71-82, J. Varenne edition, Paris, 1960. For the Vedic accentuation of the text, for its Indian interpretation and for the *gāyatrīs* in general, see ed. of Swami Vimalānanda, Madras, 1957, I, 22-23, pp. 43-56.
10. Sanjukta Gupta, *Lakṣmītantra*; *a Pāñcarātra text*, Leiden, 1972, chap. 31, 33-36, p. 172.
11. N.R. Bhatt, *Ajitāgama*, Vol. I and II, Pondicherry, 1964-67. A reference to the *gāyatrī*: XXVI, 32 (variant adding *tritayam* which can suggest the association of the classical formula with ṚV., I, 99, 1 and ṚV., VII, 59, 12, as in *Tripurātāpinyupaniṣad* 2-4, but which can also correspond to the division in three propositions with three verbs of the new *gāyatrīs*—*Vṛṣabhag*. XXVII, 103, *Gaurīg*. XXVII, 207; *Skandag*. L, 13 and 69.
12. *Somasetudīkṣita*, *Śrīcidambarakṣetrasarvasvam*, Rājamahendravaram, 1977.
13. We mention ṚV., I, 99; VII, 59, 12; *Taittirīyabrāh*., 2.8. 8.1 to 3; ṚV., I, 90, 6 to 8; *Taitti. Br*., 2.7.16.4.; ṚV., X, 121, 10.
14. *ṚV.*, I, 164, 20-21; *A.V.*, IX, 9, 20-21; *Muṇḍ. Up*. III. 1.1-2; *Śvetāśvatarop*. IV, 6-7; *Nārāyaṇottaratāpinyup*. 1.1; *Bhavasantaraṇop*. 2.2; *Bhāg. Pur*., XI, 11, 6-7, 12, 22.
15. There exist a number of other instances of the use of Vedic formulae by means of new interpretation, regardless of its legitimacy, but accepted nevertheless, cf. for instance, J. Filliozat: *Un texte tamoul de dévotion vishnouite, le Tiruppāvai d'Āṇṭāl*, Pondicherry, 1972, p. VIII.
16. In the following order: ṚV., VI, 6.4; V, 45, 11; VI, 49, 7; VII, 95, 5; I, 164.49; Vi, 61, 14 and 61,2 (I, pp. 148-49).
17. *Tait. S*. 4.2.8.2 and A.V. IV, 11; Ṛ.V., X, 123, 6; *Taitt. S*. 3.2.5.3. and Ṛ.V. I, 91, 16; IX. 31, 4; *Tait. S*., 5.5.9.3; Ṛ.V., I, 11, 1; *Tait. S*. 2.6.8.6; Ṛ.V., V, 4.5., etc.
18. *Oṃ yad bījaṃ vedavṛkṣasya saṃpūrṇānantaśākhinaḥ / phalaṃ tasyaiva yat prāhus taṃ vande bhairavāgamam //* J. Filliozat, *Bibl. nat. Catalogue du fonds Sanscrit*, t. II, Paris, 1970, p. 7.
19. *Bibl. nat. Catalogue du fonds Sanscrit*. nos. 226, 227A, 228, 229A, 229B, 229C, 229D, 229E, 230A, 289.

20. Cf. Roger Billard, *L'Astronomie Indienne*, Paris, 1971, p. 125 and foll.
21. For instance in the collection of Mss. of the Institut Français d'Indologie at Pondicherry (RE 20 835, fol. 35-37) where are mentioned: ṚV. I, 35, 2; VIII, 44, 16; VII. 4.1; I, 91, 16; II, 23, 15; X, 9, 42; IV, 31, 1; I, 6, 3; X, 101, 1; VI, 58, 19 and TS 4.7.13.5 (references given to us by K. Srinivasacharya).
22. Marguerite E. Adiceam, *Contribution à l'étude d'Aiyanār Śāstā*, Pondicherry, 1967, pp. 106-14.
23. See esp. pp. 22 to 50.
24. Aruṇācala is the mountain, a sacred Śaiva place, Tiruvaṇṇāmalai, in South India, at the foot of which Ramana Maharṣi lived.
25. Sāyaṇabhāṣyasametā Ṛgvedasaṃhitā (*Karnāṭakabhāṣārthānuvādavivaraṇegaḷadane*) translated with Critical Notes by H.P. Venkata Rao—Mysore, Śrī Jayacāmarājeṃdra Vedaratnamālā, vol. 1-30, 1948-55.
26. *Cāmavētacaṅkitai, Cāyaṇa Pāṭiyam*; *Kācivāci uyar tiṟu Civāṉanta Yatintira cuvāmikaḷ avarkaḷāl moḻi peyarkkappaṭṭatu, moḻi peyarppāciriyariṉ patavuraiyum kuṟippuraiyum aṭaṅkiyatu*, Cennai [Madras], 1935, 2 Vols. in 8°, 790 and 1320 pp.

PART II

PHILOSOPHY, PSYCHOLOGY, YOGA

CHAPTER 18

ON 'OCULAR CONCENTRATION' IN YOGA*

(I) It has become a common practice in general works on mysticism to compare Indian mystics with those of the West. Whether they are considered insane or not, a saint Francis or a saint Theresa are saints: all their aspiration is an upsurge towards perfection, their whole life an ascent towards God. The yogins, on the contrary, would then be seen as ascetics without any ideal, seeking in the vacuity of thought and in the inertia of the body, the numbness of ecstasy. One even presumes to know the precise elements of such an ecstasy. The means for producing this ecstasy are well-known processes of hypnotism; it is, therefore, a hypnotic state. It is true that some authors distrust this theory; William James,[1] while saying a few words about yoga, does not compromise himself and quotes in a footnote a passage from Karl Kellner which states that the yogin is the opposite of a hypnotised person because the former is in full possession of himself and is not in an impressionable state. On the other hand, when one thinks of *Vedānta*, one very often recognises that Hindu mysticism reached great heights. However, that does not make us any less severe towards the yogin. A recently published booklet[2] which summarises the general trend of current opinion, declares about Yoga: 'The union of the soul with the supreme Being is achieved by relatively unsophisticated practices: one hypnotises oneself by holding some posture, concentrating one's gaze, holding one's breath, concentrating on some sacred syllable (*OṂ*); one uses prolonged fasts, solitary living, or suffering. It is from these that the Hindu fakirs were born.'

It is true that these are the methods of Yogins and one is tempted to agree with Barth that 'when these are rigorously

*Sur la "concentration oculaire" dans le Yoga, in *Yoga International Zeitschrift für wissenschaftliche Yoga-Forschung*, I, 1, Harburg-Wilhelmsburg, 1931, p. 93.

practised, they can lead only to madness and idiocy.'[3] In fact, as Barth goes on to add, Indian texts themselves sometimes depict the sage as a madman or a fool. But the text to which Barth refers[4] (*Viṣṇupurāṇa*, 2, XIII) describes the sage Bharata who has a pitiable appearance but deliberates like Nāgasena and leads the king of the Sauvīras through a brilliant discourse on philosophy, to the final liberation. After this we cannot look upon this Brahmin as a mere lunatic in a state of hypnosis. This leads us to examine the actual value of the analogy that exists between some processes of hypnotisation and some practices of Yoga. It is enough to do this in the most significant case of all, that of the fixation of thought, *dhāraṇā* in yoga, which, in some forms, is absolutely similar, it seems, to the principal process of the well-known master of hypnosis, James Braid.

(II) *Dhāraṇā* in the Yogic technique is far from being of the same importance as *prāṇāyāma*, the control of breathing, which, indeed, seems to be the first element of the system.[5] It is, however, very famous and the treatises of Yoga, whether aiming at Rāja- or Haṭhayoga, the gentle and the difficult method, never neglect it. It might even be interesting to observe its influence outside Yoga, even outside India. It is a part of the eight *aṅgas* which constitute the different 'limbs' of Yogic askesis, crowned by *samādhi*, or ecstasy, as it is commonly translated.[6]

In the *Yogasūtras*, *dhāraṇā* is depicted as the sixth *aṅga* which immediately precedes *dhyāna* and *samādhi*. It is defined by the *sūtra* III, 1: 'Deśabandhaś cittasya dhāraṇā'; the concentration of the thought on a single point is known as fixation. Vyāsa's commentary (*Yogabhāṣya*) affirms precisely that this fixation can be achieved on the navel-centre (*nābhicakra*), the lotus of the heart (*hṛdayapuṇḍarīka*), the star in the head (*mūrdhni jyotis*),[7] the tip of the nose (*nāsikāgra*), the tip of the tongue (*jihvāgra*) or an external object (*bāhyaviṣaya*), which is explained to mean an image of divinity by Vijñānabhikṣu while commenting on the *Yogabhāṣya*.[8]

The *Sarvadarśanasaṃgraha*, reproduces almost literally Vyāsa's explanations, enumerating the navel, the lotus of the heart, the extremity of the artery, *suṣumnā*, or some external object like Prajāpati, Vāsava, Hiraṇyagarbha, etc.[9]

And so we see that *dhāraṇā* can work on some material point or on a mental representation, but it is in the former instance that the hypothesis of hypnotisation has greater force; we, therefore, need primarily to look into the importance of this form of *dhāraṇā*. Apart from these texts, like the *Yogasūtras*, if we pass on to more recent treatises, this importance appears more considerable. The most material practices seem more and more advanced, as one passes from Rājayoga to Haṭhayoga, the yoga of effort, one finds everywhere the fixation on the extremity of the nose, the navel, the tip of the tongue, playing an important role in *āsanas* (postures) and the *mudrās* (gestures). The fixation of a small object is, in addition, one of the six acts of the purification of the body.[10]

The *Haṭhayogapradīpika*[11] advocates in *siddhāsana* (I, 35) the fixation between the eyebrows (*paśyed bhruvor antaram*), in *padmāsana*, and in *siṃhāsana* (I, 52), the fixing of the gaze on the extremity of the nose. The two *mudrās*, *khecarī* and *śāmbhavī* by which 'the mind dissolves and there is felicity in the void which is the pure form of the Mind',[12] are different because in the *khecarī*, the fixation is practiced between the eyebrows (III, 32 and comm. on IV, 38) whereas in *śāmbhavī*, 'the gaze is far-away without the eyes being open or closed' (Comm. on IV, 38 and IV, 36: *bahir dṛṣṭir nimeṣonmeṣavarjitā*) while at the same time aiming at an inner point (*antarlakṣyam*). The latter, according to the commentary (IV, 36), could be one of the *ādhāras* (supports) or *cakras* (circles, plexus) well-known in Tāntric anatomy. Further, the *Haṭhayogapradīpikā* mentions several times the fixation of the gaze on different points or objects; without needing to insist upon it, we must note, however, its comments regarding the *ādhāras* and about *trāṭaka*, the method of purifying the eyes. The śloka III, 73 mentions the 16 *ādhāras* that the commentary enumerates and in which we have, in addition to the different parts of the body, irrelevant for us at the moment, the navel, the heart, the nose, the bridge between the eyebrows, that is to say all the points which are most often mentioned in different texts as points of fixation. The commentary ends by saying that 'in these supports one must recognise the distinctive character of the result of *dhāraṇā*, according to the treatise of Gorakṣa.'[13] To sum up, fixation is done either on inner objects, which are important points of the Yogic anatomy, or on external objects which, as we have seen, are representations of the divinity.

As for *trāṭaka*, it consists in the attentive fixation on a focal point of small dimensions (*sūkṣmalakṣyam*) held until there are tears in the eyes (H. Y. Prad. II, 31, 32)[14]. It cures all kinds of ocular diseases.

If we pass from Haṭhayoga to the Tantras we find all the practices described in the same words and evidently deriving from similar inspirations.[15]

On its side, the *Ahirbudhnyasaṃhitā*[16] takes care not to forget the concentration on the extremity of the nose in the description of the right practices (XXXII, 61).

As a matter of fact, it is of little significance to find this process being described in texts that are more or less sectarian and esoteric and, whatever their interest, these texts do not hold the same place as the *Bhāgavadgītā* or even some Purāṇas for expressing the trends of Hindu mysticism in general. It is much more interesting to find these major tenets in a closely similar form precisely in this Gītā and in these Purāṇas. In this regard, it is strange to observe that the passage previously quoted of *Ahirbudhnyasaṃhitā* (XXXII, 60 and 61) corresponds exactly to three verses of the Gītā which describe in these terms the material duties of the yogin (*Gītā*, VI, 11 to 13)[17] '...Let him arrange a solid seat in a pure spot, neither too high, nor too low, covered with a piece of cloth, with skin and with kuśa. Seated on this seat, the mind gathered, having stopped all activity of thoughts and of the senses, may he perform yoga to purify himself. Imperturbable, holding the body, the head and the neck erect and immobile, may he fix his gaze on the extremity of his nose without allowing it to be distracted....'[18]

In addition, this passage is found with a striking frequency in several Purāṇas. The *Agnipurāṇa*[19] contains it identically (372nd chapter, 2nd *pāda* from verse 1 to the 1st p. of verse 4). The pāda quoted in note 18, is reproduced verbatim in the *Vāyupurāṇa* (XI, 16). The *Bhāgavata* mentions the same rules to be followed although not in the same terms (7, XV, 31, 32). The *Mārkaṇḍeya* also has a similar verse.[20]

The *Bhāgavadgītā*[21] refers once again to ocular concentration: 'One who shuts himself to outer sensations, who gathers all his visual power between his eyebrows, who maintains in equilibrium the two breaths, expiration and inspiration which pass through the nose, the sage, who in full control of his senses, in his consciousness and in his thought, one pointedly turned towards the liberation, is always free from desire, from fear and from anger, he is really free...' On reading these two pieces, one cannot help feeling surprised or even shocked to know that by squinting on the extremity of the nose one is aiming at the final liberation. The contrast of this prescription, ridiculous at first glance, with the solemnity of the tone full of the greatness of the tale which precedes and follows it is so intense that one would imagine interpolations to have occurred. One is completely disappointed on reading the commentary of Rāmānuja, for example, when one observes that instead of being rejected or ignored in silence[22] these two passages in question are commented upon exactly in the same spirit. It is said of the latter that it is on the extremity of the nose between the eyebrows that the gaze should be focused.[23] About the former, the editor of the commentary[24] points out that the extremity of the nose gives the direction to be followed to bring the gaze between the eyebrows (undoubtedly by raising it from the extremity to the base of the nose).

However, to be astonished for long by these contrasts betrays an inadequate knowledge of India; they occur, in fact, so regularly in texts that the surprise wears out soon and one easily tends to forget the need of explaining them. It would be useful, nevertheless, to give due regard to these instances. What on first examination appears absurd often ceases to be so when one knows it better. In the present case one must observe that the habit of detailed classification of the Hindus leads them to point out in the description of the greatest things their smallest aspects, aspects that we, on the contrary, always eliminate to emphasize the highest tendencies. It should also be observed that one cannot directly condemn the *Bhagavadgītā* and the *Purāṇas* which are similar in tone: it would be condemning the whole of India, for outside these texts that are already very widely known in the whole of Indian culture, numerous others are also familiar with the practices of technical Yoga. The *Upaniṣads* themselves speak of *dhāraṇā*; it is true that one must come down to the more modern texts to find it described in the physical details which is what specially interests us here. The *Kaṭha-Up.* merely mentions *dhāraṇā*,[25] so does the *Maitrī. Up.*[26] in an enumeration which is almost that of the *aṅgas* in *Yogasūtras*; however, the first *Upaniṣads* don't speak of it and it permits those who, on this point, are still in favour of that, to admire the purity of the earlier texts. The *Yoga-Upaniṣads*, on the contrary, contain, to a great extent, material similar to that contained in the *Haṭhayoga-pradīpikā* itself.[27]

As for the secular literature, it speaks about the same practices to the extent that it has been penetrated by Yoga or by doctrines which are influenced by it. To take but one example, it is enough to recall how Kālidāsa describes the greatest ascetic, Śiva himself, at the time when Love prepares to send forth his arrow at him and which will be the cause of his own self-destruction. Śiva is immersed in the deepest meditation, his pupils shot with fierceness: 'with his eyes which without the slightest movement (that could disturb) the row of eyelashes, taking the nose as the focus-point, (direct) downward their (visual) rays.'[28]

In Buddhism, the processes which call for the hypnotic interpretation of ecstasy, are as commonly quoted. Oldenberg quotes some precisely to show that it involves processes of auto-hypnotism. He describes flat circular forms, puddles of water, rings of fire, balls of clay, in front of which one seats oneself and fixes the image, sometimes with closed and sometimes with open eyes till one can see it absolutely clearly in front, whether the eyes be open or closed.[29] The ten kinds of *kasiṇas*[30] which represent the objects of these mystic contemplations are often mentioned in the Pāli texts, in the *Aṅguttara Nikāya*, the *Visuddhimagga*, the *Abhidhammatthasamgaha*, that is to say in the canonic writings as well as in others.[31] In any case, these processes are supposed to produce visions which we can't help judging as strange and which themselves contribute in making one believe that all these meditations are nothing but hallucinations of the sick.

Outside India, one finds these processes wherever Buddhism has spread. Tibet abounds with documentation on this subject. Fixing the eyes on the extremity of the nose (*mig gñis sna rcer phab*) is the second of the seven positions (*gnas bdun*) which the ascetic should hold to enter into meditation. The concentration on any point, on the centre of magic circles, on the burning point of an incense-stick, are described in all the books dealing with Tibetan askesis. Here it is sufficient to refer to them.[32]

However easy, though uninteresting, it might be to pile up such repetitive quotations they rightly bear testimony to the commonness of the practices of ocular concentration in all Indian as well as in all India-inspired mysticism. This commonness is such as to seem to validate in a large number of cases, the comparison with hypnosis and this is what we need to examine next.

III. We have been speaking of hypnosis in India for at least the last ninety years. In 1846, the English surgeon Esdaile, who had become well-known at the Magnetic Hospital of Calcutta, published his book, 'Mesmerism in India' and described almost all Indians as 'magnetisable'. Meanwhile the ancient mesmerism or animal magnetism became hypnotism in James Braid's book, 'Neurohypnology' (London, 1843) and this book popularised the fixation of the gaze on a shining object placed just above the eyes, as a method of hypnosis. The abbey Faria had for long used the process of the fixation of the gaze on his open hand, but, in addition, he forcefully commanded the subject to sleep. Mesmer himself in the eighteenth century hypnotised with the look and by staring at the subjects.[33] In this light it was pointed out that the magnetic passes were also conducive to the concentration of attention and it was readily believed that all hypnotism was the result of such a concentration. From here, to believe that all concentration resulted in hypnotism was but a small step and it was soon taken. Lanjuinais[34] in his analysis of the Oupnek'hat of Anquetil, while describing ascetics who contemplated within themselves the divine light by the concentrated look on the extremity of the nose, pointed out the analogy with the 'hesychasts' who concentrated on their navel. Maury[35] took up the comparison quoting references from the omphalo-psychics of Mount Athos and declared that these facts as also those of Yoga were explained by hypnotism. He even added, not without ingenuity, that 'the metal disc pierced with a hole which Philips uses in his experiments of hypnotism, reminds of the form of the organ on which the monks fix their admiring gaze.' This was not all. Father Athanase Kircher, in the 17th century, discussed the fascination that jugglers caused in the cocks by holding for some time the beak in contact with a white line that they were supposed to watch. The phenomenon was also compared with hypnotism and Maury again contributed to it.[36] At least one believed to have arrived at a scientific explanation.

On their side, the hypnotists were flattered to find in the most reputed civilisations of ancient times, India, the primitive cradle of peoples and land of mystery, the knowledge of phenomena which thrilled them. Christ himself could not resist using magnetism.[37]

Since then those who did not stop believing that hypnotism called forth supernormal forces suppressed in us by the state of waking, did not stop glorifying India even more for having known how to recognise and discipline these forces. There were others who wanted to offer a rational explanation and that is why opinions on either side varied only in detail, the hypnotic theory of Yoga being challenged only by admirers of India who were not admirers of hypnotism at the same time.

Towards the end of the 19th century, this theory was at the height of its success. At the time when the famous school of Nancy with Bernheim's help revived the old practices of magnetism, in 1893, Hermann Walter[38] published a translation of *Haṭhayogapradīpikā* and offered a detailed description of the practices, known to us as hypnosis, of the yogin. The studies made on the prodigious feats of the Fakirs by E. Kuhn,[39] Schrenk Nothring, to name only these, came to the same conclusion. Garbe fully agreed with these ideas,[40] so did Warren. We know that Oldenberg was of the same opinion. Max Müller had some hesitation but believed the question to be conclusively settled.[41] Oltramare,[42] Farquhar[43] more recently, along with many others, reached the same conclusion. In short the general unanimity became impressive. A half-hearted objection by Roncin, who observed that hysteria was diagnosed without its symptoms having been picked out[44] does not seem to have had any effect. More vehement protests like those of Kellner, which we come across in William James' quotation, made the same weak impression. Besides, it must be observed that in the mind of the Indologists who upheld the opinion that a well-defined hypnosis existed in Yoga, it did not necessarily lead to the conclusion that this was so in the whole of Hindu mysticism. This pathological ecstasy was observed only among the followers of the Tantras and the Haṭhayoga who were close to the fakirs and who were suspected sometimes more than suspected to be quacks and knaves. It was, in fact, recognised that the practices of yoga had slipped into the texts but it wasn't specified whether these practices were necessarily practiced by those who followed the texts. In other words, the concentration on the extremity of the nose was considered to be a means of pathological ecstasy in the *Haṭhayogapradīpikā* and passed unnoticed into the *Bhagavadgītā*, where the context redeemed the aberrations of Yoga.

Reduced to these proportions, the hypnotic theory of Yoga did not lack conviction and it provided a satisfactory explanation of extraordinary phenomena. It exempted one from long studies of *mystici minores*, which were not very pleasant and out of some sort of indolent philosophy one imagined oneself satisfied to declare along with Garbe and Walther, that *trāṭaka* 'musste einen hypnotischen Zustand herbeiführen' (S. und Y. 45), without sufficient consideration that despite the vast literature we possessed on it, we did not know better perhaps the hypnotic state rather than *trāṭaka* itself. Its suitability conveniently glossed over a number of shortcomings and the theory could extend its life a little longer; unfortunately, hypnotism itself did not survive. It disappeared from all therapeutics, the magazines which studied it stopped publication or else changed their name; it may still be a topic of drawing-room amusement, the treatises of psychology themselves have almost forgotten it. Some years back, the treatise of Georges Dumas could declare that it does not exist on its own outside the field of suggestion and of suggestibility (t. II, p. 941). It is true that this is not denying it, it is particularly true that its passing is perhaps not real, that it is subject to sudden lethargies from which it may wake up with a start, on the condition that it changes its name. It is fit, therefore, to discuss it as if it were still living, but this shows us already that it is not the well-known and well-classified psycho-pathological phenomenon that one could have formerly believed. Whatever we can base on it by way of theories has always something fleeting and unseizable.

There is a general objection against the identification of Yoga with hypnosis among others. Firstly, this explanation is barren since while seeming to answer the question, it discourages research on it before the research has had time to sufficiently develop itself. It is the Indologists who know about Yoga and it is the physicians who explain it; in these conditions one understands that the former, feeling that their studies could not cope with the subject, often gave it up and that certain questions, in many respects worthy of being examined on the ground of their strangeness, remain almost neglected because for a long time it was believed that their knowledge was within reach.

Finally, if all phenomena of ocular concentration is to be explained by hypnosis, it must also apply uniformly to all the mystic exercises of India[45] which are akin under one name or another, to the *dhāraṇā* of yoga, and which between themselves are however so differentiated that one is truly prevented from classifying them together by any yardstick.

These objections make the theory look less significant and not fruitful enough. If it is possible to show, besides, that ocular concentration can produce something other than hypnosis, not only in the opinion of the Hindus but even and specially in our own ideas, we will have no more reason to conserve it in addition.

IV. What, then, are the probable effects of ocular concentration? Many theories answer this question and this is not the place to examine them in detail, but it is necessary to recapitulate them in their totality.

Ocular concentration could have been considered as manifesting a cramping of the attention (Braid, Heidenhain, Bleuler, Münsterberg, Beard, etc.). When a subject has his attention rivetted on a single idea, he executes the corresponding act if the idea is that of an act, he experiences the corresponding hallucination if the idea is that of a vision. In the normal state other ideas, other representations, would come into conflict with it and would balance each other off; no single impulse would manifest. Concentration constitutes a state of monoideaism in which nothing intrudes to disturb the subject: he follows the idea to the end, whatever it might be. In these conditions, whether a hypnotist obtains the concentration of the subject on an act or on a vision, the subject will perform the act or experience the vision; he will receive, in one word, suggestions. The state in which he will find himself will be characterised by suggestibility and will be the state of hypnosis. In general, apart from performing the acts that one can suggest to him, the subject will assume the pose of sleep, having been ordered into it from the beginning of the seance. In this light, hypnotism is theoretically applicable to all, it is sufficient that one keeps concentrating one's attention with enough energy and for a sufficiently long period to fall into somnambulism.[46] In brief, the concentration of the attention is sufficient to produce hypnosis. Does it imply that it should always produce it? Certainly not. Archimedes running naked on the streets of Syracuse was in a state of concentrated attention and not hypnosis. It is insufficient to have the mind fixed, one should will to let oneself sleep. Verworn, who insisted a great deal on the importance of the will of the subject in hypnotisation, has given prominence, among other reasons, to this remark against the identification of the fascination of hens or of other animals with the state of hypnosis in man.[47] More recently, Revault d'Allonnes, among others, thinks it important to distinguish this fascination from the real attention.[48]

Whatever the case might be, if one accepts the reality of hypnosis as the concentration of attention, one is not obliged, on this basis, to accept that the *dhāraṇā* of the yogis aims only at hypnosis.

But this theory of 'over-attention' was strongly challenged, and even displaced, in the literal sense of the word, since it was countered by the theory of extreme distraction. An individual who concentrates his attention on a point, who fixes upon a brilliant object (of Braid) or on Faria's hand forgets all that surrounds him, not because his attention blows up his unmoving sensation, but because it eliminates all that is foreign to this sensation. The fatigue that comes over quickly in a state of concentrated attention is distracting. It is because of this distraction due to fatigue, illness or any other cause, that a given suggestion is experienced and executed by the subject. The hypnotist Lafontaine[49] declared that he preferred working on subjects who resisted because their fatigue coming over faster, they were the more quickly overpowered. Pierre Janet in particular has picked up this idea with much enthusiasm.[50] According to him, the hypnotisable subjects far from being concentrated are supremely distracted and it is due to this state that one can introduce ideas into them which later make them move like machines. An abnormal psychological state, which he calls 'psychological misery', when it is achieved, makes the onset of hypnosis possible through visual concentration.[51] 'The fixing upon a shining point above the eyes', he writes, 'like the contemplation of the navel by the fakirs required a prolonged effort of attention... All this is true, but let us not forget that we are not talking about normal individuals capable of prolonged resistance to fatigue and especially capable of diverting their attention as soon as they feel painfully tired. These subjects experience a decrease of the tension from the beginning of the fatigue and they become incapable of making the little effort required to turn away their gaze and thus arrest this fatigue.'[52] Now the anomaly that Janet recognises in these subjects in hysteria.[53] Ochorowicz[54] who did consider hypnotism to be an abnormal phenomenon, but not a pathological one, has strongly challenged this theory. Since then hysteria has been demolished in favour of 'pithiatism'. But, regardless of this, from the last fact, it seems quite evident that the psychological disintegration which characterises hypnosis, cannot be produced in perfectly normal subjects. Whoever adopts a theory of this kind to prove that it applies to the phenomenon of yogins would have to find, therefore, in these yogins signs of hysteria, or (since the signs have lost their interest) abnormal psychic symptoms. Roncin, as we have seen, pointed out that Kuhn, Walther and others affirmed hysteria without any conclusive proofs. It is true that some authors seem inclined to believe that hypnotism by itself is a sufficient sign to characterise the illness, but these authors fall in a 'petition of principle' and demonstrate far too easily that hypnotism is always of hysteric nature, when they have accepted that hypnotism by itself is enough to characterise hysteria. We can derive little light from this jumbled aspect of the question and let us assume, to simplify things, that all yogins could be hysterics. Would they for this reason revert to a state of hypnosis by concentrating on their navel?

Perhaps, but it does not seem that this is achieved through the process described by Pierre Janet, for it is rather difficult to agree with him that a subject could reach a state of fatigue where he would find himself incapable of diverting the gaze. It is, in fact, possible that a runner may not have the strength anymore to stiffen his muscles to stop his movement, but he cannot prolong his running indefinitely, for he will collapse with fatigue. Similarly a subject who is incapable of bearing the fatigue after a certain time might not have the strength to turn his head or eye, but the fatigue will take care in any case that it annuls the fixation upon the object. If he focuses on his navel or a fortiori on the extremity of his nose, the subject, in order to see it, must contract his accommodation (ciliary muscles, eye-lens) for focusing at short distance and his converging (internal rectus muscles of the eye) for directing his gaze on the point of focus. When fatigue comes the ciliary and the internal rectus muscles will relax by themselves out of exhaustion and will distort the vision, like the runner who is stopped by a fall. To think the contrary, it must be accepted that psychological fatigue increases the resistance of the muscles to physical exhaustion, which is quite evidently impossible.

The two apprentice yogins about whom the Abbey Dubois spoke,[55] who in their exercises could not bear the fatigue, could pass in Janet's hypothesis as normal subjects who would have the strength to withdraw at the time of the trial. To their guru they might have appeared as incapable and the guru must have been right.

However, psychological disintegration seems to be actually necessary for the production of hypnosis. As long as a subject keeps his mental syntheses, which constitute at each moment of his consciousness his own personality, firmly under control, it is quite difficult to suggest to him ideas which would be transformed into automatic impulses as would be the case with a hypnotised person. Now the training of yoga and especially of *Haṭhayoga* is an arduous training. The yogin has to follow a total physical education to perform his *āsanas* and his *dhāraṇā*. If fatigue, monoideaism and hysteria could by themselves produce hypnosis and if this hypnosis was *samādhi*, how could the texts describe *samādhi* as the state obtainable by the very few, by the best trained, by the strongest, when the ability of the weak to get tired should make their obtaining of such a sublime state utterly simple?

If these remarks are not enough to remove the hypothesis of the hypnotic nature of *samādhi*, an argument which, in fact, would require further elaboration, they do show at least that it is not all that evident. It is uncertain that the prolonged fixation of the gaze can by itself produce hypnosis, and besides a quite recent theory reads in hypnotism a more specific instance of suggestion, a suggestion of sleep leading by itself to an increase in the subject's state of suggestibility,[56] but this discussion would be a digression from our subject.

Once it is pointed out that ocular concentration can produce something other than hypnosis, we should ask ourselves as to what can that be. The simplest hypothesis and which has often been put forth about yogins is that they seek in ocular concentration only a means to concentrate the mind to make their meditation more intense. A priori, this is possible but let us look into the details.

Let us examine first the most famous process, namely the fixation on the nose. To direct the two eyes on a point as close as the nose-tip demands an extreme convergence of the ocular axes and, as we have just seen, a strenuous accommodation (for a subject of normal vision at least). Apart from being rather painful, when it is prolonged, this state of muscular contraction is not conducive to a clear vision of any object, not even of the nose-tip which is the chosen point of focus. The proximity of the point being too great, the accommodation, though contracted, is insufficient, in general, to allow a clear vision. As for the surrounding objects their images form only on the peripherical parts of the retina, since the central part is focused on the nose and its image fills it. The peripherical sensations on the retina are weaker than the sensations at the centre. In these conditions the subject makes himself almost blind to the external world and the more the inward deviation of the eyes is accentuated, the more efficient is the process. We know this from the pathology of squinting. In this disease, the squinting eye, although capable of seeing when it is isolated, doesn't see anything when the normal eye functions. When both the eyes of a squint are open together, only one, whichever is focused, is being used; the sensations of the other are momentarily inhibited or neutralised, according to a more current term. Now this phenomenon of neutralisation (suppression for English physiologists) is facilitated by the deviation of the eye and although there is no perfect proportionality between its intensity and that of the deviation, it is generally more marked in the cases of severe squints.[57] These facts clearly illustrate that the suppression of the images of the external world is facilitated by the ocular concentration on a very close point.

It would, however, seem that it is altogether unnecessary to take so much trouble to shut out the external objects when it is sufficient to close the eye-lids to be enveloped in darkness. However, it must be observed that effort, and especially vigorous effort, has its utility; it paralyses the will by occupying it fully. It also paralyses the attention which aiming at one goal, forgets the others. In these conditions, the yogin isolates himself from external incitements. 'Putting on the aspect of an idiot, of a blind or of a deaf, carrying out no exchange of any sort with anybody...' King Yudhiṣṭhira wished to be thus.[58] So was the maddened Bharata whose legend Barth used. In a previous existence the sight of a young gazelle deprived of its mother, had softened him so much that he picked it up and neglected his most sacred duties in order to look after it. Being reborn in the body of a stag he meditated upon his errors and was reborn as a brahmin. It is then that he put on the external appearance of a blindman, a deaf and a fool, an object of despise for all, inviting the world's rejection, as it were, in order to transcend it.

Through ocular concentration, not only can the yogin eliminate the vison of external objects but he can also empty his own thoughts. The distraction of the yogin who is impervious to external stimuli, is not necessarily compensated by a richer internal life. His distraction is not in any way parallel to that of a scientist having no interest in other problems than his, but a passionately personal concern in his investigating. Concentrated on a point devoid of interest, on an unchanging and characterless image (external objects such as the burning point of an incense stick, different *kasiṇas*, etc.) or on a barely visible point of focus (nose, especially the base of the nose or the bridge between the eyebrows), his attention is sufficiently absorbed by his goal in order to minimize external perceptions, but not enough to fill his consciousness with new visions. Thus it is very easy for him to perform the meditation of the void and the verse of the *Haṭhayogapradīpikā* quoted earlier rightly shows that it is such a meditation that one attains through the *khecarī* and the *śāmbhavī mudrās*.

But we need to make an important observation here. The concentration is not always directed on a common point without interest—it can be done on the image of a divinity, on a mental representation, and in this case the remarks made on voluntary blindness by the abnormal positioning of the eyes, on the meditation on the void, do not apply. Should it be accepted, then, that it implies very different processes, a spiritual concentration as opposed to a physical fascination?—Not necessarily, and, in fact, it might even be difficult to make such a radical distinction between two kinds of *dhāraṇās* which, in the final analysis, are both *dhāraṇās* and which are often found rather mixed up in the texts. One remark reconciles these opposing *dhāraṇās* and helps us to arrive at a solution. *Dhāraṇā*, in fact, doesn't seem to be a fixation only in the sense of immobilisation, but also of localisation. Thought, from the Indian point of view, is not a central power which receives external images through the senses; it moves towards the object of knowledge and perception is an active grasping (*grahaṇa*) and not a passive reception of an imprint.[59] To fix the mind is not to immobilise it inside the brain on a cerebral image, it is to stop it at the point where the object is placed. To concentrate the thought on the lotus of the heart or on the navel-disc, is not to arrest in the brain an image of the lotus of the heart or of the navel conveyed by the optical nerves, it is carrying to the lotus of the heart or the navel the visual knowledge. Now we have seen that the focal points of *dhāraṇā* were in the *Haṭhayogapradīpikā*, the sixteen *ādhāras* (supports) which are at the same time important points of the mystic anatomy and physiology of India. When the latter will be known better, it is not impossible that we might be able to understand the fixation of the *ādhāras*—now seen as the simple way of training for visual insensibility—totally differently. It is true that the Buddhist *kasiṇas* will still remain unexplained by this method, but it seems another can be found for them; it is not absolutely necessary to explain everything in the same way: theories that are much too exclusive often prove to be a Procrustean bed for facts.

The meditations said to be 'spiritual', more exactly visions, appear to be used more often in Buddhist meditations, at least in the lower stages, than in yoga. The *kasiṇas* seem rather well adapted to favour them.

It is, in fact, well-known in Europe that divining had existed since antiquity, divining by means of magic mirrors, by water-tanks, by crystal-balls (catoptromancy, lecanomancy, cristallomancy, etc...).[60] The Arabs were also familiar with these methods as testified by Ibn-Khaldoun.[61] The 'crystal-vision' of the English is well-known. These practices are current in India and we can draw parallels with greater confidence than we could with the hypnotic phenomena, between the methods of divination in Europe and their counterparts in India.[62] It is true that the hypnotic state has often been identified with that of the magic-mirror gazer, always due to the same superficial analogy, the fixation of a shining object, as *dhāraṇā*, and the fascination of the cray-fish have also been identified with that hypnotic state. It actually seems that the phenomenon primarily consists in the fact that a prolonged fixation of an object of little interest in itself gives rise to the appearance of an unclear haze in which images gradually come into focus and the interpretation of which is, for some, the key to the future. The appearance of the haze can only be explained by the fact that fatigue, as we just described, causing an automatic fall in the accommodation and the convergence, makes all vision become unclear. From the moment this haziness is produced, there being no object to occupy it, the field of the visual consciousness is free and the moment is right for a host of memories to come in the form of visions. Reminiscences have then the effect of revelations and the subconscious elements, freed by the momentary clearing away of the consciousness, crowd in, group themselves as either absurd or logical syntheses, as sometimes in dreams, and might be interpreted as visions of future events, although they are merely new combinations of forgotten memories.[63] By dint of fixing on the mirror, the subject may have a bewildered look, and show some abnormal symptoms, but this does not turn it into a state of hypnosis. He is not necessarily in a state of suggestibility, nor is he amnesic (in general) after the experience or is no more than if he had seen an ordinary dream in normal sleep. He has had visions which need not be explained by hypnotism. It seems that the

Buddhist in meditation, being concentrated on a *kasiṇa*, in fact, practices the process of divining but without divining, if one may say so. The numerous visions prescribed in the Buddhist books (dead body, cemetery, etc.) can actually be encouraged by this process which, by freeing the consciousness from real perceptions, leaves it to be occupied more easily by the contemplations sought.

It might be dangerous to emphasise it any further for the moment[64] but this proposed explanation, whether it is true or false, is an interesting one because it shows yet again that the concentration of the look can produce something other than hypnosis and this was the goal of the preceding arguments.

This done, it would be appropriate to come to a conclusion about the hypnotic theory of yoga, to examine if *samādhi* itself is actually explained by this theory, but this goes beyond the limited purpose of this study and overlaps into another subject. It is enough to observe here from what precedes that the theory in question is not as easily and successfully applicable as Maury, Walther or Garbe might have believed. The phenomenon of ocular concentration is not a simple phenomenon that can be explained by a superficial analogy with a process which itself is, in fact, rather complex. And it seems that the hypothesis of the hypnosis of yoga could be rightly classified next to those whose simplism had been rightly criticised by Masson-Oursel since 1921—intoxication (Leuba) and pathological introversion (Morel).[65]

But before closing this topic we must clarify a point that has not yet been explained. We have seen that *trāṭaka*, the fixation on a small object, prolonged till the eyes water, cured ocular illnesses and which, besides, had been interpreted as being a process of auto-hypnosis. We have to accept that here hypnosis would actually explain the fact that a curative power be attributed to this process. We know how much hypnotism was in vogue as a therapeutic, forty to fifty years ago, and it seems that we must accept that it is by hypnotism itself that a known process of hypnotisation, ocular fixation, cures the illnesses of the eye. But we know that *trāṭaka* is a part of *ṣaṭkarmāṇi* which, without really seeming to have anything at all to do with processes of hypnotisation, claim also to possess a curative power. On the other hand, *trāṭaka* seeks to obtain cleanliness (*śauca*) of the eyes and not to bring about a state in which the eye could regain its health. The assertion by Walther and Garbe is unwarranted. It is even useless, for another explanation can be given for the wonderful property of *trāṭaka*, an explanation that is perhaps a little superficial but more satisfactory. Prolonged fixation on an object is impossible in serious ocular illnesses at least in those that, on attaining the transparent regions, render the vision extremely painful. We all know how much a tiny speck of dust in the eye disturbs the vision and we understand that when we are seriously affected we are unable to follow the *trāṭaka*-treatment. However, when we enter into convalescence, it is possible to take it up as in the normal state. In these conditions, whoever is on the point of being cured will be cured if he performs *trāṭaka*, but whoever is not so easily curable, being unable to follow the treatment will fail to benefit by it and the blame will fall on him for not persevering sufficiently. In short, *trāṭaka* can be seen as a test of cure mistaken for a therapeutic process.

It is high time we finally summed up these elaborate discussions.

We observed that the identification of ecstasy with hypnosis was based on the parallel of Braid's method of hypnosis with the ocular concentration of Yoga. However, a similar analogy has also mixed up divining by mirrors and the fascination of animals with hypnosis, but actually they are all distinct phenomena and any similarity is only a superficial one, in this case that of process.

On the other hand, it is not even certain that ocular concentration, by itself, can produce hypnosis. In any case, one cannot exactly understand the method by which it would produce it and it seems that other necessary causes must be accepted: the will of the subject undergoing hypnosis, specially the particular state of psychological disaggregation. Now we cannot rightly suppose in the yogins without proof, states that we will often be reluctant to accept in our own subjects.

Besides, as the hypothesis does not seem to have been fruitful till now, it seems quite unlikely to lead us consequently to a deeper knowledge of the facts.

It is, therefore, simpler to bypass it and to accept that on the one hand, a part of the explanations that we lack must be sought in the mystic physiology of Yoga and, on the other, to recognise the fact that ocular concentration, in fact, seems to represent the material aspect, the physical element of a process of fixation of thought which does not aim at the break-up of the consciousness and the introduction in it of suggestions as in the state of hypnosis, but to attain without a more complete insensibility and within a firmer self-control.

NOTES

1. W. James, '*The Varieties of Religious Experience*', 1903, p. 401, note.
2. Roger Bastide, '*Les Problèmes de la vie mystique*', 1931, p. 32.
3. *Les religions de l'Inde*, in *Oeuvres* t. I, p. 83.
4. And to which we could add others still, such as: 'the legend of Jaḍabharata' (Bharata, the Fool) in *Bhāgavatapurāṇa* 5, IX, 3, 8, 9; 5, X, 14.—'The legend of Ṛṣabha' ibid. 5, V, 29, 30; 5, VI, 6,—Also: ibid. 1, XV, 43; 7. XIII, 10.—*Mahābhārata*, Śāntiparva, 257,—*Ātmabodha*, 52 etc.
5. Cf. P. Masson-Oursel, Sur la signification du mot 'Yoga', *Revue d'histoire des Religions*, 1913; and *Esquisse d'une histoire de la philosophie indienne*, p. 50.
6. *Yogasūtra* II. 29.
7. This expression is normally translated by 'light that is in the head', but it seems that here it is *brahmarandhra* that is meant, the opening at the crown of the head where *nāḍī suṣumnā* culminates, an opening to which the name of star can be applicable but not of light. What proves that *brahmarandhra* is meant is this list of points of fixation corresponds partially, as we shall see, with that of the *ādhāras* (*Haṭhayogapradīpikā* III, 73) of which *brahmarandhra* is a part and not the light which is in the head. *Mūrdhni jyotis* which means something quite different from *brahmarandhra* would be an error in the list.
8. Cf. Rājendralāla Mitra, *Yoga Aphorisms of Patañjali*, Bibl. ind., 1883, p. 123.
9. *Sarvadarśanasaṃgraha*, trans. by Cowell and Gough, p. 268. Cf. also commentary on Y.S. III, 1 in *Pātañjalayogasūtrāṇi*, Ānandāśrama Sanskrit Series, p. 118 (*śubhāśrayā bāhyā hiraṇyagarbhavāsavaprajāpatiprabhṛtyaḥ*). These enumerations were actually supposed to be classical; this is how Aniruddha in his *Sāṃkhyasūtravṛtti* (III, 32) refers to the list of aims of *dhāraṇā* which starts with the navel.
10. About *ṣaṭkarmāṇi* see Garbe, *Sāṃkhya und Yoga*, p. 45 and *Haṭhayogapradīpikā* II, 21 and foll. About *śauca* (cleanliness) ibid and *Yogasūtra*, II, 32 *Vedāntasāra*, 215.
11. *Haṭhayogapradīpikā*, Tookaram Tatya ed., Trans. by Srinivas Iyangar, Bombay 1893. Detailed amalysis in Roncin, *Etude physiologique sur les fakirs*, Paris 1904.
12. *Bhavec cittalayānandaḥ śūnye citsukharūpiṇi.*
13. *Teṣv ādhāreṣu dhāraṇāyāḥ phalaviśeṣas tu gorakṣasiddhāntād avagantavyaḥ.*
14. Cf. also *Gheraṇḍasaṃhitā* quoted by Rājendralāl Mitra in *Yoga Aphorisms*, pp. 117 120.

15. Cf. for example *trāṭaka* in A. Avalon *The Serpent Power*, p. 205 of the Introduction. *Khecarī*, ibid. p. 236, etc.
16. M.D. Rāmānujācārya-Schrader ed., Madras, 1916, t. II, p. 306.
17. Trans. by Emile Senart, Paris, 1922, p. 84.
18. *Saṃprekṣya nāsikāgraṃ svaṃ diśaś cānavalokayan.*
19. Chapter 374 of *Agnipurāṇa* is especially devoted to *dhāraṇā*; it describes different kinds of *dhāraṇā*, particularly the fixation on the divinities and on the anatomical points of Yoga.
20. XXXIX, 31. The same chapter mentions later (44-46) various *dhāraṇās* on the heart, throat, face, tip of the nose, between the eyebrows, the crown of the head, etc.....
21. V, 27. loc. cit., p. 81 ... *caksuś caivāntare bhruvoḥ...*
22. Some yogins today, embarrassed by these practices, thinking them linked to hypnosis and considering it with suspicion, strive to get rid of them and accuse Patañjali himself, the master of Yoga, to have given a wrong guideline. Cf. Ramacharaka. *The Philosophies and Religions of India*, London, 1918, p. 125.
23. *Rāmānuja's commentary*, trans. Govindāchārya, Madras, 1898, p. 189.
24. Ibid. p. 201, note 3.
25. VI, 11; *tāṃ yogam iti manyante sthirām indryadhāraṇām*; *apramattas tadā bhavati* 'It is the yoga', it is said of the fixation of the senses; then one is without any distraction.
26. VI, 18.
27. *Yogacūḍāmaṇi Up*. 106, about *padmāsana*; — *Varāha Up*. V, 32, etc.
28. *Kumārasaṃbhava*, III, 47 ...*Netrair avispanditapakṣmamālair lakṣyīkṛtaghrāṇam adhomayūkhaiḥ*.
29. Oldenberg, *Buddha*, p. 372 (5th ed.)
30. The word is interpreted diversely. Cf. Childers, *Pāli Dictionary* and *Dict. of the Pāli text society*.
31. See Warren, *Buddhism in translations*, pp. 281, 291 sqq.—Seidenstücker, *Pāli Buddhismus*, Munich 1923, p. 275 sqq. 285.—Roussel, *Buddhisme primitif*, p. 259 and foll.—Oltramare, *L'histoire des idées théosophiques dans l'Inde*, II, p. 361.
32. Cf. Graham Sandberg *Tibet and the Tibetans*, London, 1906, pp. 278, 281.—A. David Neel *Mystiques et magiciens du Thibet*, p. 259 sqq. 267, 270 etc. A. Neel claims that all the exercises that she describes do not aim at producing hypnotic states (p. 267) but 'aim especially at making a clean sweep of all the ordinary and routine notions, to make it clear that other exercises can replace them and that there isn't anything that is absolutely true in the ideas that we formulate according to sensations that can be substituted with other ideas.' (p. 271) But it hardly seems possible to apply such an interpretation to Indian yoga.
33. On the basis of the report submitted by Bailly to the Academy of Sciences in 1784.
34. A work first published in the Encyclopaedic Magazine (9th year), in the *Journal Asiatique* in 1823 and finally in the works of J.B. Lanjuinais in 1832. Cf. p. 345 of this edition.

35. Maury, *Magie et Astrologie dans l'antiquité*, Paris, 4th edition, 1877, p. 440. Braid himself had remarked the similarity of his process with that of the yogins and omphalopsychics, cf. Durand (de Gros) *Le merveilleux scientifique*, Paris, Alcan, 1894, p. 101.
36. Revue des deux mondes, 1860, p. 705 (Sommeil naturel et hypnotisme), Magie et Astrologie, p. 432 etc.
37. Cf. Baptiste Demole, *Traité de magnétisme pour la famille*, Geneva, 1879, p. 24 sqq.
38. *Svātamarāma's Haṭhayogapradīpikā* (die Leuchte des Haṭhayoga) aus dem Sanskrit übersetzt, Munich, 1893.
39. *Zeitschriftf ür Hypnotismus*, Berlin, 1894 and the Anthropological society of Munich according to *Revue scientifique*, 1895, 1st Semester, p. 506.
40. Garbe, *Sāṃkhya und Yoga* in the *Grundriss* by Bühler-Kielhorn, Strasbourg, 1896, pp. 45, 47, 48.
41. M. Müller, *Rāmakṛṣṇa*, 1898, p. 9.—*Six Systems of Indian Philosophy*, 1919, ed., p. 349.
42. Oltramare, *L'histoire des idées théosophiques dans l'Inde*, Paris 1906, I. pp. 331, 346.
43. Farquhar, *An Outline of Religious Literature of India*, Oxford 1920, pp. 61, 64, 211.
44. E. Roncin, *Etude physiologique sur les fakirs*, p. 144.
45. It could be said that the texts, particularly the *Purāṇas* and similar compilations are formed of elements that are very disparate and that the practices they advocate are not of general bearing; the emphasis they place, however, on teaching those that are of our interest proves nevertheless that India holds on to them.
46. It should be observed that this brief summary is not given as the actual theory of such and such author (listed in the beginning) but as a general overview of the theories of hypnosis through the concentration of the attention.
47. Verworn, Article: *Hypnose* in *Handwörterbuch der Naturwissenschaften*, Jena, 1914, t. V. Ochorowicz believes in the hypnosis of the animals but seems to be unable to prove it. *Diction, de Physiol.* by Richet, t. 8, pp. 709-78.
48. *Traité de psychologie*, by G. Dumas, t. I., p. 914.
49. *L'art de magnétiser*, 1847, re-edited 1891, pp. 43, 44. Braid himself had referred to the role of fatigue, from the beginning.
50. Les *médications psychologiques*, t. I, p. 250.
51. *Automatisme psychologique*, p. 444 sqq.
52. *Médications psychologiques*, I, pp. 278 and 279.
53. *Automatisme*, p. 445 sq. *Medications*, p. 251 sq.
54. Article: *Hypnotisme* in *Dictionnaire de physiologie* by Charles Richet, Paris, 1909 t. 8, p. 745.
55. *Moeurs, institutions et cérémonies des peuples de l'Inde*, Re-edited in 1921, t. II, p. 249 sqq.
56. We have already mentioned in this regard the opinion of Georges Dumas.

See Logre, *Traité de Psychiatrie* (collection Sergent etc.) Paris 1928, t.I, p. 414.

57. Cf. Cantonnet & Filliozat, *Le strabisme. Physiologie et pathologie de la vision binoculaire*, Paris, 1932, Chapter on neutralisation.
58. The passage quoted earlier above (MHB. XII, 257) about the legend of Bharata. See also the other references in the Purāṇas.
59. It is interesting to note, *en passant*, even though the subject deserves a special study, that this idea of knowledge placing itself in front of the object is not in as flagrant a contradiction as it would seem to appear with what we think of visual perception. We do not perceive objects through sight, within the skull, we see them at their distance in space and our knowledge takes place at the same place as the object. In other words, the visual image transported to the brain by the optic nerves is returned to its point of departure, projected or better exteriorised. We are forced to concede this in order to explain the obvious errors of visual localisation. Cf. Cantonnet, Filliozat, l.c. Vision du relief.
60. Cf. Bouché-Leclerq *Histoire de la divination dans l'antiquité*, 1. p. 84 sqq. Maury, *Magie et astrologie*, 434 etc..........
61. Ibn-Khaldoun, *Prolégomènes*, Trans. by Slane, p. 221.
62. Cf. Description of similar processes by Froidevaux, Une séance de divination à Pondichéry, in the *Acts of the* 11*th Congress of Orientalists*, Paris 1897 in the Ethnography-Folklore section, p. 271 sqq.;—L. Sorg, *Mercure de France*, ler Novembre 1906, p. 14. We know of the famous "Hindu mirror" which is used from time to time in social amusements and models of which are sold at different prices depending on the size and its probable efficiency.
63. See among other studies the one made by Pierre Janet, *Névroses et idées fixes*, Paris 1898, t. I, p. 407 sqq.
64. In fact, we must keep the goal in mind, which, often sought through these exercises, is to identify the thought with its object. This is very clumsily explained through the analogy with the processes of lecanomancy, etc. But this shows that it is not possible to explain away all the processes of ocular fixation, in and outside Yoga, by hypnosis or by any other way.
65. P. Masson-Oursel, *Doctrines et méthodes psychologiques de l'Inde*, Journal de Psychologie, Paris, 1921, p. 545.

CHAPTER 19

THE ORIGINS OF AN INDIAN MYSTICAL TECHNIQUE*

India has worked out the most systematically structured and widely-followed mystical technique yet known: Yoga. Outside India also numerous religions also possess highly developed mystical techniques. In Christianity, the most well-known is the one contained in *Spiritual Exercises* by Saint Ignatius of Loyola. Jewish, Islamic and Chinese schools sought and developed many of these techniques with much ardour. But it is only in India that the methods of surpassing the ordinary limits of the mind have been classified into a discipline which is at once so precisely determined and so widely accepted. In Christianity or in Islam, one can be a saint without following any mystical practices; in India, to whichever religion one may belong, one cannot fully become a saint without practising Yoga in some way.

Yoga is, therefore, a discipline that forms an integral part of the Indian civilisation and has shared its diffusion. Wherever Indian civilisation has reached in its vast historic expansion, towards Indo-China and Indonesia or towards Tibet, Mongolia, China, and Japan, everywhere Yoga was accepted and ardently developed. The Muslim mystics may have been known in all the Islamic countries, the Christian spiritual methods may have been taught in the whole world but their sporadic success cannot match that of Yoga. Nowhere has a foreign mystic discipline flourished so intensely as the Indian Yoga in the Tibetan schools or in the Zen Buddhism of Japan. Moreover Yoga may have influenced Chinese Taoism, the Sufism of Iranian Islam and even the Christian hesichasm of the Palamites of mount Athos. It follows that the development of Yoga is one of the principal facts in the history of mysticism.

Its importance does not stop there. The minutely determined

*Les origines d'une technique mystique indienne, in *Revue Philosophique*, 1946, pp. 208-20.

psychological training it prescribes and the psychic states that it brings about have to be scientifically examined. It is the same for the physiological phenomena it produces, for, far from being merely an intellectual discipline, Yoga is 'a technique of the body'[1] as well as of the mind. It is a widespread opinion that there are two kinds of Yoga, a spiritual Yoga which is real mysticism and a physical Yoga which can be reduced to a gymnastics. The truth is that the adepts of Yoga, the Yogins, have different preferences. All do not practice the whole Yoga; some develop it specially in order to master the mind, others seek by it the development of the body. But the perfect *yogin* necessarily combines in his practice both the disciplines, the physical as well as the psychological. The most well-known religious text in India, the one in which India commonly finds one of the highest expressions of its mystic thought, the *Bhāgavadgītā*, insists likewise, in its descriptions of the conditions of Yoga, on the physical posture and respiratory discipline of the yogin, as on his meditation.[2] Beyond its historic and religious interest the mysticism of Yoga has, therefore, another interest for both physiology and psychology.

In addition, in the Indian sense Yoga is a philosophy. Its practices are not merely empirical; they achieve psychological experiences not attempted at random but founded on theoretical ideas of psychology. These ideas themselves are part of the general systems of knowledge which are simultaneously philosophies are religious methods. From the Indian point of view, in fact, philosophy, which is an integral knowledge of the World and of the Self, is the means for attaining the supreme goal of man, 'liberation'. The human soul is none other than the universal Soul forgetting itself in a phenomenal world which is more or less illusory. When, through philosophy, it becomes conscious of this truth, it escapes from its corrupting dream to find itself in its Absolute Being.

Thus Yoga, in its most complete form, consists of a complex mixture of psychological discipline, physical training, philosophical speculation and religious method. It appears thus, from the time its existence was formally certified in Sanskrit texts. It wasn't classically described till the first centuries of the Christian era, in the famous work, the *Yogasūtras*, ascribed to Patañjali.

But the texts of Brahmanic philosophy prior to the Christian era by many centuries, the *Upaniṣads*, already mention it and give its definitions which leave no doubt that a clear form was being given to it, such as was to be elaborated later by the *Yogasūtras*.[3]

When yoga is first mentioned in the *Upaniṣads*, it seems, therefore, to have already been formed in all its complexity. It is difficult to say precisely by studying more ancient documents what its antecedents might have been. The Vedic texts do allude to practices which were later used by yogins[4] but these are basically ascetic practices which are not fully peculiar to Yoga. By themselves, these practices were not sufficient to give it a distinct form. We, therefore, may take recourse to some hypothesis to try to solve the problem of its origins.

Accustomed by the Hellenic and the Christian philosophies to treating mind and matter as opposites, we are generally led to think that in combining in its technique physical and psychic exercises, Yoga blends two opposite and originally distinct tendencies. We willingly accept that there could be nothing in common in principle between the regulation of breathing or other material practices and philosophical meditation on the soul. It is true that the mystics never completely neglect some physical observances. The *Exercises* of Saint Ignatius prescribe quite a large number of them which are often found in Yoga. They advocate for example, in addition to temperance and mortifications which are a part of the preparation for the exercises, the fixing of the vision on a chosen point[5] and the recitation of prayers regulated by respiratory movements.[6] But here, it is a question of adjuvant means, specially meant to facilitate the concentration of the attention, whereas in Yoga the role of material practices has a much greater importance. By that Yoga seems to call to mind, more than the spiritual exercises of the Christian mystics, the practices of sorcerers or Shamans who rely on physical stimulations of different kinds but generally intense, to reach supranormal psychic states. And so one can ask oneself if Yoga is not derived from an ancient shamanic technique of trance, later sustaining a much more recent philosophy of the soul. By speculating on the Absolute Self which dwells within both man and Nature, one might have sought actually to reunite oneself with him. For that, one might have taken recourse to an already known technique of communicating with the spirits.

These are but pure hypotheses but which seem to have been confirmed by archaeological discoveries of the Indus Valley. The excavations of Mohan-jo-Daro in the Sindh have, in fact, produced small plaques on which is portrayed a person with three eyes, horns of a buffalo on his head, seated in the well-known posture said to be of the Buddhas, and surrounded by wild animals. Sir John Marshall[7] thought this person represented the great Indian god, Śiva, who has three eyes, is the lord of beasts (*Paśupati* in Sanskrit) and has a bull as his usual mount. The posture described is common in the practice of yogic exercises and, in fact, Śiva is known as the prince of the yogins. Therefore, it could actually be Śiva, and a Śiva practising Yoga. The identification has found positive acceptance. It is true that Śiva does not appear very early in Sanskrit literature and the small plaque of Mohan-jo-Daro, which can be dated back to 2000 to 2500 B.C., is prior to even the most ancient Sanskrit literature, but this proves nothing. Sanskrit literature was first elaborated by the Aryans who invaded India towards 1500 B.C. These Aryans partly but very slowly adopted the gods and the practices of the aboriginals. Śiva and Yoga could be autochthonous in India since the time of the old Indus civilisation and were mentioned only later in the Sanskrit works. The time when they first appear in literature need not necessarily refer to their origin but perhaps merely to their acceptance into the Indo-Aryan culture. Yoga could not have been born in the time of the *Upaniṣads*; it would then go back to a pre-Aryan past, but it might have been accepted by the Aryan or the Aryanised milieus at the time of the *Upaniṣads*. Its resurgence from then on could have been progressive for the physical practices which are characteristic of it, become increasingly predominant in the much later texts of Yoga, particularly in those called *Haṭhayoga*.

The author of an important work on Yoga, Mircea Eliade, had supported this thesis.[8] It is plausible and attractive. It could easily explain some facts like the acceptance of Yoga in a large part of Asia where Indian culture might have discovered it, rather than propagated it, since it would have belonged to an ancient strata of pre-Aryan Asiatic culture. But one must not hide the fact that we are dealing here with a rather arbitrary theory.

Without discussing here the value of the suggested identification of the Mohan-jo-Daro figure with Śiva, one must point out that the posture of this figure is much less characteristic of Yoga than it has been suggested. It is a most common posture in India outside the exercises of Yoga, and, when yogins adopt it, it is merely as a familiar and convenient position, suitable to be held for a long time without leading to fatigue that can be distracting. It is true that the portrait of Mohan-jo-Daro seems to have half-closed eyes focused on the extremity of the nose which is a part of the exercises of yoga. But this could be a rather weak, even though clear, indication, to serve as a basis to the hypothesis that Yoga actually goes back to the time of the Indus civilisation.

In fact, it is not sufficient, in order to advance the solution to the problem of the origins of Yoga, to discover in the prehistoric iconography the portrayal of postures reminiscent of those of yogins or to observe general analogies between the acts of the latter and those of the shamanic sorcerers or even of mystics outside India. It is evident that one must first and above all study the typical elements of Yoga and determine the place they occupy in Indian culture; we can thus, and only thus, hope to find out how they originated or infiltrated into it. The discipline of yoga being simultaneously psychological and physiological, the main task that is called for is to examine its relations with the classical Indian notions of psychology and physiology.

At the outset, Yoga technically consists of a preliminary and of a strict general hygiene which could have been empirically determined; observation shows us, for example, that fasting is conducive to certain psychic states. The actual exercises begin by a method to detach oneself from the external world, by using the concentration of the attention as a means of neutralising sensory impressions. Next come meditations (*dhyāna*) on chosen objects and finally states said to be of *samādhi*, in which at the highest level, the subject no more distinguishes himself from the object, for he is detached from his own conscious personality as from the external world and has no cognition except that of the object. In the most advanced state of *samādhi*, the yogin believes to realise the most complete psychic possession of the object of his contemplation. It is true that what is meant here is not a clear knowledge which can be directly used from the moment of the *samādhi*, for the working of reason becomes inoperative at that time. It implies at least a state which leaves behind unconscious or subconscious psychic formations literally 'constructions' (*saṃskāras*), that is to say it implies a state which is recorded in the unconscious and enriches its content.[9]

The process of the workings of concentration, meditation and *samādhi* is formulated from psychological notions accepted not only in Yoga but in different philosophical schools and among medical doctors of the classical period as well. Apart from differences in detail, these notions on the structure of the psychic instrument can be described without difficulty. There are five sensory powers (*indriya*) which grasp actively, rather than receive passively, external impressions through the organs (eyes, ears, etc.). The impressions grasped are conveyed to a centralising psychic organ, *manas*, which coordinates them into sensations. Through the working of a faculty of consciousness, *buddhi*[10], the perception is then awakened and it enters the domain of thought (*citta*). In addition to the sensory and the intellectual elements related to the present, there exists in a latent state a whole accumulation of 'preparations' or psychic formations (*saṃskāras*) and of 'imbibings' (*vāsanā*) which sometimes appear to the consciousness as memories or reminiscences. Besides, the soul, about which opinions vary, is in general, the agent of psychological action; it is this which perceives, reflects, and judges. This soul possesses, either individually or in common with other souls or with the Supreme Self, the nature of an eternal being. The subconscious stock of psychic formations and latent 'imbibings', however, encloses it within a stuff of impermanence. In the ordinary life, the thousands of events of the external world, seized by the senses, put into movement a mental activity that is limited, unstable and superficial. From these viewpoints the role of yoga is twofold. Firstly, it must stop the activity related to the external events:[11] thus releasing the richer and less dispersed activity of the psychic formations and 'imbibings' of the subconscious domain. In this more private domain, sheltered from outer incidents, the soul is supposed to be able to develop a superior power, which explains the belief that Yoga confers supranormal psychic powers. But in its second role, Yoga teaches the distinction between the eternal essence of the soul and its personal stuff of unconscious psychic elements, the stuff which binds it to the external world and involves it in a succession of bodies. By that it ensures the separation of the soul, the separation that is its liberation.

There is nothing in this account which must have been borrowed from the uncivilised pre-Aryans and everyone clearly agrees with it. Besides, it is when one considers the physical practices of Yoga, such as the regulation of breath, that one most often alludes to the possibility of a borrowing from shamanism.

Many exercises of Yoga seem merely to be intended to produce physiological effects without any immediate psychological interest. Some yogins claim to be able to stop their heart at will, in particular through respiratory training. This claim has long been considered quackish. It is so sometimes, for there are impostors, but not always. Dr. Thérèse Brosse was able to, in the course of her research in India, examine a yogin who would seemingly stop his heart; auscultation could no more discern any heartbeat and the pulse could no more be felt. Only the electrocardiogram showed the persistence of minute cardiac contractions otherwise imperceptible. The subject who believed stopping his heart was, therefore, sincere and the effectiveness of of his exercises was quite remarkable because the electrocardiogram obtained was such that outside yoga such oscillation could have been observed only in a very seriously ill patient; however, the yogin produced it at will and was in perfect health before and after the experiment. The other subjects under observation exhibited less marked but confirmatory phenomena.[12] It would be very important for physiology and cardiology to know the process used for producing such results. One has not yet been able to specify it and even the technique used by yogis has not yet been studied in detail. We can at least investigate whether the yogins work in a purely empirical way to acquire supranormal physiological powers or whether they act on the basis of a theory and by it perceive a direct relation between their psychic discipline and their physiological exercises.

This discipline of respiration, they call *prāṇāyāma*. The breath is the *prāṇa* but this word does not only mean breath, it means according to Indian medical treatises, the motory element of the organism conceived in the form of wind. Indian physiology includes, in fact, a pneumatic theory similar to the one which is described in the treatise *Peri Phuson* of the *Collection hippocratique*[13] and according to which wind is in the body as in the universe, the cause of all movement and of all change. The Indian medical treatises relate to the action of wind all that we ourselves relate to that of the nervous system. All the organic activities, all driving element and all sensibility are set off by the wind which exists in the body in the form of different specialised *prāṇas*.[14] The circulation of blood, like that of all the internal fluids, depends on it[15] as does the working of sensory powers.[16] It is even identified with the Supreme Self.[17]

The medical books which propound these notions are posterior to the Christian era but these notions themselves are much older because the ancient *Upaniṣads* which probably go back beyond 500 B.C., refer to them very clearly. According to the *Bṛhadāraṇyaka Upaniṣad*, for example, breath is the only essential element for the life of the body,[18] the sensorial functions result from it, they are themselves breaths,[19] all the different forms are identified with the soul[20] and wind is the cosmic equivalent of breath.[21] The theory of the physiological function of *prāṇa* and that of its localised and specialised forms goes back, besides, much further than the *Upaniṣads*. It was already being elaborated at the time of the Vedic texts, specially the *Atharva-veda* of which a certain number of passages acquire meaning only in connection with this theory.[22]

It is, therefore, certain that prior to the era in which the existence of Yoga is for the first time certified by texts, one believed in India that the functions of the body and the workings of the mind result from the same cause, *prāṇa* or the organic breath which is identical with the soul, and the respiration of which is an aspect directly subservient to the will. In these conditions, there is no ground to think that, in order to form itself, Yoga needed to combine a shamanic technique of possession and trance with a philosophy of the soul. It is evident that in seeing the respiratory breath as the common cause of psychism and of life, the Indians have sought to produce by acting on it effects simultaneously spiritual and physical. The idea of *prāṇa* having been accepted, mind and matter were no more contradictory and the two elements of yoga, its technique of the body and its technique of the mind, were complementary applications of the same theory.

By itself, the existence of the theory however does not account for the details of the processes. But it is sufficient that it suggested taking recourse to them. Experimentation did the rest. The physiological results obtained during trials and their repercussions on the psychic state restricted the choice and guided the perfectioning of the practical methods. We owe to the existence of the theory the reasons which prompted the attempts.

Besides, the experimentation has always been done with the mind obsessed by the conception of *prāṇa*. When the yogin takes any posture or goes through a muscular training, even without an accompanying respiratory exercise, he continues to believe in the working of the *prāṇa*, because there is no movement which does not involve its action. Moreover the practice of some non-respiratory physiological techniques is explained, above all, by the theory of *prāṇa*, even when one could attribute to it another motivation. It is in this way that the cleaning of the internal organs, common in the later yoga, could only correspond to an intention of purifying more completely than by external ablutions. But the theory teaches that the internal passages should be free and clean so that the circulation of *prāṇa* is normal and classical Indian medicine ascribes the origin of psychic phenomena to be avoided such as nightmares, to the congestion of the ducts of *manas*, of the mind seen as the physical organ of centralisation of sensory impressions.[23] A technique of cleaning practised with such concepts cannot, therefore, be reduced, as one might think, to a rite of magical, religious purification; it is a physiological precaution guided by the idea we have formed of the somatic and psychic workings.

Yoga has even surpassed the pneumatism of classical medicine. Starting from the facts of the latter, it has developed them into a fantastic physiology and anatomy, inventing a whole new system of the veins of *prāṇa*.[24] This being so, the importance given to physical practices in the later texts called *Haṭhayoga*, is not the sign of a resurgence of pre-Aryan mystic rites, derived from the old, autochthonous shamanic stock. It is merely the consequence of speculations based on scientific theories accepted in that time and in the surroundings where the texts of *Haṭhayoga* were composed.

The dependence of Yoga with regard to Indian scientific ideas, however, does not exclude a *priori* that it never borrowed anything from the non-civilised. The idea itself of the role of wind in the economy and of its identity with the cosmic soul could strictly go back to the non-civilised from whom Indian medicine and philosophy, as well as Yoga, might have borrowed it. But we have no way of knowing whether this logical possibility was worked out and no necessity justifies this hypothesis. Indeed, subjects liable to demonstrate abnormal psychic phenomena, shamans and sorcerers, even gifted with a psychism that in the beginning was normal but trained to go into ecstatic states, must have frequently found themselves among the adepts of Yoga and could have played a role in the elaboration of its techniques. However, it is not to these men or to their ancestors that one will attribute the guiding conception which has presided over the creation of yoga, when one would have observed that this idea is only a psycho-physiological theory common among the classical doctors and formed among their predecessors of the Vedic era.

The assigning of the origins of Yoga to a scientific doctrine rather than to a 'savage' tradition is not without reason. It has not only the advantage of explaining the birth of the system by the mentality of the surrounding environment rather than by a hypothesis supported only by a general plausibility. It also shows a fact which we should take into consideration to decide the place to be assigned to Yoga in mysticism as a whole.

If the great role that physical practices play in the technique of Yoga could be explained by the influence of an ancient current of shamanic mysticism, Yoga would have to be classified next to this mysticism. James H. Leuba thought of looking upon it as 'an intermediary link between the intoxication of the savage and the mysticism of the higher religions'.[25] But the practices of Yoga as a whole are dominated by a psycho-physiological theory and its simultaneous reference to the technique of the body and of the mind is explained because the theory has a materialist tendency. It is actually in fact tending to materialism, if not attaining it, by treating on the same plane both somatic and psychic phenomena, by turning the nature of soul into that of one of the elements, the atmospheric wind. In these circumstances the physical exercises of Yoga are not necessarily identifiable to those of the 'savages'. The study must be taken up again before classifying Yoga next to the techniques of the non-civilised.

Leuba and other authors have considered the states of yoga as comparable to the ecstatic intoxication resulting from peyotl or hashish, even while accepting that classical Yoga does not advocate the use of narcotics.[26] But in the intoxication induced by drugs the subject loses himself in states of animal thrill which have nothing in common with the absolute mastery of body and mind which the yogin develops by a strong effort of the will. It is true that the yogin's training can be crowned with bliss without compare, but all the states of bliss are far from being comparable with one another. Besides, Yoga seeks much less to create enjoyment than to govern the subconscious and to discover behind its covering the Absolute Self. The goals of ecstatic intoxication and of Yoga are, therefore, whatever one may say, altogether distinct. As for the practical processes like the ones which actually characterise Yoga, they do not exactly seem to have been traced among the non-civilised, perhaps the present representatives of those of ancient India. It is because of the systematic nature of the exercises of Yoga that a scientific origin seems more likely than a shamanic one.

Yoga, therefore, seems to us, in all its traits, not as a primordial shamanism adopted by a mystic philosophy but as a unique example of a mystic method distinguished by a materialistic oriented psycho-physiology.

NOTES

1. According to an expression of M. Mauss, *Les Techniques du corps*, in *Journal de Psychologie*, 1935, p. 271 and foll.
2. Cf. *Journal Asiatique*, Oct-Dec. 1936, p. 628.
3. What is meant here is not the *Upaniṣads* specially devoted to Yoga and which on the whole seem to be posterior to the *Yogasūtras*. It is the ancient *Upaniṣads* that are implied, which mention Yoga at places but unmistakably (*Kaṭha Up.* VI, 10, 11; *Taittirīya Up.* II, 4; *Maitry. Up.* VI, 18; *Śvetāśvatara Up.* II, 8-13). The *Maitry. Up.* lists six articles of Yoga

the regulation of breath, the retraction of the sense-organs, meditation, the fixation of the attention, reasoning and *Samādhi* (prāṇāyāmaḥ pratyāhāro dhyānam dhāraṇā tarkaḥ samādhiḥ ṣaḍaṅgā ity ucyate yogaḥ). The *Yogasūtras* mention eight which include in addition to the six two preliminary articles (*yama* and *niyama*) and including the postures (*āsana*) in place of reasoning (*tarka*).

4. Cf. J.W. Hauer, *Die Anfänge der Yogapraxis*, Stuttgart, 1922.
5. *Three Ways of Prayer*, the second way.
6. The third way of prayer.
7. *Mohen jo-Daro and the Indus Civilisation*, London, 1931, t. I, p. 44; t. 3, pl. 98. also cf. E. Mackay, *The Indus Civilisation*, London, pl. XIII, 9.
8. *Yoga: Essai sur les origines de la mystique indienne*. Paris, 1936, pp. 12, 299 and *passim*.
9. Two principal degrees of *Samādhi* are distinguished: one conscious, the other unconscious and higher. The *Yogasūtras* define them thus: 'Because of the fact that (in one) there is reasoning, reflection, euphoria, a feeling of I am, it is the conscious. The one which requires a training to stopping (the thought) and which leaves only the "preparations", is the other (the unconscious one).' (*Vitarkavicārānandāsmitānugamāt saṃprajñātaḥ* // *virāmapratyayābhyāsapūrvaḥ saṃskāraśeṣo'nyaḥ* //" (I, 17-18).
10. From the root *budh*=, 'to awaken'. The Buddha is not exactly the 'Sage' or the 'Enlightened' as one is used to freely translating it, it is strictly the 'Awakened One', he whose opened eyes have suddenly perceived the truths of 'Buddhism'.
11. That is indeed the first goal of Yoga, the one that is sufficient for defining it. From the very first words the *Yogasūtras* state in principle that 'the Yoga means stopping the movements of the mind' (*yogāc cittavṛttinirodhaḥ* // I, 2). The *Bhagavadgītā* (VI, 20) and the *Kaṭha Upaniṣad* (VI, 10-11) agree perfectly with this text.
12. Cf. Ch. Laubry and Th. Brosse, *Documents recueillis aux Indes sur les "Yoguis" par l'enregistrement simultané du pouls, da la respiration et de l'électrocardiogramme*, *Presse Médicale*, No. 83 of 14 Oct. 1936. Cf. notably p. 20 of the offprint.
13. As we know, this treatise believes air to be the universal motor. In Nature, as wind, it is the agent of all activity including the movement of stars and the changing of the seasons. In the body it is the source of life and the cause of illness as well. It is above all the passage from *Peri Phuson* dealing with the role of wind in the Universe which echoes parallel things in Sanskrit medical literature (*Carakasaṃhitā*, *Sūtrasthāna*, chap. XII and *Bhelasaṃhitā*, chap. XVI). The theory that states that wind is the cause of the movement of stars is also part of Classical Indian astronomy, cf. *Sūryasiddhānta* II, 3 and XII, 73.
14. Cf. particularly *Suśrutasaṃhitā*, *Nidānasthāna*, chap. I.
15. Cf. *Suśru.*, *Nid.*, I, 16-17: 'The diffused breath, moving through the whole body, acts so as to carry the organic juice or to allow the circulatiou of sweat and blood'... (*kṛtsnadehacaro vyāno rasasaṃvahanodyataḥ*/ *svedāsṛksrāvaṇo vāpi*...)

16. Cf. *Caraka*, *Sūtrasthāna*, XII, 8: '...it is the master and the guide of the mind, the stimulator of all sensory power, the conveyor of the objects of all sensory powers... (*...niyantā praṇetā ca manasaḥ sarvendriyāṇām udyojakaḥ sarvendriyārthānām abhivoḍhā...*); *Bhela*, XVI, 16-17: ...it governs... the sensory powers as well as the mind and the primary soul... (*...saṃgṛhṇāti...indriyāṇi manaś caiva bhūtātmānaṃ ca...*).'
17. *Suśruta*, *Nid.*, I, 4-5; *Caraka*, *Sūtra.*, XII, 8; *Bhela*, XVI, 12.
18. *Bṛ. Up.*, VI, 1, 13.
19. I, 5, 21.
20. III, 4, 1.
21. I, 5, 22: 'Just as the Breath is the centre of these breaths, Wind is the centre of these divinities (*sa yathaiṣāṃ prāṇānāṃ madhyamaḥ prāṇa evam etāsāṃ devatānāṃ vāyuḥ*).
22. Cf. *La Force organique et la force cosmique dans la philosophie médicale de l' Inde et dans le Veda*, in *Revue philosophique*, Nov.-Dec. 1933, p. 140 & foll.
23. Caraka, *Indriyasthāna*, V. 40.
24. Cf. J. Filliozat, *Magie et Médecine*, Paris, 1943, p. 119 & foll.
25. *Psychologie du mysticisme religieux*, trans. by Lucien Herr. Paris, 1925, p. 54; cf. also p. 230.
26. Leuba mentions however (loc. cit., pp. 60-61) that the *Yogasūtras* recognise a similarity between the 'perfections' (liberation from old age and death, etc.) obtained by drugs and those that are the result of *samādhi* (which he terms 'concentration' on the lines of J.H. Woods, *The Yoga-system of Patañjali*, Cambridge (Mass.) 1914). The sūtra IV, 1 indeed does arrange the plants of virtue (*auṣadhi*) and *samādhi* in the same list of means that help us obtain the 'perfections', beside the innate quality, charms and austerities. But this in no way, implies that these methods are related or even comparable to one another. On the contrary, they are different methods for obtaining the same results. The seeking after 'perfections' is, as a matter of fact only secondary in Yoga.

CHAPTER 20

THE UNCONSCIOUS IN INDIAN PSYCHOLOGY*

The notion of the unconscious being a modern development in psychology, one could deny, a priori, the possibility of finding anything that could be an equivalent of it in the psychology of ancient India. It must however be observed that the discovery of the subconscious elements of psychism was delayed by the intellectualistic traditions rather than by a particular difficulty in knowing about their existence. It is, therefore, not surprising that in a country where intellectualism was less powerful than in the West, this discovery should have been made very early. Moreover, certain Indian philosophical concepts, said to be without any parallel in European philosophy, and which were so, in fact, at the beginning of Indological studies, become remarkably clear if we realise that they are related to the subconscious psychic being and not to the soul or the intellect.

Several authors, in particular J. H. Woods and M. Eliade, did indeed find this out while studying the concepts of *saṃskāra* and *vāsanā* in texts of yoga. In the *Yogasūtras*, in fact, while speaking about the state of *samādhi*, that is, of interiorisation for the mastery of the entire being, we distinguish two varieties of this state: 'When there is reasoning, wandering of the mind, euphoria and a feeling of the self, there is conscious *samādhi*. The other (unconscious) presupposes a training which arrests (the psychic manifestations) and which lets only the *saṃskāras* abide' (I, 17 & 18). The *saṃskāras* are thus clearly what remains in the psychism, when the consciousness is suspended. What persists thus is not the mind as an organ which would be put to rest or the soul as an entity; the term *saṃskāra* can designate neither mind nor soul. In the etymological sense, it means 'confectioner', 'he who accomplishes or perfects'. In the Brahmanic ritual it popularly

*L'inconscient dans la psychologie indienne, in Proceedings of the Xth International Congress of Philosophy, Amsterdam, 1948, t.1, pp. 267-69.

designates the sacrament which perfects the one who receives it. *Saṃskāras* are then the active, constituting elements of a psychism which is not mental. They correspond to 'psychological systems' endowed with automatism of Pierre Janet and to the organised complexes of Morton Prince and psychoanalysis. They are elements of the subconscious in their formative aspect. Similar to the complexes of modern psychology, these formative elements are themselves formed by the preceding psychic stock of experiences. That is why they are also called *vāsanā*, from a name which designates residual impregnation like that left by an evaporated perfume in a phial that had contained it.

The *saṃskāras* have an essential, common property with the subconscious, psychic formations. These dissolve, or at least cease to be active, when they are known by the person they affect. Psychoanalysis seeks to find them when they provoke pathological phenomena which disappear when the patients recognise their true reality, and it seeks to transfer them from the field of automatic activity to that of an intellectual one. Now, the *yoga-sūtras* teach that intelligence (*prajñā*), developed through a psychological discipline of *samādhi*, and become 'normal' (*ṛtambharā* 'carrier of the norm'), gives birth to a new psychic formation, 'inimical' to the others (I, 48-50). The *saṃskāras*, persisting in ignorance, are destroyed by knowledge.

It does not at all follow that yoga, which we have already compared to psychoanalysis on other grounds, is really a psychoanalysis—too many features divide them—but the conception of *saṃskāras* in *yoga* does appear to be of the same level as that of the dynamic syntheses of the subconscious being.

This finding throws light on the fundamental theories of Buddhism.

The Buddhist texts commonly distinguish in the psychic being five groups (*skandha*): form (*rūpa*, that is the sensory), sensation (*vedanā*), perception (*saṃjñā*), psychic formations (*saṃskāras*) and thought (*vijñāna*). This appears to be a complete analysis of the psychic self if one sees in the *saṃskāras* the constitutive elements of the subconscious. These *saṃskāras* are considered to be those of action, of speech, and of thought and they are numbered to be 50 or 52 comprising the diverse faculties which, in this way, are not the functions of soul but subconscious constructions which can be destroyed as they were formed and which are consequently *anitya*, 'impermanent'. It is ignorance that gives them the occasion (*nidāna*) to be produced and to be active since intelligence, when it is trained, according to *yoga*, counters them. (Buddhism makes intelligence, *prajñā*, that has arrived at awakening, *bodhi*, the condition for their destruction). They themselves find the opportunity to give birth to conscious phenomena (*vijñāna*), as they are in charge of the functions attributed to the faculties. This explains why the well-known doctrine of the twelve occasions of the production in chain teaches that ignorance gives birth to *saṃskāras* and *saṃskāras* to thought. This also explains the theory of transmigration and the fruition of the acts of one life into another.

Without concerning itself with the soul, Buddhism believes that the subconscious formations are above the dissolution of the body and pass into new bodies exactly as they were formed by the traces of previous psychic states. They continue, therefore, automatically and without the intervention of a distributive justice, through lives and activities (*karman*) which gave them birth, until man develops the intelligence about their impermanent and unreal nature and thereby extinguishes them.

However, if we admit such an explanation, it should not lead us to infer that historically the Buddhist theory is derived from yoga. We have seen first in yoga and then in Buddhism the nature of the speculation on the unconscious, but, in fact, the theory of *saṃskāras*, absent from the psychology of the *Upaniṣads* and from the works on physiology, first appears in Buddhism and only subsequently in the texts of yoga, the doctrines of which contain an elaboration which is not necessarily anterior to Buddhism.

CHAPTER 21

THE WESTERN INTERPRETATION OF INDIAN THOUGHT*

It is a question worthy of examination to know whether there exists in all human beings a unique, identical structure of the mind or are there several, distinct and irreducible to one another. In other words, it is a fundamental problem for the science of man to determine whether the differences in culture and the divergences of ideas in the great civilizations are due only to the specific circumstances of the evolution of each and whether these great civilisations can agree in their essence or whether, on the contrary, a radical difference in the nature of the minds prevents a profound, mutual understanding, forces them to find points of agreement only in superficial things, and forever stops them from understanding and appreciating each other completely.

The interpretation of Indian thought by the Westerners raises, in a precise and typical case, this important question. The very solution to this depends on the possibility of such an interpretation. It is evident that if the Indian mind and that of Europe were radically different from each other, the Westerners could not meaningfully interpret Indian thought and that is precisely what one often thinks, in Europe as well as in Asia. The debate has been going on, unchecked, for a long time, on the interpretative method to be used and on the validity of the result obtained. One has, therefore, already collected a large stock of observations, one has invented a number of arguments, defined several subjects for discussion, and it is indeed necessary to use all this material to try and combine the elements that would go into answering this question. Can the West fathom the thought of India and, if yes, how can it do so? Indian thought has continued to attract an ever-increasing number of Westerners

*Lecture delivered at the Alliance Française of Saigon in 1949 and published under the title: L'Intérprétation occidentale de la pensée indienne, in *Education* no. 15 Saigon, March-April 1949, pp. 1-16.

and it can play an ever more significant role in the universal culture on the condition that it can be universally assimilated. One must, therefore, find out whether that can truly be done, in spite of the difficulties that lie in such an evaluation, because of the vast interest it possesses in itself and because the answer will be a fundamental testimony to be included in the file of the more general problem of the oneness or the multiplicity of the nature of human minds.

In a land like Indo-China, where we see the confluence of cultural currents and in this 'Alliance Francaise', where a culture flourishes that is ready to assimilate all other cultures, an Indologist, therefore, can do no better than invite you to evaluate the chances of success of the West in its effort at interpreting Indian thought.

French culture was formed from successive assimilations and continuous synthesising. It was Gallo-Roman, Christian, Classical, European and in numerous different ways, it has exalted for two hundred years, almost even before knowing them, through a presentiment of their greatness, all the civilizations of Asia, and now that it possesses a long tradition of their studies, it is necessary that it integrate the findings about them into its own general knowledge and into the universal culture towards which it has always tended.

Ancient Indian thought is available to us in a vast literature, undoubtedly the most abundant that the ancient times have bequeathed us and although numerous translations of this literature exist, we are far from knowing all the important works through them. Moreover, many of them are mediocre and some which are excellent, are meaningful only to readers who are specially prepared.

A present body of thought which is very current, is an extension of the thinking of ancient times which it explains and comments on or which it renews by adapting it to the present-day pre-occupations. This present body of thought is often expressed in English, to reach a wider audience, not only in the world but in India itself, where different regions have distinct languages. Sometimes Sanskrit is used throughout India even as Latin was formerly in Europe when one wanted to disseminate a text in the intellectual circles of different countries.

It goes without saying that this present Indian thought, when it is directly expressed in an European language, does not pose the difficulties of the ancient thought, whose interpretation is what specially needs to be studied.

In order to proceed in the simplest possible way, we shall first consider under what conditions was Indian thought revealed to the West and what were the successive means that the West has been able to adopt to have a progressively deeper knowledge of it. We will thus review the increasing efforts at interpretation from the time of the simplest elementary contacts.

The first moderately accurate notions of Indian thought were put together by a missionary, Father Pons, at the beginning of the 18th century; but the first Indian philosophical text to be interpreted in a European language was the *Bhagavadgītā* translated by Wilkins into English at the end of the 18th century.

Wilkins' interpretation was made with the help of Indian scholars. It is correct and agrees with classical commentaries. As the text of the *Bhagavadgītā* did not present any major difficulties, it was fairly well understood and was intensely admired. It is known to be one of the most popular and remarkable texts of the tradition. This text forms a part of the voluminous epic poem of the *Mahābhārata*, a story of titanic battles between two royal families, related but sworn enemies. One is helped by Lord Kṛṣṇa who assumes the role of the charioteer of one of the heroes who belongs to this family. At the time of going into a great battle, this hero falters: 'Those there are my kinsmen, those warriors that I shall fight', he says to himself. 'I am confounded as to which is more terrible, for me to be conquered by them or to conquer them.' And thus starts a colloquy which is a complete religious teaching in itself, rather a whole philosophy of the Supreme Being, of the World and of Man. The Lord, in fact, became the hero's charioteer to be not only his guide but also of the whole of humanity towards salvation through the supreme knowledge of the Norm, of the Order of things and of Duty which is the full realisation of this Norm. The hero will have to fight because such is the Norm of the warrior. Man must fulfil the destiny which has been assigned to him, but he should fulfil it with a vision that carries him beyond the fruit of action, beyond the innumerable appearances, to the Supreme Being whom one most strive to discover, know and love in all things.

We might not have fully appreciated, when this text was offered to Europe, the secret of upliftment and energy that it contains and which turns it into a great human work. We wanted to judge it from the theological point of view, to relate it to one of the known systems of theological teachings in order to classify it in familiar categories and it was viewed mainly as a pantheistic work. On considering it from this point of view we did not misjudge its character but we saw it with too restricted a vision and we have there the first instance of an obstacle which the Western interpretation might sun into: its linking to the already known which conceals the new and the original.

A little later, a more ancient Indian thought, the purely Brahmanic thought, was, in its turn, revealed to Europe by Anquetil Duperron. Anquetil impelled by youthful zeal but carried by the light of genius left for Asia, enlisted as a soldier with the French Compagnie des Indes, in order to win for the knowledge of the world, the sacred books of India and Persia, then unknown to the world, from the hands of their followers. He came back carrying the books of Persia which he offered to Europe in a French translation and he may have received after his return the Persian translation of the *Upaniṣads* from a friend equally eager to discover the thought of Asia, Gentil, who was a French officer in the service of an Indian prince. This translation was done in the 17th century on the orders of Dara-Shikoh, the great enlightened and liberal Moghul Sovereign, whom his brother Aurangzeb, a fanatic Muslim and implacable tyrant, did not delay in overthrowing. Dara was a patron of arts, a Muslim scholar who was equally eager to learn foreign religions and philosophies, and ready to respect their greatness. He assembled Indians around him, scholars who were very conversant in Persian,—which was then the official language of the enlightened Moghul empire—, but who continued the wonderful tradition of intellectual intercourse between India and Islam which had begun since the days of the great Akbar, another enlightened but more fortunate Moghul than Dara. These scholars were well trained for their work of translation from Sanskrit into Persian, precisely because there existed in their fold and in the midst of the scholars of the Persian language who were associated with them, a fruitful tradition of intellectual interchange. Their translation was faithful, but often certain technical Sanskrit words without exact Persian equivalents were left untranslated and, for those who were not at all familiar with these expressions beforehand their text contained obscure points. Anquetil first translated this version in French and published some parts of it. But he deemed it prudent so as not to deform ideas which could already have been somewhat altered in their first translation to a foreign language, to render as literally as possible the Persian version and he thought it best to do it in Latin. It is, therefore, in Latin in 1804 that the complete European translation of the Persian version of the *Upaniṣads* appeared.

The Latin translation is a remarkably conscientious and precise piece of work and it immediately gave a lofty idea of Brahmanic thought. It showed its religious nature because it rightly showed that its teaching was aimed at Liberation by a spiritual transcendence of human limitations, by the revelations of a metaphysical knowledge which was a liberating knowledge. And Anquetil Duperron brought out the master-thought so well, the thought which had inspired the ancient Brahmanic sages and according to which spiritual union with the Supreme Being leads to identification with him, that he chose as the epigraph for his book, this very thought expressed among many others in the *Upaniṣads*: 'Quisquis Deum intellegit, Deus fit', 'He who understands God becomes God.'

Unfortunately, it was very difficult to be both literal and clear. Latin which by its freedom of word-order had lent itself with ease to being literal also, at the same time, became obscure by following too faithfully the usage of a foreign language. The technical Sanskrit words inserted without translation and some approximative correspondences between Persian and Latin words added to the difficulty of reading and understanding and Anquetil's work remained incomprehensible to many readers. While reading him we meet another obstacle, that of excessive literalness which we will find elsewhere too. In Anquetil's work on the *Upaniṣads*, this obstacle, however, did not prevent some celebrated thinkers like Schopenhauer, to have a lofty idea of Brahmanic philosophy and to find there a source of inspiration.

Shortly after the publication of Anquetil's work, progress in the study of Sanskrit in Europe soon started giving the Europeans direct access to Indian texts. A great work of setting down Sanskrit grammars and making dictionaries was then undertaken by European and Indian scholars together. One sometimes believes that philosophical and mystic India understood its texts by tradition and intuition and did not have to concern itself with an explicit grammatical analysis as the Europeans do while studying Sanskrit texts. It is a serious mistake. It is India, on the contrary, that has revealed to the European world the linguistic science by providing it with the model of its detailed and particularly penetrating analysis of Sanskrit, an analysis that had already been perfected several centuries before the Christian era.

Moreover, it is confirmed that since ancient times, the Indian students have always received a highly advanced teaching of grammar in schools. It is this very teaching by itself that has maintained the usage of Sanskrit become obsolete as a popular language since at least the 3rd century B.C., as we see from the official royal inscriptions of the period. It is certain that without the educational tradition of grammarians, the classical authors would not have been able to conserve Sanskrit and that their language would have followed the natural evolution of spoken languages which were becoming rapidly more and more variegated; this is what happened to the authors of different regional literatures.

The Sanskrit authors of philosophical or scientific texts and their commentators were all well-prepared to meet the exigencies of grammar. The Western scholars needed, therefore, to understand thoroughly these exigencies in order to understand better the mentality of the authors and to grasp all the subtleties of their expressions. A profound study of Sanskrit grammar under the guidance of Sanskrit grammarians themselves was, therefore, a great step, indirect but essential, towards the interpretation of Indian thought.

And for the same reason one of the best English grammarians of Sanskrit at the beginning of the 19th century became the first to be able to tackle the basic texts of different systems of the Indian philosophy. Moreover, the Indian scholars themselves had shown the Tibetans formerly the need of studying Sanskrit grammar in order to delve into the doctrines of India. When in the 7th century A.D., Tibet established intellectual contact with India, the Tibetans borrowed from the latter a grammatical system and subsequently translated a host of Sanskrit grammars with their most detailed commentaries and included these translations in one of their canonical compilations, next to Buddhist texts the interpretation of which was aided by a deeper knowledge of these grammars.

We see through all this the falsity of the opinion spread in some milieus today that the Western Indologists deviate from the pure Indian tradition when they study closely the grammar of the texts which they have to interpret.

However, it is quite evident that grammatical interpretation is only an indispensable means for the intelligibility of a text and that it does not lead to its comprehension. It must be preliminary and not final.

Progress in the studies of Sanskrit grammar in Europe at the beginning of the 19th century greatly advanced the knowledge of purely literary texts in Sanskrit and even enabled the tackling of texts, some archaic, in Vedic Sanskrit, and others in languages derived from Sanskrit, in Prākrit, texts for which the support from Indian grammars and commentaries was less useful, less certain or less accessible than in the domain of classical Sanskrit.

In this last domain, the full intelligibility of the religious, philosophical and scientific texts required, after the precise setting down of the literal meaning according to the grammar, the fixing of the values of technical terms and the familiarity with the ideas. The works of thought literally traced from the original texts contain the same problem as Anquetil's translation that was done from the Persian version.

For the rest, the technical and philosophical Sanskrit texts normally do not carry the full meaning in themselves. The Indian intellectual tradition is above all an oral tradition. The scriptures do not form the totality of the wisdom but its summary. A good part of the literature is an aide-mémoire and not a dissertation. The master who composed a book normally did it in such a way that it could be easily memorised and oral teaching comments on brief formulae, sometimes syncopated, sometimes even conventionally symbolic which make up the book. Often the author himself writes a commentary to his book when he wants to reach a wider public than his circle of disciples, rather than include in the book itself the explanations he gives in the form of commentary. This state of affairs is another obstacle in the Western interpretation of Indian thought.

One has tried several methods to get round this obstacle and go beyond. One of the most notable writers at the time of the beginning of the English influence in India, Ram Mohan Roy had already suggested one such method. Ram Mohan Roy was one of the first Brahmins who knew how to be Europeanised without giving up Brahmanism, one of those men who had a mind open enough to contain two cultures simultaneously and judicious enough to know how to harmonise them. Enthusiastic to learn Western ideas, he was quick to master them and did not draw back to get a profounder insight from studying not only English but Latin, Greek and even Hebrew. It seemed to him that, in the spiritual order, India and the West could be reconciled and it is to be clearly noted in passing, that his opinion in this context is competent since he knew Western thought as well as that of his country. From that time he dreamed of a sort of Indo-Western synthesis of a universal wisdom, uniting the common aspirations of India and the West, and he founded, in fact, a whole school which was at the base of a great spiritual movement, still thriving today in India under different forms. But he was not satisfied with India being able to understand Europe, Europe also needed to understand India. Ram Mohan Roy also endeavoured to bring within the reach of the European public, in very short but suggestive and clear writings, the traditional philosophy which is the culmination of Indian metaphysical thought, precisely called *Vedānta* in Sanskrit, i.e. 'Culmination of Knowledge'.

Since then, such statements or simplified translations, paraphrases, meant for Europeans, have grown infinitely in the English literature written by Indians and they have contributed very efficiently to the spread of Indian thought and to increase admiration for it in numerous Western milieus.

The action of some remarkable Indian personalities was specially successful in this matter during the whole of the 19th century and since. A great movement resulted among the disciples of the admirable mystic saint, Ramakrishna who founded the present Ramakrishna Mission which has spread to the West, both the spirit of the Master and the taste of Indian philosophy in general. One of Ramakrishna's disciples, Vivekananda, left a voluminous explanatory work of Indian thought for Westerners and which forms the lucid source from which many draw their knowledge of India. Even today, many an eminent Indian thinker publishes or leaves for his disciples to publish in an European language, his teachings, be they purely original or syncretic, combining the ancient with the modern thought of the West, or interpreting ancient Sanskrit texts. Such are the representatives of the ancient teaching of Śaṅkarācārya or people like Sri Aurobindo, Ramana Maharshi and many others. On the other hand, and as a reply to the Indian initiatives to promote Indian thought in the West, the Westerners have sometimes founded societies for the study and understanding of this thought, such as the Theosophical Society.

All these movements, greatly differing in their action and profound purpose, strive not only to facilitate the interpretation of classical Indian thought but also to introduce it in the entire life of humanity, to involve it, together with their own ideas, in the activity of modern man. We are, therefore, seeing here in their endeavours the opening of numerous spiritual channels between the East and the West but these channels are not always conducive to an objective interpretation of ancient thought. They are of great interest in themselves. They can bring about elevated spiritual realisations but they deviate from an exact comprehension of the ancient Brahmanic thought. They are the expressions of a contemporary philosophy, and not restitutions of the ancient one.

One can, however, say that numerous contemporary Indian thinkers seek to explain the ancient spirit of Brahmanism rather than to synthesise it with Western ideas. It is also often said that in this case they are the most qualified to present to the West the true significance of ancient Indian thought, since their tradition, their atavism or their genius gives them a complete understanding of this significance and their Western education makes them capable of translating, in the best way they can, into a European language the ideas they profoundly feel. There is some truth in these reflections but one must admit that, often, the task of making Indian thought accessible to the West is not without difficulty or misunderstanding, even and more so, when eminent Indian thinkers try doing so. Owing to all their originality and power, these thinkers are, in fact, tempted to choose subjects against their will, to present to the public those interpretations of Indian thought which suit their own feelings, their own pre-occupations best or those that seem to them the most apt to be clearly understood by the Westerners and they leave aside the rest. For,—and this is another difficulty of entering into Indian thought—, there exists almost always in India itself, and also in ancient India, several interpretations of the same facts.

From the time of the *Upaniṣads*, of which many parts are dialogues and which frequently present learned men of opposing doctrines, one has seen these learned men vehemently confronting, contradicting each other, arguing among themselves or indulging in mutual criticism, bearing witness to fruitful rivalries and far from repeating some creed in passivity. In the later religious and philosophic Sanskrit literature, controversy plays an important role. Beside, the many debates between great rival doctrines, Brahmanic, Buddhist, Jain, within milieus which claim to adhere to the same general doctrine, the sects or schools are many and on the basis of the same fundamental texts these suggest and defend opposite interpretations. Śaṃkara's commentary on the central text of *Vedānta*, the *Brahmasūtras*, interprets the contents of this text as advocating Absolute Oneness of Being, absolute Monism, while other commentaries see in the same data the expression of a qualified Monism, even of a Dualism. It is, therefore, impossible, by following the personal opinion of any master, ancient or modern, to presume to understand the true meaning of a text, for there exists almost always other rival exegeses which should not be rejected à priori; to state it better, India does not have only one thought but a multitude of ideas which makes Indian culture, on the whole, more living and richer, than one might believe by approaching it merely from one side.

This leads us to the arduous path, the multiple path by which it must be approached. Any text, any doctrine should never be considered in isolation. One does not know them as long as one ignores the frame-work of which they are a part, one does not know this framework as long as one does not see the whole of which that itself is a part. One is thus led to recognise more and more the necessity of possessing, even if it be to explain a detail, a general culture of India. This necessity defines the essential condition for the correct interpretation of Indian thought.

For Indian authors, this condition exists already in so far as they are familiar with their tradition, but it does not follow that Indian authors make themselves directly understood by the Westerners for whom this condition does not exist, even when the former speaks to them in Western languages.

But for Westerners, this condition itself is difficult to obtain as it demands a long study to which only a few are capable of devoting themselves. The slowness in becoming familiar with India is, therefore, another impediment to its full understanding by Westerners.

It is for us now to examine in detail what this obstacle is, why it is taking so long to overcome it; and then it will also be an opportunity to recapitulate what constitutes Indian culture.

Firstly, one needs to become familiar with the principal language of this culture, Sanskrit, to be able to read the texts directly and to eliminate the inevitable distortion that seeps into translations. One must then follow the rules of grammar of which one can be sure that they were strictly observed by the authors. In a number of cases, one must even accept to follow these authors in the etymological speculations which theoretical linguistics proves to be wrong but which were nonetheless held to be true and which have consequently affected the thought of the texts.

One must at the same time seek to place oneself in the mentality of the authors and their environment, endeavour to adapt oneself to the knowledge which they probably had brought together and according to which they reflected. For this, one must, in some way, pursue oneself the studies that they followed.

We have already said that this knowledge of grammar was profound. One must also remember that all of these authors studied logic too, the art of thinking, reasoning and drawing right conclusions. This art is called *nyāya.* It defines the criteria for truth, in different ways in fact, according to the schools. Some recognise only the observed fact, others, more numerous, accept inference, comparison, personal testimony or other modes still of arriving at a conclusion. *Nyāya* defines, in addition, modes of linked deductions and it studies the errors of judgment in order to teach the way of avoiding them. Texts, commentaries, refutations always use the principles so defined but without openly disclosing them because they are supposed to be known and for those who ignore them, the allusions that are made there, even the steps of reasoning they command, are incomprehensible.

Besides, all the Sanskrit authors absorbed during their studies traditional notions of mythology, the royal dynasties and of the structure of the world, without counting more special and less frequently taught notions of the ancient Vedic texts or of specific techniques. What are most important are the notions they have of nature, of physiology and psychology because they constitute the starting points of their speculations. Now these notions come from sciences which very early on secured an autonomy among Indian researches and which were greatly developed. They also got classified very early in well-defined systems, of which all Indian scholars, even the non-specialists, know the broad outlines and to which they implicitly refer. We cannot understand the complete import of their comments if we do not know them.

To cite but one example to demonstrate this need to know them and the wrong paths one can take if one ignores them, let us consider the well-known technique of Yoga.

We know that this technique aims at the perfect mastery of the body and the mind, a mastery which is capable of conferring superior powers or, better still, to lead to liberation through identification with the Absolute Being. This technique uses as one of its fundamental means the regulation of the respiratory breath and this is where surprise is often expressed, and unwarranted suppositions made, by those who are directly interested in yoga without taking care to study other Indian doctrines as well, doctrines which don't seem to them to be related to yoga. And the Westerners are not the only ones to belong to this category, numerous Indian authors too today work specifically on yoga without having followed the whole range of the ancient teaching. Now these texts of yoga do not explain why the regulation of breath is prescribed by them. The explanation is implicit for them as it is found in the texts of physiology and that is where one has to look for it.

Without doing so, one has often supposed that regulation of breath was an empirical process inherited from ancient prehistoric shamans using physiological means to enter into trance and it was believed that yoga originated from a deliberately invented prehistory whereas the explanation is very simple.

Ancient Brahmanic physiology, systematised in medical texts universally accepted in the ancient times, shows that life consists of breaths circulating in the whole body and of which the respiratory breath is only a part, directly under the control of the will. It was, therefore, absolutely natural that one sought to modify vital phenomena, to indirectly dominate them, by controlling the functions of the body, that is, by acting on the respiration. On the other hand, the psychology in ancient scientific texts served as a basis for ideas current in the ancient Brahmanic societies and this psychology showed that the phenomena of thought rested on breath, or the soul could be said to be composed of air. It follows that it was common knowledge that working on the breath of the body was highly conducive to controlling the spiritual state and the doctrines of yoga are founded on this basis which is always present though never explained. One gets lost in conjecture when one considers them without being familiar with the ideas of those very men who formerly conceived and expounded these doctrines. It is, therefore, through a study of the ancient knowledge of the authors of the texts that one must look for the explanations of their thought and it is only there that one can find them.

The difficulty in knowing, in this way, the entire tradition of Indian learning, in understanding properly even a single text is very great. Still it is not enough to overcome it. One must also know Indian History, general and regional history, Indian law and Indian society. In other words, the totality of Indology which cannot be set out in detail without suffering some distortion.

This is not strange in the least, nor exceptional. If a European philosopher can fruitfully read a text of Plato either in the original or in a translation, it is simply because he has imbibed, from his customary educational upbringing, from his being placed in the tradition of Western culture, the ideas which are not referred to in the text and which are, however, necessary to its understanding. Therefore, it is not astonishing at all that one needs to possess India's culture in order to understand her.

In these conditions, one may, however, say that the knowledge of Indian thought is restricted to a very small number of Westerners. If it is a question of an indispensable knowledge for a profound elucidation of the texts, this is true. Similarly, a deep comprehension of Plato is restricted to only a small number of Hellenists. But if it is a question of a more general knowledge, it can certainly be acquired at lesser expenses. The difficulty comes only from the fact that carrying out endless new researches, the indologists, much too few still, have not always been able to provide translations with commentaries and with descriptions of doctrines which would be necessary. But this is only a temporary difficulty. It will be resolved by the increasing contribution made to indology by a growing commitment of individuals to learning, impelled by the already widespread knowledge and by the ever more greatly felt necessity of integrating the thought of Asia with a universal humanism.

It, however, still remains to be seen, when all the difficulties have been overcome, whether the integration will actually be feasible. In enumerating the dangers, obstacles and the sluggishness, we have not found any which arise from the very structure of Indian thought. However, one can still suspect that there exist such obstacles. What means do we possess of being sure that they do not?

Some authors, either in India or in the West in certain milieus, indeed claim that they do exist. They readily confront the materialist tendencies of the Westerners and the spirituality of India, they deem that the latter reaches summits which the matter-of-fact mind of the rationalist and scientific West cannot attain. If it were so, one should deplore it, not only for the sake of the West but also for India herself whose doctrines could not have a universal value and would remain confined to a greatness which, from outside, one could feel, admire and measure only through prejudice.

Fortunately, it seems that it is not so. It is false that India knows only spirituality and the West only materialism. Both mingle and agree between themselves more frequently than one would believe at first sight. One needs only the patience to compare them and to harmonise them and there exist conclusive proofs of their mutual understanding.

We have already noted in passing that Indian thinkers having a grasp of both Indian and Western thought, like Ram Mohan Roy, have not found any incompatibility between them.

On the other hand, Westerners are not the only foreigners to India who ever attempted to interpret its thought. Indian culture is one of the most widespread in the world: it has traversed the whole of Eastern Asia and it has been absorbed in its entirety by a number of different races. This cannot be better observed than in Indo-China. It is, therefore, truly a universally intelligible culture. It is true that some say that Asian races can, in fact, understand it easily but that the mind of the Westerners has become too different for the culture to be accessible to it. One could ask these to consider the works of those indologists who, in order to complete their studies of India, take recourse to the data that the Tibetans or the Chinese have translated from Indian languages. If they study these works, they will arrive at the conclusion which obviously follows. The Tibetans and the Chinese made of the same Sanskrit texts versions which exactly correspond to each other and also to those that the Western idologists, on their part, can make of the same Sanskrit texts. The same methods of interpretation that the Indian scholars had formerly passed on to the Tibetans and the Chinese and which we Europeans too have drawn from the scholarly traditions of India, lead to the same results. Therefore, we in the West actually do understand Indian doctrines as the Asian scholars have understood them and as the Indians wanted them to be understood.

And so we can conclude: an interpretation by the Westerners of Indian thought is, no doubt, full of difficulties and impediments, since we must assimilate a vast culture from which we cannot divorce it. We do not, however, mean a delimited and heterogeneous or limited thought which must remain forever hidden, a treasure of no use to humanity as a whole. On the contrary, we mean here a thought which has a universal value which will reward all our endeavours at its discovery and validation.

CHAPTER 22

CONTINENCE AND SEXUALITY IN BUDDHISM AND IN THE DISCIPLINES OF YOGA*

THERE ARE DIFFERENT ANSWERS to the question whether continence is advocated out of fear of sexuality or because it seems to be an aid in mystical life; the answers, although they differ according to the different forms of Buddhism and the different disciplines of yoga, are always very clear-cut.

In ancient Buddhism, it is indisputable that there exists a fear of sexuality and that the advocacy of continence is unambiguously absolute. What's more, in strict theory, the involuntary thoughts that are contrary to continence should not even exist. It is not enough to reject them, they must not even come into being. On the one hand, the minutest disciplinary precautions are taken to remove any opportunity for their occurrence among the monks and on the other, the aim is the elimination of the possibility of their emergence in the mind, and this is especially the goal of the technique of psychic reformation which is the crux of the Buddhist method of salvation.

We might think that a parallel exists between the Buddhist belief that sexuality is a great danger and the important Brahmanic notion that absolute continence is a condition for the acquisition and the containment of higher powers conferred by asceticism. In that case, one could wonder whether sexuality is condemned in itself or whether it needs to be simply avoided for fear of losing those energies which, on the contrary, continence would help to conserve.

The Brahmanic belief, according to which, the act of sexuality entails a drop in the general energy-potential, comes across in numerous legends about ascetics immersed in a rigorous discipline of austerities (*tapas*) in order to acquire extraordinary powers

*Continence et sexualité dans le bouddhisme et les disciplines de Yoga, in *Mystique et continence*, Etudes carmélitaines, Paris, 1952, pp. 70-81.

but who lost all the benefit of these austerities at the slightest sexual desire. From this point of view, the danger of sexuality and that of anger, another violent emotion, are identical for ascetics. In the *Rāmāyaṇa*, Viśvāmitra loses the effect of a thousand years of askesis, the first time, when he lets himself be seduced by the nymph Menakā, and the second time, by losing his temper against the nymph Rambhā who had also come to seduce him. It is only after a third askesis of a thousand years that he attains his inmost aspiration, as soon as he becomes fully the master of all his impulses (I, LXIII-LXV). It is then not a conscious reflected desire that is harmful but an involuntary impulse. The sexual impulse and the movement of anger are denounced not in themselves but as hindrances in self-mastery. In the legend of the god Śiva who during an askesis does not suffer any loss of energy, while, in fury, he burns to ashes the god of Love who has come to tempt him, and then proceeds to marry Umā, the contradiction of this fact is only apparent. In this last act, Śiva does not yield to an impulse, but acts in a state of personal detachment: 'For me there are no activities that are directed at myself', Kālidāsa makes him say.[1] Furthermore, despite the superiority of continence, the union of the two gods (Śiva and Kṛṣṇa) with their consorts is raised as a symbol of a mystic union (the Song of Jayadeva, *Gītagovinda*, is comparable in this respect with the *Cantique des Cantiques*).

Continence, therefore, continues to be advocated in the classical Brahmanic legends not out of fear of sexuality but for the conservation of potential and this was so right from the ancient Brahmanic period when the Brahmanic student (*brahmacārin*) was supposed to respect chastity during the entire course of his spiritual training. Only when this training was over, was marriage officially prescribed. Whosoever desired to lift himself above the ordinary human level, spiritually and materially, had to follow the path of continence.

From the Buddhist point of view, psychophysiological discipline demands absolute chastity and can confer extraordinary powers quite similar to the ones often sought by Brahmanic askesis. One can, therefore, be led to believe that both in Buddhism and Brahmanism, sexuality is prohibited principally as a cause of a loss of potential energy.

However, a deeper investigation shows that it is not so. Firstly, the extraordinary powers for the realisation of which continence would be indispensable, play only a secondary role in Buddhism. The fact of their quest cannot explain the condemnation of sexuality which is more severe than in Brahmanism. Then and above all, the Buddhist notion about the necessity of continence is a consequence of the theory itself which sees man as entangled in an existence of suffering and seeking ways of salvation.

Whatever may have been the origin of the belief in transmigration, it is explained in the following manner in Buddhism, as can be easily gathered from classical Buddhist sources.

After any act of the body, of speech or of thought, an act that is marked by a certain psychic participation, the agent of the act is no more the same as before. The action leaves an imprint on him, an imprint that retains a part of the action that provoked it. The accumulated traces go to make an unconscious, psychic stock, some elements of which eventually reappear in the memory, but which above all go into the making of individuality. This stock is organised by coherent and dynamic constructions (*saṃskāras*) which quite resemble the 'complexes' of the unconscious in modern psychology. This stock does not constitute a person, a unitary being but an aggregate which practically takes the place of a person since it is individual. At death, this aggregate does not get dissolved and wanders about until it finds an opportunity to reincarnate in an embryo, in correspondence with the inherited potentialities of acts that slowly formed him and gave him a certain orientation. These potentialities will from now on tend towards fulfilment in a new existence, in a new body that has already been selected and which would become an instrument of realisation. Such is the productive mechanism of transmigration and the most dynamic active traces left by acts in the transmigrating psychic stock are desire and passionate impulse.

Now, the transmigration that takes place in this way is bad. The false personal entity which is nothing more than an amalgamation of the consequences of acts, does not benefit from the nature of the Absolute Being but endlessly experiences suffering linked to this conditional existence, which even if relatively happy, is interrupted by death. Salvation would mean an end to this vain and cruel chain of successive lives. It can be achieved by stopping this accumulation of the traces of action in the psychic stock and by neutralising those that already exist and are active. It will mean the extinction (*nirvāṇa*) of their activity. Desire, a major cause of this activity, should not merely be suppressed but be eliminated altogether. If it still occurs, even only accidently and only to be suppressed, it is because desire is still active in the unconscious psychism and that the goal of Buddhist discipline has not been reached. It is not guilty in this case but it is a sign of imperfection and a cause of tainting as it can leave in the psychic stock a new trace, a new seed for yet another reproduction eventually.

From the Buddhist point of view, then, desire is a major enemy. Continence is an absolute necessity, even an accidental temptation should be rendered impossible. The Buddhist sage should not only resist it but he should not even get to know it.

This standpoint is well illustrated by the notion of the purity of Buddha's mother and by the story about a great schism in the 4th century B.C.

The Buddha is not supposed to have been born from a virgin as was believed by St. Jerome; his mother was the wife of King Śuddhodana. But she conceived in an immaculate way. This happened during a period when his mother practiced chastity; the conception took place by a miraculous descent into her womb.[2] It is moreover believed, in principle, that the mother of a Buddha cannot inspire the slightest desire in those who behold her.[3] There does exist a total incompatibility between the Buddhist idea of perfection and sexuality.

The history of the great schisms in Buddhism imputes the responsibility for one of these, which took place a little over hundred years after the Buddha's passing, on someone known as Mahādeva.[4] The orthodox schools consider this Mahādeva too have been an old criminal who had converted insincerely and who was the author of five scandalous propositions. The first was that a Buddhist saint (*arhant*), in principle, rid of all trace of action that could entail a rebirth and continuing to live only to exhaust a residue of potentiality born from previous actions, could still be tainted by wet dreams. Temptation in dreams and its consequences did not seem culpable to Mahādeva and, therefore, not contrary to purity which should characterise the saint. No doubt, the orthodox did not consider them any more culpable in themselves, but they maintained that they were a sign of a persistence of impurity in the residual stock.

Below the Buddhist saint, there, however, exist the multitudes who can only move slowly, across numerous lives, towards salvation, and who can direct their psychic stock transmigrating towards increasingly favourable or pleasant rebirths, only by right conduct, good deeds and by hearing the law. For these, continence, however desirable, is not yet indispensable. It is even considered normal that in certain divine existences which we obtain justly through an acquisition of merit, continence is not observed and that Buddhist ethics is possibly practiced in order to become worthy of such existences.

The legend of the Buddha's half-brother, Sundarananda, is a clear illustration of these facts. Sundarananda, who had been made into a monk against his will, on the very day of his wedding, misses his beloved. He is led by the Buddha on a celestial journey during which he first perceives a female monkey horribly burnt by fire and then the nymphs of a paradise. He admits that these nymphs prevail as much over his beloved as she did over the female monkey, and he accepts his monastic state in order to merit a rebirth among the nymphs. In fact, he takes up the Buddhist discipline so well, that his heart changes and he renounces all desire, momentary or reflected, in order to set out on the path of salvation. That is exactly where the Buddha wanted to lead him. The fact, however, remains that he first offered continence not as an absolute ideal but as some sort of a 'deposit' of enjoyment at a high interest. By doing this the Buddha accepted (and the common disciples ordinarily admitted too) that it was legitimate to desire as heavenly delight that which was condemned as human gratification, if not to attain saintlihood then, at least, on the lower levels of the Buddhistic discipline.

According to the Buddhist idea, these same joys are ordinarily part of the lot of beings who take birth as gods and goddesses. In the tiered heavens the union of two beings is more and more refined and distant until it is reduced to the enjoyment of a gaze but this union is part of divine felicity. In the worlds which are above the human one, up to a certain level, where one is under the sway of the god Māra who is Love and Death together, which culminates above the whole cosmic domain of desires—before arriving at worlds free from desire and even from perceptibility—continence is not a necessary virtue. Obviously, the Buddhist saints, beginning with the future Buddhas, who in spite of their being established in a paradise of the world of desires, are immune from all impurity. But for inferior gods, the absence of continence is the rule.

This absence is a proof, in them as in men, of a persisting impurity and attachment to the process of existence, but the consequences of actions do not have the same importance for gods as for men. In non-human births, in fact, there is merely a realisation of the consequences of the accumulation in the psychic stock of traces linked to previous actions, there is no accumulation of new traces. It is only in human rebirths that actions leave traces, because, there exists ideation or mentalisation (*cetanā*) only there, the transformation of perception into thought along with the recording of the latter.[5] The gods enjoy for some time a felicity attained by virtue of the orientation of their activity during past human lives and as gods they are not responsible for either their loss or their salvation. For both, there is needed an entry into the human condition which is the sole determinant. Desire or sexuality do not really exist among the gods as among men because there is no psychic control over sensations. And despite the freedom allowed to gods, sexuality and desire continue to be formally prohibited for men. Sexuality can still enter the life of one who is distantly interested in moving towards liberation but for one who really walks on the path it is to be feared and stifled above all else.

The counterpart of this principle of orthodox Buddhism is provided by a sort of a Buddhism of counter-current, that of the *Tantra*. Buddhism has tended increasingly, in the course of its evolution, to depreciate the phenomenal world in order to battle against attachment of which it is the object. It has ended up in denouncing all things as devoid of an essential nature and reduced to representations without any objective basis, comparable to optical illusions. As a result, anything that belongs to existence stems from a truth of appearance called the truth of enveloping (*saṃvṛtisatya*) and not from Absolute Truth (*paramārthasatya*). He who understands this realises immediately that, in reality, there is neither suffering, nor salvation, neither good nor evil, nor even the Buddha's teaching. He attains directly through this sort of gnosis, Absolute Truth, by discovering the insignificance of the cosmic illusion in which the ordinary being thinks itself to be imprisoned.

On this basis, some sects pushed its consequences to a point where it was considered necessary, in order to establish their mastery of the universal illusion, to deliberately violate the laws of common morality. Their incorruptibility, they thought would be as much demonstrated by this tainting as the proof of incombustibility is demonstrated by the test of fire, or better still, their upliftment beyond the pure or the impure. They followed, then, the contrary of all the Buddhistic prescriptions and developed sexual practices.

One can naturally interpret their theoretical intentions as a retaliatory backlash of the libido—or passions, if one prefers—against the severe constraints of orthodox morality. But such a cursory explanation would be inadequate.

Firstly, the violations of morality do not merely consist in allowing free-play to impulses. These violations are based on certain procedures into which the adept is initiated by the master and they generally take place only after a probation of asceticism which is intended to bestow a kind of immunity against the consequences of such violations. This can, in fact, be interpreted as a vestige in the licence of the orthodox constraint. In addition, despite his disdain for the phenomenal world, the adept should continue to be sufficiently self-controlled to respect certain social obligations. Practically, it is impossible to have total freedom of impulses when one lives within the framework of society. It is to be remembered, above all, that self-mastery is the essential element of the psychophysiological techniques of *yoga* to which the Buddhist techniques are related. The influence of these techniques intervenes, then, to discipline the activity and to give it another significance than the one found in the ordinary libertine.

Moreover, a good part of the violations remains purely mental and constitutes a simple psychic exercise. This is especially so with the violation of the law against murder. It is possible that followers of the *Tantra*, sometimes or even often, did really commit murder;[6] however, the strict teaching of the *Tantra*, restrained by social conscience, advocates that we only imagine it. In the course of an exercise said to be of 'creation' (*bhāvanā*, a psychic creation), the adept imagines, for instance, a god in a terrible form uniting with a goddess who represents that god's energy. He then creates in his mind hatred for the god, love for the goddess, sees himself killing the god and himself uniting with the goddess in his place.[7] While doing this, the adept must not only imagine the characters clearly—something which is facilitated for him by the contemplation of a painting or a statue depicting them—, but he must, moreover, visualise and live the scene as if it was real and from the viewpoint that everything in the world is but a psychic representation is it actually real. Imagination then is truly an act of 'creation' which is as fully efficacious as if the imagined act was really performed.

In such a creation, the adept while placing himself above all morality by thinking of the crime, takes upon himself as much energy as possible by putting into play the two major impulses of hatred and love. What occurs here is not merely a violation of interdictions that to the ordinary person are absolute, so as to assert oneself as supremely perfect and untouched by the consequences of the gravest of mistakes; there is, in addition an attempt at channellizing potential energy and, to some extent, a sublimation of suppressed energies, since a precise symbolism virtually transmutes these energies into an élan towards the supreme status of the Buddha.

Sexual union, according to this symbolism, represents in fact, the union of Intelligence (*prajñā*) with the Means of realisation (*upāya*), in order to produce the thought of Awakening (*bodhicitta*), by which one becomes the 'Awakened One', a Buddha. Thanks to this symbolism an activity which, even when it is reduced to its mere imagination, can lead to the downfall of an uninitiated person by increasing his unconscious psychic stock, for the initiate becomes a measure of salvation. The horror of sexuality is turned to a sublimating use.

However, this kind of sublimation is still looked upon with

great suspicion and the doctrine of the *Tantras* has been decried in orthodox milieus, Buddhist as well as Brahmanic. The practice of *Tantra*, always seeking the loathsome and the disgusting, naturally was accused of unleashing perversities under the false guise of a symbolising doctrine. It is, however, accepted without much hesitation that the good faith of a number of Tantric adepts and authors was sincere but an aberration in good faith is also not uncommon.

In any case, the practices of Buddhist *Tantra* are similar to certain practices of *yoga* in India.

Yoga, which is a rigorous mental and physical discipline, and whose starting-point seems to be in the physiological experiments tried out on the basis of an ancient pneumatic doctrine,[8] consists, in its essential form, in a voluntary stopping of the impermanent phenomena of consciousness (*cittavṛttinirodha*), in order to assume positioning (*samādhi*) over an unconscious, stable base, so as to attain the self within, which is free from the phenomenal self.

It is evident that in such a discipline, the attitude vis-à-vis sexuality should be, like in ancient Buddhism, strictly restrictive. Any impulse capable of disturbing the self-mastery and producing active elements of the phenomenal world we strive to get rid of, is necessarily to be eliminated. But, beside this ideal discipline of *yoga*, there are others which are connected to it by the general technique (attitudes, respiratory exercises, psychic concentration, etc.) which are also part of *yoga* and which, besides, have different aims. These *yogas* do not simply aim at the return of the self to its Absolute Being above the phenomenal world, but to the mastery of the phenomenal world itself, seeking power either for itself or, lifted by a higher ideal, for rising beyond the phenomenal reality. For the general goal, in principle, is the same in classical yoga and in the others. The difference lies in that the former raises one above a phenomenal reality which has been extinguished while the others above a reality that is kept under control. The former represses all those energies which seem external to the Absolute Self, the others strive to channelise them. These consider the energies in fact, to be less alien to the self than would seem, because they connect them to this self, the sole existing entity, by looking upon them as fleeting visions. They are not averse to making use of them, on the condition that they clearly discriminate them from the Absolute which underlies them, that they do not let themselves be carried away by them as if they were fundamental realities. There exists then the same difference between these *yogas* and classical *yoga* as between orthodox and Tantric Buddhism and this difference lies in a restoration of the value of phenomenal energies. The feared and suppressed sexuality in classical yoga and orthodox Buddhism is then restored in its new function, in view of or under the pretext of a higher utilisation.

Meanwhile *yoga*, even the classical one, as defined and described in the *Yogasūtras* of Patañjali, does not dread sexuality as much as ancient Buddhism did. If it does strictly prescribe continence it is not just out of fear for the deadly traces left by a free play of sexuality on the transmigrating self, it is also for the sake of accumulating energy. The *Yogasūtras* are quite clear in this regard: 'When continence is established, there is gain of energy'.[9] It does say 'gain' because it is not merely an economising. Virtuous abstinence from the act procures, in spiritual value, at least, the totality of energy whereas the act itself would only help one gain a part of that energy. The context confirms this. The sentence that precedes it is in fact: 'When there is firmly established the absence of stealing, then all the jewels are at our disposal'.[10] The virtue of sincerity, therefore, guarantees fully, in absolute right if not in practice, the obtaining of the fruit which it prohibits to seek in a wrong way. The impulsive urge fails and renunciation gains precedence. The virtue of continence is founded on this principle in classical *yoga*.

In the other forms of yoga, especially in *haṭhayoga*, the 'yoga of force', and mostly in the *yogas* of the Hindu *Tantras*, analogous to the Buddhist *Tantras*, the virtue of continence is similarly advocated for attaining perfection but once this perfection is attained, the adept can, as in the Buddhist *Tantras*, give up without any danger of a fall, the practice of abstinence which placed him above ordinary morality. It is here that sexuality is employed, in principle sublimated through a symbolism.

Sexuality intervenes less than in the Buddhist *Tantras* but often in an analogous way, at times, in actual fact, at others, as a psychic representation. There exists a particular theory that states that in the lower part of the back, there sleeps a coiled serpent, an energy called *kuṇḍalinī*, which must be awakened and made to rise to the summit of the head in order to unite with Life (*jīva*) and this union represents in the microcosm that is man, the cosmic union of Śiva and His Energy (*śakti*).[11] This view, by itself, makes a mere theoretical allusion to sexuality. But in other texts, the techniques become purely sexual. One of them consists in the combination of a manoeuvre for shuting off the cavum by rolling back the tip of the tongue towards the throat (*khecarīmudrā*)[12] along with the performance of a sexual act without any ejection or with an ejection that is followed by re-assimilation; this last act is also practiced separately (*vajrolī-mudrā*).[13] In these techniques the elements of symbolism are numerous. It is in this way that the secretion of the cavum closed off by the tongue symbolises the lunar nectar of immortality and the flesh of the tongue itself, the meat of the cow, which is to be virtually consumed,[14] whereas in Hinduism there is no stricter prohibition than the consumption of cow-meat.

To this symbolism, other considerations are added in order to encourage the pursuit of such practices. The symbolic union of Śiva and Energy should take place within the microcosm that is the body, if it aspires to reflect a union which occurs in the macrocosm. Moreover, the conservation or the re-assimilation of the seminal fluid is motivated by a distinct notion. It is accepted, in reality, that it depends on the mind (*cittāyatta*), that life (*jīvita*) depends on it, and that, in consequence, one must protect it along with one's mind with the same mindfulness.[15] The yogin who gives up continence and does not pay heed to the moral standpoint, having transcended it, seeks however, not to lose any of its presumed benefits and means to express the same mastery of self-control over the act he consents to, as the one he exerts over the mind through *yoga*.

Through all these practices, whether sexual or other, the yogin seeks to develop a blissful awareness of control of the universe and a realisation of the Absolute Self. At first, he overcomes the dangers of sexuality by the practice of asceticism, then he uses the former in order to invoke the great cosmic mystery of the fusion of the universal energy with the supreme principle. Thus, he believes to have reversed his earlier ordinary attitude to sexuality. Earlier he was its slave but now after having conquered it he becomes its master in order to make use of its potential energy at will.

But it should be remarked that historically such a framework of ideas on continence and sexuality does not derive only from speculative thought within the schools *of yoga.* There are noteworthy antecedents in Brahmanism. One of the principal ancient *Upaniṣads*, the *Bṛhadāraṇyaka-upaniṣad*, contains actually a passage (VI, 4) that describes the rites of sexual union founded on a symbolism of the woman representing the materials of a Vedic sacrifice and the semen which is considered to be the essence of essences (*rasa*). A basic difference has already been established, as it will be later in both *haṭhayoga* and the Hindu and Buddhist *Tantras*, between ordinary sexual union which is unprofitable and the one practiced by the one initiated in symbolism which is beneficial. The initiate who in the beginning, as a Brahmanic student, observed continence is now liberated from it. He has been taught a rite and a formula for the recuperation of potential energy in case the purity of the act is marred. Such a recuperation is already a first form of the kind *haṭhayoga* and *Tantra* strive to realise by physiological techniques. One must not, therefore, see in *haṭhayoga* and *Tantra* a mere spontaneous reaction against the prescription of continence out of fear of the dangers of sexuality and a desire to place the adept above morality even while allowing him to make use of sexual energy for symbolically sublimated ends. One should trace in it an echo of a Brahmanic notion about the licit and beneficial utilisation of sexuality in a certain symbolism after having mastered it in continence.

Our findings can be finally summarised in the following way. In the ancient orthodox forms of Buddhism, continence was conceived to be an absolute necessity for fear of the peril that sexuality attached man to existence. In classical yoga, it was advocated to remove all that disturbed self-mastery and to gain in energy by the practice of renunciation. In *haṭhayoga* and in Hindu and Buddhist *Tantra* sexuality was considered to be utilisable as a source of power and spiritual energy, once it was conclusively mastered instead of it becoming master, thanks to a theoretical symbolism of sublimation which was drawn to a large extent from the Brahmanism of the *Upaniṣads*.

NOTES

1. *Svārthā na me kāś cit pravṛttayaḥ, Kumārasambhava*, VI, 26.
2. Cf. A. Foucher, *La Vie du Bouddha*, Paris, 1949, pp. 39, 46 and notes pp. 356, 357.
3. *Dīghanikāya*, t. II, p. 13 (*Mahāpadānasutta*).
4. Cf. P. Demiéville, *L'origine des sectes bouddhiques, Mélanges chinois et bouddhiques*, t. I, Brussels, 1931-32, p. 30 and foll.
5. There are exceptions. The legends about the previous lives of the Buddha speak of his acquiring merit through heroism for other creatures, even in the animal existences he goes through, and it is certain that this is a merit which increases his perfection on the path of salvation but he is also an exceptional being.
6. Actually in our time: the Kalmouk lama, Dambin-Jansang, who played a great part in Mongolia at the end of the last century and the beginning of the present, is known to have executed after the capture of Kobdo in 1912, Chinese prisoners according to Tantric rites. Cf. R. Bleichsteiner, *L'Eglise jaune*, Paris, 1937, p. 120.
7. *Caṇḍamahāroṣaṇatantra*, IV, 18 and foll., 33 and foll. (Ms. Bibl. Nat. Sanskrit fol. 13a 14b).
8. *Les origines d'une technique mystique indienne. Rev. Philosophique*, April-June 1946 p. 208 and foll.—Now, I would be inclined to do away with the term 'mystic' which is commonly used and accepted but which is unclear and has the disadvantage of suggesting a kinship with spiritual attitudes which actually have nothing in common or comparable, and which subsequently lead to strenuous but vain discriminating speculations.
9. *Brahmacaryapratiṣṭhāyāṃ vīryalābhaḥ*, II, 38.
10. *Asteyapratiṣṭhāyāṃ sarvaratnopasthānam*, II, 37.
11. *Gheraṇḍasaṃhitā*, III, 39-41.
12. *Haṭhayogapradīpikā*, III, 32-42 and commentary of Brahmānanda on 86; *Dhyānabindūpaniṣad*, 83 and foll.; *Yogacūḍāmanyupaniṣad*, 57 and foll.
13. *Haṭhayogapradīpikā*, III, 83-91. The last manoeuvre is physiologically possible by a pumping of the bladder, which certain *haṭha-yogins* demonstrate with the help of water. The non-ejection is due to a flowing towards the bladder. A similar manoeuvre is conceived for the woman reabsorbing her secretions (*Haṭhayogapradī.* III, 99. 103). The manoeuvres for non-ejection are also well-known in the Buddhist *Tantras.* Cf; M. Shahidullah, *Les chants mystiques, de Kanha et de Saraha*, Paris, 1928, pp. 11, 17.
14. *Haṭhayogaprad.*, III 47-49.
15. *Ibid.*, III, 90 and the commentary of Brahmānanda.

CHAPTER 23

THE LIMITS OF HUMAN POWERS IN INDIA*

INDIA IS THE COUNTRY par excellence for the study of the limits of human powers, as much on the physiological level as on the psychological one. In fact, India has evolved since ancient times and in an altogether unique way, highly developed techniques of body and mind that aim at attaining powers or superhuman psychic states, surpassing at least the average human level. For long considered mysterious or purely quackish, these techniques have hardly begun to be studied scientifically. Fortunately they have remained sufficiently alive to enable continuous study in a fruitful way. They are characterised by the production of determinable and not incoherent phenomena which can be reduced to a great number of types that always remain the same. We can, therefore, hope that an accurate study of the conditions they bring about will enable us one day to establish the laws for the production of such phenomena. For the moment, in this study, we are at the first stage of the enquiry, in order to prepare a basic documentation.

We find that there are two categories of phenomena: some somatic, the others psychic. They sometimes appear separate, and at others concomitant. Most often, they both occur, at least in their higher form of realisation, in subjects who possess the knowledge of the traditional theoretical explanations and interpretations which accompany the techniques of their production. These explanations and interpretations cannot be taken as such; even when they are rational, as is often the case, modern physiologists and psychologists inevitably judge them to be arbitrary and simplistic. This does not justify their being ignored and it is equally incorrect to say that their interest is merely historical. They come in, in fact, as psychological components in the web

*Les limites des prouvoirs humains dans l'Inde, in *Limites de l'humain*, Etudes Carmélitaines, Paris, 1953, pp. 23-38.

of conditions for the realisation of such phenomena. Whether right or wrong, the faith of the concerned persons in these interpretations later makes of them the motives that animate them, that elicit their effort and give a direction to its modalities. They are authentic integral parts and in consequence, unimpeachable, of the mechanism of the phenomena. On verification, the importance of their role can be found to be minimal in a host of cases, but the existence of this role, however, should never be ignored. We shall not, therefore, separate the phenomena, which will be briefly reviewed here, from the traditional conceptions, whether rational or mystic, which determine and guide their research.

Moreover, the data supplied by tradition about the facts which interest us, provide us with valuable inventories to be compared with the indications given by observers of all times, though they are occasionally superficial as well as one-sided either due to credulity or incredulity. Finally, the nature of psychic powers, which cannot be observed directly, can only be known by the traditional indications and by the testimonies of those who have consecrated themselves to acquire them. Such testimonies are valuable for the light they throw on the data supplied by ancient texts and, when they can be obtained directly from a subject under observation, they are indispensable in pointing the actual state of his particular psychism, a state which can differ from the one foretold by ancient tradition. But, precisely in case such differences do come up, the present testimonies would not suffice without a first-hand study of tradition in order to lead to a general knowledge of facts that are so strongly stamped by this tradition. Besides, modern explanations can be influenced by the European culture of those who offer or translate them and by the effort at adapting the ideas to the understanding and sometimes to the taste of Westerners who are strangers to Indian culture. Whereas the traditional texts which have the advantage of not having been composed to suit our purpose, must, therefore, continue to be our principal sources until more in-depth enquiries are carried out.

The extraordinary powers which have been observed in India since ancient times can be brought down to three categories:

they describe feats of asceticism, spectacles of miraculous appearance or acts which in normal circumstances are impossible.

The spectacles of miraculous appearance take place in conditions which are similar to exhibitions of prestidigitation and in fact, undoubtedly, consist in similar exhibitions. If the latter touch the limits of human powers, it is due to the consummate skill that they testify. Its most well-known manifestations are the rope and the mango-tree tricks. In the first, the performer throws a rope in the air and it seems to rise into the sky. His assistant, on being scolded, escapes by climbing up the rope; the performer follows him as well, and both disappear; the performer kills the assistant and throws his dismembered limbs which fall before the spectators, after which the performer and the assistant reappear. Observers who have photographed this trick affirm that the photographs reveal that the performers of the trick do not leave the ground and that the rope remains at their feet. It would, therefore, be a question of collective illusion but the production of such an illusion would, by itself, be a most remarkable feat. The trick of the mango-tree consists in planting a mango-seed, making it germinate and then grow into a young mango-tree in a few seconds under a veil, revealing in succession the different phases of the operation. Ordinarily it would be explained as a trick of prestidigitation, where one substitutes successively a germinated seed and young mango plants at different stages of growth. Similar tricks, and that of the mango-tree certainly, could in ancient times have passed off as miracles demonstrating the saintliness of those who accomplished them. The Great Chronicle of Ceylon, the *Mahāvamsa* (5th century A.D.) recounts that Mahinda, the harbinger of Buddhism in Ceylon in the 3rd century B.C., produced from the seed of a mango that the island-king had just eaten, a big mango-tree. (*Mah.* XV, 41-43)

The feats of asceticism are more widespread and are better testimonies of the attaining of the limits of human powers. They have continued to astonish observers right from the time of Alexander's Greeks not by the miraculous character of the performed acts, but by the extraordinary mastery of the body and will which they revealed. Aristoboulos was filled with astonishment at seeing an ascetic who impassively exposed himself to the sun and to the rains of the end of the Indian spring-time, and another who stood all day on one foot, his hands in the air, carrying a long pole (Strabo, *Geogra.*, XV, 1, 61). Several other Greek authors were stupefied by the ease with which certain sages burnt themselves alive (ibid., 65, 68, 73), Megasthenes did declare that suicide was considered a folly by others (ibid., 68), but we know that even today it can be committed consciously, in virtue of some premeditated, religious convictions and unrelated to any pathological impulse, among the Jains for example.[1] Such suicides are explained as the result of a training in a long and rigorous discipline of detachment from the self, a discipline which neutralises the instinct of survival and, therefore, willingly places the one who observes it in a psychic state similar to the one that is accidentally or pathologically realised in a grave psychological crisis. The superhuman capacity of giving oneself up to a slow and painful death corresponds then to a dehumanisation that is willed and trained for.

As for the ascetic practices of exposing oneself to the blazing sun, sometimes by positioning oneself, in addition, between four fires, or taking and holding some extremely painful postures, they have been well documented since the ancient Brahmanic literature, in the same way as the vow of silence. Numerous have been the ascetics at all times who took similar postures, keeping their arms raised until overcome by cramps or muscular atrophy, or who clenched their fist until the nails dug into the hand, or who hung themselves by the legs, bearing heavy chains, etc.[2] These practices, touching the limits of human possibilities of maceration, constitute feats of extreme endurance and are the fruit of systematic training. They are called *vratas*, 'observances' or 'vows'.

The aim of such vows is neither atonement nor sacrifice but, in fact, the acquisition of merit, of the right to the benefit sought. They are effective due to the direct extraordinary consequence of the power they attest and set in motion or because of the gods being moved by this power to act according to the ascetic's aspiration. In the legends contained in the epics and the *Purāṇas*, Brahman is specially pleased with asceticism, *tapas*, literally 'heat', thus called for reasons that are not totally clear but most probably it refers to the form in which the creative energy of

Brahman, as Prajāpati, the creator, was conceived. Pleased, Brahman grants the wishes of the victorious ascetic. One of his characteristic states of being, according to the Buddhist texts, which on this point are more accurate testimonies than the Brahmanic ones, is in fact 'joy' (*muditā*) and the *Yogasūtras* (II, 33) explain that it is merit (*puṇya*) that produces this state of joy. Now, askesis is one of the principal sources of merit, the heroic source. The merit which is won from it is automatically gained as soon as it is accomplished and this happens independently of the moral value of the goal aimed at. Those who imperil the entire universe as well as the gods have the same right, like the saints, to the fruit of askesis. The gods can merely skilfully escape the consequences of such askesis, when they are unable to arrest its consequences before they reach their target.

An important author of the 16th century, Vijñānabhikṣu, classifies in the same category the realisations obtained by askesis and those obtained from *bhakti*, devotion (*Yogasārasaṅgraha*, end of III). In all likelihood this is so because devotion, like askesis, pleases the divinity and calls down its grace. But on the spiritual plane devotion, like endurance on the physical, must go to the extreme of human possibilities, whether divine grace helps it or not before rewarding it.

Acts surpassing the normal faculties result from extraordinary powers, *aiśvarya*, also called *siddhi*, 'realisation, success'. The latter are classically divided in eight categories:

1. *aṇiman*—reduction of the body to the size of the atom.
2. *laghiman*—making oneself light, levitation.
3. *mahiman*—expansion of the body to the extreme.
4. *prāpti*—attainment of all things, for example touching the moon with the finger.
5. *prākāmya*—irresistibility to the will, allowing one for example to plunge into the earth as if into water.
6. *vaśitva*—to avail at one's will of material things and non-submission to others, power of free use of all that exists.
7. *īśitṛtva* or *īśitā*—mastery of the production, disappearance and transformation of things.

8. *yatrakāmāvasāyitva*—faculty of changing things according to one's will to the image that we give to it, for example turning poison into nectar or vice-versa.

Except for slight differences, this list is the one agreed upon by the commentators of *Yogasūtras* (III, 44 or 45 depending on the editions). Another more ancient list is given by the physician, Caraka, who sums up, on his part, the powers of the yogins:

1. *āveśa*—entry into the body or the spirit of another
2. *cetaso jñāna*—knowledge of the mind of the others
3. *arthānāṃ chandataḥ kriyā*—acting at will on objects
4. & 5. *dṛṣṭi* and *śruti*—extraordinary sight and hearing
6. *smṛti*—the power of calling everything to the mind
7. *kānti*—extraordinary beauty
8. *iṣṭato'darśanam*—becoming invisible at will

(*Śārīrasthāna*, I, 138)

The Buddhistic canon in Pāli which is even more ancient, prior to the Christian era, enumerates the *iddhis* (Sanskrit: *ṛddhis*) 'advantages', which are powers for multiplying oneself and resuming one's 'one'-ness, of appearing and disappearning, of passing through walls, plunging into the earth, walking on water, moving in space, touching the sun and the moon, acting at will with the body right up to the world of Brahman.

According to the tradition of yoga, one either possesses these powers from birth or one obtains them from plants having special qualities, or incantations, or asceticism, or the 'positioning of psychism' *samādhi*, the essential act of yogic discipline (*Yogasūtra*, IV, 1). It is among gods that these powers manifest from birth; they are obtained from plants, among the asuras or Titans (Vācaspatimiśra on *Yogas.* IV, I; *Yogasārasaṅgraha* end of III). They are, therefore, divine, half-demoniac, magical, divinely accorded to the ascetic's merit or conquered by yoga, which is a natural psycho-physiological technique.

Most of them are known only through legends but certain realisations of yoga resemble some among these. In a good number of cases, their authenticity is far from being systematically proved; however, besides the fact that a certain number of observations and photographs exclude quackery and even prestidigitation, the authenticity of realisations surpassing those of normal present physiological life has been established by the works of Therese Brosse.

The latter have established, beyond the truth of some exercises which seem to imply a voluntary control of the neurovegetative system and which were often examined, an astonishing influence of the will on the cardiac and respiratory rhythms as well as consequently, on the organic interchanges. A simultaneous recording of the pulse, the respiration and the electro-cardiogram has, in fact, been able to discover objectively such a phenomenon.[3]

The case of yogins, sometimes wrongly designated as 'fakirs'[4] who claim to bury themselves alive without harming themselves is well-known. The observers have vacillated between the belief that what was in question was a miracle and the conviction that they were witnessing a trickery. Today we can glimpse in the light of the observations made by Therese Brosse that one can voluntarily slow down one's rhythm of life. The yogin proceeds, at first, through a training for the regulation of respiration which following long and deep inspirations, culminates in extended phases of total retention or only allowing for a very superficial respiration. This is what in Sanskrit is called *kumbhaka*, a phase wherein the subject is like a 'jar' (*kumbha*) full of air, between the phase of *pūraka* 'filling up' and that of *recaka* 'emptying'. Retention in its initial stage is accompanied by a tightening of the muscles which is followed by a relaxation. These physical conditions are linked to an intense psychic concentration in three successive stages which Therese Brosse defines, on the basis of what she has been told, as a tremendous concentration on the chosen object, an easy and joyful contemplation of this object and an identification of the self with it.

These stages are effectively characterised in quite an analogous fashion by the *Yogasūtras* (III, 1-3). They are *dhāraṇā* 'fixation', which is the mind's hold on a single point, *dhyāna* 'meditation', consisting in a one-pointed orientation of the mind's energy on this point and *samādhi* 'poise' or 'positioning' of the mind, consisting in the appearance (*nirbhāsa*) of the sole object, an abstraction made of all the consciousness of the psychic operation itself, that is to say it is a question of meditation without the consciousness of meditating and where only that object is visible on which the mind is totally concentrated.[5]

These three operations together are the 'control' (*saṃyama*) *Yogas*, III, 4). Such a control can be exerted on widely different objects. It is said to help us acquire numerous extraordinary powers. To begin with, these powers are of knowledge. The mind knows an object not with the help of reason, from outside, but in its own nature by intimate participation, by entering the object itself and identifying with it. Thus according to the *Yoga-sūtras*, the control over the sun leads to the knowledge of the worlds, the control over the moon leads to the knowledge of the system of the stars (of which the moon is king), etc. (III, 25, 26, etc.) By participating in the object one is introduced into the entire field of the object; the control over the relation of hearing and of space, which is the universal field of sound, leads to divine hearing (III, 40). The boundless knowledge thus obtained allows us to perform extraordinary acts; the different *siddhis* are the result of a victory over the elements (*bhūtajaya*), a victory obtained by 'control over the gross (outer appearance), the form itself, the subtle, the relationships and the finality' (III, 43-44 or 44-45 depending on the ed.), that is to say over the manifestations, the intimate nature and the law of things. The extraordinary powers sought by yoga are, therefore, not miraculous in the sense of a suspension of the laws of nature, but they are deemed to be realisable through a higher and even integral knowledge of the laws of nature.

It seems that, in the cases studied by Therese Brosse, it is the organs of the body that were controlled, particularly the heart and in the mind of the subjects this control was to give them mastery of these organs through a 'stationing' within them, which was equivalent to an introduction of the will in the heart of their natural movement. Whatever the case may be, the results obtained were the following: in an extreme case in which the subject was performing an exercise similar to the one by which he could get himself buried in a very small space and which he thought would lead to the stopping of his heart, there followed the stopping of the heartbeats, disappearance of the pulse at the radial, persistence of a faint sphygmographic recording at the humeral region, and such a pronounced low voltage on the electrocardiogram that it ended in a levelling off and a complete disappearance of all waves, only very faint fibrillations giving evidence of the persistence of an extremely reduced cardiac contraction. These phenomena could be produced at will, in a subject who showed before and after the exercise, normal electrocardiograms and normal cardiac movements.

The physiological process of these phenomena has not yet been recognised, except for some references made on the effects of the respiratory regulation which plays a fundamental part in the exercises of yoga. Besides certain changes in the oxygenation of the blood caused by a slowing down of the respiration and the retention of breath, electrostatic phenomena have been mentioned. Inspired by the works of A. L. Tchijevsky and L. L. Vassilliev who conclude that there is an acquisition of a negative potential by the surface of pulmonary air-sacs during inspiration, G. du Puy-Sanières has suggested interpreting the retention of breath by yogins as something that increases the negative potential and consequently modifies the pH of the blood.[6]

In any case, the field of study to be undertaken on these subjects is vast and numerous other phenomena entirely different from those we have just described are open for observation. The heat produced in the body by exercises of yoga is such that it enables certain yogins to live naked in the snows or to dry by that heat soaked icy blankets. A. David-Neel briefly described some of the processes employed to produce this hyperthermia in Tibet (in Tibetan: *gtum-mo*, pronounced 'toumo'). These processes involve muscular effort (which however, cannot obtain extended results like the ones we observe), respiratory actions, naturally essential but still not well-defined and 'mental creations' of fire.[7]

The exercises said to be of *haṭhayoga*, some of which are also found in other forms of yoga, can be more frequently observed. These exercises, many of which have health or bodily feats as their aim but indivisible, in principle, from their spiritual realisation, consist in the taking of complex postures,[8] along with the regulation of breath and a voluntary control over muscular movements which ordinarily are involuntary. The most striking among these movements are those that are concerned with individual muscles that normally function only in groups and which bring into play the smooth muscular fibres.

All these movements seem at first sight to imply an extraordinary power of control either of functional muscular synergies or of the neuro-vegetative system. The power of contracting individually such muscle implies the dissociation of certain habitual functional synergies, but which are not always automatic and indissoluble. Frequently the contracting of cramps occurs, selectively on groups or parts of muscular groups and even on a portion of a section of the same muscle, independently of the coordinated contractions that occur in normal movements. The unilateral, alternate contraction of the rectus abdominal muscles combined with a deep drawing in of the abdominal wall outside the abdominal rectus muscles constitutes an exercise that acts mechanically on the digestive tracts, particularly on the stomach, the small intestine and the colon, specifically to provoke the intestinal peristalsis. The individual contractions of muscles of the dorsal region or of the limbs, are produced, in general, in the form of spasmodic jerks while the surrounding muscles are in a state of high tension. The triggering of the spasmodic jerks in these conditions appears to be indirect, and is achieved as a consequence of the effort in retaining a group of postures, rather than direct and resulting from a centrifugal influx towards a specific muscle.

The exercises which put into play the smooth muscle fibres, normally not subject to the will, are the pumping and the rejection of fluid by the urethra or the rectum. At least the unusual capacity of practising thus an injection into the bladder or an intestinal cleaning is ordinarily interpreted in yogins as implying an extension of the control, which is normal to the striated fibres, to the smooth fibres. Ch. Laubry and Therese Brosse have adopted this interpretation.[9] Although repercussions of cortical activity on the neuro-vegetative system are certain,[10] it doesn't however seem to prove that the power of making the bladder and the rectum draw in liquids is no other than a power of direct control over the smooth musculature. These phenomena are not produced during the respiratory and muscular rest-period but during efforts at putting into play the abdominal wall and the diaphragm, as the alternating contractions of the rectus abdominal muscles, though in a manner much less apparent externally. To demonstrate that a voluntary action is obtained directly on the smooth fibres it must, therefore, be proved that it is necessary to eliminate the external mechanical action of the intestinal mass, moved by the wall and the diaphragm, on the bladder and the rectum functioning like rubber pears.

It is true that in the case of the rectum, the hypothesis of such an action is disputable because the rectum, unlike the bladder, would be like bottomless pear. One must at least admit that it is the whole of the big intestine, closed at its origin by the ileo-caecal valve, which functions as a pear. The quite considerable amount of water that can be absorbed, in certain cases, will, in fact, justify this hypothesis. But a possibility remains that the combined action of the contractions of the diaphragm, of the abdominal wall, of the levator ani muscles, even of the psoas, (the subject executes this squatted in a tub or sometimes employing a connula but always in the same position), indirectly sets off anti-peristaltic movements. In any case for the yogin the drawing in of water by the rectum seems more difficult than drawing it in by the bladder.

In the case of the bladder, a text that describes a preparatory technique for the drawing in of the liquid by the urethra rightly seems to justify our hypothesis regarding the functioning of this bladder like a pear. This technique is indeed one of blowing in air into the bladder of which the relative distension should facilitate the functioning of the pear pressed and released alternately. The text is a commentary of the classical treatise of *haṭhayoga*, the *Haṭhayogapradīpikā*. The latter states (III, 86):

'Carefully, by means of a pipe, one should blow air slowly into the cavity of the thunderbolt.'

The commentary explains that the 'cavity of the thunderbolt', (*vajra*) is the urethral passage and adds:

'Here is the method for the realisation of *vajrolī* (an exercise for drawing in water by the bladder): a smooth pipe of lead, suitable for insertion into the urethra, fourteen-finger (across) long. On the first day, it is introduced to the length of one finger (across). Two fingers on the second day. Three, on the third. And thus progressively one goes on increasing. When twelve fingers' length is inserted, the urethral passage is cleaned. One gets another similar pipe made, fourteen-fingers (across) long, with a curved end two-finger long at the top opening. This pipe should be inserted up to twelve fingers' length. One should keep the two-finger curved end outside, the opening facing upwards.

Then one takes a blow-pipe like the one used by goldsmiths in order to blow fire, and one joins the blow-pipe to the pipe's opening. Then one blows through it into the urethra. In this way the cleaning of the passage is right. Thereafter one should practice drawing in water by the urethra....

However, the distension of the bladder with air does not seem to be indispensable for all the yogins who practice drawing in by the bladder. We have ourselves observed one of them operating without any prior injection of air. If such an injection had taken place prior to our presence it must have been done over half an hour before, the yogin having executed during this interval of time other different exercises before this suction by the bladder. New and more precise studies than those already conducted so far become necessary.

Beside the physical powers of *Haṭhayoga* which have been much witnessed, although insufficiently studied, we possess some data on more extraordinary phenomena which as yet remain completely unexplained. Here is a description accompanying a series of photographs which are quite exceptional,—of a case of levitation which is of the second kind of extraordinary powers in the classical Indian list reproduced above.

The case in question was witnessed, quite by chance, by an English planter of South India, P. T. Plunkett, and it was described in an English magazine for its readers.[11]

The feat took place in the full sun of half-past noon in an open area that was eighty feet in radius in all directions. The witness points out that the sun was directly overhead in such a way that no shadow could play any part. The longish shadows that are visible on some of the published photographs show that, in reality, the sun was not at its zenith at all and the date and place of this event not being given, it is impossible to ascertain whether the time given is quite accurate. But even if the time and the position of the sun were to be incorrect, it is quite clear that the falling shadows could not assist any attempt at trickery.

The yogin covered a pole of about three feet length with a piece of white linen. Then enveloping himself in another piece of linen, he positioned himself stretched out, holding the pole standing vertically on the ground with the right hand, circumscribed within four poles planted in the ground at the centre of a circle drawn by water ad inside which entry wearing leather shoes was forbidden (fig. 1). A piece of canvas covered the poles which formed a tent over him. His exercise then took place away from the view of spectators and sheltered from the hot sun. After a certain time which is not specified, the tent was removed and the yogin was seen lying almost horizontally in the air, his eyes closed, the right hand leaning on top of the pole without any visible effort. He remained in that position for about four minutes (fig. 2, 3), after which the tent was replaced. The witness not only photographed the phenomena but verified that there was no other support besides the pole on which he had laid his hand, by passing a cane above, under and around the yogi's body. Under the replaced tent, one could see his silhouette through the thin cloth. He remained in the air for about another minute, then he started to move and slowly to come down, maintaining the horizontal position. His descent lasted five minutes. When the tent was removed once again after he had come down to the ground, it was found that he was in a near corpse-like state of stiffness.

A verification of the photographs reveals that before the ascent and at the beginning of his state of suspension in the air, the yogin had a normal expression on his face but that signs of considerable fatigue soon appeared and some movements took place: the turban fell off, the features became taut, the hand which at first rested on top of the pole on the fingers and the extremity of the palm, rests later on the middle of the palm and the fingers come down vertically to the top of the pole, as if the hand had consolidated its grip. However, we did not see in this, a sort of clutching on to the extremity of the pole. In the conditions visible on the documents, the pole could not, in any case, serve as a point of support which in normal conditions would be considered sufficient for a body—even a stiff one—to hoist itself leaning on that single point, or to even hold itself in equilibrium. In fact, this pole, which is not stuck into the ground, is slightly inclined towards the yogin, the centre of gravity is thus very much off the narrow base of support offered by the lower end of the stick on the ground. Though due to the presence of the stick the phenomena cannot be looked upon as an exercise in levitation, in these conditions everything happens as if the body, by becoming light, was holding itself in the air and by its contact prevented the stick as well from falling. At least the hypothesis of lightening the body comes at once to mind even though it seems very unlikely in the present state of our knowledge. It is in this light that we can consider the phenomenon, at least for the time being, as one related to levitation. Another hypothesis, not very satisfactory either, is that of rediation issuing from the body and which lifts it from the ground without affecting the cloth that envelops the yogin and which hangs normally; this radiation cannot be felt by the cane passed under the yogin's body. The existence of photos excludes the possibility of collective illusion affecting the spectators or if this hypothesis were to be admitted then the photographs have been very skilfully tricked. In any case, the last photograph (fig. 5) shows the yogin after the exercise, the turban having been replaced on his head and an expression of great exhaustion visible on his face. Any way we try interpreting the phenomenon, the yogin executed a tiring exercise during which he willingly went into a state of total muscular rigidity and for the spectator he accomplished a feat that corresponds to a phenomenon of levitation according to the traditional Indian classification.

All the human powers of a physical kind or, more generally, all those that are executed by the organs of action and the senses are proofs of a supreme mastery of the body as well as of the mind as organ of knowledge. However material they may be, they demand some degree of psychic, if not spiritual, culture. In reality, as well as in Indian psychology, the body does not clash radically with the mind in totally independent acts. Even for those who seek to escape from the self to beyond nature, to abide in the Self that transcends the phenomenal world, physical feats of self-control can be a preparation for the control of the body and the mind in order to free oneself from the slavery to the senses. Meanwhile, the powers in question do not go beyond the stupefying tour de force. Many Indian doctrines consider them to be only hindrances for the one who seeks the true liberation and it is indisputable that the capacity to move this or that muscle which ordinarily is insensitive to selective stimulus or even to hold oneself in the air for a few minutes, are absurd compared to the boundless freedom of the self sought by the lofty Indian doctrines of liberation.

The Jains practice yoga, under the name of *cāritra*, but prohibit the seeking of extraordinary powers. Buddhism does admit the legitimacy of their acquisition and praises the demonstration on some important occasions of these powers which legend attributes to the Buddha and to the saints. But it denounces their use especially with the intent of astonishing the public. As for classical yoga, it is far from converting them into a supreme end: 'They are from the point of view of the mind poise (*samādhi*), accidents (*upasarga*) and from the angle of the dispersion of consciousness (*vyutthāna*), they are perfections', say the *Yogasūtras* (III, 36 or 37). As extraordinary acts on the plane of phenomenal activity, they are merely hindrances to taking the position of supreme poise which is what *samādhi* is for the mind. Tradition too, through Vācaspatimiśra and Vijñānabhikṣu, discourages from hankering after them or if they do occur, its advice is to simply ignore them.

The supreme power that is sought through Yoga in general by all Indian religions, is that of liberation from the phenomenal world, material as well as spiritual, in which we are involved to such an extent that one is not one's true self in the fulness of one's own being but a self that is influenced and veiled by the activity of nature. It is necessary for attaining this liberation to arrest the natural vital activity and to cultivate a sense of identity with the Absolute, Universal Self. Obtained through a psychological training in which philosophical meditation acts like an instrument along with physiological and psychic workings of yoga, this state does not imply either death or inertia or even unconsciousness. It is compatible with ordinary life, the 'living liberated one' (*jīvanmukta*) continuing to participate in it but no more reducing its involvement to the personal self which binds us to empirical existence and burdens the pure existence of the Self with the jumble of traces left by the psychic experiences one goes through. These experiences continue but they do not find a 'self' to cling to and to mark with their imprints.

The power to raise oneself thus, at the very heart of social life, at the giving up of all egoistic enjoyment of acts, is one of the cardinal aims envisaged in India and even today India reveres a few 'living free', liberated individuals; and the extent of their influence and the poise of their lives are subjects of great awe and admiration for many Westerners.[12]

For the future, an accurate study of their psychism, to which some offer themselves willingly, is necessary along with a study of the theories from which they derive their inspiration and which are attested to in two types of literature: one that is ancient and original and is about their tradition, elaborated by and for their milieu itself; the other, contemporary, written and distributed by them and mostly by Westerners, in European languages, meant for contemporary foreigners, without always keeping in mind the former type of literature or its actual purport.

This enquiry, based on the processes of modern psychology, is beginning in India. Maryse Choisy has recently published the first results of these beginnings.[13] Prof. Fr. Spiegelberg of Stanford University and M. Choisy herself have respectively put Swâmî Śivânanda, a 'living liberated' yogin to the test of Rorschach and to TAT. Their findings have been absolutely remarkable, certifying the exceptionally eminent nature of the Swâmî. Prof. Spiegelberg observed quite correctly that this Swâmî could not actually be subjected to a normal analysis and this for the time being seems to be the most noteworthy conclusion for us. The significance of the tests can only be relative to the categories of persons for whom their value was established. In a milieu which is different from those where the texts were carried out, a new, preliminary standard becomes necessary. This has not been done so far, it seems, and it will require an examination of a number of the yogins' answers. The current interpretations are perforce premature.

In the ink-spots of the Rorschach test and the tables of TAT, the Swâmî saw symbols of concepts of yoga with which he was deeply familiar and which he usually looked for in different forms, driven precisely by the habit he had acquired from the literature of this yoga. It is, therefore, difficult to admit that his answers, reproduced in the published report, reveal any great originality, as Prof. Spiegelberg (p. 602) thinks. The professor was in fact so struck by the reactions of the Swâmî that he wrote: 'We're obliged to agree with his interpretation of the ink-spots,

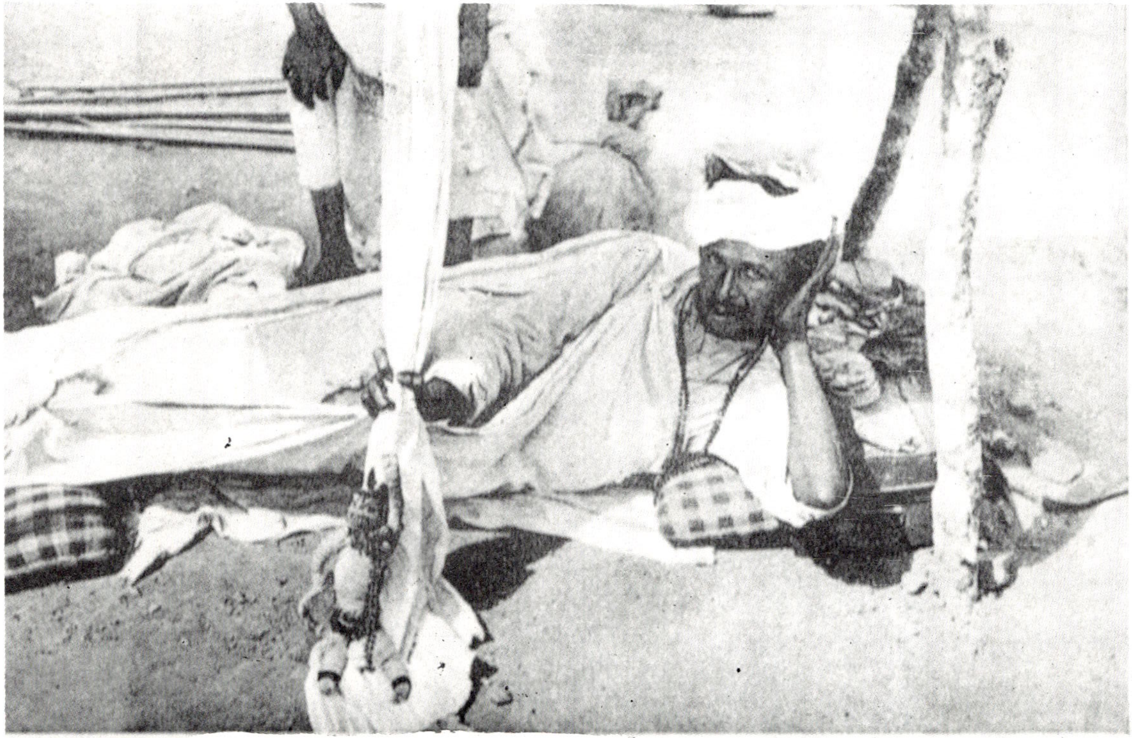

Fig. 1—État au Moment de Commencer L'exercice. (Just before starting the Exercise)

Fig. 2—Exercice en Cours (The Exercise in Progress)

Fig. 3—Exercice en Cours
(The Exercise in Progress)

Fig. 5—Immédiatement Après L'exercice
(Just after the exercise)

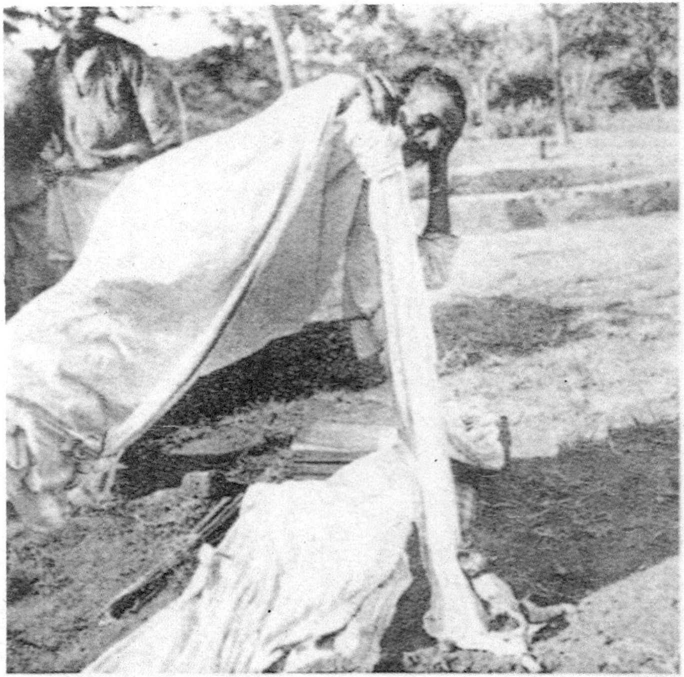

Fig. 4—Vers la Fin De L'exercice
(Towards the end of the exercise)

for which he has found more meaning than all the interpretations submitted so far. It is so because the Swâmî knows the *sat* behind the *bhava* (read 'the Absolute Real' behind 'Existence') and within the *Bhava* of all reality and consequently in those ink-spots among other things.' For us, the examined subject did not really project an expression of his personality but he converted the psychologist. In order to appreciate his originality, it may have been necessary to compare his answers with those of the subjects of the same culture. However, the skilful manner of giving these symbolic interpretations is evidently greatly commendable. On either side of the test of Rorschach, we find, in fact, two confirmed symbolists, one brought up on Indian tradition and trained to give systematic, symbolic interpretations, the other led by psychoanalysis to accept them. However, this does not take away from the usefulness of the published reports to furnish elements for the new standardisation necessary for a valid utilisation of the tests. The exceptional cases, being on the fringe of the human level in matters of psychic achievements, may remain for a long time outside the reach of any 'testing' which can be applicable only for the average achievements. But all the reactions need to be recorded precisely for the psychological documentation and it is clear that the powers at the limit of the human level will not be known in general, unless their nature is well-determined in India where they have been developed with such intense interest, as much on the physical as on the psychological level.

Note on the photographs:

The subject seems to be sleeping in the air, without any support: the folds of his dress fall normally under him. His feet, not visible on fig. 2, are free (see fig. 3). The pole on which he leans is not stuck into the ground and is inclined towards him (fig. 3). He is, therefore, not supported by this pole and only leans on it like on a walking-stick.

At the lower end of the pole Fig. 1 reveals a sort of a doll, which like him is wearing a rosary. The use of the rosary, generally of 108 beads, is common especially among the Śaivas. As the subject was not interrogated, since there isn't any sign of what he said, the importance of this doll as well as the reasons for covering the stick with a piece of linen are not known. The fact that the subject had delimited an area in which he was to do his exercise, prohibiting entry into this area wearing leather footwear, suggests that he was operating within a *maṇḍala*, a sort of an occult area of space into which a divinity is said to operate. One could suppose that the doll represented for him some such divinity. However, dolls like the one seen here, although they are sometimes mentioned in texts on occultism do not generally play any such role. The texts on yoga which allude to phenomena of levitation do not mention any magic procedures for their realisation by the yogins and even in a general way by men. Besides they are very sober about talking about such extraordinary feats as the one performed here, which stun the public, and most often they disapprove of them. In the present case, fresh enquiries need to be made to find out the psychological state in which the subject performs these feats.

NOTES

1. Cf. L. and M. —S. *Renou, Une secte religieuse dans l'Inde contemporaine*, in *Etudes*, March 1951, pp. 350-51. All killing being prohibited in the Jaina religion, here a passive suicide through starvation is meant.
2. Cf. among others J. Campbell Oman, *The mystics, Ascetics and Saints of India*, London, 1903.
3. Charles Laubry and Therese Brosse, *Documents recueillis aux Indes sur les "Yoguis" par l'enregistrement simultané du pouls, de la respiration et de l'électrocardiogramme*, Presse Médicale, No. 83, Oct. 14, 1936.
4. The arab designation for '*fakīr*', 'poor', was applied by the Indian Muslims to all those who practice a life of renunciation, yogins, ascetics and even quack mendicants.
5. It is clear how inaccurate the translation of the term *samādhi* as 'concentration' (J.H. Woods, *The Yoga-System of Patañjali*, Cambridge, Mass., Harvard Oriental Series, 1916), or 'trance' is (Rāma Prasada, *Patañjali's Yoga Sūtras*, Sacred Books of the Hindus, Allahabad, 1910.) Ch. Laubry and Th. Brosse (p. 14 of the offprint) have very rightly stressed that the psychic states in question have nothing to do with the passive states of trance.
6. *Note sur l'action physiologique de le rétention volontaire du souffle*, in *Revue de Pathol. Comp. et d'Hyg. générale*, No. 482, Nov. 1936, and *La modification volontaire du rythme respiratoire et les phénomènes qui s'y rattachent* ibid., No. 486, March 1937 (the texts mentioned about Indian tradition are not authoritative).

7. *Mystiques et magiciens du Thibet*, Paris, 1929, pp. 218-31. J. Bacot, *Le Bouddha*, Paris, 1947, p. 97, n. 1.
8. Recent descriptions in Hubert Risch, *Le Haṭha Yoga, Exposé sommaire de la methode, Quelques expériences physiologiques et applications thérapeutiques.* Thesis of the Faculté de Médecine de Paris, 1951 (useful hints on the physiological results of postures and different movements, the information on Indian doctrines is of unequal value.)
9. Loc. cit., p. 8 from the offprint.
10. Ch. Laubry & Th. Brosse had themselves given excellent examples before their work on Yoga: *Interférence de l'activité corticale sur le système végétatif neuro-vasculaire*, Presse Medicale, No. 84, Oct. 19, 1935.
11. *The Illustrated London News*, 6 June 1936, pp. 993-95. The document was kindly made available to me by Jacques Bacot.
12. An interesting recent testimony: Roger Godel, *Essais sur l'expérience libératrice*, Paris, 1952.
13. *Psyché*, No. 70-71, Aug-Sept. 1952 (Special number on India).

Chapter 24

THOUGHT AND EFFICIENCY IN ANCIENT INDIA*

The 18th century in France began taking an objective interest in the culture of ancient India. But in the beginning of the 19th century this culture was extolled throughout Europe, for its ancient poetry, for the freshness of a still immaculate natural state that its wisdom had helped to preserve. Today India is glorified for her spiritual pre-eminence, for a supreme mastery over natural instincts. In short, Indian culture was formerly admired for being in front, being the vanguard of civilisation and today its charm lies in being beyond it, in having surpassed and mastered it. The second feature is more justified than the first. The belief in the primitive nature of Indian culture finally yielded to an objective enquiry into things which was always pursued regardless of the opinions of the time. The realisation of the value of Indian thought has been, on the contrary, the result of this very objective enquiry.

India has naturally acknowledged with joyousness the positive response shown to her. However, sometimes, she finds the response inadequate and at others, she is overwhelmed. We need to understand the Indian reaction in both the cases.

On the one hand, a son gets easily annoyed that his mother is not considered to be the most beautiful woman and some see in the Western indifference—sometimes, alas, in the contempt—vis-à-vis Indian culture, a motivated unjustness. Most often this is due to ignorance; in any case, it is ignorance, or a limited and biased knowledge which veils the real significance of this culture, both in the past and the present, where its influence abides, latent, in all the countries it has indelibly marked in former times.

On the other hand, the tributes paid to India often make of her a country that is idealised, a country of supreme wisdom, but

*Spéculation et efficience dans l'Inde ancienne, in France-Inde, no. 14, 6 May 1954, pp. 1-2.

of wisdom, not of realism: whether she is extraordinarily ancient or, on the contrary, brilliantly disenchanted, as long as she exists, she will never be like any other nation. However, she seeks to be modern, she strives to solve her social and economic problems, her problems of life, and not only the universal metaphysical ones. The latter, she has already solved, but their solution, even if it serves in any possible situation the one who possesses it, it is not accessible to the population in its entirety which is struggling with the present: the child who cries of hunger cannot, like the sage, take recourse in the transcendent. And India does get annoyed by the fact that some imagine her to be fully recomforted by the law of the impermanence of things every time the monsoon fails. Similarly, she gets upset when others find her to be unconcerned with pragmatic problems or incapable of solving them. In fact, she has often suspected even the admirers of her thought. She suspects that they glorify her past hypocritically, just to keep her entrenched there, and they praise her eternal wisdom only to divert her from administering herself in a practical way.

Some of her children continue to think that she must discard her traditional thought which withholds her from following the present universal trend of civilisation and she must consecrate herself exclusively to modern researches and to practical efficiency to which she can perfectly adapt herself whenever she wishes to.

But is there really a contradiction in her mind between thought and pragmatism? We should hope that the future answers this question but we shall not be present to hear the answer. It is to future generations that it will reveal whether India will be able to succeed in reconciling the dream and the goal, meditation and action, its own culture and modernity. The present is full of contradictions and one-sided and unusually chaotic: the so-called present realities are, to a great extent, made up of a residual subsisting past and an awaited future. It does not have its own existence, it is reduced to a moving point of the junction of what has been done and what will be done. The past remains to be questioned and it clearly shows that, in her ancient tradition, India already knew perfectly how to reconcile thought and pragmatism.

The Indian doctrine of the emptiness of things is the one

which strikes most the European who is attached to the world where he lives, the scientist who holds the observed phenomenon, the tangible matter to be reality itself. When India—Buddhism and Vedānta together—propounds that this visible matter is merely an illusion and that reality, on the contrary, lies in the absolute unknowable Self, she does seem to withdraw from life and refuses to join the world-movement and one expects to see her scorning both action in this world and knowledge of it. One readily believes that it was her philosophy that made her defenceless against invasions in former times and that the science she possessed was rudimentary or borrowed science. In fact, the causes for the events of political history are not so simple and India has a vast scientific and technological literature, the bulk of it being original.

It could no doubt be said that she wasn't entirely faithful to the attitude of disdain of her philosophers for this lower world. This is certain, but we can add that her philosophers themselves did not always renounce worldly action and the knowledge obtained through observation and they could do this without contradicting their theory that the world is merely a dream.

One of the most radical 'nihilists' as we commonly call them, the philosopher Nāgārjuna, lived probably in the 2nd century. He believed all to be 'void' and one might think that the vacuity of the universe turned him away from thinking about it. However, he devoted himself to a huge work of exegesis on sacred texts in which he gives proof of a very extensive Indian scientific culture. Moreover, many concordant traditions attribute to him special studies of purely rational medicine, as well as alchemy and magic. Even if one wished to believe that these traditions are not authentic, one is forced to admit that those who propounded it did not judge it improbable that a sane person could have proclaimed the vacuity of things and at the same time sought to know them through all possible means and to act upon them. The Chinese Buddhist pilgrim Hiuen-Tsang who came to India in the 7th century, did not disbelieve this and he was thoroughly competent in the field of Buddhist philosophy. This is so because, in fact, there does not exist any contradiction in the attitude of someone like Nāgārjuna. The vacuity that he denounces is a 'vacuity of the being-in-itself', not of the empirical existence. The phenomenon which takes and loses form, which appears and disappears, is not endowed with the plenitude of the being-in-itself, an existence independent of other phenomena. But it has a relative existence. It is not more stable and more definitively real than a dream but, as long as one is in the dream there is no reason not to enact it and not to control its play.

Similarly, the great thinker of Vedānta, Śaṃkara, at around 800 A.D., actually carried on the speculation on the Absolute Being to the point of turning the world of phenomena into a mirage, but the tradition around him is full of his battles, his feats, his activity at the heart itself of this mirage, perhaps only to be able to propound better the doctrine which denounced that mirage. Long before that, the *Bhagavadgītā* had preached simultaneously the duty of action, to fully realise the human condition in which one is placed, and the upliftment of the soul beyond the affective fruit of action, a feeling of success or failure.

Therefore, Indian spirituality never intended to condemn pragmatism in the midst of the workings of matter. It meant only to go beyond it, through the means of a meditation which sets forth an ideal superior to those of the world, without annulling them, and which inspires serenity before the phenomenal. If she wishes, India can, therefore, truly act socially, scientifically, practically in relation to life and in total pragmatism and, what is more, it can do so without giving up in her thought a blissful enjoyment of the ideal of the Absolute.

CHAPTER 25

YOGA AND ITS UNDERLYING DOCTRINE*

The study made of the relationship between yoga and hesychasm underlined a number of parallels in the external practices as well as in the sensory results of these practices though at the same time it highlighted some of the fundamentally divergent qualities. If anything was borrowed it happened indirectly and only through the Iranian Sufis. In any case, this interchange was very partial and had a bearing on a superficial aspect of yoga only, on yoga in its practical aspect. The deeper motivations of yoga are unknown to the Hesychasts who have their own drawn from the Judaeo-Christian tradition going back to the Bible. The doctrinal foundation that is characteristic of yoga is totally absent from the Hesychasts.

In fact, Yoga is not merely a technique although its technical aspect is the most visible. Its underlying doctrine is as indispensable to its nature as its practical working. It is this underlying foundation that we shall try to examine today.

It is constituted of elements provided by the Sāṃkhya doctrine as well as by the physiological and psychological doctrines of *Āyurveda*, together with the actual results of yogic experiences. One cannot speak of yoga in its full sense when this doctrinal background is not included: we only have the practical operations of yoga, a practical utilisation of its doctrines which even when absent from the minds of the practitioners, do not in any way lose their importance as the basis of all their particular techniques.

Meanwhile, there are many who believe yoga to be constituted only by its methods, losing sight of the basis on which the method stands. There are three categories of authors who think that yoga is a technique and nothing more: either outsider observers, or some theoreticians who believe in extra-doctrinal

*L'arrière-plan doctrinal du Yoga, in *Entretiens 1955*, Pub. I.F.I. no. 4, Pondicherry 1956, pp. 13-20.

origins of yoga, or else yogins themselves who, as pure practitioners, received from the guru, from generation to generation, an initiation into the techniques only with a view to obtaining specific results without bothering about the doctrinal basis or the historic origins.

For a study of the doctrines, we need not go into the affirmations of such yogins who themselves do not give any importance to them. As pure practitioners they obtain results that are in themselves valid but ignore the texts or the traditions which have preserved these doctrines or some traces of them. The opinions of outsider-observers are all the more to be ignored as unworthy of examination. They have studied neither the theory nor the practice of yoga but only seen it in its external appearance in the course of chance meetings. Nevertheless their judgments are accepted by many authors. Abbé Dubois is one of them whose famous work constantly re-edited, describes a whole pile of facts which arc exact but he describes them merely from the outside and his only concern is to inform the average European with his opinions. Jacquemont is another example; he too completely misunderstood yoga and mixed up the yogins with ordinary beggars who wander about in places of pilgrimage seeking only to attract pity by maceration or by their infirmities.

We must, however, examine the opinions of those theorists who believe in an extra-doctrinal origin of yoga. They do admit doctrinal elements in yoga but think them to have been superimposed over a primitive, prehistoric base constituted by magic or shamanic technique. It is the ethnologists in general who, while intending to record merely facts, in reality interpret them on the basis of some general theories. It is in this way that one hopes to find hints of the existence of yoga from the time of Harappa and Mohenjo-daro. One of the figures represented on the seals of Mohenjo-daro is seated in a posture that is reminiscent of the yogin's. The position of the body, the direction of the eyes, and the fact, in addition, of being surrounded by animals have led one to believe that it is Śiva Paśupati who is represented, performing an exercise of yoga. However, as the most ancient Vedic texts do not make any mention of yoga, we can easily conclude that yoga was a prehistoric Indian practice which was not known by the Aryan invaders, the authors of the Vedas.

The practices here would then be anterior to the theories and they are compared to the practices of shamanism. The word shaman is tunguz but it is generally used to designate men who among the peoples of Upper Asia, function as entranced divines, counsels and doctors. The practices undertaken by these shamans are bodily practices and lead them notably to an increase in the volume and acceleration of breathing. These practices are intended to bestow on them magic powers, that of 'rising towards the sky' being one among many and symbolised by a whole ritual of ascent.

Now, in yoga too there are practices that lead to the obtaining of extraordinary powers, although only in a secondary way. This has induced some to think that there is a close relationship between the two kinds of techniques: both demand efforts that are of a physical nature, both are based on a regulation of breath, both achieve exceptional results.

Meanwhile, the milieus in which shamanism developed were not very civilised. Shamanism would, therefore, correspond to an ancient state of human evolution of which it was a late offshoot and witnessed equally what yoga might have been at the beginning of Indian history. It would follow that yoga in India was first a group of practices to which subsequently some doctrines were appended.

All this, of course, appears as pure hypothesis. It is incorrect to speak of yoga before the essential characteristics of yoga are gathered. If we make a closer study, the suggested parallels fall away. Thus the shamans lose control over themselves, either during or at the conclusion of their trances, whereas the yogins train to exert a total containment and control of their organism and of their mind. Moreover, the shaman does not strive to achieve, outside his shamanic practices, an ever-greater control over the self unlike the yogin who seeks to keep that poise even during the intervals between the exercises of yoga. Lastly, it is hard to talk of a yoga that is pre-doctrinal when in numerous texts, yoga appears precisely only along with its doctrinal base. And this is all the more difficult as these doctrinal elements are mostly present in the oldest documents and as it is only in a much more recent period that yoga is described in the texts as being more distant from doctrines. On the other hand, we can ask ourselves whether shamanism itself, like the word 'shaman', is not a defective borrowing from an Indian tradition. In fact, we know that an ancient name *Śramaṇa*, applied to a category of Indian religious men who were far from necessarily being yogins, might be at the origin of the word *shaman*.

We cannot thus talk of yoga before the yoga in its actual sense without taking the risk of mixing it up with certain ascetic or psychophysiological practices which do not have its exact particularities, particularities which can be accurately pointed out thanks to the classical texts of which the *Yogasūtras* of Patañjali constitute a sort of catechism or memento, summing up in brief formulae the preceding theories, and the commentaries of which provide the doctrinal tradition.

The elements of yoga consist essentially in eight *aṅgas* or 'articles', classically enumerated in the *yogasūtras* and which culminate in 'yoking' certain physical and psychic faculties, or rather, in their perfect 'adjustment'.

These eight *aṅgas* are:

1. The *yamas* or restraints: not to kill, not to lie, not to steal, to observe continence, not to commit an act of 'total appropriation' (*aparigraha*), that is to free oneself from all attachment that could act like a 'tied knot' of recall and would ultimately prevent the yogin from retaining his autonomy.

2. The *niyamas* or disciplines: to be trained for cleanliness (*śauca*), to be satisfied with what one has (*santoṣa*), to bear pain (*tapas*), to repeat texts committed to memory (*svādhyāya*), to offer oneself to the Lord (*Īśvarapraṇidhāna*).

3. The *āsanas* or helpful bodily postures.

4. *Prāṇāyāma* or the discipline of the breath leading to a physiological state in which breath is retained, on the one hand, and to a psychological state in which the external sensory impressions are eliminated, on the other.

5. *Pratyāhāra* or the retraction of the powers of sensation and of action, of the *indriyas* (*Jñānendriya* and *karmendriya*). What is meant is a gathering up of the functions that are naturally turned towards the outside, this gathering up is symbolised by the tortoise retracting its limbs. This stage seeks to immunise the yogin from external influences, and consequently eliminates the reactions to such influences.

6. *Dhāraṇā* or the fixation of thought by means of a concentrated attention, as if the mind was reduced to a single point (*ekāgracitta*).

7. *Dhyāna* or meditation: voluntary meditation and even a discursive intelligence putting into play all kinds of representations.

8. *Samādhi* or 'putting into position': the most important word in yoga which designates the culmination of all the rest. This term has been translated in the most diverse and sometimes incorrect ways. One particular translation of the term is 'ecstasy' which is altogether different from it if one considers that yoga seeks to develop an exclusively inner concentration. The word *Samādhi* has even been correctly defined, notably by Mircea Eliade, as 'enstasy' rather than 'ec-stasy'. The word signifies exactly the act of 'positioning', *dhā*, 'completely' *sam-ā*, the mind on an object. Must we conclude then that this last stage is merely a culmination of the preceding one, or that it is its complement, being nothing more than the fulfilment of meditation. In fact, the 'position of the mind' obtained through *samādhi* is not just a focalising of the thinking activity, a crowning of conscious meditation. The Indians discovered the unconscious very early on and they believed that establishing one's psychism on an object consisted first in fixing one's conscious attention on it; but they concluded that a total 'positioning' implied a focalisation not simply of consciousness but also of the unconscious, in short, of the whole psychic being. This explains the sequence of three terms that correspond to three distinct stages, of which the first is the endeavour at fixation (*dhāraṇā*), the second is the conscious attention developed by meditation (*dhyāna*), the third is the final stage in which the total psychic self finds itself to be in total identification with the object of contemplation, for the consciousness itself is extinguished after it has directed the integral psychism on to the point where it must 'position' itself. These three terms, although distinct, constitute then a unique operation which is described as *saṃyama*, 'mastery'.

Saṃyama leads one to have exceptional powers, powers of action and of knowledge which far transcend the ordinary human possibilities.

The powers of action are the least important. Their pursuit is considered rather as a hindrance to an integral realisation of yoga. That is why they are presented more as potential: the yogin feels their presence in him without feeling a need to exercise them. What is indisputable is that the yogin must not be attached to them, otherwise he would be unfaithful to his initial intention of keeping out all feeling of appropriation. When, however, the yogin wishes to experiment with them, he often does it subjectively: he has, for instance, the sentiment that he might be able to fly, he feels lifted up and transported in the air, without, however, appearing to others to have left his seat. There's a whole category of yogins, meanwhile, that practices certain material realisations which, although more or less controversial, have been ascertained by a large number of external witnesses. But for the yogin who operates only on a mental level, the consciousness of a realisation that we shall call subjective has the same value as its actual realisation: the objective act and the subjective sensation of the same act intermingle. In the opinion of certain yogins who believe the phenomenal world to be a well-structured dream, perception has as much value as fact, what one would call the illusion of action is of the same nature as what one would call phenomena since everything is essentially psychic. An acknowledgement by a third party, which characterises empirical phenomenon, has no importance for the yogin who denies an objective existence to everything including the third party. We find this especially in the Buddhist yoga of the *Yogācāras* who are also *vijñānavādins*, those who propound that the world is nothing but thought and for whom our representations themselves are insubstantial: at that moment dream is identified with reality and the feeling of flying is identical with actual flight in space.

The powers of knowledge, much more important, are in their essence subjective and because of their nature are free from the objection which says that they cannot be objectively ascertained. But they are, for all practical purposes, incommunicable and cannot be transcribed to a level that is accessible to others. The guru can well guide his disciple until the latter can feel something similar to what he knows to be *samādhi* but he cannot describe what he feels to be his own experience of it. In fact, here, it is not only the clear consciousness of the yogin that takes position on the contemplated object but the whole of his psychic being, including his unconscious psychism, enters into play as well.

We may ask ourselves then: How does the yogin know in his consciousness that his unconscious knows? The answer is that he knows he has an unconscious and that before putting it into play alone, by excluding the consciousness, he experiences the existence of a precise moment where he has adequate residual consciousness in order to be able to judge that in the following moment his unconscious psychism would go out seeking its perfect 'adjustment' with the object that had been fixed, before the stopping of the consciousness and on which he had directed his attention and his meditation and on which he had even begun to 'position' himself quite fully.

This is because there are actually two degrees of *samādhi*: the *samādhi* qualified as 'with knowledge', *saṃprajñātasamādhi*, and then the *samādhi* that is total, called 'without knowledge', *asaṃprajñātasamādhi*. The *Yogasūtra* (III, 9) has the following description of what happens in the state of *samādhi* without knowledge:

> *vyutthānanirodhasaṃskārayor abhibhavaprādurbhāvau nirodha-kṣaṇacittānvayo nirodhapariṇāmaḥ.*
>
> 'The subjection and manifestation (respectively) of two kinds of psychic constructions, one of the waking state and the other of the ceasing (of consciousness), are the development of the state of ceasing (of consciousness) consequent to the thought (present) at the moment of the ceasing (of consciousness).'

The *saṃskāras* are constructions that remain stored in the unconscious as traces of previous psychic actions, they are unconscious thoughts, 'engrammes' or 'complexes' (without any psychoanalytical nuance). They are either imprints or traces constituting the unconscious residue of each psychic action, which is expressed by *vāsanā* signifying 'perfuming' (such as the perfuming of a phial by a fragrance), or in a more dynamic sense expressed by the word *saṃskāra* which is more frequent, an active 'construction' and the source of impulses which intervene into one's conduct even beyond the control of consciousness. These mental constructions that become unconscious but were recorded during a fully conscious state, have to be mastered in *samādhi*. The whole practice of yoga aims at this. Thus, according to our text, the mastery of the thoughts recorded in the conscious state and the manifestation (which is simultaneous) of thoughts that continue to exist during the ceasing of the consciousness, are what develop and continue in the state of ceasing which follows the thought produced at the moment of ceasing. Thus the unconscious continues to operate in the line of the last thought produced before the ceasing and it does this thanks to the pre-established psychic constructions.

What follows from all this is that India knew about the unconscious and had a very clear perception of its importance. It also follows that the Indian theories studied before the discovery of the unconscious in Europe were not really understood by the Westerners. Yoga, nevertheless, did endeavour to control the Unconscious itself, keeping in view not merely the conscious and controllable thoughts but also the unconscious. These notions explain the doctrine, so well-known and so misunderstood, of the *karman*. According to it—in it conceptions of yoga coincide with those of *Sāṃkhya*—there remains after the death of every being, something that is individual, the psychic body, *liṅgaśarīra* or *sūkṣmaśarīra*, the carrier of the seed of later existences which must fulfil, thanks to a new material body, the potentialities that have been accumulated by the psychic constructions. It follows that the *karman* is much more a natural, psychic determinism than a sort of application of a distributive justice that would reward each one according to his merits, even if such an interpretation was given in numerous Indian circles. It is quite certain that here, it is not a question of a primitive thought but of speculations arrived at through philosophical reflection.

Besides, neither is the technique of breathing a practice that goes back to a prehistoric origin. It appears clearly that it was sought because of certain ancient, physiological theories which see breath as both the somatic and psychic motor which allows one, when it is controlled, to regulate everything that depends on it. This conception is implicit in the ancient medical doctrines in India which are pneumatist like the Greek. All of ancient physiology and psychology were based on the belief that the vital motor was the breath and it was natural to try and act through the respiratory mechanism on all the breaths. Some real experiments were conducted on the basis of this doctrine, experiments of which the aim was to govern the organism and which ended in significant discoveries of physiological and psychological effects. If it is true that the techniques of yoga have been able to develop freely even by breaking away from its doctrinal background, it is not in any way less true that these techniques flowed out from it.

CHAPTER 26

THE NATURE OF YOGA IN ITS TRADITIONS*

Yoga is more well-known than it is understood. It attracted the mistrust of 19th century rationalism to begin with. The naturalist, Jacquemont, in 1830, dismissed it as quackery and nothing more. The philosopher, Barthélemy Saint-Hilaire, in 1860, considered it to be one of those obscure subjects where one should not seek to bring clarity. Many think that since then it has never emerged from such sweeping condemnations. The Indian yogin or fakir is still looked upon with suspicion: half-ascetic, half-conjurer, he lives on the credulity of the masses who are mesmerised by his awe-inspiring self-mortification, irrespective of whether it is genuine or affected, and by his extraordinary tricks.

Many, on the contrary, consider it with great enthusiasm. The mystic and 'irrational' character that they attribute to it has made them look upon it as a means for rising above the petty realisations of 'official science', as a means for communicating with the great initiates or for stepping into their omniscient and secret world.

Lastly, its double aspect of psychological method and physiological training, or better still, its psychosomatic techniques have attracted, on the one hand, psychoanalysts and psychologists like Jung, who, in addition, was interested by its symbolic aspects, and on the other, a group of people in search of health and mental and physical attainments.

But a basic research, which should describe the phenomena of yoga with precision, independent of all speculation or hasty utilisation, has remained till today partial and sporadic.

The task of such a research is, however, considerable and it is two-fold. It must, on the one hand, study the entire tradition of

*First published in Th. Brosse, *Etudes instrumentales des techniques du yoga*, E.F.E.O., Paris, 1963, pp. I-XXVIII.

yoga, its raison-d'être, its nature and its purpose for those who invented it and those who practise it, and, on the other hand, its psychological and physiological effects. In these conditions, this research is simultaneously interlinked to several very distinct human and biological sciences. Philology and history are necessary for the study of written sources and of all documents related to its origin, to its utilisation and spread of theories and their practice in the course of time within the culture of Indian civilization, as well as in distant places that came under its influence. The study is philosophic to the extent that the theory expounds a cosmology and a conception of Man. It is religious in that yoga offers to the human individual a means of salvation. It is sociological insofar as it introduces models of behaviour in different societies and more particularly in certain communities. It is psychological, biological, physiological in the mechanisms that it brings into play.

It is, therefore, not surprising that the complexity of the task requiring such different bases that no scholar can presume to fully master, should have discouraged many a scholar and especially those who lacked a certain level of competence in fields that were so foreign to theirs. However, every scholar can, at least, get on with the research in the field he is familiar with and contribute his observations to the vast file of enquiry which needs to be prepared at present.

Today, the first elements of this file can be the results of those studies on yoga which are mostly concerned with the documentary sources, its origins, a description of its practice, its philosophical or religious significance and its kinship or presumed kinship with the practices of other countries. To this we must add a small number of studies on the respiratory alternations during the yogic exercises, on intestinal movements and especially on the circulatory phenomena.

These studies have been carried out to greatly varying levels and their value is evidently disputed. Even if Dr. Therese Brosse was able to prove, through the simultaneous recording of the pulse, the respiration and the electrocardiogram, the physiological authenticity of phenomena that were previously considered impossible or suspect, even if the listing—if not the final interpretation—of documentary sources is quite through and the most important practices of yoga can be described fairly well in their external aspects, there still exists a lot of arbitrary speculation or total ignorance about many other aspects and significances of yoga. The very nature of yoga as well as its origins and its various affinities continue to be a few of the inadequately answered question because of arbitrary working hypothesis.

Some scholars themselves, who have deeply studied the problem, get carried away into making similar hypothesis. Every time this happens because of an absence of a very precise definition of yoga. A very common definition is the one found in Patañjali's *Yogasūtras*, the primary classical manual, 'Yoga is the stopping of the movements of the mind'.[1] But as the word yoga usually takes a much wider connotation in several other contexts this definition seems too restrictive and refers essentially to the final state that is reached after doing the exercises prescribed in the manual. This is the definition of the 'royal yoga', *rājayoga*, as it is conceived in this manual and not of yoga in general. The latter includes many more forms such as *haṭhayoga*, 'the yoga of effort', in which a physical training consisting of complex bodily postures is added to a psychic exercise, *layayoga*, 'the yoga of dissolution' which by means of a series of repeated representations applied to the constituents of the body, psychically dissolves the material stuff which makes up this body and envelops the *ātman* or 'being-in-itself', there is *karmayoga*, 'the yoga of action', *bhaktiyoga* 'the yoga of devotion', which respectively set into motion an activity of right conduct and ritual and a fervent surrender to the Supreme Being. In addition, yoga is part of Buddhism as well as of ancient Brahmanism and its present form, Hinduism ('Hindu' being used as opposed to the Muslim religion since its establishment in India). Yoga is practiced even in certain unorthodox Muslim groups close to Hinduism. It is still practised in order to attain non-religious and technical realisations such as extraordinary knowledge and power, as an auxiliary even in technical study and training. In short, the word yoga can designate any discipline that makes us capable of some mastery. In fact, that is the actual meaning of the word which signifies 'bring under a yoke, adjustment, adaptation'.

But the various kinds of aptitudes sought to be developed in

India through yoga led some sociologists to try and relate it to other means, used by other civilizations, for attaining some of the same ends. And so there exists a current theory expounded mainly by Mircea Eliade,[2] that believes yoga to have issued from the same tradition as shamanism; this tradition is said to go back to pre-history in Asia and we also find its parallel in south America. The theory is quite attractive but it widens the significance of yoga to such an excessive degree that it deprives Indian yoga of all its uniqueness in its major forms. In order to base it on a hypothetically reconstituted prehistoric movement it, moreover, completely overlooks the intellectual tenor of the cosmophysiological and psychological speculations that suffused it at the time of its appearance, as is testified by the ancient documents that have come down to us.

In fact, the theory of the emergence of yoga and shamanism from a commonstock can hardly be sustained by the fact that the Siberian shaman, like some yogins, seeks to rise above the ordinary human powers and operate there according to some traditional rules; or that he takes on in society certain responsibilities that are often analogous to those of yogins. Actually in their essential nature the shaman and the yogin differ with each other more than they resemble. The qualification of a shaman rests on predestination, it is revealed through a psychic crisis and completed by initiation. The making of a yogin rests on a training which although empirically tested, is based on some rational doctrines of psychophysiology. It is in the conclusion and not in the origin of their activities or only in certain forms of these activities, that the shaman and the yogin seem to resemble.

The theory of a common pre-historic substrata does lean on an archaeological hypothesis which at present is in vogue like the theory itself. Among the representations engraved on the seals of the proto-historic civilization at Mohenjo-daro there is one of a figure surrounded by wild animals, donning a head-dress made of buffalo horns and squatting with thighs flexed in the horizontal position and stretched apart to the maximum in such a way that the two soles of the feet touch. Sir John Marshall saw figured in this the supreme divinity of Śiva Paśupati in a yogic pose. Some feminine figures are supposed to correspond to a mother goddess which is quite easily identified with the companion goddess of Śiva. As Śiva and the goddess generally belong to Hinduism and not to the Vedic religion brought in by the so-called 'Aryan' invaders during a time when the Indus civilization was already quite old, it is tempting to believe that they already existed as part of a pre-Aryan substrata revealed by the archaeological remains of the Indus and among which we can recognise their representation. But the clues brought forward to justify this identification are such that they make it suspect. Śiva's mount is a bull and this feature has no connection with the fact of donning a buffalo-horn head-dress. As Paśupati, lord of the animals, he is the compassionate cowherd of men who are compared to cows of a herd, whereas the Mohenjo-daro figure is surrounded by beasts. Śiva is undoubtedly the master of yoga and even if the god of Mohenjo-daro had actually been Śiva, its representation would not prove in any way that he was immersed in yoga or that yoga was a practice of the proto-historic Indian substrata prior to the erudite culture which bears testimony to it. In fact it would be a most superficial vision of yoga if we inferred its practice on the mere basis of a posture it described. Now the posture depicted at Mohenjo-daro is not even a posture of yoga. Not only is this sitting position on the ischium with outspread thighs and legs folded-up generally very common in India but what is more, this particular position is found not among the postures prescribed for yogis but among certain artisans like cobblers who by adopting this posture hold the shoe in a vice-like grip between their soles. The posture of the Mohen-jodaro god is, therefore, far from possessing a specific identifiable significance.

In any case, a scientific view of yoga can follow only after its existence and its character have been conclusively known.

In a proper study of yoga even those exercises should be set aside which like yoga, are well documented in the Indian society itself and related to it, but which tradition however fails to include in its description of yoga. We refer to certain ascetic practices said to be of *tapas* through which the body trains itself to bear abnormal conditions for as long a duration as possible. For example, it is a kind of an intense warm-up (the word *tapas* in fact signifies, in its strict sense, 'heating') with five fires: the subject positions himself at the centre of a square marked by four braziers, with the sun above his head. But *tapas* also consists in holding certain painful positions for a long time: arms raised, standing on one leg, etc. These exercises of physical endurance, highly valued and widely practiced in India (they astonished Alexander's companions in the 4th century B.C.) have this in common with yoga: both seek to master the will and the elementary physical reactions. They are also interrelated by a very clearly stated intellectual motivation. Whatever may have been their primary origin, which remains veiled in the darkness of the past, they were not meant to be feats which merely sought to elicit admiration. We observe that they were valued in the Brahmanic world which was preoccupied with dissociating the inner being, the essential base of psychic individuality, from bodily attachments. The being-in-itself, *ātman*, is a part of Being in general, the universal Being whose essence consists in simply being. The body, or even the bodies that the being can successively inhabit belong to the changing and perishable world, to a modality of accident, not to the world of the permanence of existence considered in itself. This is what justifies the presence of the endeavour to master and ward off all accident so as to be firmly established in one's own being.

But, if mastery of the will and of natural external reactions connects the exercises to yoga, the latter in its specific form, comprises much more: a more scientific and subtler method of gaining this lasting and total mastery of the psychic and physical individuality.

We know, thanks to Buddhist texts primarily, that from the 6th century B.C., India was experimenting with a number of methods to liberate the Self from the tangles of the phenomenal world. This is recounted to us by the description of the efforts made under a succession of masters by the one who was to finally awaken himself unhelped to a clear consciousness of a new method, the 'Awakened One' in the highest sense of the word, the Buddha. It is true that these texts have not been accurately dated, no more than the orthodox Brahmanic ones which constitute the Upaniṣadic literature. But they originate from among numerous Buddhist sects which branched off very early on and they agree on the essential points, especially as regards the list of methods and philosophical ideas during the time of Buddha, i.e.

at the end of the 6th century and at the beginning of the 5th. Their tradition, therefore, surely goes back to that period for it does not seem probable that after their fragmentation, these sects agreed to rewrite the Master's biography.

The oldest documentary evidence on yoga, in the strict sense of the term, are not descriptive but are composed of references to its doctrines and to its practice as they are defined, in the subsequent classical expositions such as the *Yogasūtras* and they use the same terminology. From thence, yoga is understood as a technique for the control of the body and mind. Its basic means on the physiological level are the 'regulation of breath', *prāṇāyāma*, and on the psychological level, 'meditation', *dhyāna*. The theoretical conceptions to which their practice corresponds stand out in *Āyurveda*, the medical science of that time.

The oldest periods of Sanskrit literature had already revealed how important the research on *prāṇa* or breath was. It is not only the respiratory breath that is meant. The respiratory breath is but a form of the driving (motory) element, not merely of the animal body but of the entire universe as well where it moves in and puts in motion all things, in the form of the all-pervasive wind. In the body too all the movements are controlled by an inner circulation of the wind or the breath. Physiology, or rather, cosmo-physiology is, therefore, pneumatical as it was, for a number of Greek philosophers as well.

The five breaths are life or its pre-requisite and instrument. Deglutition, the digestive transit, excretion, the movement of limbs are the result of different breaths as are speech and digestion as well. This last is a kind of 'cooking' that occurs by the action of breath on the fire whose presence in the body is known by the heat therein. Through the external respiration there is an interaction of the breaths of the body with the wind in the cosmos.

Wind or breath, as the universal motor, is also the carrier of sensation and thoughts. If sight, for instance, is produced by the contact of a fire that issues from the eye and illuminates the objects for it, a sensation of 'seeing' is experienced in the consciousness because this sensation like others (*vedanā*) is conveyed by a breath to 'the seat of the mind' (*manas*)—the central organ of perception (*saṃjñā*). This central psychic organ of the body is located at its anatomical centre—the heart linked by channels to all the parts. The heart has the shape of a lotus-bud, that is turned upside down on its stem (the aorta). When it is contracted, the mind is inactive and this is what happens in sleep. In the state of wakefulness, the lotus of the heart opens up and consciousness emerges.

There lie in the passage of the major channels where breath moves organic liquids which convey sensory impressions to vulnerable points, the *marmans* (which if wounded can be fatal or may paralyse a part of the body by interrupting the flow of breath which lends it movement and sensitivity). The *marmans* are deep-seated organs and the axillary, cervical, inguinal regions, etc., where the bundle of nerves and vessels level out towards the surface of the body. Indian medicine includes also the heart and the navel among these.

According to these ideas, it is obvious that if one wanted to act on the functions of the organism, that is on the inner breaths that activate them, one could attempt to do so with the respiratory breath linked to the inner breaths but controlled by the will; this explains the popular practice of *prāṇāyāma*, the 'regulation' or even the 'blocking' (*āyāma*) of breath (*prāṇa*). This exercise consists mainly in slowing down the respiratory rhythm through gradual training and in the retention of breath. It is, therefore, a process that aims at stopping, as far as possible, the psychic and organic reactions of which breath is the agent. This is done so as to stabilize the individuality in a state which is closer than usual to the permanence of the inner being. Actually it is foremost a means of stabilizing the psychic activity and more commonly of the focusing of the attention. In addition, the relationship between the breaths, the organs and the mind, led one to believe that the will of the mind nourished by the breaths could, in its turn, influence the activity of these breaths through the organism. From this stems the belief that the yogin can direct his inner breaths at will and an extensive research into the physical attitudes and training is associated with regulated psychic operations.

At the same time, in India, the analysis of the workings of the mind was perfected to a remarkable degree of precision and it was accompanied by equally precise theoretical speculations which were generally accepted in all the circles as scientific facts, regardless of the different religious beliefs.

Among elements of psychic workings, besides sensations and perceptions, the following were enumerated: thoughts (*citta*), ideas or knowledge (*vijñāna*), imagination (*kalpa*) and psychic 'construction' (*saṃskāra*). The meaning of this last element (the word is masculine) is fundamental to Indian psychology. It includes the unconscious mechanisms of psychism whose elements are provided by the traces of past actions accompanied by ideation which are still retained in him. When this idea was discovered in Europe at the beginning of the 19th century, it was not clearly understood, as European psychology, at that time, looked upon the unconscious simply as the state in which the soul is inactive. The interpretations that were given by it then continue even today, to confuse the understanding of the theory of *saṃskāras*. However, as elucidated in the Brahmanic texts in Sanskrit as well as in Buddhist texts both in Sanskrit and in Pāli, this theory can be summarized down to a few quite simple principles. There is in the consciousness (*buddhi*), a grasping (*grahaṇa*) of new cognitions (*anubhava*) or the presence in the mind (*smṛti, manasi karaṇa*) of recollections, old *anubhavas* which were retained by memory (*smaraṇa*). Every action accompanied by an ideation (*cetanā*), whether the latter is voluntary or accidental, leaves thereby an imprint on the psychic individuality. But this imprint is not merely a 'picture-memory'. It is not characterised only by eventual recall to the consciousness, it leaves an imprint on the psychic individuality or, more literally, it 'perfumes' it (*vāsanā*).

Opinions have differed on this psychic individuality. For some, it is a specific entity, a carrier of *vāsanās*, a subject of sensations and perceptions and an agent of ideas: in short, a person (*pudgala*). For others, it is only a collection (*skandha*) of accumulated *vāsanās*, self-organised into constructions which are known as the *saṃskāras*. This psychic individuality does not constitute a person either but a constructed (*saṃskṛta*) individuality, as a chariot, for instance, is an assembly of parts and forms a coherent individual whole, not a personal one. According to the first theory, that of the person, the *vāsanās* also organise themselves into *saṃskāras* but these have the person as their substratum, whereas according to the second theory, it is the collection of *saṃskāras* which itself forms the firm nucleus of the psychic individuality where the occasional group of appearances (*rūpa*), sensations, perceptions and ideas arise. Both these theories were debated among the ancient Buddhist schools. They differ, as is evident, not in the psychological analysis, but in the answers they give to the ontological problem regarding the nature of psychism: is it a person or a psychic conglomerate? The Brahmanic schools took this ontological speculation further, by stating beyond the psychological phenomenism, the being-in-itself, the *ātman*, which, despite a temporary phenomenal individualisation, remains co-essential with Universal Existence. They too followed the same psychological analysis. As for the popularly held belief of the transmigration of souls, they too gave the same scholarly explanation, based on these very ideas.

The psychic individuality, whether it is an autonomous person or a conglomerate of psychological events, and whatever is its relation with the being-in-itself, does not dissolve during the decomposition of the body. The psychic constructions, the *saṃskāras*, which themselves constitute this individuality or link themselves to it, and which remain during the life of the body, outside its consciousness and above the vicissitudes experienced by the body by their nature are not subject to the slavery to organs. The death of organs, therefore, does not entail theirs. Now, these *saṃskāras* are seen to be during life itself not just the inactive remnants of past psychological experiences but active agents of the individuality's reactions. The latent tendencies are contained in them (*saṃskāras*) and they emerge in their time. As physical death does not change their nature, they wander invisibly like an airy spirit, a *gandharva*, approaching living beings whose activities have some affinity with their tendencies and they take on a body among them when a sexual union between these beings gives them a chance. Thus, *saṃskāras* being the product of psychic actions, reincarnation, in the final analysis is the natural consequence of actions done in a previous incarnation. The fruit of action is thus reaped by the psychic individuality, in the course of its transmigrations through the effect of a psycho-physiological mechanism and not because of the decrees of an external justice.

In this conception of natural determinism, man was the master of his destiny; through the practice of a psycho-physiological discipline, yoga, and by the mastery of the organic breaths and of meditation, he ruled the vegetative and psychic functioning, forming the desired *saṃskāras* and with them compensating for the others.

Outside yoga, strictly speaking, but within theoretical ideas of similar content and through a discipline of action and thought, the ritualistic Brahmanic circles established, in addition, a method of conditioning the *saṃskāras.* They widen the meaning of the word to designate certain ceremonies which we ordinarily translate as 'sacraments', in a superficially accepted analogy of those of Christianity. These ceremonies indicate the stages in the training of an orthodox Brahmin. If the very first ceremonies have purely ritual value, applicable to young children, the others can be effectively fulfilled only after each period of a minutely organised education that ensures the formation of psychic constructions, the *saṃskāras* necessary for a full-fledged Brahmin. It is the preliminary discipline not the final ritual which essentially operates and achieves the state which is sealed by the conclusive rite.

It seems, then, that the moment one refers to the doctrines of the milieus which practice it, we are no more obliged to sustain our understanding of yoga by taking recourse to the unknown subjects of pre-history, or by the uncertainty of a presumed mysticism. Thus it seems to us that we have here a polyvalent technique of mastering the body and mind, whatever one may seek to do with them. But the mastery of the body is limited by the play of physiological possibilities. A yoga that aims only at that is incomplete and inferior. The marvellous powers such as levitation which it is said to confer are devalued and the seeking after them is often openly denounced. It is the mastery of psychism culminating with its being 'fully set in position' *samādhi*, which is its ultimate goal.

The term *samādhi* has been the subject of several contradictory interpretations in a good number of books on yoga. Some translate it as 'ecstacy' as if yoga were mysticism and that mysticism necessarily ended in 'ecstacy', but without taking into account the real nature of such a state where the subject does not have the slightest feeling of being transported out of himself but, as we shall see later, stabilises his thought and his innate psychic inclinations, by even removing, at the ultimate stage, all representation. Mircea Eliade much more rightly suggests 'enstasy'. Nevertheless, psychic stabilisation, even while being an internal state, can work on an exterior object. Translations such as 'concentration' or 'meditation' are applicable only to the preliminary stages. 'Contemplation' implies the persistence of an observing consciousness whereas in total *samādhi* this stage is surpassed as well.

The most ancient Buddhist texts describe four levels of meditation (*jhāna*, Pāli equivalent of *dhyāna*). These levels correspond to a successive elimination of intellectual phenomena and sentiments in order to leave, in the end, nothing but psychic tranquillity. At the first stage, one shuts oneself out in advance to the proddings of external senses. What is left is reasoning (*vitakka*), reflection or wandering of thought (*vicāra*), the feeling of joyousness (*pīti*) and that of well-being (*sukha*). At the second stage, reasoning and wandering of thought are removed; at the third, joyousness goes out and there remains only the sense of sheer well-being. At the fourth, finally, this too disappears in its turn and gives way to imperturbability (*upekkhā*). These degrees are temporary phases of exercises.

Samādhi goes further, it is fully achieved by realising a permanent state of psychism, including the unconscious movements. A long Buddhist text from the beginning of our era, devoted to the *Samādhirāja* 'king among samādhis', defines it as the final establishment in a tranquil certainty, that all things of the sensible world are devoid of their own being, which is the major theme of the philosophical school from which this text is taken. In a psychism, established thus in certitude, nothing exists that could disturb it, no idea has any consistency. One who has reached this stage and who himself is nothing but the certitude of the void, can truly encourage men with his speech itself but it is only as appearance at their disposal. In the endeavour towards a similar state, what is important are mental creations (*bhāvanā*) of the elements of this certitude and the exclusion of all other preoccupation (*cintā*): in short, systematic indoctrination. Physiological exercises are absent: we limit ourselves to the renunciation of the goods of the world and to leading a life of solitude in the forest.

But generally in yoga physiological technique is linked to a psycho technique even if it be as an auxiliary. Most often, they are not thought to be capable of being effective, one without the other, taking into account the theoretically expounded and empirically proven interdependence of the functions of organs and of psychology. Yoga is then essentially a psychosomatic technique.

In the classical form of the *Yogasūtras*, this technique consists of eight elements:

The first two are preliminary. They are the *yamas* and the *niyamas*, the restraints and disciplines which prepare, through a general regulation of diet and conduct, the psycho-physiological conditions necessary to the undertaking of the psychosomatic exercises during the rest-period of the organic functions and the sensibility.

Strictly speaking, the exercises begin by the taking of a posture, *āsana*, that is stable and conducive to concentration and helps one to step back from eventual sensory stimuli. The most common postures are not among those that can be adopted only after a special training and which belong to some specific forms of yoga. They are, on the contrary, positions that are very common in Indian society and which can be held for a long time without any effort. The great texts most universally accepted, like the *Bhagavadgītā*, do specify that above all, one should be in a comfortable position. The Westerners who want to practice yoga by blindly imitating postures that are comfortable for Indians but painful for them, adopt the wrong approach. The Chinese Taoists who borrowed a good number of elements of yoga from India for their own practices and substituted certain Indian postures with those that without being uncomfortable for them had the same effect on their bodies. They adopt the sitting position on a seat and leave the one which consists in sitting cross-legged on the ground or on any other flat surface.

But what is meant is not postures of a general loosening of contractions. One must be in a vigilant state of mind that is in full readiness to take up the exercises. A supine position proper to sleep is forbidden.

In the most well-known *āsana*, which has several different types by variations in the positions of legs and hands; the trunk is erect, is slightly bent forward, the chin down and the eyes converging on the tip of the nose, between the eyebrows or on the navel.

The attitude is essentially one of self-concentration.

Once the static attitude is taken, there comes the action of general conditioning of the functions through a regulation of breathing, *prāṇāyāma.* After inspiration or 'filling up' (*pūraka*), which normally is not forced, there follows a prolonged retention (*kumbhaka*, the word strictly signifies a 'jar' to which the immobilised chest is compared).

The modern theorists of yoga have observed for a long time that outside all specific exercises, an attitude of concentration and effort are often spontaneously accompanied by a retention of breath. Here, yoga merely puts into play a common psycho-physiological process. The expiration of 'emptying' (*recaka*) is finally done slowly. It could be followed by a duration of thoraxic immobility. It is this time that some yogins, examined by Dr. Th. Brosse, call the 'external *kumbhaka*' in contrast to the normal *kumbhaka* which is then designated as 'internal *kumbhaka*'. The respective durations of the three periods are controlled as one progressively trains oneself to prolong the retention of breath and its controlled expulsion. They generally are in the proportion of 1-4-2. Thus is achieved a kind of controlled tension of the general activity of the subject who is now ready for specific psychosomatic operations.

It is here that the exercises can differ depending on the ultimate aim sought. In the *Yogasūtra* tradition, the following four stages are exercises that have psychic aims.

There comes first 'retraction', *pratyāhāra,* which deals with sensory and motory activities, the subject refraining from voluntary observation, shutting his attention to all possible external stimuli and maintaining immobility.

This shutting out of the attention does not, however, seem to be an independent process of a willed neutralisation of the perception which would be specific to yoga. It is rather the consequence of setting into motion the operation that follows 'retraction' and in fact overlaps into it: 'fixation', the *dhāraṇā* of the attention. This operation consists in reducing thought to a single point (*ekāgracitta*), to the one-idea concentration.

From now we are at the stage of meditation, *dhyāna*, on a selected theme. Strictly speaking, it is the intellectual activity that provides the material for corresponding psychic constructions, of *saṃskāras* that are no more accidental and caused by fortuitous representations, but predetermined by a deliberate choice. Thus the psychic content, until now guided by consciousness, ceases in the state in which he is so placed and this is the 'position of psychism', *samādhi*.

There are two stages of *samādhi*. In the first, the last organised psychic constructions which lead one to this stage persist, and it is called the *saṃprajñātasamādhi*, the 'conscious position of psychism'. In the second and final stage, the constructions are given up and *asaṃprajñātasamādhi* is achieved, the 'unconscious position of psychism',[3] where the psychic individuality remains immobile and isolated in the contents that they constructed for it.

The deep psychic individuality formed by *saṃskāras* constitutes the 'subtle body' (*sūkṣmaśarīra*), as opposed to the 'gross body', the material body. The subtle body is also called *liṅgaśarīra*, 'the body of signs' because the *saṃskāras* which form it, constitute the latent forces which, by becoming active, provide the signs of its life and that of the material body it animates. In Indian psychology the *liṅgas* are in fact the signs and manifestations of vegetative and psychic life.[4]

The last three operations of the classical practice: fixation, meditation, position constitute together *saṃyama*, mastery. This mastery is psychic but conditioned by the somatic preparation and it is effective on the gross body through the subtle body where it is established.

This mastery can also be applied to powers of action and knowledge depending on the object on which our concentration has been fixed. Among these powers of action we find the extraordinary capacities which are discouraged. Among the powers of knowledge are included, theoretically again, the intimate understanding of things, of the luminous celestial bodies for instance, through a rigorous adaptation of the perceiving psychism to the object (and it is in this sense that one can speak of contemplation in *samādhi*). But a total mastery of knowledge is the merging of oneself in Universal Being, absolute and immutable, hidden behind the phenomenal aspect of Nature.

In classical scholasticism the relation between *Puruṣa* the self, the Man par excellence, with *Prakṛti*, Nature, is defined by a doctrine of the analysis of natural facts said to be of 'numbering', *sāṃkhya* and this explains the oft-mentioned affinity between *sāṃkhya* and *yoga*.

The question about the extraordinary material powers: making oneself small like the atom or infinitely large, walking on water, holding oneself in the air, etc. poses a difficult problem which we cannot avoid by simply negating the possibility of such facts. If we cannot truly admit their reality, as affirmed by legend and theoretical nomenclature or as apparently testified to by observation, we should at least ask ourselves on what the belief in them is founded. Those among the masters of yoga who discourage all seeking after them, would not fail to challenge their true reality, or to denounce them as false or illusory, if they deemed it worthwhile to do so.

It is certain that faith in the omnipotence of a god, of a demon, of an extraordinary man or as in yoga, of a technique of mastery, this faith that ultimately becomes a fixed absolute attitude, can be enough to sustain a popular belief in the exceptional without the support of any personal proof. But what can we say about the yogins who claim to be capable of such prodigious powers? To accuse them of bragging or quackery would be too facile a way of dismissing the question of their psychology. It is true that some among them are false and pretentious and impostors; their enemies don't hesitate to denounce them as such. The Buddhist texts are full of this kind of accusations against 'heretics', but it is selected miracle-mongers who are condemned while in others their sincerity is not questioned.

The task of scientific investigation which in these conditions seems to be indispensable, appears to be twofold at the very outset. We must record, if the case demands, all the facts of an extraordinary nature which we meet or which are reported to us with some documentary precision. We must also seek to understand how these facts are judged by the believers vis-a-vis their mentality, i.e. keeping in view their intellectual training, their acquired knowledge and the circumstances of their personal experience. We can understand another person only by knowing the cultural background that conditions his judgments. It is not enough to criticise the judgments in the light of our own ideas, ignoring the motivations and the circumstances which gave them birth.

The first task can rarely be accomplished because of the very uncommonness of observable cases and the ambiguities that are left in the rare reports, which are accompanied by something other than unverifiable affirmations.

Sometimes it is possible to give an explanation to an apparent extraordinary feat by a simple objective interpretation on the basis of the description of the facts that go into its making. It is in this way, that an alleged method of cure for ocular problems called *trāṭaka*, is described as consisting in fixing the look on a point very close-by until the eyes start watering. But as long as the problem is still present, the patient will not be able to do this. He, therefore, gives up this 'fixation' and is reproached with not having followed the treatment sufficiently. It is from the moment that this painful irritation has been removed that the exercise can be done as in the normal state. Here, therefore, we see a test of cure being wrongly mistaken for a theraphy.[5]

At other times we are unable, at least so far, either to accept or prove as false the apparent extraordinary feat. Sometime back a truly astonishing observation was published with a great deal of photographic illustrations. It was about a case of levitation: holding the body in the horizontal position above the ground with the only support of a pole placed on the ground.[6] The conditions of the experiment done under full sun in a vast open area, shuts out the hypothesis about using the common method employed in the circus of supporting from above with a string that is hidden by the play of projectors and shadows. The author of this observation declared that he had checked with a cane under the body to ensure that there was no support below. There isn't any shadow or trace on the ground of such a support. The hypothesis of extremely clever photographic tricks is no doubt admissible while that of collective illusion is set aside by the photographs themselves. Great effort on the part of the 'performer' is visible on the successive photos which show him with his hand contracted on top of the pole and exhausted within a few minutes. This shows that there wasn't really an elimination of all the effect of weight from the body, but it does not explain at all either the phenomenon or its appearances. The hypothesis of multiple photographic montage combined to create the illusion of real, successive phases, implies that what was intended was an untrue report of a prodigious feat that had already been spoken of much before photography came into existence. Whatever the case might be, from this observation or pseudo-observation, we must in similar cases note down the affirmations and the documents supplied, while waiting to be able to make its criticism, either justifying the facts or showing their insignificance. And now we are reverted to our second task, to the need for studying the reasons that go to form the opinions in India about the genuine, illusory or presumed achievements that are attributed to yoga.

It is clear that such exploits, seen or heard recounted, obvious or not, as the one that has just been described, give in the public mind currency to the belief in extraordinary powers. But what needs to be mainly studied is the belief of those who themselves practice yoga and one must study these not in the *rājayoga* of the *Yogasūtras* which dissuades the seeking after powers, but in *haṭhayoga* which permits it and especially develops such somatic techniques.

Haṭhayoga comes into the picture later than *rājayoga* in literary references and expositions. It uses the same elements of technique but static postures are practiced with considerably more elaborateness and different techniques of physiological action are added to it. It bases itself, in addition, on new symbolist, physio-anatomical concepts and it emerges from a great movement of the evolution of religious aims and the evolution of attitudes to the world and to life.

The old Vedic religion and ancient Brahmanism founded on the Vedas about 1500 B.C., were religions aiming at the proper functioning of the cosmic order and at the attainment of all kinds of prosperity. They set *bhukti* as their goal, 'enjoyment', this enjoyment being legitimate in the right, universal Order (*dharma*). Brahmanist thought, having discovered the Being-in-itself, immutable behind the inconsistency of natural conditions, had striven to disengage from these conditions the psychic self in order to allow it to unite, by means of a complete adaptation through the intelligent technique of yoga, with this Being-in-itself. It was a religion of *mukti*, of 'liberation'. Similarly, although without setting the Being-in-itself as the goal to be attained by the psychic self, ancient Buddhism and Jainism had preached, from the 5th century B.C. onwards, certain methods of liberation. The Right Order was not merely universal prosperity but a higher Order of escape out of such prosperity, of its misfortunes and its transitoriness. Parallelly, certain theistic movements submitted the Order to a Law of God who, as a manifestation in nature of the Being-in-itself in a sovereign form, and compassionate to men, was the thinking soul of the Universe as the human psychic being was the thinking soul of the body. The individual soul's love for this God was the soul's path leading up to him and a step towards the Being-in-itself of whose reality he was an approximate representation in this world. Whatever the devotees may have called God, either Śiva or Viṣṇu, or conceived him in yet other aspects, these were all religions of *bhakti*, of 'devotion'. Yoga, used then as a method of orientating the psychic being towards God, took the form of *bhaktiyoga*, of the 'yoga of devotion'.

Around and during the first centuries of our era, many different currents divided themselves in this group of movements which, whether old or recent, were greatly active, sustained by teeming literatures of scripture and exegesis that affected, directly or indirectly, a great part of the peoples of India. The currents that have prevailed among them are: on the one hand, a more promising Buddhism than the old tradition and which proudly labelled itself 'Mahāyāna', i.e. the 'Great Way of Progress', on the other, Hinduism which has reigned over all the others to this day and from which the immense majority of yogins come. These two currents were so powerful that they lent to India a force of cultural expansion in Asia similar to that of Hellenism in the West, and perhaps even greater still.

Even prior to these currents, the ancient Buddhist schools which, in fact, had continued to exist simultaneously with the new ones, and Brahmanic sciences and techniques, had begun to spread and subsequently renewed themselves by a succession of prolonged contacts, towards Upper Asia, China and Southeast

Asia. But it is mostly the Mahāyānic and Hindu currents that conquered all of Eastern Asia and the Southeast. Buddhism established itself in Upper Asia, China, Korea, Japan, Tibet and from thence in Mongolia. Buddhism and Hinduism established themselves together in Indo-china and Indonesia. All these Indian influences abroad were especially transmitted through Sanskrit literature that was translated everywhere, Sanskrit having become for India what Latin had been for Europe: a means of unifying the general culture and the vehicle for propagating its ideas.

The techniques of yoga had an important role in all these countries and naturally, according to the principles borrowed from the heart of the milieus who propagated them, before pursuing their own development in China and in Japan.

In order to restrict ourselves to the place they held and to the ideas that impelled them in India, we must consider them at the heart of Mahāyānic Buddhism and above all in Hinduism.

Two kindred convictions inspired the two principal philosophic tenets of the Mahāyāna. One which has already been referred to, was that all things are devoid of an essential self. For the *śūnyavādins*, 'those who speak of the Void', the Right Order of things was not the Order of nature but the very principle of the emptiness of an essential being in the Order of nature. Such was the Supreme Truth veiled for the ignorant man by a truth of envelopment (*saṃvṛti*): the perceptible world. The other conviction, that of the *vijñānavādins*, 'those who speak of the representations', was that the sensible world reduced itself to a group of psychic representations without a corresponding objective substratum. The arguments for dismissing perception as the irreproachable proof of the existence of a corresponding objective substratum, were taken from illusions and dreams. It did not follow that the apparent or the 'knowable' (*jñeya*) was totally non-existent but that its representation was not the faithful image of the external Reality and that it was founded on a fundamental psychism (*ālayavijñāna*). An extremely elaborate psychology was developed to explain this or, better, to ascertain 'the fact of being thus', what was called *taṭhatā*.

In the two conceptions, the world was actually pictured as a waking dream that was collective and coherent since it depended on a structure which is common to all psychic individuals who as individuals also enjoyed a certain latitude to some specific representations. Yoga was then a technique of handling such representations, especially for 'those who speak of representations' and who were also called the 'practitioners of yoga', *yogācāra*. For both, samādhi consists in firmly establishing not merely consciousness in these convictions, but the unconscious as well which is always filled with the repetition of such notions. The most essential use of *bhāvanā* or psychic 'creation', enables one to replace the spontaneous formations of daily life with selected and well-determined ones which have neither more nor less external, objective basis as the involuntary, ordinary perceptions, in short, formations that have the same empirical reality. The authors, fully permeated with these ideas, therefore, spoke commonly of voluntary psychic experiences of *bhāvanās* exactly as they did of experiences that were involuntary, without giving them any lesser relative reality. Whether a *bhāvanā* aimed at an extraordinary feat, such a consciously sought feat would be an event of the same order of reality as any accidental, natural event. The practitioner of yoga would testify in all good faith to having experienced it by his own power and the believer would admit its possibility, since for him, the possibility is in harmony with the natural order of things as he has learnt to know it. Neither will require an objective proof, as we understand it, since both deny that a representation can have an objective, absolute basis and our proof would only be another representation.

Brahmanic philosophy, on its parts, has developed similar views. In the 9th century, the great philosopher of the school of Vedānta, Śaṅkara, stressing the ontological analysis more than the psychological one but without distancing himself from the fundamental traditions of the latter, explained the external world as the phantasmagoria of a cosmic illusion, *māyā*, veiling the Absolute Being, the Unique Reality. He reiterated this so much that he was sometimes accused by others of being a Buddhist in disguise. The latter, without discounting the primacy of the Absolute Being, allowed the participation of the relative in the Absolute Being's reality and conceived it as being immanent in the phenomenal.

Yoga was considered by all to be a supreme method of conditioning the knowledge of accepted viewpoints. It has, thus, with its basis of psychological and physiological concepts, fully permeated Brahmanism that went on evolving more and more towards the seeking of liberation through knowledge and devotion.

This Brahmanism became the most eminent religious system of all India, what we conveniently call 'Hinduism', through a reassimilation and development of the ancient Vedic ideal of the organisation and the enjoyment of the empirical world, *bhukti*. This happened during the centuries around the Christian era and in circumstances that remain unclear to us,—as the ancient documents which could have illumined the first attempts at this reassimilation were retouched or replaced in such a way that we possess them only to the extent and in the form in which they won wide acceptance. This reintegration, accompanied as well by an integration of popular, local elements which were certainly important but difficult to distinguish, was the reintegration of a general tendency and also of certain Vedic texts and practices but not of the great Vedic ritualism itself.

Vedic recitation is the only thing that has been conserved to this day on the fringe of new beliefs and practices. Thanks to the inevitable seriousness of the study and the automatism it achieves, it can be related to the yogic discipline, piling up selected *saṃskāras* in the psychic self.

In the technical literature of Hinduism, however, in its 'Traditions', *āgama*, or 'Texts par excellence', the *Tantras*, there dominates a group of prescriptions of rituals, of conduct and of yoga proper, all founded on the doctrine and aiming at the total assimilation of it by the psychic individual. The rituals consist essentially in the invocation of energies and temporal manifestations of Divinity and of its worship. It ensures temporal prosperity and well-being while waiting to be delivered from the temporal. It is in this way that it re-establishes enjoyment even while it prepares one for knowledge.

This ritual too, like Vedic rituals, bases its effectiveness on formulae or *mantras* which precede, accompany or replace any operation. It uses certain Vedic *mantras* and exalts the primordial sound, OṂ, the essence of all speech, but introduces a mass of new formulae of adoration and the graphic depiction of these formulae arranged in symbolic diagrams (*yantra*) and organised spaces (*maṇḍala*) which are symbolic as well. It puts the adept in contact with all the energies of the world, thanks to a double symbolism which integrates these (energies) to the formulae on the one hand, and to physio-anatomical elements of the body on the other. Thus the activities of the universe and the essence itself of the universe are found again in the psycho-physiological complex of the organism of which yoga is the instrument of mastery.

The relatively later Buddhist sects too set out analogous rituals prescribed in similar works also called *Tantras*.

This had led to the current notion of a 'tantrism' conceived as a specific, religious form, branching out in different kinds of tantrism, Shaivaite, Buddhist and subdivided further into numerous schools. What is meant is rather a mode of practice based on a common *Weltanschauung* which is adopted by the various religions and disciplines of escape striving towards transcendent knowledge, beyond the mastery of things and of oneself. Depending on what a Hindu or a Buddhist mainly devotes himself to: intellectual thought, adoration or techniques of rites and conduct, he is a philosopher, a devotee or a tāntrika, but that does not make him any less of a Hindu or a Buddhist, and his predilection for one particular religious attitude, whether it is spontaneous or dictated by teaching, seldom totally excludes the others.

The common *Weltanschauung* is the inheritor of cosmo-physiological Brahmanism—the system of interrelating the macrocosm to the individual microcosm—and carries on the Upaniṣadic thought, narrowing down endlessly the diversity of things by establishing equivalences between them, and yoga remains the instrument of mastery.

But beside its psychosomatic principles and techniques, a magical element is often introduced in this yoga, to the extent that it accepts irrationally conceived connections and self-operating formulae, that is to say when realisation does not wait any more for a gradual increase of empirical and inductive knowledge and rushes up to surpass it. The limits of psychic and physiological possibilities and its nature of practical discipline have, however, greatly maintained yoga in its field of psychosomatic technique. It's the cosmo-physiological thought that diverged the most from the science of natural observation and provided yoga with an arbitrary system of anatomical and physiological representations.

The old 'pneumatism' is preserved and so is a notion of the principal seats of breaths, of which six coincide with the *marmans*, the vital points[7]. These seats of breaths (*prāṇāyatana*) are: head, throat, heart, navel, rectum and bladder. But the new anatomy of yoga which used to consider the spine as the microcosmic equivalent of the mountain Meru, the axis of the universe, located the six seats of breaths in front of this mountain at their respective levels; they were thought to be linked to allow for the circulation of these breaths, by an uninterrupted channel, *suṣumnā*, which was itself framed by two other channels *iḍā* and *piṅgalā*, representing the paths of the Moon and the Sun which gravitate around Meru, and anatomically these channels begin at the nostrils. By extending to the six seats of breath, the name of 'lotus' which earlier was applied to the heart and the name of 'circle' which belonged to the navel, they are all designated as 'lotus' (*kamala*) or 'circle' (*cakra*).

Several authors, ill-informed about the origin of their conception in Indian medicine, wished to trace it in the modern anatomy of the nervous system which they thought was discovered by yogic intuition and they identified them with the sympathetic plexus. We need not consider this identification which is in fact, contradicted by the localisations ascribed to these 'lotuses' in the texts that describe them. But the guidance of such an imaginary representation serves as a mental scheme to the yogins endeavouring to lead within the body by their thought, the organic breaths that they think to be linked to their respiratory breath and subjected to *prāṇāyāma*.

In the Shaiva cosmophysiology (often accepted also outside the Hindu circles where Śiva is seen as the Absolute Being), Śiva or the embodied manifestation of Absolute Being, is seated in the head in a lotus, the 'Thousand-Petalled Lotus' which dominates the other six, whereas Cosmic Energy (*Śakti*) rests on the lowest of the lotuses of the body, *mūlādhāra* or the 'receptacle of the base'. She (the Energy) is there in the form of *kuṇḍalinī*, the 'coiled', coiled like a sleeping serpent and rooted to the densest matter. In effect, the 'receptacle of the base' corresponds in the body to the element earth, the grossest in nature. It is pulled out of sleep, and activated by yoga. From then on, it rises up the *suṣumnā* through the higher lotuses which represent ever subtler elements: water, fire, wind, space and mind, before achieving union with the Absolute Being in the lotus where it culminates. With the psychic creation of the feeling of successive gathering of the organic breaths at every level and of their upward ascent from one stage to the next, the yogin collects his energies in the *kuṇḍalinī* and follows it in its ascent culminating in the attainment of union with the Absolute and then the psychic self can go out of the body through a symbolic opening located at the summit of the skull and called the aperture of Brahman, *Brahmarandhra.*

This essentially psychic operation demands a psychosomatic conditioning that takes a long training to get formed. This training, which is that of *haṭhayoga*, contains the same elements as of *rājayoga* but under a multiplicity of precise and much more elaborate forms. It is *haṭhayoga* that provides to modern physiological research the maximum material for study.

The postures, *āsanas*, are more numerous and often more complex. They are executed in well-defined attitudes, in general difficult to take and to hold and some of which are called *bandha*, 'bonds' and some others *mudrā*, 'seals'. Both center the organism in a characteristic situation that corresponds to a symbolic state or that aims to act on an organ or a function.

One of the main instances of a *mudrā* is the *khecarīmudrā* where after its strings have been gradually severed by small repeated cuts over a long period and after it has undergone long and progressive manoeuvres of elongation with joint exercises of stretching the soft palate, the tongue can be turned over in the cavum. And example of a *bandha* is the *uḍḍiyāna bandha* which is executed by an expiration forced to the extreme with a vigorous contraction of the abdominal rectus and the lifting of the ribs by a contraction of the scapulo-cervical group of muscles. Such exercises are among those that produce the most important physiological phenomenon, such as the restriction of cardiac movements. We know since long that some yogins in India are known to bury themselves alive for quite a long time. It was thought for a long time that this could be possible only through trickery and some attempts did effectively expose it. But Dr. Therese Brosse[8] was the first to show in 1936 that the electrocardiogram recording of the yogin in conditions that were similar to those of the burial experiment, proved the faculty of the yogin to achieve, at will, a state where circulation is greatly reduced and thereby also the fact that certain exercises of yoga have an intense, physiological action.

In addition, a number of auxiliary or special techniques were experimented with and are employed in *haṭhayoga.* A later, classical manual, the *Gheraṇḍasaṃhitā* (I. 9 & foll.) enumerates these techniques in a series called the seven *sādhanas*, 'realisations' or 'practices'. These realisations are: *śodhana*, purification; *dṛḍhatā*, firmness obtained from the *āsanas*; *sthairya*, immobility due to the *mudrās*; *dhairya*, steadfastness due to retraction; *lāghava*, lightness (the sensation of being light, alert) through a control of the breath; *pratyakṣa*, clear perception through meditation; and *nirlipta*, suppression of the affections by a position of psychism.

The practitioner, *sādhaka*, achieves the last six realisations through the classical methods of yoga. But purification is done by six different methods: *dhauti*, the cleaning of natural cavities; *basti*, rectal injection or intestinal mobilisation without injection; *neti*, the passing of a muslin cloth through the nostrils into the cavum and the mouth; *laulikī*, a strong mobilisation of the stomach and the intestine through alternating contractions of the abdominal rectus, this operation is elsewhere called *nauli*; *trāṭaka*, the fixation on a near object until eyes begin to water and *kapālabhātī*, cleaning of the *cavum* with water absorbed either through the nostrils or through the mouth, or else through an uninterrupted breathing with forced expiration.

In practice, the rectal as well as bladder cleaning can be done without any other instruments of injection except a probe. The yogin can be trained, in fact, to suck in water through voluntary bladder or rectal pumping with the help of a simple probe or by directly dipping the outer orifices. These exercises have been said to set off a voluntary action of fine fibres but it seems more probable that it is the vigorous and combined contractions of the muscles of the abdomen, pelvis, and the diaphragm, contractions that are followed by their loosening, which enable the yogin to act on bladder and rectal cavities as on rubber-pears. Similar contractions and expansions are necessarily a part of the technique employed.[9]

The unilateral alternating contractions of the abdominal rectus, which normally act as one, are part of the isolated contractions of muscles or of a groups of muscles that the yogins manage to achieve, often at will, by dissociating a number of customary synergies.

If these techniques are often described in Indian treatises, it is done very briefly and physiological observations which have been made so far remain rudimentary. They are very often repeated without any additions and the field is open to a number of biological and physiological investigations which would enable a detailed analysis of phenomena, of their conditions and their results.

For the time being, Dr. Therese Brosse has done well to gather the totality of her experiments and findings which were mainly carried out on respiratory and cardiac rhythms. The yogins' exercises have been described as they were presented to her and the corresponding explanations reproduced exactly as they were offered by the yogins or by the English works to which they themselves had referred. These exercises, explanations and books do not always agree with the descriptions and theories of the original Indian treatises. It has appeared indispensable to us not to separate what the yogins under observation do from what they think they are doing. At the documenting stage in which we find ourselves, we must, along with recording the physiological phenomena that they accomplish, take down the accompanying ideas they express. This does not desist us from comparing the facts and what is said with the testimony of the written tradition; but by substituting now the data from the latter, even the most well-founded data, according to the indications of the subjects under study, we would be substituting the thoughts of their predecessors, or of different schools, to their own, and we would break the psychosomatic unity that is to be studied.

One must not, however, try to shy away from the difficulties that exist in finding the correspondence of the psychic activity with the observed or recorded somatic phenomena. The yogin's verbal description of the states of his mind is sometimes incompatible with the exercise he undertakes. Sometimes words fail him, especially in a foreign language like English, to describe states that do not correspond to the usual feelings or else the translation is inadequate. In some cases, the given explanations are deliberately simplified in the hope of making them intelligible to non-yogin observers, whether foreign or Indian. At other times, the yogin has been trained by the master to practice on indications that are not explained but passively followed. If he gives explanations then, they do not correspond to a personal attitude that is put into practice in the exercises, but to facts that have been learnt independently and which may not be adequate. On the other hand, the exercises that are presented may not be correctly executed or be incomplete. The results obtained in this way do not fully reflect the results that would ensue from a perfectly executed exercise. It is for this that Dr. Brosse has taken care to note down, as often as possible, the conditions of the yogins' preparation for the exercises they were to accomplish. For every technique that is described, the results should be taken as those derived from observation or from their recording in each given case and yet these results must not be taken as the only possible results of the technique under study.

We are at the indispensable stage of rudimentary observation, not yet at the stage of laying down the laws of yoga.

Observations and recordings, in relation to subjects who are normal or ill, alien to yoga and to India, were used with the intention of comparing the precise objective data collected by them with that supplied by the yogins. But the general assimilations of techniques and theories to which writers of books on yoga often revert have not been examined here. They would have been out of context in a compilation of observations.

In fact, they are often misleading because of their superficiality; they make comparisons with analogies that are external to the subject and do not sufficiently examine in their real nature or their cultural context either yoga or the techniques that are compared to it. It is for this reason that since the beginning of the 19th century, parallels have been drawn between yoga and *hesychasm*, the contemplative path of Oriental Christianity leading to a beatific state and using notably flexible positions of the body, a slowing down of the breath, a concentrated visual fixation on the navel and the repetition of a short prayer to the Christ by visualising him in the heart. But M. Eliade has cautioned against too hasty an identification[10] and J. Monchanin has made a lucid comparison of these two disciplines which shows them in their respective traditions and thereby, in their autonomy.[11] The comparison of facts of a similar nature is always legitimate, but their general interpretation demands a complete study not only of these facts but also of the conditions of their execution. It demands this especially in regard to the psychic concomitants of somatic exercises, concomitants which can provoke, if they differ from one school of training to another, through the action of psychism on physiological functioning, divergent results in each one for the same exercise.

The danger of error in such assimilative interpretations of the methods belonging to two fields that are foreign to one another, is to be avoided, especially by the historian and the therapist. For the historian, because it confuses him with regard to some human activities and thereby misrepresents them. For the therapist, because it encourages him to apply on his patients borrowed techniques which are truly valid only on subjects of an altogether different psychological make-up. Now, the books that popularise yoga, especially those that describe its body-techniques, but leave out its psychological aspect or extol a vague and mysterious 'spirituality', still enumerate endlessly the curative or hygienic effects of each exercise of yoga. The Indian texts themselves do extol the soothing and therapeutic qualities after a brief description of the exercise to be practiced but the principles of general preparation and the preliminary conditioning are taken to be already known and followed. Each exercise is separately described in its particularity but is not practiced all by itself. It is a part of a whole discipline to be taken up together.

However, a detailed observation of the phenomena of yoga, to the exclusion of their being put into practice, should be analytical, ready to take down simultaneously the greatest number possible of their manifestations. We can then compare the observed results with those of similar psychosomatic techniques practiced in other systems. These comparisons can reveal the common basis of psychosomatic reactions which can be that of exercises done with different aims. These comparisons can, in a more general way, discover some laws of automatic causation of certain phenomena, either independently of the psychic preparation of the subject or conditioned by a specific preparation. The comparative investigation of the phenomena of yoga and of other psychotechniques is, therefore, likely to inform us about certain workings of psychosomatic phenomena and certain precise relationships between some psychic tensions and physiological reactions.

In this regard, comparative studies of the processes of yoga, on the one hand, and those of Schultz's autogenous training on the other, can be useful. Jean Bruno has already written a pertinent introduction.[12] Schultz[13] himself made comparisons with yoga as well as with different facts of religious or ethnic psychology.

Autogenous training, 'concentrative self-relaxation' (we should rather say 'self-relaxation through concentration', is above all a therapeutic method; yoga is first a technique of mastery of healthy psychism. The former aims to reduce painful pathogenic tensions, the latter is for conditioning the mind in conformity with a philosophic ideal of the relationships between the individual and the universal being and to the phenomenal modalities of existence. The former is applied mostly on sick people, the latter excludes them, at least from its highest strivings and if it advocates, in its aspect of *haṭhayoga* especially, a number of techniques as curative, it is to clear the 'royal path' of all intervening psycho-physiological obstacles.

Moreover, autogenous training with its aim of including a state of general relaxation, takes as its starting point a suggestion of relaxation initially localised which gradually becomes more general. This suggestion, first made by the doctor, is subsequently taken up by the subject himself who, in this training, becomes his own instructor although still guided by the doctor. This method was born from hypnosis and more specifically autohypnosis inducing techniques. Now if yoga requires instruction from a master, from an experienced guru and his continued guidance, it still strives for an autonomous mastery setting into motion tensions that are often extreme, as much on the psychic level as on the physiological one. That is why the legitimacy of often clubbing together in the past yoga and hypnosis was notably challenged, as Jean Bruno[14] tells us, by Eliade and Hauer and by us. But as J. Bruno very rightly remarks too, the hypnosis that is seen as opposed to yoga is the one where the subject relinquishes all personal will in a state of quasi-sleep in order to give himself up to the suggestion from outside or just retains that amount of will which is needed to execute the suggestions that are received. But if the hypnosis is seen as a specific state of the will where the subject applies himself to conform himself to a method of psychic and physiological training that has been learnt, then yoga is certainly an auto-hypnosis of this kind. The difference between the subject submitting himself to autogenous training and the yogin following a prescribed discipline is, therefore, not in the basic mechanism that is put into play, it pertains only to the goals set at the beginning: relaxation or mastery.

We can also observe that the relaxation of autogenous training is not without elements of tension and that yoga, in order to consolidate the mastery, leaves out the tensions which could be perturbing. The 'relaxation' that is brought about by autogenous training is not a state of pure passivity but the result of a systematic, channelised activity. Relaxation is obtained by means of concentration, by creating a calm and steady movement of attention and by focusing of that attention after alternating intentions of loosening and tautness. The 'relaxation' is not total, it is achieved less by the cessation of all activity than by a change of activity, by its orientation on the prescribed exercises of calming down. It is easier to achieve it in this way, through reorientation rather than total abstinence, as this gives free vent to emotional movements and to the established tensions. Similarly and more intensely, by forcefully fixing the attention on some particular point or theme which, as a matter of fact, can be tranquility, 'insensibility', 'unconsciousness', the exercise of yoga orientates all psychic activity in one direction and relaxes it in all the others. *Pratyāhāra*, the retraction of sensory and motory activities is a general 'disconnection' which is the consequence of a deliberately selected connection.

In addition, a good number of elements of both the techniques are truly analogous, such as setting into motion, in comparable conditions, the same natural, psychosomatic mechanisms.

We shall take only two examples: first, the concentration on the heart and on the solar plexus and second, the convergence of the eyes towards the mid-forehead. The first are part of the lower cycle of Schultz,[15] the second, of the higher cycle.

Concentration on the heart consists in becoming aware of the heart-beats and the representations of the heart and its action, the representations that are derived from memories of anatomical drawings and impressions gathered while doing the exercise. This can enable us to control the heart and this control is expressed in a voluntary change of the pulse-rate, just by concentration on an idea assisted by the repetition of a formula which is inductive, but without the interference of eventually perturbing affective factors. Similarly, concentration on the solar plexus is done by directing one's attention on the epigastrium by a mental visualisation of the solar plexus based on anatomical plates and even by producing imaginary images.

The aims here are limited to the training to be undertaken voluntarily in the state that is expressed in this formula: Ich bin ganz entspannt, 'I am totally relaxed'; once automatism is obtained through training, this formula is enough to produce this state at once. From the point of view of yoga, the final aim to be attained is much more complex but one finds similarly a process of psychosomatic action through mental concentration on organs along with a concrete although arbitrary visualisation of a structure and function that are ascribed to them.

A specific example cited in a *Upaniṣad* of yoga[16] can reveal the kind of representation in use based on the philosophical and physiological ideas of the country:

93\. 1. I shall now expound the ultimate knowledge of the Self (Ātman). In the seat of the heart there lies the eight-petalled lotus. In its center, forming a circle, there exists the form of the Jīvātman,[17] of luminous shape and of the size of an atom. In that all is founded. That knows all. That does all. All that occurs is according to his free vision, thus; I am the doer; I am the enjoyer; I experience pleasure, I experience pain; I am the one-eyed, the lame, the deaf, the dumb, the lean, the corpulent.

2\. When, it rests on the Eastern petal,—the Eastern petal is white—, then, as a consequence of the inclination for devotion, psychism is in the Right Order (Dharma).

3. When it rests on the South-eastern petal,—the South-Eastern petal is red—, then psychism is prone to slumber and weariness.
4. When it rests on the Southern petal—the Southern petal is black—then it is prone to hatred and anger.
5. When it rests on the South-Western petal—the South-Western petal is blue—then it is prone to evil acts and violence.
6. When it rests on the Western petal—the Western petal is the colour of crystal—then it is prone to play and amusement.
7. When it rests on the North-Western petal—the North-Western petal is the colour of ruby—then it is prone to travel, movement and detachment.
8. When it rests on the Northern petal—the Northern petal is yellow—then it is prone to happiness and love.
9. When it rests on the North-Eastern petal—the North-Eastern petal is the colour of lapis lazuli—then it is prone to generosity: giving etc.
10. When it leans on the joints of the petals, then there is the rousing of the great maladies: of vāta (wind), pitta (bile), śleṣman (phlegm).
11. When it stands in the centre, then it knows all, it sings, dances, recites and creates bliss.
12. When the eyes are strained, then in order to remove the strain it draws a first circle and plunges in the middle. The first circle is the colour of the bandhūka[18] flower, then the state of sleep follows. In the state of sleep, there is the state of dreaming. In the dream-state, it indulges in the imagination, of having seen, heard and inferred events, etc. then there is great fatigue.
13. To alleviate fatigue, it draws a second circle and plunges in the middle. The second circle is the colour of the indrakopa insect. Then follows the state of slumber and in that state of slumber consciousness is connected with Parameśvara the isolated one. It assumes the form of

permanent wakefulness; therefore, there is realisation of the form of Parameśvara.[19]

14. After having drawn a third circle, it plunges in the middle. The third circle is the colour of ruby. The fourth state follows. In the fourth state, it is connected with the isolated Paramātman; then it takes on the form of the permanent wakefulness. Then:
"One should slowly cease from mental action by an intelligence firmly held and having fixed the mind in the Self one should think of nothing at all" (*Bhagavadgītā*, VI, 25).
15. Then, after having united the prāṇa, and the apāna, it sees the entire universe in the form of the Ātman. When this state beyond the Turīya is attained, then all forms assume the form of Ānanda. It is beyond all pairs of opposites. It lasts as long as the body endures. After this there is liberation consisting in what is told to be the realisation of the Paramātman himself. This is the means of seeing the Self.

If the chosen themes of ideation in autogenous training are very different from those in yoga, it is, however, clear that the two methods use common psychosomatic processes which unfortunately remain unexplained, as does the physiological action of the attention directed towards a part of the body and focused there not only by the repetition of suggestive formulae but also by visualisations of anatomy and of functionings which do not correspond at all to any reality (even with European subjects who may have been shown anatomical plates).

Focusing the eyes on the mid-forehead is a physical means that is employed, as Schultz pointed out, in most ancient techniques of concentration or hypnosis and it plays an important part in the experiences of the higher cycle of autogenous training increasing considerably the relaxation (*Entspannung*). It seems to us to be a typical example of 'reorienting tension'. The selected tension, and which must be strong, for the movement is contrary to the usual, ocular synergies,[20] possesses a great part of the general energy at the expense of the other tensions in progress. It even suppresses natural reactions, as in the case cited by

Schultz,[21] of a subject who was insensitive for a long time to a burn while doing this exercise.

In yoga, focusing the look on the tip of the nose or, as in Schultz' prescription, between the eyebrows, is quite a common practice. But this practice, the psychotechnical efficacy of which is verified in this manner in autogenous training, has much deeper motivations in yoga. It is greatly valued by a philosophical system which uses it to put its ideal into practice.

The celebrated *Bhagavadgītā*, popular all over India and where the embodied Supreme Being himself speaks in order to instruct a human hero, clearly shows the place of this ocular exercise in the method to turn the psychic self towards the universal substratum of existence, towards its own self-existent being, freed from the natural propulsions in order to abide in its immutable essence only.

In a passage, it associates it with the cutting off from the external world which corresponds to the retraction (*pratyāhāra*) of classical yoga, and to the slowing down of the breath (*prānāyāma*) as the preparation to achieve peace (*śānti*):

V, 27. Having put outside of himself all outward touches and concentrated the vision between the eyebrows and balanced[22] the prāṇa and the apāna moving within the nostrils.

V, 28. Having controlled the senses, the mind and the understanding, the sage devoted to liberation, from whom desire, fear and wrath have passed away, is over liberated.

V, 29. When a man has known Me as the Enjoyer of yajña (the sacrifice) and tapas (askesis), the mighty Lord of all the worlds, the Friend of all creatures, he travels to the peace.

And a little further, while enunciating the supreme endeavour at liberation at the moment of death, the message of the *Bhagavadgītā* uttered by God continues:

VIII, 10. To Him the supreme Puruṣa attains he who at the time of departure is with motionless mind, armed with the strength of yoga, united with bhakti and the breath entirely drawn up and set between the eyebrows.

VIII, 11. That which the knowers of Veda speak of as the

Imperishable, that into which the Yatis enter when they have passed beyond the passions and for seeking which they practise Brahmacarya, that status I will declare to thee with brevity.

VIII, 12. All the doors of the senses closed, the mind shut in into the heart, the breath gathered up into the head, he who, established in the concentration of yoga.

VIII, 13. Utters the single syllable OṂ and remembers Me when he goes forth, abandoning the body, he attains the supreme soul.

Here, the same technique is, at first, briefly indicated, then repeated, with more precision although in an extremely condensed summary. By exercising control over the openings of the body, we shut the body to external stimuli and abstain from all outward action. Blocking the mind in the heart which, according to ancient Indian, medical physiology, is its natural seat, and then localising the breath in the head, corresponds to two exclusive and successive representations of the vital breath as they are gathered in the heart, then at the top of the forehead, and suggest the description by the yogin of an ascending transfer of its vital activity conceived as breath, passing through the middle of the eyebrows, that is from one to the other of the higher centers of *haṭhayoga.* On VIII, 10 Śaṅkara gave the following commentary: 'having at first subjected the thought to the will within the lotus of the heart, and then having directed the breath between the eyebrows through the ascending channel, thanks to a method of controlling the levels,[23] having established it well, being without any distraction...' Ānandagiri has commented on the same passage by using the technical terminology of *haṭhayoga*: 'after having blocked *iḍā* and *piṅgalā*, the two channels which issue from the heart, on its right and its left, it is from the tip of this heart through the *suṣumnā* channel normally pointing upwards, that having driven the heart's breath, having brought it to the portion of flesh resembling a suspended breast at the throat,[24] having then inserted it between the eyebrows, being without distraction, once issued from the opening of Brahman...'

In the commentaries on Verse 12, Śaṅkara and Ānandagiri have taken up the same explanation and Madhva observed that when the breath is in the head, the seat of the mind is not in the heart for according to the yoga of Vyāsa, that is to say Vyāsa's commentary on the *Yogasūtras*, 'where there is the breath, there is mind, there is life and there the superior (self).' The control of the vital breath does not consist only in controlling the respiration, *prāṇāyāma*, but consists also in guiding mentally through the body an ideal representation of the breath according to the ancient Indian medical physiology which makes of it the common motor of all psychic or somatic activity.

We shall remark, on our part, that concentrating the vision between the eyebrows is explained by Ānandagiri in his comments on the *Bhagavadgītā* V. 27-28, as aiming at avoiding distraction (*vikṣepaparihārārtham*) and that according to the commentaries of Śaṅkara and Ānandagiri in VIII, 10, it is when the breath is brought by thought between the eyebrows that the yogin is said to be without distraction. The ocular exercise in question is, therefore, in yoga, as in autogenous training, a process of the concentration of the attention. But being valued as it is in yoga thanks to the lofty significance of the whole technique of which it is a part, it takes on a much more psychosomatic importance. That is why yoga can provide to the psycho-physiological observation an exceptional field for its rich and wide-ranging effect of its techniques. That is why too, that physiological operations, respiratory exercises, postures, attitudes, muscular training, having no importance by themselves, the precise psychological motivations and backgrounds of these operations should be more and more studied parallelly with the operations themselves.

Until now, studies on yoga, when they have been complete, and except for some enigmatic cases which require a deeper observation, these studies have hardly revealed phenomena that were different from all the known ones. But known phenomena are described in yoga more clearly than elsewhere and do not appear only in haphazard cases. They can be reproduced in some specific conditions. They reveal the physiological effects of the discipline of the mind together with the discipline of the body. They constitute, therefore, an entire system of psychosomatic experiences of which numerous examples have been given in the present work which opens the field to a general enquiry.[25]

NOTES

1. *Yogaś cittavṛttinirodhaḥ*, Y. s., I, 1.
2. *Le Chamanisme et les techniques archaiques de l'extase*, Paris, 1951; *Le Yoga, Immortalité et Liberté*, Paris, 1954, incidentally a very richly documented work; Mr. Eliade did not take up this theory again in his last book, *Patañjali et le Yoga*, Paris, 1962.

   J.W. Hauer tried to trace the first yogins in the fold of those that the *Atharvaveda* called the *vrātya* and who seem to belong to the fringes of orthodoxy. But the references that are made about them do not reveal anything characteristic of yoga and Hauer goes as far as to write that 'the manner of being and the occupation of this group of *vrātya* are ancient proof not only of yoga in India but also of dervishism and of sufism.' (*Der Yoga, Ein indischer Weg zum Selbst*, Stuttgart, 1958, p. 37). This is mixing up everything and completely ignoring the gap of twenty centuries. On the arbitrariness of Hauer's theories and interpretations, see Paul Hacker, *Orientalistische Literaturzeitung*, 1960, Nr. 9/10, columns 521-28.
3. Others call them *savikalpasamādhi* and *nirvikalpasamādhi* respectively.
4. *Kāśyapasaṃhitā*, Hemrāj Śarmā ed., Bombay, 1938, p. 45. Cf. J. Filliozat, *L'apport de l'étude des religions de l'Inde à la science de l'homme*, in *Archéologie religieuse*, suppl. to *Numen*, VII, 1955, Leiden, p. 118. In *Śvetāśvatara-Upaniṣad*, I, 13, *liṅga* is the sign that reveals the invisible form of fire (smoke, according to Śrīraṅgarāmānuja's commentary (17th century) in a comparison of the fire contained in the rubbed wood that produces it with the *ātman* concealed in the body.
5. Cf. J. Filliozat, *Sur la "concentration oculaire" dans le yoga*, in *Yoga* I, 1, 1931, pp. 93-102. But ocular concentration has another aspect with which we shall deal later on.
6. *The Illustrated London News*, June 6, 1936, pp. 993-95. Cf. J. Filliozat, *Les limites des pouvoirs humains dans l'Inde*, in *Limites de l'humain*, *Etudes carmélitaines*, Paris, 1953, pp. 23-38. Professor Jean Lhermitte, who accepted some miracles summarily set aside this observation on the basis that in other cases in India, the trick is exposed; cf. *Le Problème des Miracles*, Paris, 1956, p. 195. He thought (p. 192) that by taking this example, I intended to show that 'levitation might enable man to reach the limit of human power without transcending it'. It is indeed regarding the limits of human power in techniques of yoga that I had cited the case but as an example of the unexplained relationship of some aspects that are considered to be in Indian tradition at the limit of human powers. This strange observation should had to be studied although it did not claim to demonstrate anything.
7. This notion is explicit in classical *Āyurveda* which is a rationalist system of medicine. Cf. *Carakasaṃhitā*, *Śārīrasthāna*, VII, 9; *Aṣṭāṅgasaṃgraha*, *Śār.*, V, Ganesh Sarma ed., t. I, p. 223, 1.17 and foll.; *Aṣṭāṅgahṛdaya*, *Śār.*, III, 13.

8. Charles Laubry and Therese Brosse: *Documents recueillis aux Indes sur les "yoguis" par l'enregistrement simultané du pouls, de la respiration et de l'électrocardiogramme*, Presse Medicale no. 83, of October 14, 1936.
9. Cf. *Limites de l'humain*, pp. 31 and foll.
10. *Le Yoga, Immortalité et Liberté*, p. 78.
11. *Yoga et Hésychasme dans Entretiens* 1955, Publ. de l'Institut Français d'Indologie, no. 4, Pondicherry, 1956, pp. 1-10.
12. *Yoga et training autogène*, in *Critique*, August-September 1960, 159-160, pp. 781-807. Contains a critical bibliography of the subject.
13. Johannes H. Schultz: *Das autogene Training* (*konzentrative Selbstentspannung*), 10th ed., Stuttgart, 1960. The French adaptation by Dr. R. Durand de Bousingen and Y. Becker, *Le Training autogène. Méthode de relaxation par autodécontraction concentrative*, 2nd ed., Paris, 1960, is unfortunately abridged, especially as regards the comparative observations which have been removed.
14. *Yoga et training autogene*, pp. 792 and foll.
15. *Le training autogène*, pp. 34 and foll.
16. *Dhyānabindūpaniṣad*, 93.
17. The *jīvātman* corresponding to a vegetative soul which would, in fact, be the embodied manifestation of the being-in-itself and which is the nucleus of psychic individuality. It is his psychic self in the state of waking, in the hypnagogic states, in sleep and in the essence of his nature which the yogin reviews one after the other.
18. *Pentapetes phoenica* Linn. But this plant has varieties which are distinguished precisely by the colour of the flowers.
19. That is to say that consciousness, *buddhi*, exists always in its nature of seeing entity, but it does not exercise this function in relation to worldly visions as it does not project any image there; the Supreme Lord, *Parameśvara*, when he is 'alone', *kevala*, absorbed in his pure nature, being self-existent, bare of all imaginable aspect. However, as the Supreme Lord, he is the sovereign of the world. If he is untouched by the 'sensible' aspects that belong to this world, he is not yet the pure, Absolute Being, he is relative to the world forever, he potentially contains the vision of the world. The consciousness of the living Self continues to be Consciousness when, on ceasing to operate in the world, it is reduced to its fundamental nature which is but one with the Supreme witness.
20. In rest, the eyes are divergent (normally, and not just with the short-sighted as it seems to be suggested in *Training autogène*, p. 137). When working, the convergence is easier and of the maximum wide amplitude in the downward look than in the upward one. In addition, the convergence is linked to the capacity of accomodation; that is why it is more difficult in the short-sighted who do not make use of this accomodation than in the hypermetropes and the emmetropes, cf. A. Cantonnet and J. Filliozat, *Le strabisme. Sa rééducation. Physiologie et pathologie de la vision binoculaire*, Paris, 1932, p. 96 and foll. The English translation is by Max Coque, *Strabismus, its reeducation: The Physiology and Pathology of Binocular vision*, London, 1934, p. 84 and foll.

21. *Training autogène*, p. 137.
22. 'equalled' according to the more current sense of the word *sama* and the interpretation of the philosophers Rāmānuja and Vedāntadeśika among others; 'stopped' by the *kumbhaka* according to most of the commentators, notably Madhva, Jayatīrtha, Veṅkatanātha, Vallabha, etc.... The great philosopher Śaṅkara (8th-9th century) does not give, in his commentary, any precise notions on this point, but Ānandagiri (app. 1200) belonging to his school and one of the annotators of his commentary, interprets it as 'having stopped it with the *kumbhaka*'. Śaṅkara described the whole exercise as a *dhyānayoga*, 'yoga of meditation'.
23. Ānandagiri takes *bhūmi*, translated here as 'level', in its most common meaning of 'earth' and he believes that what is implied is a mastery of each of the elements (earth, water, fire, air, space) to which the lower circles of *haṭhayoga* are actually respectively related. This interpretation is natural from the point of view of *haṭhayoga* but both the interpretations come down to the same thing, the elements referred to being superposed in the body in the form of the circles which correspond to them.
24. 'Adam's apple' is meant. This comparison figures in an enumeration of the same levels in *Taittiriyopaniṣad* I, 6.1.
25. We deeply thank all the yogins who took interest in an objective verification of their techniques, and thereby made our study easier and also explained their understanding of the subject. We thank specially Mr. Mahesh Ghatradyal for his valuable collaboration.

CHAPTER 27

THE CONCEPTION OF TIME AND SPACE IN THE INDIAN WORLD*

The knowledge we have of Indian thought is based on a great abundance of documents spread over several centuries from the Vedic era up to the present, as Indian civilisation and tradition are still very much alive. About the Indian ideas on time and space, we can, therefore, derive notions borrowed directly from the Indians of today and we can also draw a lot of information from their traditional literatures.

These literatures start with the Veda but there is no reference to time and space except occasionally in the *Ṛg Veda* in its most ancient part, but in the *Atharva Veda* on the contrary, there is a whole hymn, among others, devoted to *Kāla*, Time. In this hymn, time is described as an entity which dominates everything and particularly the whole succession of events, all creation, all preservation of things in their state and subsequently their destruction. Besides, this idea which is set out very simply everywhere, is to remain very important in Indian thought as a whole: time is always said to be the great master of all things and particularly of all that is concerned with life and the evolution of phenomena.

Everywhere in Sanskrit literature, the word *kāla* is in fact used very currently with the same meaning that we give to the word time. In this case, for once, words which are mutually translatable, are actually equivalent. The idea that time wears out everything, allows all things to be born, to endure and then to dissolve is a current idea which is expressed by idioms that are completely identical to those that we possess. To say that an object has outlived its utility, or that a man has ended his life, one says he has lived out his time.

As for the conceptions of space called *ākāśa*, or else *diś* in the

*Le temps et l'espace dans les conceptions du monde indien, in Revue de synthèse, XC, July-Dec., 1969, pp. 281-95.

sense that we shall speak about presently, there are similarities though not perfect equivalences with what we call space. The Sanskrit terminology is a bit more detailed than ours, it has a slightly larger vocabulary and consequently enables us to distinguish between the different aspects we attribute to space.

But what needs to be said at once is that in India speculation on the notions of space and time has been multi-faceted. And it began very early because besides a philosophical speculation, there was also, and at its very base, a naturalist representation of the world. Already in a text which is part of one of the *Brāhmaṇas* and which is itself a well-known *Upaniṣad*, we observe something very significant. The *Upaniṣads* are texts which seek to equate, to compare and even to assimilate, whenever possible, different notions. These are texts where, startings from observable phenomena, one seeks to turn them into coordinated representations. And this coordination consists first in establishing links between the facts being studied. There are some sort of records of debates between philosophers in the *Upaniṣads*, and we have in the *Bṛhadarāṇyaka Upaniṣad* a passage that deserves our attention. Here a woman philosopher, Gārgī, questions Yājñavalkya, a famous philosopher. She asks him among other things, this: that which is found beyond the sky, beneath the earth, between the earth and sky, and that which constitutes the sky and the earth themselves, that which, on the other hand, is called present, past and future, upon what is it warped and woven? That is to say on what does it rest, on which organised substance is based not merely the sky with the earth, but the totality which goes beyond the earth and the sky and which simultaneously is to be considered either as an accomplished past, or as existing in the present or as something that must exist later. We see, here, Gārgī referring to the universe and she considers it in its spatial as well as in its temporal aspect. Yājñavalkya answers: all this is warped and woven on space, *ākāśa*.

The translators, in this text and very often in other texts, translate *ākāśa* as ether. I have done it myself at times, but I believe it is wrong; if one considers the scientific Indian theories which compare the human body, the microcosm, to the universe, the macrocosm, we find that they establish relations between the constitutive elements of the body and those of nature, which are five, and which are found, on the basis of their theories, both in the world and in the human or animal body. These elements are the same as the four elements recognised by the Greeks, and the first Greek philosophers who came in contact with India during the expeditions of Alexander, particularly Megasthenes, noticed this at once: they declared that the Indians were familiar with their elements, they reproached them with positing a fifth element, because the Greeks obviously thought they were the only ones to know the truth. These elements, starting from the heaviest, are earth, water, fire, wind,—here one has to say wind; it's air for the Greeks but in India it's wind and we shall soon examine why—but the Indians add one more, space. Now, many translators thought that one had to follow the analogy with the Greeks as far as possible, and as one already had four Greek elements, it was thought that the fifth, ether, should be added because the Greeks include it. But it is not so; in fact, we learn from the correspondence that is posited in books of ancient Indian physiology, the following equivalences: to the earth of the cosmos correspond the bones and the muscles, the solid parts of the body; to water correspond the fluids; to fire corresponds the animal heat; to the wind corresponds breath, it means wind and not air as a chemical substance. It means air in movement which is absolutely distinct, in the whole of Indian philosophy, from inert air. Wind has the characteristic of being tangible, it is through movement that one feels the wind, it's not in static air that we can feel it. Consequently, it refers to the wind. As to space, *ākāśa*, it is found in the human body in the form of the cavities in certain organs such as the stomach, etc. As a consequence it does not mean ether, it simply means void. It is, therefore, in the void, on the void that everything rests, and it is empty space that contains the world according to Yājñavalkya's first answer. But Gārgī is not satisfied, she resumes, saying: but space itself, *ākāśa*, on what does it rest? Then Yājñavalkya gives her the final answer: it rests on the *avyakta*, that is to say the Imperishable, on the Being that has no definition, which is neither big nor small, which is neither long nor short, which has no form, no smell, no taste, no dimensions, which is simply Being. And here we already have the reference to pure Existence, according to the most ancient Indian philosophy to which we have access. We have here, the formulation of the idea that there is a world with concrete evolving forms which are contained in a void which is a vessel, and undergo successive changes which account for a past, a present, and a future, but that all this is supported or englobed by the fact of existing, otherwise it wouldn't exist. And this fact of existing is the unique Being, absolute but formless, without any specific delimitation, the essence of which has the unique characteristic of being pure Existence.

Therefore, on the one hand, there is a Being easily distinguishable, which is simultaneously transcendent and inclusive of the world but as regards space and time they are aspects of that which man perceives. At the outset, it is the Indian scientists that best described and specified these aspects. One very often forgets while studying Indian philosophy that to study any philosophy in depth, one must possess quite a precise idea of the general culture of the philosophers who propounded it. For they do not have the habit of repeating in their specialised expositions all that went into the making of their intellectual heritage, all that is the common heritage of the whole milieu. And if one sticks strictly to the texts in which they have set forth their particular rational expositions, one misses the implicit, latent knowledge of their culture which conditions a good part of their thinking. Moreover one must remark that Indian philosophers have based all their previous teaching, all their basic culture on notions that are partly scientific, which claim to be rational explanations, rational representations at least, of the facts of nature. Since the *Veda*, we have numerous, frequent testimonies of the existence of a will to understand the world, and we know that Indians accepted, from the time of the most ancient texts that they have left to us, the existence of a general, universal law of nature. They called this law *ṛta*, or else *dharman* or *dharma* which is the second name which gained currency later. It means the normal order, the truly right order. It is contrasted by its opposite which is depicted by the disturbance of the natural order of things. But the existence of a natural order of things, which, although very clear, can undoubtedly be disturbed, is well-established. And it was well-established in India probably because of the importance of the regular phenomenon of monsoon; all over the world various peoples clearly observe the periodicity of days and nights, and even of the celestial phenomena of the lunar phases and other less evident celestial phenomena, but they do not always have the chance to perceive a direct link, a concomitance at least, between the celestial phenomena which recur periodically and the phenomena of the terrestrial world. Now in India, the monsoon breaks out on a more or less fixed date which is foretold, which can be foreseen by the calendar, which is based on the periodicity of the celestial movements. And one sees that if the monsoon comes on the normal date the prosperity and even the indispensable conditions required for the life of the people are obtained, but that, on the contrary, if there is a disparity between the time indicated on the basis of the regularity of the astral positions, and the metereological phenomenon of the monsoon, one will have a disturbance and one concludes from this fact that the whole of human life is linked to the movements of nature which are regulated by celestial movements. A method was established, a method quite efficient, and in fact, even striking, striking because of the early point in time in which it was devised, to establish a precise calendar. But then, at once, a fact emerged. It was realised that the moon completed a revolution in one month. Even the length of the lunar month was determined very early on. A certain number of months, twelve in general, though not always, a certain number of lunar revolutions occur within the time of a solar revolution. Later, it was observed that there were other revolutions of other planets, like Jupiter, for example, which has a complete revolution of a different duration (12 years). But above all, it was observed that by comparing the revolutions of the sun and the moon, a certain number of solar years had to elapse so that one could have in an integral number of solar years an integral number of lunar years at the same time. And a common period conceived of the two series of revolutions, that of the moon and the sun, was a period at the end of which the positions of the moon and the sun, after an integral number of complete revolutions for each of these celestial bodies, are found to be the same in reference to fixed celestial points.

It was, therefore, conceived that there were movements in space which could be complete without having the same duration, and this drew the attention of the existing concordance, and also the positioning that is produced, between time and space. The astronomers, in the classical text of the *Sūryasiddhānta*, begin by defining time.

There are two kinds of time. There is a time which is a universally known entity—in fact it is to this entity that a hymn of the *Atharva Veda* had already been composed—which is responsible for the fact that we represent things either as past and gone, or as present, or as future. It is a general, vast and continuous entity, and which is not directly related to astronomy. What is of interest to it is the time which can be measured. And in this time, we again distinguish two kinds: time which is *mūrta*, that is to say with a form, and time which is *amūrta*, that is to say formless. The time with form is duration, definable through a comparison with a phenomenon whose duration is precisely known. For example, respiration, the normal time of respiration is universally known, it is a time, a duration which is marked by respiration. The blinking of the eyes is a shorter duration. There are longer durations, such as those which are marked by the return of day after night, or else the periodic returns of the phases of the moon, or again the periodic returns of the sun to the same constellations, and so on. This, then, is the time which is represented in the space where we live. But there is a time that is formless, it is time that is too small to be measurable at the scale of human perception, or on the contrary, that is too great. But astronomy needs this time, and we can calculate it starting from durations defined in comparison with known durations. And by subdividing mathematically these known durations, one can imagine shorter durations that are not directly perceptible.

In any case one considers the relations of space with time by merely examining the displacements that the mobile stars make in reference to fixed points that one has chosen as points of reference. And one measures the spatial displacements through corresponding times. Space itself is divided in angles, measured in degrees, minutes, seconds or in equivalent units. And for mathematical need or convenience, or because of having inherited the sexagesimal system we count 360° in a circle, etc.

The scientific conception of space and time, beside the popular conception of the entity-time as all-embracing is one that is natural to all Indians, whether philosophers or not. And in the ancient Indian civilisation, the conceptions of astronomers had greater influence than the much more advanced data of astronomy have on us today. The astronomers have developed astronomy considerably, but the notions on the stars, and particularly the dependence of our life on the movements of stars is eliminated by the use of watches and calendars. We do not need to think about the phases of the moon, individually we don't need to be capable of reading a solar dial, or to watch the sky to know the date on which a meeting is to take place. On the contrary, in ancient India when there were neither time-piece nor calendars—distributed to us by the postman at the end of every year—it was necessary that in every village there be people capable of fixing the dates for ceremonies no doubt, but also for commerce, festivals, fairs and any other kind of gathering. It was also necessary that all know, at least in an elementary way, how to fix divisions of time. Consequently, the importance of the divisions of time and the influence of the knowledge and ideas of astronomers were very widespread, particularly among Indian philosophers, but even among rural and other peoples of India. One must, therefore, always bear in mind while studying the conceptions of philosophers of space and time in particular, the fact that they are familiar with the conceptions of astronomers —without their saying so because all are familiar with them, and it is these that were actually fundamental.

And these were the conceptions that gained currency in the ideas of ordinary cosmology, accepted by all who were not specialists of astronomy, and who generalised the notion of different times englobed one into the other and each effecting a complete movement in space. The relativity of duration was very soon established and very commonly accepted, or rather, even if those who really conceived it were few, they diffused it everywhere.

Even as the moon completes several revolutions while the sun completes one, in the same way one finds that one can count the lunar movement as days, but as days which will not have the same duration as that of solar days. One also finds that a sidereal day, that is to say the time which elapses between two identical celestial positions, is different from the civil day, of the time determined by the rising and setting of the sun. And one also thought of the solar year as only one day which would be divided into two parts, like the civil day, that is to say in what is actually called day and night.

The proper day lasts six months, which corresponds to the apparent movement of the sun from winter solstice to summer solstice. Then the sun seems to rise every day from a little more towards the North and the days slowly grow longer and the luminous intensity of the sun is greater. One believes these six months to be one day of the gods, for the gods dwell in the Northern hemisphere and are settled at the North pole, from where they rule everything. And from the summer solstice to the winter solstice, the sun follows a reverse path: it goes to the South to finally stop at the winter solstice in the South, and consequently in the dominion of those who are opposite to the gods, and whom, because of that, in short, we call demons. But it is the demons of the south who receive the sun, while the gods of the North receive it less. Consequently, one thinks that for both there is a division of the solar year into a night and a day, but what is night for the gods is day for the demons, and vice-versa.

It was observed very early on that if one considered all the celestial movements as a whole, and not harmonise only an integral number of lunar revolutions with an integral number of solar revolutions, one had to greatly extend the period that is called *yuga* to take into account all the revolutions, so that this period be defined as the time elapsed for an integral number of revolutions of all planets in a way that they are all able to return to the same point which was their starting point. One needs an extremely long period for that and it was finally calculated to be four million three hundred and twenty thousand years. This duration has been considered as being only an element of the life of the being who has organised the world, and one must count only twelve thousand divine years in the four million three hundred and twenty thousand human years. The repercussion of these calculations which have a wrong but rational astronomical basis, on which one cannot elaborate now, was that one considered supraterrestrial worlds to exist, heaven in particular, or else hells, subterrestrial, where duration was not the same as on the earth. One conceived this without effort when one realised that there could be a complete revolution, a unit of activity of another dimension, according to the beings in question. For example, a complete revolution of the moon is shorter than a complete revolution of the sun. But for each it's a complete revolution. So, staying in heaven or staying in hell could also be considered as a life, but the duration need not be the same. And in the Buddhist texts there is an example which had formerly struck La Vallée-Poussin very much; as a result of the form given to her psychic individuality which, after death, turns—for it does not die—towards a new incarnation, a lady who had been virtuous, without attaining immediate liberation, was born in a paradise. There she played with other gods, since she had become a goddess for the same reasons as they. But the force which had carried her to this paradise was exhausted and she, therefore, died in paradise and returned to earth. She resumed a life of virtue similar to the preceding one, became very old, died a second time on earth and returned to paradise, where she rejoined her companions of play who had not noticed her absence. The Buddhists want to evaluate the time passed in paradise. This time is so pleasant that one does not feel its duration. It is when one is on the earth that one feels the duration of time because there one is miserable and therefore one feels it even more in the hells. I must admit that I don't exactly know the feelings of people who abide in the hells; it is described as being extremely painful and we are told, for example, that so-and-so fell in hell after committing some sin, for sixty thousand years; but it means human years, and one cannot say how long these sixty thousand years seemed to him to have lasted. But, in heaven, time doesn't pass for the gods.

And this has spread in the popular minds extremely varied notions of time which are not objective, which are merely the result of the feeling of time that man can have. And this has led to the propounding of a Buddhist philosophy which we shall take up in a moment. But, before that, one must explain what is the usual doctrine of the classical Brahmanic philosophy. This philosophy is expounded particularly in the works which one designates under the generic name of *Nyāya* and *Vaiśeṣika*. These are texts which deal with logic but which apply logic for definition, for the characterisation of all things and this logic consists in using correctly the concepts which one is working on, after one has properly defined them, to draw conclusions and to understand the structure. In any case this philosophy roughly distinguishes in general seven *dravyas*. One normally translates *dravya* by substance, and it is in fact a translation which is correct in many cases; the texts of pharmacy talk of *dravyas* and their *guṇas*, that is to say of substances and their properties. But it does not follow that *dravya* always designates a material substance and only a material substance. However, it actually designates a material substance, even in this case, for we have, in the list, earth, fire, water, wind, void, that is to say space, as we have already noted, and then we have another space which we call *diś*. But *diś* designates especially the directions, east, west etc.: it is, therefore, orientations, parts of organised space, which have their fixed directions. It is something different from *ākāśa*, which, itself, is the void containing the whole universe. *Ākāśa* is the containing void, *diś* is organised void. But we immediately see a difference: the word *dravya* cannot be always translated by 'substance'. It is indeed substance when it is applied to earth, water, fire, because one can say that these things are substances, but orientation in space is not a substance and one has other substances or so-called substances that are listed which are not substance any more in the sense we understand it. But what is important for us above all, at present, is that there is among the *dravyas* with which we are concerned, in the classical philosophy, *ākāśa*, which is void, *diś*, which is organised void, and *kāla* which is time. All three are defined as being unique, all-penetrating, omnipresent, permanent. Permanence, omnipresence and uniqueness are the three qualities of these three elements that constitute the universe.

But the Buddhists themselves have a philosophy which does not accept this homogeneity and this continuity either in time or in space. One should know that Buddhist philosophy is one-sided; all philosophies could, in fact, be thus, but often they strive only to prove the personal opinion of the philosopher, and are partial only to that extent. But the philosopher's intention is to seek the truth. Among Buddhists also it is truth that is sought, but what is mostly sought is the conditioning of the mind and psychism of the followers one wants to liberate from the world, and to whom one must depreciate and belittle the world so that they renounce all attachment to it. In these conditions, one has insisted, since the origins of Buddhism, on the impermanence of things; a thing has no value if it is not real forever. But it was not sufficient, for it is true that to those who said that the wealth of the world was perishable, the following remark was made: yes, but precisely, as long as one has it, all the more reason do we have to enjoy it. Now, the Buddhists wished to establish rationally an elimination of all continuity and all stability of the world. For this reason, they observed a difference which they stressed, between the picture we have of the world, either a spatial one when we consider a host of things which are in fact different, or the temporal one which we have when we review the same pictures successively. We can very well understand today and even formerly one could understand with the help of a scroll of painting, as with a film today, that we have a series of pictures which occupy a space if we consider them all together; and put end to end, the scroll has a definite length. However, one can also divide space in an infinite number of small bits till there remain only points and in the same way can one divide time. We can, in fact, divide time as the astronomers do, without stopping at the physical possibility of its expression, but ideally sub-dividing it more and more, almost infinitely, passing from *mūrta*, time with form, to *amūrta*, time without form.

Consequently, Buddhist philosophers made use of an indefinite sub-division which the astronomers visualised, to reduce time as well as space to infinitesimal quanta.

And then they declare that an instant of time or space, called *kṣaṇa*, will be found to have its own individuality; such an instant is placed, either in space or in time, before or after, to the left or the right of similar others, or between its neighbours. Consequently, it is different from the latter, it has, therefore, an existence which belongs to it but it is totally impermanent, purely momentaneous. And this division of space and time that was propounded by the astronomers as an arbitrary division, made for analysis and for scientific purposes, is, on the contrary, considered as the essential, fundamental nature of the constitution of space, time and matter. Space and time, for Buddhists who strive to belittle the world, are basically made up of juxtaposed instants. Consequently; there is a change in the perception; when we perceive a continuous space or else a continuous duration we are merely under an illusion, we do not see the divisions that are there and we have a series of pictures running in our mind and which give us the illusion of continuity where, in fact, there is none.

This Buddhist attitude is better understood if one refers to the general idea that Buddhists, and for that matter, even the Brahmanic philosophers too, formed about the consistency of the external world. Indian psychology, in general, accepts the fact that what we see of the world outside is not the external world itself; what reaches our consciousness is that which the senses bring to us about the external world. But our picture of the external world is basically a subjective picture conditioned by the senses, and even by the physiological condition of the senses. When we see a strand of hair or flies in a bowl that one tries to remove without success, it actually indicates an illness of the eye which projects an appearance of hair or flies, when in reality there are none. On the other hand, when one touches the eyes while looking in front, one sees double, one sees two moons for example, two moons exactly alike, one knows that one of them does not exist, but it is exactly the same as the one considered to be real. Consequently this leads us to doubt the existence of the moon as we see it. It is possible that an objective, external world exists, but in any case we can only reach it through our own representation of it. And the Buddhists, in these conditions say with the philosophers that the world is a well-knit dream, an illusion, and they also state that one should not be attached to this illusion, to these dreams, to this continuity; they are, in fact, when we analyse it the way we have just discussed, juxtapositions of momentary and basically perishable things.

This doctrine did not prevail and what is most important in the Indian conceptions of space and time, is, in fact, that they are considered as permanent settings. But what is certain is that the permanent and unique milieu that time and space represent and even the specialisation of space into directions, is real and practically should serve in the exercise of life in the world and in the conception of the natural order of things. This *ṛta* or *dharman* which we said was conceived by the Indians in the ancient past, depends on the existence of space and time. But space is contained in an infinity and its existence suggests the general universal existence. As for time, it is co-extensive with space but, in fact, it exists only in the form of successive, simultaneous movements in space; they are successive for example for each star that moves but they are simultaneous for all the stars together. And time has neither beginning nor end, it is essentially cyclic and absolutely eternal. However, there can occur a reabsorption of the whole world and consequently of time and space, whose pure and simple existence is not perceptible unless it is expressed in the form of a differentiated world. But the numbers that one uses to mark the duration of the world show that the Indians imagined it to be a length which almost touches the conception of infinity. One has even reproached them with this because, when in the 18th century, Indian philosophy was discovered, in Europe the idea was current that the world was six thousand years old; and the world was thought to be finite. When Buddhists and Brahmanic philosophers propounded that there were billions of years and billions of worlds and that all was being perpetually renewed, they were thought to be excessive and they were accused of extravagant folly because they did not know what the Europeans knew so well, that is to say that the world was six thousand years old and it was finite. Today we would condemn them no more and in any case we still see them today as more preoccupied than we ourselves are, in general, to make practical use of time and space.

There is one specially striking fact which strikes us while in India or in a country of the Indian world, the world influenced by India: that not only do the peasants have more ideas on the stars and celestial movements than city-dwellers as is still sometimes the case in our country, but also that one does not like to use very much the words 'left' and 'right' to indicate positions with reference to oneself; one is always oriented in space, and you will be directed to go towards the west or the east; one will not say that a door is to my right or to your left, but rather that it is towards the east. And thus, man sees himself as being part of nature and not as an independent being.

CHAPTER 28

THE OEDIPUS COMPLEX IN A BUDDHIST TANTRA*

THE *Caṇḍamahāroṣaṇatantra* (CMT)[1] is one of the texts that have given a bad name to 'Tantrism' and which were instrumental in spreading the idea that the *Tantras* were the products of a ritualistic, impassioned and magic-oriented reaction against the great orthodox religions of knowledge, renunciation and devotion. There is no doubt that it claims to take a stand that opposes traditional Buddhist ethics, by prescribing obscene scatological practices and imparting formulae for black magic, charms and control over others as well as formulae against ordinary ailments. It is also certain that it is in no way unique and that a number of other texts designated as *Tantra* contain similar teachings. It would be most incorrect to look upon it as characteristic of Tantric literature which includes, in fact, treatises on the religious techniques of various religions: Śaiva, Vaiṣṇava, Jain and Buddhist; treatises on philosophical doctrines, usually classical and orthodox and having the utilisation of concrete religious practices, symbols and formulae in common. The theories and practice of the CMT correspond to a particular current of speculation and conduct which do not characterise the whole of *Tantra*.

The most salient feature of the theory of CMT is its emphasis on sexual union as the supreme realisation, especially when it is practiced in conditions which could set in motion the most violent psychological states, such as the state of consciousness of moral censure (consciousness of incest or of the ignominy of woman) or of repulsion (consuming excrements).

Sometime everything seems to be prescribed as happening in a state of meditation (*dhyāna, bsam-ba*) or of a mental creation (*bhāvanā, sgom-pa*) where feelings of love and hatred, that

*Le complexe d' Oedipe dans un tantra bouddhique, in Etudes tibétaines dédiées à la mémoire de Marcelle Lalou, Paris, 1971, pp. 142-48.

correspond to the 'Oedipus complex', are evoked. Thus, in chapter 4 (*devatāpaṭala, lha-ñid kyi rim par phye-ba*) the yogin seats himself in a pleasant surrounding and with the right positioning of the mind (*samāhita, mñam gžag*), mentally creates the four modes of benevolence (*maitrī, byams-pa*), compassion (*karuṇā, sñin-rje*), contentment (*muditā, dga' = ba*), imperturbability (*upekṣā, btaṅ-sñoms*). Then he creates in his heart a 'germ' (*bīja, so-bon*), rising up with Lotus, Moon and Sun and invokes Caṇḍaroṣaṇa arisen in front with rays of light, pays him homage in his mind, confesses his sins, congratulates himself for all his merit, takes the triple refuge, begs and asks for guidance, takes merit upon himself, takes the vow (of bodhisattva), turns his thought to Awakening, bows down and reabsorbs this representation with rays of light (*raśmibhiḥ saṃharet punaḥ, 'od-zer rnams kyis slar yaṅ bsdu*). He then practices meditation on the void, thinks of himself as having for his own being the thunderbolt which is the knowledge of the void (*oṃ śūnyatājñānavajrasvabhāvātmako'ham*, reproduced without translation in the Tibetan editions). He pictures his own body as being transparent, similar to space and reduced to the duration of a second. He must invoke the *bījas* of the elements and conceive a square pavilion with four gates, eight pillars, in which the eight-petalled lotus has bloomed and he must meditate on Akṣobhya coming out of the lotus and united with Māmakī. The text then continues thus: (IV, 16-19).

'16. Thereupon, the master-yogin must draw near by a conjunction (of the kind) of the entrance into a star,[2] his thought absorbed in this (Akṣobhya's) head, (turned) towards Māmakī's organ.

17. Then, transformed into spermatic fluid, he must fall into the latter's organ. Thereafter, in the fulfilled form of Caṇḍa, he must emerge from the organ,

18. and he must kill the father, Akṣobhya, with a sword, then let him be eaten by Māmakī and make her conceive what she has absorbed of the father.

19. Then, having held Māmakī, the mother, he must make love to her; he must visualise himself in meditation embraced by her in Dveṣavajrī's own form.

Dveṣavajrī is the vajrayoginī associated with the vajrayogin

Krisṇācala. In addition, there exist four other vajrayoginīs associated with four vajrayogins who are enumerated at the very beginning of the first chapter. These vajrayoginī-vajrayogin couples are: Śvetācala and Mohavajrī, Pītācala and Piśunavajrī, Raktācala and Rāgavajrī, Śyāmācala and Īrṣyāvajrī. The five vajrayoginīs correspond to the emotional states that inspire the violation of the five Buddhist precepts: *Moha*—to the erring that inebriates, *Pisuna*—to calumny which is against sincerity, *Rāga*—to passion, *Īrṣyā*—to envy which incites to theft, *Dveṣa*—to hatred which impels to kill.[4]

The text goes on to describe the form the yogin assumes by identifying himself with Caṇḍamahāroṣaṇa or Kṛṣṇācala, then the placing on an ideal *maṇḍala* of the four vajrayogins and the four vajrayoginīs (other than Kṛṣṇācala and Dveṣavajrī who are at the centre) on the cardinal and intercardinal points according to the arrangement already described in chapter two (*maṇḍala-paṭala*).[5] After this, the four vajrayoginīs, described as goddesses (*devī*, *Lha-Mo*, *śloka* 27), invite him, each one with a song in apabhraṃśa which the Tibetan version reproduces in the original before translating it. These texts have come down to us in an uncertain form in the manuscript material which we have consulted but the Tibetan version is of assistance in the effort at a provisional restoration, a restoration that can be ameliorated by the scrutiny of other manuscripts and by new studies.[6]

Song of Mohavajrī (placed at the S.E.):

Text accompanying the Tibetan version (TV):

> *pahu*[7] *maitritu bibajjaa hohi mā*[8] *śunnasahāba*[9]
> *khyab-bdag byams-pa rnam spaṅs nas / stoṅ-pa'i raṅ bžin du ma mjad*

Skr. mss.: *paṭṭa*[10] *maitrītu*[11] *vivajjia*[12] *hohi maṇḍalasahāva*[13]
Restoration: *pahu maitrītu vivajjia hohi mā śunnasahāba*
(Sanskrit: *prabhu maitrīto vivarjya bhava mā śūnyasvabhāvaḥ*)

TV: *tojju bioe phitā mi sabba jagahi babhaba*[14]

> *khyod daṅ rnam bral bdag 'gum pas /' gro kun stoṅ par ma bjad čig /*

Skr. mss.: *tojju viyoe phiṭṭa savve 'hi tāba*[15]
Restor.: *tojju bioe phiṭṭā mi sabbajagahi* (*vibhavaḥ*?)
(Sanskr.: *tvadviyoge *sphiṭṭāsmi sarvajagadbhir* (*vibhavaḥ?*))

'O Lord,[16] do not become, by rejecting benevolence, of the very nature of void'

In the separation from you[17] I am lost[18] with all beings: it is the privation of existence[19]

Song of Piśunavajrī (placed at the S.O.):

TV.: *mā karuṇaciya phiṭṭahi pahu mā hohi tu śunna /*
sñiṅ rǰe'i sems bral bdag 'gum pas / khyab bdag stoṅ par ma mjad čig /

Skr. mss.: *mā*[20] *karuṇācia iṭṭahi*[21] *pahu*[22] *mā hohi tu śunna*[23] /
Rest. : *mā karuṇācia phiṭṭahi pahu mā hohi tu śunna*
(Skr.: *mā karuṇācitta sphiṭṭa prabhu mā bhava tvaṃ śūnyaḥ*)

TV: *mā moju dehasu dukkhia*[24] *haijība bihunna /*
bdag gis lus ni sdug-bsṅal-bas / 'cho-ba daṅ bral ma mjad čig //

Skr. mss.: *mā mojja*[25] *dehasu dukkhia aho ihaï*[26] *jīvavīhunna //*
Rest.: *mā mojju dehasu dukkhia haï jība vihunna //*
(Skr.: *mā maddehasya duḥkhena jahi jīvaṃ vidhūtam //*)

'O you who have the spirit of compassion, do not kill, Lord, do not become the void! Do not strike a despondent life with the pain of my body!'

Song of Rāgavajrī (placed at the N.O.):

TV.: *kīpa*[27] *tu haripa*[28] *pitohi aśunnahi karapi*[29] *pabeśa /*
či ste mkhas-pa khyod ñid ni / dga'-ba spaṅs nas stoṅ-par ma' ǰag /

Skr. mss.: *kīsa*[30] *tu harisa vihohi*[31] *aśunnahi karasi paveśa /*
Rest.: *kīsa tu harisa vihohi aśunnahi karasi paveśa /*
(Skr.: *kīdṛśaṃ tvaṃ harṣaṃ vibhava na śūnye karoṣi praveśam*)

TV.: *tojju nimannana*[32] *kariḍā / maṇi*[33] *acchaï loāśeṣa //*
'jig-rten ma lus-pa rnams daṅ / bdag gi[34] *yid ni khyod la sdod*[35] *//*

Skr. mss.: *tojju nimanteṇa*[36] *karia*[37] *maṇe*[38] *acchaï*[39] *loāśeṣa*[40] //
Rest.: *tojju nimantena karia maṇe acchaï loāśeṣa*) //
(Skr.: *tvannimantena kṛtvā manasy āsati lokāśeṣam*)

'Create, thou, some joy! Where void is not, you make your entry; moving at your call, the totality of the worlds are founded on my Mind.'

According to the Tibetan Version: 'If you do not enter the void since you are wise, after having abandoned felicity, all the worlds and my mind rest on you.'

Song of Īrṣyāvajrī (placed at the N.E.):

TV.: *yobanavantim*[41] *upekhea*[42] *niṣphala*[43] *śunnae diṭṭha*[44] /
laṅ cho[45] *daṅ ldan btaṅ-sñoms-pa'i / mig ni stoṅ-pa 'bras*[46] *med čan /*

Skr. mss.: *yovanamantim*[47] *upekhim*[48] *niṣphala śunnae uṭṭi*[49] /
Rst.: *yovanamantim upekhia niṣphala śuanae diṭṭhi /*
(Skr.: *yauvanamatīm upekṣya niṣphalā śunyā dṛṣṭiḥ*)

TV.: *śunnasahāba bigoia karahi tu moe samaghiṭṭha //*
stoṅ-pa'i raṅ bžin ñid spoṅs la / bdag la mñam-ñid sbyor-bar mjad //

Skr. mss.: *śunnasahāva*[50] *vigoia*[51] *karahi*[52] *tu moeṃ*[53] *samaghiṭi*[54] //
Rest.: *śunnasahāba bigoia karahi tu moeṃ samaghiṭṭi //*
(Skr.: *śūnyasvabhāvaṃ viguhya kuru tvaṃ mayā samaghṛṣṭim*)

'When she despises the one who is youthful, without fruit and vacant is the sight.
Having hidden the very nature of void, offer yourself with me to mutual rubbing!'

Tibetan: 'The look of indifference towards she who has youth, is empty, has no fruit. Having rejected the very nature of the void, accomplish for me mutual union.'[55]

The text then continues in Sanskrit, specifying that the yogin, after having heard this as in a dream (*svapnenaiva idaṃ śrutva*), must meditate on himself in sexual union (*samputātmakam*)[56], kill Śvetācala and take possession of Mohavajrī and in the same way kill one after the other Pītācala, Raktācala and Śyāmācala, then take possession of Piśunavajrī, Rāgavajri, Īrṣyāvajrī. After having made love to the four goddesses he must remove the whole *maṇḍala*.[57] The subsequent text puts the yogin in correspondence according to his complexion with women of similar complexion, in the actual order.

Chapter seventeenth, *pratītyasamutpādapaṭala*, after a classical exposition of this *pratītyasamutpāde* and of *skandhas* as well as their removal, deals with the formation of the elements of *pratītyasamutpāda* (*avidyā* etc.), then with fate and the action of the psychic individual in the state between death and the successive birth. It goes thus: 'Stationed in one spot, the being in the intermediary existence, with that which begins with *avidyā* and ends with the six sensory supports, watching the triple world, sees passionate men and women. Thus, excited by the actions done in the preceding life, he will be born into the same caste as the woman and man he has seen indulging in pleasure: an intense contact with them will follow. Thereupon, if he must become a man, then he will see himself in the shape of a man. He becomes intensely passionate towards his future mother, he feels great hate towards his future father, and passion and hatred come up because of a sense of pleasure and pain. He may then think: "In what form shall I indulge in sensual pleasure with her?" The sensation of pleasure and pain maddens him. Then, driven by the gusts of his past actions, with a great lust, he exclaims: "I like her" and utters in pain: "Who is this man who makes love to my woman?" Having slipped through the head of the future father as through an entrance into a star,[58] by establishing his thought as well-settled in this man's sperm, he sees himself making love to his future mother. He takes upon himself the basic cause of pleasure. Then merging with the sperm, ejecting passionately out of the father's *vajra* through the *avadhūtī*[59] passage, he settles down through the *vajradhātvīśvarī* passage which lies in the cavity of the lotus, in the pelvis, in the passage of birth. Having reached the interior by a secretion, he becomes a life. Successively called *kalala*, *arbuda* (ball), *ghana* (density), *peśī* (flesh), in nine or ten months, he emerges through the passage he had entered: birth occurs.

Or else if the being must become a woman, then it falls passionately in love with its future father and the hatred is directed to the future mother. Thus it sees itself in the shape of a woman. Having slipped in through the head of its future mother, it immerses itself in the sperm when it drops into the lotus, it remains in her passage of birth. Then it emerges in the way described before: it is born'.

In spite of the mediocre condition of the textual tradition of the CMP and thanks to the Tibetan version which allows the restoration at a number of places, these texts are clear by themselves. Their general doctrine, which links it to the doctrine of the union of the *prajñā* and the *upāya* and thus producing the *bodhicitta* (cf. Inde Classique, To. II, p. 594 and foll.) is expressed with conciseness and clarity. This justifies Csoma's opinion in his *Analyse du Kandjour* (Transl. by Feer. Ann. du Musée Guimet, II, Paris, 1881, p. 299) according to which 'it's an excellent *tantra* of which the text is good and fluent', although Csoma did not see or did not point out the erotic symbolism and prescriptions which are one of the chief characteristics of the work.

APPENDIX: A SPECIMEN OF THE TEXTS

The sanskrit text has been established on the basis of three manuscripts: BN = Bibliothèque Nationale *Sanskrit* 18 (J. Filliozat, *Catalogue du fonds sanscrit*, Paris, 1941, p. 9); SA = Société Asiatique C 13 (J. Filliozat, *Catalogue des mss. sanscrits et tibétains*, J.A., 1941-42, p. 16) and T = Tokyo University Library, Sanskrit 70 (Seiren Matsunami, *A Catalogue of the Sanskrit mss.*, Tokyo, 1965, p. 30). The manuscript of the Société Asiatique, in mediocre nāgarī and that of Tokyo (dated saṃvat 934=1813 A.D.), in beautiful Nepālī abounds in mistakes which in other passages are often the same and suggest that both are copies, at least in parts of an already flawed original. Only the significant variants are listed here. The Tibetan text has been established on the Snar-thaṅ and Peking editions of the Bibliothèque Nationale which only differ on slight variants.

IV. 16. *Saṃkramet tatra yogīndras tasya mūrdhavilīnena* /[60]
tārāsaṃkrāntiyogena māmakībhagacetasā //
de la rim bžin rnal-'byor dbaṅ / de yi sbyi-bo la thim nas /
skar-mda' ji bžin sbyor-ba yis/ māmakī yi bhagar bsam //

17. *tataḥ śukrarasībhūtaḥ patet tasyā bhagodare* /
niṣpannañ caṇḍarūpan tu niḥsarec ca bhagāt tataḥ //
de las khu-ba ro mñam gyur / lhuṅ gyur de yi bhaga'i naṅ/
gtum-po'i gzugs su gyur nas ni / bhaga'i mtha' las ṅes
byuṅ nas //

18. *hanyāt khaḍgena cākṣobhyam pitaram paścāt prabhakṣayet*/
māmakyā pitatas tañ ca bhakṣitaṃ vai prakalpayet //
mi bskyod pa la[61] ral-gri yis / bsnun nas phyi nas rab tu
bza' /
māmakis kyaṅ de las de'i / śa za-bar ni rab tu bsam //

19. *tato hi māmakīṃ*[62] *gṛhya mātaraṃ saṃprakāmayet* /
tayā cāliṅgitaṃ dhyāyed dveṣavajrīsvarūpataḥ //

de phyir māmakīs gzuṅ nas / ma daṅ yaṅ ḍag rab 'ḍoḍ bya /
des kyaṅ 'khyud par bsam bya ba / že ldaṅ[63] rdo-rǰe ma vi gzugs //

NOTES

1. The title in fact is Ekaravīra or Ekallavīra, the 'Unique Hero', which is an appellation of Caṇḍamahāroṣaṇa, in Tibetan *Gtum-po-khro-bo-čhen-po.*
2. The comparison with 'the entrance into a star', *tārāsaṃkrānti* (Cf. see also below, p. 434) has been taken from the popular notion in astrology and astronomy, of the entry of the sun into the successive signs of the Zodiac marked by the determining stars. Such comparisons are found elsewhere in Indian literature. Cf. for example P.E. Dumont, L'*Iśvaragītā*, Baltimore, Paris, 1933, pp. 142-43, (st. XI, 34) and p. 192 and foll. The Tibetan version does not translate *Tārāsaṃkrānti*, very strictly. The term *skar-mda'* which it uses corresponds usually to *ulkā*, 'meteor', and it says: 'through a conjunction like that of a meteor'.
3. See further a similar text and its 'complements' which are found in Chap. XVII.
4. Cf. about these vajrayoginīs, Bhattacharya, *The Indian Buddhist Iconography*, pp. 60-61.
5. There are several arrangements: Śvetācala and Mohavajrī can move to the centre, and so can Pītācala, etc. (II, 26).
6. We give first the text that accompanies the Tibetan version, then that of the Sanskrit manuscripts, an attempt at reconstruction and we give the probable Sanskrit equivalents below. For the explanation of the abbreviations see Appendix which lists our sources.
7. Snar-thaṅ: *Bahu.*
8. Pekin: *ma.*
9. Pekin: *pahāba.*
10. SA: *khaḍga.*
11. SA: *maitītu.*
12. BN: *vivarjjia,* T: *vivarjjitaa.*
13. BN: *maṇḍalu,* SA: *ṃaṇḍalaṃ.* The form *maṇḍala* given by the three manuscripts is clearly the result of a simple confusion in Nepāli script between *ṇḍala* and *śunna.*
14. Pekin: *babhāba.*
15. SA: *viyoeṃ hiṭṭa sarvaṃ 'hitābaḥ,* T: *vicāśrīhaṭṭa sarvva 'hitāva.*
16. The variant reading *paṭṭa*, 'diadem, turban', could be explained if necessary as an elliptical apostrophe: 'You, who don a diadem'.
17. Cf. Mahārāṣṭrī *tujjha(ṃ)*, Hemacandra *tujjha* (ablative and genitive case), Hybrid Sanskrit *tuhya(m)* (genitive). The variant reading *viyoeṃ* is possible (instrumental in *eṃ*, 'through separation').
18. de SPHIṬṬ 'to kill', Pkr. *phiṭṭa* is translated by *bhraṣṭa* in Seth, *Pāia-sadda-mahaṇṇavo. Mi,* cf. ardhamāgadhī *mi*, Skr. *asmi.*

19. Tib: 'do not render all beings superfluous!'
20. T: *nā.*
21. SA: *dgahi.*
22. T: *pahū.*
23. BN: *śunnā*, T.: *gunna* (confusion in ancient scripts of śa and ga).
24. Peking: *kria.*
25. BN: *morjja*, T.: *māja.*
26. SA: *sūdūṣki' aho a ihai*, T.: *sasuḥṣki aho ihaī.*
27. Snar-thaṅ: *kāpi.* Read: *kīsa*, *pa* results from the confusion in 'khyug yig between *pa* and *sa.*
28. The same confusion. Read: *harisa.*
29. Pekin: *karipi*, read: *karasi.*
30. T.: *kisa.*
31. SA: *vibhohi.*
32. Pekin: *nimaṇṇaṇa.*
33. Snar-thaṅ: missing.
34. Pekin: *gis.*
35. Pekin: *stod.*
36. BN: *nimantaṇa.*
37. T: *aria.*
38. BN: *maṇu.*
39. SA: *pucchaī.*
40. BN, T: *śedha.*
41. Snar-thaṅ: *yobanavinnam.*
42. Pekin: *upekhaa.*
43. Snar-thaṅ: *naṣphala.*
44. Snar-thaṅ: *diḍtha.*
45. Pekin: *'cho.*
46. Pekin: *'bral.*
47. BN, T: *-manti.*
48. SA: *upekṣim khi.*
49. SA: *śunneedidvi*, T : *dradvi.*
50. SA: *sunna-*, T : *-sahāve.*
51. SA: *ligoia.*
52. T: *Kahi tu.*
53. T: *mae*, SA : *mova.*
54. BN: *samadyiṭṭi*, SA: *-ḍḍhi.*
55. *mñam-ñid sbyor-ba* corresponds to *samayoga*, not to *samaghṛṣṭi.*
56. The Tibetan translator has read *saṃyuta*, for he translates *bdag ñid yaṅ dag sbyor de la* (Pekin.: *las*).
57. 36. *anurāgya caturdevīḥ saṃharet sarvamaṇḍalam/lha mo bži la rǰes čhags pas dkyil-'khor thams-čad yaṅ dag bsdu. Yaṅ dag bsdu* supposes a variant *saṃkṣipet*, 'let him reduce'. In the śloka IV, 7, the Sanskrit similarly corresponds to the Tibetan *bsdu.* In both cases the final meaning is the same : 'remove'.
58. Cf. below, n. 2.
59. IX, 19-20 defines the three channels as *avadhūtī* (*kun'dar ma*), medial

placed on the left of *lalanā* (*brkyaṅ*) and on the right of *rasanā* (*ro-ma*). In the first the wind mixes with the sperm which falls from the head through the opening of the *vajra* into the *bhaga* of the *woman*. The relevant channels are well-known under other names in a number of Northern Tantras, in the Śaiva Āgamas of the South, in the principal texts of Haṭhayoga (*Haṭhayogapradīpikā*, *Gheraṇḍasaṃhitā*) as well as in the Vaiṣṇava texts of the *Pañcarātra* and in a number of *Upaniṣads*. These other names are *suṣumnā* for *avadhūtī*, *iḍā* for *lalanā*, and *piṅgalā* for *rasanā*. But *avadhūtī*, *lalanā* and *rasanā* are the names mentioned in the Buddhist texts since the *Saddharmapuṇḍarīka* (cf. Edgerton, Buddhist Hybrid Sanskrit Dict.)

60. T: saṃkramya tatra yogīndras tasya murdhāvalena ca / SA...mūrddhavilena ca / BN: ...murddhavilena ca / 'through the opening of the head', but the Tibetan version employs *thim* which corresponds to *vi-Lī*.
61. Pekin: ni.
62. BN and T: *māmakī gṛhya*, Tib: *māmakīs*.
63. Pekin: *sdaṅ*.

CHAPTER 29

THE PSYCHOLOGICAL THEORIES OF INDIA*

WHAT I WOULD LIKE to sum up for you is a study of the concepts created to represent psychic mechanisms throughout Indian civilisation. The import and particularly the unity of these theories of psychology has long been ignored. In fact, when they were discovered, a little before the middle of the 19th century, European psychology was primarily intellectualist. It wasn't quite ready to understand the Indian expositions and especially to perceive behind the allusions in texts that were frequent, what these theories could be, of which we did not yet have a complete description.

We were at once struck by the quite considerable number of words that were part of the Sanskrit vocabulary on psychology. We endeavoured to translate these words, although gropingly, without any clear guide. We ended up with all sorts of translations which eventually led to a great deal of confusion. And the blame for this confusion was squarely placed at the door of the Indian philosophers themselves, who, however, were not responsible for the lack of understanding in their regard.

And then, gradually, the different categories of Indian philosophy, the different schools got to be known better and today we are able to understand that, in addition to the special fields in classical philosophy determined by the educational principles of the Indians themselves—some which are considered orthodox while others are heterodox—there is a general knowledge as well, a general and scientific culture which belongs to the whole of India, which is common to all philosophers and religious seekers, irrespective of the sect or the time to which they might belong.

*Lecture delivered at the Société française de philosophie on 26 February, 1972 and published under the title, Les théories psychologiques de l 'Inde, in Bulletin de la Société française de Philosophie, July-Sept., 1972, pp. 73-96.

This is what we can observe if, while comparing the different data about psychological phenomena from the different texts we discover a certain homogeneity and unity in the representation of things. So common is this way of looking at things that most of the time the philosophical writings that deal with specific aspects take this outlook for granted. And it is this that often conceals it as it remains implicit.

But we have a specially significant source from the scientific and philosophical field in order to study the question that we have selected. It is not strictly philosophical; it is from the field of medicine, a whole group of medical theories by which the Indians sought to understand not only the functioning of the body but also the functioning of the mind, the functioning of the whole man since in their view there never was any opposition between body and mind. They conceived very early on that there existed a being, which they called *sattva* and which was composed of a physical, corporeal part and a unity of a psychic nature. In a stricter sense, this psychic nature is also given the name of *sattva.* This unity that only manifests itself as involved in a body and thereby forms with it a new unity, that of the living being, may be, though not necessarily according to all the philosophies, inhabited and controlled by what is called a self, *ātman*, well-known in all the Indian philosophies but whose existence is denied by some.

The theories of medical doctors, therefore, involved the study not only of illnesses and medication but also of man's total structure, including the spiritual being or, more precisely, the psychological being. They did this even more as they needed to study not merely the physical or even the mental disturbances, but also its normal constitution: what we call 'Indian medicine' is, in fact, an original system of medicine, called *Āyurveda* (= the knowledge related to longevity) which consequently extends its scope far beyond a simple treatment of illnesses. We have to understand the way normal life functions in order to be able to take adequate measures to maintain it in its normal state or to bring it back to normalcy when it goes out of it.

We find, then, this field of medicine to be an extremely special one. Moreover, the medical doctors are free from all religious concern while writing their technical texts and they have openly professed that there are several ways of treating the sick: first, one which consists in uttering magic formulae, one which consists in administering magical drugs, one which consists in invoking supernatural forces for their benefit. But it consists equally, and for the medical doctors which is of the greatest and perhaps sole import, in the medicine based on what is called *yukti*, that is right adjustment—we must understand it to mean a rational representation of the mechanism of the production of phenomena which enables us, on the basis of the knowledge of a symptom or a group of symptoms, to determine not merely the nature of the malady, according to what we remember of similar clinical cases, but above all what is its probable origin, what changes in diet and circumstances could have brought it about. Examples of this *yukti* are given in the experimental medical science which are, in fact, hypotheses, starting from all we already know, and which are constructed on the basis of such data about the occasional phenomena we are confronted with.

Indian doctors—and I speak of the treatises of Caraka and Suśruta which were written at the beginnings of the Christian era—in wanting to affirm better the rational nature of their method, have included in their expositions, notions of logic and in Caraka's case, a veritable treatise on logic so as to provide the apprentice-doctor and the doctor himself, the means, the elements of reasoning which can assist him in establishing the prognosis and the diagnosis. It is utterly exceptional to find in the history of medicine a treatise on logic in the midst of other more strictly medical teachings. But it is the peculiarity of Indian science to have wanted to affirm and clearly proclaim the necessity, most certainly in reaction against elements that are animated in an altogether different way, of a logical adjustment for the understanding of phenomena and then to pertinently act on them.

We find, then, in these texts, elements that shall help us to understand how the Indians visualised psychological mechanisms in a strictly rational way. It is stated that the living being is composed of the five elements of Nature which, in addition to the four elements known by the Greeks, include a fifth which is space, vacant space. But, at the same time, a sixth element which is the psychic element and is called *cetanā*, also enters into its composition. It is this whole composed of five material elements and the psychic element which constitute 'man'.

Starting from this very general definition, our authors analysed in as much detail as was possible for them, the psychological phenomena. We mentioned earlier that some philosophers, and perhaps even the bulk of them, admit that in addition to the six elements that constitute the organism, there is a seventh one which is the being-in-itself and which is the self, *ātman*, an ontological substratum of all things and which operates sometimes as a simple guarantor of existence, sometimes as a soul that is itself a portion of the Transcendent Self. But independently from this notion of the *ātman*, which in any case remains foreign to the elementary constitution of man and the psychic being, we have in this psychic being the following elements: first, the elements of perception which correspond one to one to the elements of Nature, that is to say to earth, water, fire, wind (the moving air is meant) and to the void. To these elements correspond respectively the eyes, ear, etc. but for the Indians it is clear that these organs converge all their information to one centre. There exists a treatise on logic which isn't composed, as a matter of fact, in a medical spirit, but which is very well-known, the *Nyāya-sūtras*, according to which the right eye recognises that which was seen by the left and reciprocally, which proves that there is a central organ to which the different external organs convey the knowledge they acquire, and this helps us to understand that after one eye has seen a certain form, the other eye can recognise it again. Because, in reality, it is neither the right nor the left eye which knows, it is the agent that is behind and that receives the impressions from both the eyes. It is this inner agent that also collects all the other elements that come from the other senses and it is known as the *manas*. We can translate *manas* conveniently as 'mind', remembering, however, that the meaning we give to it is not quite the same as that which is given to the mind and that there are numerous and widely different conceptions of 'mind', even when it is used in the French language. One can keep this term once we have understood well what is meant, namely, the centralising organ of all sense-data.

Whatever it may be, the *manas* or the mind, the centralising organ of all perception is also a sorting and classifying centre of these perceptions. It is this centre that stores traces of all these perceptions and it is here that the most original and fundamental element of Indian psychological theory comes into the picture: How does the psychic individuality store all the experiences that it goes through? Especially, how does it form itself through the accumulated and organised mass of the psychic experiences it has had?

There are two kinds of perception: one is called *anubhava*, that is the perception one has for the first time. This perception will remain stamped in the *manas*. Later, other similar perceptions will follow and if they are precisely similar then they would attach themselves to the first and thus consolidate and reinforce it. The perceptions accumulated thus would lead to the birth of another series of knowings which will no more be new cognitions but unconscious accumulated knowledges that can reappear to the consciousness as memories or as new combinations. And that is why at the beginning of the 19th century this was not understood; we failed to see that the Indians had perceived that there was a psychic being that later we were to call the unconscious, and about which we did not have the slightest notion at that time, this centre being quite other than a mere storehouse of memory. *Manas*, in fact, is not only a storehouse in which the results of the phenomena of perception pile up one on top of the other not only a sorting organ, it is also an organ of judgment and elaboration of thought. It is in the *manas* that the accumulated material is judged. And when the judgment of *manas*, which is, therefore, automatic and unconscious, reaches its term, then there is the birth of what is called *buddhi*, strictly 'the awakening', that is consciousness which arrives at *niścaya*, decision or conclusion.

It is, therefore, with the help of a great amount of material that has been accumulated as a result of all the psychological experiences that have occurred, as well as because this mass is organised by the spiritual organ, that a psychic individuality gets formed. It can be conceived as the personal substratum of a soul or as self-existing without constituting a person. And there exists a clarifying metaphor in this context, both in Buddhism and in Hinduism, the metaphor of the chariot.

This comparison is made by those who hold that the soul does.

not exist or that if it exists, then the soul is, in any case, totally detached from the individuality. The upholders of this theory make the following comparison: A chariot is composed of elements, wheels, shaft, etc. All these elements, when well-adjusted, lend individuality to the chariot. Even if a chariot is built on the same model as another, it will be an individual chariot, since, even though the structure might be identical with other chariots, its wood would be slightly different, the accidents it may have had would be different, one wheel might be smoother than other: it will, therefore, have its own unique characteristics. It would possess a technical individuality but none would think this chariot to be a person, a body carrying a soul. It has no soul; all it needs to fulfil its function of a chariot is that all its composit parts be well-combined.

Whatever solution we may offer, then, to the metaphysical problem of man, either as a spiritualist or as a materialist, that is of little consequence, as regards the simple understanding of the functioning of the self or the psychic individuality. There is a theory that say that there are a number of doors that open out to the outer world, but here, a point of contention lies in finding out whether the outer world is objective or illusory, etc. But whether it be illusory or not, there is, in any case, a perception and even an infinity of perceptions of what we call the outer world. These perceptions recorded in the *manas* come into being in the following way. There is yet another comparison which enables one to understand the way in which one represents facts to oneself. When a perfume has been poured into a phial and then removed, there remains for a long time in the phial, a 'trace', a 'fragrance', and this is what in Sanskrit is called *vāsanā*. Similarly, when a psychological phenomena has taken place, there remains a *vāsanā*, a permanent trace in the *manas*, that is the psychic individuality that evolves within the *manas*. The organisation of these traces, *vāsanās* which can be controlled by the will or the intelligence, by the consciousness, but which can also be automatic if the consciousness is negligent, will end in real psychic constructions, *saṃskāras*. In these conditions, the psychic individuality will not merely be a treasure-trove, a storehouse of old psychic phenomena, it will be a unifying, structured element constituted by all these traces which, in fact, are not simply inactive traces but which remain dynamic, which carry in them not only the memory of their activity but also that of the received perceptions.

And all this will serve to resolve a number of problems that crop up in this philosophy as a whole, without forgetting that the techniques of salvation would, obviously, take these conceptions into serious consideration. Among the philosophical theories which can be explained on the basis of psychological conceptions we can first quote the theory about language and the aesthetic theory. For the Indians it is actually a most important preoccupation to understand why and how speech, which is sound, produces states of consciousness; how a sound can have meaning from a psychological point of view, not only individually but also in combination with other sounds in order to produce a whole intellectual process. Well, this is easily explained when one refers to the commonly accepted theory, namely that there exists within each psychic individuality a great quantity of material which can become active again, return to the consciousness and which can resonate to new external stimuli. If, therefore, an association of ideas has formed between certain sounds and concepts, as can be easily imagined, subsequently it would suffice for the sound to be heard again to make the concept reappear. And so on.

It is the same with the theories on poetics. The question to be asked is how not only the sounds of words but also inarticulated words and certain rhythms can produce aesthetic emotions. To which the answer would be: because there already existed a whole set-up of pre-established resonators in the form of *vāsanās* and *saṃskāras* within the psychic individuality and it is all this that enters into resonance at the time of a new external stimulus. This leads to many other consequences and particularly practical consequences. First, if one believes like a number of religions of India, and probably the majority of them, that the psychic being does not die with the decaying of the body, it shall be admitted that since it is animated by the traces of the old activity that produced it, it may tend to, once released from the body, to take on another one in order to realise its potentialities. And consequently it would be possible to determine by regulating his meditations, the manner in which one could constitute or recondition his own psychic individuality. In order to convert him to a religion one could undoubtedly offer to him arguments that logically he could accept, or seduce his consciousness by making him feel, for instance, the insecurity of his human condition and by promising him a better one; one could move him in the name of charity vis-à-vis other beings, etc. But all this could very well clash against an already formed block which would precisely be a block of *saṃskāras* that form the psychic individuality. Thus, in order to make a deep conversion, to reform the very substratum —what is sometimes called *āśrayaparāvṛtti*—we must take recourse to a psychological method. That which has anarchically constituted, at the mercy of circumstances, the psychic individuality, could be undone or reformed, by virtue of a disciplined method. And that is the reason we see that even the philosophers who have written exclusively on metaphysics, have almost always, revealed, in one way or another, a surprising attachment to purely material practices, to the repetition of certain formulae while doing the humblest of daily chores. If we revert to their conceptions of the structure and constitution of their own psychic individuality, we realise that they could not neglect anything. If one wishes to transform his being into a being that comes close to the divine ideal, then one would have to re-mould his psychic individuality entirely, that is, one must not only meditate in all circumstances—it is impossible to meditate philosophically all the time—but one must also shut oneself out from all arbitrary and disturbing thoughts during the physiological exercise of living. One must, at the same time, naturally, strive to collect all one's attention on selected themes of meditation which would help in leaving positive traces within the psychic individuality and eliminate the negative ones.

There are yet other practical applications, much simpler and extremely important, of the psychological doctrines of India. I did not mention Yoga while speaking just now about the efforts required to transform an ordinary psychic individuality into a new one. Naturally yoga is the most well-known method for realising this, but yoga also claims to train certain psychological faculties, such as the development of an attention that is more sustained or making much clearer representations of things that one believes in. The reasons for believing that yoga can really obtain such results are many, including psychosomatic reasons over which we cannot linger today. We do not consider, as some texts would like us to believe, miraculous results that would open us out to extraordinary revelations in the field of scientific knowledge: in fact, it is shown to us, for instance, that through the concentration of both the attention and the meditation, on the basis of an accurate technique, it is possible to obtain a very precise knowledge of physiology, or of astronomy or the system of the world. Unfortunately, what is set forth to us as the result of the yogin's discovery by means of so-called direct visions of things, is nothing else but a classical exposition either of Indian medicine or of Indian astronomy, which deserve merit and are rational but which are now old and unfortunately wrong. Yoga, therefore, cannot furnish anything else besides a more intense vision of something that was already known to us, or it can also enable us to obtain significant intellectual capacities within a meditation that shuts us out to external disturbances.

To conclude, I would merely like to give an example of the pedagogical consequences of these Indian theories, according to which we can model our being as we wish. In the end, one is less attached to the belief that heredity decides everything and arranges absolutely everything in advance, than in many other countries where they don't have conceptions related to individual psychic constructions. In Indian theories of psychology, heredity does, in fact, provide a human organism, but not a psychic individuality, a pre-determined soul because one can constitute one's psychic individuality the way one wants to, this psychic individuality being dependent on the psychological experiences encountered in life. Thus, in order to form a scholar, a pandit, a pedagogical method is used which has been condemned outright for a long time in the West but nevertheless produces absolutely remarkable results. One must start with the child as soon as he is able to speak or recite something, around the age of three, depending on his development. He starts by repeating some ethical stanzas in Sanskrit, for instance. At the age of four or five, when he knows two or three thousand such stanzas, he is taught the dictionary by heart without any explanation. One has thus programmed him as one programmes these days a computer; a considerable amount of material has been put into him, texts and words; after some time grammar is introduced. And then finally everything is explained. And when we explain, understanding is very quick. When we try to explain something to a European child to whom we have taken care not to teach anything for fear of turning him into a parrot and for fear of obliterating his innate gifts of intelligence, we find he has nothing on which he can rationalise other than that which we provide him at the last moment. We also give him books, we buy him a dictionary which remains in his library; he must then look up the word in it and while reading a text he has to stop at every word in order to understand what the word means in that particular text. The European child is very gifted, he does a lot of work but the young Indian on being given a sentence, either recognises it at once because he knows it already or he has immediately, without any delay entailed by his searching, the ready-made solution to his problems of meaning.

On the other hand, we see in this exercise, his memory being developed in a way that is absolutely astonishing for us. He is capable of not only having this memory, this capacity of recording and remembering but, what is more, an incredible amount of memories that are present simultaneously in his mind. At the same time, he can become capable of remaining alert to everything that happens on the outside (this is developed by a special training but it is done always with a view to applying these theories and it is subsequently empirically tested. Competitions are held to pick out who is able to compose, in a given limited time, on a given subject a certain number of verses and be able to say at the end, after having composed these verses, how many times such and such person came into the room, how many times he heard the bell strike during the composition, etc. All this has to be present in his mind simultaneously, his attention has to be focused on a great number of simultaneous representations, and even when unconcentrated it cannot lose its precision.

This pedagogical method does not always succeed but it generally ends in offering to the intelligence in the field of *buddhi*, of the consciousness, a large quantity of material, all ready and which it is most convenient to have at one's immediate disposal instead of being obliged to look for it.

These are some of the observations I wanted to make on these Indian theories of psychology, emphasising the fact that we are far from what we usually think, that the Indians are mystics who believe exclusively through intuition in all sorts of divinities and who have no logic. In truth, they have constituted a fundamental psychology which is already quite subtle and they have successfully put their theories into practice thus combining theories that may not have been completely right with the test of experience which, in any case, rectifies the errors of the theories and, in the end, proves to be effective.

Chapter 30

VISIONS OF THE SPIRITUAL SEEKER OF INDIA*

The literature of India, right from the most ancient one, that is Vedic scriptures, abound in references to visions, some of which are spontaneous and others induced. The latter are induced, as in several other countries, by psychotropic substances, particularly hallucinogens, or by some physical techniques (dances, etc.). But in India they are produced selectively by psychosomatic techniques of yoga.

Whether induced or not, most of the visions of which we are speaking, are not those of spiritual seekers and, therefore, in principle, we don't need to dwell on them, notably visions which are induced by the India cannabis or by opium are not relevant to our study. Those, however, arising out of the use of psychotropic drugs, despite their condemnation by yoga, are found sometimes to facilitate the exercises of these spiritual seekers. We cannot, therefore, neglect them altogether.

In any case, since the time of the *Ṛg-Veda*, visions of different kinds have played an important role in Indian religion. Firstly, the Veda itself, made up of a collection of texts, is considered not to be a product of man, as the compiled texts are eternal and were discovered by the Ṛṣis or 'seers'. The vision of which we are speaking is not merely optical, for the Vedic stanzas are considered to be spoken not written words. Therefore, what is meant is becoming clearly conscious. In fact another name for the Vedas is Śruti or 'hearing'.

It is sometimes difficult to decide whether the seers who revealed the Vedas were human or divine, but the superhuman faculties are conceived to be an extension of the human ones. The visions regarding the gods bear testimony to men's belief in visions. They are sometimes induced indirectly, as is the case with

*Les visions chez les spirituels indiens, in *Nouvelles de l'Institut Catholique de Paris*, 1976-77, Feb. 1977, pp. 145-55.

Vasiṣṭha who, while being a legendary Ṛṣi, was also the ancestor of a sacerdotal line. The hymn VII.88, in fact, evokes a personal vision of Vasiṣṭha who is inspired by the God Varuṇa. Other visions are more directly imputed to spiritual seekers, the *kavis* or inspired poets and more particularly to the *Sūris* or sages and to men united with God (*naro devayavo*). These last two categories which practically overlap are devotees of Viṣṇu, a God who is invoked less often than the gods of the forces of Nature but who is superior to them because he could cross the natural world in three steps and transcend it with the third one, the supreme abode:

'Behold the acts of Viṣṇu, by which we have clearly seen the contracts (which are the laws of nature). He is the friend to be associated with Indra (divine Force of nature). The sages (*Sūris*) regard always the supreme abode of Viṣṇu as we behold the eye which is manifested in the sky (the Sun). This abode the admirable, enlightened sages set aflame (illumine), which is the supreme abode of Viṣṇu. (ṚV I. 22, 19-21)

This supreme abode is visualised by the spiritual seekers themselves and they strive towards it in view of the greatness of Viṣṇu who alone dominates all:

'May the mighty thought go to Viṣṇu who resides in the mountain, who travels far, the sole man who has measured the long, common vast sojourn, in three steps!

'He whose three steps full of nectar (*madhu*) intoxicate their own nature without being exhausted, it is He alone who has triply maintained the Earth and the Sky, and all the worlds.

'That which is dear to Him, the Way, may I attain, there where men united with God (*naro devayavo*) are inebriated, for such is the companion who travels far. In the supreme abode of Viṣṇu is the fountain of nectar.' (ṚV I. 154, 3-5)

The nectar, according to tradition, is 'the sweet, divine nectar of Immortality'. Its name, *madhu*, in classical Sanskrit, means 'honey', but can also mean a fermented liquor. Some regard it as *Soma*, the drink which represents on the Earth the fecund waters of Heaven. It is obtained on the Earth by squeezing some plants whose identification is still in doubt. But the *madhu* of Viṣṇu, even if it has been represented down here as an intoxicating drink, in the supreme abode, in the transcendental world, is the element which intoxicates with a spiritual bliss, that is apparently already, the bliss of the devotees of classical Vaiṣṇavism right up to our day.

There exists however in certain ancient forms of Vaiṣṇavism, especially in that which is dominated by devotion to a particular form of Viṣṇu, Balarāma or Saṅkarṣaṇa, traces of a practice of self-intoxication brought about by an alcoholic liquor. In classical Vaiṣṇavism this practice is excluded.

It is the same in classical Śaivism, elder brother of Vaiṣnavism. Fundamentally the two religions don't differ, each accepting at the essential level of the Universe, One Entity, a Supreme Godhead, a Unique, Cosmic Reality that some see manifested in the world under various aspects in the name of Viṣṇu and others see in the name of Śiva.

Among the faithfuls of both these religions, some of the most exemplary devotees known to tradition are frequently visionaries. Besides the works traditionally ascribed to them, we also have more or less legendary biographies that are sometimes fantastic, especially with regard to their supposed period, but sometimes they are verifiable by historical points of reference which, in their turn, are guaranteed by epigraphical data. Thanks to the internal criticism of the texts it is at least possible to fix their relative chronology. In any case, whatever may be the validity of the legendary tales about them, those bear testimony to the beliefs of which they are the objects.

The textual sources which inform us are either in Sanskrit and, in that case, belong to the general Pan-Indian literature, or in regional languages, principally, among the older ones, in Tamil and in Kannaḍa, which are Dravidian languages of the South.

The *Mahābhārata* and the *Purāṇas* are the major Sanskrit sources. In Tamil, the works of the Vaiṣṇava devotees, the Āḻvārs, form the collection which has been extensively commented upon. Those of the Śaiva devotees, the Nayanmārs, we have other collections which have been less dwelt upon. These Tamil texts generally belong to the period from the 5th to 10th or 11th century.

In Kannaḍa, there exists, besides the works of the spiritual seekers of the Vīraśaiva community which was formed in the

12th century with Basava, a noteworthy collection of texts and biographies, the *Śūnyasampādane* by Allāma Prabhu. The more recent literature in Bengali, Marathi, Hindi, Gujarati etc. abounds in texts inspired by visions. Some of these texts originate in milieus where Indian and Sufi traditions have mingled thus giving birth to an Indo-Muslim spirituality.

In Sanskrit texts which are common to the whole of India, accounts of visions are frequent. Some of them are well-known. For example, a text from the Vedānta or 'the end of the Veda', the *Kaṭha Upaniṣad,* describes Naciketā's vision of the world of Death. In the *Mahābhārata,* the *Bhagavadgītā* describes the vision in which the Supreme Being appears before the eyes of the hero Arjuna. In a number of tales, the Supreme Godhead or gods appear before men, particularly before ascetics whose zeal they wish to reward. These ascetics are not always real spiritual beings. Some utilise asceticism for some end, in order to win the ultimate reward of power and extraordinary boons.

Gods make themselves visible to human beings whom they wish to support or guide but they do this not necessarily in dreams or in waking visions. They do it then by assuming the forms of various human or even animal beings. But then it is no more a question of the visions of spiritual seekers. The people to whom they appear do not even always recognise them in their disguised appearance.

On the other hand, we often hear of divine apparitions and revelations that take place in dreams in order to assist the devotees.

We also know of instances of revelations to men by beings other than gods. For example, we know the story of Nāthamuni, a Vaiṣṇava of South India around the year 1000, who, on hearing by chance some devotional songs of the greatest of the Āḻvārs, Nammāḻvār, was filled with admiration and faith and went to the place where the poet had lived, at the southernmost part of the Tamil country. There he could gather only a preserved part of the texts but by repeating them over and over again he received the help which Nammāḻvār himself came to offer him by revealing the rest of his works.

However apocryphal the story of this adventure may be, it proves that in the environment in which it originated, they normally accepted the possibility of revelatory visions of this kind. Moreover, if we admit the hypothesis that Nāthamuni himself claimed to have received the revelations, we would not be obliged to doubt his good faith. Obsessed by the incessant repetition of the texts that enthused him, Nāthamuni could have involuntarily produced them himself by the very same inspiration of content and style, and been led to truly believe that he had got a revelation from the poet, the spirit and legend of whom constantly occupied him.

The technique of yoga, however, is reputed to enable one to obtain visions and extraordinary knowledge. Some of these visions occur automatically in the course of exercises, others are voluntarily sought and methodically induced.

The phenomena which are automatically triggered are essentially sensorial and principal among these is the vision of a light that is usually blue. It is obviously related to the reactions of the nervous system to the physiological modifications, notably in the hematocritic field, which yogic exercise brings about, especially by breath-retention. The other relative sensorial phenomena are auditory: it is the noise of echoing resonances such as of bells, of the conch, of the sea, of the rumbling of thunder, the trumpeting of elephants, the sound of the flute, or the drone of insects (*Tirumantiram* 606-07). The setting off of these visions and hearings occurs in the state of *dhyāna* or 'meditation' and if, however, it is reflective, the form itself of these visions and these hearings is, in part, probably determined by notions previously acquired. It is, in fact, traditionally accepted that knowledge is light and the Supreme Entity that it seeks is also Light. The indefinite resonance of the sea or of the conch is, on its part, a manifestation of the fundamental, eternal Sound which is represented by the syllable OṂ. But it is at the same time the symbolism of light and the reality of the visions of coloured lights, which are of the greatest importance and which have been most frequently mentioned in the works of the spiritual men of India right from the beginning uptil now. Faith in the light assists and psychologically prepares the visions which are to follow, even if they are physiologically induced.

But this phenomena is not peculiar to India alone. The vision of colours—and in this case it is green colour—is found also in the works of Iranian sufis of whom a study has been made by Henry Corbin.

What is characteristic of India is the instrument that is made available by the technique of conditioning and psychological orientation called yoga, to the Indian spiritual seeker.

The visionaries of every country see—sometimes in fantastic setups—only those beings and things which conform with the customary representations of their own environment, or they have visions of things that come into their ken accidentally. Their visions draw sustenance from their own ordinary or exceptional world, but they don't open them to others' worlds. And because they are in concordance with the beliefs of their immediate environment, they seem to confirm the objective reality of these beliefs.

What yoga adds to the nature of visions is the possibility of selecting them in advance and to realise them with accuracy and force.

Despite a widespread but ill-founded opinion, Indian thought, guided by the classical teachings of the common culture, isn't purely intuitive and imaginary. On the contrary it seeks to be rational. Logic as well as grammar are at the base of all classical Sanskrit teaching. These teachings are, in theory, reserved for Brahmins, the class which essentially upholds knowledge, but in fact they have always been more widely known. Beyond the social classes and diverse religions, there exists a general Indian culture which founds itself on the observation of important natural facts and attempts to construct a rational representation out of it. In the domain of psychology, reflection on the mechanism of thought on the formation of the psychic individuality was remarkably and advanced quite early on. It should be mentioned here that at the time when Indian ideas began to be known to the Western world in the first half of the 19th century, they were misunderstood and the notion of the unconscious, although present in India, was not yet even conceived in Western philosophy. Now, on the one hand, the general ancient Indian culture established a link between the cosmos and the microcosm that man is supposed to be; and on the other, it integrated the essential self, the *Ātman* of each individual human being, into that One Self of the Universe, *Paramātman* or the Supreme Self. The latter, though in essence transcending the cosmic body, is empirically manifest in it, like the individual self is manifest in the human body. In these conditions, God is not only the allpowerful king of the human Universe; He also rules in the multiple manifestations at the heart of the world; and that gives rise to an apparent polytheism in the terrestrial order. But God is also beyond the world (*para*), in the transcendental world: the One Being, Pure Being, Consciousness and Bliss (*Saccidānanda*), or simply the Undifferentiated Being.

At the edge of the Transcendent and of the cosmos there lies the Form of Godhead who is Being-Consciousness-Bliss and who looks upon the universe in sovereignty but with compassion for the suffering of the spiritual beings caught up in physical individualities and constituting by this involvement the empirical 'beings' (*sattva*) that are subject to birth and death.

All the metaphysical schools did not accept the real existence of an ontological self, of a soul in the beings, but they did accept by necessity the distinction of a psychic element from a somatic one even while looking upon both as necessarily linked in the living being. And most of the schools also declared that at the dissolution of the body, the psychic individuality does not necessarily dissolve. In fact, it could be recognised to be created by the traces left by the psychological experiences gone through, whether these traces join themselves to one soul or they stick together to form one specific individuality like the composite elements of a car are put together without there being any soul.

In any way, the psychic individual forms a subtle body (*sūksmaśarīra*) as opposed to a gross body (*sthūlaśarīra*) which decomposes at the time of death. The traces of events and psychological acts are called *vāsanā*, literally 'perfuming': they retain the natural dynamism of acts (*karman*) which set them into motion or record them; and their groupings according to their affinities and reactions, were psychic constructions or *Saṃskāras*, lending to the psychic individuality its particularity as well as their motory force and reaction. This psychic self continues to live in the corporeal individuality. This explains at the same time memory and the activity of the living, particularly its attachment to a specific environment. This attachment, at the time of the body's death, could induce the subtle body to look for another one to fulfil its aspirations in another life. It was in this way that the mechanism of transmigration was understood, whatever may have been the real origins of its conception, origins which haven't been certified yet and which continue to remain an object of speculation.

The constitution of human psychism understood thus, it was clear that left to itself without any discipline, it was a plaything of the circumstances of life which sustained it haphazardly with its successive states of consciousness. But it also became clear that by choosing one's states of consciousness one could become master of one's final constitution. It is this choice that is given to us by the technique of Yoga. And it is this technique that was utilised and heightened by the spiritual seekers conversant with its concepts and which was taken as an example even by those who were unconcerned with those concepts but set before them the ideal of rising towards God which the same concepts elaborated upon.

The technique of yoga is psycho-physiological. Firstly, it imposes conditions of hygiene and of ethics, then exercises for the mastery of the body so as to better control the attention, especially by holding certain physical postures (*āsanas*) and above all by the control of breath (*prāṇāyāma*), followed by exercises which were strictly psychological: the neutralisation of the external sensory stimuli which perturb (*pratyāhāra*) the concentration of the mind and its fixation (*dhāraṇā*), meditation (*dhyāna*) and the stable positioning (*samādhi*) of all the psychic activities on the object chosen by the consciousness until the extinction of the very consciousness of the act of seeking it.

The combination (saṃyama) of the last three operations gives a particularly clear consciousness of the object, naturally before the extinction of the consciousness of seeking it; this extinction however, is not aimed at necessarily or if it is then it is only in the final stage when the chosen object of consciousness is undifferentiated Being.

It is taught that this combination of all the psychological steps gives an immediate vision of the reality sought. If this occurs over celestial bodies, the vision obtained will be of the structure of the Universe, if it occurs over the body, it will be of the constitution of the body, etc. Now, the descriptions of realities thus seen in Yoga coincide perfectly not with the observations of modern science but with the classical teachings of ancient Indian science. We find that the yogin has a vision of only that which he has learnt, more perfectly so in the solitude of his contemplation than he can through ordinary study. As far as the body is concerned the vision obtained is not even always that of the classical specialists of ancient Indian Medicine. It is more commonly a representation that belongs strictly to the tradition of the yogins, especially those whom we call the *siddhas*, the 'Perfect Ones'. This representation mingles with notions of classical origin and with speculation that is based on the interpretation of empirical findings in the course of yogic exercises; and the whole establishes a symbolic correspondence between the conception of the universe and the theoretical elements of the corporeal microcosm.

The Siddhas, often reputed to be the most exalted of spiritual seekers, look down on ordinary science, taking God and the highest hierarchy of His manifestations in the Universe as objects of their visions. This vision relies on knowledge (*jñāna*), knowledge par excellence, of the conception of God and of the individual self, and this vision, chosen on the basis of this conception itself, goes to confirm and set it off in all its symbolism of light. It is here that recourse is sometimes taken to some psychotropic drugs to facilitate the desired visions. But the practice is condemned and it should indeed be, as it goes against the very method of yoga. As yoga, in its authentic form, endeavours to keep out states of consciousness born from an external source in order realise the mastery of the body and the embodied spirit, and favours a willed spiritual choice of the content of consciousness and of the conclusive conditioning of the unconscious individuality, it cannot substitute the free will of the yogin with an externally induced intoxication. The mastery of the spirit is the prerogative of the yogin not that of a drug.

The content of the visions controlled and intensified by yoga is very varied. With the spiritual seeker they are not concerned only with the supreme divine representation in his luminous symbolism, any divine manifestation can take place in its proper climate. The various aspects of such a manifestation correspond to their description in devotional and iconographical texts. The liturgical hymns of praise abound in literature and describe or evoke the concrete forms that are later recreated by art. The link between the hymn and the image is often direct when the poet has eulogised a specific divine aspect venerated in a particular sacred place. We even have very numerous stanzas called *dhyānaśloka*, 'stanzas of meditation' which specify the character of the divine image for the use of artists and visionaries.

In the philosophic milieus where the plenitude of the being is denied to the phenomenal being and the latter is made to be an illusory construction, the visionary representations are considered as basically equivalent to the perception of this world. Illusory as both are, external perceptions and imaginary projections are both of the same nature. The difference is that the perception of the external world is experienced whereas the vision that is externally constructed is selected, it is a *bhāvanā* or a 'creation'.

The abundance and the popularity of this literature and these images give ample material to the spiritual seekers of India to nourish the visions to which their faith leads them. For them these visions occur all of a sudden, as it happens everywhere in the world but India, on the contrary, has been blessed, in addition, with a veritable technology of visions.

CHAPTER 31

SCIENCE AND YOGA*

TODAY WE TEND TO think that science is what is based on the evidence of reason and yoga is what is based on intuition.

This way of looking at things is modern because the modes of knowledge spoken of in the Indian tradition do not include intuition. In fact, different philosophical schools, mainly those said to be of 'logic' enumerate a certain number of means of knowledge. Some even accept only fact and pure and simple observation, such as *Āyurveda.* To this fact are added the knowledge obtained from classical science and finally inference, that is to say the perception or concept of signs implying the existence of certain phenomena, even when the latter are not being observed.

Comparison or analogy are also means of knowledge but the physicians refused to accept analogy as it could be misleading, therefore, not to be used by scientists since the physician seeks to be rational in his science.

One of the most ancient Indian medical texts, the 'Caraka *Saṃhitā*' points out that there exist several modes of the research of healing:

— through prayers to a divinity
— through magical formulae and acts
— through *yukti* which signifies adjustment, that is to say the seeking of the causes of the illness, the laying down of an etiological diagnosis and the understanding of the development of the pain from a condition of health.

This rational research is, therefore, absolutely in accordance with the present-day methods of modern science. We too seek to observe all possible phenomena, to understand how they are produced, to form a possibly valid hypothesis, at least temporarily, in keeping with all the known facts and disagreeing with none.

*Summary of a lecture delivered in 1979 in Paris, published under the title "Science et Yoga" in *Yoga et Vie*, no. 22, Paris, Dec. 1979.

This hypothesis can, however, in a certain manner, be considered as an intuition because, from a certain number of disparate facts, an intellectual endeavour strives to perceive behind the complexity of phenomena and their diversity, the law which will allow him to explain the coherence of their formation. However, here we are talking about scientific procedure, and we find that since the ancient times Indian science has always followed the same path.

When we study the yogins of ancient times, we observe that they started from the ideas formulated by the scientists of the *Āyurveda*, the ancient Indian medical science, and they surpassed it, as they sought, beyond the easily attainable knowledge, to free themselves from the human condition and to attain the knowledge of the Supreme Being.

A whole range of relations with the phenomenal world have been built around this Being, most often called Śiva, as also relations between this phenomenal world and man who presents a microcosmic form similar to that of the infinite Being. When man, this microcosm, becomes conscious of the fact that he is contained by the same Being as the whole of Nature, he seeks to unite with it. But he must do this in the present body, subject to a multiple bondage, exposed to illness, old age and death, a body which, in any case, is impermanent and opposed to the Absolute Being which, on the contrary, is permanent, eternal and infinite.

It is, however, impossible to come out of the human condition and approach the divine state by using physiological means. It is thought which should act and it is bound to a body. But for the ancient Indian science, 'wind' which blows in and animates the universe, animates also the body and the mind of man. Thanks to this wind, the sensations seized by the sensorial organs are directed to the heart, the seat of the mind, and they allow a complete knowledge of the object. *Manas*, or the spiritual organ, gathers all the perceptions which then join the consciousness or the *Buddhi*. The image and the abstract thought, perceived or conceived, imbue the psychic individuality; it is *vāsanās* that, united together, make up the *saṃskāras* which are capable of promoting new activities in our consciousness, either appearing in the form of memories or in the form of impulses which drive us to act.

The Indians had, therefore, discovered this mechanism which by and large corresponds to our conception of the subconscious.

For a long time, European psychology was exclusively intellectualist. If it accepted memory, it believed specially in intelligence and beyond it in an entity always called soul.

We all know of the existence of the pineal gland which can be considered as the remnant of a third eye which is that of knowledge. This gland was not known and is never mentioned in the ancient Indian texts of anatomy. It is Descartes who spread the idea that this gland could contain something that was superior to intelligence. According to him the soul is unique and its seat is the only impair organ of the brain.

Whatever it might be, it is certain that the psychological analysis made by the Indians was remarkable for that ancient age and yoga relied on it from very early on.

The greatness of India lies in having given to man, by means of a very advanced system of psychological analysis, the possibility to rise above the human condition, acting on the known psychic mechanism. Yoga takes the credit of inventing and perfecting the method allowing the conditioning of the psychism thanks to physiological and psychological techniques, because there is no opposition between the substance of the body and the substance of the soul. It is, therefore, possible to do away with the bondage of the senses and to attain the Absolute Being.

The Indians who had observed the concomitance of the ceasing of breath and of the intensification of the attention, developed the *Kumbhaka* or the power to stop the functioning of the respiration. Thus by means of *prāṇāyāma*, one could attain higher stages in the practice of yoga, particularly the *pratyāhāra* or the retraction of senses. This leads to meditation and then to *samādhi.*

For the point of view of modern science, yoga, concerns two different but complementary sciences:

—**Psycho-physiology**. If physiological phenomena are most easily studied on yogins, the psychological phenomena are very much less so. They can't, in fact, be communicated at the moment when they are being experienced, since the yogin is then cut off from the external world. Even later, it is extremely difficult to analyse the exercises or the experiences which, by definition, are personal and isolated;

—the study of the tradition. We mean here all the ideas that the yogins profess and which must be examined by very simple methods.

When phenomena produced by yoga are observed, present science does not hesitate to accept them.

I think it will be unwise for yoga to seek to establish too precise a relationship between its facts and modern science because it would stop at a science known to be provisional, that is to say much superior to what it was a hundred years ago, but much inferior to what it will be in the coming centuries. But an explanation of the phenomena of yoga must be attempted with the help of the provisional knowledge of modern science.

It can, therefore, be concluded that yoga brings to modern science very vast notions and it would be most profitable for scientists to devote themselves to its further study.

SCIENCE AND YOGA*

In ancient times, it did not occur to anyone to draw parallels between the science developed by yoga and other sciences, except for the very ancient Indian medical science called *Āyurveda* which signifies the knowledge which bestows or preserves longevity.

Today, it is believed that there exists a considerable and fundamental difference of method between modern science and yoga. And this difference consists in the fact that science seeks to base itself on evidence and reason, whereas yoga bases itself on intuition.

Such an outlook on things is modern: it did not find any acceptance in the ancient times because the modes of knowledge which are listed in the Indian tradition do not include intuition. In fact, different philosophical schools, especially the schools said to be of Nyāya, that is to say Logic, declare that there exist a certain number of means of knowledge which they have enumerated: some accept only evidence, observation, pure and simple. But others admit that there exist two, three, four or five means of knowledge.

*Science et yoga, in *Yoga et Vie*, no. 28 June, 1981.

Āyurveda accepts only the evidence that is obtained by observation. In no science can anybody reconstitute exclusively with his reason and his senses the whole of science. One is obliged, in every case, to inherit from preceding savants even if we realise that they are mistaken and their theories must be changed. There is, therefore, evidence or the reasons obtained and finally inference.

Anumāna corresponds to what we can call the hypotheses on the formation of things. In fact, there are some which are always associated with certain phenomena and we can, when we perceive these signs without perceiving the producing phenomenon itself, judge that this phenomenon exists because it is manifested by a sign which necessarily is always linked to it.

Let us take, for example, the smoke on the mountain: its presence proves that there is a fire, although this fire is not visible. This is *inference*.

Other theories also work as a means of knowledge: through comparison or analogy. But physicians have refused to accept analogy as a valid means of knowledge. They believe that analogy is as misleading as it is conducive to conviction and that as a consequence, it should not be employed by the scientist since the physician seeks to be rational in his science.

There is a major text in one of the oldest collections of Indian medical texts called the *Caraka Saṃhitā* which indicates that there are several ways of looking for the cure of a sick person.

One can seek the cure through prayers to a divinity. One can seek this through magic formulae and acts. But one can also seek the cure of a person through what is called *yukti*, which means adjustment, and when one becomes conscious of *yukti*, this means that one becomes conscious of the adjustment of things in nature which explains the event in question. An etiological diagnosis is sought to understand how the illness might have developed. And this rational seeking is altogether in accordance with the researches of modern science. We too seek to observe all the possible phenomena, to understand how these phenomena were produced, to form a hypothesis which should, in order to be accepted as valid, at least temporarily, be in concordance with all the known facts and clash with none.

From a certain standpoint, this hypothesis can be considered as an intuition. From a certain number of jumbled facts, an intellectual effort is necessary, from our side, to try to imagine behind the complexity of the phenomena and their diversity, the law that can explain the coherence of their formation. But it is always the question of a scientific process and it is found that since the ancient times, in Indian science, this same process has been followed.

Now, when we observe, not the yogins of today and their theories, but the yogins of ancient times—and this is certified by a good number of texts—we observe that in some cases they started from ideas formed by rationalist āyurvedic scientists, but they did not follow *Āyurveda.* They thought that they had to surpass them. *Āyurveda* is an extremely limited method as regards the results and did never fully satisfy those who sought, beyond the easily acquired knowledge, the evident observation, to have the supreme knowledge, nor those who wanted to free themselves from the human condition to rise to a higher state, if not to the state of the Supreme Being.

This Being is most often called *Śiva.* And a complete exposition was elaborated about the relation between the supreme Being and the phenomenal world, between this phenomenal world and man who represents for those who share this faith, a microcosmic form but similar to that of the Infinite Being. The moment this microcosm becomes conscious of the fact that he is sustained by this same Being as is the whole of nature, he can seek to unite with this Being and should seek to do it by means of this body which is constrained to a great deal of servitudes, which is exposed to disease, old age and death and which, in any case, is impermanent and in this way contrasts with the Absolute Being who himself is, evidently, permanent, eternal and infinite.

How does one succeed in coming out of the human condition in order to approach the divine state? It is impossible to do it uniquely through logical means. It is thought that must act. But thought is body and Indian science, following an ancient hypothesis, thinks it to be wind, the same wind that blows in the universe, that in the form of internal breath of the body animates it as the wind animates the universe. Now this wind which animates the body is also the wind of the mind. It is thanks to it that the sensations gathered by different sensorial organs are transported by canals to the heart, the seat of the mind: *manas*, which brings together all the different sensations, censures their cohesion and enables one to form a total image. This *manas* can be directed, it can focus its vision on anything. When sensorial phenomena take place, they are recorded by the *manas* and thus go to the consciousness which is called *Buddhi* (or awakening, becoming conscious).

Not only is there consciousness, there is also an imprinting on the psychic individuality of the image or the abstract thought which was perceived or conceived, this is what is called *vāsanā*, 'perfuming' which imbues the psychic individuality. The individual is not the same after this experience. Something has been added to his psychic individuality. This 'something' does not remain isolated. The different *vāsanās* are found, they link themselves and form what are called *saṃskāras* (construction). They are not simply constructions or imprints because they often result from a movement and they retain a dynamism inherited from this movement. They are, therefore, capable of triggering new activities in our consciousness, either by appearing in the form of memories or in the form of impulses which drive us to act in one way or another.

The Indians had discovered this mechanism which roughly corresponds to our conception of the subconscious that has lately appeared in Europe. It is certain that the psychological analysis that was made by the Indians was a remarkable analysis for the time when it was founded and very early Yoga leaned on this rational psychological science of India.

And it is on this very science that it bases itself because it is only in India that it found its moorings, that is in the same place, in the same culture or region where precisely there existed an advanced psychic knowledge, more advanced than in any other civilisation of the ancient world. This is why India was the seat of the birth of Yoga.

It is India's greatness to have made a psychological analysis far in advance of other countries, and to have based on it possibilities of raising oneself above the human condition. In fact, from the representation made of the psychic structure and mechanism, found to be quite correct, one could actually act on it in stead of letting it get haphazardly moulded through psychological experiences that it encountered, either by accident or,—and this is more serious—, through ill-natured psychological experiences.

Thus one could control thought by a total discipline which itself, when rightly directed, is capable of moulding the psychic individuality in an ideal way. Each one's psychism could be conditioned by a regular method and it is this method that yoga was credited with having invented and perfected. Surely, thought had to work internally since it is involved in the body; it only functions through the mediation of the senses or even if it can cut itself off from the data supplied by the senses it cannot, in any case, cut itself off from the latter. There is a representation of the world or a representation of one's self or, at its highest, a representation of pure self.

It is, therefore, internally that one should seek to perfect thought that inhabits the body; from this arises the technique of yoga which is simultaneously a physiological and psychological technique. There is no opposition between the substance of the body and the substance of the soul. It is behind the existence of matter, the existence common to all beings and things: that of the Supreme Being.

Consequently, by means of psychological techniques, it is possible to abolish the servitudes of the senses in order to emerge into this Being that one can conceive but whose conception and specially whose realisation is ruffled by the difficulty of being involved in the world. Certain methods, practices and particular postures (*āsanas*) were also sought and with great success. Principally a respiratory discipline was used, a technique of breathing which is so common and natural to all human beings. In fact, when one is very conscious, when one is concentrated, one holds one's breath, one stops breathing.

There also takes place the phenomenon of the breath arrested through the effect of a sudden inrush of emotion; it is particularly interesting to observe the phenomena of the temporary physiological stopping of respiration. The Indians observe the concomitance of the stopping of respiration and the intensification of attention. To cultivate the power of attention, the power to stop the respiratory functioning is developed, it is called *kumbhaka*.

There are several kinds of *kumbhaka* depending on whether the stopping of respiration is done with filled lungs or emptied lungs. All these things are of great interest to modern science.

Let us see now how yoga could be understood from the standpoint of modern science which is quite foreign to the fact of the production of these ideas and these techniques. How can it be considered? From the standpoint of scientific investigation it is actually concerned with two different but complementary sciences. There is first the psycho-physiological aspect: the phenomena produced by yogins must be studied. The physiological phenomena are most easily recognised because they are communicable. On the other hand, the psychological phenomena are much more difficult to recognise because they cannot be communicated and the yogin, while he conceives the states he sought, cannot stimultaneously describe them precisely because he is closed to the external world and has no contact with it. It is only later that he might be able to express something about his experience and might also be able to say how he himself arrived at this result through some exercises, so that others by imitating him, may arrive at it as well. But it is impossible to communicate to others an explanation of the exercises which, by their very definition, are personal.

There is also another aspect which makes yoga an object of scientific enquiry and that is its historic tradition, it is all the ideas that the yogins still profess and which ought to be examined by means of a very simple method that we have and which the scientists of ancient India also possessed. To do this, we must first study all the facts because, as we have said earlier, the condition of scientific knowledge is, above all, the knowledge of all the facts once we have their complete statement. If one analyses these facts correctly, there is little reason for not arriving at an apparently valid solution.

When the tradition of yoga is examined, we discover, quite often, a discordance between what this tradition teaches and what one observes in reality. Consequently, one is really obliged, not to assert that the tradition is false but to observe that it has not been proved and that in order to record it as a scientific fact, one must wait for it to be actually observed.

It is sometimes said that official science refuses to accept theories which are scientific (their own): this is wrong because official science does not stop demolishing old theories, it cancels out the former interpretation if new facts come into its ken.

When phenomena produced by yoga are observed, there is never any hesitation to accept an observation but when there is hesitation—and it is here that there have often been disagreements, affirmations without proof—one cannot accept them.

I think it is imprudent for yoga to seek to have too precise a correspondence between its own facts and modern science because —at that moment—it will stop at a science that we know is temporary. If through yoga, an idea can be had of the actual reality, it cannot be the present scientific representation because we know that it is not true: it is temporary. It is much superior to what it was a hundred years back but much inferior to what it will become during the following centuries.

As a result, if one wants to compare the explanations of ancient yogins and modern scientists, it must be understood that the yogins evidently could not know the present truth. On the contrary, modern science, basing itself on its knowledge, seeks to explain the phenomena of yoga by a study of the physiological phenomena that are most accessible to us. As for the psychological phenomena, they can only be known from the yogins themselves or through personal practice, even though one may not be able to explain its results.

As regards the Indian texts that deal with its thought, it is not enough to make grammatical and semantic translations of them but they need to be studied in the cultural background of the author. If one truly seeks the understanding of these texts, the whole culture of the author's country needs to be studied and assimilated in order to form an exact idea of his thought.

However, it is clear that yoga opens out to science a vast field of scientific enquiry and scientists should explore and study it in a greater degree than has been done until now.

CHAPTER 32

YOGA AND PSYCHOTROPIC SUBSTANCES*

AT THE BEGINNING of this century, the well-known American psychologist, James H. Leuba gave an important place to yoga in his book *The Psychology of Religious Mysticism.* He was familiar with yoga thanks to James Haughton Woods' translation of the *Yogasūtra*: published in 1914 at Cambridge (Massachusetts) according to which he was convinced that the thought of India had taken a very different course from the ones Western thought took. We see today that speculative divergences between yoga and our thought were merely apparent: Woods rightly understood the Sanskrit phrases but neither he nor his Indian interpreters found the appropriate words in English to render the technical Sanskrit terms of psychology.

The psychologist who was depending upon this translation could only get an incomplete idea of the exact content of the *Yogasūtras.* He made up for it by superficial analogies with Western facts or others furnished by ethnology. Above all, he was convinced that yoga essentially consisted in liberation from suffering and that its crowning achievement was in the ecstatic beatitudes that are similar to certain intoxications obtained by drugs. He recalled the frenzied and licentious festivals of the 'savages', as well as the ecstacy of the Christians as analogous, observing, in fact, in all these enthusiasm and sentiments of bliss or of certitude, merely illusions and hallucinations. Others have sought in some psycho-pathological states the causes of Indian philosophical doctrines which render the phenomenal world into an illusion. They forgot, then, that the philosophical representations in question and the emotional states and certainties of the yogins are obtained, not unexpectedly and haphazardly, but through consciously undertaken discipline and training, normally under the guidance of a master, and in logical concordance with the premises set forth by the ancient science.

*Le yoga et les substances psychotropes, in *Yoga et Vie*, no. 26, Dec. 1980.

The ultimate psychological states which the yogins attain are extreme and undefinable sentiments for others but they are not 'intuitive' as it is often said because, even though they are suddenly perceived, they were prepared by the traditional discursive knowledge or else they are not concerned with the actual Indian methods of yoga.

The *Yogasūtras* point out the results of *saṃyama*. It involves the simultaneous workings of three operations of yoga: fixation on an object, meditation and a stable positioning of the mind (*dhāraṇā*, *dhyāna*, and *samādhi*).

There follows a plenary knowledge (*jñāna*). By *saṃyama* on the Sun we gain the knowledge of the world, *saṃyama* on the Moon gives us knowledge of the stars, *saṃyama* on the Pole gives us knowledge of the movements of the stars, *saṃyama* on the navel gives us knowledge of the distribution of different constituents of the body. Now the traditional commentaries describe in what these plenary branches of knowledge of the real consist and they are in concordance with the teachings of the treatises of astronomy and of the medicine of traditional Indian science which was the truth of the time (III, 26-29).

In these cases, therefore, we have to deal with exceptional achievements of education and not with intuitions.

But *saṃyama* does not only produce intellectual notions.

When *saṃyama* is directed on the pharynx (III, 30 *kaṇṭhakūpa*, literally 'the well of the throat'), it arrests hunger and thirst; it acts, therefore, on affective sensations. It also helps us to attain psychic conditions and visions: on the 'canal of the tortoise', *kūrmanāḍī*, it ensures the immobilisation (*sthairya*) of thought; on 'the light in the head', *mūrdhajyotis*, it brings about the sight of the *siddhas*, mythical beings endowed with magical powers who move between the sky and the earth. But the organs in question belong like the *siddhas* to an ideal and traditional knowledge which results from the initiation of current ideas in the surrounding intellectual milieu.

The 'canal of the tortoise' would be in the lotus of the heart and the tortoise symbolises stability. This again is a notion that flows from a teaching.

As for the real intuition, it is accepted in the same text (III, 33) as capable of succeeding the *saṃyama* which gives the sight of the *siddhas*. It is called *pratibhā* and tradition defines it as a knowledge that is not taught (*anaupadeśikam jñānam*). It is sudden and can produce 'everything', that is to say the sight of the past as well as that of the future. It is a prelude to a complete knowledge of thought in the *saṃyama* of the heart, its seat (*hṛdaye cittasaṃvit*, III, 34). Other kinds of *saṃyamas* are known to give extraordinary powers, the *siddhis*.

All these phenomena, experienced or expected, produced by the *saṃyamas*, are the result of the will involving techniques mastered to achieve very specific results.

It is evident that there is nothing in them comparable to intoxications produced by drugs.

It is true that *Yogasūtras* (IV, 1) claim that the extraordinary powers can be obtained through drugs. But here is the sūtra: 'The extraordinary powers come from birth, from drugs, formulae, askesis and *samādhi*.'

However, only *samādhi* is part of yoga. The use of drugs (*oṣadhi*) according to the tradition of the commentators of the *Yogasūtras* is the practice of the *asuras* or demons. The *siddhis* obtained through the *saṃyama* of yoga do not in any way depend on it. There are human *siddhas* who in view of the *siddhis* use all the known or imagined processes including the yogic technique of *samādhi*, but when they do not use this technique exclusively, they do not operate as *yogins* but as alchemists, magicians or ascetics.

The fundamentally psychological nature of yoga which aims at the mastery of the psychic individuality by using the physiology of the material body where it is incarnated, necessarily excludes the use of psychotropic substances.

This use, precisely, supposes the abandoning of this mastery to give away the psychic individuality to the specific haphazard action of a toxic.

An intoxication automatically produced by a foreign substance, instead of helping in yoga, would falsify its method and bring about its loss.

Peyotl, for example, fills the eyes with wonder during the time of its action and it is known that some exercises of yoga produce visions of coloured light. Some may think that in the final account regarding the two visual perceptions without object, one is faced with phenomena of the same order. One of them is triggered off by an exogenous biochemical action, the other by an endogenous one of the psychosomatic exercise of yoga. Therefore, the difference would only be in the origin of a sensorial stimulus that determines comparable results. But the conditions of the production of these results are themselves not comparable.

Besides, the collective and ceremonial seeking of peyotl ends in the hallucinatory vision. In yoga, visions are a sign of a stage crossed during an exercise which does involve the organism and its reflexes, but is in no lesser way led by consciousness and logic towards a specific knowledge.

The Buddhists, who are specialists of the theory of transmigration being the consequence of acts, teach that the instinctive acts, devoid of ideation (*cetanā*), as those of a tiger killing its prey, do not bring about retribution. That is not the case with the absorption of intoxicating substances which is forbidden as it is in yoga, because that would be conscious.

A recent theory which gave rise to sharp controversies, sought to identify the *soma* plant of the ancient Vedic times with the fly-agaric mushroom used today by the peoples of Siberia as a hallucinogen. The very elaborate theory refutes many objections but is silent about the description given by Suśruta's book on medicine according to which the plant puts out every month fifteen leaves which it loses regularly! In any case, it is a celestial plant of which there are on the earth only symbolic substitutes which have no use in yoga.

Finally, the use of Indian hemp is well known and it is quite common in North India, even among some religious sects but that too has no use in yoga.

Babar, conqueror of India in the 16th century, wrote his memoirs wherein he recounts that while travelling in the country in the evening at the time of the execution of some Hindus, he used to take along with his followers some Indian hemp in the form of electuary to start the night, but the well-being of a roughneck soldier is not that of the yoga of knowledge.

It is not intoxication but the mastery of the driving breath of thought which gives the real intoxication, that of knowledge. This is what the yogin and poet Tirumular expressed in Tamil. (*Tirumantiram* 566) calling this breath 'horse': 'If one rides the horse which surpasses the bird, palm wine should not be consumed. By itself (the breath), it will give intoxication, it will make one walk trippingly, it will stop torpor: it is for those who have the knowledge that we have spoken the truth!'

CHAPTER 33

PSYCHIC TENSIONS AND YOGA*

PSYCHIC TENSION or *stress*, meaning thereby the psychosomatic response to this tension in the organism, is today the object of deep research in neurophysiology and biological chemistry. Numerous kinds of this stress automatically and unconsciously affect the organic functions and the general equilibrium of health. These efforts are produced by mechanisms that are progressively discovered. They depend largely on psychic stimuli or inhibitions produced in or below the cerebral cortex. These phenomena induce or abstain from inducing, through the cerebral systems of transmission, elaboration and equilibration, humoral secretions that themselves incite and regulate other secretions. There results the triggering of a chain of multiple organic functions. The initial stimuli do not all result from psychological phenomena responding to different psychic perceptions and actions or reactions. They can, in turn, be induced by humoral phenomena concerning the cortical and sub-cortical centres and notably the frontal lobe which is the psychic centre. All this, naturally in regard to genetic conditions and susceptibilities, is of a complexity, which, in its mechanism and evolution as well as in its interactions is at once totally bewildering, when we think of it, and marvellous in its apparently simplest results.

The psychic functions and the vegetative functions are not mutually independent. For example, the frontal lobe is connected to the system of hypothalamus which plays a major role in the regulation of numerous organic activities. Thus the frontal lobe can exert an inhibiting effect on hypothalamic stimulus of secretions of saliva or the gastric juices. The effect can also be arrested by different emotions, from which their commonly observed variations result, specially as regards the salivary secretion, in relation to certain psychological states.

From the study of intricate psychosomatic phenomena it results

*Tensions psychiques et yoga, in *Yoga et Vie*, no. 31, Paris, March 1982.

that the more the study advances in its biochemical analysis of new humoral factors, the more pharmacology can prepare new products to stimulate or reduce their effects, which explains the present proliferation of chemical medicines. Contrary to the beliefs of some zealous supporters of phytotherapy, these chemical medications are not antagonistic with natural medications which too are chemical in their nature. The most efficient ones in both types are poisons which should only be used in the right cases and the right doses, determined by an experimental biological pharmacodynamic study and not merely on the basis of traditional reputations or those reputed to be traditional. Modern pharmacology in fact, seeks through its analysis of medicinal plants, natural chemical models which it can itself reproduce in a systematic way.

Apart from prejudices which sometimes make us suspicious of chemical medications, some psychologists, psychoanalysts or psychiatrists do not favour the use of these medications in either normal or pathological psychology. They believe that the medications are not topical and that to psychological phenomena, one should essentially apply direct psychological action rather than an indirect one based on the working of a still mysterious humoral chemistry.

In fact and in practice, it is necessary to have a full choice of all the possible therapeutics used, according to the cases, single or combined.

Here yoga can and ought to come into these therapeutics today.

A recent work of Professor K.N. Udupa, director of the Institute of Medical Sciences at the Hindu University of Benaras and rector of this University, deals with disorders of stress and their control through yoga (*Disorders of stress and their management through Yoga: A study of neuro-humoral response*. Benaras Hindu University, 1978).

First, he expounds on the state of our present knowledge of anatomy, of the physiology of the brain and of neuro-endocrinology, the neuro-humoral response to stress and the psychological factors of stress. These are partly genetic when they answer to hereditary, psychosomatic dispositions but they also depend largely on environment as soon as the individual is formed and psychogenous experiences have been encountered.

A simplified example: the image of a scene of violence formed on the retina is transmitted by the optic nerve to the occipital lobe, from there it moves to the frontal lobe where (according to predetermined arrangements) an emotive pressure is produced which, through hypothalamus, will induce a discharge of catecholamines and of cortisol. This discharge, on the shock of the rebound, will augment the activity of the stimulated frontal lobe. The repetition or the recollection of similar scenes of violence will be able to bring the accidental stress to a chronic state, which explains the later somatic consequences in different organs.

The experimentation of certain stress-patterns on animals has been able to lead to numerical evaluations of their biochemical effects. For example, repeated electroshocks bring down by 33% the rate of acetylcholine in the cortex, the thalamus and the hypothalamus. It is also known that the decrease in the rate of the acetylcholine in the brain corresponds to its increase in the blood. The decrease in the brain is accompanied by phenomena of nervousness and, at the same time, the increase in the blood stimulates the activities of thc organs and the tissues.

It is clear that similar observations proceed from chemical therapeutics. But this does not mean that psychological and psychosomatic disciplines of yoga can and should be used as therapeutic means. They allow us to counter or to substitute in the consciousness, and from there in the unconscious, psychological situations that are involuntarily experienced in states which are chosen and produced through a regulated training.

Two-thirds of the work following the exposition on neurophysiology, are devoted to the researches and observations made at the Institute of Medical Sciences of Benaras. The studies are made on famous yogins but more so on volunteers who apply themselves to different exercises of which the effects need to be tested.

The principal physiological aspects of yoga are, of course, *āsanas* and *prāṇāyāma*; its psychological aspect is meditation with its different levels and aims. In practice 'bio-feedback' is used, that is to say an exercise in which through voluntary action one manages to act on functions that are normally involuntary.

Effects of this type obtained through yoga had already been brought to light since 1953 by Thérèse Brosse who was the first to demonstrate with the help of the electrocardiogram the validity of yogic experiments formerly regarded as illusory.

The physical ailments in which the methods of yoga had been studied at Benaras were mainly arterial hypertension, different cardiac troubles, bronchial asthma, ulcer of the stomach, ulceral colitis, thyrotoxicose, diabetes, osteoarthritis, nervousness and some other troubles or illnesses.

In a number of cases, particularly in the beginning and in acute or sub-acute cases, tranquilising remedies were used or some others like *Terminalia emblica Lin* (the emblical mirobalan imported from India, in the old European pharmacopoeia which is cholagogue and diuretic in value). The importance of meditation and also religious convictions was recognised but does not as yet lend itself to an easy experimentation. The study of these powerful means of application of thought does not belong only to the physician, nor only to the yogin or the devotee. It should be the object of a specific research. But the works concluded at present open up new paths of research, simultaneously in Yoga, Medicine and Psychology.

INDEX OF NON-INDIAN WORDS

abstentions (five obligatory) in Buddhism 194 sq
amidism 106
Anquetil Duperron 314
Arya Samaj 262
ascetic practices 344
Aurobindo 262, 319

Barthélemy Saint-Hilaire 216
Bergaigne 219
Bibliothèque Nationale at Paris 260
Brahma Samaj 262
Braid (James) 270
breaths 323
Brosse (Thérèse) 376, 400
Buddhism 20, 308 sq, 329 and *passim*

Caldwell 210
caste system 177
charity 3 sqq
Christians in India 131
compassion 14
complexes 308, 329
continence 327 sqq
contradiction (principle of) 216
Cosmas Indicopleustes 132
cult of Siva 187, 190

Dara-Shikoh 199 sq, 228, 314
Dayananda Sarasvati 262
Deguignes 167
desire 329 sq
divining 285
docetism 127 sqq
Dravidians 179
Dubois (Abbé) 216, 366

education 254 sq
electrocardiogram (of yogins) 299
Eliadex (Mircea) 296, 378, 386
Esdaile 275

fire-walking 112
Fleury 217

Gentil 314
grammar 316 sq

heart 382
hero stones 151 sq
hesychasm 365, 402
hesychasts 275
Hinduism 396 and *passim*
honour 146
hypnosis 270 sq
hysteria 280

imagination 334
intuition 462 sq

Jacquemont 366
Janet (Pierre) 280, 308

king (divine nature) 53-56, 62
Kircher 275

Lévi (Sylvain) 216
Loyola (Saint Ignatius) 295

malabar rites 220
memory 448
Mohan-jo-Daro 296, 366, 378
Morton Prince 308

Oedipus complex 430
Order (Right universal) 61 sq

pandit 447
panegyrics 55
pedagogical method 447 sq
perception 443
Persian Church 132
Polo (Marco) 135, 144
prestidigitation 343
propagation of the Buddhist Law 63
prosopon 133
psychoanalysis 308
psychotropic substances 451

Ramakrishna 319
Ramana Maharshi 262, 319
Ram Mohan Roy 318
retribution of acts 14
Rorschach test 356 sq

schisms in Buddhism 330 sq
Schopenhauer 315
Seleucus 64
self-immolation 91 sqq
sexuality 327 sqq
shamanism 367, 378
soul 56 sq
Spiritual Exercises of Saint Ignatius of Loyola 295
Strabo 64 sq, 107, 135
suicide 135 sqq, (by the hero) 145 sqq, 153, (expiatory) 144

Tamil literature 20 sq and *passim*
Tantrism 397
Thomas (the Apostle) 131
transfer of merit 197, 242 sq
translation 217
transmigration 193, 221, 329

unconscious 307 sqq, 369 sqq
untouchables 178
Upanishads 49 sq, (yoga in) 295, (translated by Anquetil Duperron) 315

Vallée Poussin (la) 216, 240
vedic rite 187, 190
Vivekananda 319

Ward 216
Wilson (H.H.) 165

Yi-tsing 41, 44

INDEX OF INDIAN WORDS

agnikārya 260, (-paddhati) 261
Atharvaveda 414
anubhava 443
annasūkta 260
abja 204
araṇa 240
arhant 11, 330
Allamaprabhu 210, 229
avatāra 129
Aśoka 11, 61 sq
asaṃprajñātasamādhi 371, 389

ākāśa 416
āgama 68, 175, 256 sq and *passim*
ācārya (vaiṣṇava) 25
Āṇḍāl 36 sq
ātman 221
Ānandagiri 410
Āyurveda 381, 461 and *passim*
āśrayaparāvṛtti 446
āsana 368, 387, 399
Āḻvār 23 sq, 83 sq

indriya 298

uḍḍiyānabandha 399
upāya 334
upekṣā 5

Ṛcaka 261
ṛtambaharā 308
Ṛṣabha 288
Ṛṣi 451

eruvai 190

aiśvarya 345

karuṇā 5, 7
Karnāṭaka 87
karman 221, 372
karmayoga 377
Kalabhrar 184
Kaśyapa 11
kasiṇa 374
Kātyāyanī (vrata) 38
kāla 414
Kālidāsa 138
Kuṭumi 184
kuṇḍalinī 337
Kumāra (Skanda) 38
Kṛṣṇa 38
Kṛṣṇabhakti 22 sq
Koṅkaṉar 210
Koṟakai 184
kṣaṇa 425
Kṣemadattaparivarta (Samādhirāja 33) 92 sq

khecarīmudrā 337, 399

gāyatrī 257 sq
Guruparamparāsāra 81 sq
Govindācārya (Ālkoṇḍavilli) 79

Gheraṇḍasaṃhitā 400

cakra 398
Caṇḍamahāroṣaṇatantra 429
cāritra 355
cittar 210
Cidambarakṣetrasarvasvam 259
cinmātra 44
Cilappadikāram 149 sqq
centanā 332
Caitanya 85
caitya 115

Jaṭilaparāntaka 184
Jaḍabharata 270, 288
jīvanmukta 355

Jñānadeva 87

tantra 69, 227, 256 sq, 332, 334
tapas 327, 344 sq, 379
Tirukulattar 178
Tiruppāvei 37 sq
Tirumaṅkaiyāḻvār 246
Tirumūlar 210, 229
Tiruvāymoḻi 26 sqq
Tiruviḷaiyāḍalpurāṇam 22
Tiruvembāvai 38, 40
Tissa Moggaliputta 63
Tolkāppiyam 145
trāṭaka 286, 391

dānapāramitā 102
dikkālādy ... (Nītiśataka of Bhartṛhari 256) 43 sq
diś 424
Durgā 149
Dramidopaniṣad 28
dravya 424

dhamma 61, 65 sq
dharma 245, 250
Dharmaśāstra 177
dhātugarbha 93
dhāraṇā 270, 369, 388
dhyāna 369, 381, 386, 389, 455
Dhyānabindūpaniṣad 406 sqq

Nammāḻvār 24
nalam (tamil) 29 sq
navagraha 261
Nāgārjuna 363
Nāthamuni 25 sq, 454
Nālāyiradivyaprabandam 26
niyama 368, 387
nirmāṇakāya 128
nirvāṇa 330
Nyāyasūtra 442

Paṭṭiṉapālai 237 sq
pattidāna 244
paramārthasatya 333
Parāntaka Neṭuñcaṭaiyaṉ 184
Palyākacālai Mutukuṭumi 184 sq
Paśupati 296
Pārameśvarāgama 72
pāśupata 243
Piḷḷeiyār 38
puṇya 233 sq
Puṟanāṉūṟu 148 sq, 183
prajñā 308, 334
praṇava (in Vākyapadīya) 45
pratyāhāra 368, 388
praling 57
prāṇa 381
prāṇāyatana 398
prāṇāyāma 368, 381 sq, 388
prāyopaveśana 138

Buddha 6, 128 sq, (his mother) 330
Buddhaghosa 105
Buddhadatta 184 sq
buddhi 298, 443
Bṛhadāraṇyaka Up. 416
bodhicitta 334
bodhisattva 14 sq
brahman 52
brahmacārin 328
Brahmaloka 138, 141

bhaktiyoga 377, 393
Bhagavadgītā 313, 409
Bhartṛhari 41 sqq
Bhāgavatapurāṇa 22, 79 sqq
Bhāgavatamāhātmya 21, 22, 79 sqq
bhāvanā 334, 395
Bhaiṣajyarājapūrvayogaparivarta (Saddharmapuṇḍarīka 22) 92

Majma-'al-Baḥrain 200 sq, 228
Maṇipravaḷam 25
manas 298, 442 sq
Manu 177, 179
Manusmṛti 147
marman 382, 398
Mahākarmavibhaṅga 245
Mahādeva 330
mahāprasthāna 137
Mahābhārata 108 sq, 147
Mahāyāna 393 sq
Mahārāṣṭra 87
Mahāvastu 237 sq
Māgha 147
māhātmya 173
muditā 5
Murugaṉ 38
mūrti 130, 133
Meykaṇṭa Tēvar 76
Maitrī 3, 5, 7, 9 sqq

yama 368, 387
Yājñavalkyasmṛti 147
yukti 441, 461, 465
yoga 323 sqq, 335 sq, 346 sqq, 377, 447, 456 sqq and *passim*
Yogasūtra 5, 307 sq, 355 and *passim*
yogācāra 370, 377, 395

Rājadharmaparva of Mahābhārata 52 sq
rājayoga 377
Rāmānuja 21 sq, 178

layayoga 377

liṅga 57 sq
liṅgaśarīra 389

Vakkali 103 sq, 153
vajrolīmudrā 337, 351
vāsanā 221, 298, 307 sq, 444
vijñaptimātra 44
Vijñānabhikṣu 345
vijñānavādin 394
Villiputtūrār 112
Viśvāmitra 328
Viṣṇu 452
vīrakkal 151 sq
Vīraśaiva 178
vetavēlvittoḻil 190
Veda 219 sq, 253 and *passim*
Vedāntadeśika 29, 81 sq
Vēḷvikkuṭi (chart) 184
Vyāghrīparivarta (Suvarṇabhāsasūtra 17) 92
vyūha 128
vrata 344

Śaṅkara 395, 410
Śūnyavādin 32
śodhana 400
Śaiva Āgamas 67 sqq and *passim*
Śaivasiddhānta 178, 213
śramaṇa 368
saṃlekhanā 143
saṃvṛtisatya 333
saṃskāra 221, 298, 307 sq, 329, 372, 383, 396, 444
satipaṭṭhāna (smṛtyupasthāna) 118
satī 110 sq, 135
satyavacana 242
Sanatkumāra 38
Sangam 148
samādhi 100 sq, 297 sq, 307 sqq, 369, 371, 385 sq, 389
Samādhirāja 386
Samudrasaṅgama 200 sq, 228
saṃprajñātasamādhi 371, 389
Sarasvatīsūkta 260
Sāyaṇa 219
siddha 206 sq, 228
Siddhas 459
siddhi 345
Sundarananda 331
Sūryasiddhānta 420
Skandha 308
sthalapurāṇa 173
svādhyāya 254

haṭhayoga 377, 399
Haṭhayogapradīpikā 351